Naruto: The Official Character Data Book

Masashi Kishimoto

Translation/JN Productions
Lead Design/Sam Elzway, Izumi Evers
Design/Lauren Doolan, Amy Martin, Gerry Serrano
Manga Lettering/Sabrina Heep
Editorial Consultant/Mari Morimoto
Copy Chief/Rebecca Downer
Editor/Joel Enos

NARUTO [HIDEN · SHA-NO SHO] © 2008 by Masashi Kishimoto
All rights reserved.
First published in Japan in 2008 by SHUEISHA Inc., Tokyo.
English translation rights arranged by SHUEISHA Inc.

The reader survey and fan-submitted portions of this book are data
from polls that were conducted in Japan.

Printed in the U.S.A.

Published by VIZ Media, LLC
P.O. Box 77010
San Francisco, CA 94107

SHONEN JUMP Profiles Edition
10 9 8 7 6 5
First printing, January 2012
Fifth printing, November 2015

RATED T FOR TEEN
ratings.viz.com

VIZ media
www.viz.com

THE WORLD'S MOST POPULAR MANGA
SHONEN JUMP
www.shonenjump.com

SJ PROFILES

D0048527

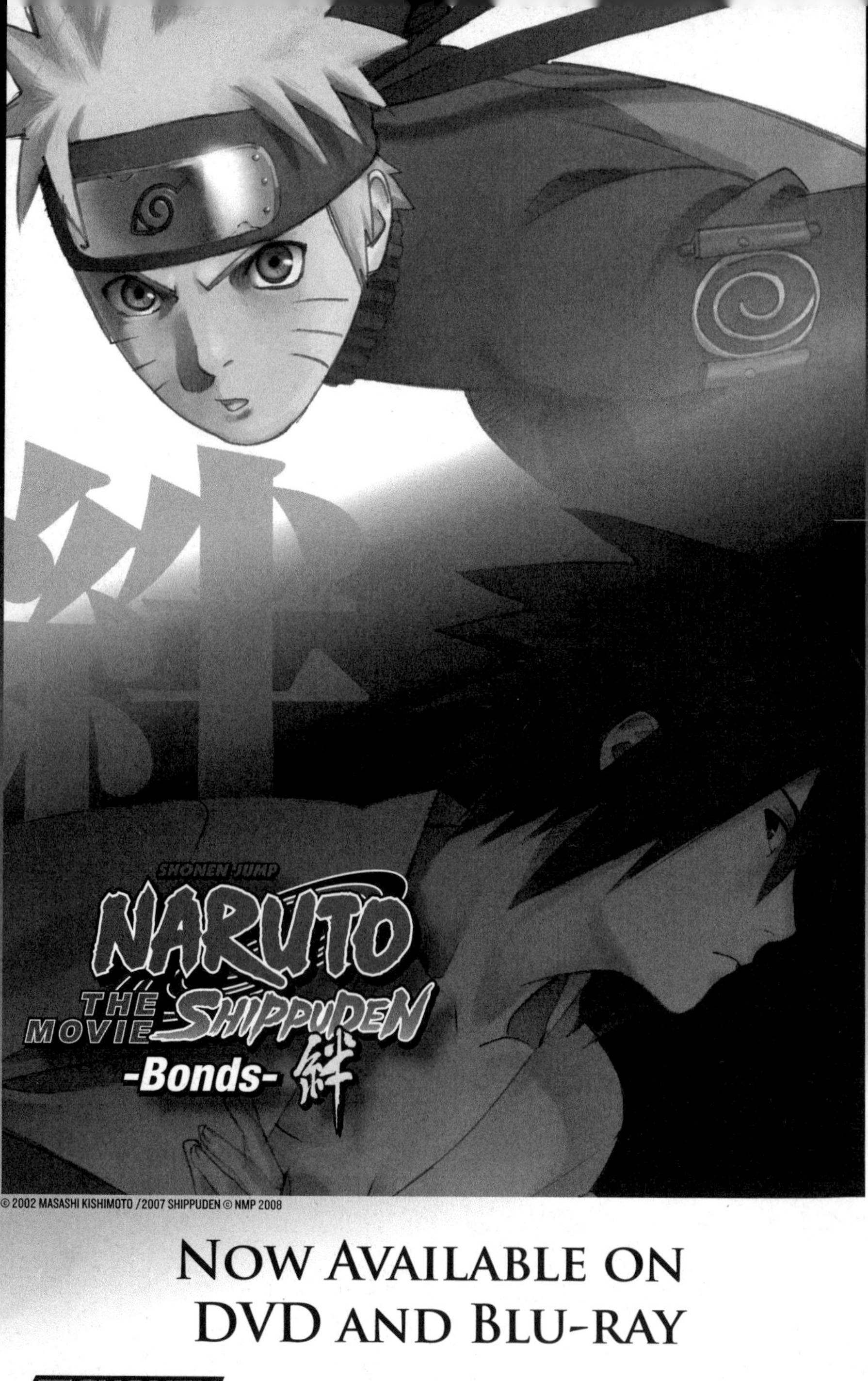
SHONEN JUMP
NARUTO
THE MOVIE
SHIPPUDEN
-Bonds- 絆

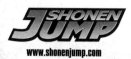

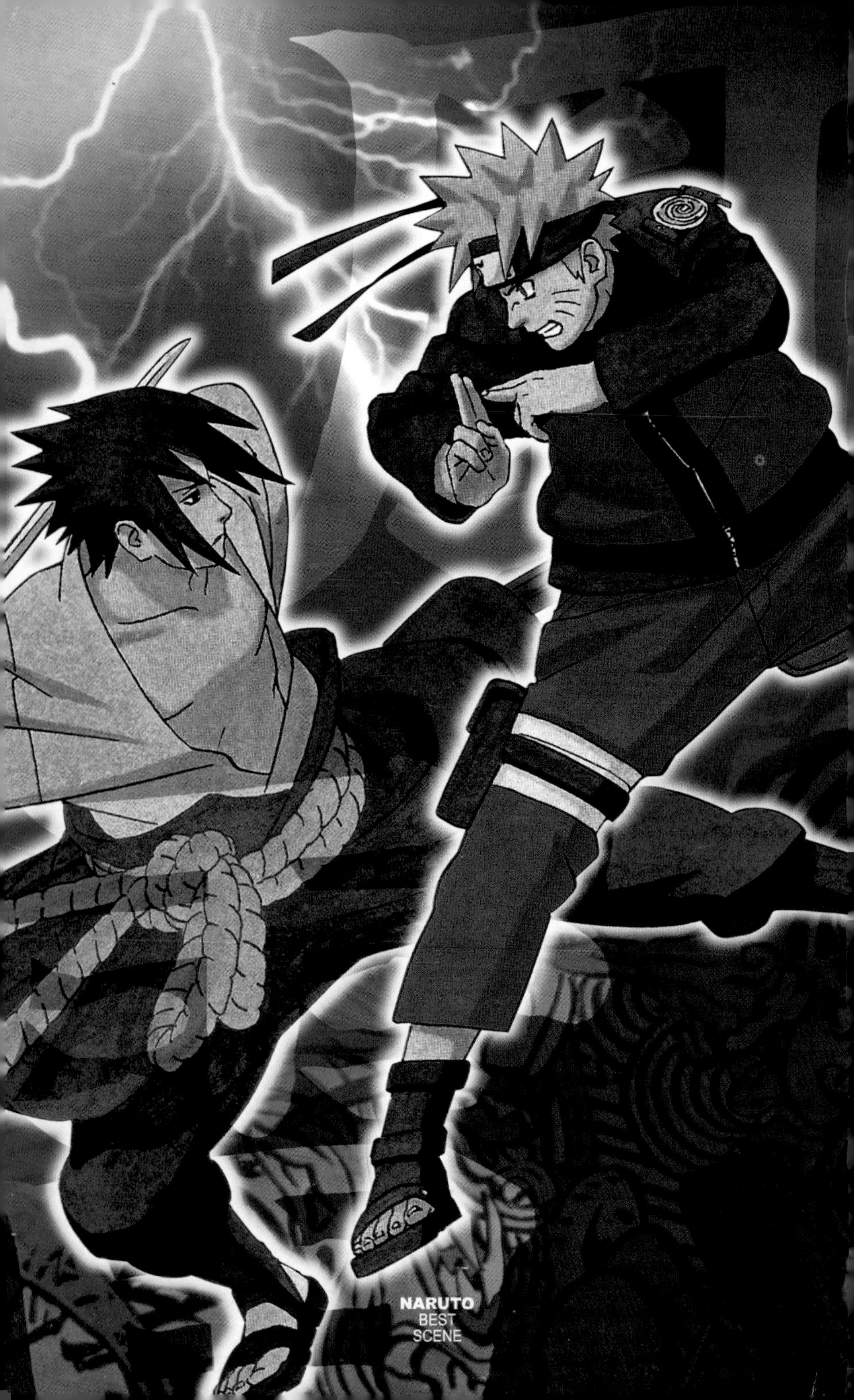
NARUTO
BEST
SCENE

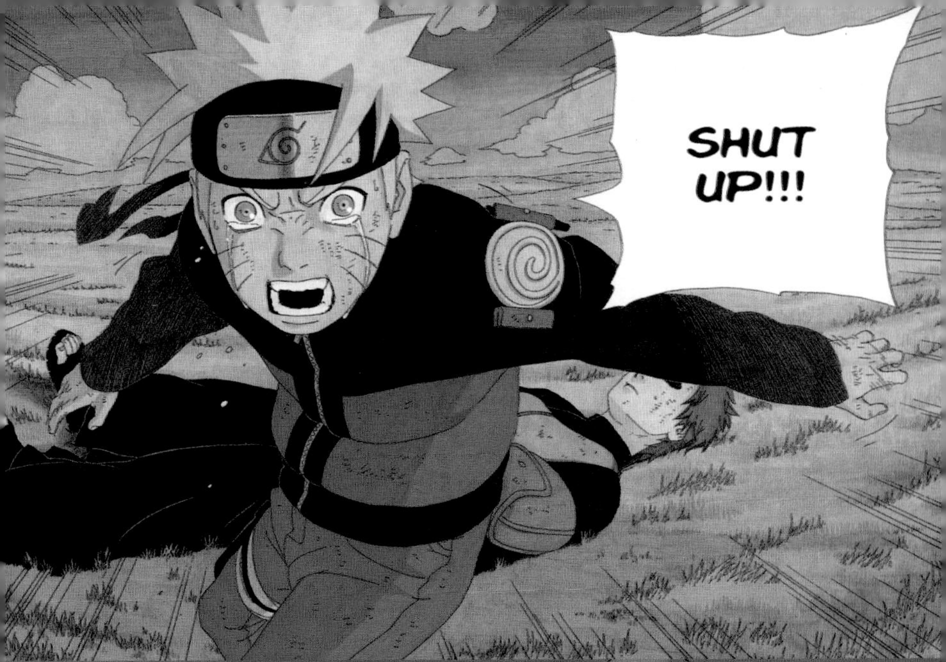
SHUT UP!!!

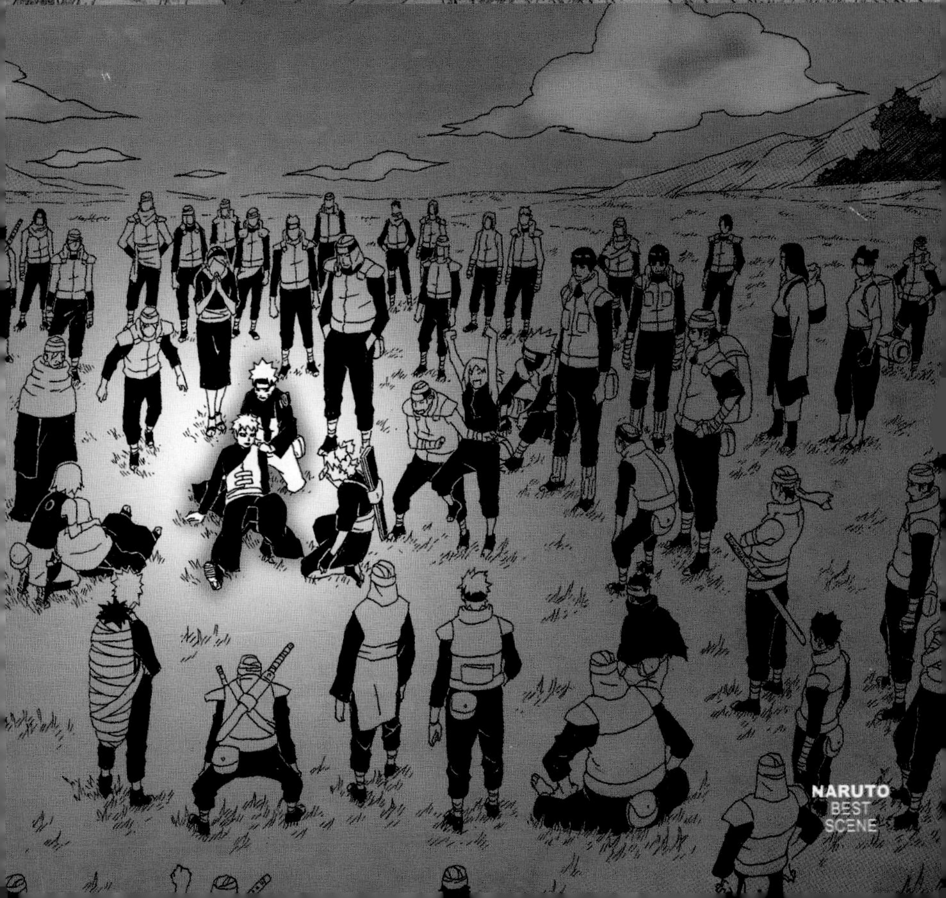

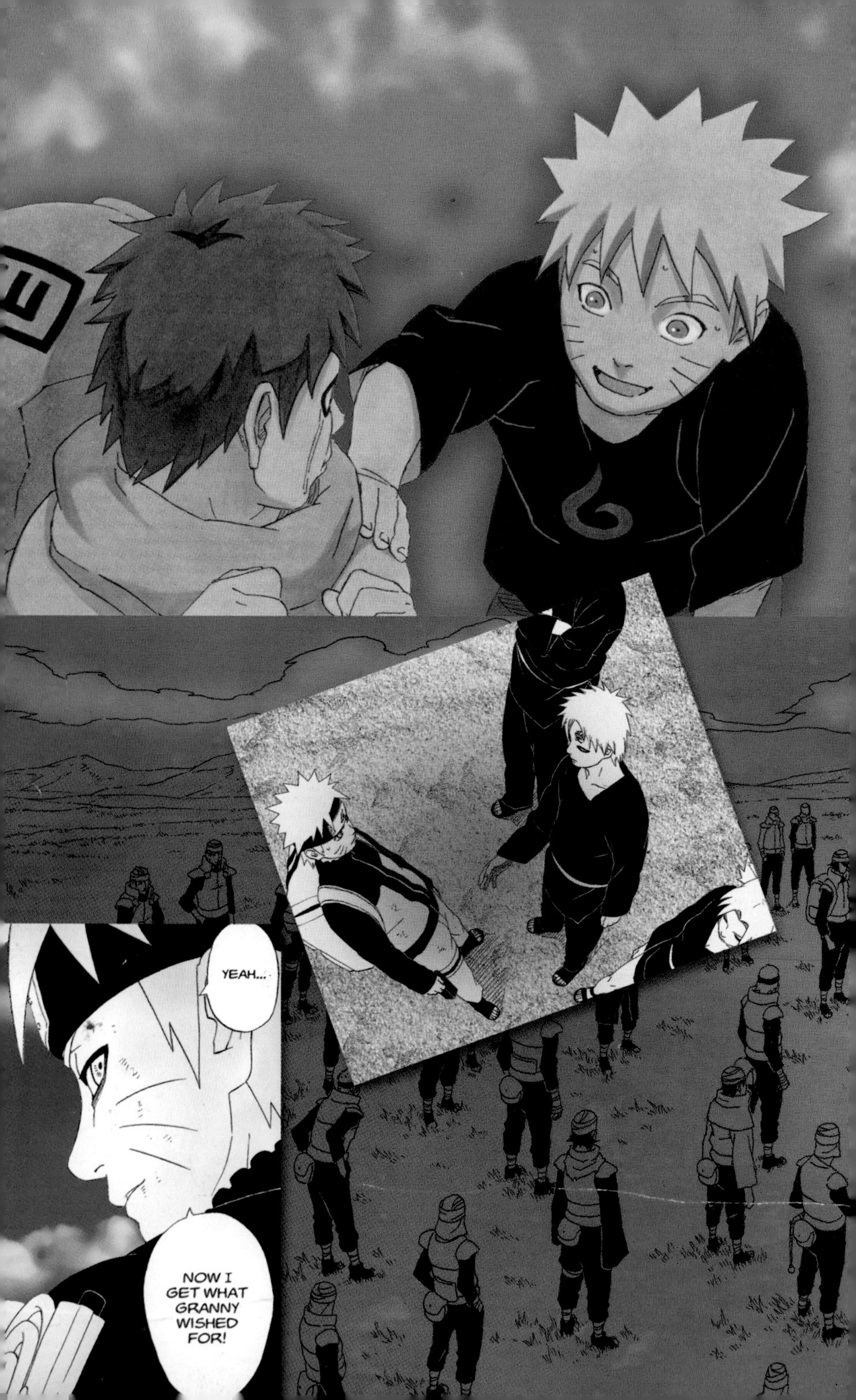
YEAH...
NOW I GET WHAT GRANNY WISHED FOR!

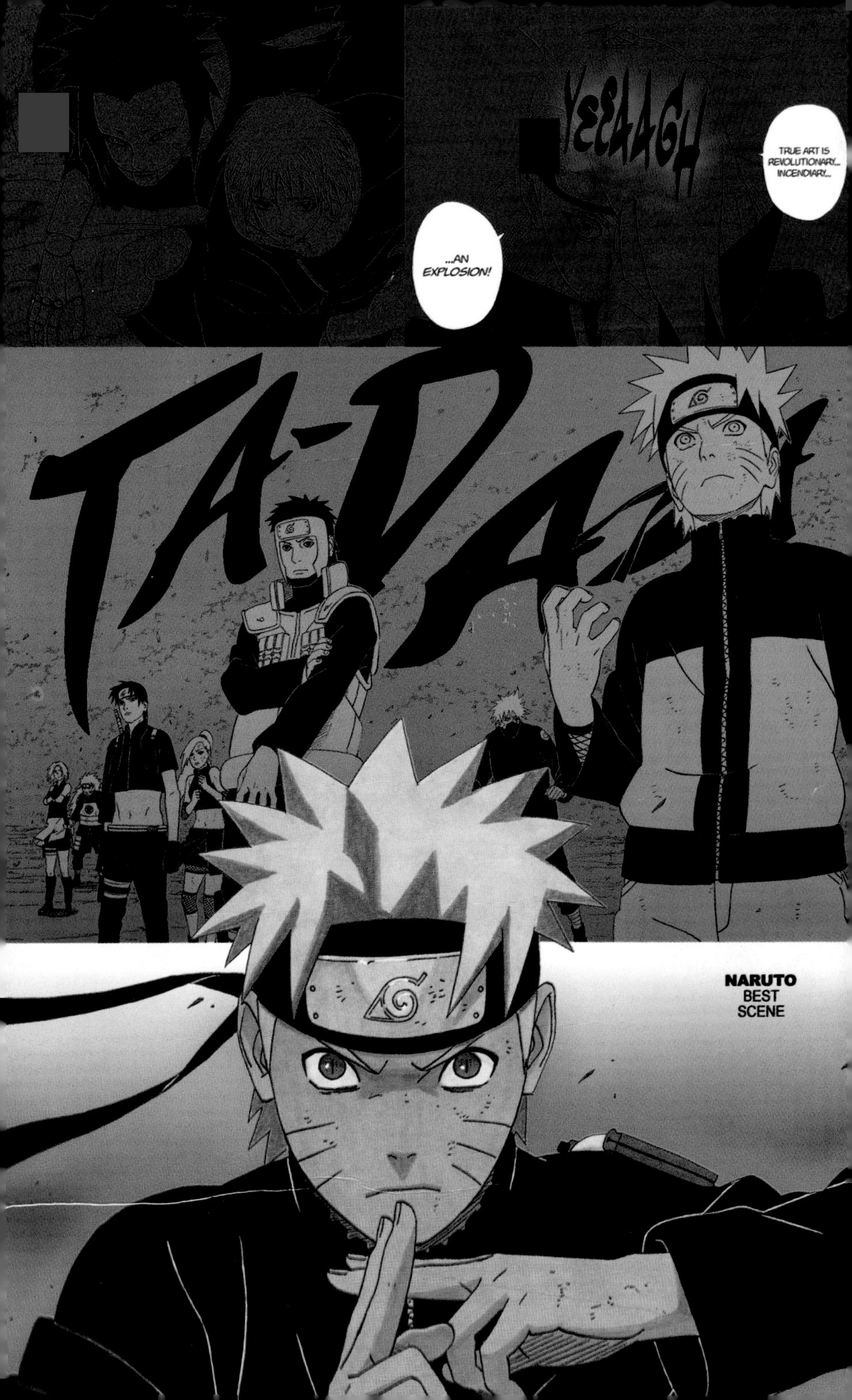

TRUE ART IS REVOLUTIONARY... INCENDIARY...
YEEAAGH
...AN EXPLOSION!
TA-DA
NARUTO BEST SCENE

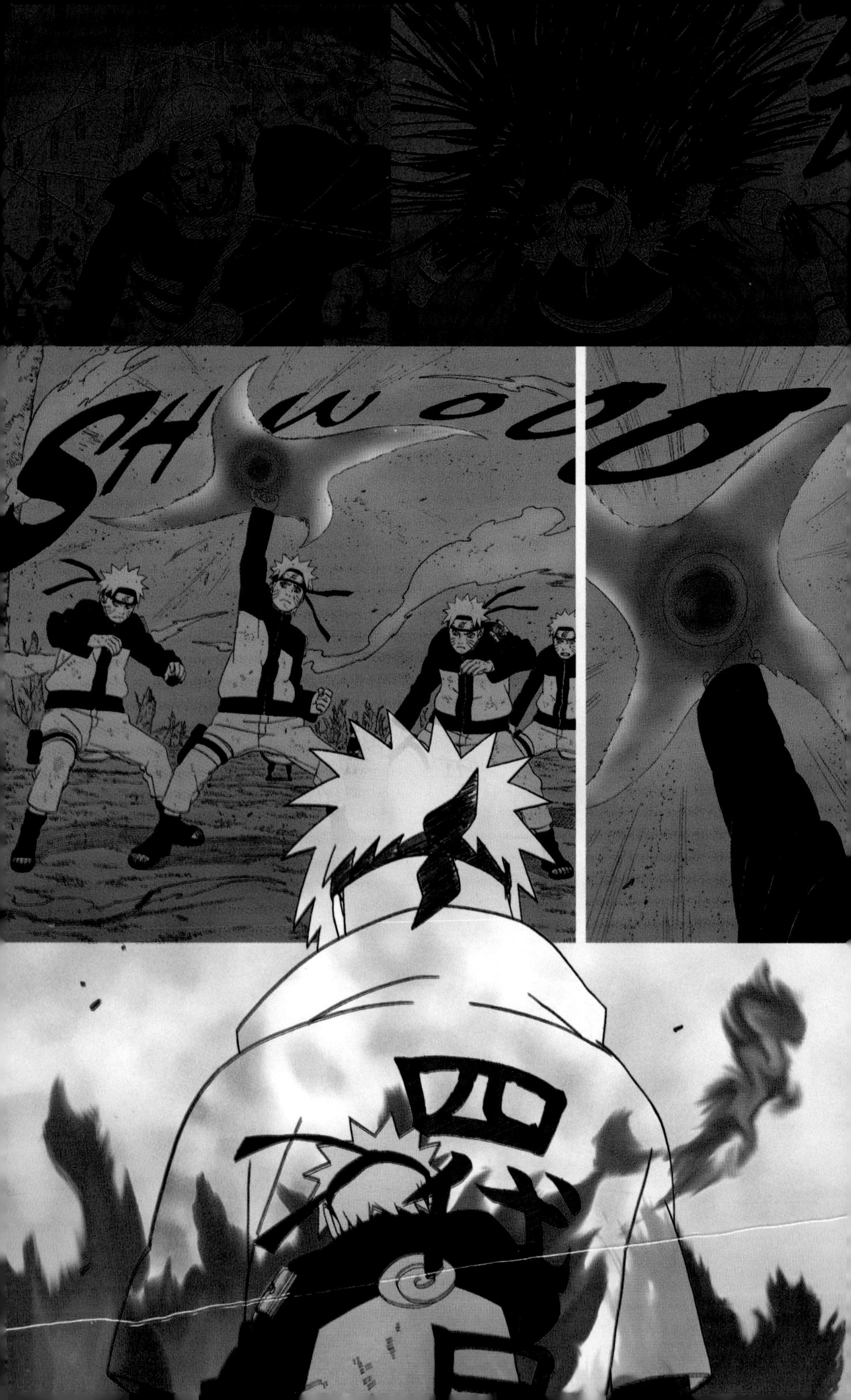
SHWOOOO

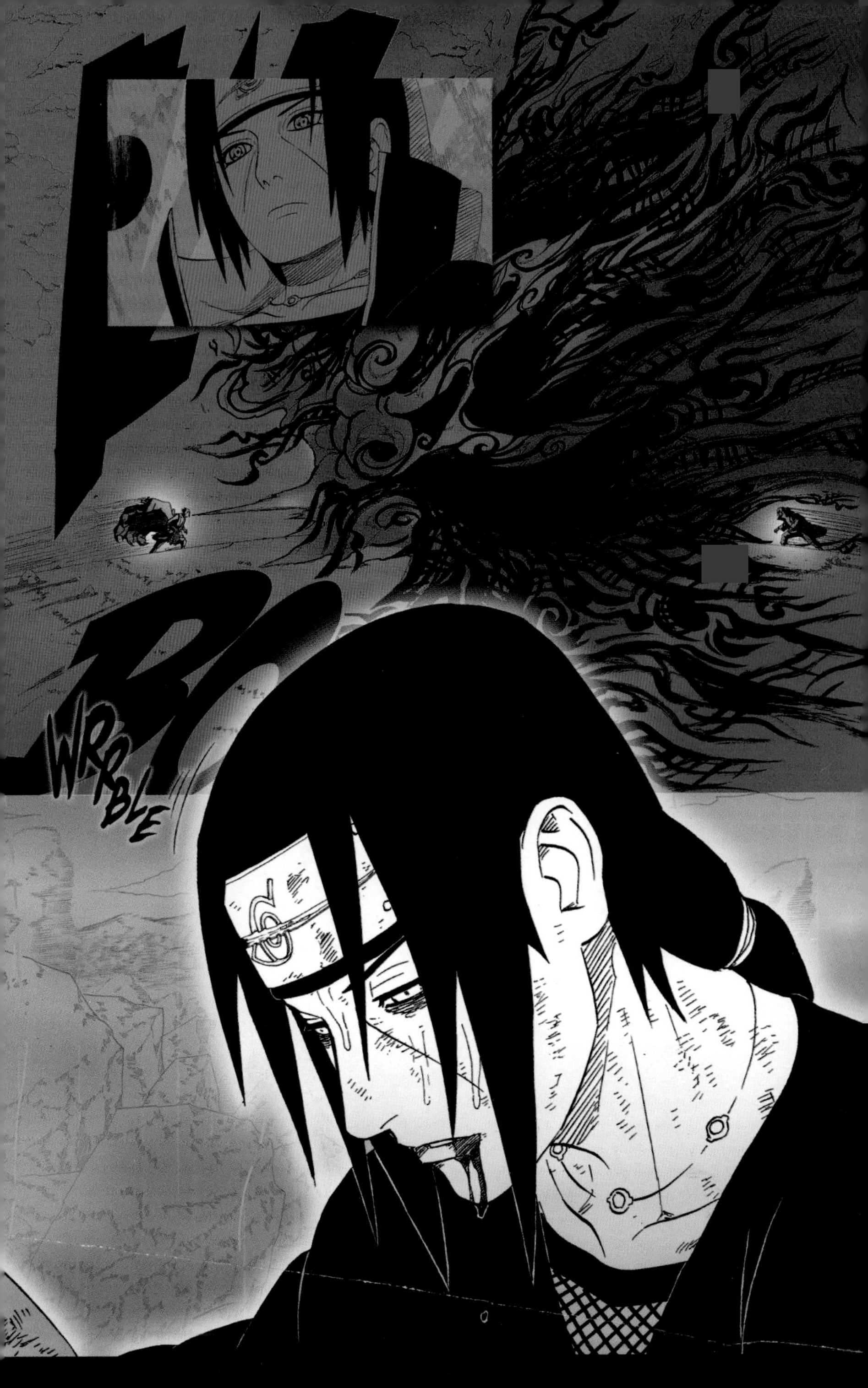
WRRBLE

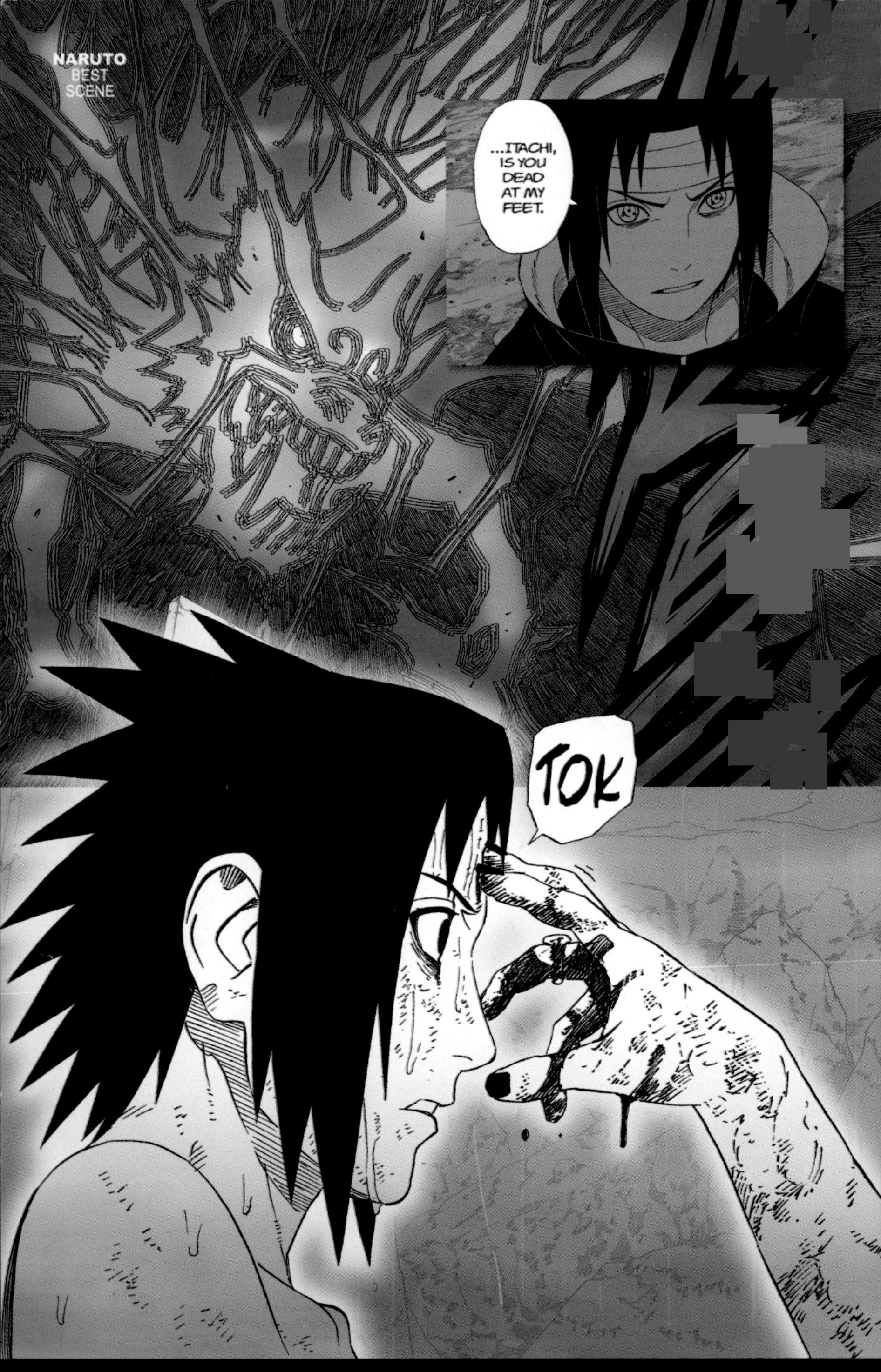
NARUTO
BEST
SCENE
...ITACHI, IS YOU DEAD AT MY FEET.
TOK

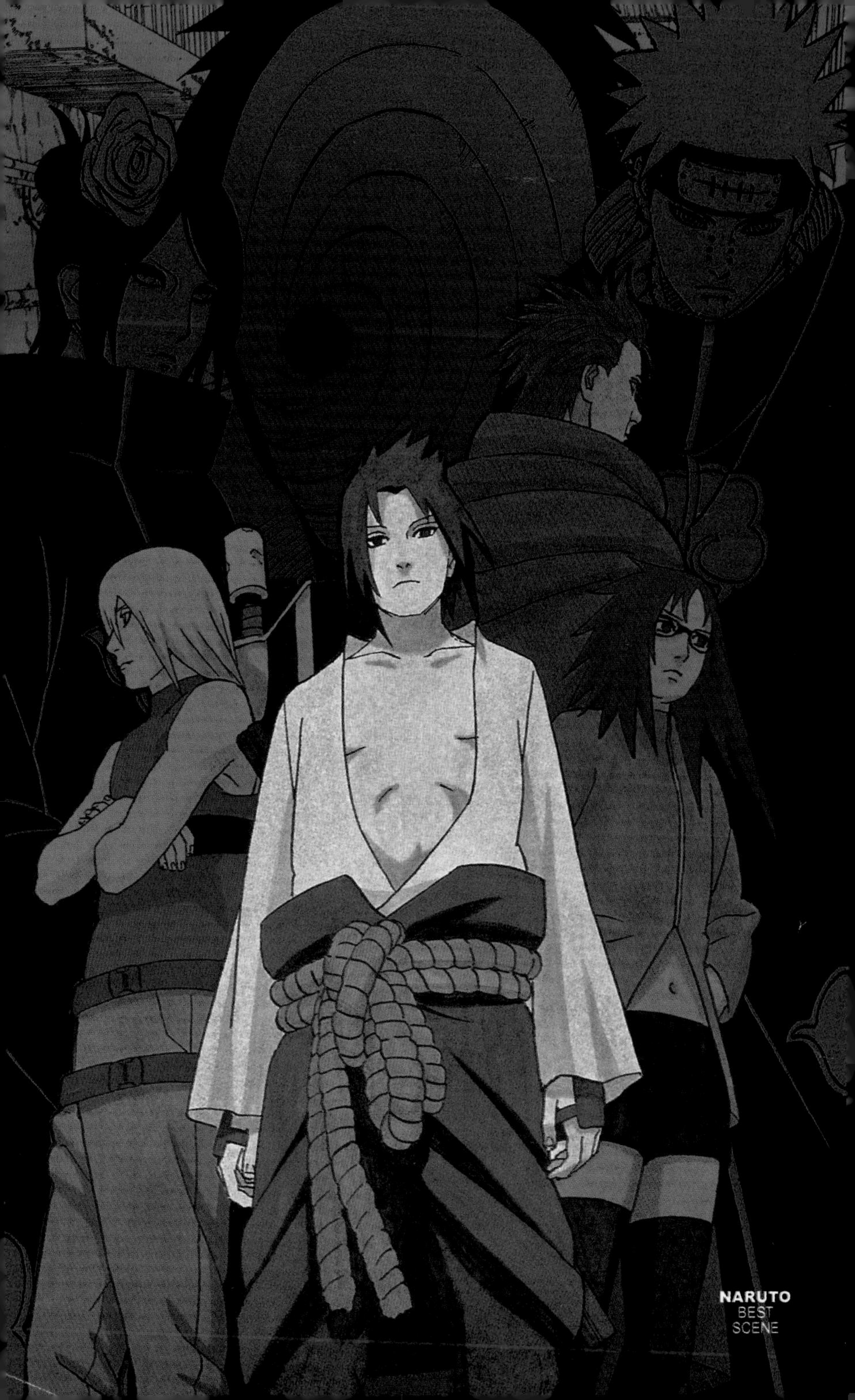
NARUTO
BEST
SCENE

者の書

Secret Files

Naruto: The Official Character Data Book

Secret Files

**Naruto: The Official
Character Data Book**

TABLE OF CONTENTS

Character Data
Naruto and company are analyzed from various angles. Find out secrets you never knew!

Reader Survey
Readers responded enthusiastically to the *Weekly Shonen Jump* magazine poll! Check out how readers voted!

The Konoha Collection
Untold mysteries of the ninja world revealed!

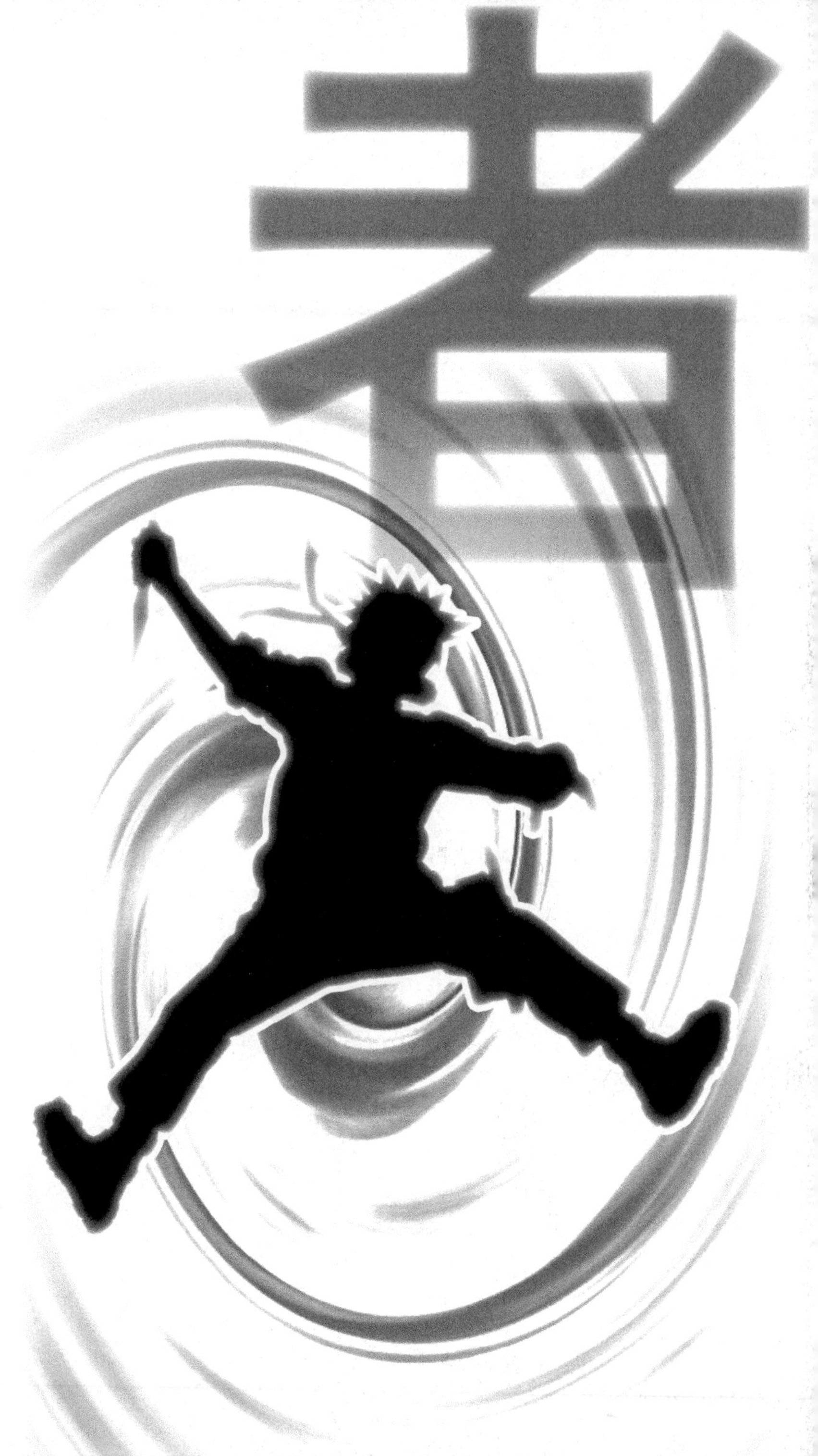
者

Shinobi Data

In the shadows of a turbulent world
Walked one hundred thirty-two shinobi
Whose tread left not a trace

【SHINOBI DATA】 –How to read data–

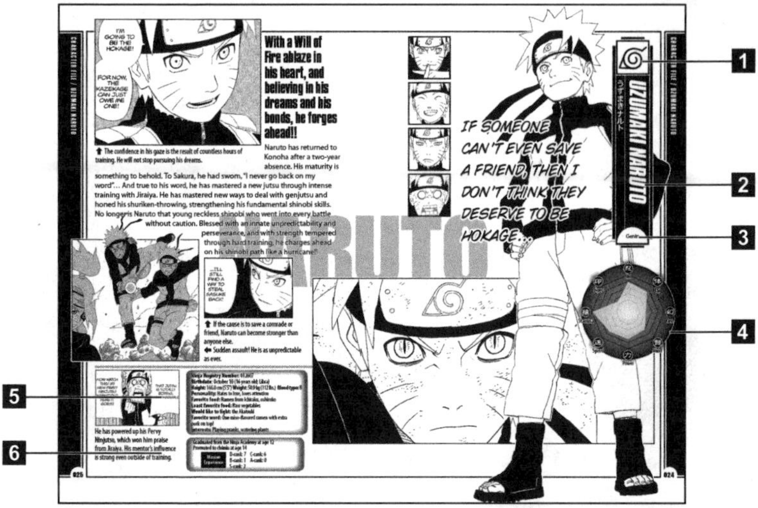
I'M GOING TO BE THE HOKAGE!
FOR NOW, THE KAZEKAGE CAN JUST OWE ME ONE!
With a Will of Fire ablaze in his heart, and believing in his dreams and his bonds, he forges ahead!!
The confidence in his gaze is the result of countless hours of training. He will not stop pursuing his dreams.
Naruto has returned to Konoha after a two-year absence. His maturity is something to behold. To Sakura, he had sworn, "I never go back on my word"... And true to his word, he has mastered a new jutsu through intense training with Jiraiya. He has mastered new ways to deal with genjutsu and honed his shuriken-throwing, strengthening his fundamental shinobi skills. No longer is Naruto that young reckless shinobi who went into every battle without caution. Blessed with an innate unpredictability and perseverance, and with strength tempered through hard training, he charges ahead on his shinobi path like a hurricane!!
NARUTO
If the cause is to save a comrade or friend, Naruto can become stronger than anyone else.
Sudden assault! He is as unpredictable as ever.
He has powered up his Pervy Ninjutsu, which won him praise from Jiraiya. His mentor's influence is strong even outside of training.
IF SOMEONE CAN'T EVEN SAVE A FRIEND, THEN I DON'T THINK THEY DESERVE TO BE HOKAGE...
UZUMAKI NARUTO
1
2
3
4
5
6

4 Skill parameter

忍 NIN - STEALTH
Symbolizes one's knowledge and proficiency in ninjutsu.

体 TAI - BODY
Symbolizes one's knowledge and proficiency in taijutsu.

幻 GEN - ILLUSION
Symbolizes one's knowledge and proficiency in genjutsu.

賢 MIND
Symbolizes wisdom. Indicates the level of knowledge and IQ.

力 POWER
Symbolizes physical strength, one's physical and muscular power.

速 SPEED
Symbolizes speed, quickness of movement and reflex.

精 STAMINA
Symbolizes the level of one's stamina or spiritual power, the foundation of chakra.

印 SIGNS
Symbolizes one's knowledge and proficiency in seals.

*These parameters are based on a shinobi's past performance. Skill levels are always changing.

5 Profile 1

Pertinent information about a character and his/her nature.

6 Profile 2

Mission experience and history.

1 Village emblem

Identifies the affiliation of a shinobi. The emblems of each village are illustrated below. A rogue shinobi is identified with his former village emblem, non-shinobi and unknown persons are identified with a "—."

The Village of Konohagakure	The Village of Sunagakure	The Village of Otogakure	The Village of Kirigakure	The Village of Amegakure
The Village of Kumogakure	The Village of Takigakure	The Village of Kusagakure	The Village of Ishigakure	The Village of Yugakure

2 Name of character

3 Shinobi rank

The icon that signifies a shinobi rank. The grades are as follows: genin, chûnin, special jônin, jônin, Anbu Black Ops, and Hokage. Rogue shinobi, those who have resigned or whose rank is unknown, unranked shinobi and other non-shinobi persons are identified with "—." Shinobi who are killed in the line of duty retain their rank at the time of their death.

*The Village of Amegakure does not have an academy, so a genin rank does not exist. It is marked with a "—."

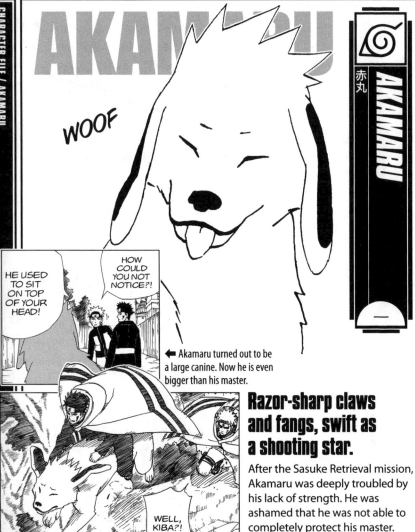

AKAMARU

赤丸 AKAMARU

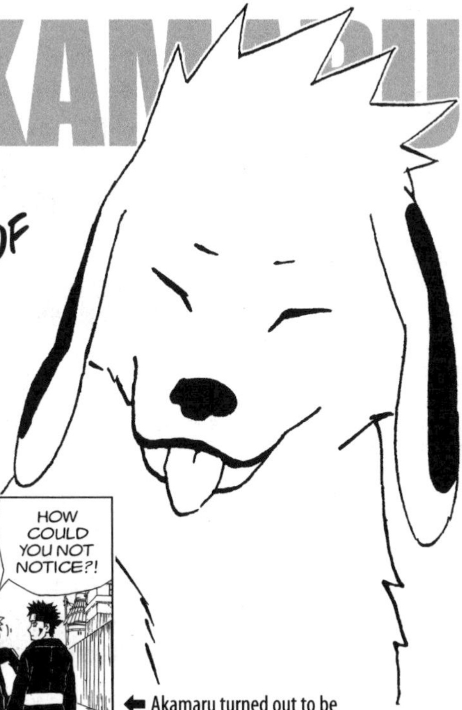
WOOF

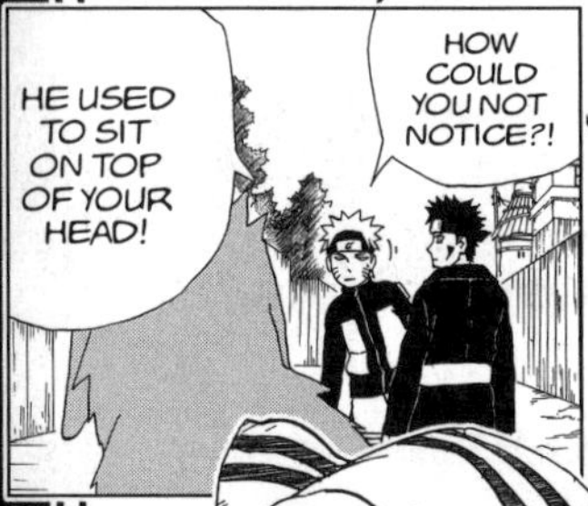
HOW COULD YOU NOT NOTICE?!
HE USED TO SIT ON TOP OF YOUR HEAD!

⬅ Akamaru turned out to be a large canine. Now he is even bigger than his master.

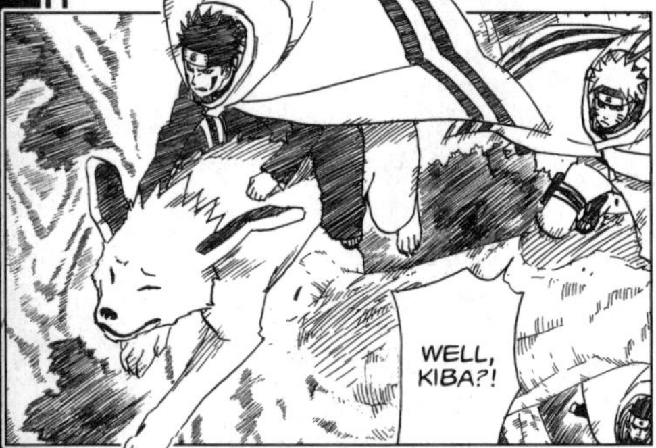
WELL, KIBA?!

⬆ The roles have switched. Kiba used to carry Akamaru, but now Kiba rides on Akamaru. With his sharp sense of smell and kido power, he usually leads the charge during a mission.

Razor-sharp claws and fangs, swift as a shooting star.

After the Sasuke Retrieval mission, Akamaru was deeply troubled by his lack of strength. He was ashamed that he was not able to completely protect his master.

Grow strong with Kiba and guard him! In the three years since, Akamaru has made this his mission in life and trained hard. The once little puppy has grown into a true protector.

Birthdate: July 7 (7 years old; Cancer)
Height: 127.2 cm (4'2") **Weight:** 80.5 kg (177 lbs.) **Blood type:** ?
Personality: Action-oriented, beastly
Favorite food: Dog food prepared specially by Kiba
Would like to spar with: Kuromaru

AKIMICHI CHOJI

秋道チョウジ

Chûnin

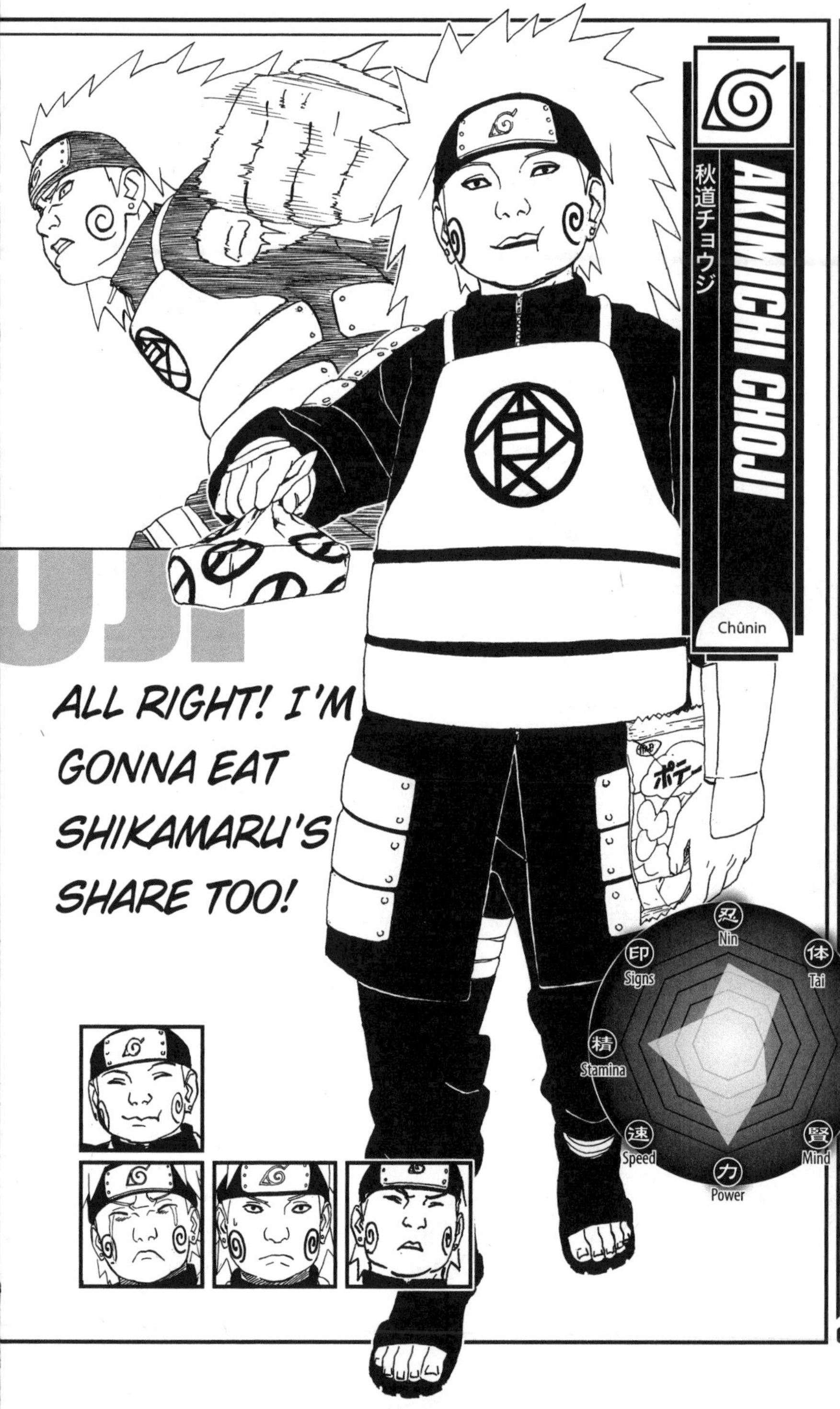
UJI
忍
Nin
体
Tai
幻
Gen
賢
Mind
力
Power
速
Speed
精
Stamina
印
Signs

ALL RIGHT! I'M GONNA EAT SHIKAMARU'S SHARE TOO!

Power honed by an insatiable appetite. He fills his belly and swings hard!!

Roughly three years earlier, Choji ingested the secret pellets of the Akimichi clan. Since then, he has been plagued by a new curse known as Rebound… As he grows in maturity, so does his weight. And his increasing girth can hardly be described as pleasingly plump. However, the battle that day gave Choji enormous confidence. He, too, had the strength to save his friends. That is the reason why Choji continues to train, and eat…believing that eating is a source of pride to the Akimichi clan.

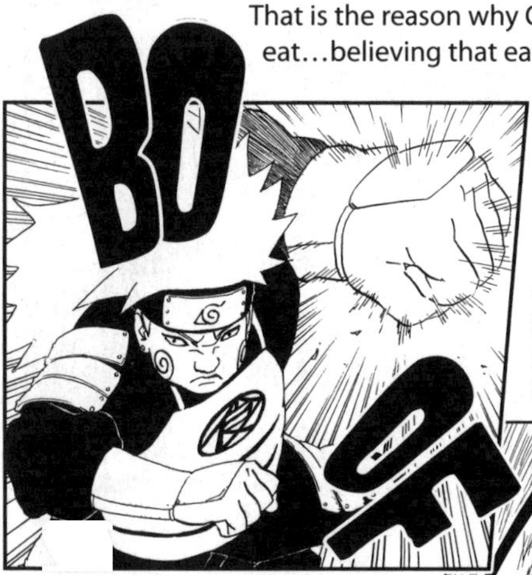
BO
OF

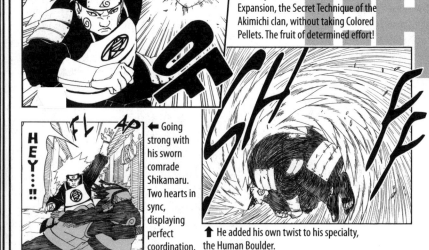

⬅ Choji masters the Art of Partial Expansion, the Secret Technique of the Akimichi clan, without taking Colored Pellets. The fruit of determined effort!

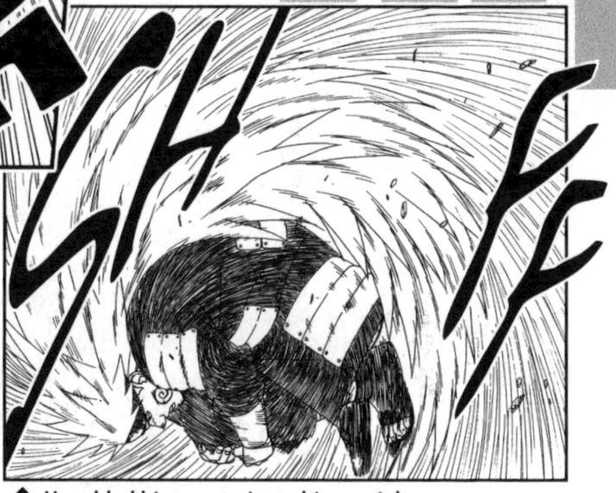
SH
FF

⬆ He added his own twist to his specialty, the Human Boulder.

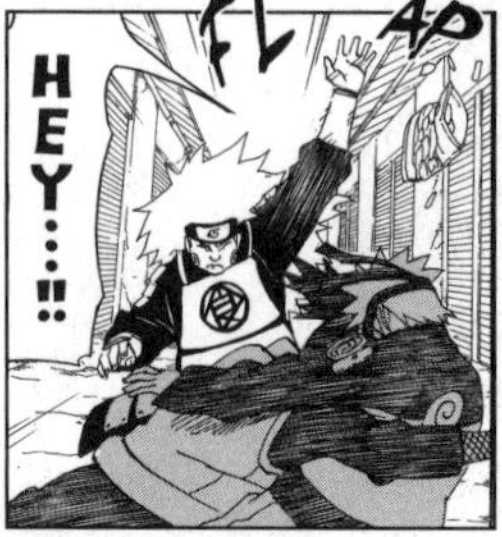
FL
AP
HEY…!!

⬅ Going strong with his sworn comrade Shikamaru. Two hearts in sync, displaying perfect coordination.

Ninja Registry Number: 012625
Birthdate: May 1 (16 years old; Taurus)
Height: 172.3 cm (5'8") **Weight:** 87.5 kg (193 lbs.) **Blood type:** B
Personality: Glutton, easygoing
Favorite food: Candy and chips to snack on, Korean BBQ
Least favorite food: Anything he cannot eat
Would like to fight: Anyone, as long as they give him food
Favorite word: meat
Interests: Buying food and eating it right away

Graduated from the Ninja Academy at age 12
Promoted to chûnin at age 14

Mission perience		
	D-rank: 17	C-rank: 13
	B-rank: 6	A-rank: 3
	S-rank: 0	

The gentler the person, the greater his wrath. One must never, ever utter that rude three-letter word in front of him (or any other word that might mean "not skinny"!).

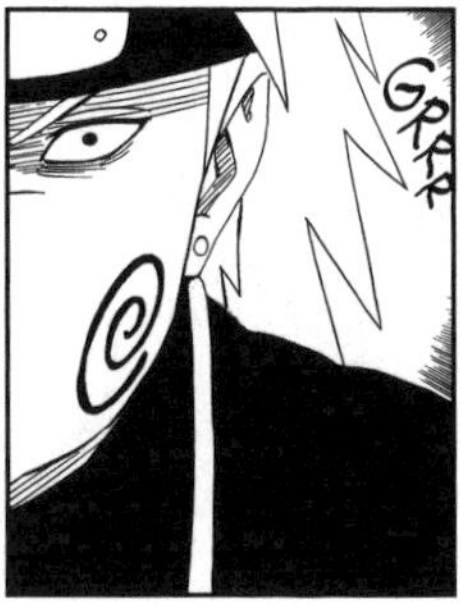
GRRR

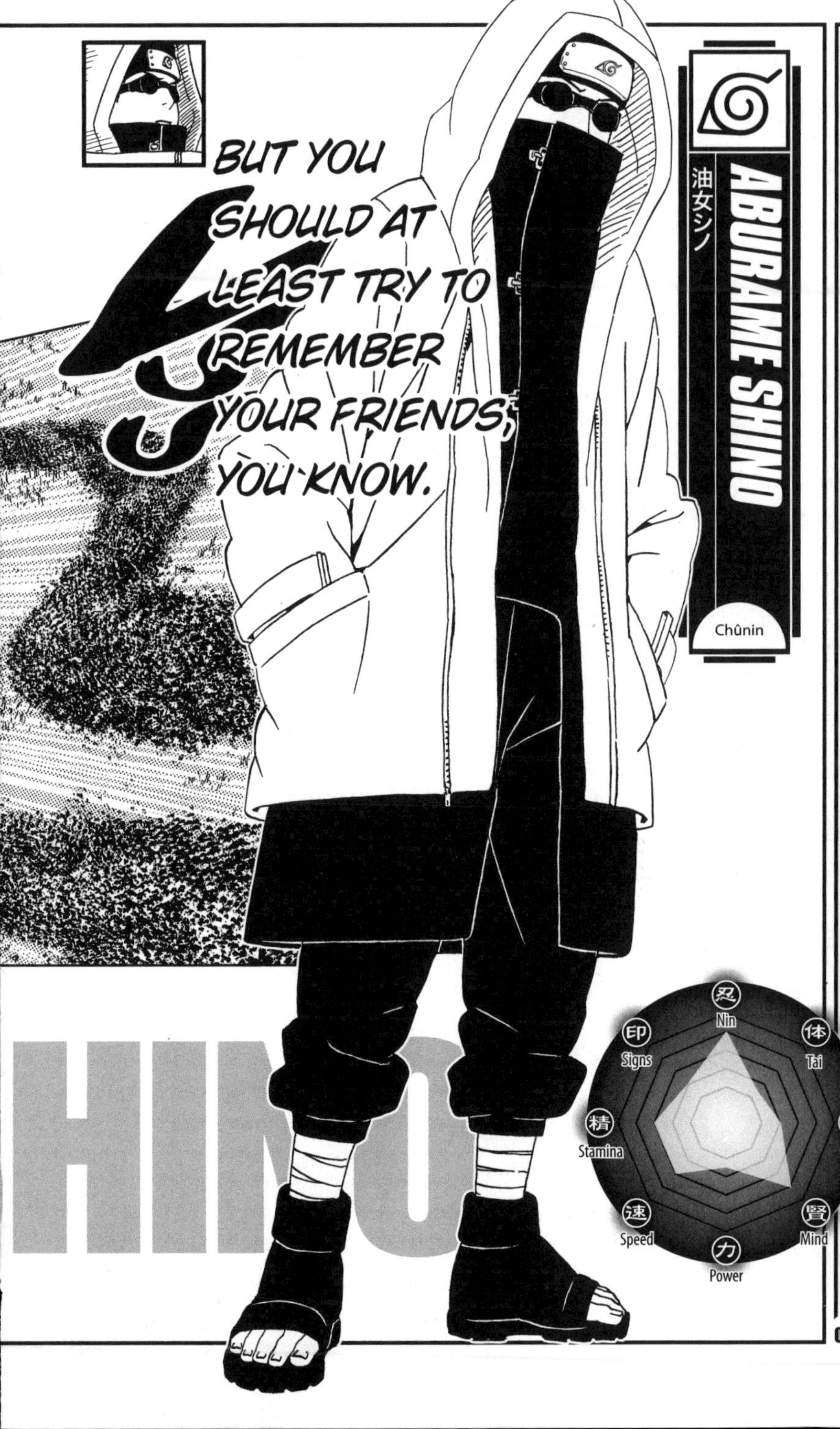
ABURAME SHINO
油女シノ
Chûnin
BUT YOU SHOULD AT LEAST TRY TO REMEMBER YOUR FRIENDS, YOU KNOW.
忍 Nin
体 Tai
幻 Gen
賢 Mind
力 Power
速 Speed
精 Stamina
印 Signs
HINO

Though he is shy and quiet, the swarming beetles inside him stir his true feelings!

DISPERSE.

To the Aburame clan, being silent is their way of communicating with the beetles that reside in their bodies. The rich dialogue Shino has had with his beetles these past few years has strengthened their bond.

↑ Communicating daily garners results. The ability to control those loyal beetles as his clones...

As a result, his hijutsu has matured and reached the ultimate level of perfection. The beetles carry Shino and his comrades to victory in battle and instill fear in their enemies. It is the destiny of members of the Aburame clan to feel uncomfortable speaking to humans. Despite that, Shino quietly fulfills his duties. It is how he lives up to his creed of *action before words*.

GO.

...WHILE IN ACTUALITY, HE CAUSED YOU AND YOUR JUTSU TO PASS THROUGH HIM.

SO IN SHORT, HE JUST MADE IT LOOK LIKE HE EVADED IT AND YOU...

← A man of few words, he can focus on a battle situation and analyze it. He towers above the rest in this skill.

...NARUTO.

YOU RECOG-NIZED KIBA RIGHT AWAY...

His destiny makes him feel isolated from others. But he will speak his mind when you least expect it!

Ninja Registry Number: 012618
Birthdate: January 23 (16 years old; Aquarius)
Height: 175.1 cm (5'9") **Weight:** 56.6 kg (125 lbs.) **Blood type:** AB
Personality: Austere, secretive, poker-faced
Favorite food: A salad with wildflowers and field greens, gourd-melon
Least favorite food: Food with strong odors
Would like to fight: Someone strong
Favorite word: trump card
Interests: Observing insects (monitoring their condition)

Graduated from the Ninja Academy at age 12
Promoted to chûnin at age 14

Mission Experience	D-rank: 17	C-rank: 17
	B-rank: 9	A-rank: 1
	S-rank: 0	

INUZUKA KIBA

犬塚キバ

Chûnin

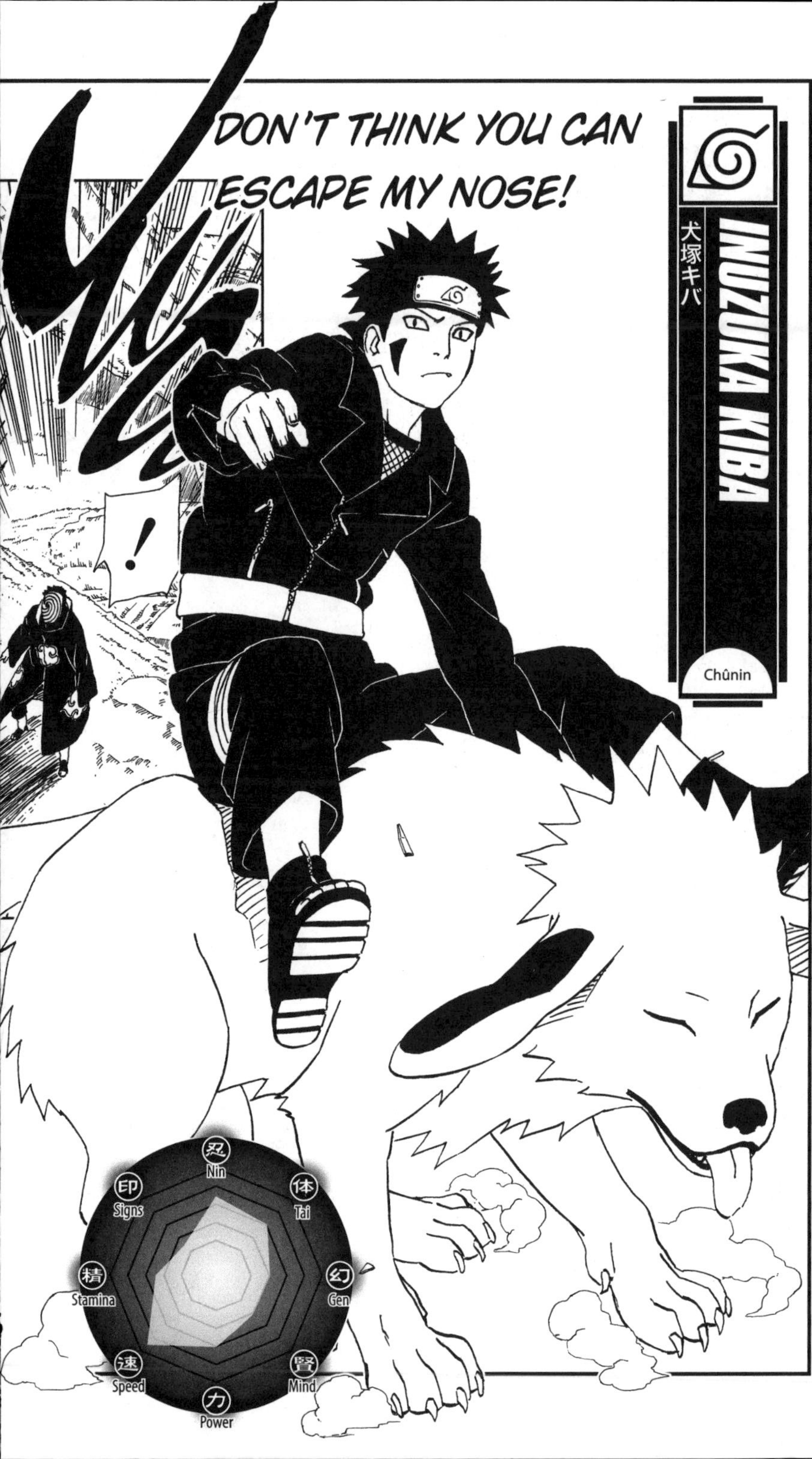
DON'T THINK YOU CAN ESCAPE MY NOSE!
!
忍 Nin
体 Tai
幻 Gen
賢 Mind
力 Power
速 Speed
精 Stamina
印 Signs

A loyal ninja hound, and fangs that will rip through the air at super speed!

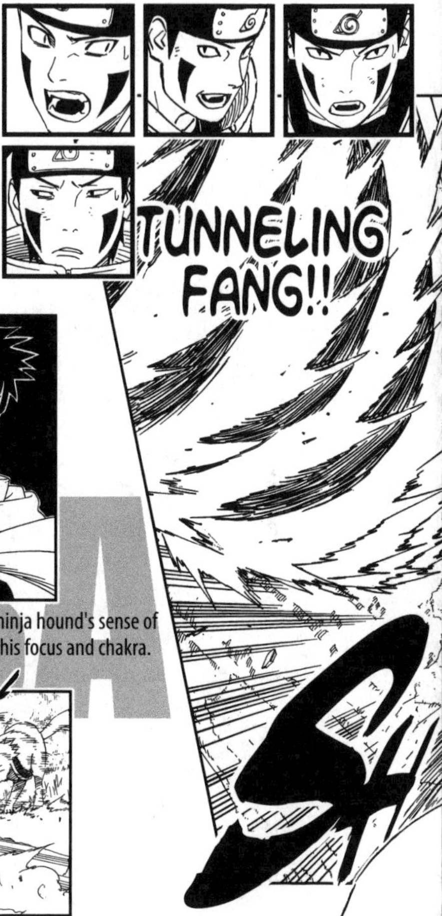
TUNNELING FANG!!

After the Sasuke Retrieval mission, Kiba had one thought in mind. He had to be strong enough to fight alongside his partner, Akamaru, as well as protect him. Since that time, Kiba has continued to strengthen his body and sharpen his already keen instincts of the wild, a characteristic unique to his clan. Living with that need to protect over these past three years has given Kiba a new weapon for his hurricane wolf fangs.

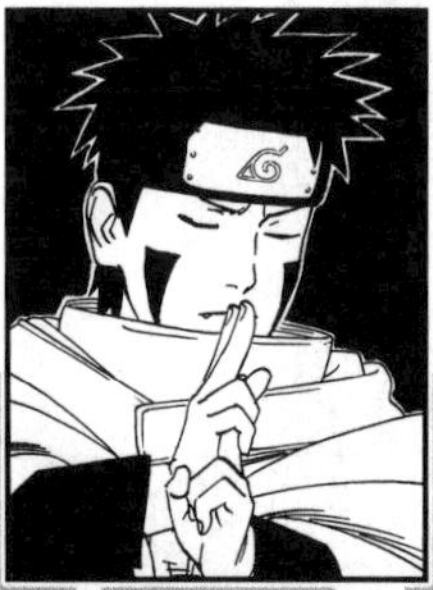

⬆ He can surpass a ninja hound's sense of smell by intensifying his focus and chakra.

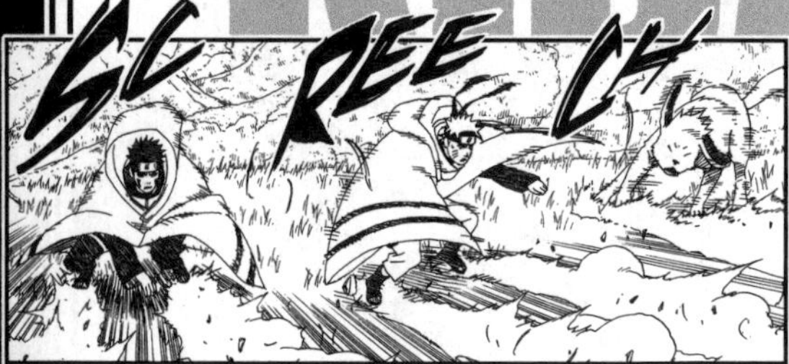
SCREECH

⬆ Kiba is now able to take impromptu action with someone other than Akamaru. He can execute a perfect attack formation even with Naruto, in spite of the short amount of time Naruto has been back home.

Ninja Registry Number: 012620
Birthdate: July 7 (16 years old; Cancer)
Height: 169.1 cm (5'6") **Weight:** 52.5 kg (116 lbs.) **Blood type:** B
Personality: Action-oriented, short-tempered, wild
Favorite food: Beef jerky, gristle
Least favorite food: Soft foods that you cannot sink your teeth into
Would like to fight: Uzumaki Naruto
Favorite word: Akamaru
Interests: Taking Akamaru for a walk

Graduated from the Ninja Academy at age 12
Promoted to chûnin at age 14

Mission Experience		
	D-rank: 21	C-rank: 19
	B-rank: 8	A-rank: 2
	S-rank: 0	

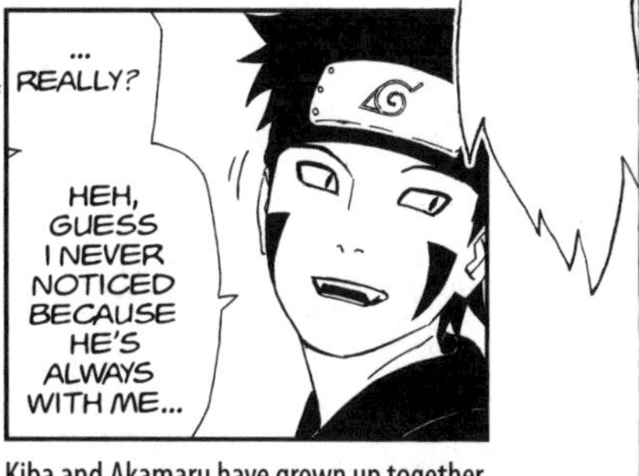
...REALLY?
HEH, GUESS I NEVER NOTICED BECAUSE HE'S ALWAYS WITH ME...

Kiba and Akamaru have grown up together. Even if Akamaru matures into an adult hound, their love will never change.

NARUTO... IT'S A WONDERFUL NAME.

うずまきクシナ

UZUMAKI KUSHINA

Ninja Registry Number: ?
Birthdate: July 10 (? years old; Cancer)
Height: 165.0 cm (5'5") **Weight:** 47.0 kg (104 lbs.) **Blood type:** B
Personality: Tomboy, hates to lose
Favorite food: Shio ramen
Least favorite food: Bitter-tasting food, coffee
Would like to fight: No one in particular
Favorite word: Never say die
Interests: Chit-chats, playing pranks

Graduated from the Ninja Academy at age ?
Promoted to chûnin at age ?

Mission Experience	D-rank: ?	C-rank: ?
	B-rank: ?	A-rank: ?
	S-rank: ?	

KUS

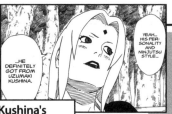

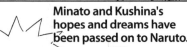

⬇ With Minato, she envisioned peace in her village. The light of her life was her son, Naruto, to whom she passed on her optimism.

YEAH... HIS PER-SONALITY AND NINJUTSU STYLE...
...HE DEFINITELY GOT FROM UZUMAKI KUSHINA.

⬅ Skilled in ninjutsu and more spirited than a man, even the Three Great Shinobi had heard of her prowess.

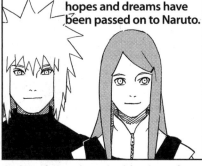

Minato and Kushina's hopes and dreams have been passed on to Naruto.

She dreamt of a future for her unborn child. This red-haired kunoichi who could rival a man.

A former kunoichi from the Land of Eddies, she gave birth to Naruto. Having grown up during the turbulent civil war years, Kushina fervently wished for days of peace and calm. After meeting her life companion and bearing his child, Kushina should have found peace.

However, due to the Nine-Tailed Beast, that peace was shattered. So it was to Naruto that Kushina entrusted her dream of the future and her indomitable spirit.

Collection ... Number 1

Konoha

UZUMAKI NARUTO

HOW HE GOT HIS NAME

I REALLY HOPE MY SOON-TO-BE BORN CHILD...
...CAN BECOME A SPLENDID SHINOBI JUST LIKE THIS MAIN CHARACTER!

⬆ Named after a shinobi literary hero, Naruto is destined to walk the same path!

⬇ He got his name from Jiraiya. Perhaps his love of ramen can also be traced to his name?

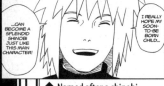

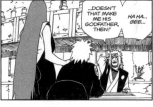

HA HA... GEE...
...DOESN'T THAT MAKE ME HIS GODFATHER, THEN?

Naruto: This is the name used by Jiraiya, who would become Naruto's teacher, for the hero of his autobiographical novel. Deeply impressed by the hero's never-say-die attitude that was so like Jiraiya's, Minato and Kushina asked to name their son Naruto with the hope that he would inherit the hero's traits.

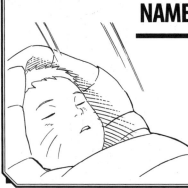

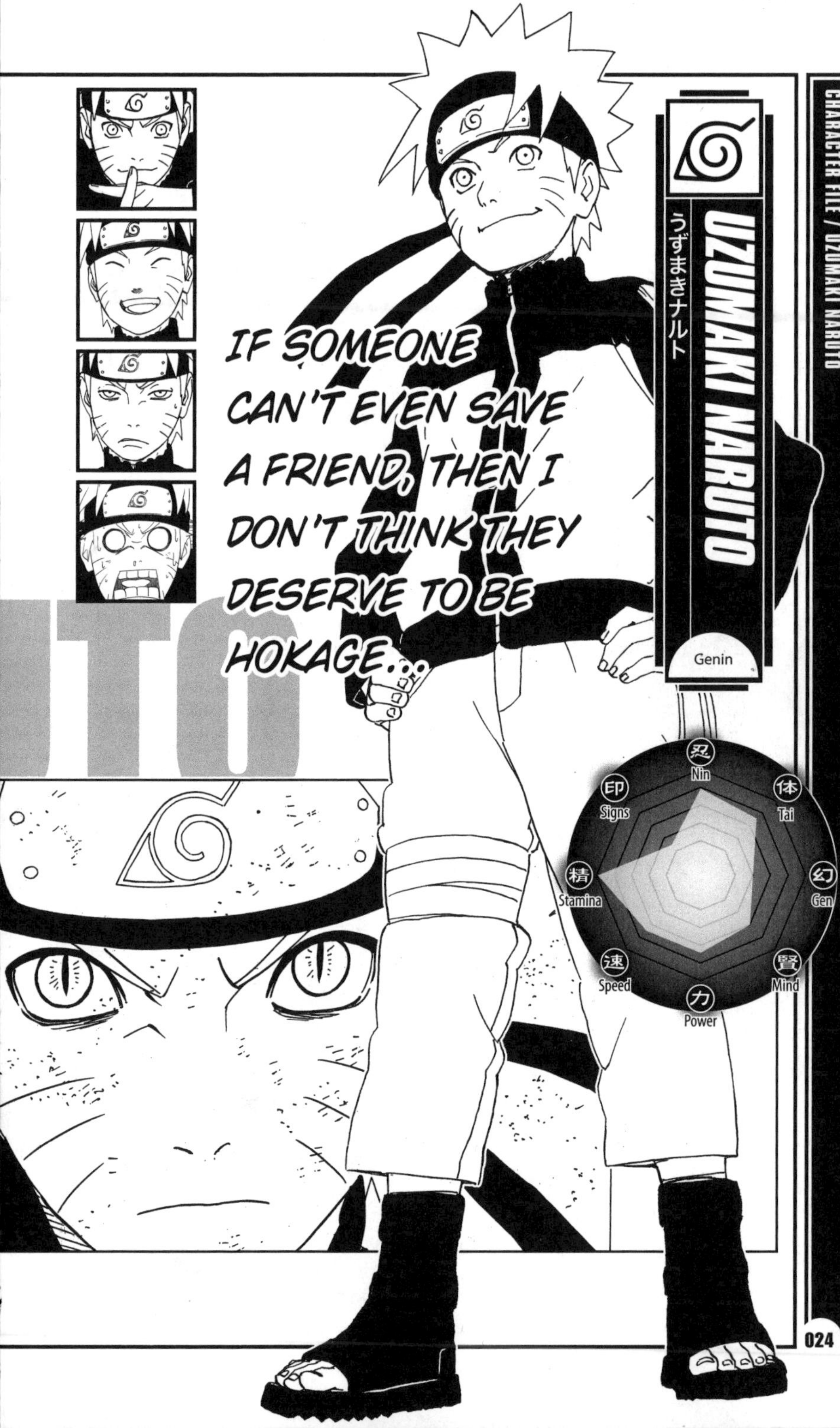
UZUMAKI NARUTO
うずまきナルト
Genin
IF SOMEONE CAN'T EVEN SAVE A FRIEND, THEN I DON'T THINK THEY DESERVE TO BE HOKAGE...
忍 Nin
体 Tai
幻 Gen
賢 Mind
力 Power
速 Speed
精 Stamina
印 Signs

I'M GOING TO BE THE HOKAGE!

FOR NOW, THE KAZEKAGE CAN JUST OWE ME ONE!

⬆ The confidence in his gaze is the result of countless hours of training. He will not stop pursuing his dreams.

With a Will of Fire ablaze in his heart, and believing in his dreams and his bonds, he forges ahead!!

Naruto has returned to Konoha after a two-year absence. His maturity is something to behold. To Sakura, he had sworn, "I never go back on my word"… And true to his word, he has mastered a new jutsu through intense training with Jiraiya. He has mastered new ways to deal with genjutsu and honed his shuriken-throwing, strengthening his fundamental shinobi skills. No longer is Naruto that young reckless shinobi who went into every battle without caution. Blessed with an innate unpredictability and perseverance, and with strength tempered through hard training, he charges ahead on his shinobi path like a hurricane!!

…I'LL STILL FIND A WAY TO STEAL SASUKE BACK!

⬆ If the cause is to save a comrade or friend, Naruto can become stronger than anyone else.
⬅ Sudden assault! He is as unpredictable as ever.

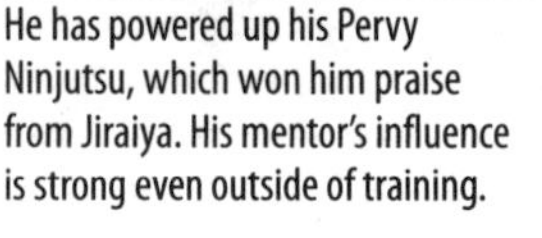

NOW WATCH THIS! MY NEW PERVY NINJUTSU INVENTION!! HERE IT GOES!!

THAT JUTSU IS TOTALLY BORING, KONOHAMARU!!

He has powered up his Pervy Ninjutsu, which won him praise from Jiraiya. His mentor's influence is strong even outside of training.

Ninja Registry Number: 012607
Birthdate: October 10 (16 years old; Libra)
Height: 166.0 cm (5'5") **Weight:** 50.9 kg (112 lbs.) **Blood type:** B
Personality: Hates to lose, loves attention
Favorite food: Ramen from Ichiraku, oshiruko
Least favorite food: Raw vegetables
Would like to fight: the Akatsuki
Favorite word: One miso-flavored ramen with extra pork on top!
Interests: Playing pranks, watering plants

Graduated from the Ninja Academy at age 12
Promoted to chûnin at age —

Mission Experience		
D-rank: 7	C-rank: 1	
B-rank: 2	A-rank: 6	
S-rank: 0		

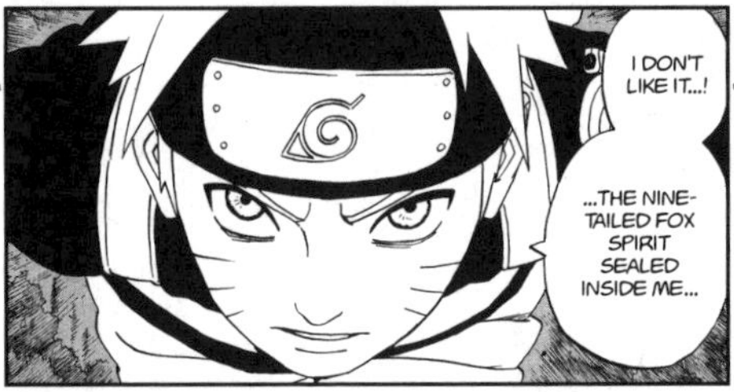
I DON'T LIKE IT...!
...THE NINE-TAILED FOX SPIRIT SEALED INSIDE ME...

⬆ Filled with rage when he learns the reason why the Akatsuki is after him.

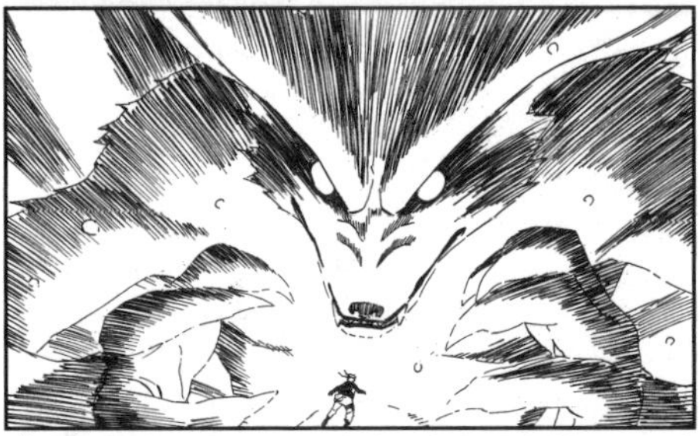

⬆ A jinchûriki is destined to clash with the Tailed Beast inside him for all eternity.

The sorrow of one who harbors a Tailed Beast.

《Jinchûriki》

Those with a Tailed Beast sealed inside suffer the same fate regardless of the village they live in. Naruto was shunned and lonely. So he knows firsthand how badly Gaara feels. It doesn't matter that Naruto is Leaf and Gaara is Sand. Naruto's only wish is to save Gaara from the darkness and to share the happiness he himself has now found, the same way Naruto's teacher, Iruka, saved him when he was a child.

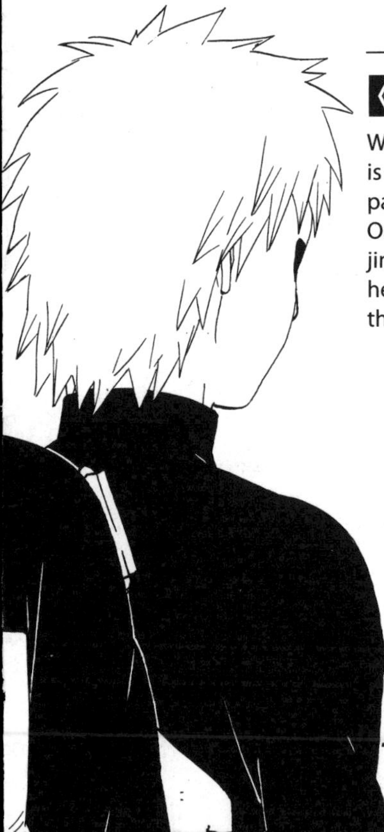

《Shared Pain》

When Naruto hears that Gaara is Kazekage, he is genuinely happy. When faced with Gaara's passing, Naruto cries real tears of deep sorrow. Only a jinchûriki can truly understand another jinchûriki. Only one who has shouldered the heavy burden since childhood can comprehend the other's joys and sorrows.

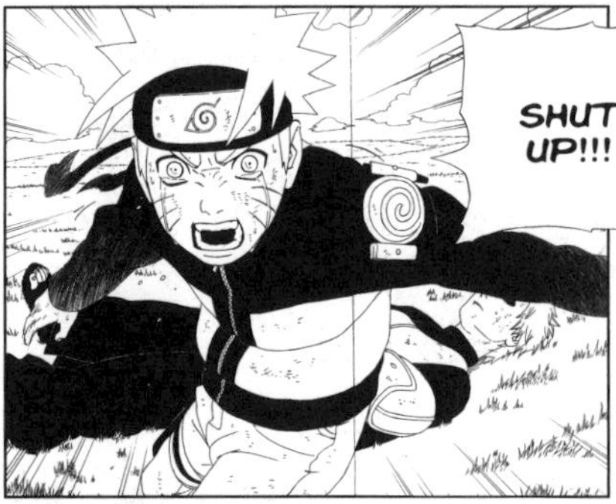
SHUT UP!!!

⬆ Naruto feels the pain of Gaara's death as if it were his own.

➡⬇ The warmth one feels from Naruto is closer to the warmth of a family member than a comrade. His unending kindness touches the hearts of many.

YOU HAD US WORRIED...!

A friendship without barriers clears the way for a new future.

...

《A strange power》

Alongside both Leaf and Sand ninja, Naruto runs to save Gaara. Naruto has the power to bring people together. He can get along with anybody, even if he's battled them before. His friendship is without prejudice and goes beyond national borders, spreading and instilling hope. He understands the lonely and cherishes the bonds between people. Because of that, Naruto is able to touch the hearts of many.

《Entrusted with the future》

The Great Ninja Wars and Operation Destroy Konoha! Leaf and Sand have engaged in battle time after time. But their fates are ultimately tied to the same fate. It is Naruto's destiny to shine the light on that future that both villages must forge.

YEAH...
NOW I GET WHAT GRANNY WISHED FOR!

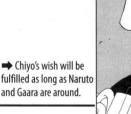

➡ Chiyo's wish will be fulfilled as long as Naruto and Gaara are around.

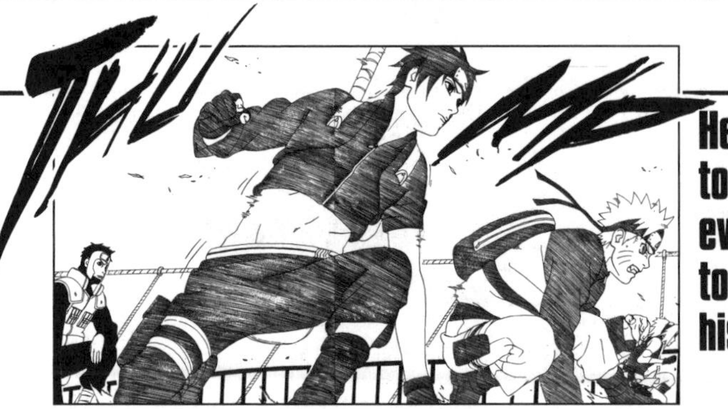
THUMP

He is willing to risk everything to protect his bonds.

⬆ Teamwork is the key to success on a mission. He brushes off uncertainty and keeps looking straight ahead.

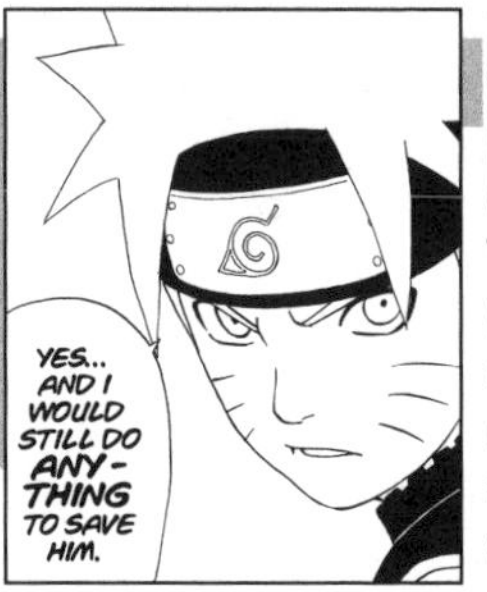
YES... AND I WOULD STILL DO ANY-THING TO SAVE HIM.

《 Team Kakashi 》

The new Team Kakashi! Naruto rejects new member Sai. He still believes that Sasuke is the only third member of the team. Naruto understands the true nature of teamwork but refuses to acknowledge Sai who is insulting to the team and disdainful of the missing Sasuke.

⬆ Teamwork is the key to success on a mission. He brushes off uncertainty and keeps looking straight ahead.

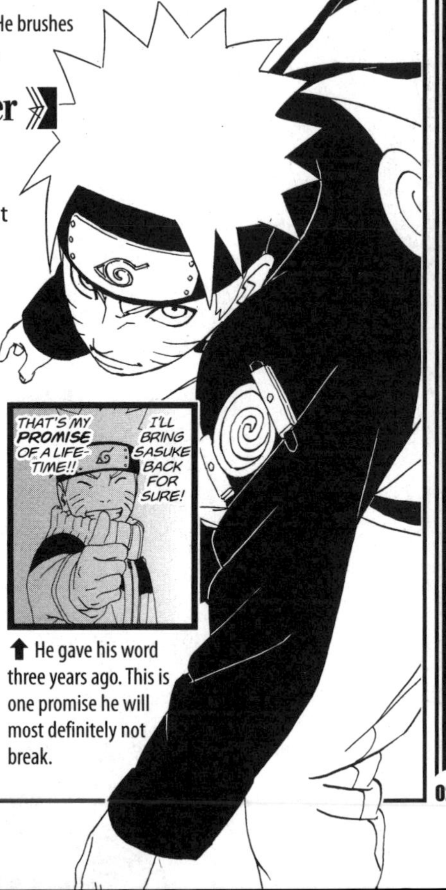

《 A Forbidden Power 》

Through his training with Jiraiya, Naruto learns how to control Nine Tails' strength. But it simply has too much power to be completely dominated.

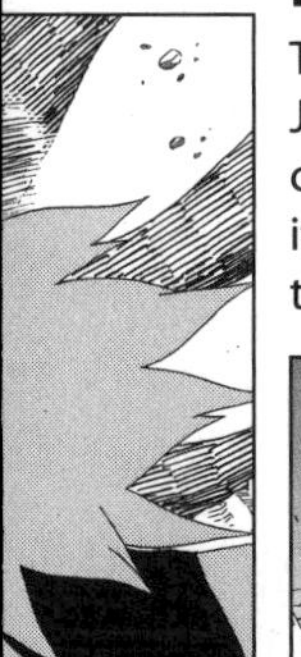

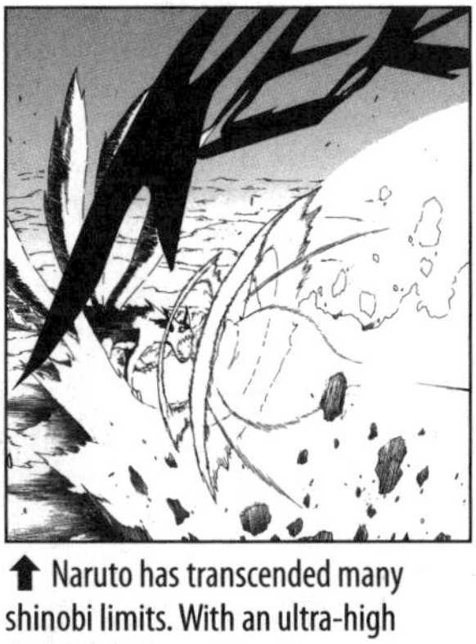

⬆ Naruto has transcended many shinobi limits. With an ultra-high density chakra cannon, he can now turn almost anything in his line of sight into dust and ash.

I'LL BRING SASUKE BACK FOR SURE!
THAT'S MY PROMISE OF A LIFE-TIME!!

⬆ He gave his word three years ago. This is one promise he will most definitely not break.

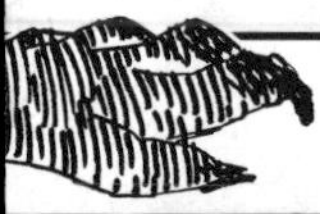

《Impatience》

He is in a rush. He feels pressured. Almost immediately Orochimaru undergoes his next reincarnation. And Sasuke is still just beyond Naruto's saving grasp. Naruto must reach out to the power of the Nine-Tailed Fox.

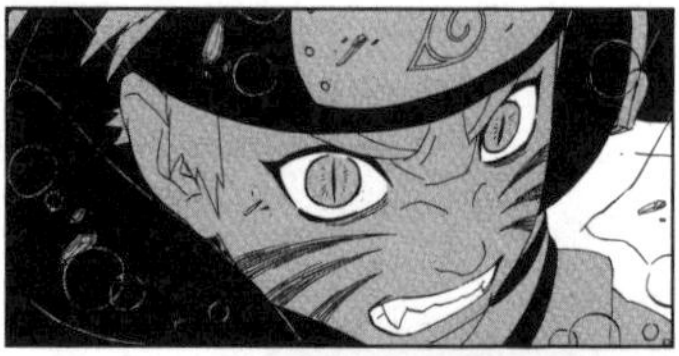

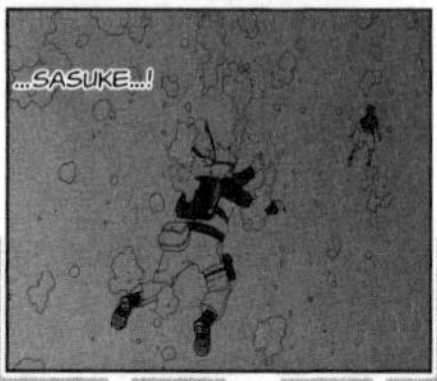
...SASUKE...!

⬆➡ He still lacks power to save Sasuke.

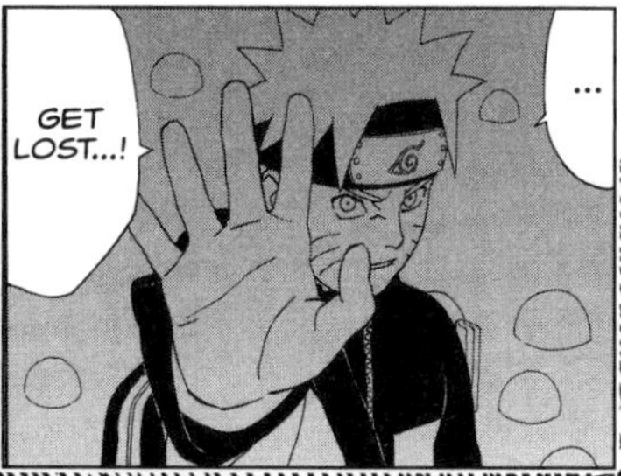
...
GET LOST...!

⬆ When the Nine-Tailed Fox seeks to break the seal once more, Naruto rejects it of his own free will.

《Real Strength》

The power of Nine Tails' fourth tail, a double-edged blade that hurts even his own body. After hearing the truth from Yamato, Naruto makes up his mind. He will never use this power again. In order to protect the people dear to him, he decides to trust his own chakra, which will hopefully make him able to endure the destructive chakra of Nine Tails.

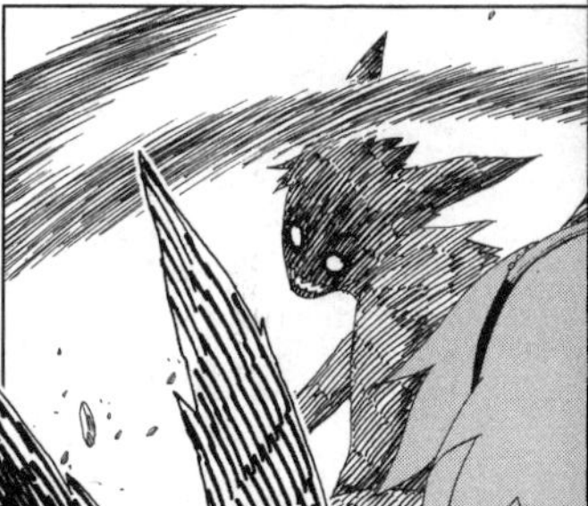

➡ His inner self collapses, and he destroys all that come into his view.

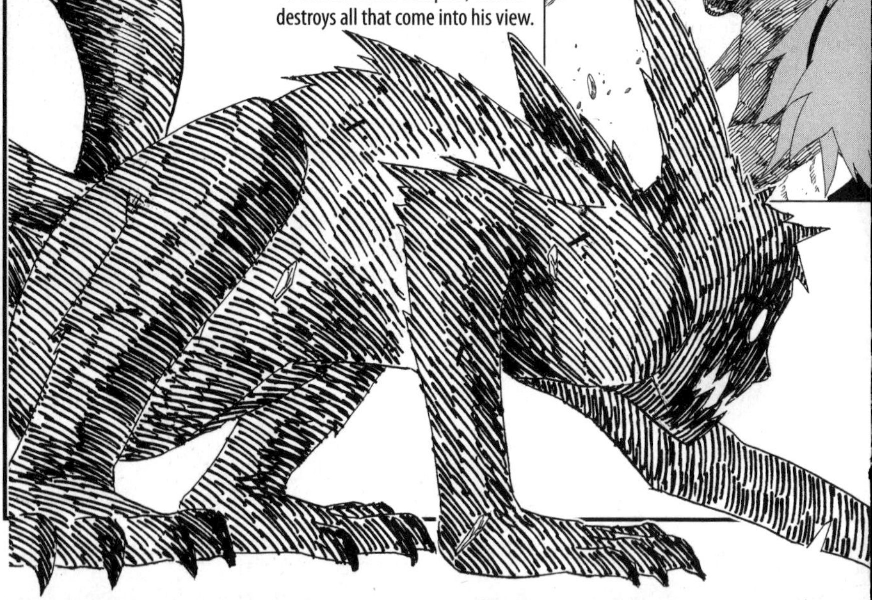

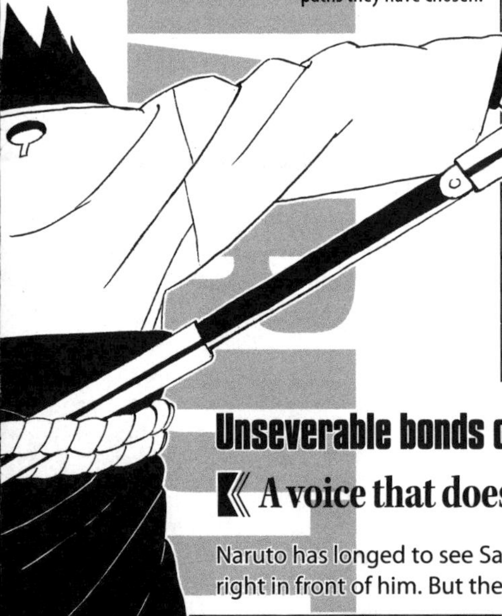

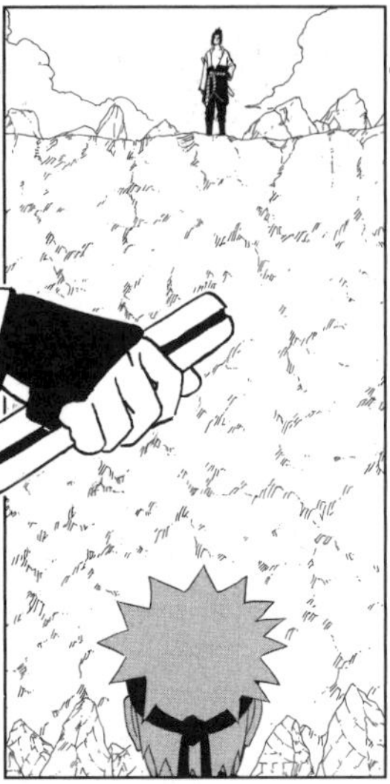

➡ Sasuke towers over Naruto as if to show the distance between the paths they have chosen.

Unseverable bonds of the heart.

《A voice that does not reach far enough》

Naruto has longed to see Sasuke again. And now here he is, right in front of him. But the distance between them has grown even more. Naruto still has faith that Sasuke feels the bond with his friends. After all, Sasuke didn't kill him in the battle at the Final Valley. Yet Sasuke heartlessly points his blade at Naruto. Is Naruto too late to save him? No! He cannot give up. He made a promise!

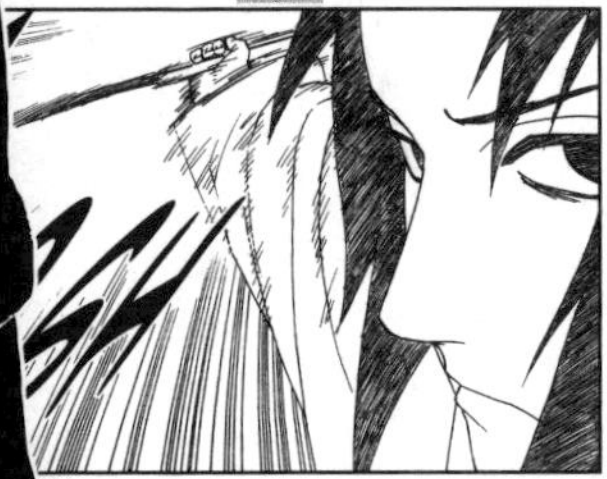

⬆ Sasuke's eyes have become even colder. He aims his blade at Naruto without hesitation.

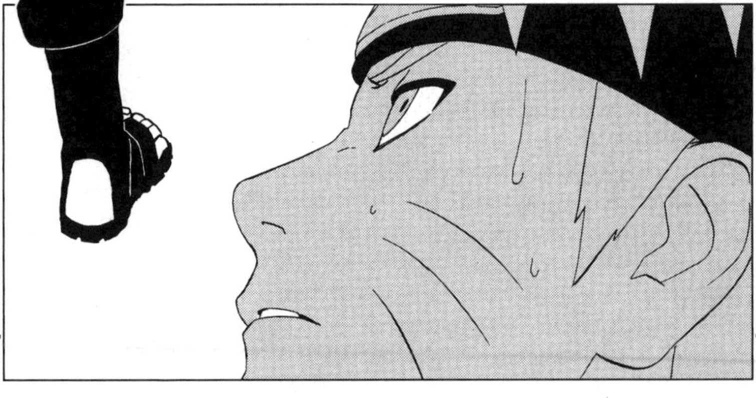

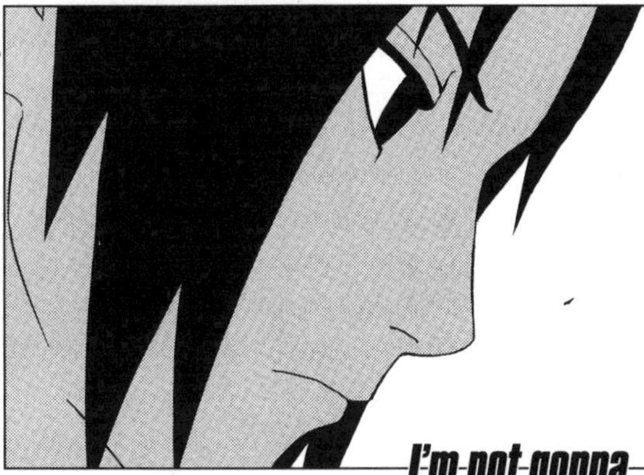

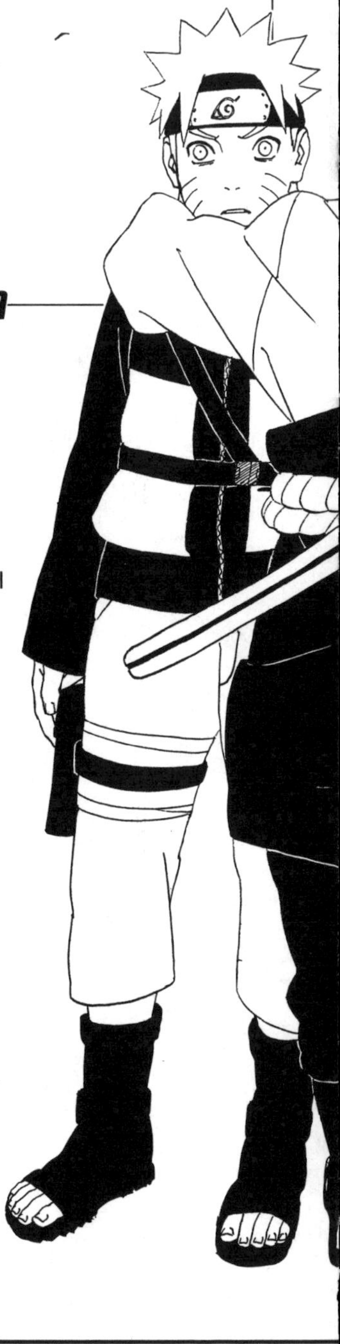

I'm not gonna give up. Naruto's shinobi way.

⬇ Naruto is able to persist because of his friends' loyalty.

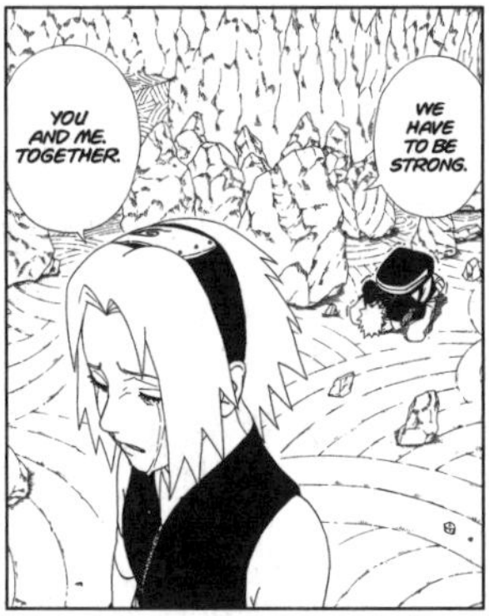
WE HAVE TO BE STRONG.
YOU AND ME. TOGETHER.

《 Hope 》

The Sasuke Retrieval Mission is over. But Naruto is more determined than ever. He has to get Sasuke back on his side. Backed by friends and comrades, Naruto burns with fighting spirit. The only way to save Sasuke is to never give up.

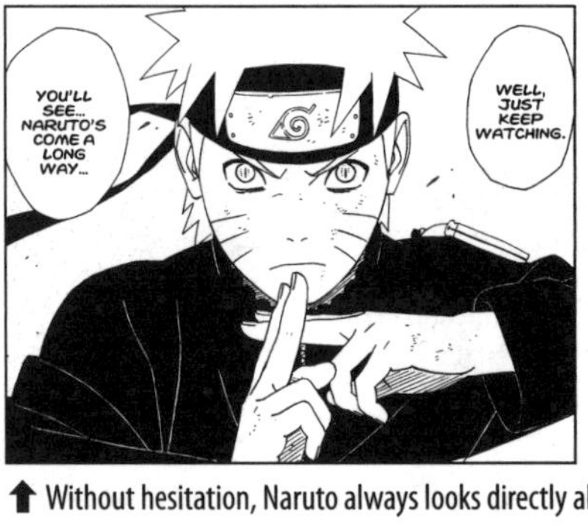
WELL, JUST KEEP WATCHING.
YOU'LL SEE... NARUTO'S COME A LONG WAY...

⬆ Without hesitation, Naruto always looks directly ahead!

A hint of a legend

VWEEN

➡ He challenges himself to perfect a new jutsu that even the Fourth Hokage could not master.

《 Training 》

Kakashi's idea, the Shadow Doppelganger Training Method, is ideal for Naruto, who possesses an enormous amount of chakra. He mastered change in chakra nature, which normally requires years of training, in just two days.

NARUTO

《 Sasuke 》

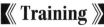

Having a good rival can be a motivating force to grow faster. The existence of the genius Sasuke, who is always ahead of him, has made Naruto more passionate about training. And that has made his abilities blossom.

BUT THAT'S THE POINT...
...SASUKE'S THE ONE I'VE GOTTA CATCH UP TO!!

⬆ Because Sasuke exists, Naruto can become stronger.

《 The shinobi who will surpass the Fourth Hokage 》

To this day, no one had used this ultimate, yet incomplete, jutsu. Not even the Fourth Hokage could perfect it. But Naruto has honed it to the point of actually using it in a fight... The loser at the Academy is about to evolve into a shinobi who will be the next generation's guiding force.

BOF BOF BO

⬆ He quickly puts into use his Shadow Clone Jutsu, which can store his experience.

RAAGH!

⬆➡ The rasen which the Fourth Hokage created has been passed on to his son and swirls like a storm.

UCHIHA IZUNA

うちはイズナ

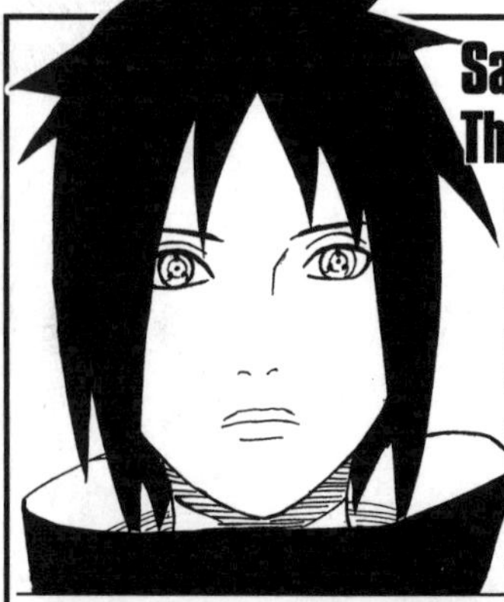

Sacrificed for his clan. The pillar of the Uchiha clan.

His older brother, who is the leader of the Uchiha, loses his eyesight—which signifies ruin for the clan. Silently and without hesitation, Izuna presents his own eyes. For a member of the Uchiha clan famous for its ocular ninjutsu, this act is tantamount to complete self-destruction.

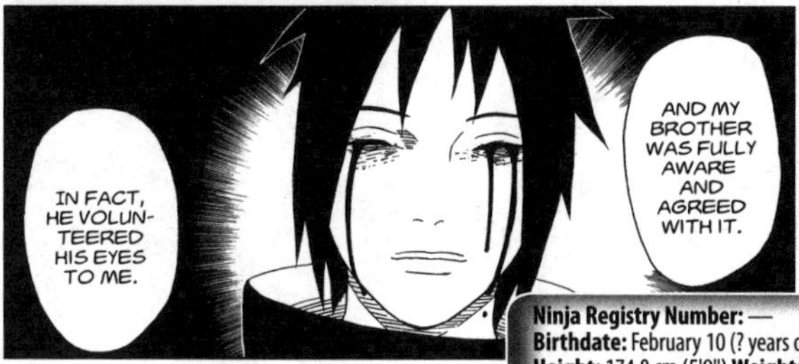
AND MY BROTHER WAS FULLY AWARE AND AGREED WITH IT.
IN FACT, HE VOLUNTEERED HIS EYES TO ME.

⬆ Izuna, who gives his eyes to his older brother, eventually dies in battle.

Ninja Registry Number: —
Birthdate: February 10 (? years old; Aquarius)
Height: 174.8 cm (5'9") **Weight:** 55.9 kg (123 lbs.) **Blood type:** O
Personality: Devoted, peace-loving
Interests: Training with older brother

Collection ... Number 2

Konoha

THE MANGEKYO SHARINGAN BLOOD-STAINED DESTINY

There is only one way to keep from going blind. That is to steal a new Mangekyo Sharingan from a clan member. Madara resorts to this abominable act. The Mangekyo Sharingan, a cursed ocular ninjutsu only obtainable through great sacrifice.

⬇ Both these gifted brothers became enlightened with the Mangekyo Sharingan.

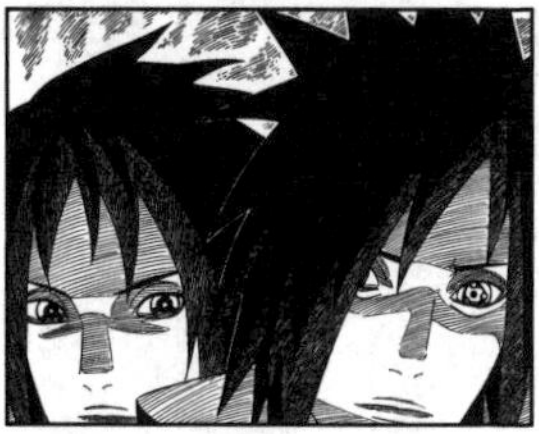

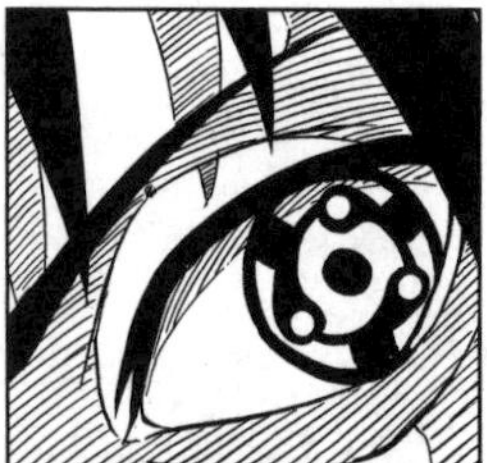

⬅ Using his younger brother's eye, Madara obtained an everlasting Mangekyo Sharingan.

Through the entire history of the Uchiha clan, it was rare for a member to be able to wield the Mangekyo Sharingan. It hides a power that is frightening, as are the risks. With every use, it robs the sight of the caster. One cannot fathom the anxiety of suddenly going blind that the user of this powerful ocular ninjutsu feels.

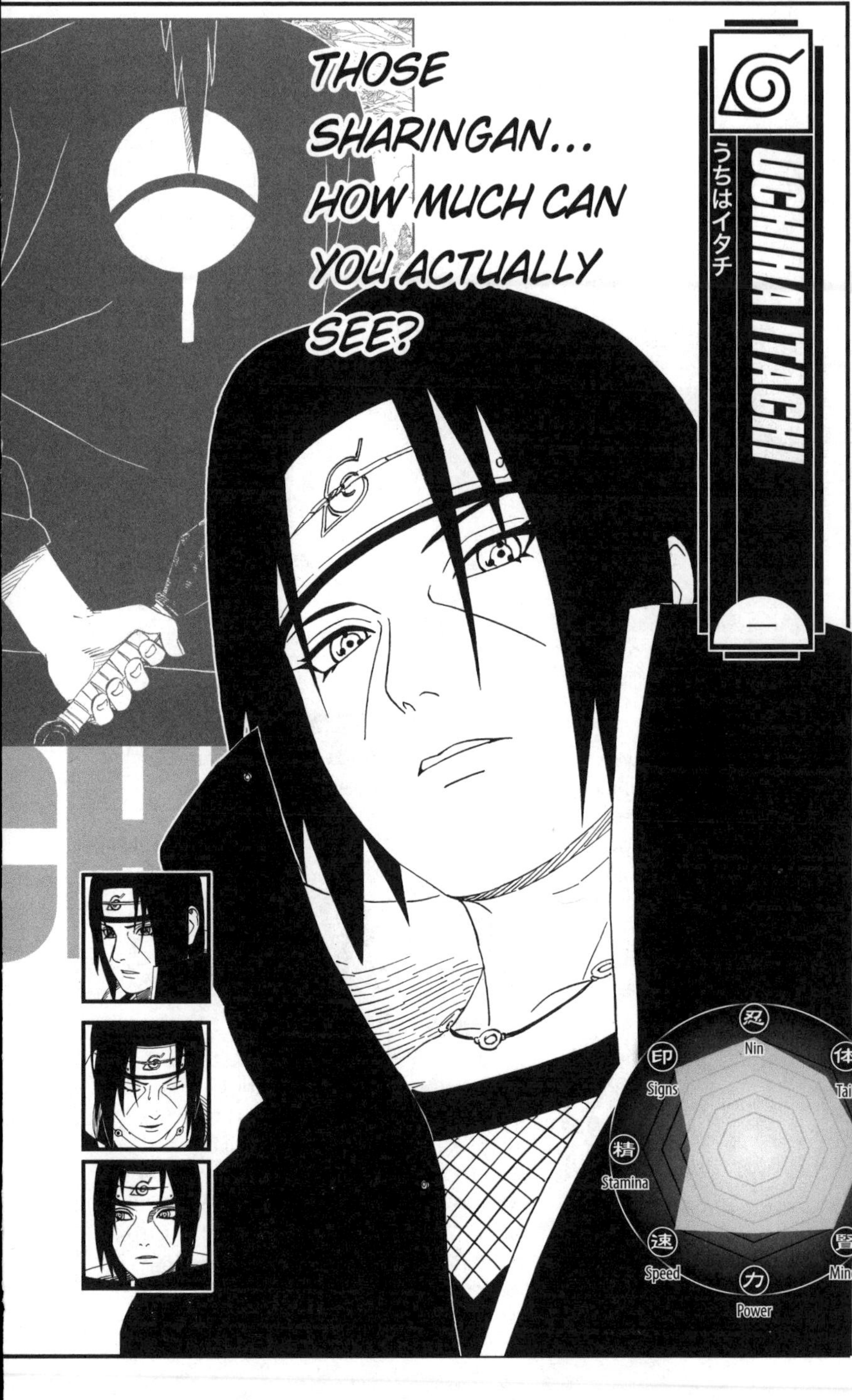
UCHIHA ITACHI
うちはイタチ
THOSE SHARINGAN... HOW MUCH CAN YOU ACTUALLY SEE?
忍 Nin
体 Tai
幻 Gen
賢 Mind
力 Power
速 Speed
精 Stamina
印 Signs

Viewing the past, present and future through scarlet eyes. He hides his long-cherished wish and spins a yarn of truth and lies.

"He is indeed my son." To his father, the head of the Konoha Police Force, he was a constant source of pride. "He's so distant." His younger brother idolized him, but at the same time, couldn't repress the stirring of jealousy inside him. His genius, which was the envy of the clan, destined Itachi to a harsh fate. Because he was naturally gifted, he was chosen to become a spy. His sharp

intelligence allowed him to give even the most minute detail new perspective. But this ability ultimately caused him to commit grave and harsh acts. He was, without a doubt, a hero. But he would never attain fame.

He was too kind to be a shinobi. That he chose to live as a ninja because of that kindness is the ultimate irony.

⬆ He awakened the Sharingan at the age of eight. How much grief has been reflected in those eyes?

⬅⬆ Ocular ninjutsu and genjutsu go hand-in-hand with Sharingan, but he was also highly skilled in taijutsu and ninjutsu.

...EVERY SINGLE ONE OF US GOES THROUGH LIFE DEPENDING ON AND BOUND BY OUR INDIVIDUAL KNOWLEDGE AND AWARENESS.

AND WE CALL IT REALITY.

Itach's view of life and death are rooted in the harsh experiences he's endured.

Ninja Registry Number: 012110
Birthdate: June 9 (21 years old; Gemini)
Height: 178.0 cm (5'10") **Weight:** 58.0 kg (128 lbs.) **Blood type:** AB
Personality: Loving brother, self-sacrificing
Favorite food: Rice balls (with konbu), cabbage
Least favorite food: Steak
Would like to fight: Uchiha Sasuke
Favorite word/saying: Peace
Interests: Café-hopping

Graduated from the Ninja Academy at age 7
Promoted to chûnin at age 10

Mission Experience	D-rank: 53	C-rank: 152
	B-rank: 134	A-rank: 0
	S-rank: 1	

Everything was for his younger brother and the village... The truth of the tragedy revealed.

Treading a thorny path between conflicting sides.

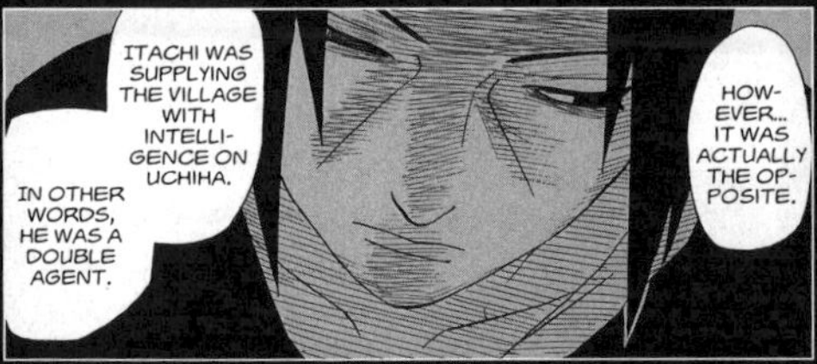
HOWEVER... IT WAS ACTUALLY THE OPPOSITE.
ITACHI WAS SUPPLYING THE VILLAGE WITH INTELLIGENCE ON UCHIHA.
IN OTHER WORDS, HE WAS A DOUBLE AGENT.

⬆ The village or the clan. Reason or sentiment. The greater good or self-respect. Itachi was torn between conflicting beliefs.

The source of Itachi's suffering goes back in history to the time of Konoha's founding to the dispute between the Senju clan from which the First Hokage hailed and the Uchiha clan led by Madara. Even as a day of unification approached, there was hidden mistrust between the two. Suspecting the Uchiha of rebellion, the village orders Itachi to spy on the clan. Meanwhile, learning of the government's mistrust, the Uchiha order Itachi to investigate the village. Each side has its own sense of justice and pride. Caught in the middle of this chasm, the young shinobi's heart was torn apart...

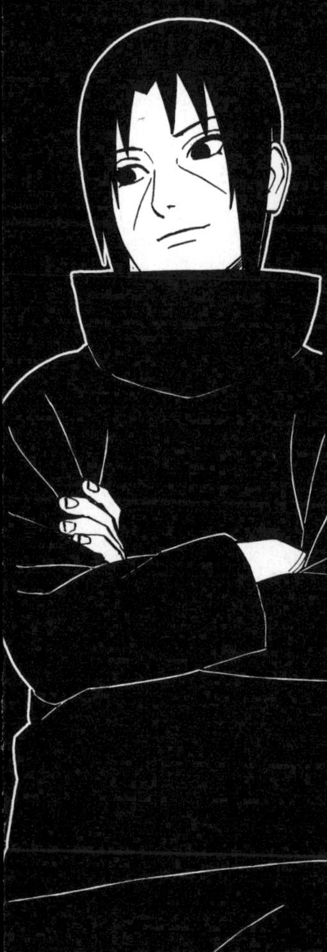

Suspicion breeds an Uchiha rebellion

At first, it was simply a case of neither side liking the other. However, when by coincidence or inevitability, a calamity called the Nine-Tailed Fox attacked the Leaf Village, many believed that it was a man-made disaster caused by the Uchiha, and their suspicions turned real.

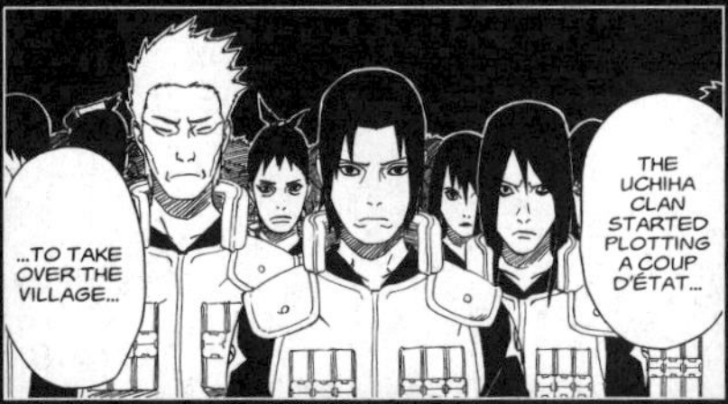
THE UCHIHA CLAN STARTED PLOTTING A COUP D'ÉTAT...
...TO TAKE OVER THE VILLAGE...

⬆ The Uchiha plotted to take over the village that had doubted and persecuted them. Itachi and Sasuke's father, Fugaku, stood at its helm.

Love plants the seeds of a nightmare.

The village or his family.
Itachi, who desired peace more than anyone else, was faced with a heartless choice. For peace in the village, rather than for peace in the world, Itachi carried out the annihilation of his clan. But he could not bring himself to kill his younger brother Sasuke. Itachi told Sasuke that he himself was the traitor. He carved the mark of a rogue shinobi onto his headpiece and left the village alone, taking the secret designs of his clan, as well as the unjust suspicions of the village, with him. He did this to shield Sasuke's eyes from their evil. He shouldered the "truth" of what happened, leaving his brother with the fabrication of a proud and noble clan.

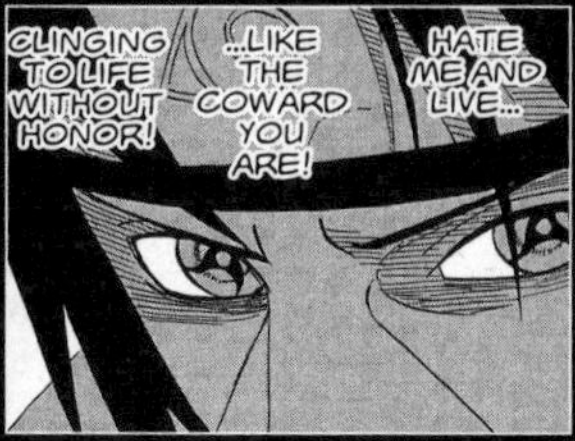
HATE ME AND LIVE...
...LIKE THE COWARD YOU ARE!
CLINGING TO LIFE WITHOUT HONOR!

←↓ Inducing Sasuke to hate him was also in order to make a hero out of him.

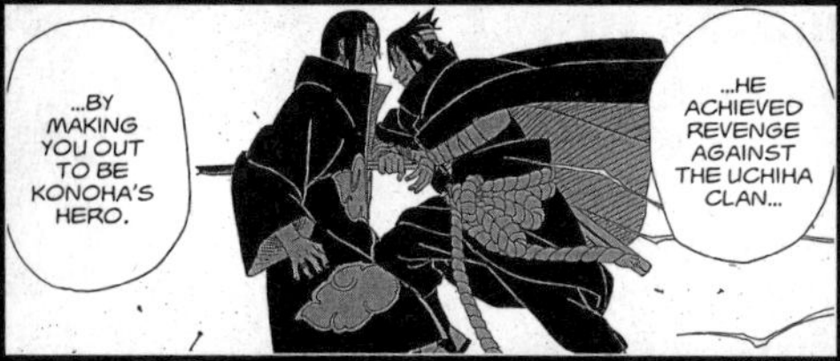
...HE ACHIEVED REVENGE AGAINST THE UCHIHA CLAN...
...BY MAKING YOU OUT TO BE KONOHA'S HERO.

He existed in the world of the dark, but he still yearned for home.

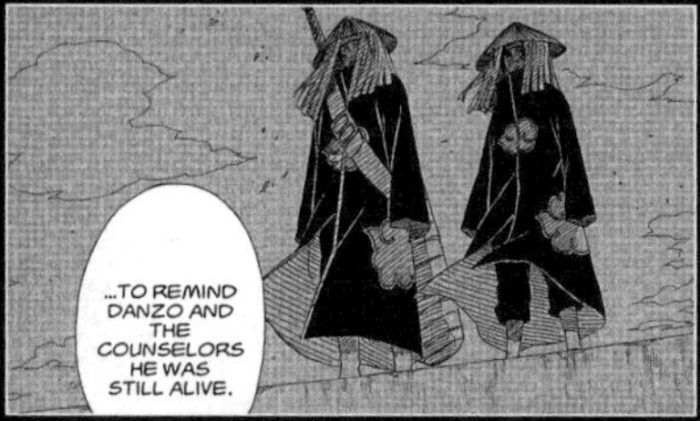
...TO REMIND DANZO AND THE COUNSELORS HE WAS STILL ALIVE.

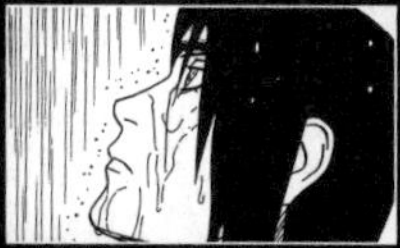

←↑ Although he played the part of an enemy in the village and was treated with disdain, his most fervent wish was its stability.

Itachi joined the Akatsuki, which posed a threat to Konoha, so that he could keep an eye on its movements from the inside. Although he was cloaked in ebony and scorned as the incarnation of evil, Itachi's heart overflowed with thoughts of the village and his brother.

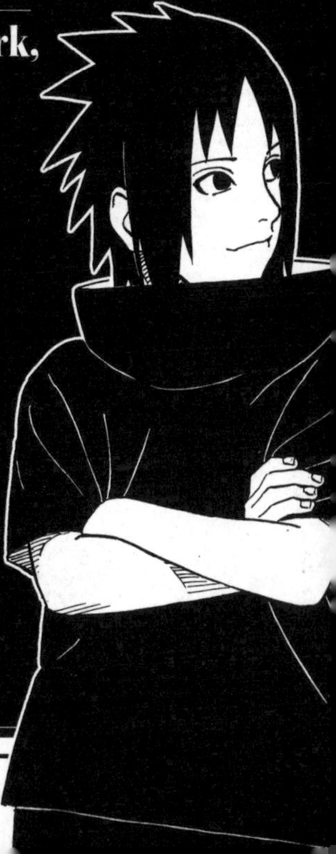

Shouldering the hidden truth about the carnage, he sacrificed his life as a rogue shinobi.

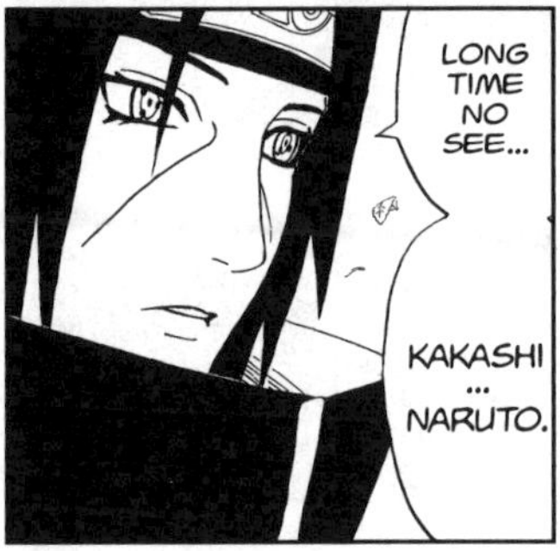
LONG TIME NO SEE...
KAKASHI ... NARUTO.

《A member of the Akatsuki》

In order to keep Sasuke believing in his pretense, Itachi had to remain the scoundrel rogue shinobi who was after Naruto. That is why he participated in the Akatsuki missions. And now, that is his reality.

⬅ By going after Naruto, he fools the Akatsuki. At the same time, he is able to follow the movements of the village.

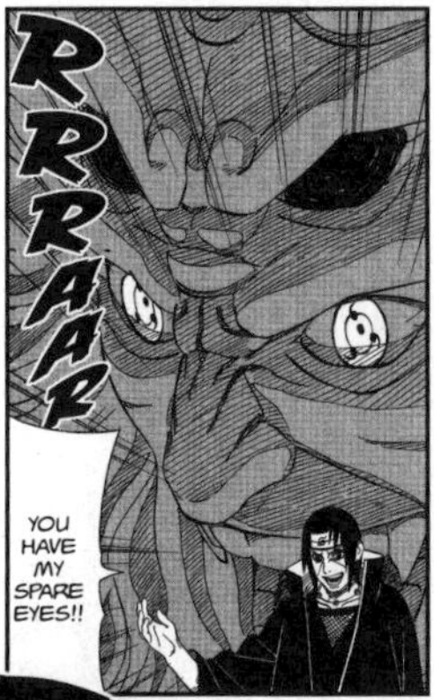
RRRAAR
YOU HAVE MY SPARE EYES!!

⬆ He uses genjutsu to rile Sasuke. But even that is an illusion.

《Two brothers make a vow》

The day of revenge abruptly arrives for Sasuke. For Itachi, it is the day he promised would come on that tragic night. That night when he lost his dreams and his future... Itachi entrusts all of that to Sasuke and smilingly bids farewell to his younger brother.

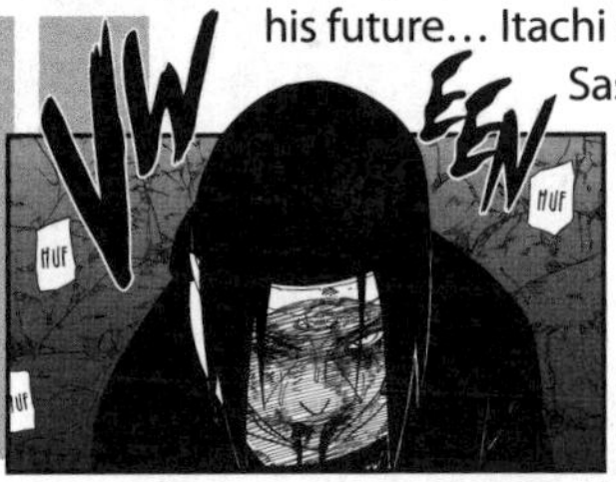
VWEEN
HUF
HUF
UF

⬆⬇ His fingers reach out to gouge out Sasuke's eyes, but instead they brush his forehead lightly, just as he used to in the past.

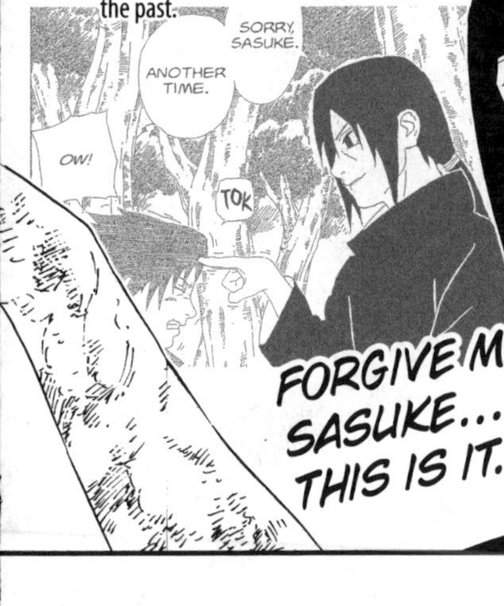
SORRY, SASUKE.
ANOTHER TIME.
OW!
TOK

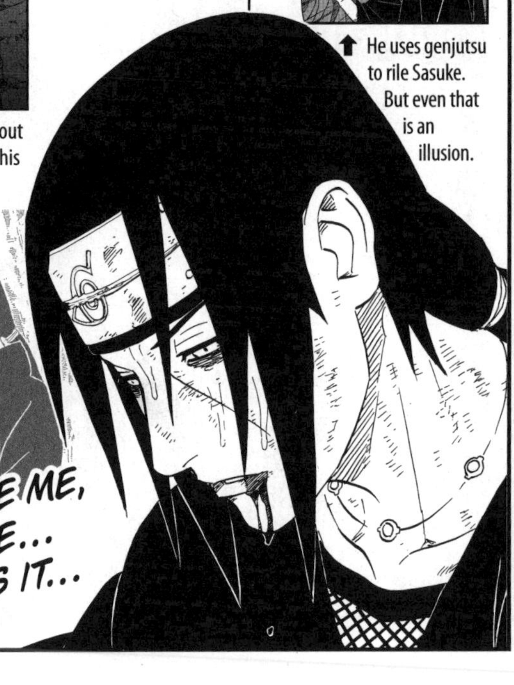
FORGIVE ME, SASUKE... THIS IS IT...

...FINALLY, IT EMERGES ...

Knowing his mission and sensing his life coming to an end, he leaves his dreams to dawn with the next generation.

↑ ↓ Orochimaru's fate is sealed by the very sword he sought.

EH?

《Completion》

Driven by revenge, Sasuke devotes himself to a wicked power. Freeing him from the clutches of evil is what Itachi likely perceived as his final mission... He pushes Sasuke to the limit in order to reveal the snake and completely seal it with the sacred Ten-Handed Sword. With this, he puts an end to Orochimaru's deep-rooted delusions about the Uchiha body.

《Naruto》

While operating within the Akatsuki, Itachi verifies one thing. Naruto is the only one who can save Sasuke and the village. That is why he entrusts Naruto with his feelings. Together with his great hope...

...I'LL SAY IT AGAIN.
I JUST WANT TO TALK.

↑ What kind of future did Itachi's eyes see in Naruto?

《Mangekyo Sharingan》

In sacrificing himself and having his brother witness his death, Itachi is able to bequeath his Mangekyo Sharingan to Sasuke. "I'll always be there." Itachi wanted to make sure that even after death, he could protect Sasuke.

← What future is reflected in the eyes Itachi bestowed upon him? Is it hope? Or...

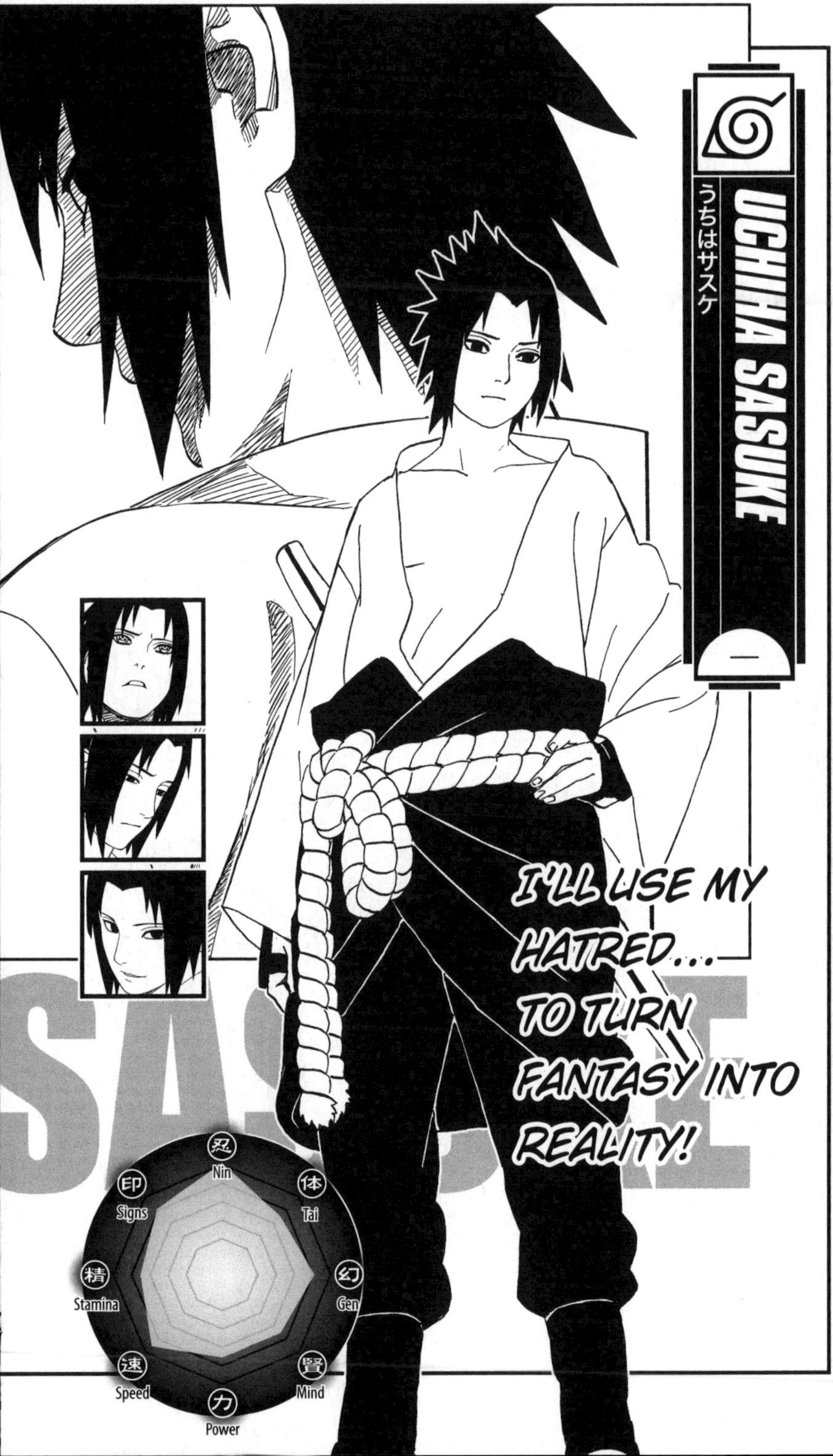
UCHIHA SASUKE
うちはサスケ
I'LL USE MY HATRED... TO TURN FANTASY INTO REALITY!
忍 Nin
体 Tai
幻 Gen
賢 Mind
力 Power
速 Speed
精 Stamina
印 Signs

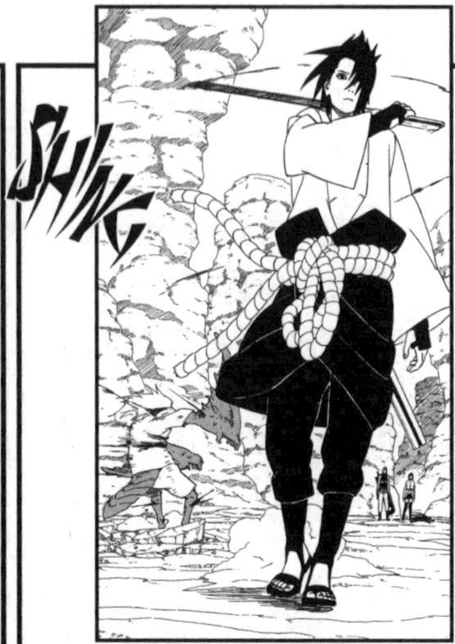
SHING

⬆ Three years have passed since he left the Leaf Village. Now Sasuke radiates an aura as steely and frightening as a sharp blade.

Casting off the dark shroud from his heart, the Uchiha hawk is ready to spread its wings.

Sasuke is consumed by the desire for revenge. He abandons everything that could be a burden to him and rejects warmth and tranquility. It will be a dark and gloomy road, and like the Hebi, the snake, after which he names his new team, he will crawl on the earth as he hunts down his prey.
When Sasuke achieves his long-cherished desire for revenge, he discovers the truth. That truth then sends him into a spiral. But now the young hawk soars through the skies, surveying all below him with Sharingan eyes. What lies ahead is another bloodstained road of carnage.

➡ Blessed with innate shinobi talent, Sasuke's fighting skills have improved even more rapidly during the years since he left the village.

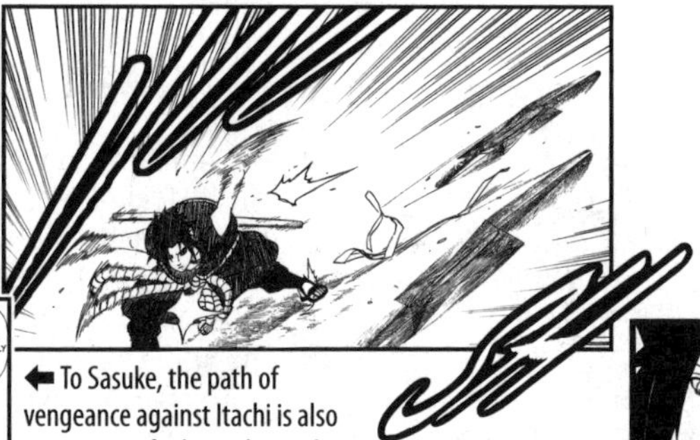

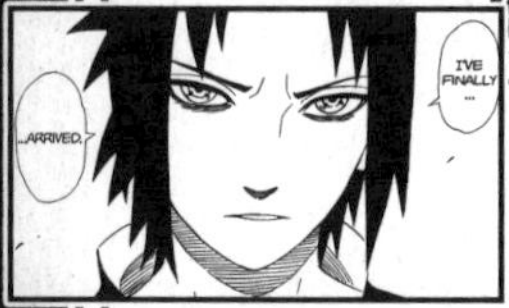
I'VE FINALLY...
...ARRIVED.

⬅ To Sasuke, the path of vengeance against Itachi is also a journey to find out the truth about his clan.

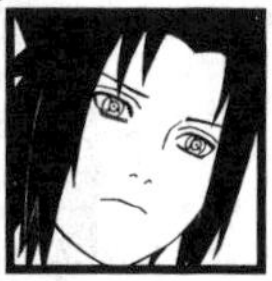

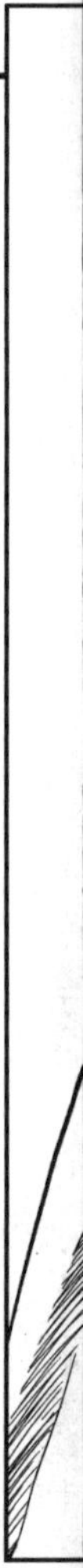

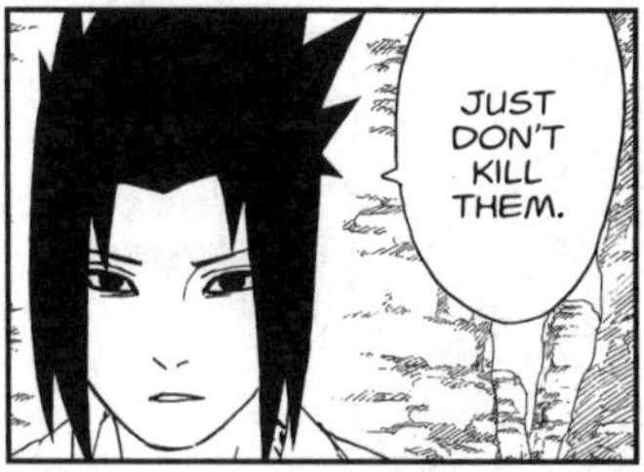
JUST DON'T KILL THEM.

He is not the type to destroy life unnecessarily. Does an innate gentleness still flow deep in his heart?

Ninja Registry Number: 012606
Birthdate: July 23 (16 years old; Leo)
Height: 168.0 cm (5'6") **Weight:** 52.2 kg (115 lbs.) **Blood type:** AB
Personality: Cool, acts tough
Favorite food: Rice balls (with okaka), tomatoes
Least favorite food: Natto beans, sweet things
Would like to fight: The top echelon of Konoha
Favorite word: Power
Interests: Taking walks

Graduated from the Ninja Academy at age 12
Promoted to chûnin at age —

Mission Experience		
	D-rank: 7	C-rank: 1
	B-rank: 2	A-rank: 6
	S-rank: 0	

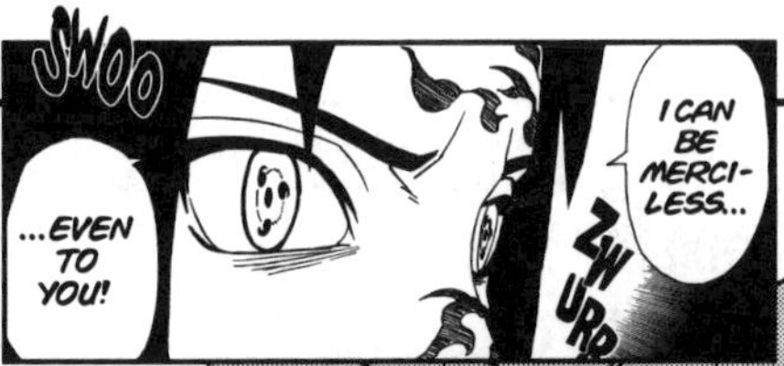
SWOO
I CAN BE MERCI-LESS...
ZWURR
...EVEN TO YOU!

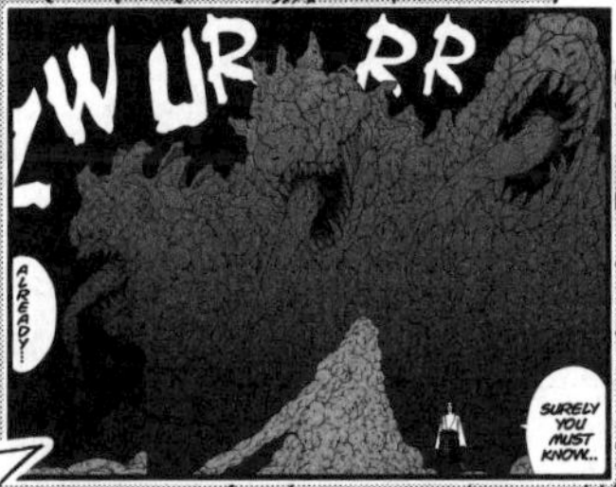
ZWURRR
ALREADY...
SURELY YOU MUST KNOW...

⬆➡ Turning his back on Orochimaru's power, Sasuke leaves forcibly. Even the Transference Technique is powerless against the power of the Uchiha.

The time has come! The noble hawk swallows the snake and leaves the nest!!

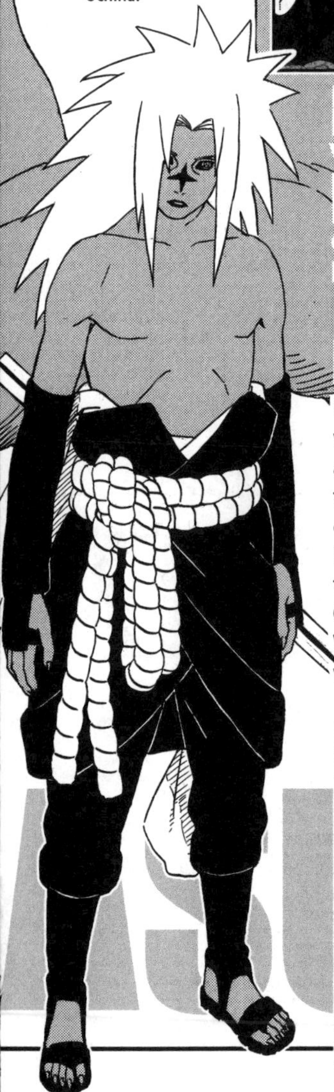

《Rebellion》

His notoriety as a rogue shinobi growing, Sasuke rushes to Orochimaru's side in order to carry out his revenge. But this ninja who abandoned his village has not gone so far as to lose the pride of a powerful clan. Even as he trains under Orochimaru, he despises his maliciousness and waits for the opportunity to revolt. And when Orochimaru misreads Sasuke's progress, that day finally comes.

《The power of the White Snake》

From the moment Orochimaru sees Sasuke's body with its Sharingan, he feels it is his dream vessel, and he anxiously waits for the day to administer the Transference Technique. But his greed comes crumbling down because the vessel he seeks is too flawless. The noble blood that courses through Sasuke gives him a power that is beyond Orochimaru's imagination. And Sasuke captures the White Snake's powers along with its poison fangs which thirst for that blood.

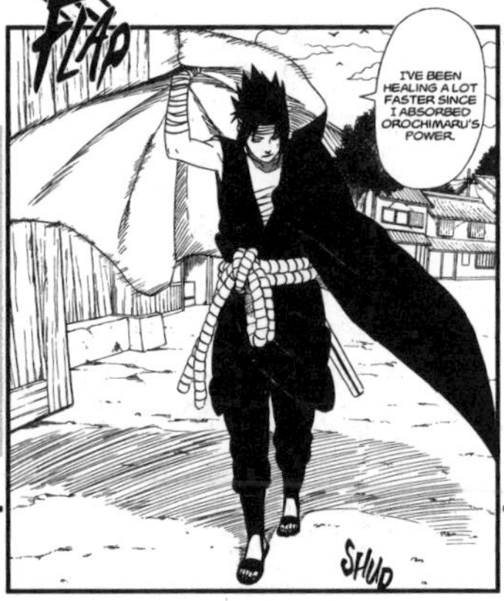
FLAP
I'VE BEEN HEALING A LOT FASTER SINCE I ABSORBED OROCHIMARU'S POWER.
SHUP

⬅ The White Snake's power has given Sasuke the added benefit of a miraculous recovery speed.

Severed bonds and new relationships. All for the purpose of bringing down his brother.

《 Reunion 》

As painful as losing a part of himself, Naruto must face that he is losing his friend. Since leaving the village, Naruto continues to pursue him. Still, even though it is their first reunion in three years, Sasuke's heart doesn't soften. Bonds which cause confusion must be severed. An avenger needs only one connection—the one with hatred toward his older brother…

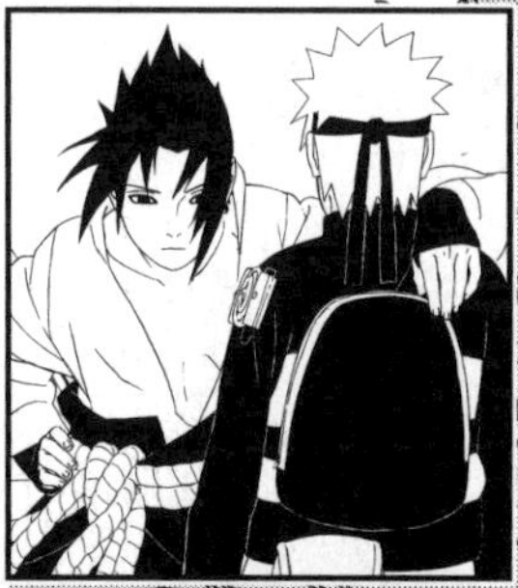

⬅ Sasuke is extremely brusque even in front of Naruto. This is his way of informing Naruto that the time for revenge has arrived.

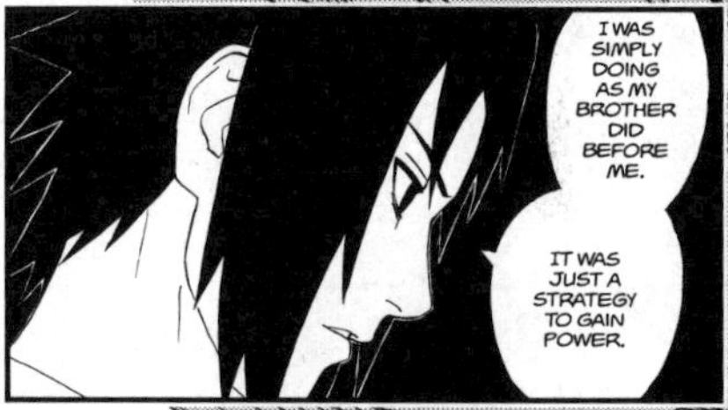
I WAS SIMPLY DOING AS MY BROTHER DID BEFORE ME.
IT WAS JUST A STRATEGY TO GAIN POWER.

➡ His unwavering determination is another indication of his decision to part from them.

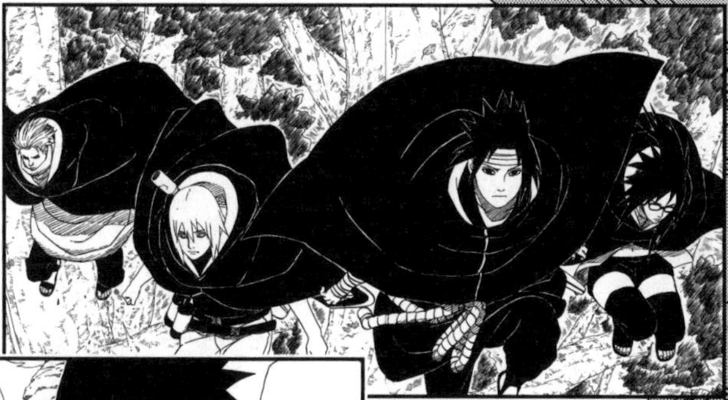

⬅ Each one in Hebi has a special ability, such as sensory detection or close-range combat, making them ideally suited to take independent action.

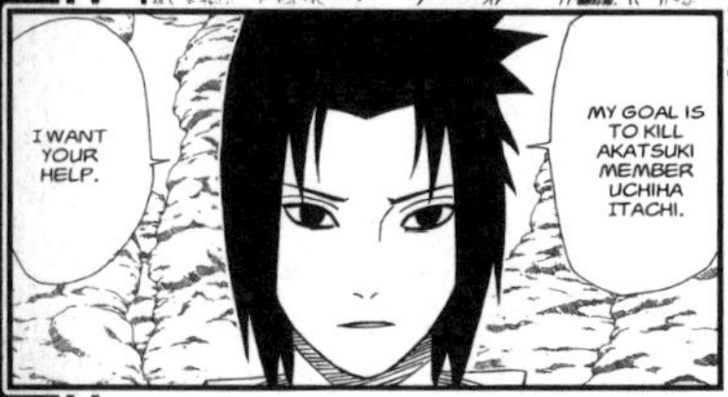
MY GOAL IS TO KILL AKATSUKI MEMBER UCHIHA ITACHI.
I WANT YOUR HELP.

《 Hebi is formed 》

Sasuke severs all unnecessary bonds in order to become stronger to carry out his revenge, but he takes another action toward fulfilling his goal… He gathers new members to create new ties. However, although team Hebi was formed solely for the purpose of defeating Uchiha Itachi, the members who join up do so only after weighing the merits and demerits of the cause. So there is a delicate balance holding up this castle in the sand. Anything could tip the scale and force the team to break up. The only thing that keeps them united is their reverence toward Sasuke and his absolute authority.

Fighting skills from devoted training! His power exceeds even that of the Akatsuki!

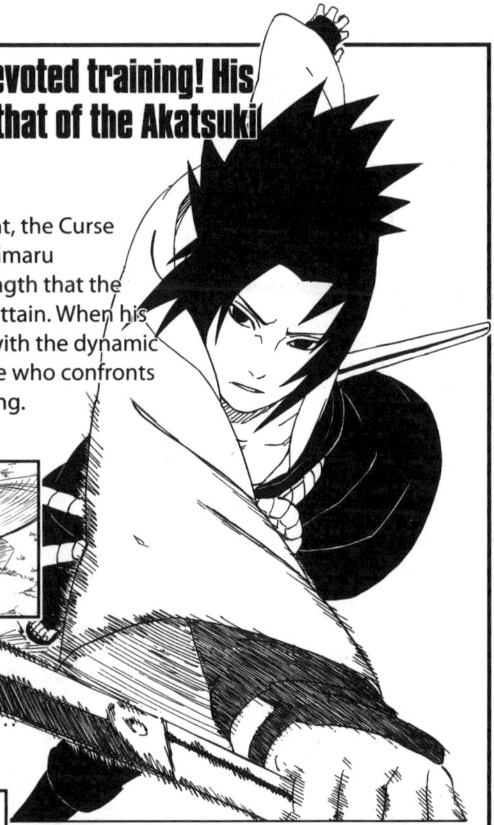

《Godlike speed》

Together with his inborn talent, the Curse Mark placed on him by Orochimaru empowers Sasuke with a strength that the average shinobi could never attain. When his amazing speed is combined with the dynamic vision of his Sharingan, no one who confronts Sasuke stands a chance of living.

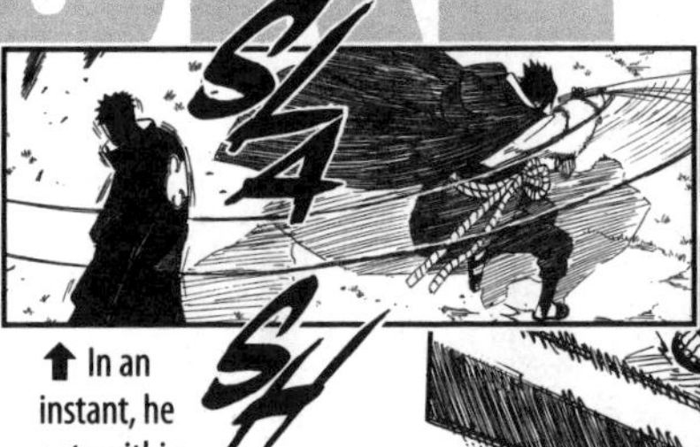
SLASH

⬆ In an instant, he gets within range of his opponent, brandishing his sword... His speed takes away the breath of even the Akatsuki members.

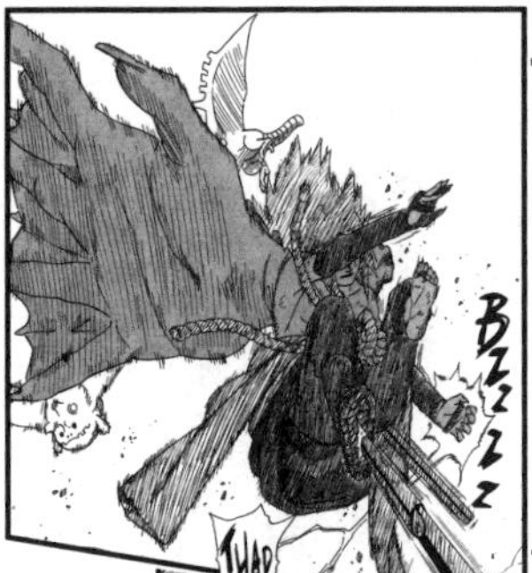
BZZZZ

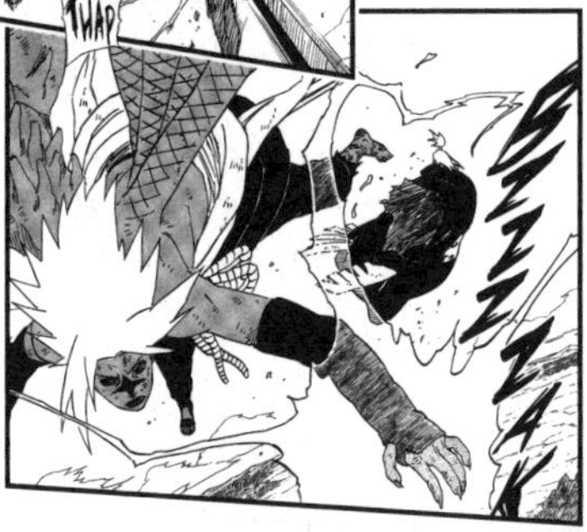
THAP

⬆➡ Victory is the only word he sees. Hence, he is able to see the path that leads to it.

《Tactics》

Sasuke's tactical skills and battle sense showcase his resourcefulness as a shinobi. He maintains his calm in battle and has a keen ability to observe and analyze an opponent's power.

Then he selects from his wide repertoire of skills and ninjutsu the one which will be most effective. When necessary, he will even allow himself to be injured—receive a flesh wound, have a bone broken. It is this resolve and ability to act which puts Sasuke in a special class of shinobi.

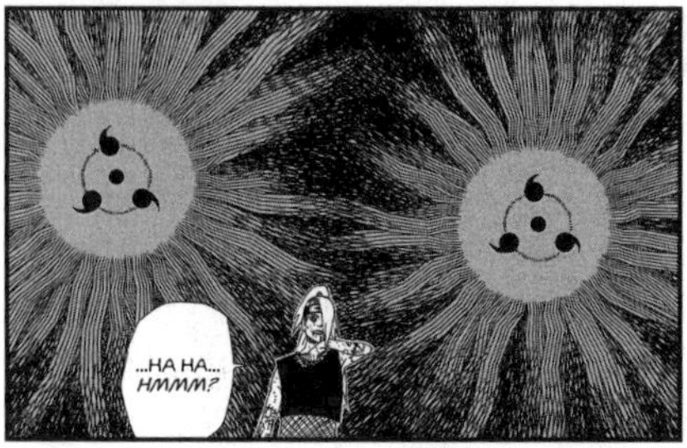
...HA HA... HMMM?

⬆ Whatever trick the opponent attempts, whatever strategy he uses will never work before Sasuke's eyes.

The cursed bloodline makes enemies cower.

《All-seeing》

The Sharingan is the symbol of the all-powerful Uchiha clan, and its power is also the cause of the tragic fate of this bloodline. Sasuke takes pride in possessing the Sharingan and utilizes its full potential in battle.

He reads the way a foe weaves a seal and determines its change in chakra nature, then decides on the range of attack from the color of the chakra. And always, his defeated opponents are reflected in his eyes...

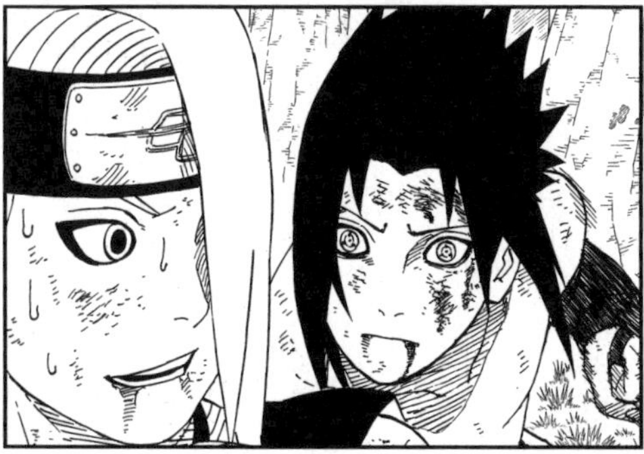

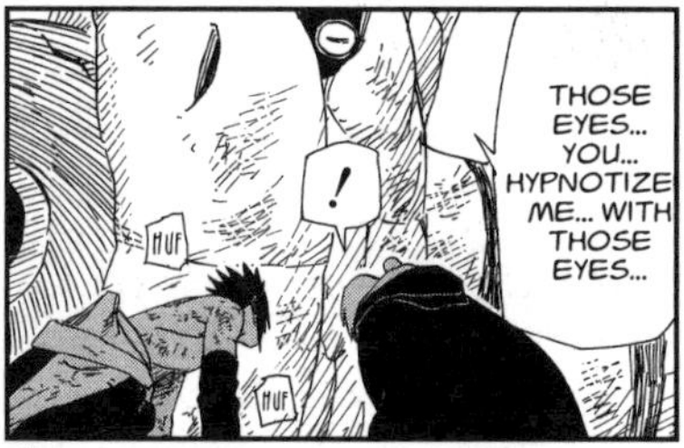
THOSE EYES... YOU... HYPNOTIZE ME... WITH THOSE EYES...
!
HUF
HUF

⬆ The utmost limit of the Sharingan which once was able to control the Nine-Tailed Fox. One can get a glimpse of it in Sasuke too, when he controls Manda.

《Ocular power》

Why is the Sharingan so feared, even by the people of the Leaf Village? The main reason is its ocular power that can tame even the Tailed Beast. As Sasuke awakens to his powers as an Uchiha, so too does that cursed power that dwells within him.

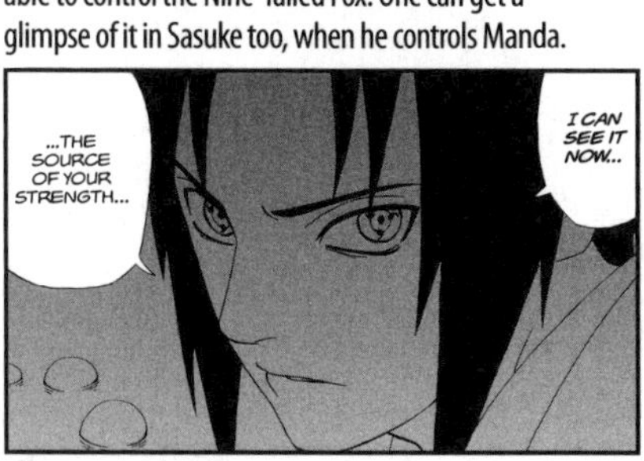
I CAN SEE IT NOW...
...THE SOURCE OF YOUR STRENGTH...

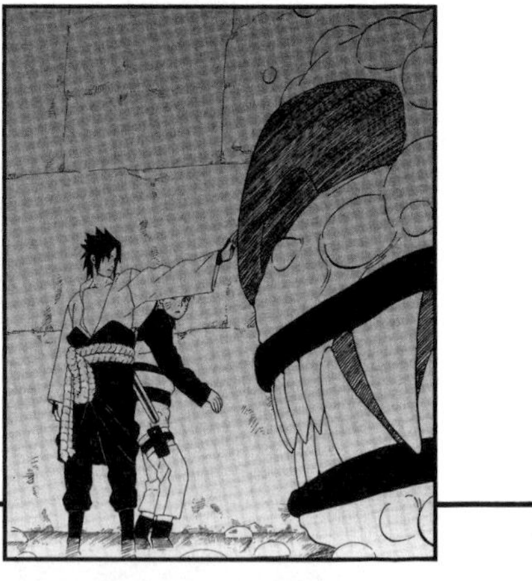

⬆ ➡ Sasuke's ocular powers can even capture the Nine-Tailed Fox Spirit that dwells in Naruto's body. Its sinister power prompts Nine Tails to remember Madara.

《Fantasy and reality》

Sasuke's goal to bring his brother down consumes him; he feels it even more strongly now than as a boy, when Itachi took everything from him. When they meet again, it is with blades and countless genjutsu, each with a desire to fulfill their wish, that is, to make a fantasy of the other's wish and destroy him. But fantasy becomes mired with reality in the fight. But for Sasuke, there is only one reality. The tragic events of that day and the hatred he feels for Itachi.

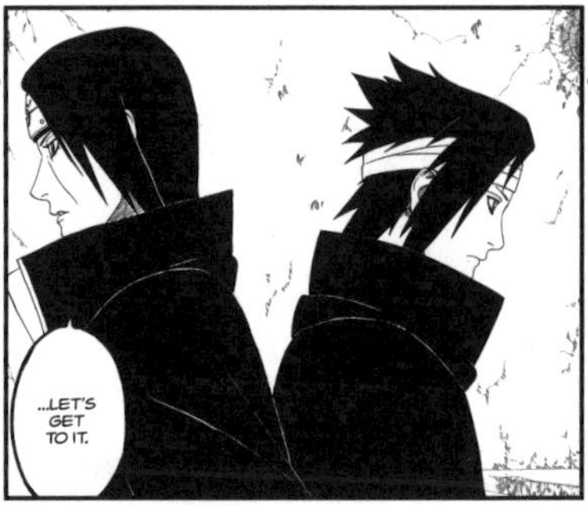
...LET'S GET TO IT.

⬆ The two Uchiha brothers walk separate paths, but destiny lures them into a fight.

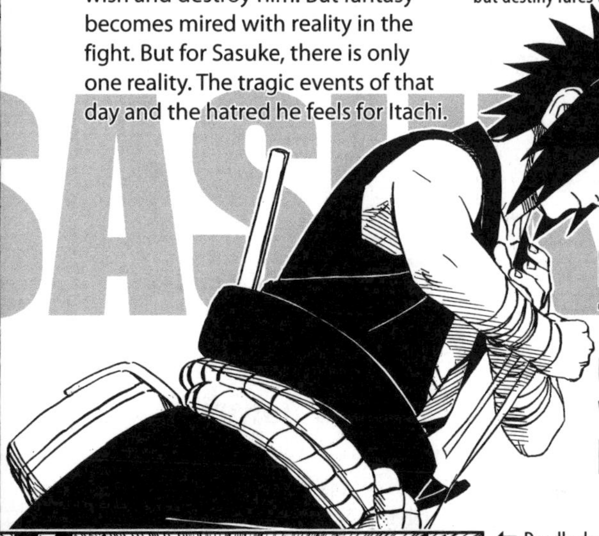

Reunion of Brothers That will be the day of the death match when he lays his life on the line!

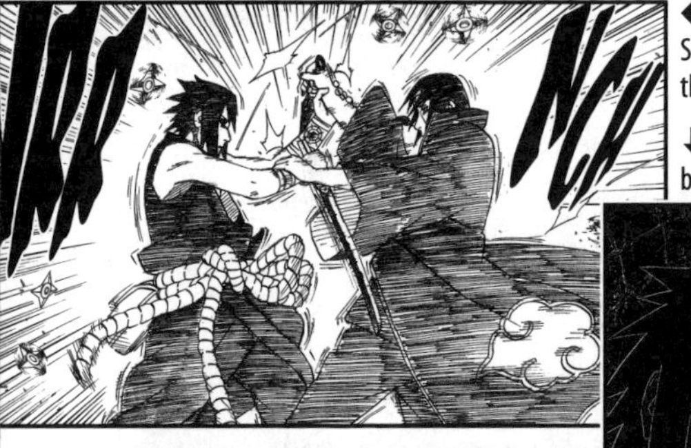

⬅ Deadly daggers fly and swords clash. Simultaneously, both men cast genjutsu. And the ultimate battle unfolds.

⬇ Sasuke is driven into an eternal hell created by the Mangekyo Sharingan. . .

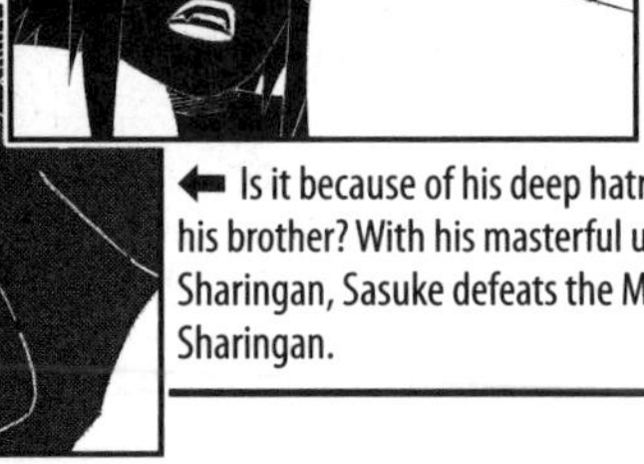

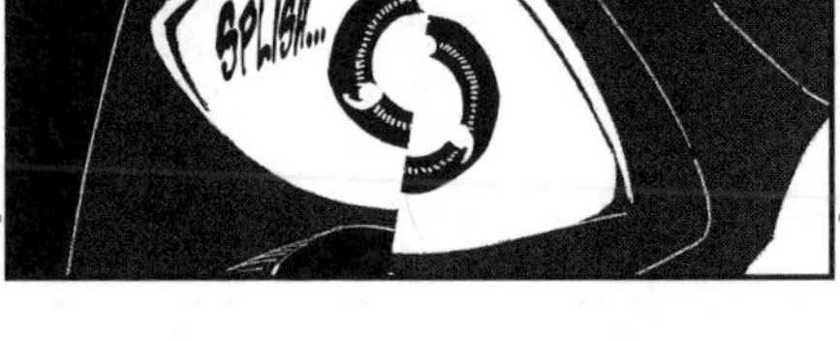
SPLISH...

⬅ Is it because of his deep hatred toward his brother? With his masterful use of the Sharingan, Sasuke defeats the Mangekyo Sharingan.

《Conclusion》

In his quest to bring Itachi down, Sasuke abandons his village, friends and mentors. His trump card, the Kirin, consists of the Uchiha Fire Style jutsu combined with a Lightning Style jutsu taught to him by Kakashi. Sasuke intends to use this to settle it all. But Itachi also wishes to end their long feud and counters with the hidden jutsu, Susano'o.

The end of vengeance– What lies ahead is another blood-tainted journey of retribution.

...TO CREATE A LIGHTNING STYLE JUTSU!
CHIRP
CHIRP
CHIRP

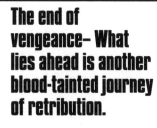

⬅ Sasuke yells out, "This is my final attack," and a thousand birds begin to chirp on cue.

KRSH

⬅ After a desperate fight, Sasuke falls to the ground alongside his fallen brother. A cold rain washes away the enmity of the brothers.

《Trust》

Vengeance is achieved. But when Sasuke learns the cruel truth, that his brother really loved him, he is consumed with loss. His vengeance is not sweet. It is colored by tears of regret and the pain of pure desolation.

⬇ With the power of his brother in his eyes, and the will of his brother in his heart, Sasuke vows to destroy the village that betrayed his brother to begin with.

HE WANTED TO FREE YOU OF THE CURSE MARK AND OROCHI-MARU...
...BY CAUSING YOU TO LOSE THE ONE YOU WERE CLOSEST TO... THE BATTLE WOULD THEN AWAKEN YOUR MANGEKYO SHARINGAN.

⬆ Itachi's purpose was not only to give his brother power, but to free him from Orochimaru's Curse Mark.

...TO DESTROY KONOHA!

UCHIHA MADARA

うちはマダラ

—

⬆ Through his rivalry with Senju Hashirama, the shinobi he admired, Madara became stronger.

⬆ With the Mangekyo Sharingan, he takes the reins of power and works to protect his clan.

The man who stole his younger brother's Sharingan and who waged nothing but war— This is how the world judged Madara. No one understood all that he did out of grief for his clan's fate. In anger and despair, Madara bares his fangs at Konoha. What is Madara planning after losing to Hashirama? No one really knows.

BUT ITACHI HAD EVEN PICKED UP ON THAT.
HE OF ALL PEOPLE KNEW OF MY EXISTENCE.

⬆ After dropping out of the record books, Madara puts on a mask and moves into action as Tobi.

In his eyes lie the true Sharingan Calamities ready to wreak vengeance on Konoha.

Ninja Registry Number: —
Birthdate: December 24 (age unknown; Capricorn)
Height: ? **Weight:** ? **Blood type:** ?
Personality: Militant, ambitious
Favorite food: Inarizushi
Least favorite food: Shirako
Would like to fight: The top echelon of Konoha
Favorite word: Win hands down
Interests: Falconry

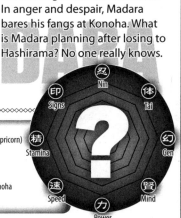

忍 Nin
体 Tai
幻 Gen
賢 Mind
力 Power
速 Speed
精 Stamina
印 Signs
?

UMINO IRUKA

うみのイルカ

Chûnin

Every student is his pride and joy Following the light of the burning Will of Fire.

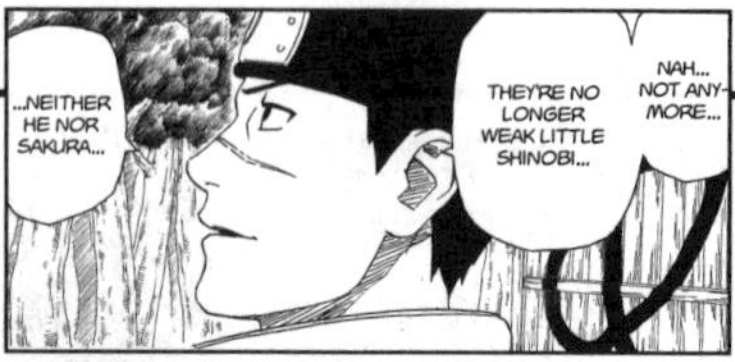
NAH... NOT ANYMORE...
THEY'RE NO LONGER WEAK LITTLE SHINOBI...
...NEITHER HE NOR SAKURA...

⬆⬇ Strict at times and gentle at others. He gazes upon his students intently.

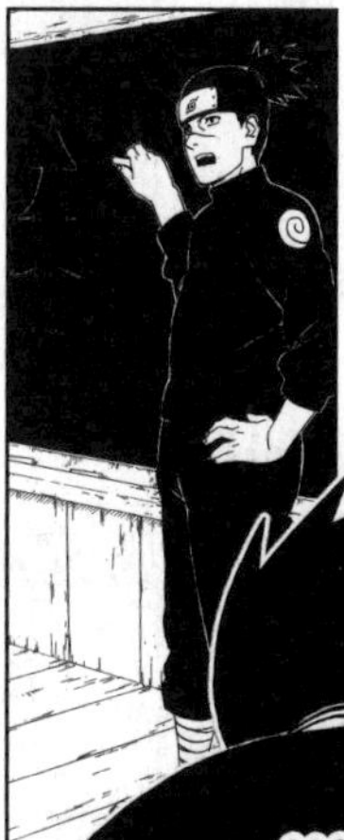

Every day as an Academy instructor, Iruka picks up his blackboard pointer. The first thing he teaches is the importance of comrades and the great history of Konoha and those who came before them. In this harsh shinobi world, what must be cherished?

For Iruka, the answer is every student that he has taught. Even Naruto who has mastered sophisticated jutsu and is rapidly becoming stronger is "one who must be protected" forever.

IRUKA

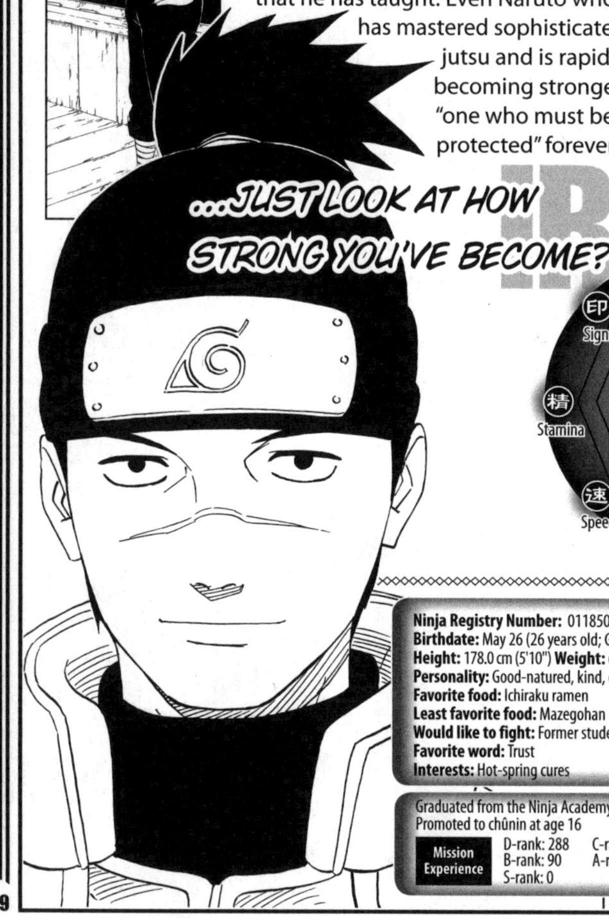
...JUST LOOK AT HOW STRONG YOU'VE BECOME?

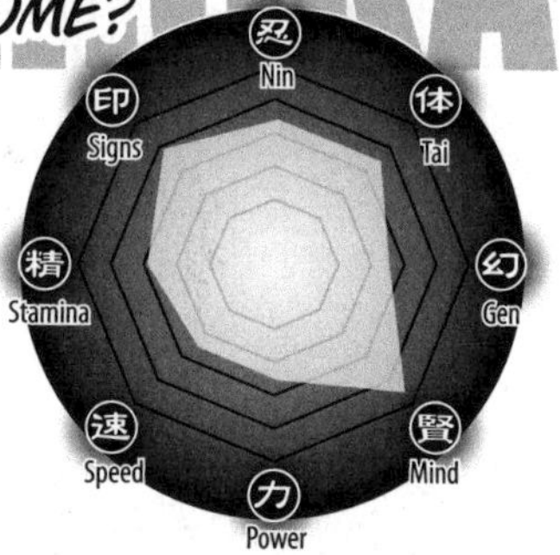
忍 Nin
体 Tai
幻 Gen
賢 Mind
力 Power
速 Speed
精 Stamina
印 Signs

Ninja Registry Number: 011850
Birthdate: May 26 (26 years old; Gemini)
Height: 178.0 cm (5'10") **Weight:** 66.2 kg (146 lbs.) **Blood type:** O
Personality: Good-natured, kind, optimistic
Favorite food: Ichiraku ramen
Least favorite food: Mazegohan
Would like to fight: Former students he mentored
Favorite word: Trust
Interests: Hot-spring cures

Graduated from the Ninja Academy at age 11
Promoted to chûnin at age 16

Mission Experience		
	D-rank: 288	C-rank: 183
	B-rank: 90	A-rank: 12
	S-rank: 0	

EBISU

エビス

Special Jônin

He guides the young seeds entrusted to him by the previous Hokage.

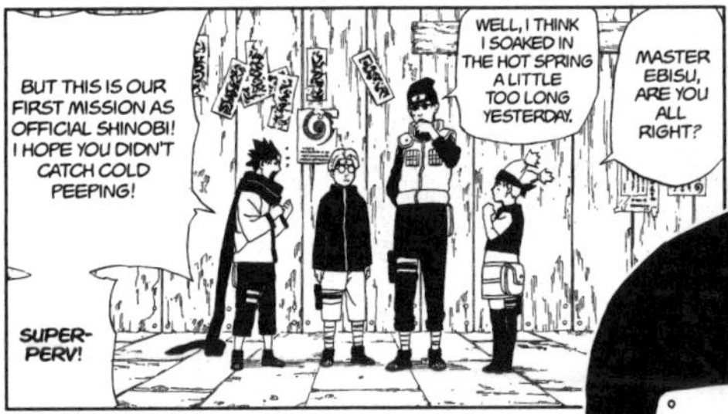
MASTER EBISU, ARE YOU ALL RIGHT?
WELL, I THINK I SOAKED IN THE HOT SPRING A LITTLE TOO LONG YESTERDAY.
BUT THIS IS OUR FIRST MISSION AS OFFICIAL SHINOBI! I HOPE YOU DIDN'T CATCH COLD PEEPING!
SUPER-PERV!

⬆ Affectionate, calm, quick-tempered. His pupils, each of whom possesses individual traits that he respects, show various faces.

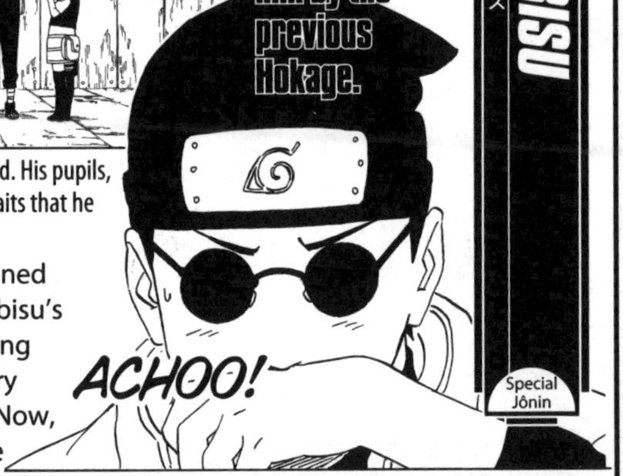
ACHOO!

A shinobi's talent is determined by his lineage... That was Ebisu's belief. However, after meeting Naruto, he realizes that every child has infinite potential. Now, instead of teaching only the elite as a household tutor, he is an instructor at the Academy. He thinks of all students, not only Konohamaru, as potential Hokage candidates.

Ninja Registry Number: 010777
Birthdate: March 8 (32 years old; Pisces)
Height: 181.4 cm (5'11") **Weight:** 67.5 kg (149 lbs.) **Blood type:** A
Personality: Confident, a bit pervy
Interests: Mentoring elite ninja

EBIZO

エビゾウ

While his older sister is impulsive and quick to act, Ebizo throws off the enemy with carefully planned strategies... In the previous war, the Sand was feared because of his brilliant mind. That mind is as lucid as ever and still going strong.

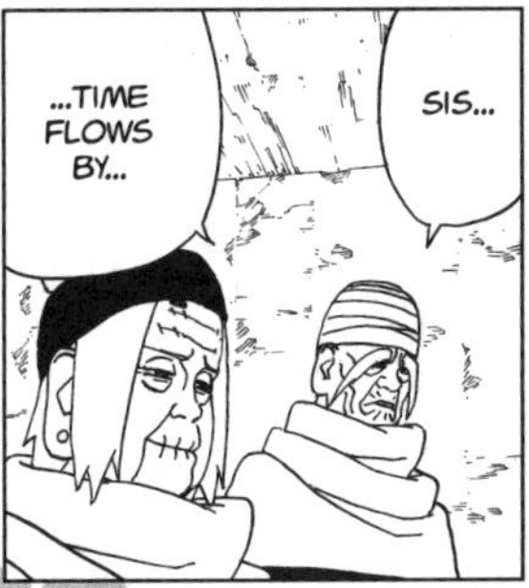
SIS...
...TIME FLOWS BY...

⬆ Witnessing the villages set up a system of cooperation, he feels the coming of a new age.

The unexpected can never shake his stout heart. This imperturbable old man of the Sand.

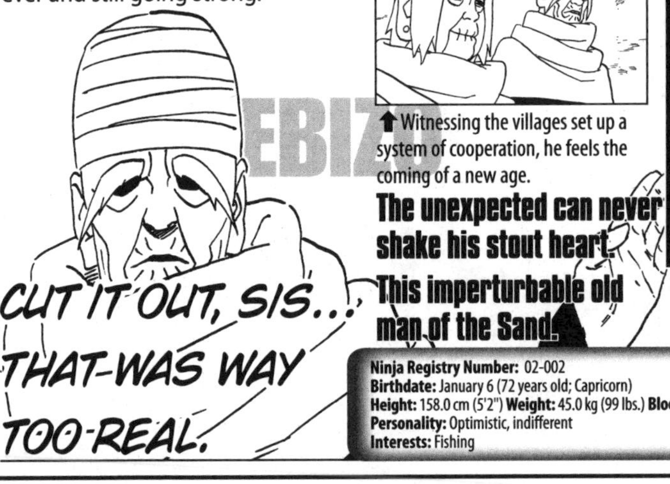
CUT IT OUT, SIS...
THAT WAS WAY TOO REAL.

Ninja Registry Number: 02-002
Birthdate: January 6 (72 years old; Capricorn)
Height: 158.0 cm (5'2") **Weight:** 45.0 kg (99 lbs.) **Blood type:** B
Personality: Optimistic, indifferent
Interests: Fishing

GREAT TOAD SAGE

大ガマ仙人

The high priest of Mount Myoboku dreams a vision of the future.

Mount Myoboku, the headquarters of the toads, has greatly influenced the shinobi world since ancient times. The Great Toad Sage, rumored to be several thousand years old, sits at the peak of the mountain. His warm smile is unassuming and may belie the power he possesses. His enormous amounts of chakra allow him to see the future in visions.

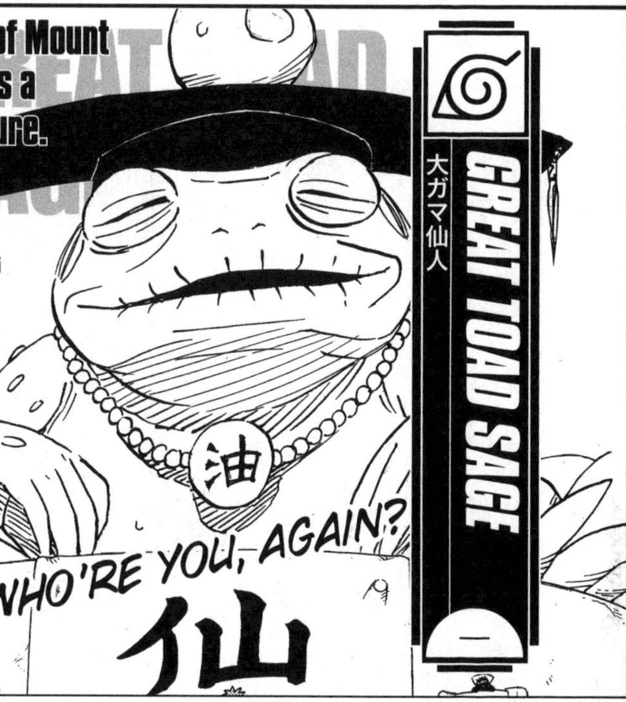
油
WHO'RE YOU, AGAIN?
仙

Collection ... Number 3

Konoha

THE MIRACULOUS PROPHECY OF THE GREAT TOAD SAGE

The prophecies that the Great Toad Sage makes from his dreams are distinctly different from other forms of divination. In his deep sleep, his eyes transcend time and space and see fragments of the future. His forecasts have always been 100 percent accurate.

Just once, the Great Toad Sage saw his own future. It was one that would affect the course of the world of the shinobi. In several centuries, a youth would appear at Mount Myoboku and he would bestow the power of the toads unto him, so that he could witness the future he dreamed.

⬇ Absolute predictions. The Great Toad Sage himself trusts the future in his dreams.

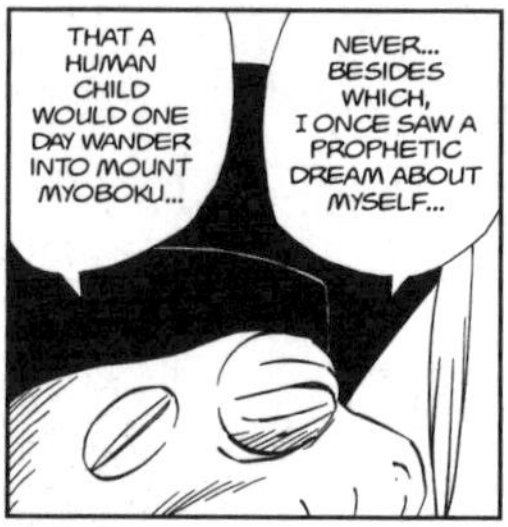
NEVER... BESIDES WHICH, I ONCE SAW A PROPHETIC DREAM ABOUT MYSELF...
THAT A HUMAN CHILD WOULD ONE DAY WANDER INTO MOUNT MYOBOKU...

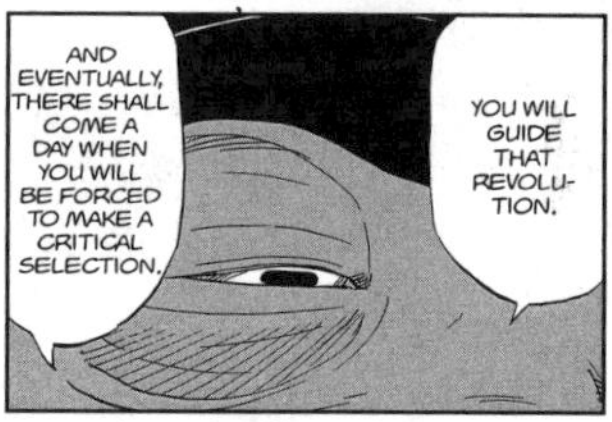
YOU WILL GUIDE THAT REVOLUTION.
AND EVENTUALLY, THERE SHALL COME A DAY WHEN YOU WILL BE FORCED TO MAKE A CRITICAL SELECTION.

⬅ He has fragmentary dreams... he cannot foretell the exact details of the future.

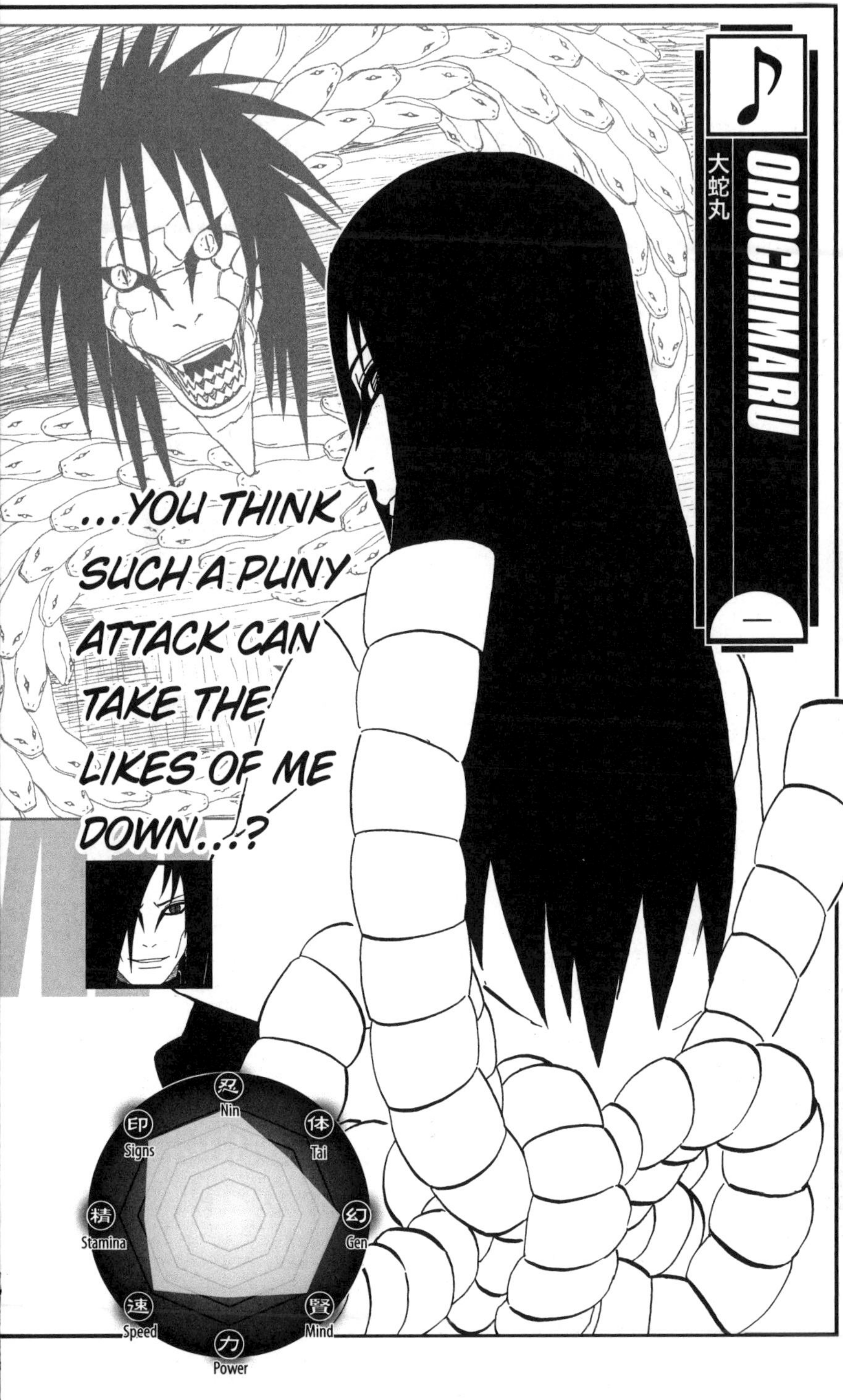
OROCHIMARU
大蛇丸
...YOU THINK SUCH A PUNY ATTACK CAN TAKE THE LIKES OF ME DOWN...?
忍 Nin
体 Tai
幻 Gen
賢 Mind
力 Power
速 Speed
精 Stamina
印 Signs

The bewitching serpent who made his way through a world of unrest, devoting himself to greed and desire.

Orochimaru had gained fame as one of the Three Great Shinobi. The "Professor" of the group, the Third Hokage, said of him, "All of my knowledge is still no match for his talent." But this hero had fallen off the path of glory long ago. His fame turns to notoriety, and his genius turns to evil and corruption. He has a mad thirst for chaos in this world and eternal life, and even if his physical body should rot, he will continue to roam the earth, claiming countless victims as well as devoted followers.

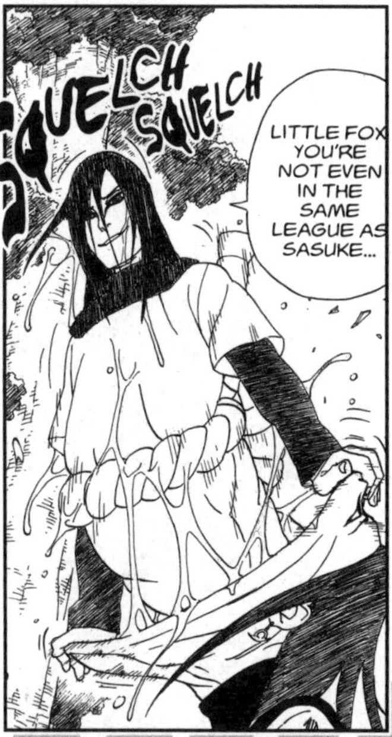
SQUELCH SQUELCH
LITTLE FOX YOU'RE NOT EVEN IN THE SAME LEAGUE AS SASUKE...

⬆ Orochimaru has reincarnated himself many times. To him, the life and death of a person, the giving and taking of life, is nothing but an amusement.

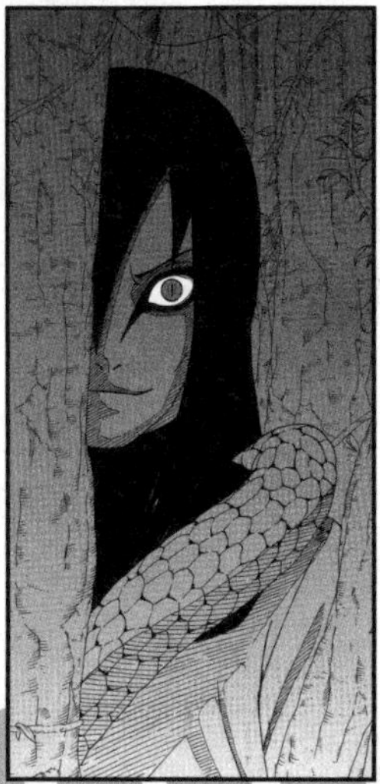

⬅ When Orochimaru targets something he desires , he will show the persistence of a snake and the ferocity of a beast.

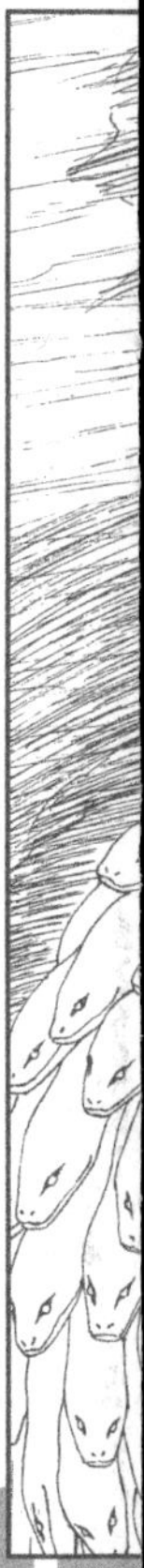

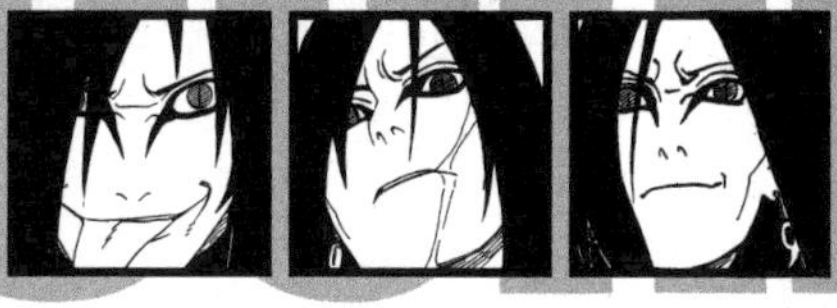

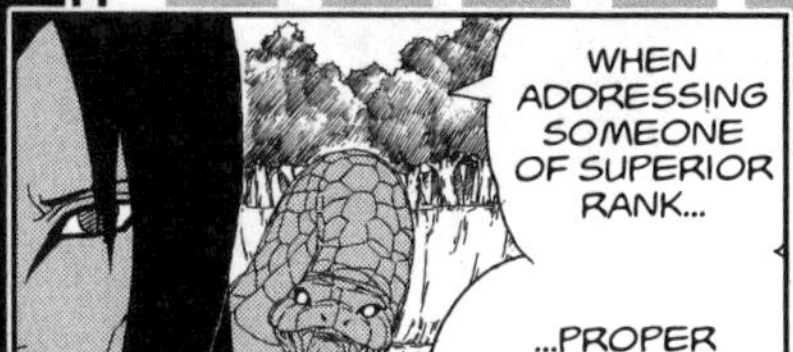
WHEN ADDRESSING SOMEONE OF SUPERIOR RANK...
...PROPER ETIQUETTE DICTATES YOU FACE THEM DIRECTLY.

⬆ He rarely expresses his fury, but every word he utters is filled with pride and confidence.

Ninja Registry Number: 002300
Birthdate: October 27 (54 years old; Scorpio)
Height: 172.0 cm (5'7½") **Weight:** 57.3 kg (126 lbs.) **Blood type:** B
Personality: Ambitious, cruel, egotistic
Favorite food: Eggs
Least favorite food: Cold food
Would like to fight: One who possesses an unknown jutsu
Favorite word: Destruction, chaos
Interests: Developing new jutsu

Graduated from the Ninja Academy at age 6
Promoted to chûnin at age ?

Mission Experience		
	D-rank: 16	C-rank: 332
	B-rank: 521	A-rank: 491
	S-rank: 108	(Konoha days)

Even as a child, he was obsessed with rebirth.

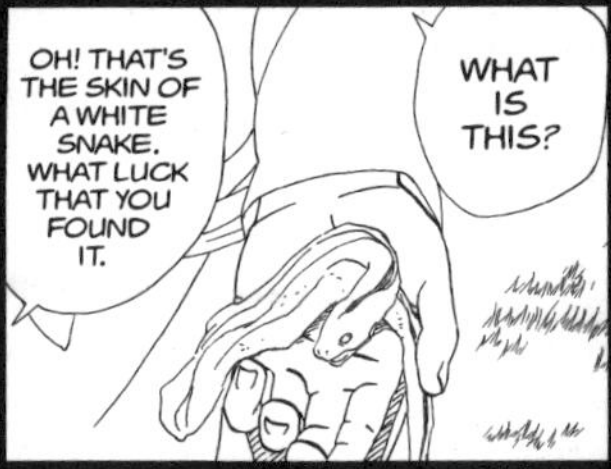
WHAT IS THIS?
OH! THAT'S THE SKIN OF A WHITE SNAKE. WHAT LUCK THAT YOU FOUND IT.

A childhood experience greatly influenced Orochimaru's fanaticism in rebirth. He discovered the molten skin of a white snake near his parents' grave. Could it be that a pure-hearted wish gave rise to his ambitions…?

⬅ The molted skin of a white snake is a symbol of rebirth carved deep into a young boy's heart.

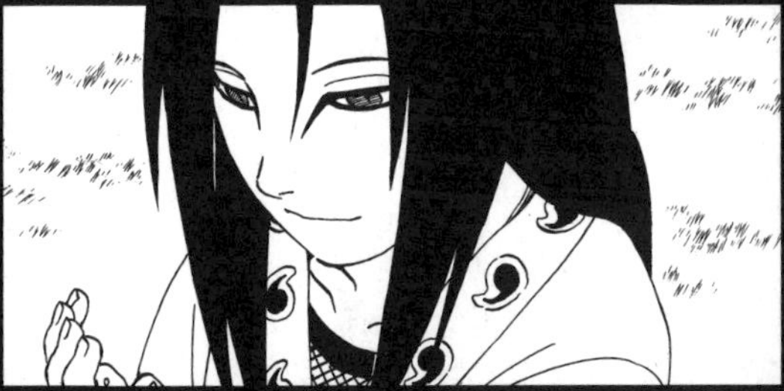

⬅ In this smiling figure with molted skin in hand, there is not a hint of the wickedness that exists today.

Immoral transference is repeated in his desire for life eternal.

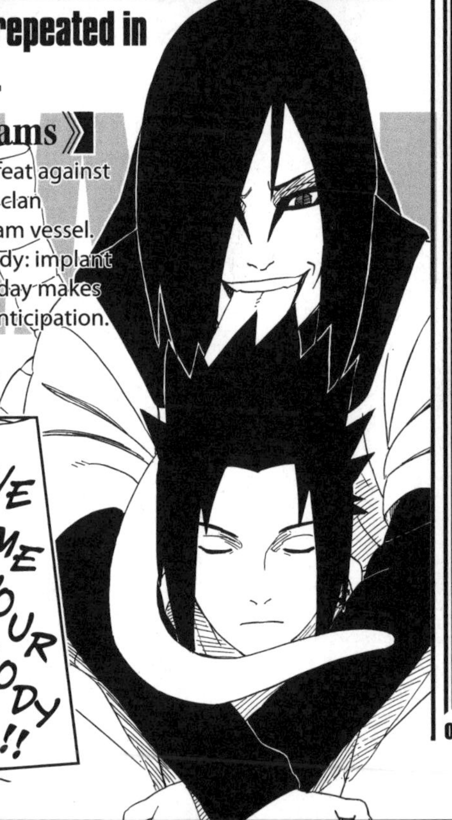

《 The vessel of his dreams 》

From the day he suffered a total defeat against Itachi's eyes, the body of an Uchiha clan member became Orochimaru's dream vessel. What he would do with Sasuke's body: implant his soul into it. The thought of that day makes Orochimaru tremble with joy and anticipation.

⬇ Orochimaru shows his true form and attacks Sasuke, whom he hopes to make his vessel.

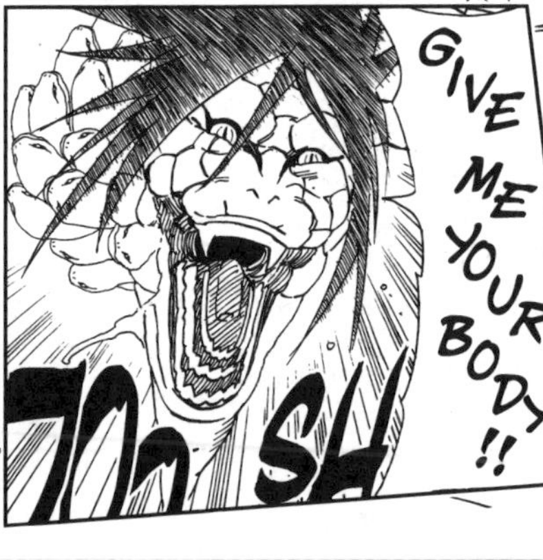
GIVE ME YOUR BODY!!
ZOOOSH

《The Transference Technique》

Orochimaru became too devoted to his desires and overly confident in his intelligence. His impatience clouded his vision… The moment of transference to Sasuke should have been the realization of all his dreams. But the one who took control of Orochimaru's special space, which no one could breach, turned out to be his vessel—Sasuke's soul.

Predator and prey—those stricken by the power of the great snake.

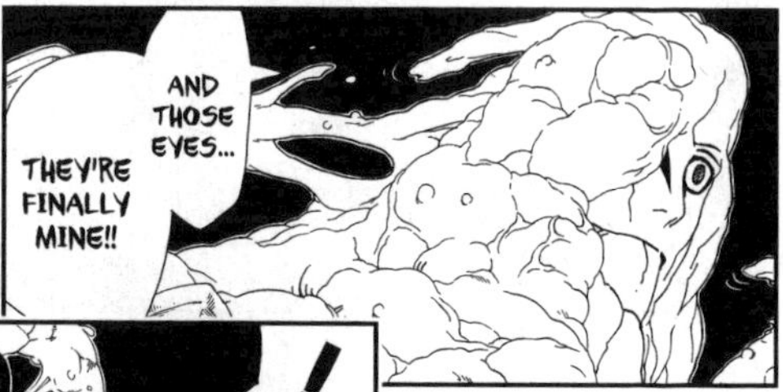
AND THOSE EYES...
THEY'RE FINALLY MINE!!

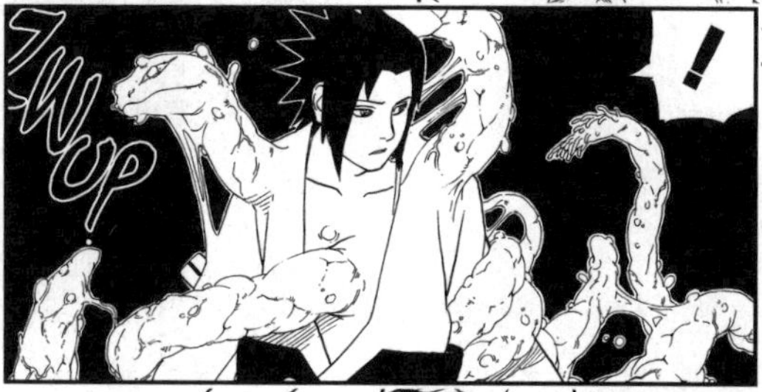
!
ZWUP

←↑ Although touted as a genius, even Orochimaru could not comprehend the power of Kekkei Genkai. This is why he tried to obtain the Sharingan through transference.

《Crushed ambition》

Orochimaru plots his revival even as he is deprived of a body. But his tenacity is crushed by Itachi's Totsuka Blade. Now, only traces of his ambition remain inside Kabuto's body.

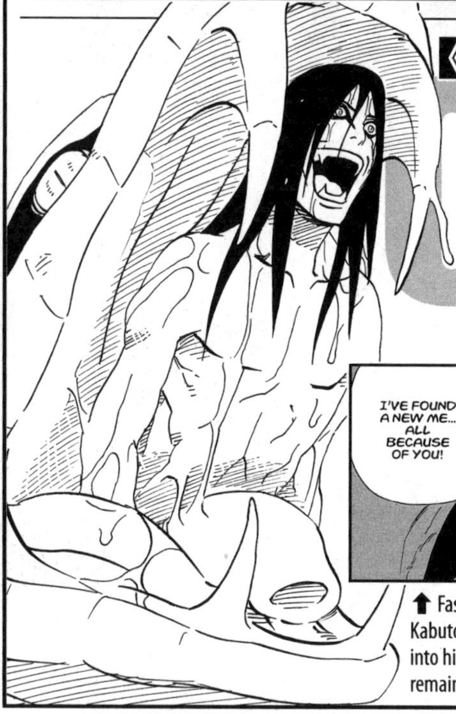

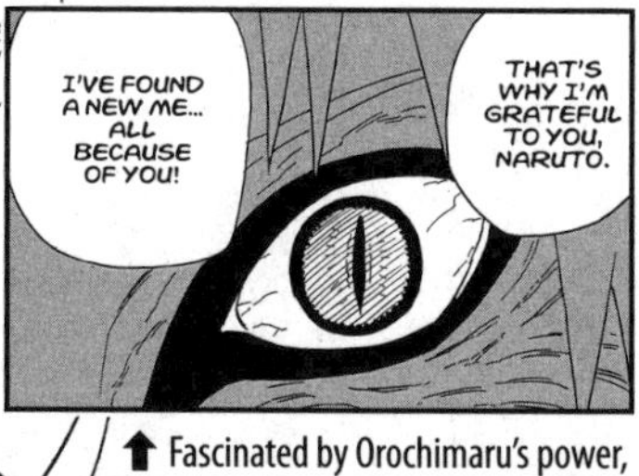
THAT'S WHY I'M GRATEFUL TO YOU, NARUTO.
I'VE FOUND A NEW ME... ALL BECAUSE OF YOU!

↑ Fascinated by Orochimaru's power, Kabuto implanted Orochimaru's cells into his own body. Is it Kabuto that remains? Or…

KAKUZU

角都

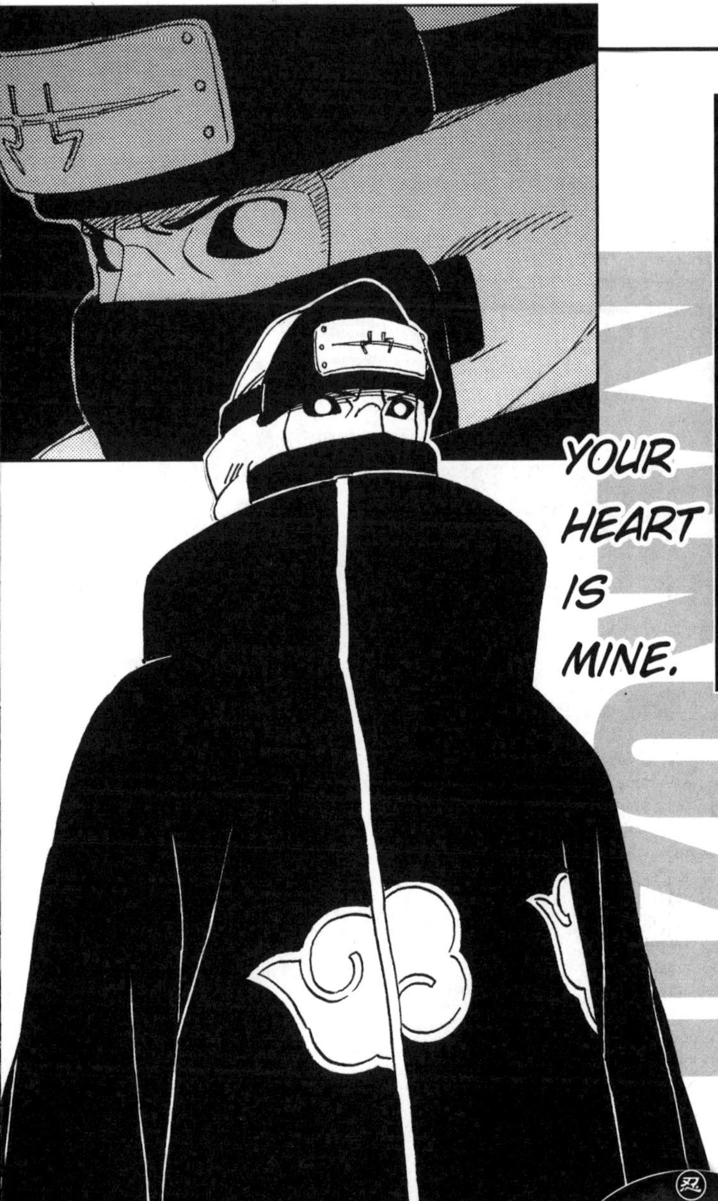

YOUR HEART IS MINE.

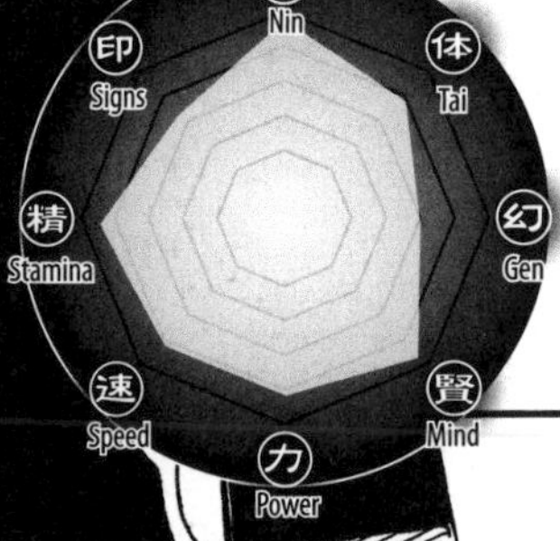
忍
Nin
体
Tai
幻
Gen
賢
Mind
力
Power
速
Speed
精
Stamina
印
Signs

THE FIRST HOKAGE...

← As if they have a mind of their own, Kakuzu's tentacles squirm and wriggle.

Robbing hearts and stitching life into himself... the immortal warrior races across battlefields.

The impetus that got Kakuzu to find a way to cross through time was around the dawning of the hidden villages, just as they were being formed. One of the elite of the Village Hidden in the Waterfalls, Kakuzu is assigned to a mission to assassinate the Hokage. However, he suffers a loss in the face of a Wood Style hijutsu and escapes. He barely makes it out alive. When he returns to his village, he is showered with dishonor and severe punishment. Bitterly angry over this unfair treatment after having risked his life for his village, Kakuzu breaks out of his cell. He takes with him the village's prized forbidden jutsu and the hearts that he carves out of the village elders.

PFOF SHRE

← He is immortal, using the lives of others as provisions. He has already scaled the boundaries of man.

THE MISSION IS ABSOLUTE.

ENOUGH, HIDAN.

Kakuzu is relentless. The passing of years has greatly decreased his connection to humanity. But sometimes traces of the once-honorable samurai surface.

Ninja Registry Number: —
Birthdate: August 15 (91 years old; Leo)
Height: : 185.0 cm (6'1") **Weight:** 63.2 kg (139 lbs.) **Blood type:** A
Personality: Short-tempered, methodical
Favorite food: liver sashimi, monkfish liver
Least favorite food: Kuri Yokan
Would like to fight: Someone at the top of the most-wanted list
Favorite word: Prepare well and you have no worries.
Interests: Reading (Antiquarian books)

Graduated from the Ninja Academy at age ?
Promoted to chûnin at age ?

Mission Experience	D-rank: ?	C-rank: ?
	B-rank: ?	A-rank: ?
	S-rank: ?	

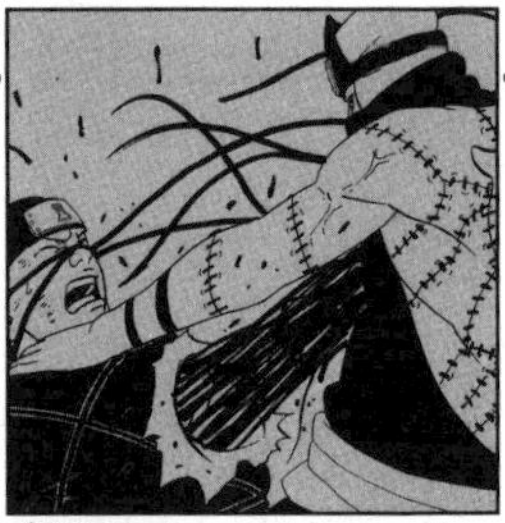

⬆ He butchers and gouges, then forms masks. The powers of the strong become part of Kakuzu.

《Masks and hearts》

There are countless scars and stitch marks on Kakuzu's body. It is evidence of the untold times he has returned from the threshold of death. After he steals a heart and converts it into a mask, he mutilates himself in compensation. It is a never-ending cycle of conflict and death… It can be said that this is the history of the shinobi world.

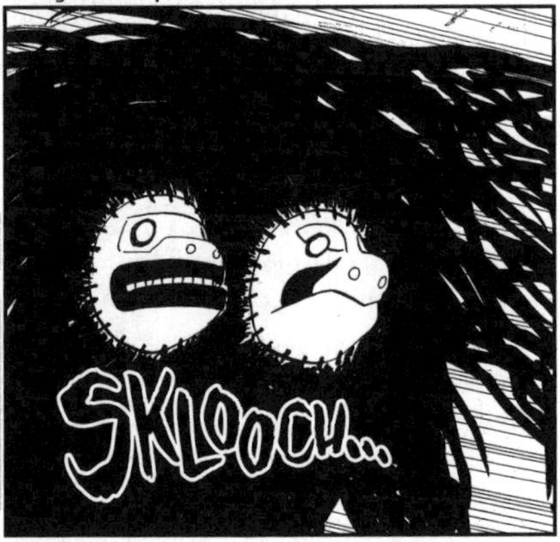
SKLOOCH...

⬆ His masks have many properties in order to utilize an opponent's abilities.

He possesses overwhelming battle experience, having crossed swords with even the First Hokage.

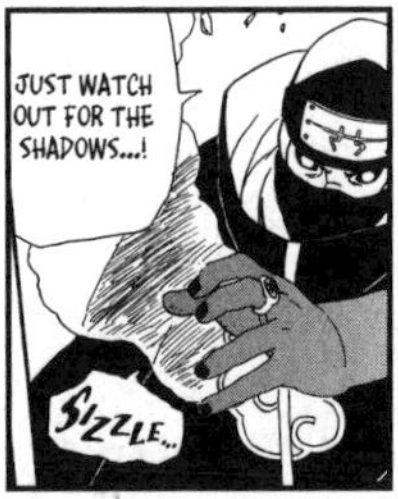
JUST WATCH OUT FOR THE SHADOWS...!
SIZZLE...

⬆ Stored memories of near-death battles make Kakuzu act with prudence.

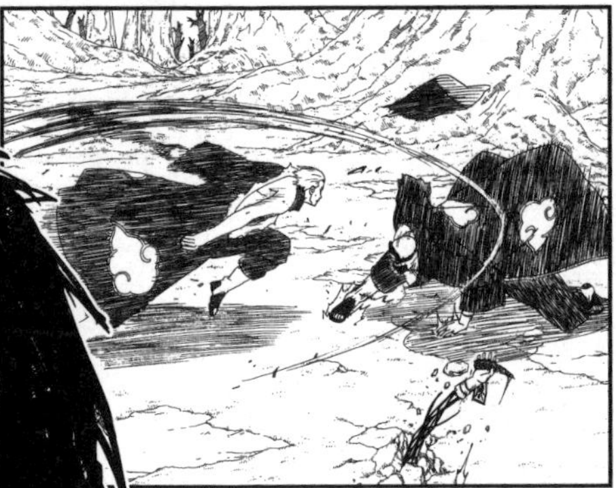

⬅ He will analyze an opponent's power and work out a strategy on the spot.

《Power of analysis》

He has walked the path of a shinobi for a long time. That he has lasted so many years is due to the ability to observe those who are strong. And as he tenaciously clings to life, he has honed his analytical skills to determine whether a heart is worth taking or not.
Kakuzu's abilities, backed up by extensive knowledge and experience, and grounded on cooperative strategizing, is especially useful in two-man cell operations, which is the standard for the Akatsuki.

Deliberate and careful.

《Cool murderous intent》

It is said that until he found a partner who wouldn't die, Kakuzu slaughtered every partner he had and cut out their hearts. This only shows that beneath his cool demeanor and mask, Kakuzu hides a seething anger…

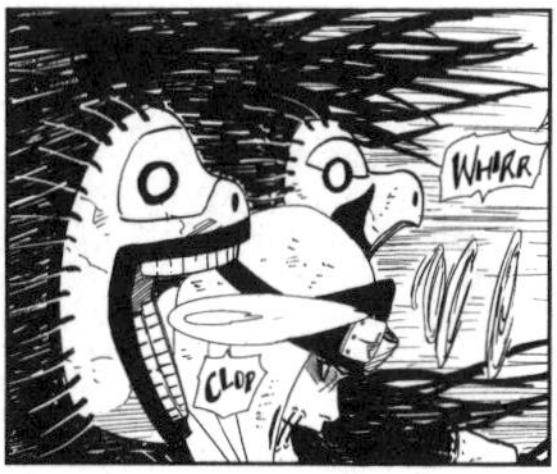
WHIRR
CLOP

⬆ He has turned the hearts of his butchered partners into masks too.

《The Akatsuki's treasurer》

After his escape from the Village Hidden in the Waterfalls, Kakuzu did not join any organizations and made a living as a bounty hunter. His reason to oversee the Akatsuki's finances is directly linked to his ability to survive.

In working for the organization, it is his job to find those with a high bounty on their heads, which equates to someone strong. It is the perfect setup for him to look for strong hearts.

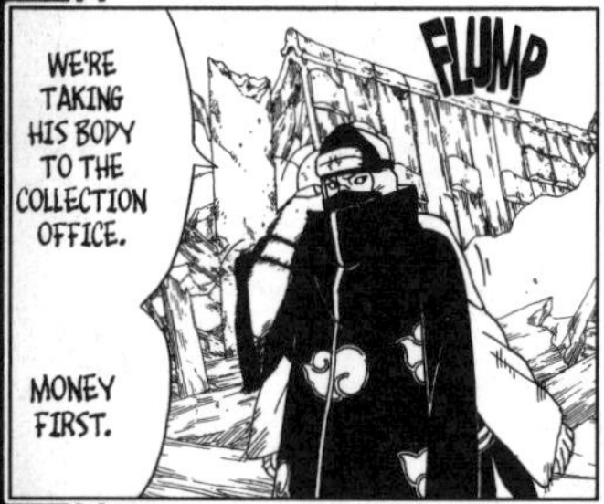
FLUMP
WE'RE TAKING HIS BODY TO THE COLLECTION OFFICE.
MONEY FIRST.

⬆ His contract with the Akatsuki is one of mutual interest.

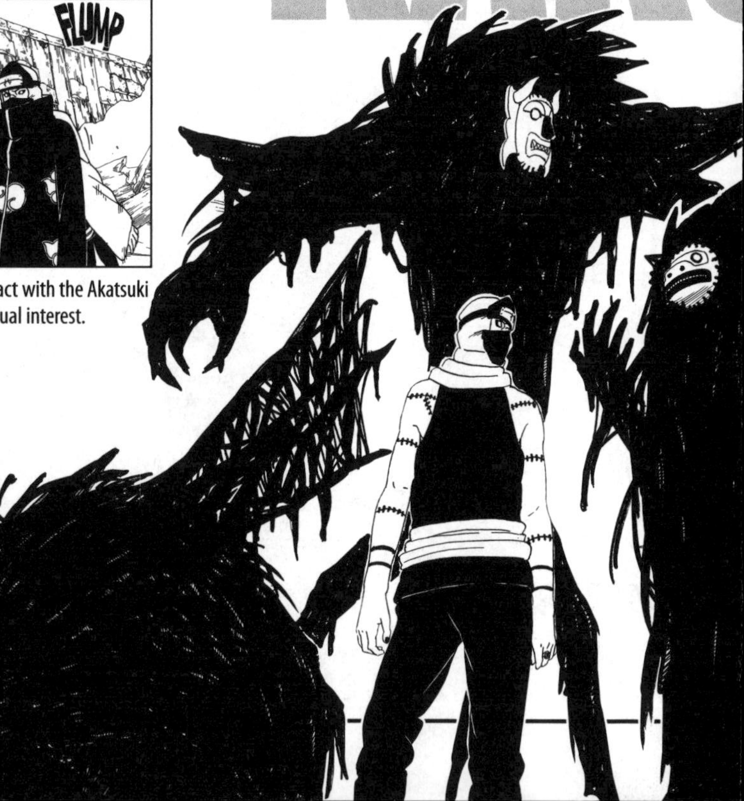

FIFTH KAZEKAGE • GAARA

風影（五代目・我愛羅）

Kazekage

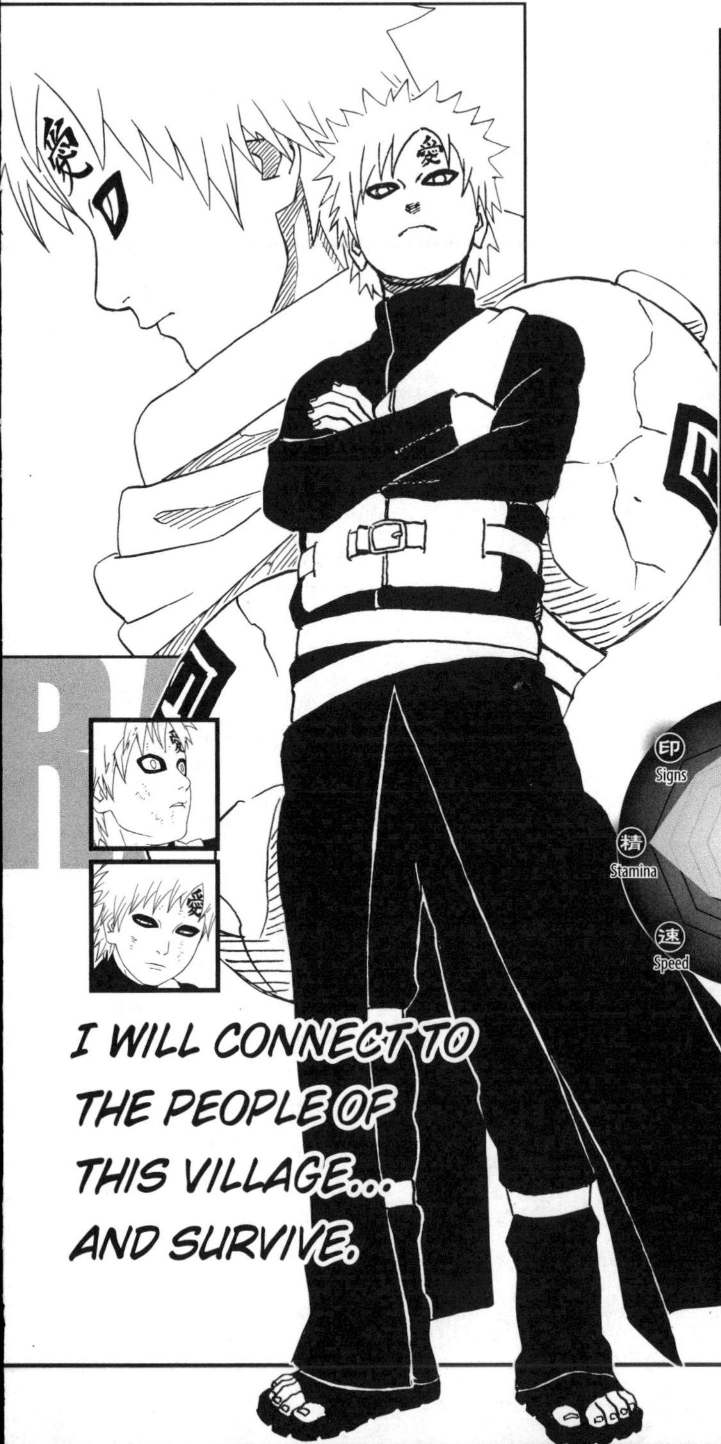

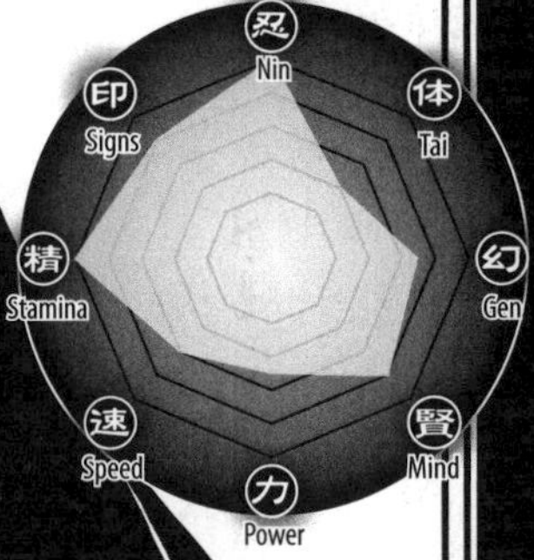
忍
Nin
体
Tai
幻
Gen
賢
Mind
力
Power
速
Speed
精
Stamina
印
Signs

I WILL CONNECT TO THE PEOPLE OF THIS VILLAGE... AND SURVIVE.

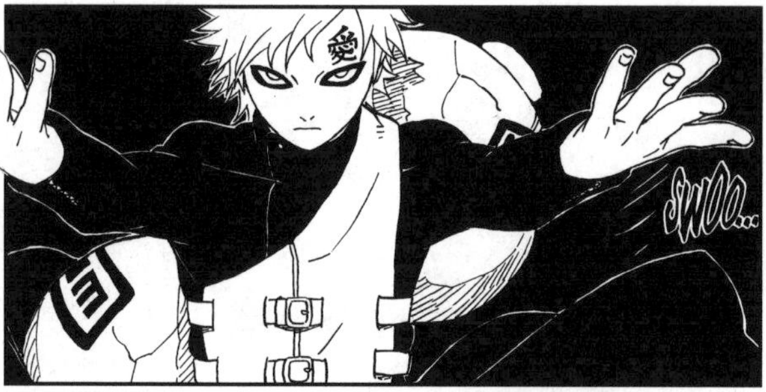
SWOO...

⬅ The assassin's dagger that killed many in the past is now a powerful shield that protects his people.

From a military weapon to guardian– He protects his people with an unwavering will.

Out of convenience, the village placed Shukaku inside him. And from the time he was born, he was shunned as a feared military weapon. That was the scope of Gaara's existence in Sunagakure. It was not a path he desired or chose…but a sad destiny crafted by others. Despite that, he made the decision to change himself; to open the eyes of the villagers and form a bond with others. The Fifth Kazekage. Through pain, he gained strength, and a young, new leader was born.

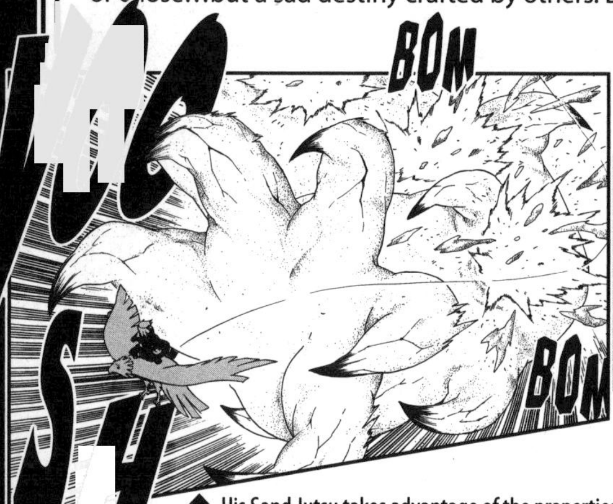
BOM
BOM

⬆ His Sand Jutsu takes advantage of the properties of the earth and grows ever more powerful.

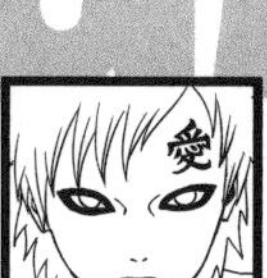

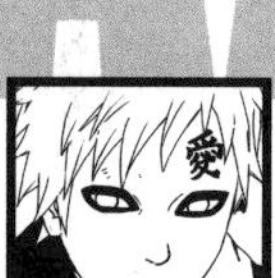

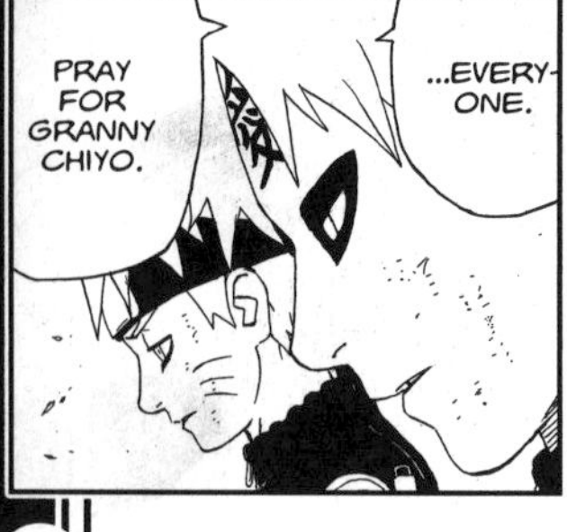
PRAY FOR GRANNY CHIYO.
...EVERY-ONE.

⬅ He always acts with propriety. To Chiyo, who restored his life, he offers the highest level of respect.

Ninja Registry Number: 56-001
Birthdate: January 19 (16 years old; Capricorn)
Height: 166.1 cm (5'5") **Weight:** 50.9 kg (112 lbs.) **Blood type:** AB
Personality: Calm, fearless
Favorite food: Gizzards, Tan Shio
Least favorite food: Sweet bean jelly, marron glacé
Would like to fight: Will fight anyone in order to protect his village
Favorite word: Love, future
Interests: Growing cacti

Graduated from the Ninja Academy at age 12
Promoted to chûnin at age 14

Mission Experience		
	D-rank: 0	C-rank: 9
	B-rank: 8	A-rank: 14
	S-rank: 3	

The friend he found through the chaos shows him a new path in life.

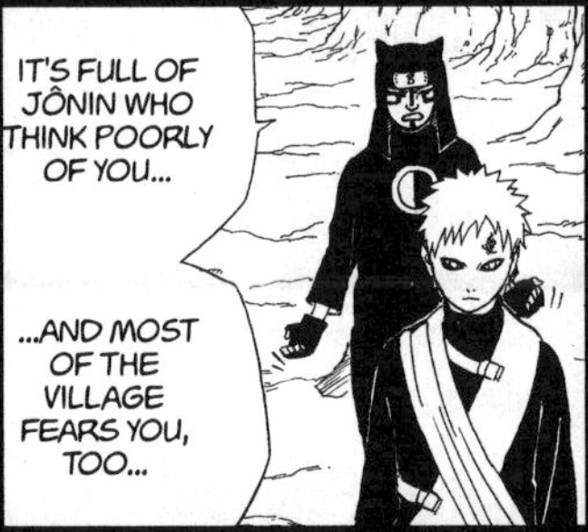
IT'S FULL OF JÔNIN WHO THINK POORLY OF YOU...
...AND MOST OF THE VILLAGE FEARS YOU, TOO...

Despite being in the same circumstances, Naruto has lots of friends. This was a bright light of hope for Gaara.

Realizing that one's destiny is his own to create, Gaara lets go of his resentment towards the past. And he decides to walk the same path as Naruto and dream of the future.

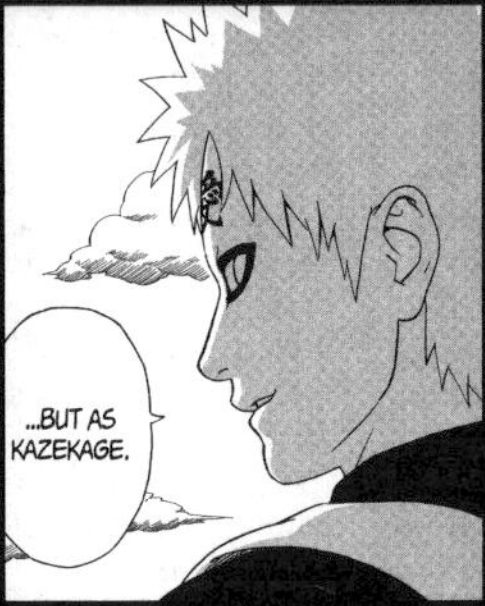
...BUT AS KAZEKAGE.

➡ Although grateful for Kankuro's kind concern, Gaara resolves to take on the difficult duties of the Kazekage.

The sand that the Kazekage hurls–it is sand to protect his village!!

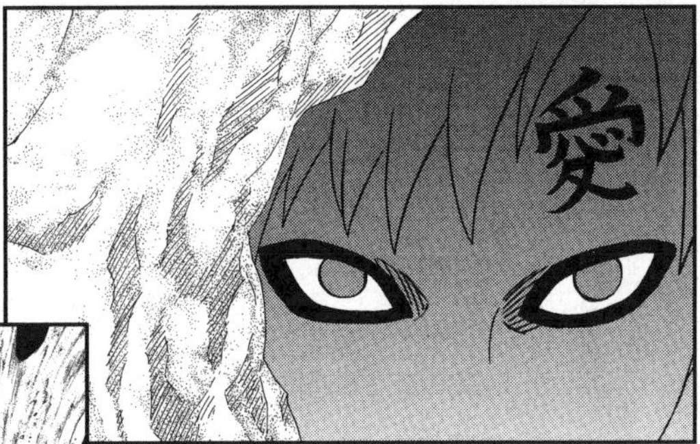

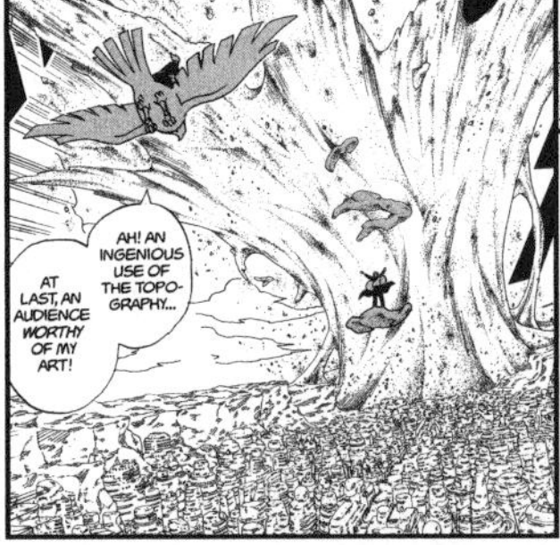
AH! AN INGENIOUS USE OF THE TOPO-GRAPHY...
AT LAST, AN AUDIENCE WORTHY OF MY ART!

⬅⬆ His purpose is not to kill, but to protect the village. Hence, Gaara's foremost principle is to capture assailants, not to kill them.

《Those he must protect》

The Gaara of today does not consider a battle an opportunity to take the lives of those he confronts. Protect the lives of those who live in his village from outside enemies and make their daily lives joyful... To Gaara, that is the true battle he faces as the Kazekage.

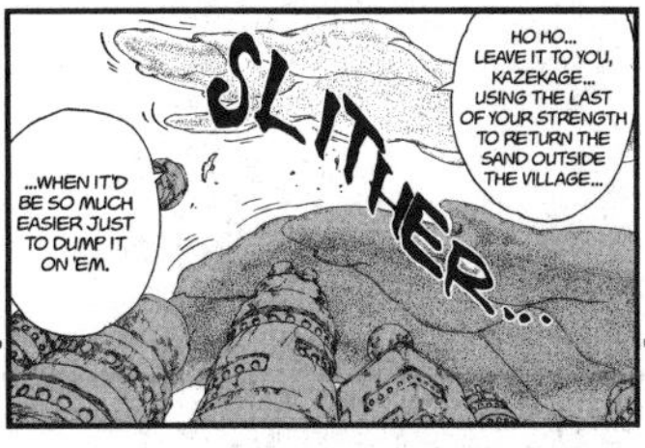
HO HO... LEAVE IT TO YOU, KAZEKAGE... USING THE LAST OF YOUR STRENGTH TO RETURN THE SAND OUTSIDE THE VILLAGE...
...WHEN IT'D BE SO MUCH EASIER JUST TO DUMP IT ON 'EM.
SLITHER...

➡ Even if he sustains severe injuries, he will protect the village.

A discovery made–a friend makes it worth being alive. I am valued!!

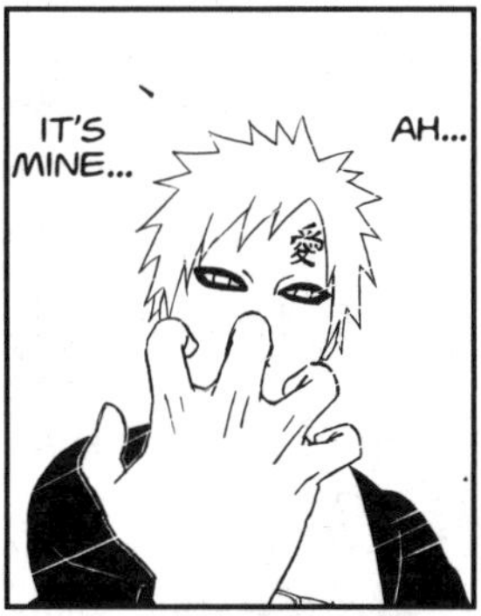
AH...
IT'S MINE...

➡ In his fading consciousness, Gaara asks himself, "Was I ever necessary?"

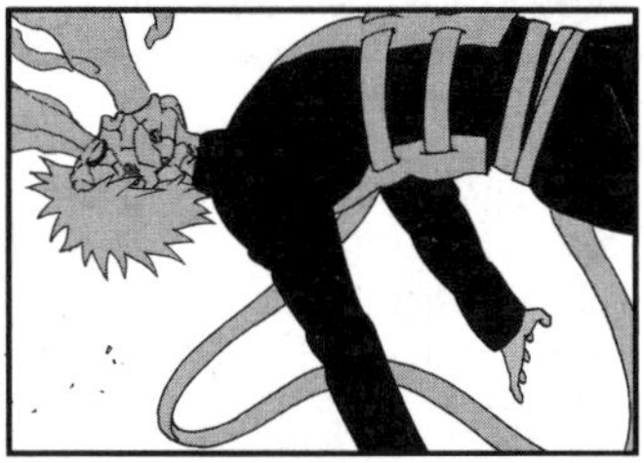

⬆ Gaara is a jinchûriki. If Shukaku is extracted from him, the only thing that lies ahead for Gaara is death.

《Insignificant》

The Akatsuki extract Shukaku, and Gaara hovers near death. As he feels his life ebbing, he questions the meaning of his existence. Is he actually insignificant…

Although he strived to be someone needed by others, Gaara is at a loss about the uncertainty of his existence. "Just who am I?" Just then, as if in answer to his question, Gaara hears his name being called and his shoulder being touched!!

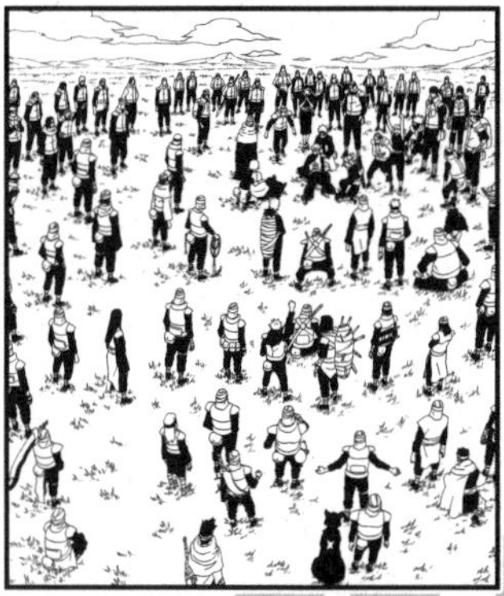

《A bond with another》

The voices calling to him in the dark—they are the voices of his friends, and the people of his village. Feeling the warmth welling up inside him, Gaara comes to a realization. People are defined by their bonds with each other.

⬅ The villagers all rush to Gaara's aid and validate the reason for his existence.

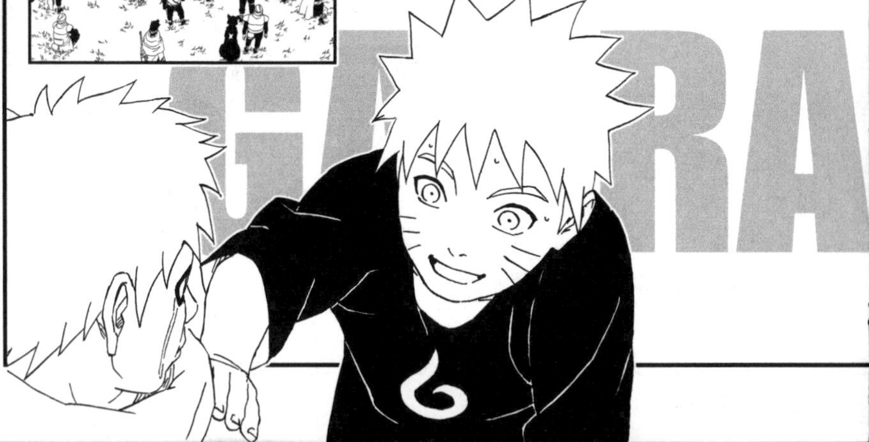
GAARA

ONE AFTER ANOTHER FELLED BY AN ASSASSIN'S BLADE: THE CURSED LINE OF THE KAZEKAGE

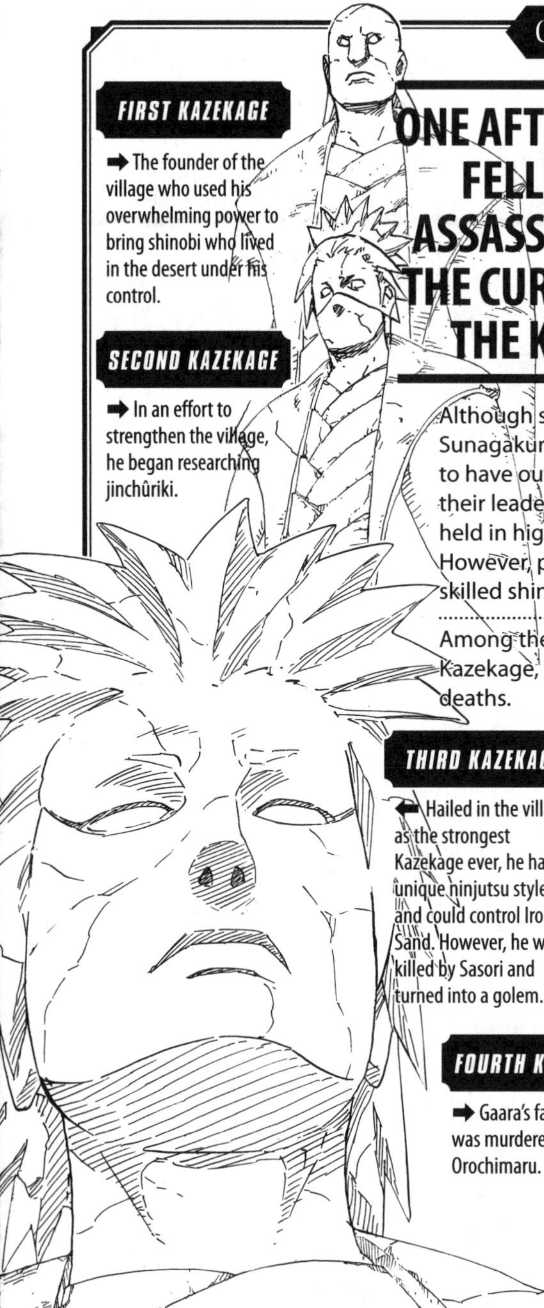

Although small in scale, Sunagakure was acknowledged to have outstanding shinobi. And their leaders, the Kazekage, were held in high esteem by other lands. However, producing so many skilled shinobi came with a price…

Among the generations of Kazekage, many have met untimely deaths.

FIRST KAZEKAGE

➡ The founder of the village who used his overwhelming power to bring shinobi who lived in the desert under his control.

SECOND KAZEKAGE

➡ In an effort to strengthen the village, he began researching jinchûriki.

THIRD KAZEKAGE

⬅ Hailed in the village as the strongest Kazekage ever, he had a unique ninjutsu style and could control Iron Sand. However, he was killed by Sasori and turned into a golem.

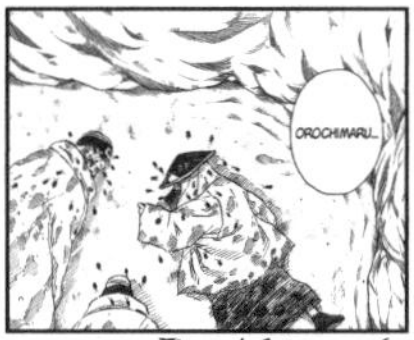
OROCHIMARU...

FOURTH KAZEKAGE

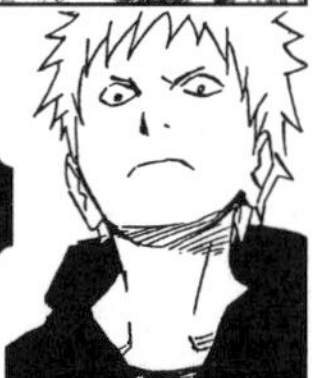

➡ Gaara's father. He was murdered by Orochimaru.

GAMAKEN
ガマケン

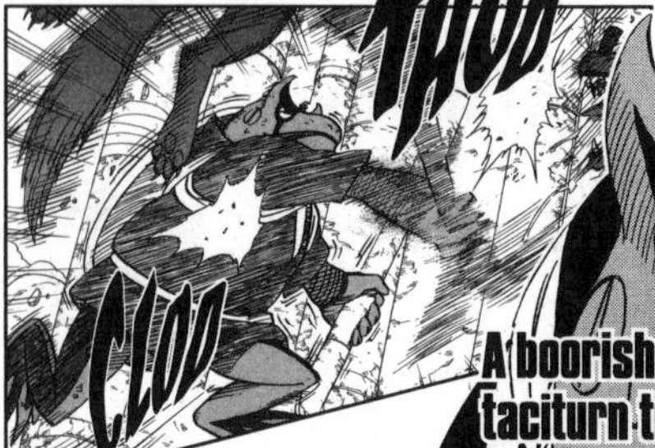
THUD
CLOP

⬆ Apowerful direct attack! Gamaken shows off his true worth!

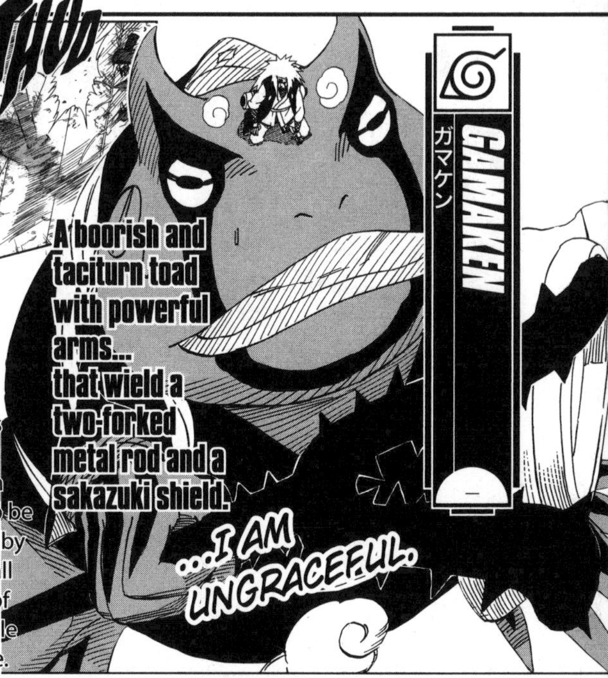
A boorish and taciturn toad with powerful arms...
that wield a two-forked metal rod and a sakazuki shield.
...I AM UNGRACEFUL.

He is a giant toad who boasts arms as strong as Gamabunta and relies exclusively on taijutsu in battle. While he tends to be "ungraceful," he is loved by all who affectionately call him "Ken-san." In times of need, he is always reliable and rushes to the rescue.

GAMAKEN

KAMIZUKI IZUMO
神月イズモ

Chûnin

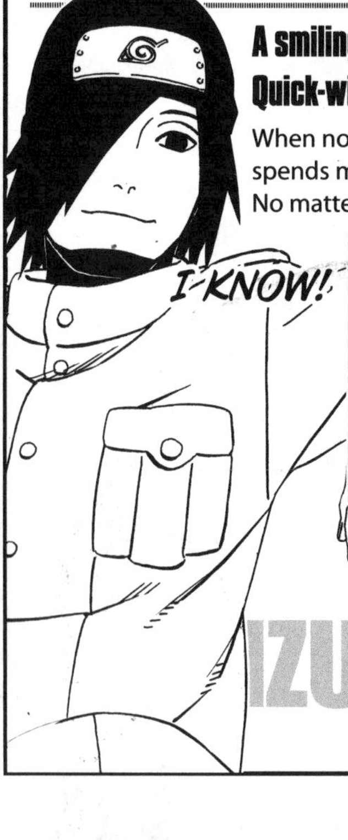
I KNOW!

A smiling face brimming with confidence–
Quick-witted, he always has a comeback.

When not on a mission or training, Izumo spends most of his time organizing data. No matter what the situation, he is able to produce pertinent information and make precise judgments. This is possible only because of his diligent efforts behind the scenes.

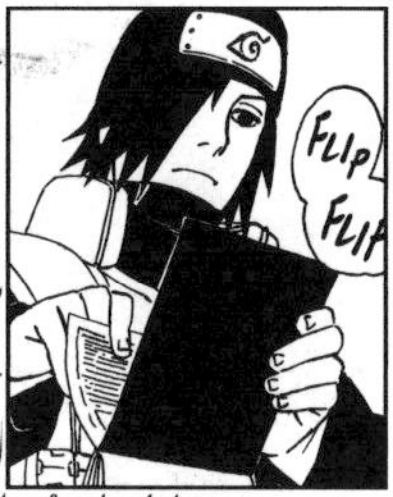
FLIP
FLIP

⬆ He wins not with strength, but intel. This is a form of nindo.

IZUMO

Ninja Registry Number: 012049
Birthdate: November 25 (28 years old; Sagittarius)
Height: 169.0 cm (5'6½") **Weight:** 58.0 kg (128 lbs.) **Blood type:** A
Personality: Fastidious
Interests: Hagane Kotetsu

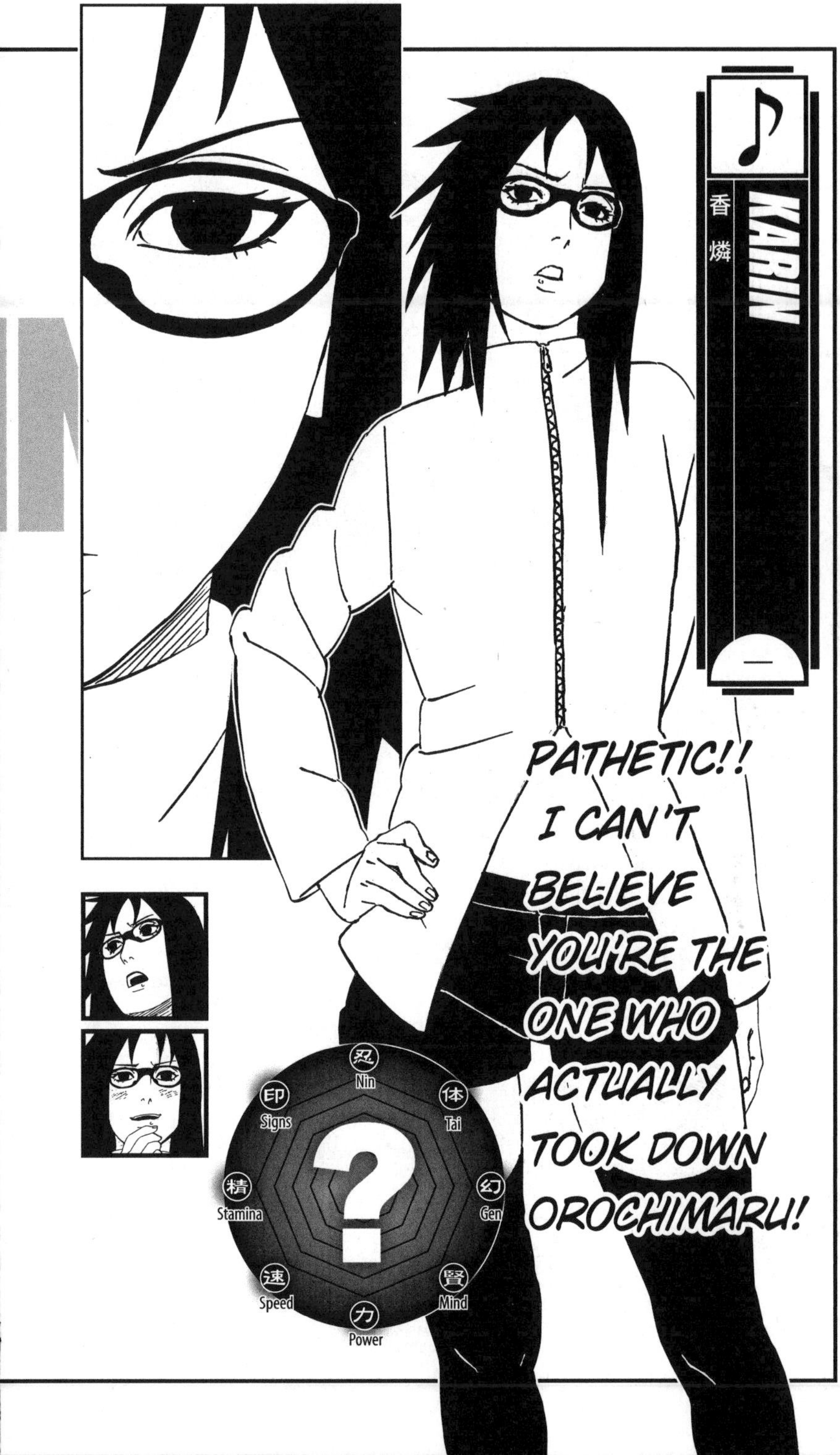
KARIN
香燐
PATHETIC!! I CAN'T BELIEVE YOU'RE THE ONE WHO ACTUALLY TOOK DOWN OROCHIMARU!
忍 Nin
体 Tai
幻 Gen
賢 Mind
力 Power
速 Speed
精 Stamina
印 Signs
?

Her cold eyes can see for thousands of miles, and her heart belongs to the Taka.

⬇ Not only is she able to use sensory skills, but Karin has extensive knowledge at her disposal. With this, she comes up with brilliant strategies that contribute to the mission.

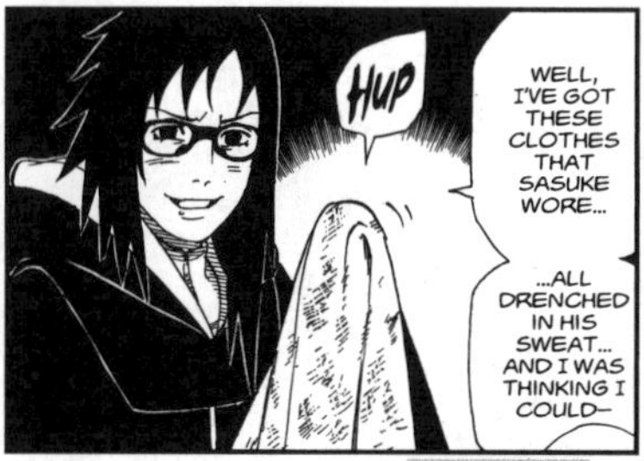
WELL, I'VE GOT THESE CLOTHES THAT SASUKE WORE...
...ALL DRENCHED IN HIS SWEAT... AND I WAS THINKING I COULD—
HUP

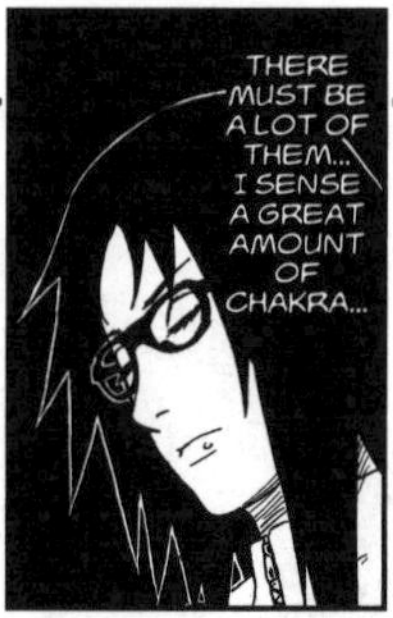
THERE MUST BE A LOT OF THEM... I SENSE A GREAT AMOUNT OF CHAKRA...

⬆ In chakra type and quantity, Karin was born blessed with sensory powers that surpass ocular jutsu.

Once, in a village destroyed by the fires of war, a young girl stood, totally unscathed. She said, "I knew a lot of people were approaching." This is how Orochimaru came to bring Karin to Otogakure. Karin began serving the Sound with her sharp sensory skills and clear thinking. However, although she was Orochimaru's subordinate, she never felt any loyalty to him. She continued because of her love for Sasuke. Then Orochimaru died, and Sasuke stood before her. Why is she so obsessed with him?

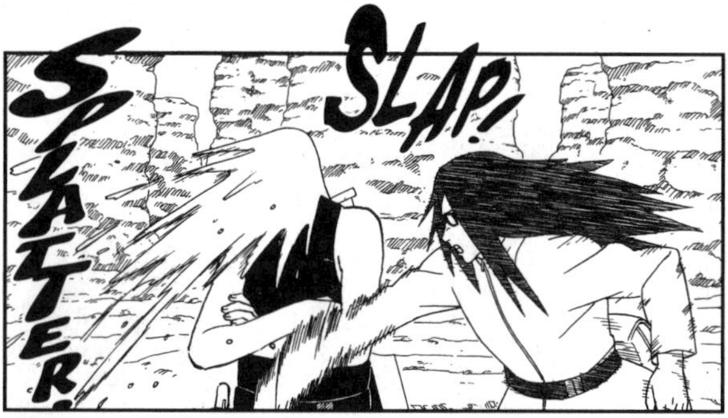
SLAP!
SPLATTER!

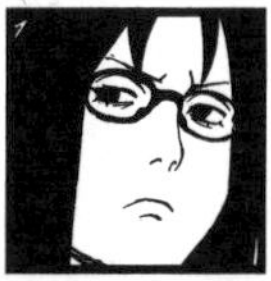

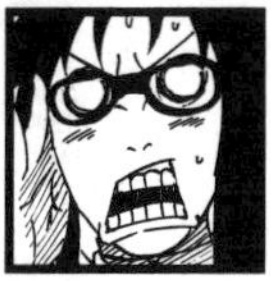

⬆ She has confidence in her fists too! She never backs down!

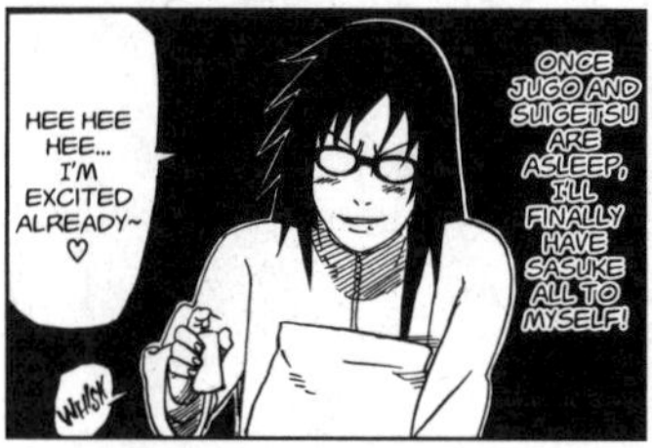
ONCE JUGO AND SUIGETSU ARE ASLEEP, I'LL FINALLY HAVE SASUKE ALL TO MYSELF!
HEE HEE HEE... I'M EXCITED ALREADY~ ♡
WHISK

⬆ Behind her usual moody demeanor, Karin conceals a dangerous love for Sasuke...

Ninja Registry Number: —
Birthdate: June 20 (16 years old; Gemini)
Height: 162.6 cm (5'4") **Weight:** 45.8. kg (101 lbs.) **Blood type:** AB
Personality: Headstrong, eccentric
Favorite food: Okonomiyaki
Least favorite food: Boiled gyoza
Would like to fight: Hozuki, Suigetsu
Favorite word: A woman's resolve can smash boulders.
Interests: Collecting perfumes

Graduated from the Ninja Academy at age —
Promoted to chûnin at age —

Mission Experience		
	D-rank: 25	C-rank: 16
	B-rank: 7	A-rank: 2
	S-rank: 0	

KANKURO

カンクロウ

Jônin

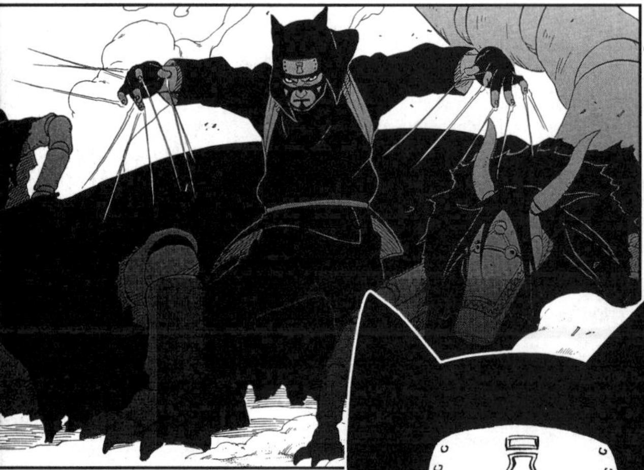

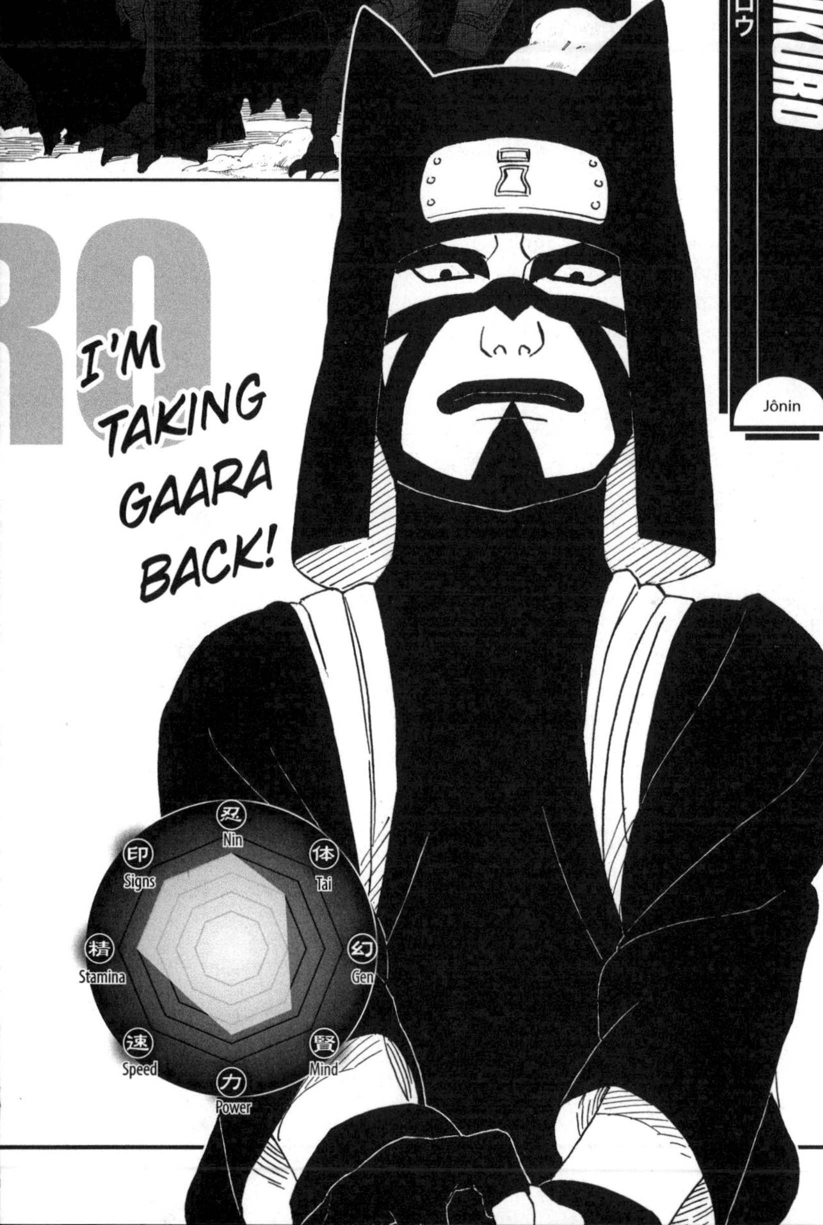
I'M TAKING GAARA BACK!
忍
Nin
体
Tai
幻
Gen
賢
Mind
力
Power
速
Speed
精
Stamina
印
Signs

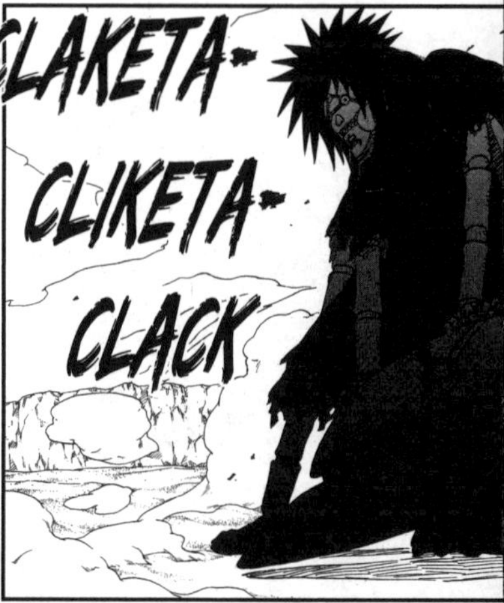
CLAKETA-
CLIKETA-
CLACK

In just three short years since he took his first Chûnin Exam, Kankuro has advanced to becoming a Sand jônin with his gruesome puppet mastery! His ability has given him confidence, and he takes pride in his skill as a puppeteer. Until now, Kankuro's goal in battle has been to fascinate his foes with his skills. But the passage of time has greatly changed the reason he fights.

Although he still hosts Shukaku inside him, Gaara has reformed his way of life. Seeing his little brother's growth despite being a symbol of fear forces Kankuro to re-evaluate his own role as a big brother. His new golem, Sansho'uo, the Salamander, is impregnable. It is Kankuro's first jutsu to be used to protect. And the reason for obtaining it is none other than his desire to protect his little brother who has become the Kazekage.

The puppet master fascinates with a supreme performance of the dance of terror!!

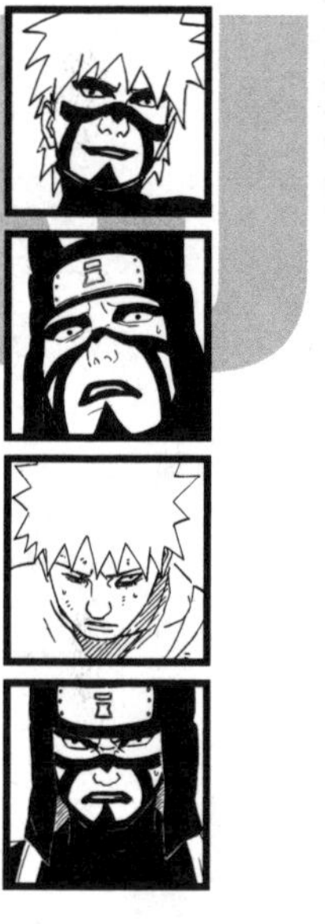

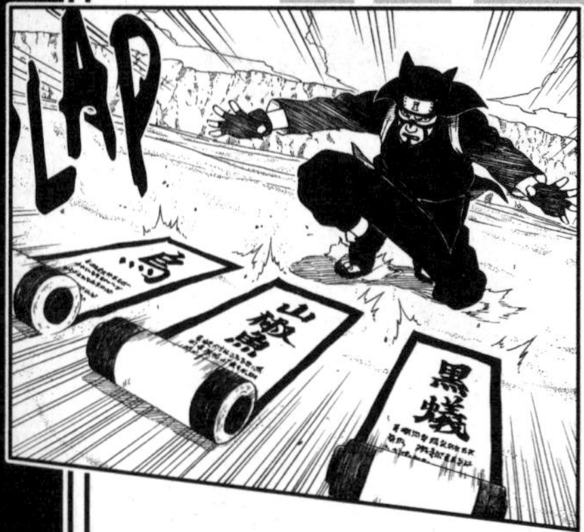
CLAP

⬅ Kankuro summons his golems, three at once, in a performance that even Sasori of the Red Sand praises.

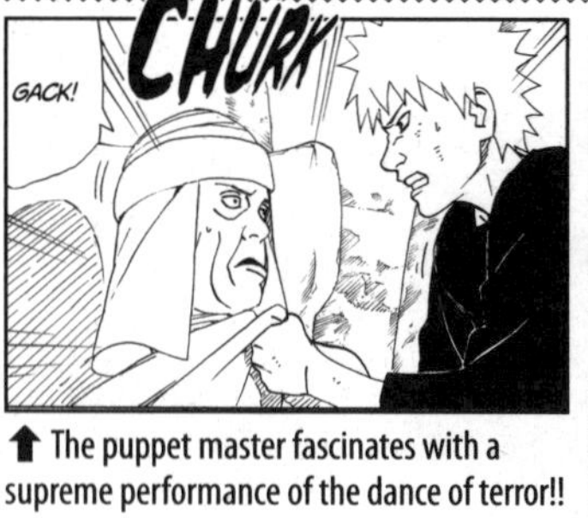
CHURK
GACK!

⬆ The puppet master fascinates with a supreme performance of the dance of terror!!

Ninja Registry Number: 54-002
Birthdate: May 15 (18 years old; Taurus)
Height: 175.0 cm (5'9") **Weight:** 61.2 kg (135 lbs.) **Blood type:** B
Personality: Scheming
Favorite food: Hamburger steak
Least favorite food: Spinach
Would like to fight: Anyone but Gaara
Favorite word: Never pass up a golden opportunity.
Interests: Collecting marionettes

Graduated from the Ninja Academy at age 12
Promoted to chûnin at age 16

Mission Experience		
	D-rank: 0	C-rank: 9
	B-rank: 10	A-rank: 23
	S-rank: 1	

NINE-TAILED FOX SPIRIT

九尾の妖狐

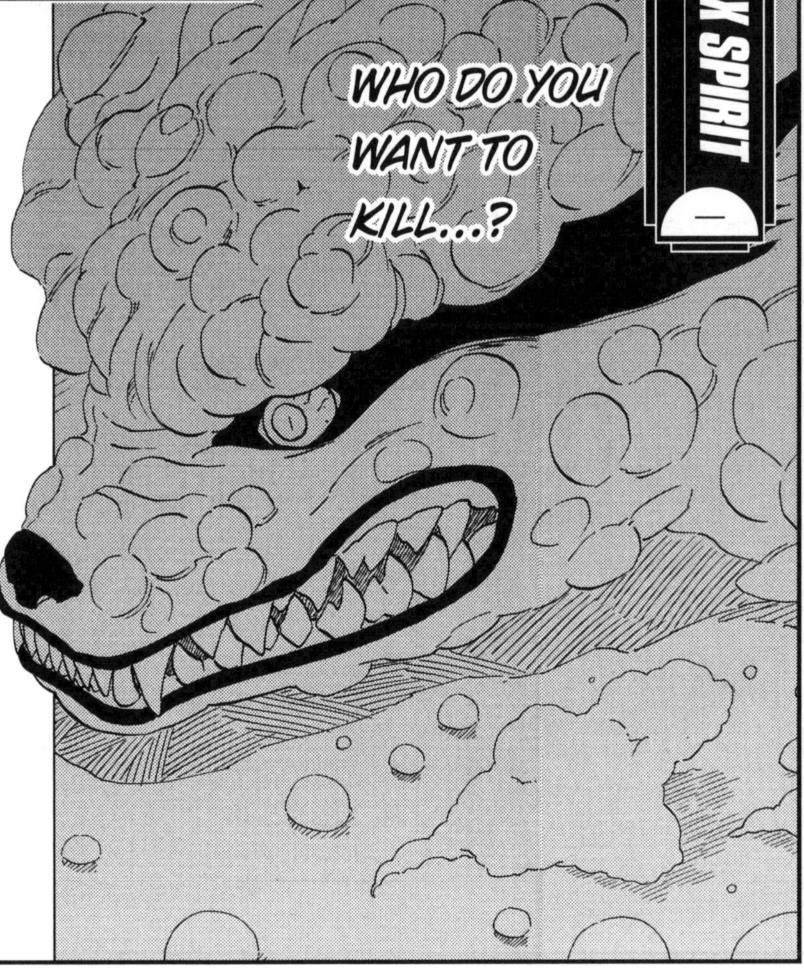
WHO DO YOU WANT TO KILL...?

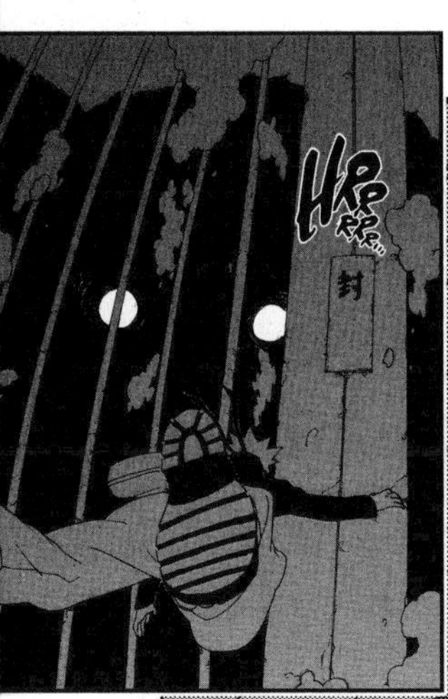
HRRRRR...
封

YOUR OCULAR POWERS AND THAT VILE CHAKRA YOU EXUDE...

D... ON'T... KILL... NA... RUTO...

⬆ Nine Tails knows about the Uchiha clan's past as well as Naruto's secret. Just what is this truth…?!

Sealed inside Naruto is a powerful force that could easily turn the world to ash.

During crucial periods in history, this Tailed Beast would appear suddenly and destroy everything in sight. The Akatsuki and countless strong men like Uchiha Madara have long tried to obtain its powers. Presently, Nine Tails is sealed inside Naruto. But it bides its time, waiting for the opportunity to take over Naruto's body and resurrect itself. There was a time when it was possessed by Uchiha Madara's eye. However, right now, there is no one who can control its chakra.

Collection ... Number 5

Konoha

THE FACT THAT HE SPLIT THE NINE-TAILED FOX SPIRIT'S POWER INTO YIN AND YANG...
...AND SEALED THE YANG HALF INSIDE NARUTO WAS TO PURPOSELY LEAVE HIM NINE TAILS' CHAKRA.

⬆ The Fourth Hokage sacrificed his life and used the Reaper Death Seal to seal the Yin chakra of the Nine-Tailed Fox Spirit.

The jutsu used to seal Nine Tails inside Naruto's body has been weakening, making it more difficult, year by year, for Naruto to suppress it. However, there are many mysteries behind this jutsu, and only the Fourth Hokage who placed the seal knows the truth hidden in it.

Why did the Fourth Hokage seal only half of Nine Tails' chakra, the Yang chakra, inside Naruto? Only Naruto, who was entrusted with the key to the seal, can unravel the mystery his late father left behind.

THE FOURTH HOKAGE'S TRUE INTENTION: THE MYSTERY BEHIND THE SEALING OF THE NINE TAILS

...THAT HAPPENED WHILE TRAINING NARUTO...
...WHEN THE FOURTH TAIL OF THE NINE-TAILS' CHAKRA EMERGED.

➡ It is impossible to completely suppress the Nine Tails' power, the force of which overflows into Naruto himself.

GEROTORA

ゲロ寅

WHAT DO YOU MEAN BY SUMMONING ME?!

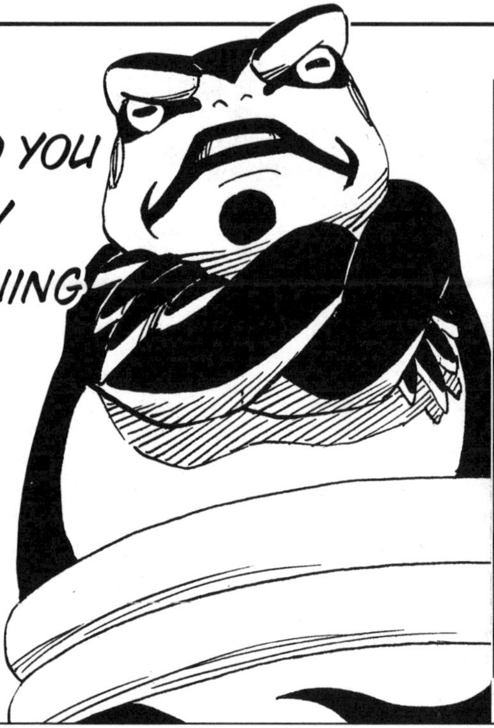

The scroll toad who holds the key to a detestable power.

Gerotora was born into this long-respected line of scroll toads, which store seals and seal formulas in their bellies. He's known for being tough and reliable.

During the Nine Tails' attack on Konoha, the Fourth Hokage entrusted him with the grave responsibility of guarding the key to the Eight-Signed Seal, which he placed on Naruto's stomach. For nearly 16 years, he has fervently fulfilled his duty.

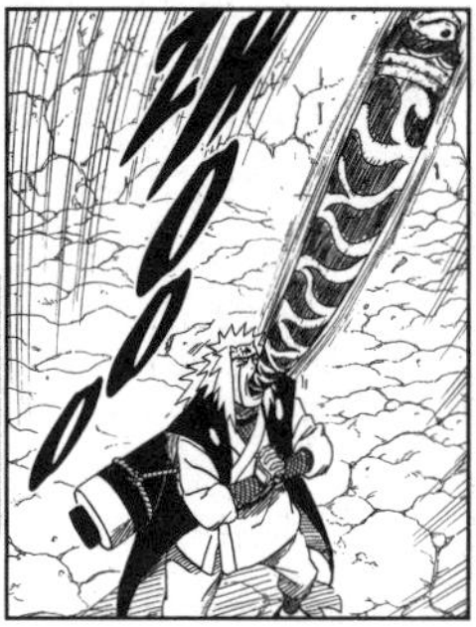

➡ Just before the battle which would claim his life, Jiraiya summons Gerotora who has been kept in safe storage.

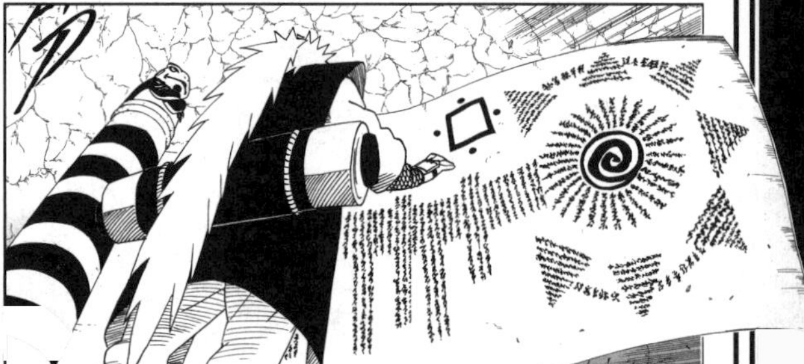

➡ The Five-Pronged Seal is used to release and confine Gerotora.

ELDERS
ご意見番

The village leaders who watch over the village and offer their advice.

Here are the two elders who observe everything that happens in Konoha and exert considerable influence on its governance. They feel that the present Hokage, Tsunade, is too inexperienced and often take issue with her. However, they do this only out of love and concern for their village.

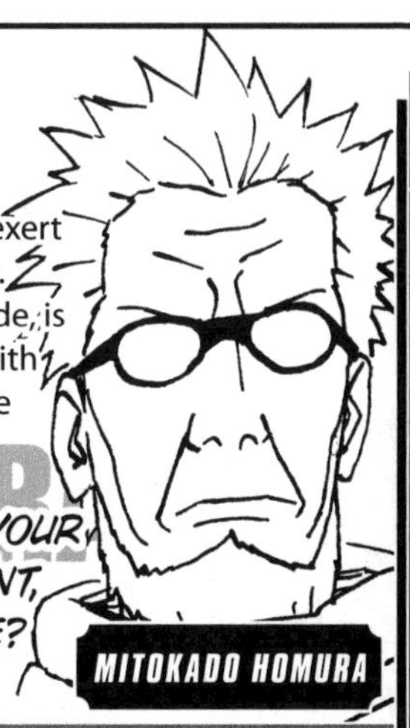
THAT IS YOUR ARGUMENT, TSUNADE?
MITOKADO HOMURA

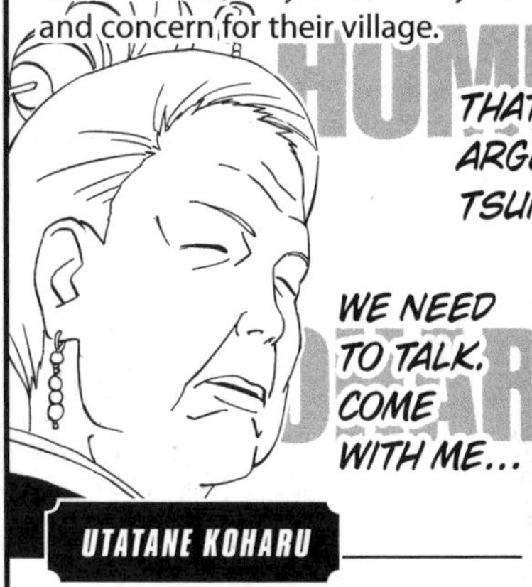
WE NEED TO TALK. COME WITH ME...
UTATANE KOHARU

UTATANE KOHARU
Ninja Registry Number: 000256
Birthdate: September 1 (72 years old; Virgo)
Height: 153.0 cm (5'0") **Weight:** 46.3 kg (102 lbs.) **Blood type:** A
Personality: Group-oriented, modest

MITOKADO HOMURA
Ninja Registry Number: 000293
Birthdate: May 8 (72 years old; Taurus)
Height: 166.0 cm (5'4") **Weight:** 55.2 kg (121 lbs.) **Blood type:** A
Personality: Authoritarian, cool

—

KONOHAMARU
木ノ葉丸

Genin

A budding leaf that will grow into a tall tree.

He is the grandson of the Third Hokage, and having graduated from the Academy, he has set out on the path of the shinobi. He belongs to a cell commanded by Ebisu, his former tutor, and has been going on low-level missions. His goal is to become the Hokage someday.

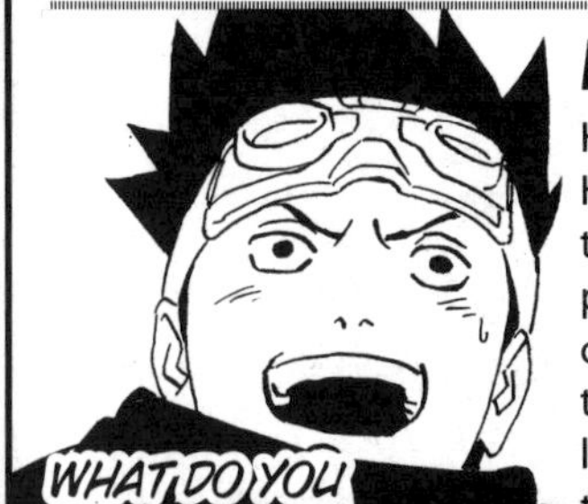
WHAT DO YOU THINK?! I GOT THE BOING-FWHHT-BOING PART DOWN NOW, EH?

➡ These days, he has progressed to the point where he can use Shadow Doppelgangers. However, there is a slight problem with how he uses them...

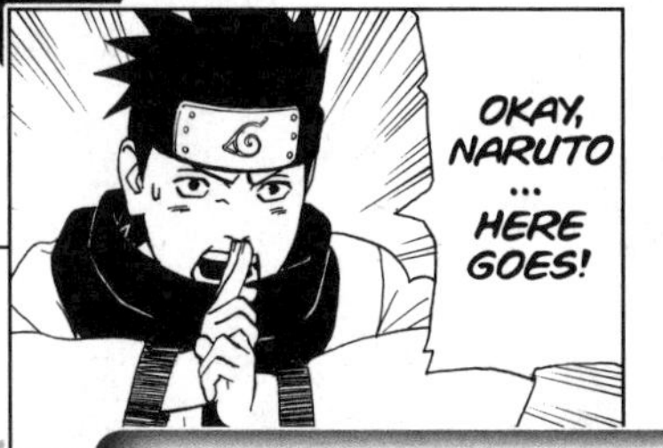
OKAY, NARUTO ... HERE GOES!

Ninja Registry Number: 012707
Birthdate: December 30 (12 years old; Capricorn)
Height: 141.1 cm (4'7½") **Weight:** 36.9 kg (81 lbs.) **Blood type:** B
Personality: Impatient, hates to lose
Favorite word: There is no shortcut to becoming the Hokage.

KONAN
小南

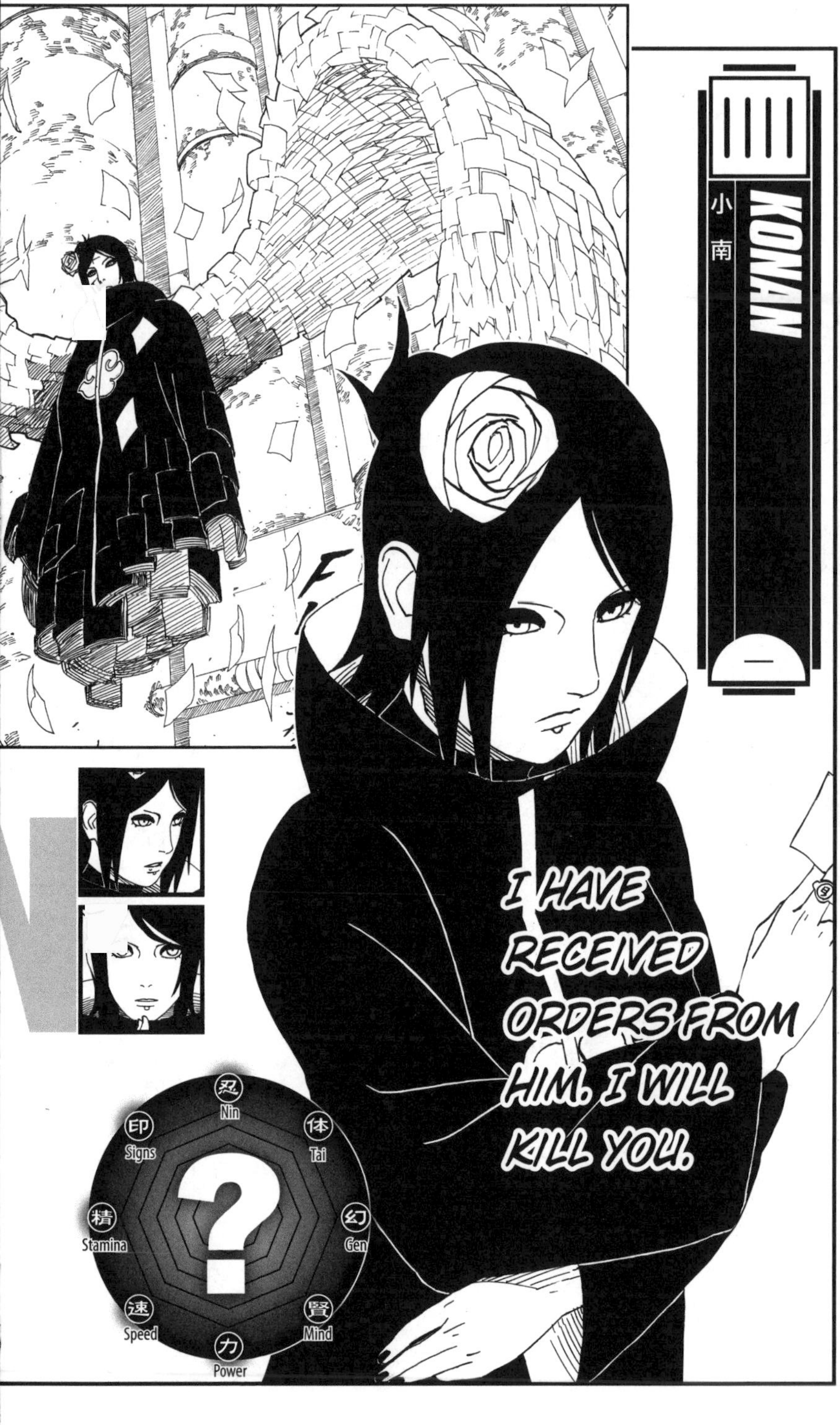
I HAVE RECEIVED ORDERS FROM HIM. I WILL KILL YOU.
忍 Nin
体 Tai
幻 Gen
賢 Mind
力 Power
速 Speed
精 Stamina
印 Signs
?

MASTER, YOU KNOW NOTHING ABOUT WHAT HAPPENED TO US AFTERWARDS...

This strange, fascinating disciple... Will she play a song of joy or sing of destruction?

← What is it in her past that makes Konan want to change the world even with extreme means?

Like a shadow, Konan always stands by Pain, the leader of the Akatsuki and the Rain. The villagers reverently refer to her as the Angel. She reveres Pain and will not hesitate to murder people if Pain so orders. When she was a child, Konan trained under Jiraiya. This girl, who had not only shinobi potential, but a kind heart…

Why did she end up joining such a dark organization? The answer lies hidden within a paper blizzard, beyond the reach of human eyes…

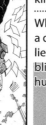

UNNH...

⬆ Konan uses an original jutsu in which she changes her body into paper. There is splendor in the way she fights, but also a sense of transience.

HERE.

THANK YOU...

⬆ As a child, Konan loved origami and was very friendly to others.

Ninja Registry Number: —
Birthdate: February 20 (? years old; Pisces)
Height: 169.4 cm (5'6½") **Weight:** 45.3 kg (100 lbs.) **Blood type:** O
Personality: Calm and collected, kind
Favorite food: Grilled fish
Least favorite food: Fried chicken
Would like to fight: Those who defy the gods
Favorite word: Orderliness
Interests: Origami, pressed flowers

Graduated from the Ninja Academy at age —
Promoted to chûnin at age —

Mission Experience	D-rank: 0	C-rank: 65
	B-rank: 161	A-rank: 85
	S-rank: 30	

SAI

サイ

Anbu

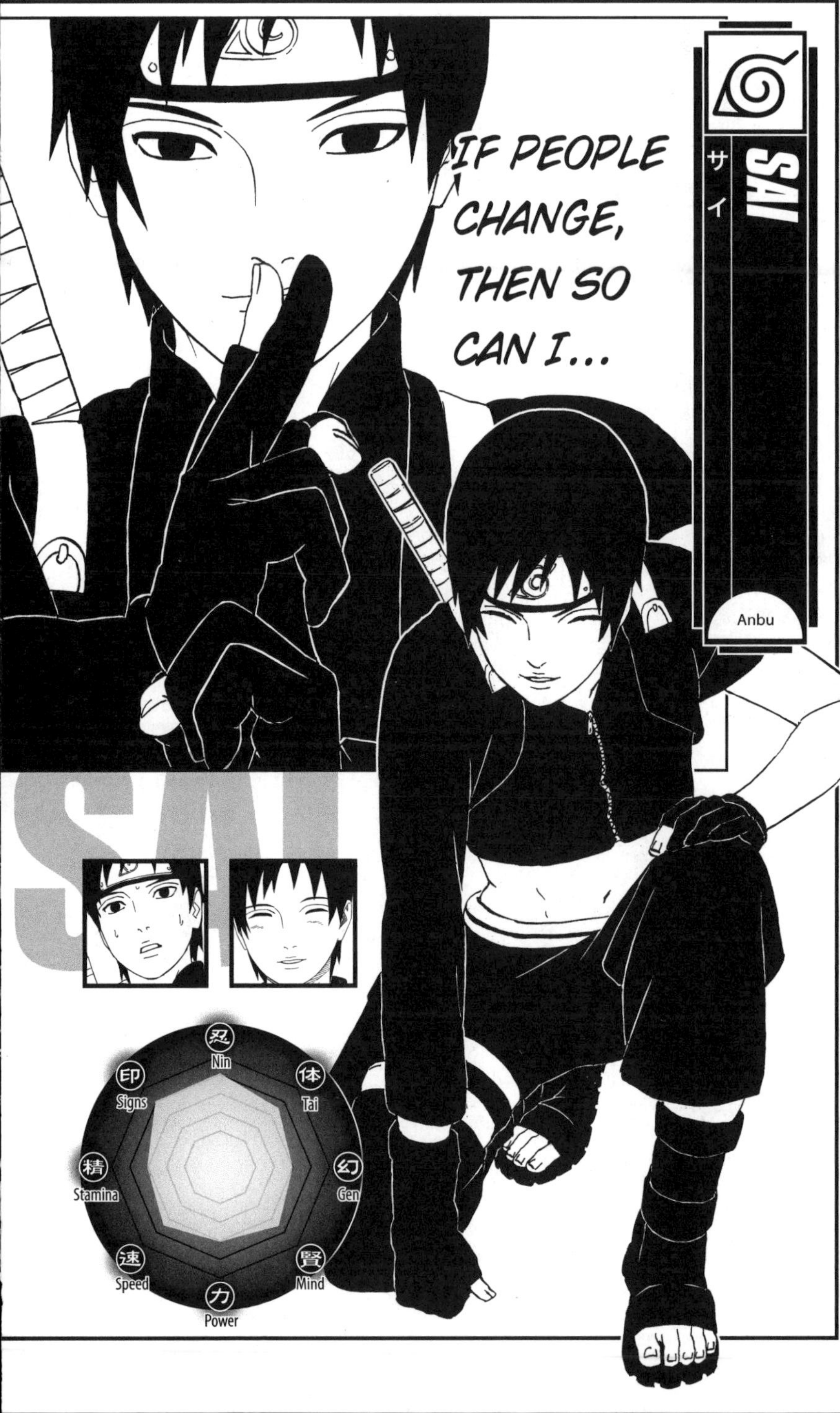
IF PEOPLE CHANGE, THEN SO CAN I...
SAI
忍 Nin
体 Tai
幻 Gen
賢 Mind
力 Power
速 Speed
精 Stamina
印 Signs

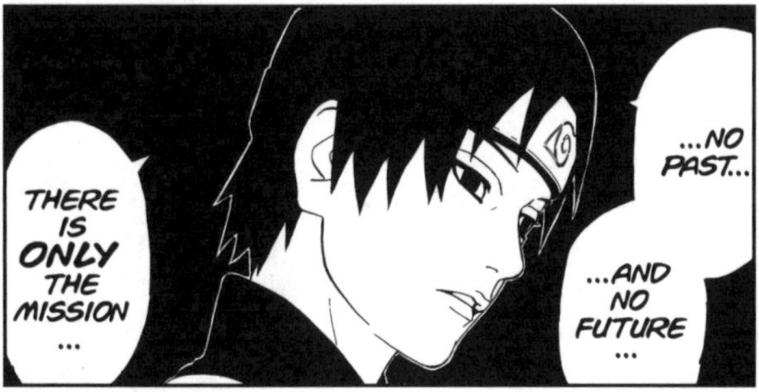
...NO PAST...
...AND NO FUTURE...
THERE IS ONLY THE MISSION...

The finishing touch... A still heart makes his brush and ink come alive.

⬆ Abandoning everything that one would cherish, Sai focuses on his missions for the Anbu Black Ops.

After war had torn apart his family, young Sai was taken in by the Foundation and trained to carry out missions without a shred of emotion. Meeting Naruto changes all that. Although he is confused, Sai gradually gives in to his feelings, proving they were not gone, but simply buried deeply by his training.

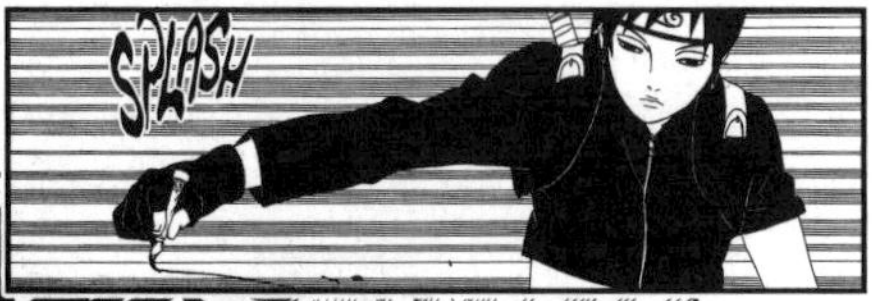
SPLASH

The only friend Sai ever had was his late older brother, Shin. To Sai, his friendship and new bond with Naruto is a new beginning.

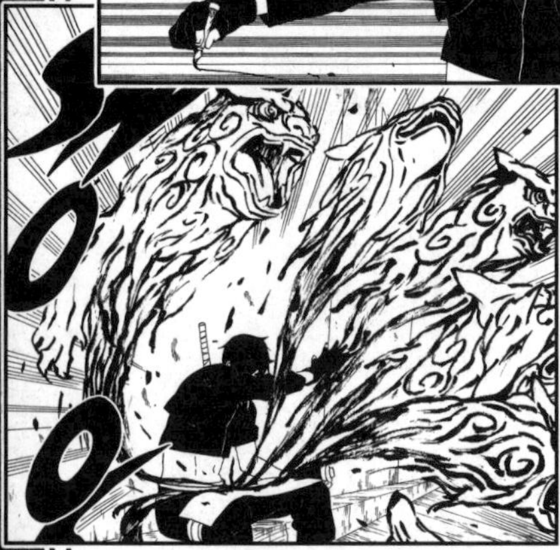

⬅ He can control at will any beast he paints. This is possible only because of Sai's artistic sensibilities.

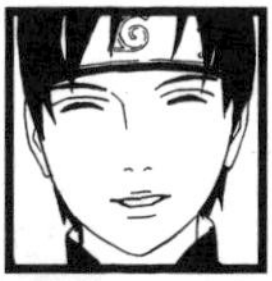

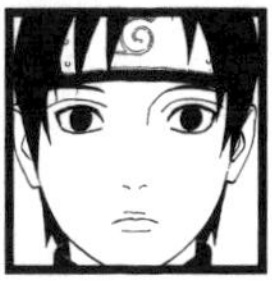

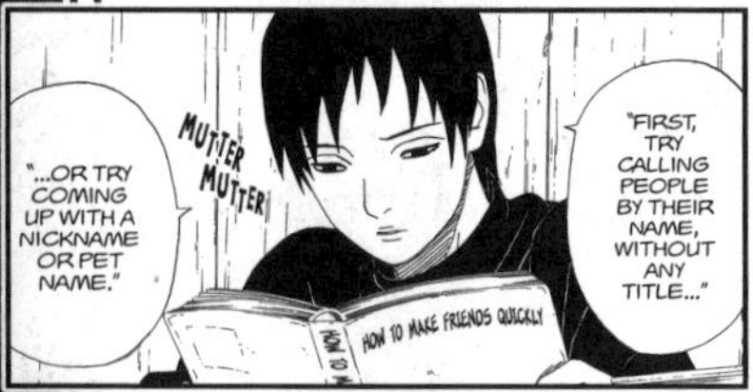
"FIRST, TRY CALLING PEOPLE BY THEIR NAME, WITHOUT ANY TITLE..."
MUTTER MUTTER
"...OR TRY COMING UP WITH A NICKNAME OR PET NAME."
HOW TO MAKE FRIENDS QUICKLY

⬆ Sai finds friends and tries to learn about social relationships through books. However, he has quite the opposite results with Sakura.

Ninja Registry Number: 012420
Birthdate: November 25 (17 years old; Sagittarius)
Height: 172.1 cm (5'8") **Weight:** 53.3 kg (118 lbs.) **Blood type:** A
Personality: Honest, docile
Favorite food: Tofu (firm)
Least favorite food: Mitarashi dango
Would like to fight: Hatake Kakashi
Favorite word: Friends
Interests: Drawing, calligraphy

Graduated from the Ninja Academy at age 9
Promoted to chûnin at age 10

Mission Experience		
	D-rank: ?	C-rank: ?
	B-rank: ?	A-rank: ?
	S-rank: ?	

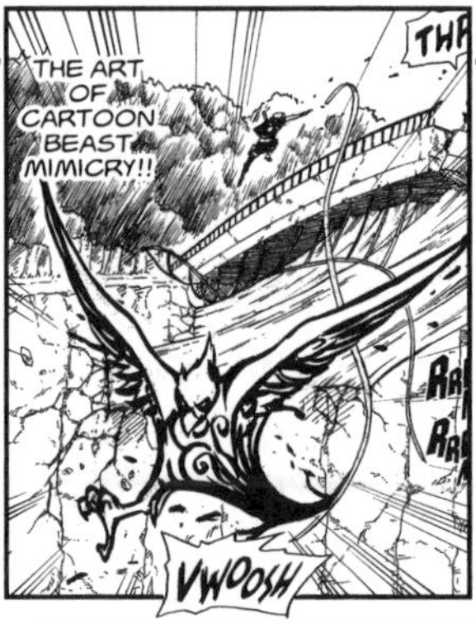
THE ART OF CARTOON BEAST MIMICRY!!
THP
VWOOSH

He executes clandestine missions with a cold and crafty gaze.

《Cartoon Beast Mimicry》

If he paints a bird, he can fly through the air. If he paints mice, he will have additional help in an investigation. With just one jutsu, Sai is able to adapt to every situation he must face on Anbu Black Ops missions.

《Top Priorities》

Sai grew up in the Foundation. Accomplishing a mission is the only thing he truly understands. Even if he is part of a team, he exists only to make sure the mission was a success. At least, that was true till he met Naruto…

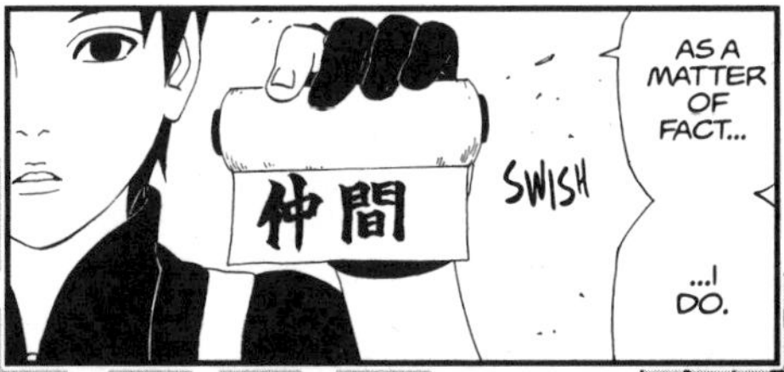
AS A MATTER OF FACT...
...I DO.
SWISH
仲間

⬅ He may know a word, but its meaning is lost on him.

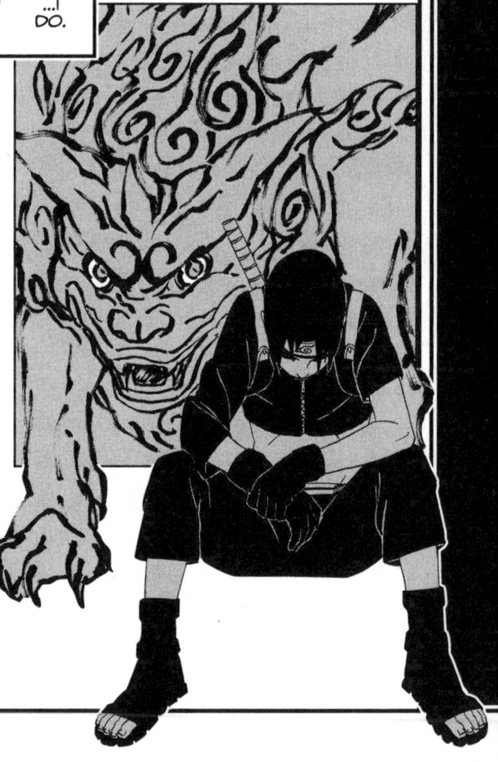

《Top Secret Mission》

Sai becomes part of Team Kakashi, but he also is given one more mission by Danzo. In order to fulfill his mission, Sai deludes friend and enemy alike. And the reason he tracks Sasuke is not to rescue him, but to assassinate him.

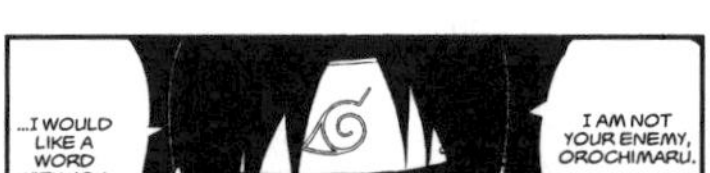
I AM NOT YOUR ENEMY, OROCHIMARU.
I AM AN ENVOY FROM DANZO. AND ON HIS BEHALF...
...I WOULD LIKE A WORD WITH YOU.

⬆ He breaks away from Team Kakashi to make direct contact with Orochimaru. However, this action is also a ruse to hide his true mission.

Bonds drive a wedge into a heart of ice.

《Bonds》

Sai's older brother Shin also grew up in the Foundation. The friendship Sai shared with him was the last thing he knew about being connected to others. After Shin dies, Sai abandons his feelings and all ties he ever had. However, he meets Naruto who reminds him of Shin, and once again, his yearning for a friend surfaces and grows stronger.

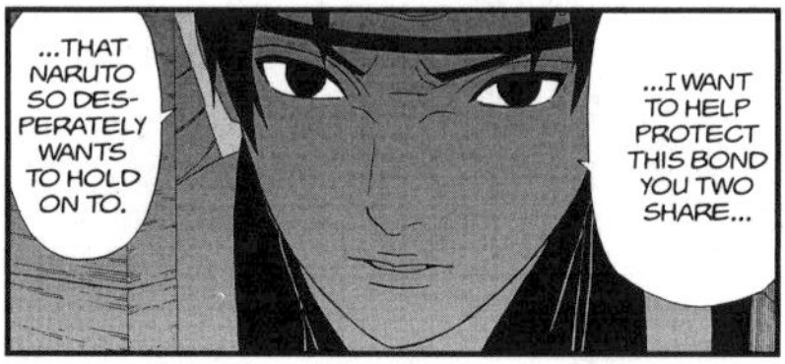
...I WANT TO HELP PROTECT THIS BOND YOU TWO SHARE...
...THAT NARUTO SO DESPERATELY WANTS TO HOLD ON TO.

⬅ He abandons the mission for which he even betrayed his comrades.

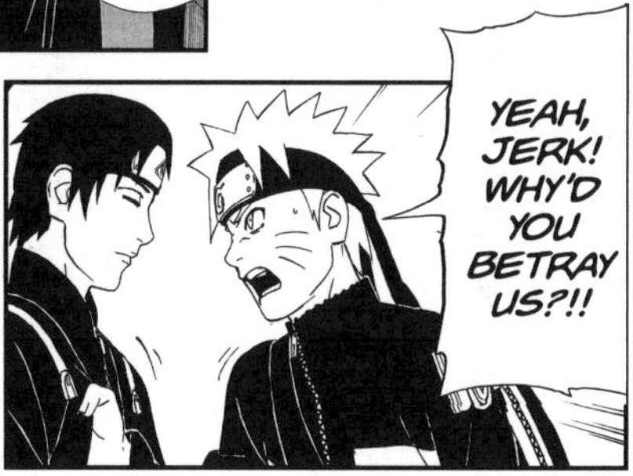
YEAH, JERK! WHY'D YOU BETRAY US?!!

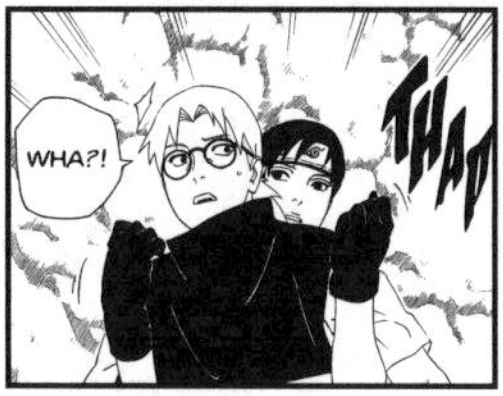
THAD
WHA?!

⬆ Despite the fact that he is in the midst of an infiltration, Sai revolts against Kabuto.

《Friends》

Sai respects Naruto's will more than his assigned mission. This signifies that he has forged a true bond with the members of Team Kakashi, and is proof that Sai now understands the meaning of the word friends.

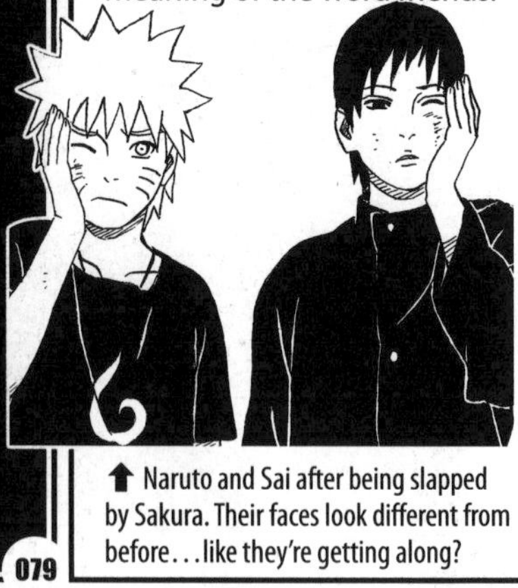

⬆ Naruto and Sai after being slapped by Sakura. Their faces look different from before... like they're getting along?

《Picture Book》

Sai had created a picture book to memorialize his bond with Shin and he keeps it with him all the time. But having discarded his emotions, Sai is unable to paint the last page. When that last page is filled, it will mean that Sai has formed the bond of friendship again.

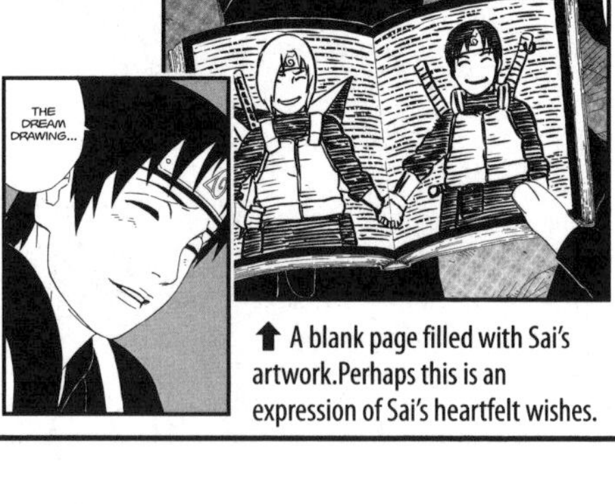
THE DREAM DRAWING...

⬆ A blank page filled with Sai's artwork.Perhaps this is an expression of Sai's heartfelt wishes.

SASORI

サソリ

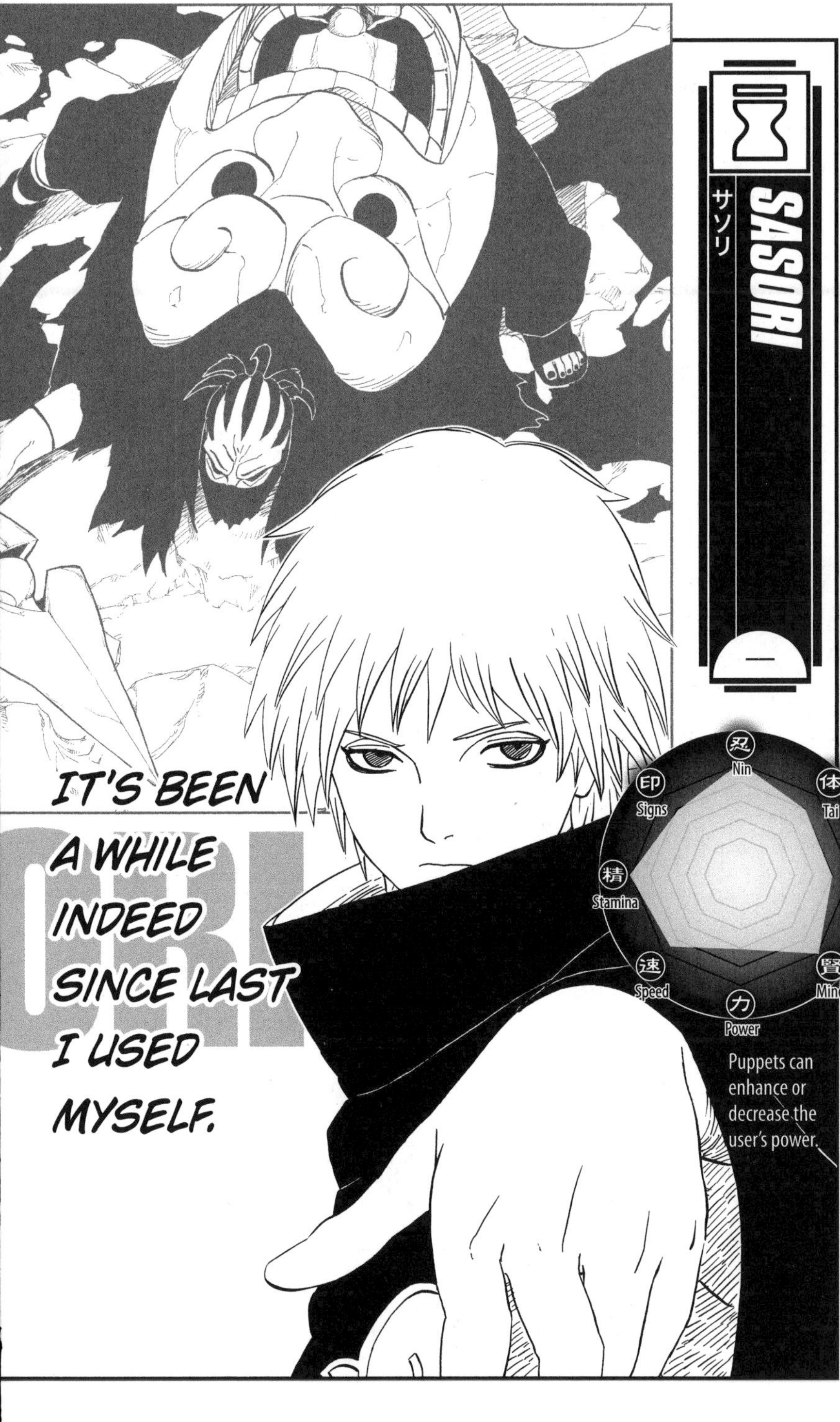
IT'S BEEN A WHILE INDEED SINCE LAST I USED MYSELF.
忍
Nin
体
Tai
幻
Gen
賢
Mind
力
Power
速
Speed
精
Stamina
印
Signs

Puppets can enhance or decrease the user's power.

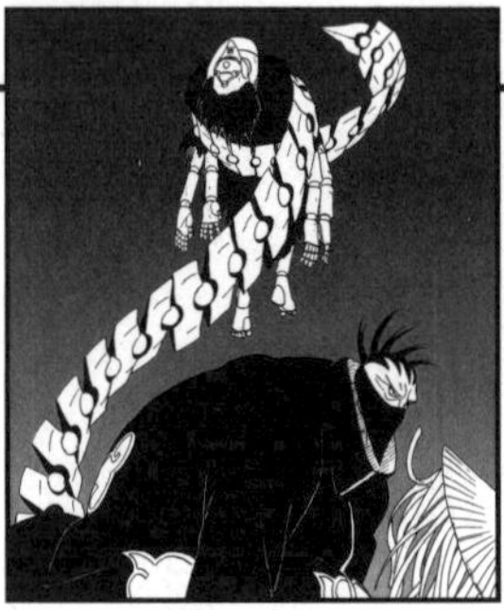

Discarding his human body, this puppet master is also a puppet himself.

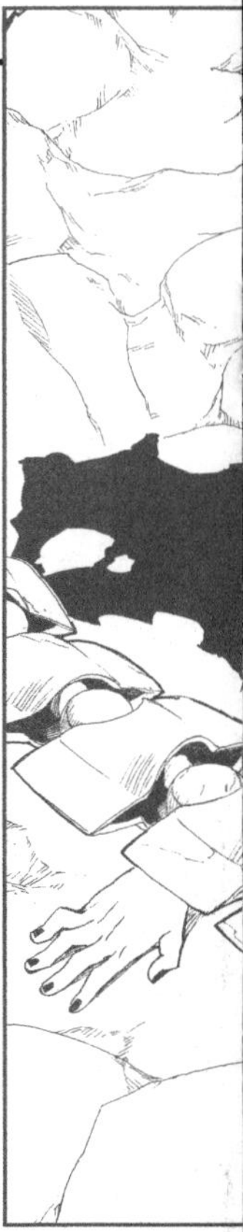

⬆Sasori's talent makes even Kankuro's puppetry seem amateurish.

After losing his parents, Sasori had only his creations to keep him company. His talents were incredible, but he soon reached the limits of making ordinary puppets. Sasori turned to the macabre, using the dead to create new puppets. Eventually, he turned himself into a puppet as well. What lies ahead for Sasori who has gone beyond the boundaries of reason?

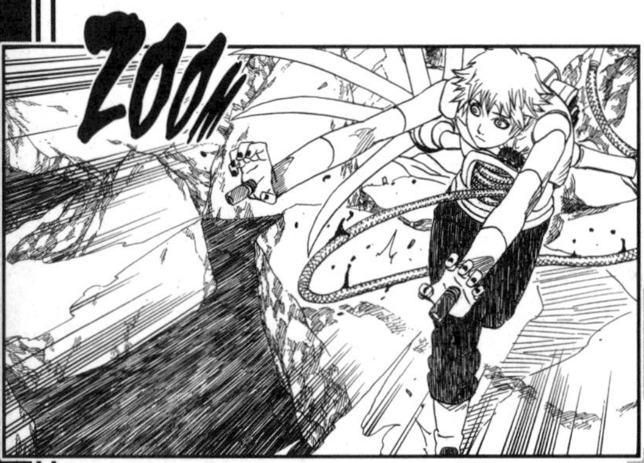
ZOOM

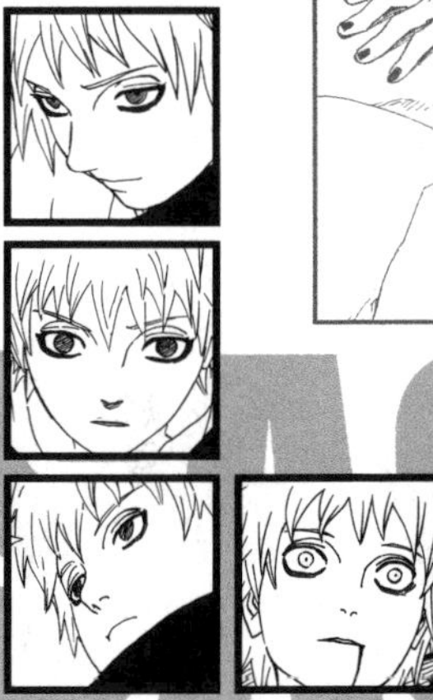

⬆Sasori can no longer be considered human.

According to Sasori, beauty that never decays is the ultimate art. His view of art differs from Deidara and results in occasional tension between them.

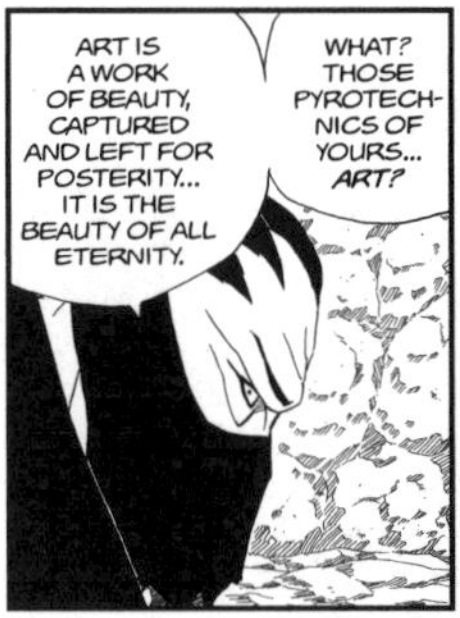
WHAT? THOSE PYROTECHNICS OF YOURS... ART?
ART IS A WORK OF BEAUTY, CAPTURED AND LEFT FOR POSTERITY... IT IS THE BEAUTY OF ALL ETERNITY.

Ninja Registry Number: 33-001
Birthdate: November 8 (35 years old; Scorpio)
Height: 164.1 cm (5'4½") **Weight:** 47.3 kg (104 lbs.) **Blood type:** AB
Personality: Cautious, individualistic, impatient
Favorite food: Does not find food necessary
Least favorite food: Does not find food necessary
Would like to fight: Monzaemon, the first puppet master
Favorite word: Everlasting beauty
Interests: Remodeling his collection

Graduated from the Ninja Academy at age 7
Promoted to chûnin at age 8

Mission Experience		
	D-rank: 5	C-rank: 12
	B-rank: 16	A-rank: 29
	S-rank: 10	

Puppets – The supreme art and the embodiment of his power and desires.

《The Third Kazekage》

It was only natural for Sasori, who desired superior puppets, to set his eyes on the Kazekage, who was called the strongest shinobi. A difficult opponent, defeated and then turned into a puppet, is pure ego gold for Sasori.

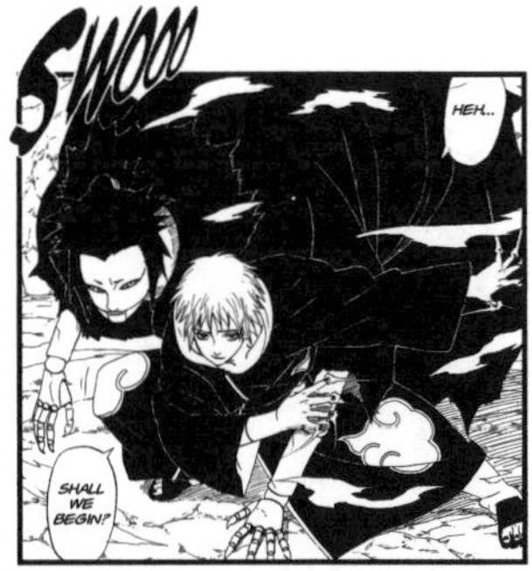
HEH...
SWOOO
SHALL WE BEGIN?

⬆ He can still wield his Iron Sand Jutsu, his specialty when alive, as a puppet.

《Hiruko》

Using Hiruko, which is an armor as well as a weapon, creates a safety buffer that allows him to focus on fighting. The ability to fight without injury is an aesthetically beautiful style of battle.

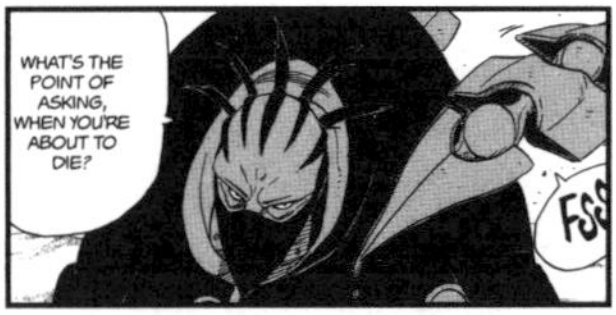
FSS
WHAT'S THE POINT OF ASKING, WHEN YOU'RE ABOUT TO DIE?

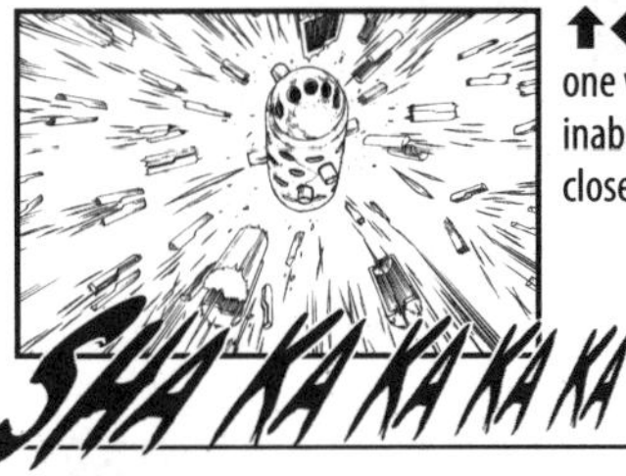
SHA KA KA KA KA

⬆⬅ A puppeteer's one weakness is the inability to engage in close combat.

《Father and Mother》

The first puppets Sasori creates are of his parents. He wants to feel their embrace once more. But his puppets did not speak and their hands were cold, and Sasori did not find fulfillment. So Sasori abandoned the puppets that were made in his parents' likenesses and left the village.

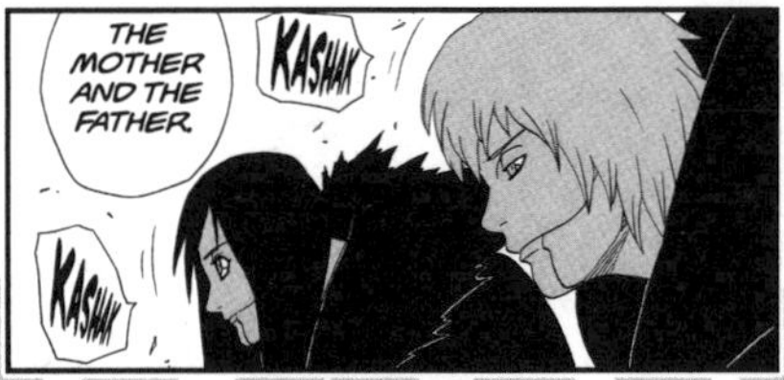
KASHAK
THE MOTHER AND THE FATHER
KASHAK

⬆ Sasori, who had discarded all emotion, attacked even his parents' puppets.

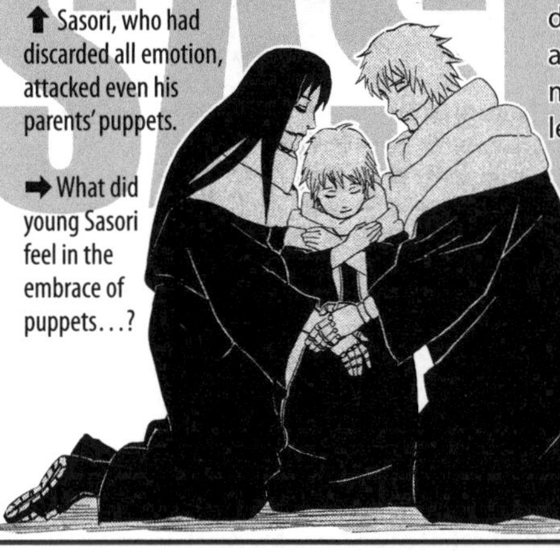

➡ What did young Sasori feel in the embrace of puppets...?

He abandons his humanity and gains a puppet's body that feels no pain.

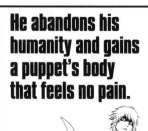

《 Self 》

Sasori, who ranks at the top of puppeteers, puts absolute trust in one golem…that is himself. In his search for the supreme puppet, Sasori chooses to turn himself into one. A puppet that will never decay and can be repaired over and over again. And he embeds countless tricks into his body. He has turned himself into a power that can only be termed extreme. Those who confront him will know only disappointment because attacking him is useless.

⬆ Even if he is broken apart, his body is indestructible. This is the power that Sasori has pursued.

《 A nucleus that is living flesh 》

Sasori's body is indestructible. However, in order to create chakra, human flesh is essential. This is Sasori's one and only weakness. During his battle with Chiyo, just before he attacks, that tight squeeze he feels in his nucleus is his parents. Although he had abandoned his body and his heart, Sasori was not able to completely turn himself into a puppet.

⬆ His body was controlled through the nucleus. If the nucleus is lost, he is a mere shell.

SARUTOBI ASUMA

猿飛アスマ

Jônin

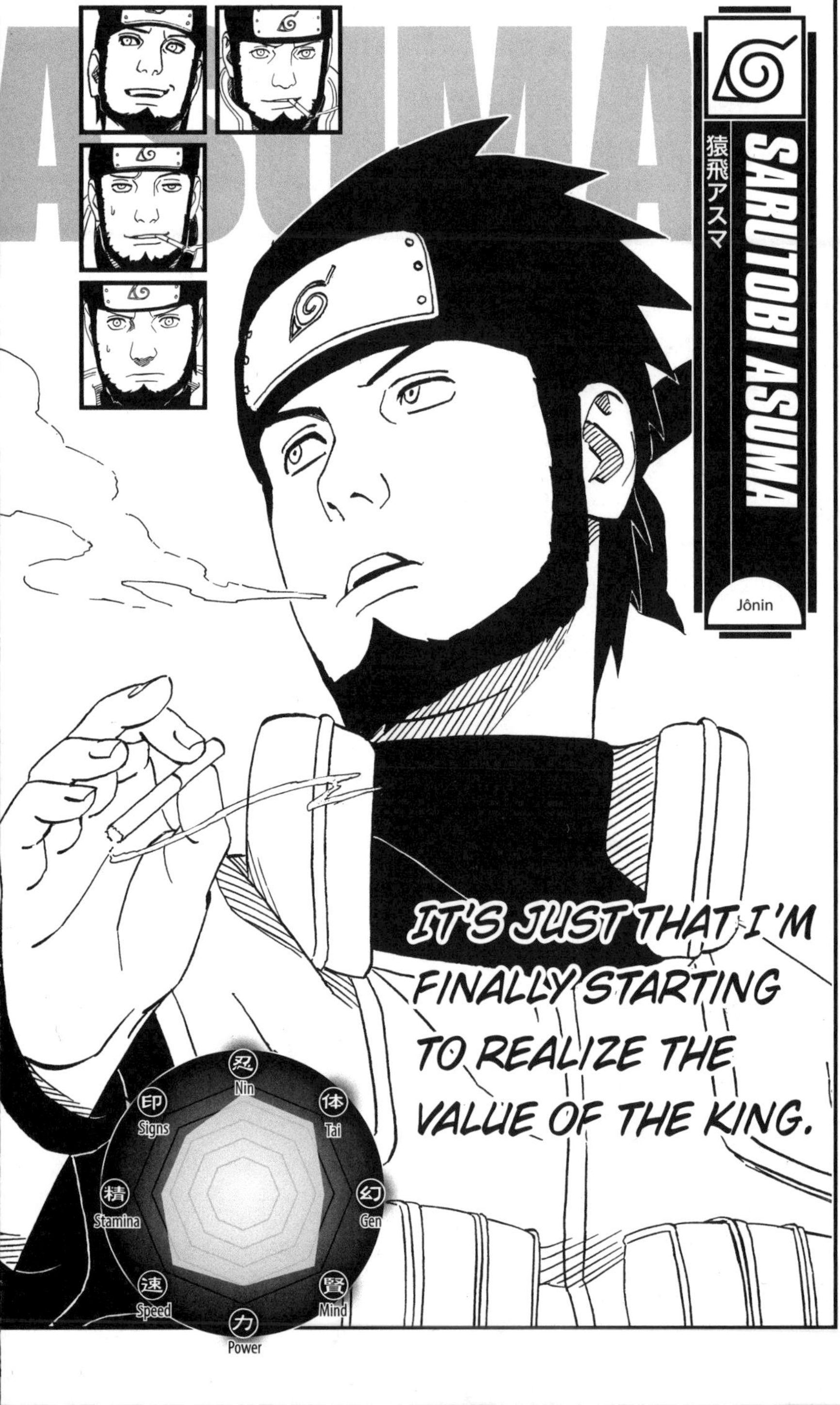
IT'S JUST THAT I'M FINALLY STARTING TO REALIZE THE VALUE OF THE KING.
忍 Nin
体 Tai
幻 Gen
賢 Mind
力 Power
速 Speed
精 Stamina
印 Signs

WE ALREADY KNOW YOU USUALLY OPERATE IN PAIRS.
I WAS PLANNING TO TAKE DOWN ONE OF YOU FIRST, THEN CAPTURE THE OTHER...
...BUT I GUESS THAT'S GOING TO HAVE TO CHANGE...

⬅ A chakra blade is Asuma's calling card.

A strong warrior who wields shining blades of the wind. His will is reflected in his rising smoke.

A Konoha jônin who possesses the Wind chakra nature, no one is more skilled in close-arm combat. But few are aware of Asuma's past. His relationship with his father Hiruzen was always one of admiration and discord.

In search of the meaning of his father's words that the Hokage is not the most precious thing in the village, Asuma leaves the village and becomes a wanderer. But those days come to an end with his father's death and the birth of a new life. And Asuma's will is ignited, never to wane again.

DON'T YOU UNDER-STAND?! THIS IS THE BEST PLAN WE'VE GOT RIGHT NOW!!
THEY'RE FAR STRONGER THAN EVEN ME...!
IZUMO, KOTETSU, YOU TWO ASSIST SHIKAMARU AGAINST THE OTHER AKATSUKI.

⬆ He boasts a power that is immense, but he never underestimates a thing. As a cell commander, he explains every plan with utmost care.

WHO'S IT FOR?!
ER, NO ONE IN PARTIC-ULAR...

⬆ A bouquet of flowers for his loved one. Much to his chagrin, his pupil teases him.

Ninja Registry Number: 0108829
Birthdate: October 18 (31 years old; Libra)
Height: 190.8 cm (6'3") **Weight:** 81.6 kg (180 lbs.) **Blood type:** 0
Personality: Easygoing, blunt
Favorite food: Sausage, buckwheat noodles with grated yam
Least favorite food: Asparagus
Would like to fight: Nara Shikamaru at Shogi
Favorite word: Take that back!
Interests: Shogi

Graduated from the Ninja Academy at age 9
Promoted to chûnin at age 12

Mission Experience		
	D-rank: 111	C-rank: 193
	B-rank: 217	A-rank: 178
	S-rank: 20	

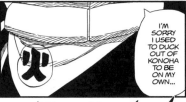

I'M SORRY I USED TO DUCK OUT OF KONOHA TO BE ON MY OWN...

During the unceasing passage of time, a man realizes his purpose in life.

↑ It has never left his side—the proof that he was one of the Guardian Shinobi Twelve.

《Climbing Silver》

During the destruction of Konohagakure, Asuma's father Hiruzen, the Hokage, stood at the forefront of battle and was killed. Seeing how his father had lived and died, Asuma discovers a beam of light inside himself.

What is truly precious is neither position nor country. When he becomes a father himself, this spark of light, his will, which he discovered three years ago, will give him the answers he needs.

↑ The vanguard attacks the enemy lines. Trusting their comrades at the rear, they boldly charge forward.

《Cell 10》

Nara Shikamaru, Akimichi Choji, and Yamanaka Ino make up Konoha's Cell 10, Asuma's first three pupils since returning from his wanderings. They are the next generation of Konohagakure. For the first time, Asuma realizes that here are the ones to whom he can entrust his will.

《Will of Fire》

As a shinobi of Konohagakure, as a teacher... Asuma chooses death and that vision is burned deep into his pupils' eyes. Although his body is no more, his will continues to burn, illuminating the village. And his spirit will be inherited by the king, the most precious piece, which represents all the future generations. He dies believing that.

← Asuma has a warmth that is both kind and strong. Asuma's will shall be passed on to the next generation, and to future generations...

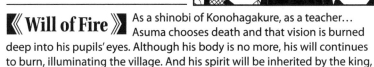

SHIZUNE

シズネ

Jônin

Tsunade's right-hand woman.

She can vie for a spot as one of the top two medical ninja in Konoha, and she is the Fifth Hokage's right-hand woman. She understands Tsunade's personality and tends to her needs amicably and with care. Trusted by the village's top officials, she is allowed to attend meetings between the Hokage and her advisors.

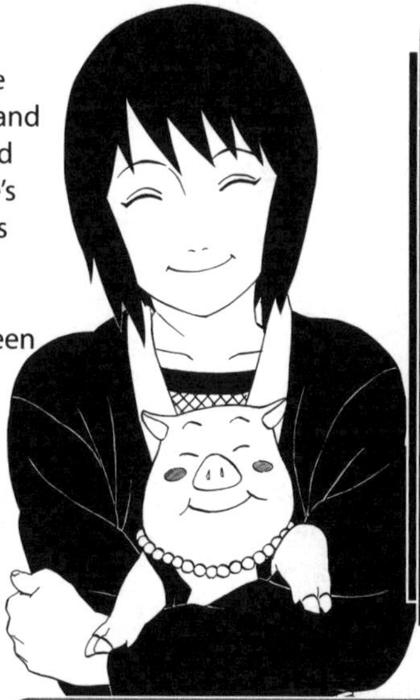

➡ No matter whom she is speaking to, she will express her opinion. It is this attitude that has earned her Tsunade's trust.

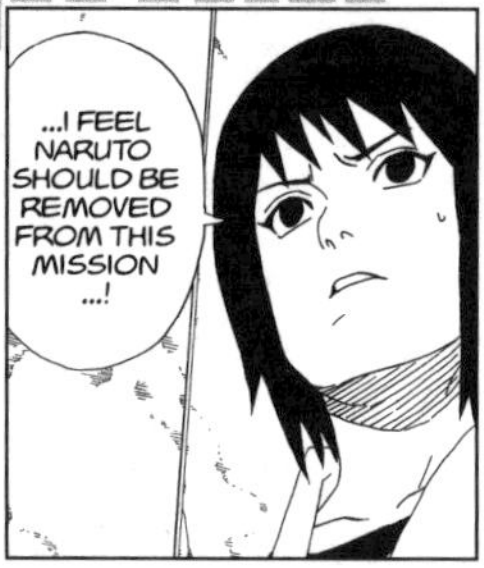
...I FEEL NARUTO SHOULD BE REMOVED FROM THIS MISSION ...!
LADY TSUNADE...

Ninja Registry Number: 010800
Birthdate: November 18 (31years old; Scorpio)
Height: 168.0 cm (5'6") **Weight:** 49.2 kg (108 lbs.) **Blood type:** A
Personality: Worrisome
Interests: Visiting cultural heritage centers

⬇ During battle, she will analyze the situation instantly and become a command post that plans the best strategies.

SHIMA

シマ

The gutsy toad sage who can war with words.

She is Fukasaku's wife as well as one of the two exalted toad sages who can succeed the Great Toad Sage. Honesty is her policy, and she is always straightforward, calling the shots as she sees it. As such, she is the beloved Mother of the Toad's Way.

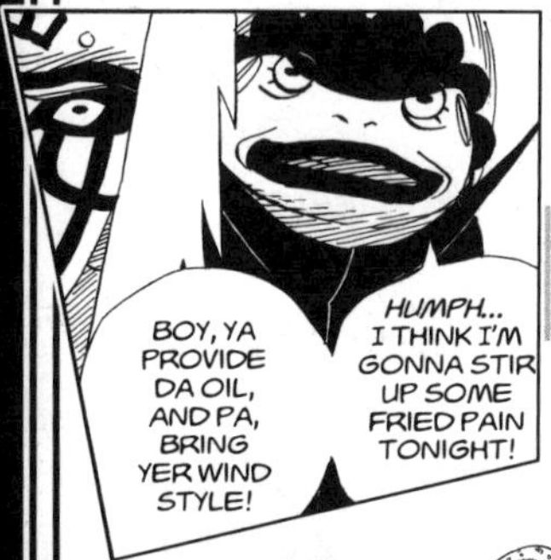
HUMPH... I THINK I'M GONNA STIR UP SOME FRIED PAIN TONIGHT!
BOY, YA PROVIDE DA OIL, AND PA, BRING YER WIND STYLE!

➡ On the battlefield, she puts her sensory skills to work to capture the enemy.

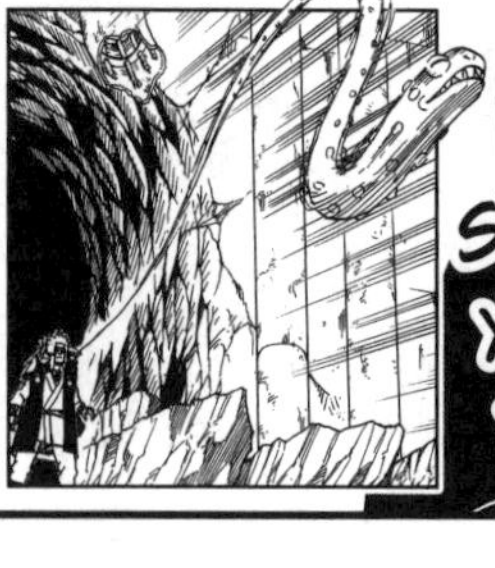

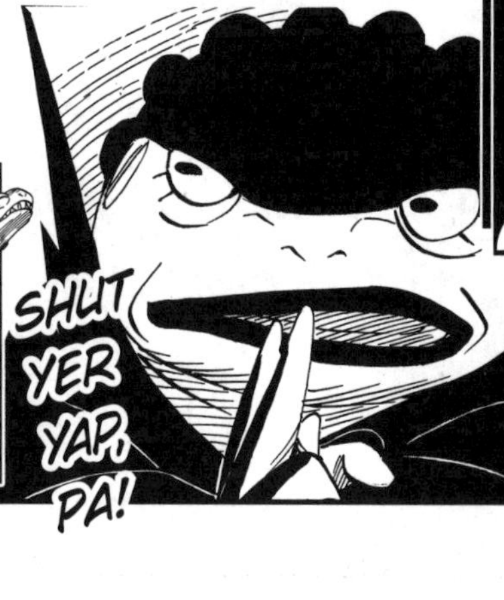
SHUT YER YAP, PA!

♪

JUGO

重吾

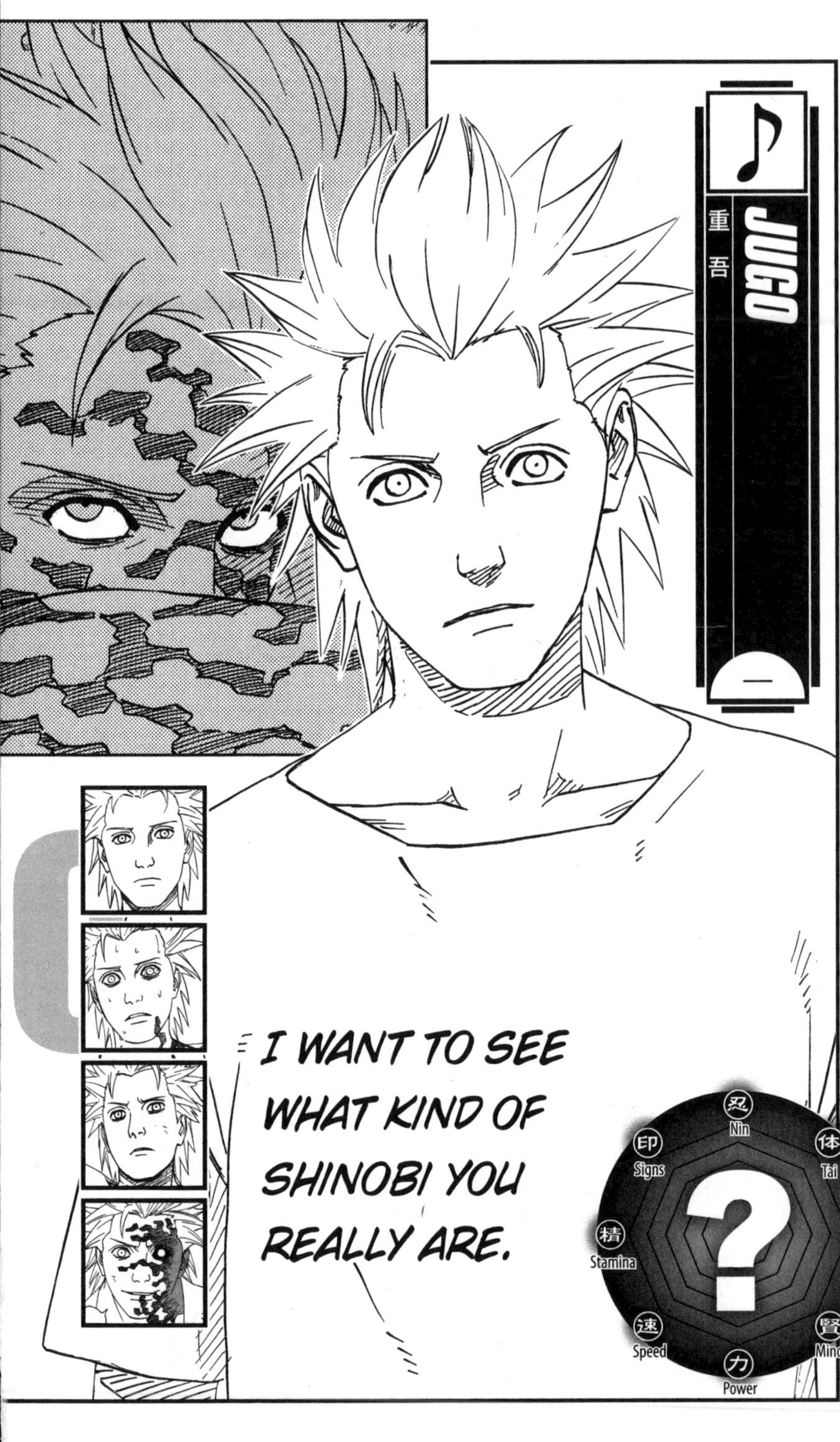
I WANT TO SEE WHAT KIND OF SHINOBI YOU REALLY ARE.
忍 Nin
体 Tai
幻 Gen
賢 Mind
力 Power
速 Speed
精 Stamina
印 Signs
?

HAVEN'T SEEN A COPYCAT THIS GOOD SINCE KIMIMARO!!

HE'S STRONG!!

◀ Athirst for blood. The black curse that is to blame and that causes his physical self to transform is something even Jugo himself fears.

With a strength and fury that cannot be held in check, Jugo was first to be given the curse mark.

He is usually very quiet, but when angered, Jugo will attack even humans. Thus, he was feared as the Scale in one village. Cursing his fate, he secluded himself in a cave. The one who saved him was Kimimaro, the lone survivor of his family. At his suggestion, Jugo seeks out Orochimaru's human experiment facility, and there, the curse mark is born. But time passes and Kimimaro dies, and Orochimaru dies. Once again, Jugo conceals himself. Then a friend shines light into the cave, asking Jugo to entrust his life to him. In deference to Sasuke's power, the Scale comes out of the cave.

I DON'T WANNA GO OUTSIDE... PLEASE JUST LEAVE ME ALONE!

I DON'T WANNA KILL ANY MORE PEOPLE!

◀ The sudden desire to kill that occurs without warning and the guilt that overwhelms him have shut down Jugo's heart and isolate him from the outside world.

LET ME ASK YOU LITTLE ONES...

⬆ The normal Jugo is gentle and loves nature. It is why his urges weigh on him so heavily.

Ninja Registry Number: —
Birthdate: October 1 (18 years old; Libra)
Height: 202.1 cm (6'7½") **Weight:** 75.8 kg (167 lbs.) **Blood type:** AB
Personality: Laid back, timid, brutal
Favorite food: Small fish, milk
Least favorite food: Chicken
Would like to fight: No one (usually). Everyone (during his manic stage)
Favorite word: Samadhi
Interests: Frolicking with birds, a walk through the woods

Graduated from the Ninja Academy at age —
Promoted to chûnin at age —

Mission Experience	D-rank: 0	C-rank: 0
	B-rank: 0	A-rank: 0
	S-rank: 0	

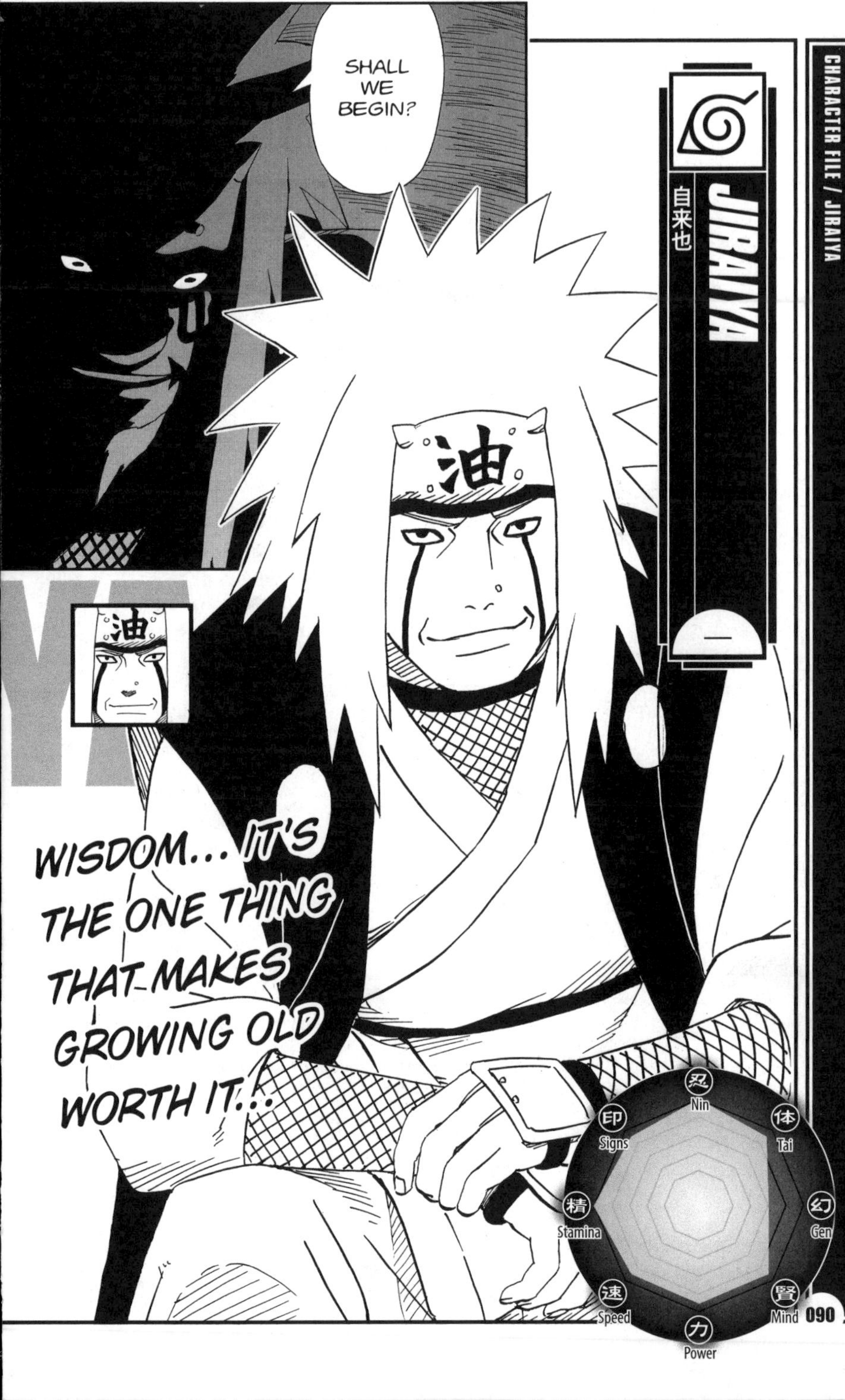
SHALL WE BEGIN?
WISDOM... IT'S THE ONE THING THAT MAKES GROWING OLD WORTH IT...
JIRAIYA
自来也
忍 Nin
体 Tai
幻 Gen
賢 Mind
力 Power
速 Speed
精 Stamina
印 Signs

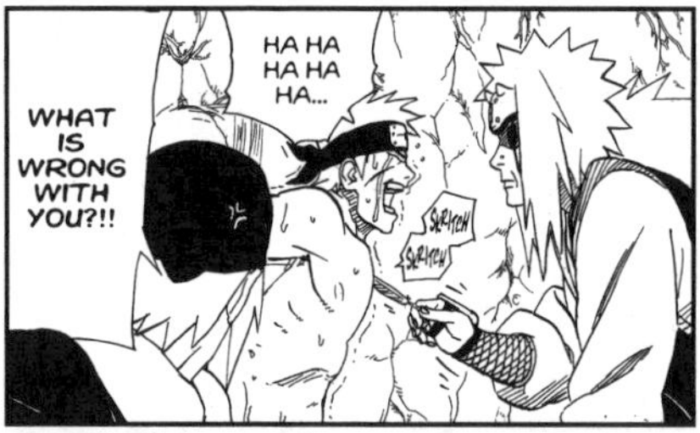
HA HA
HA HA
HA...
WHAT IS WRONG WITH YOU?!!
SKRITCH
SKRITCH

⬆ Jiraiya has been working in intelligence for many years. He has very original ways to make people talk without resorting to killing.

The Toad Sage hurls his lion's mane in a stirring rendition of the Kabuki dance.

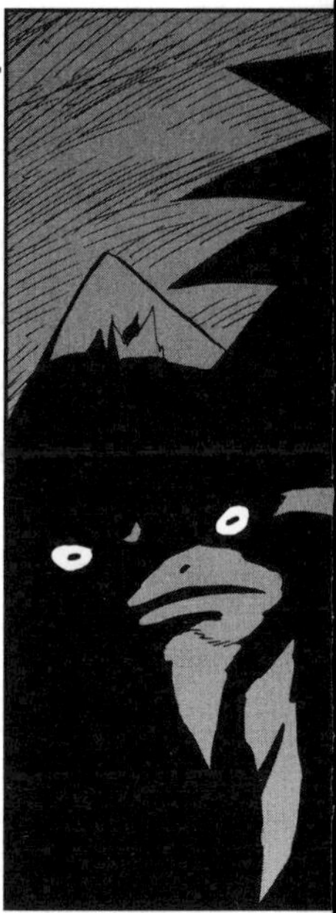

A teacher to the Fourth Hokage, one of the Three Great Shinobi, a toad sage. Jiraiya's amazing prowess has made him a living legend in Konohagakure. However, he does not accept such accolades because he does not believe he deserves them. Jiraiya's true story is a secret.

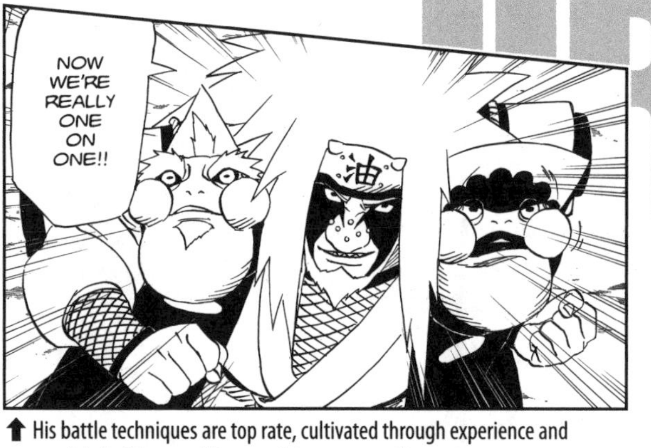
NOW WE'RE REALLY ONE ON ONE!!
油

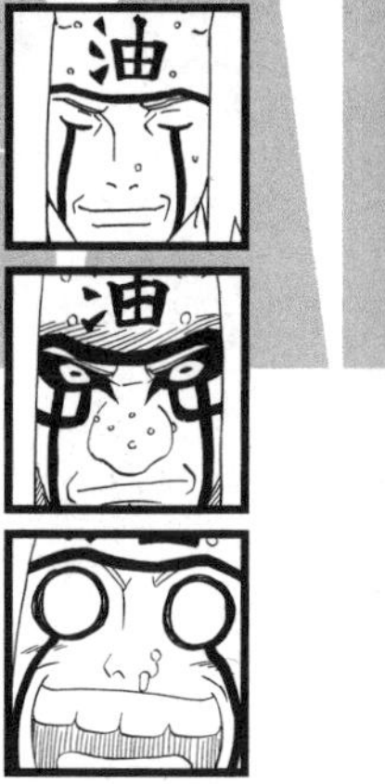
油
油

⬆ His battle techniques are top rate, cultivated through experience and resourceful. And they get him out of the worst predicaments.

➡ Even in the midst of a death battle, he promises to entertain. He finds inspiration in himself.

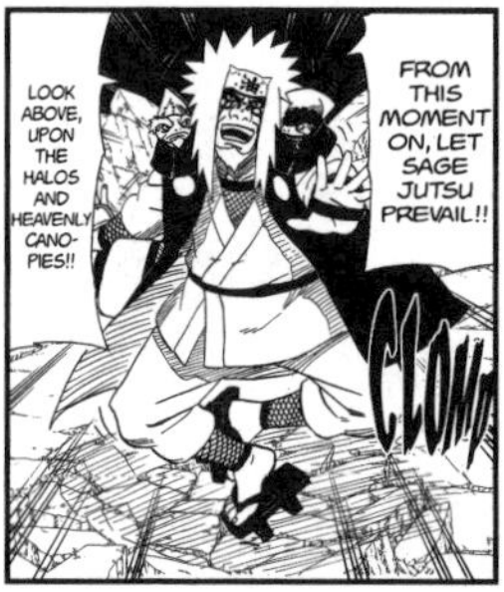
FROM THIS MOMENT ON, LET SAGE JUTSU PREVAIL!!
LOOK ABOVE, UPON THE HALOS AND HEAVENLY CANOPIES!!
CLOMP

Ninja Registry Number: 002301
Birthdate: November 11 (54 years old; Scorpio)
Height: 191.2 cm (6'3") **Weight:** 87.5 kg (193 lbs.) **Blood type:** B
Personality: Lecherous, carefree
Favorite food: Garlic with shiso leaves, deep-fried chicken
Least favorite food: Kiwi fruit, gratin dishes
Would like to fight: Uzumaki Naruto
Favorite word: Freewheeling
Interests: Research (Peeping)

Graduated from the Ninja Academy at age 6
Promoted to chûnin at age ?

Mission Experience	D-rank: 58	C-rank: 345
	B-rank: 684	A-rank: 614
	S-rank: 138	

He entrusts the main stage to the next generation while he dances in the shadows.

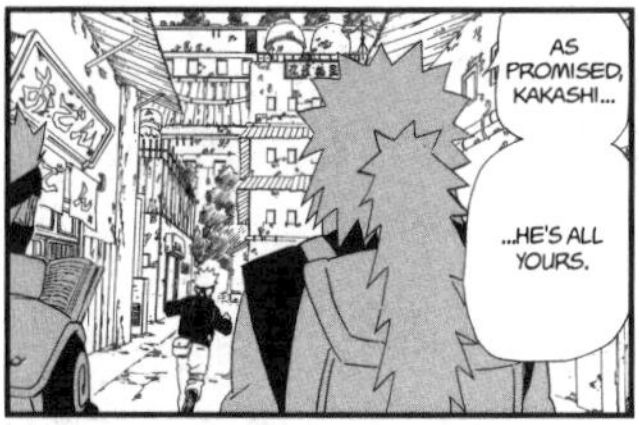
AS PROMISED, KAKASHI...
...HE'S ALL YOURS.

⬆ From the teacher's hands into those of his superior. It is Jiraiya's way of acknowledging Naruto as a fully grown man.

《Homecoming》

Naruto's training travels are done and Jiraiya returns to Konoha after two and a half years. He leaves his pupil under Kakashi's care and disappears into the shadows to resume his intelligence work.

This activity would also include searching for the bond between Naruto and Sasuke, as well as his own bond with Orochimaru.

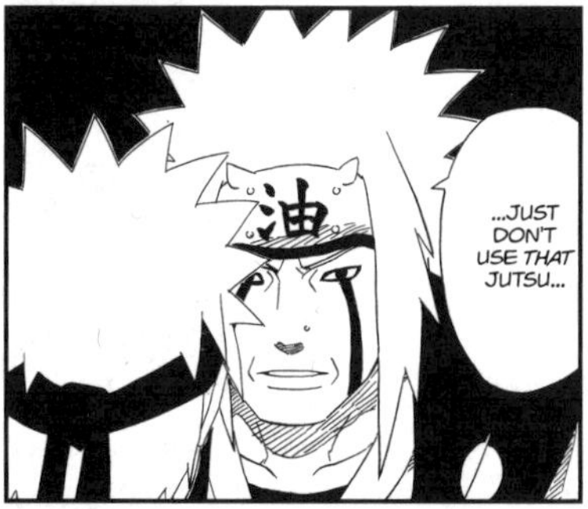
...JUST DON'T USE THAT JUTSU...

⬆ The calamity that slumbers inside Naruto. Although he recognizes Naruto's abilities, it is still a cause for concern.

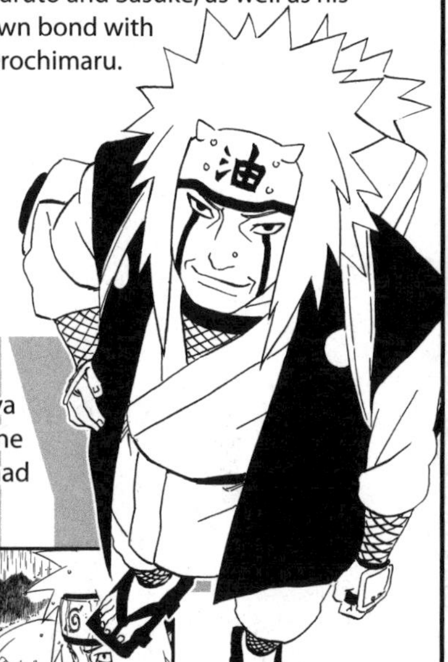

《Three Great Shinobi》

Once upon a time, Orochimaru and Jiraiya were actually friends. They were two of the Three Great Shinobi of Legend. That he had been unable to stop Orochimaru's madness fills Jiraiya with regret. It is why he turned down the position of Hokage and supports his village from the shadows.

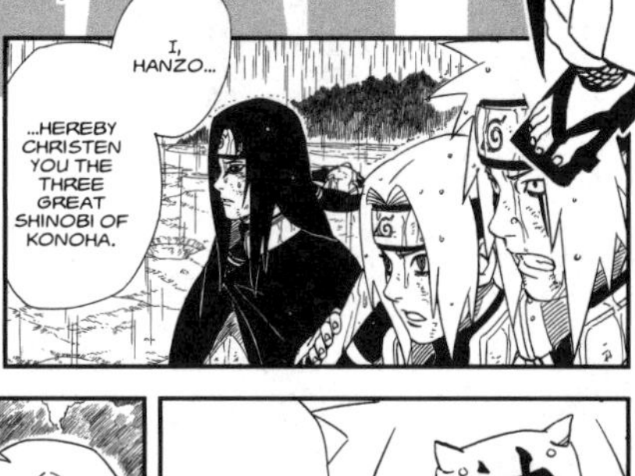
I, HANZO...
...HEREBY CHRISTEN YOU THE THREE GREAT SHINOBI OF KONOHA.

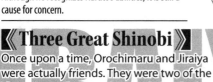

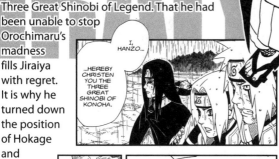

⬅ The three of them had crossed through scenes of carnage together. Their bonds have not faded.

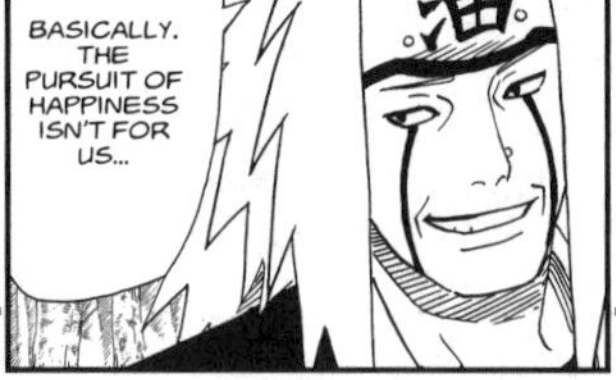
BASICALLY. THE PURSUIT OF HAPPINESS ISN'T FOR US...

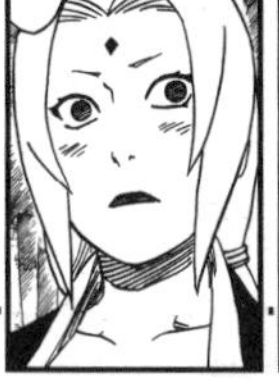
...

⬅ He has been continually rejected by Tsunade. Despite the passage of time, his love for her never waned. But a sophisticated man does not let his feelings show.

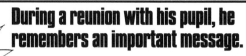

During a reunion with his pupil, he remembers an important message.

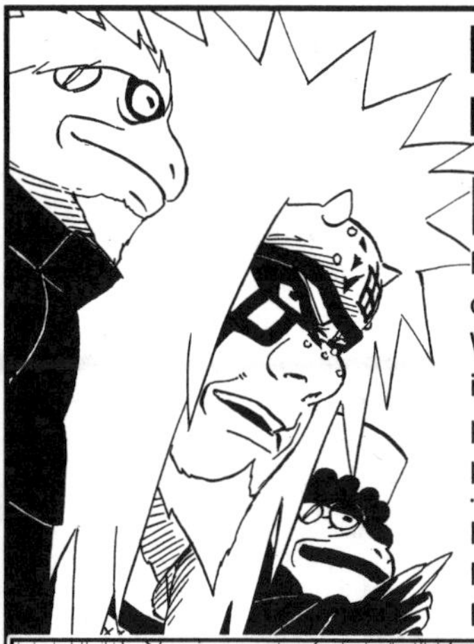

《Chance meeting》

Pain, the one who rules the Akatsuki, that dark cloud hovering over the shinobi world. When their confrontation comes, Jiraiya looks into Pain's eyes and is reminded of his former pupil Nagato. He is the boy who swore to protect his friends.

He had overcome pain, and Jiraiya believed Nagato could be the one to guide the world. But Jiraiya is shocked to see him so changed. It makes Jiraiya painfully aware of how he has contributed to this and how heavy are the chains of fate.

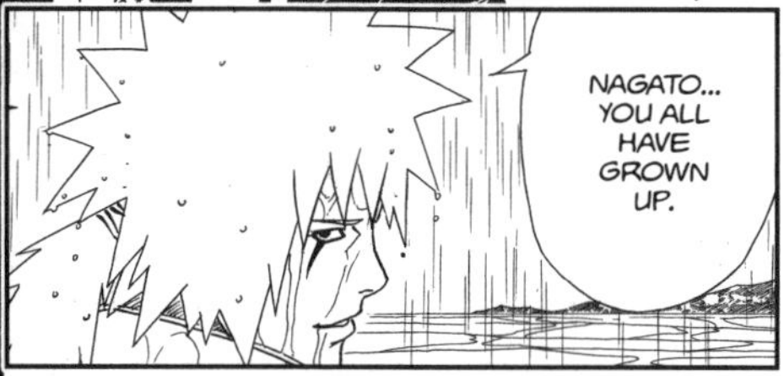
NAGATO... YOU ALL HAVE GROWN UP.

⬅ Does his Kumadori represent the tears he cries for his fallen or lost comrades such as Orochimaru?

⬇ He had been told about a choice, and that time is now. Jiraiya comes to a decision in order to protect the shinobi world.

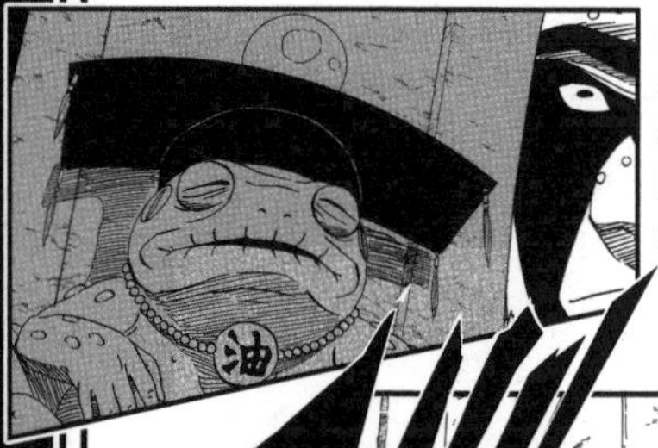

《Prophecy》

In the midst of his battle to the death, Jiraiya recalls the Great Toad Sage's prophecy that a "disciple will one day bring about a great change to the world of shinobi." But the path Pain walks will not bring prosperity. So Jiraiya casts his former pupil into oblivion.

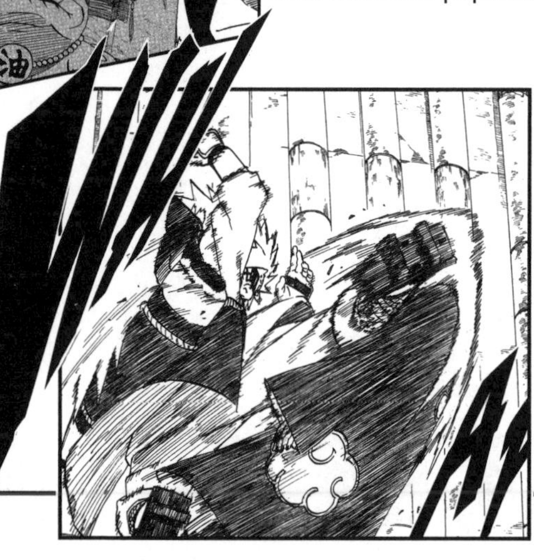

⬅ Jiraiya hardens his resolve and attacks, and destroys Pain's eyes...

His beloved pupils teach him to never give up his shinobi way!

《One who resists and endures》

Jiraiya is filled with regret that he could not save Minato and his own teacher… That he could not stop Orochimaru. Jiraiya begins to lose hope over what he feels is a wasted life. But wracked with pain, with wounds covering his body, two of his pupils make him remember what is the most important thing to a shinobi. Namely, to resist and endure.

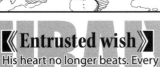

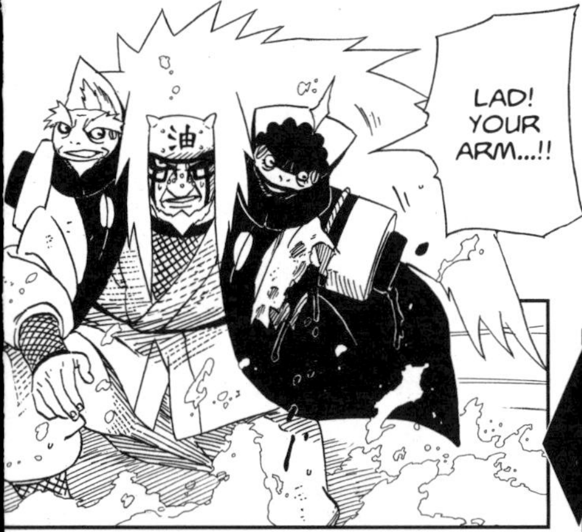

LAD! YOUR ARM...!!

⬅ He has lost his left arm and is in no condition to fight. Still, Jiraiya refuses to stop.

THUD

⬆ All together, the Pains attack. With their assassin's daggers, they pierce Jiraiya's body, then his heart.

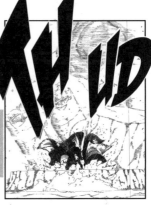

《Entrusted wish》

His heart no longer beats. Every cell in his body has given up living. Still, Jiraiya refuses to give up. He knows the truth… Through sheer will, he writes on Fukasaku's back, fingers shaking, so that he can entrust it to his last pupil and the Child of Prophecy, Uzumaki Naruto.

With this the "Tale of Jiraiya the Gallant" comes to an end. However, the new tale that Jiraiya intended to write is just beginning.

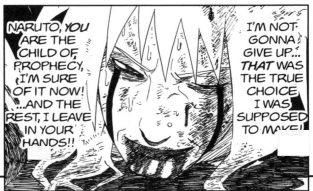

⬇ Just before dying, Jiraiya makes his final choice. His smile reflects his faith in the one he has entrusted.

I'M NOT GONNA GIVE UP... *THAT* WAS THE TRUE CHOICE I WAS SUPPOSED TO
NARUTO, *YOU* ARE THE CHILD OF PROPHECY, I'M SURE OF IT NOW! ...AND THE REST, I LEAVE IN YOUR HANDS!!

SHIN

Anbu Black Ops

Impulsive and guileless, he was the maverick of the Foundation.

Shin was a war orphan recruited by the Foundation. He and Sai shared similar circumstances and grew up together, forging a strong bond. Passionate and disorganized, he did not fit into the Foundation and died young...

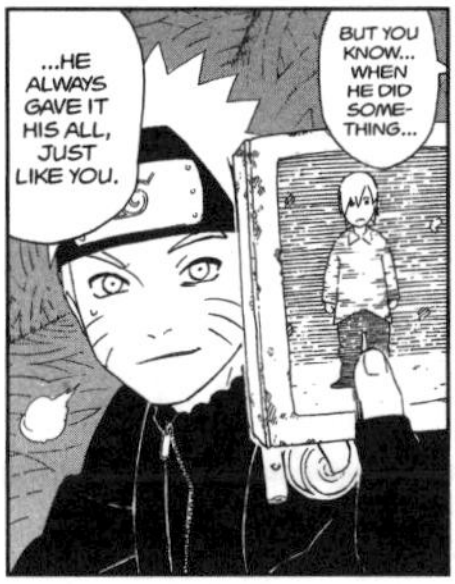
...HE ALWAYS GAVE IT HIS ALL, JUST LIKE YOU.
BUT YOU KNOW... WHEN HE DID SOME-THING...

⬆ Vestiges of Shin remain only in Sai's picture book. That is the fate of those in the Anbu Black Ops.

SHIN

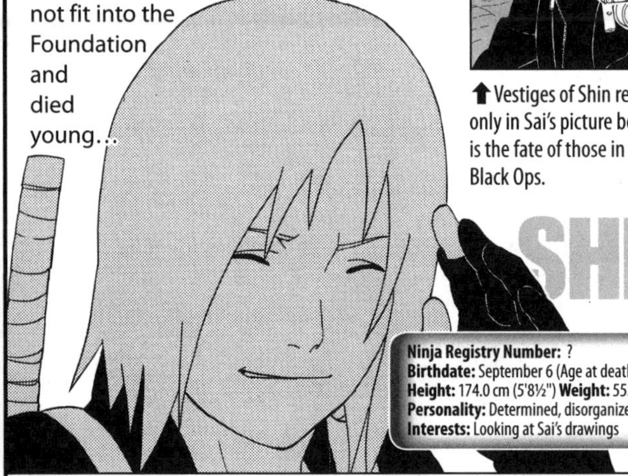

Ninja Registry Number: ?
Birthdate: September 6 (Age at death unknown; Virgo)
Height: 174.0 cm (5'8½") **Weight:** 55.4 kg (122 lbs.) **Blood type:** B
Personality: Determined, disorganized
Interests: Looking at Sai's drawings

Collection ... Number 6

Konoha

THE TRUTH OF THE FOUNDATION AS TOLD IN A PICTURE BOOK

According to Sai, Shin's death is officially due to illness, but the truth is shrouded in mystery. From the drawings in Sai's picture book, it is possible to surmise that as part of training to shut down emotion, the young trainees were forced to engage in a killing spree.

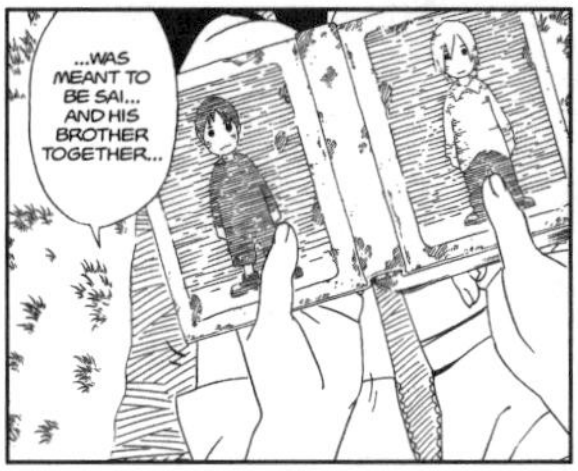
...WAS MEANT TO BE SAI... AND HIS BROTHER TOGETHER...

⬆ Do the drawings in Sai's picture book give a clue to his childhood training?

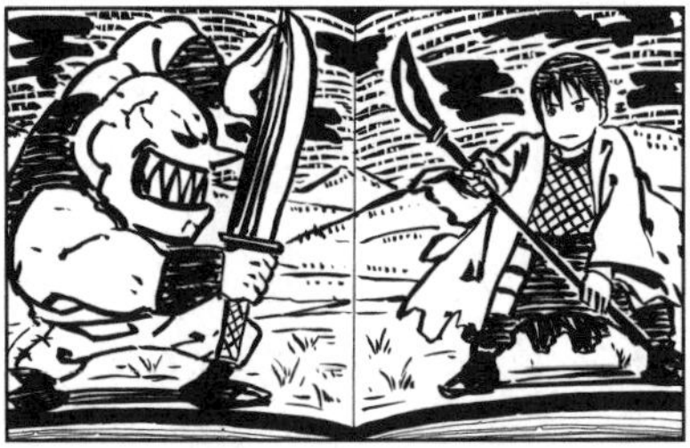

➡ The two steal their opponents' weapons and move in for the win.

ZETSU
ゼツ

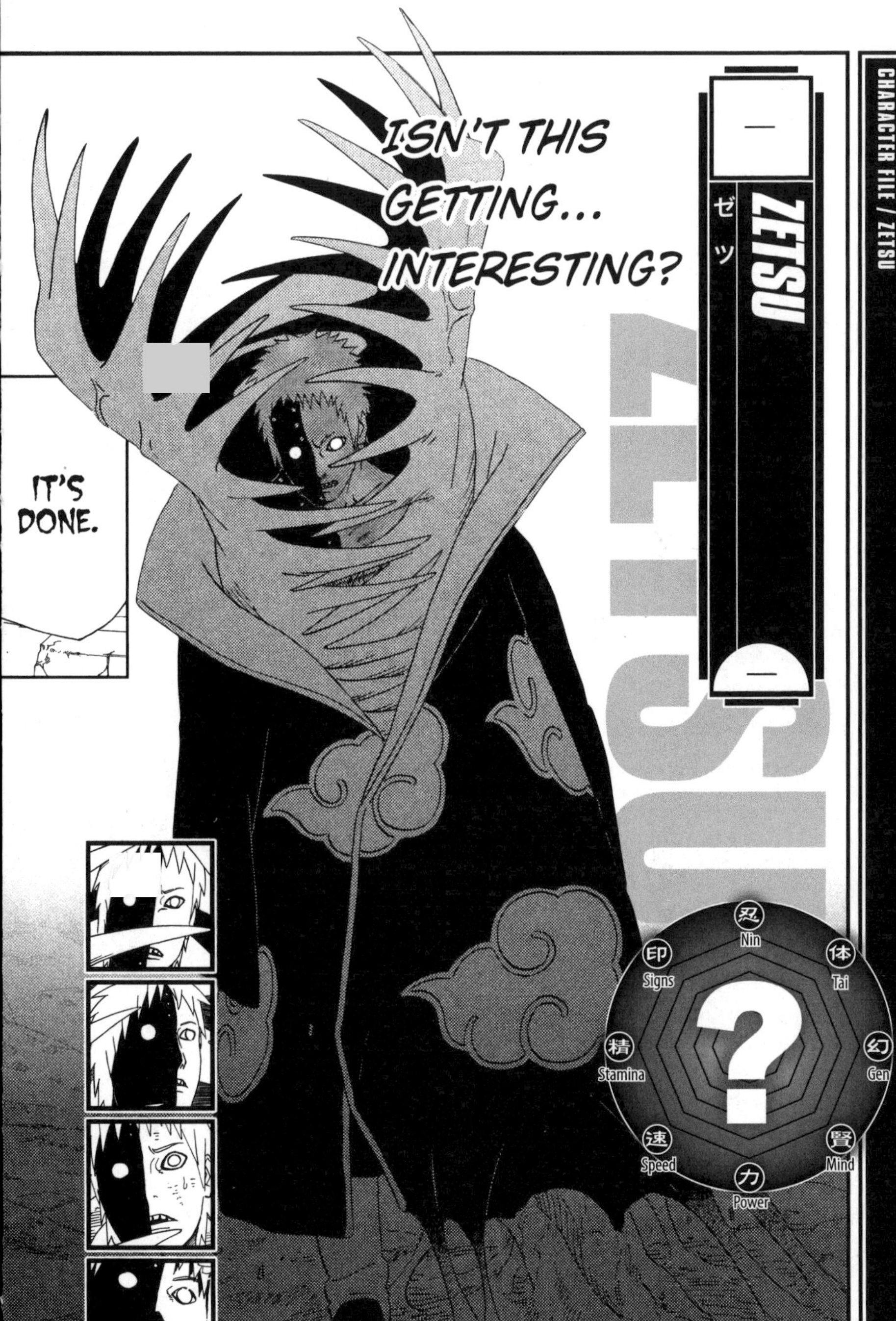
ISN'T THIS GETTING... INTERESTING?
IT'S DONE.
忍 Nin
体 Tai
幻 Gen
賢 Mind
力 Power
速 Speed
精 Stamina
印 Signs
?

Enveloped by a uncanny appearance he goes deep into the ground to record every sound!

His outer shell is a carnivorous plant, and he has two distinct personalities who converse with each other. Everything about Zetsu is unusual and even among the Akatsuki, he is especially ghastly. He has witnessed the major battles in the shinobi world.
After he meets Madara, the mastermind behind the Akatsuki, he is given the duty of recording all battles. Despite questioning Madara in detail about his motives, Zetsu continues to head to the battlefield. Is it merely because it satisfies his curiosity?

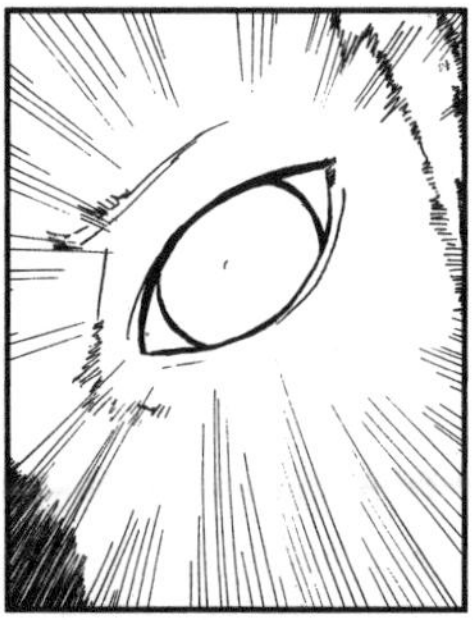

➡ Zetsu has the ability to put up a warning system over a vast area. It is not known whether this is ninjutsu or an individual skill.

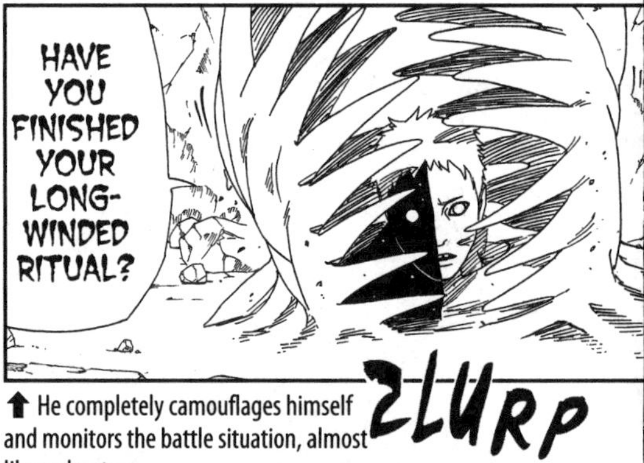
HAVE YOU FINISHED YOUR LONG-WINDED RITUAL?
ZLURP

⬆ He completely camouflages himself and monitors the battle situation, almost like a phantom.

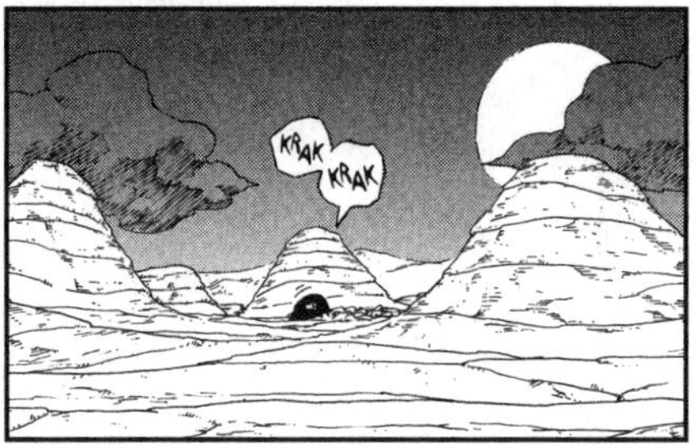
KRAK
KRAK

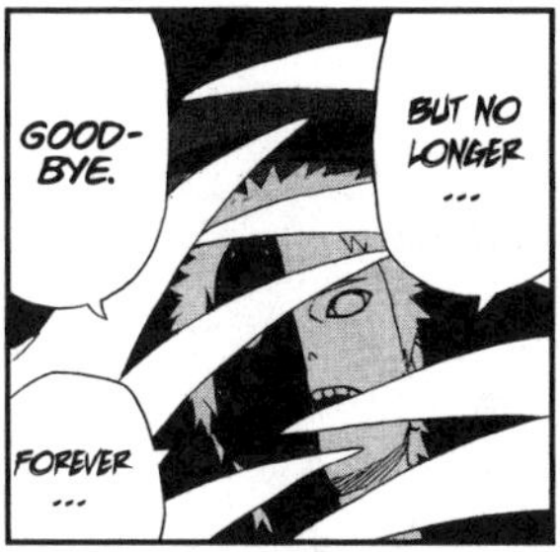
BUT NO LONGER ...
GOOD-BYE.
FOREVER ...

⬆➡ He oversees the disposal of sacrifices. The outer shell leaves no evidence whatsoever.

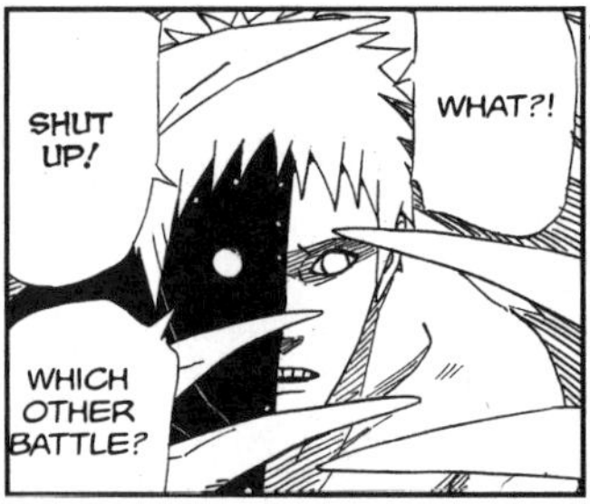
WHAT?!
SHUT UP!
WHICH OTHER BATTLE?

⬆ He is full of curiosity and thoroughly enjoys analyzing the battle condition in detail.

Ninja Registry Number: ?
Birthdate: ?
Height: 177 cm (5'9½") **Weight:** ? **Blood type:** B
Personality: Flippant (half of him), analytical (other half of him)
Favorite food: Things to gnaw on
Least favorite food: Konjac gel, Jello
Would like to fight: Someone worth biting into
Favorite word: Unbending independence (self-reliance)
Interests: Observing unique shinobi

Graduated from the Ninja Academy at age ?
Promoted to chûnin at age ?

Mission Experience		
	D-rank: ?	C-rank: ?
	B-rank: ?	A-rank: ?
	S-rank: ?	

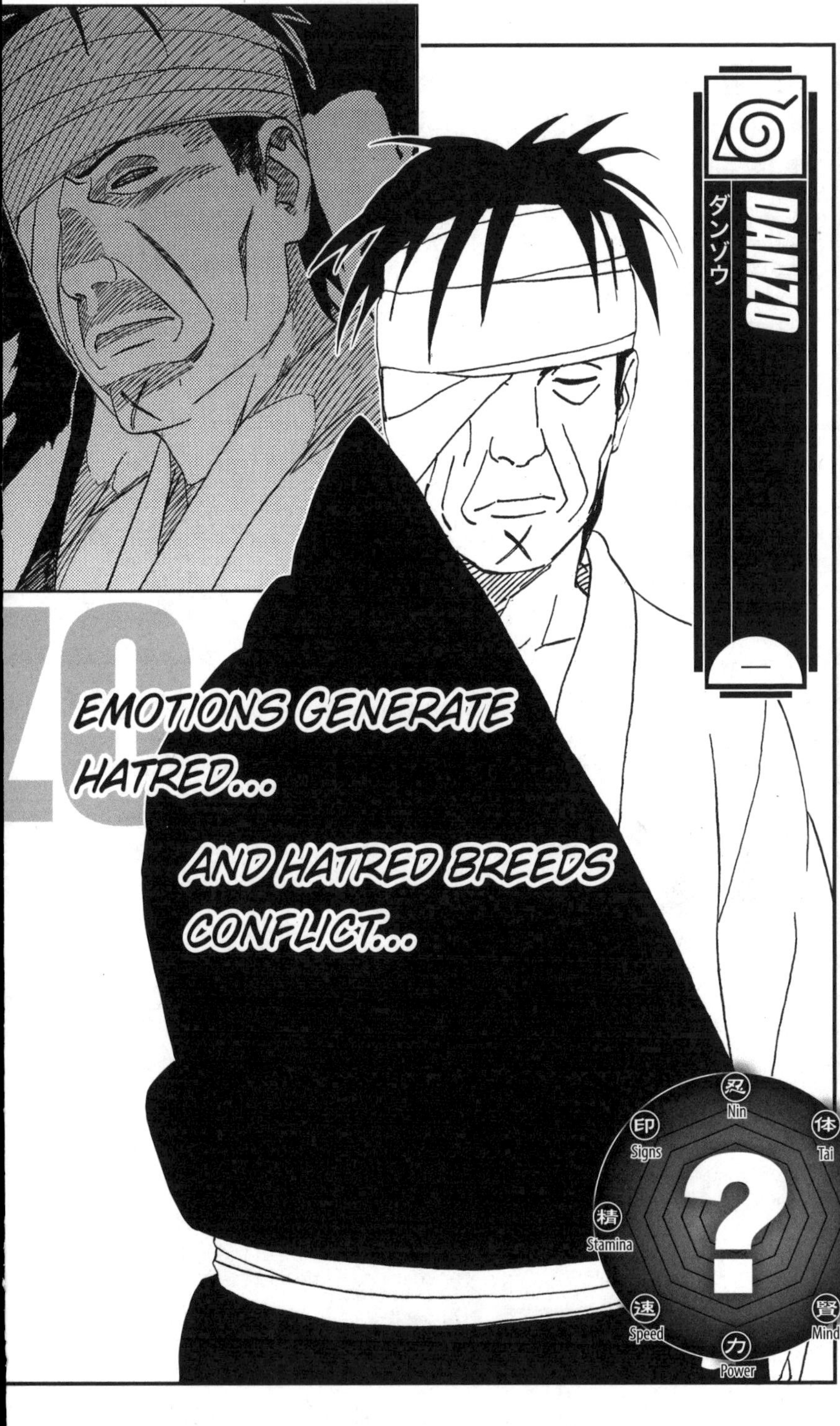
DANZO
ダンゾウ
EMOTIONS GENERATE HATRED...
AND HATRED BREEDS CONFLICT...
忍 Nin
体 Tai
幻 Gen
賢 Mind
力 Power
速 Speed
精 Stamina
印 Signs
?

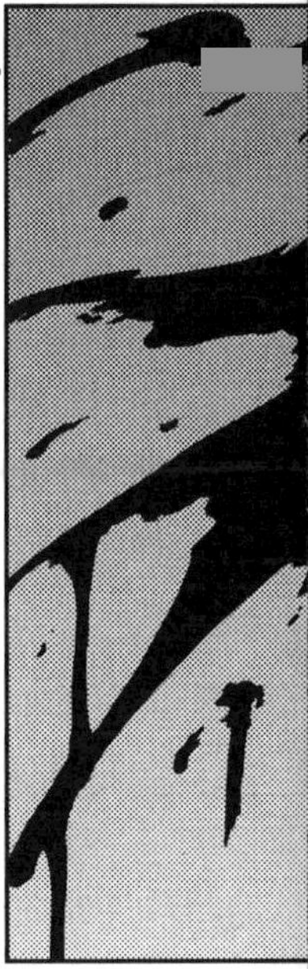

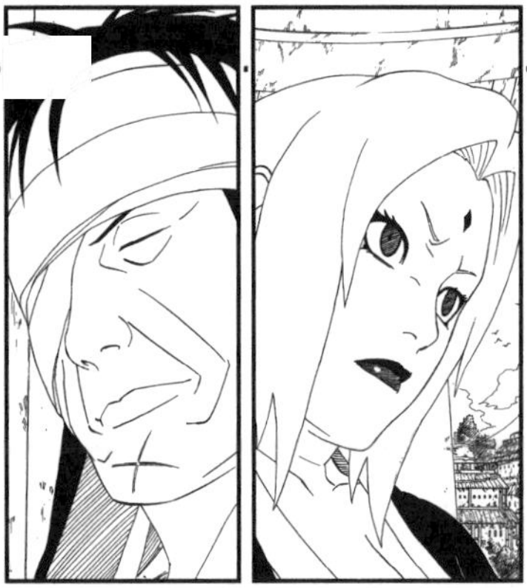

The shadow of Konohagakure–He supports the Hokage from underground.

➡ When Naruto returns to the village after more than two years away, Danzo, the leader of the Foundation, also surfaces and reveals his face. Tsunade, the granddaughter of the First Hokage, who carries on the will of the previous Hokage, and he have a stormy relationship.

In the past, Danzo and Sarutobi Hiruzen had vied for the Hokage's seat. To him, a ninja serves the will of the village and the land. That is why, after failing in the succession, he forms the Foundation, which reports directly to the Hokage. He trains shinobi who will be loyal to him and controls Konoha's underground. The Third Hokage is no longer alive. The Foundation that worked to support him…what influence do they now exert?

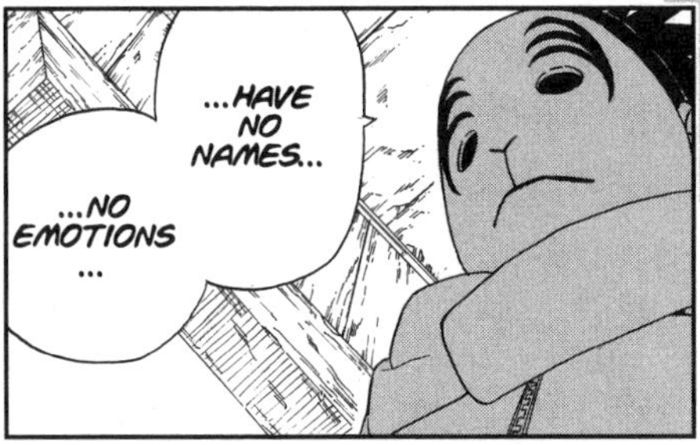
...HAVE NO NAMES...
...NO EMOTIONS ...

⬆ The mission of the Foundation is pounded into the shinobi. They do whatever Danzo orders, serving as silent vessels, dominating the shadows of Konoha.

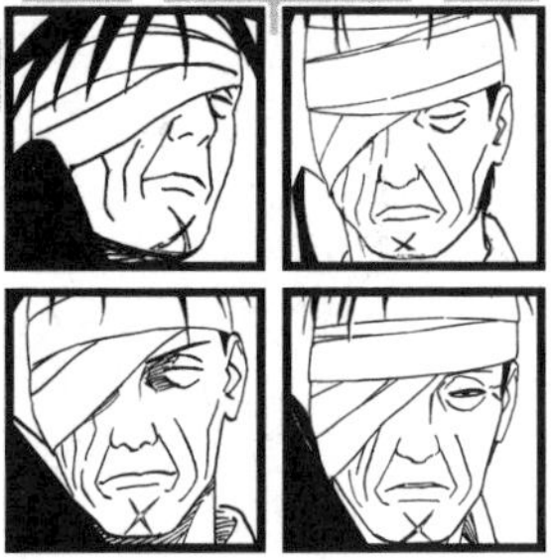

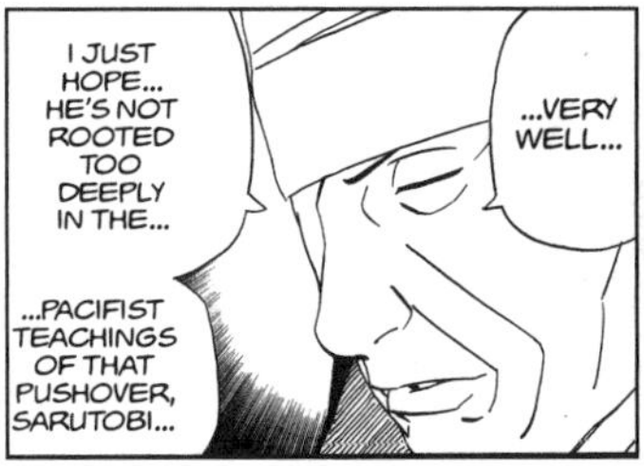
...VERY WELL...
I JUST HOPE... HE'S NOT ROOTED TOO DEEPLY IN THE...
...PACIFIST TEACHINGS OF THAT PUSHOVER, SARUTOBI...

⬆ The Taka has the stamp of Konoha on it. What kind of future do his eyes see…?

Ninja Registry Number: 000272
Birthdate: January 6 (72 years old; Capricorn)
Height: 170.0 cm (5'7") **Weight:** 52.7 kg (116 lbs.) **Blood type:** AB
Personality: Ambitious, secretive, unyielding
Favorite food: Hijiki, genmaicha
Least favorite food: Warabimochi
Would like to fight: No one in particular
Favorite word: Indomitable
Interests: Appreciating famous pictures, keeping a diary

Graduated from the Ninja Academy at age ?
Promoted to chûnin at age ?

Mission Experience		
	D-rank: ?	C-rank: ?
	B-rank: ?	A-rank: ?
	S-rank: ?	

CHIYO

チヨ

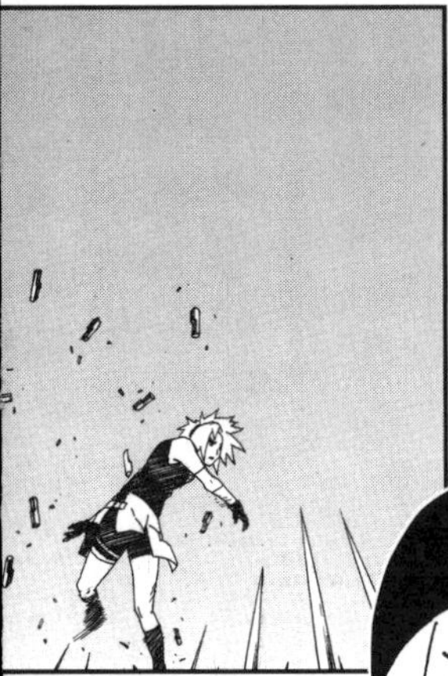

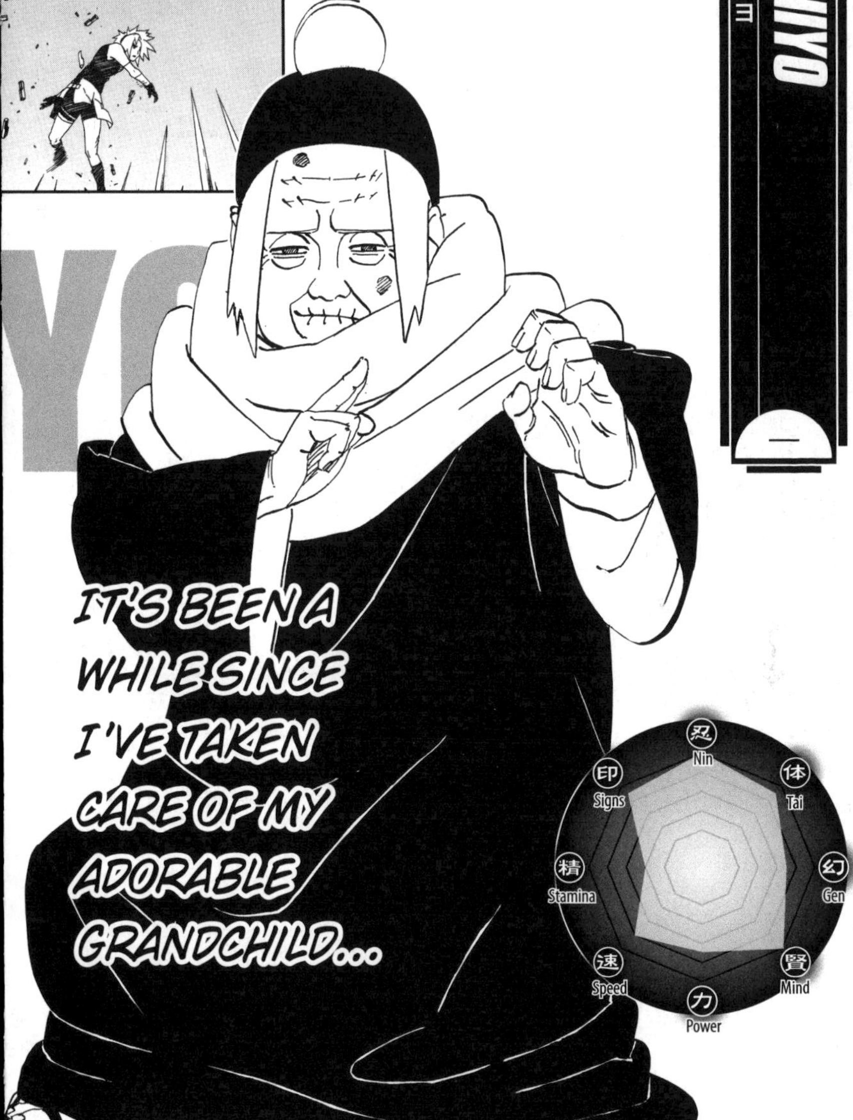
IT'S BEEN A
WHILE SINCE
I'VE TAKEN
CARE OF MY
ADORABLE
GRANDCHILD...
忍
Nin
体
Tai
幻
Gen
賢
Mind
力
Power
速
Speed
精
Stamina
印
Signs

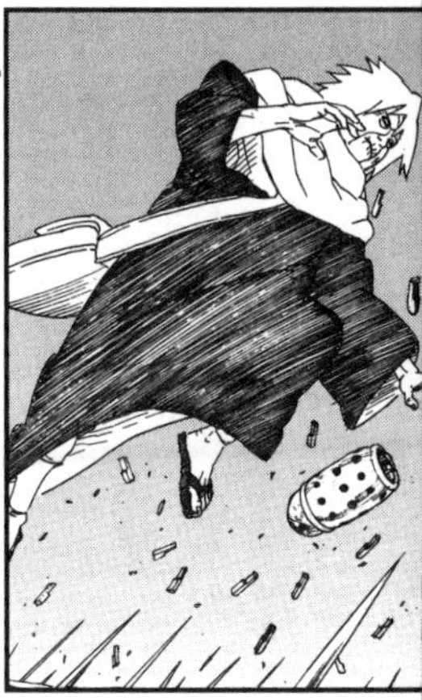

Even when bombarded by the sands of fate, this flower does not wilt.

Long ago, the young kunoichi Chiyo amazed shinobi from foreign lands with her extraordinary skill in medical ninjutsu, taijutsu and puppet jutsu. Today, she is an advisor to the Suna, but would probably prefer to be fishing with her younger brother. The wars that dragged on for many years have turned her bitter toward foreign lands, as well as her own village. And at her advanced age, she is resigned to waiting for death to take her quietly.

But one day, unexpected visitors fuel the fire in her once more. He is none other than Konoha's White Fang, the one who took her son's life and Princess Tsunade who gave her so much hardship. They were the descendants and pupils of her sworn enemies. They were shinobi of the next generation, reminders of how much time has passed for her. This serves to jolt Chiyo back into action.

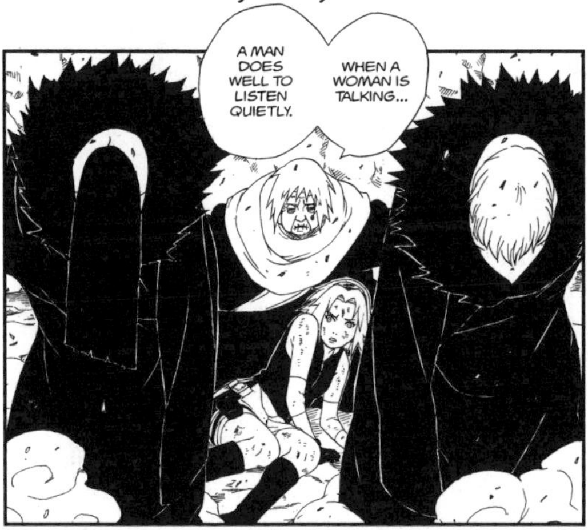
WHEN A WOMAN IS TALKING...
A MAN DOES WELL TO LISTEN QUIETLY.

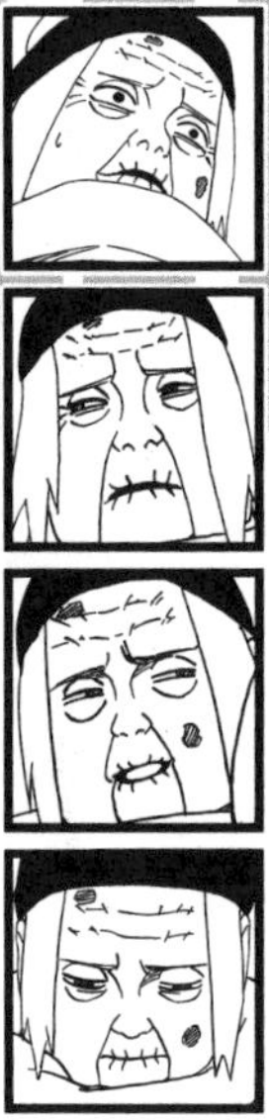

⬅ She controls her puppet jutsu with her fingertips. A miracle art that is deeply ingrained in her, she gives not even a hint of weakness.

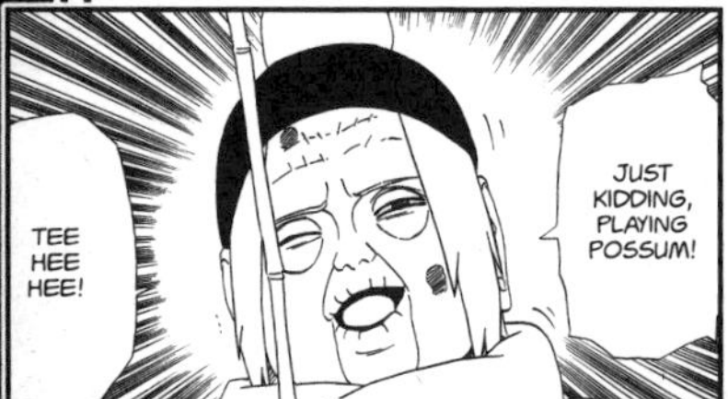
JUST KIDDING, PLAYING POSSUM!
TEE HEE HEE!

⬆ Women must be courageous and charming. She has a playful side that belies her age.

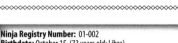

Ninja Registry Number: 01-002
Birthdate: October 15 (73 years old; Libra)
Height: 149.1 cm (4'10½") **Weight:** 39.1 kg (86 lbs.) **Blood type:** B
Personality: Easily jumps to conclusions, mischievous
Favorite food: Bean cuisine, potatoes
Least favorite food: Sashimi
Would like to fight: White Fang of Konoha
Favorite word: Battle-tough
Interests: Pretending to be dead, pretending to be senile, fishing

Graduated from the Ninja Academy at age ?
Promoted to chûnin at age ?

Mission Experience		
	D-rank: ?	C-rank: ?
	B-rank: ?	A-rank: ?
	S-rank: ?	

The young shinobi make Chiyo see beyond the hatred to the time of her spring.

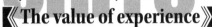

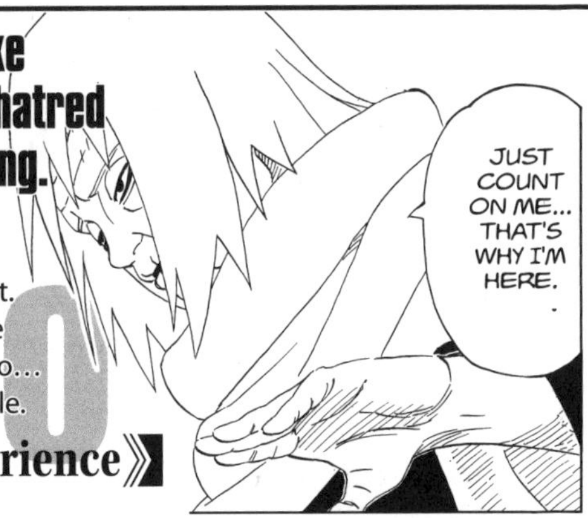
JUST COUNT ON ME... THAT'S WHY I'M HERE.

Princess Tsunade was once a bitter enemy. Now her pupil, Sakura, is an ally she must trust. Seeing her struggle ignites the kunoichi fighting spirit in Chiyo… Chiyo has been in many a battle.

《The value of experience》

Her vast experience and keen instincts honed over the years serve as ideal partners, and she turns them into weapons, displaying a force that shines on the future of the shinobi.

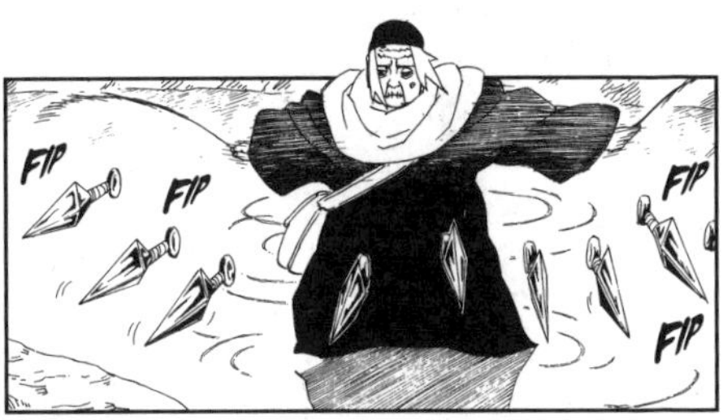
FIP
FIP
FIP
FIP

➡ The puppetry she used to protect is used by those she taught to tear the future apart.

《Regret》

Sasori was her grandson. She taught him puppetry to help ease his grief over losing his parents. To protect their village, Chiyo sealed a Tailed Beast in Gaara and turned him into a military weapon. Her past actions, done to protect, come back to haunt her and end up actually posing a threat to those she wishes to save. In giving her life, Chiyo finds redemption. Her expression at the end is one of peace, of one who has found closure in the past and is hopeful for the future.

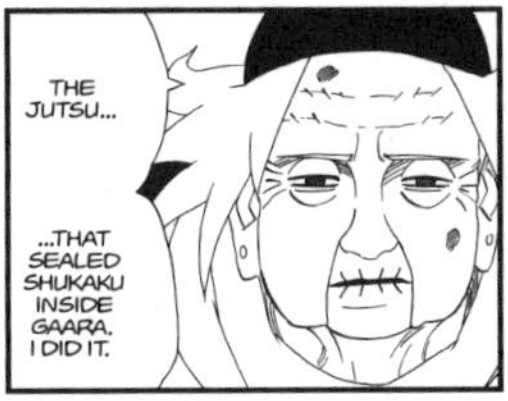
THE JUTSU...
...THAT SEALED SHUKAKU INSIDE GAARA. I DID IT.

➡ For the sake of the village, she had sealed the darkness herself. The burden of this sin quickens Chiyo's resolve.

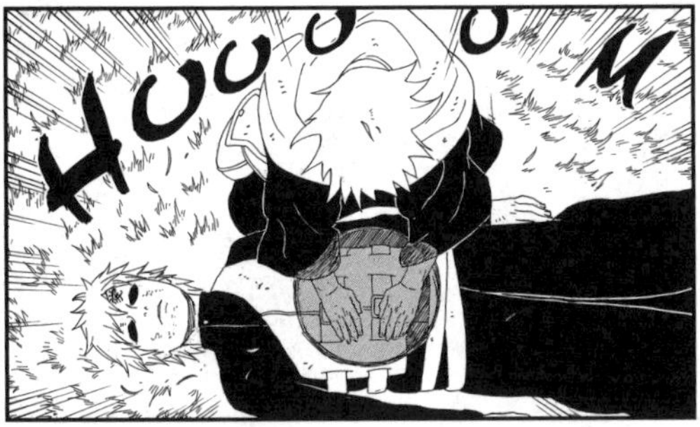
HOOOOM

⬅ A jutsu in which one gives one's life to bring back the dead. Chiyo broke taboos to develop it for her grandson's sake. But now, it will save the village…

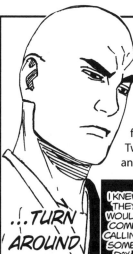

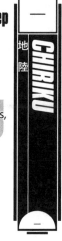

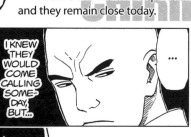

...TURN AROUND AND GO HOME!

CHIRIKU

地陸

A ninja monk who possesses the gift of the sages and strives to keep peace in the land.

Chiriku is a monk of the Fire Temple in the Land of Fire. No one in the temple comes even close in strength to this former member of the Guardian Shinobi Twelve. He and Asuma are past compatriots, and they remain close today.

...
I KNEW THEY WOULD COME CALLING SOMEDAY, BUT...

⇧ He maintains contacts in the outside world and is up to date on all the activities of the Akatsuki.

Ninja Registry Number: —
Birthdate: July 1 (31 years old; Cancer)
Height: 179.0 cm (5'10½") **Weight:** 59.1 kg (130 lbs.) **Blood type:** A
Personality: Sincere, straightforward
Favorite word: Sarutobi Asuma

Collection ... Number 7

Konoha

THE GUARDIAN SHINOBI TWELVE

A shinobi organization under the direct control of the feudal lord of the Land of Fire, they serve as his bodyguards. Skilled shinobi are gathered from around the land, then hired into service. Today, the Shinobi Guardian Twelve have been disbanded, but its members are well-known shinobi.

➡ They are hunted for their fame as well as the bounty on their heads on the black market.

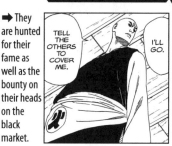

I'LL GO.
TELL THE OTHERS TO COVER ME.

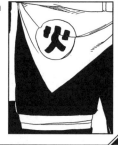

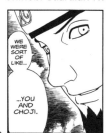

WE WERE SORT OF LIKE...
...YOU AND CHOJI.

⬅ Birth and upbringing matters little to him and he shares a close friendship with Asuma.

➡ The waistcloth with the crest of the Land of Fire is proof of membership in the Guardian Twelve.

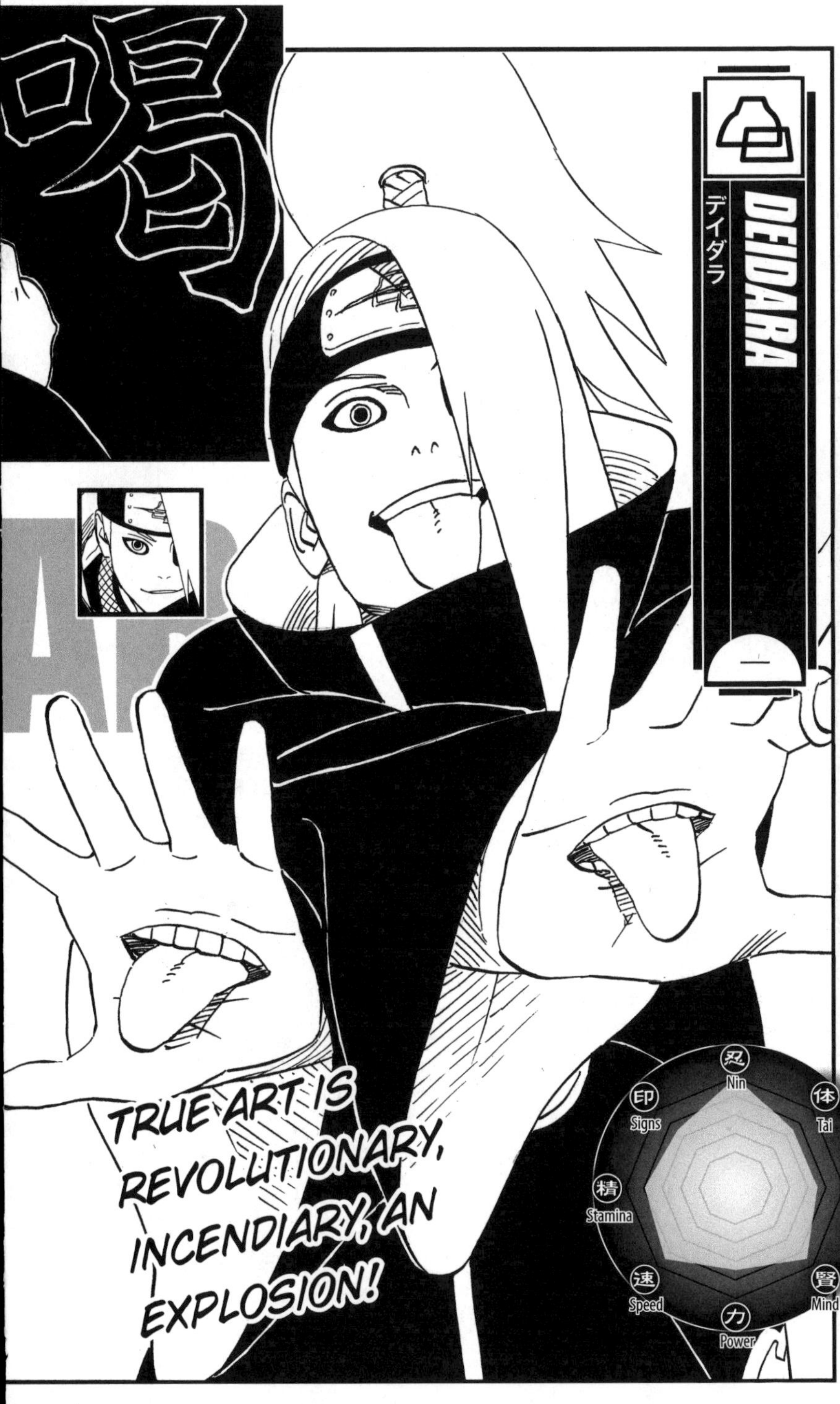
DEIDARA
デイダラ
TRUE ART IS REVOLUTIONARY, INCENDIARY, AN EXPLOSION!
忍 Nin
体 Tai
幻 Gen
賢 Mind
力 Power
速 Speed
精 Stamina
印 Signs

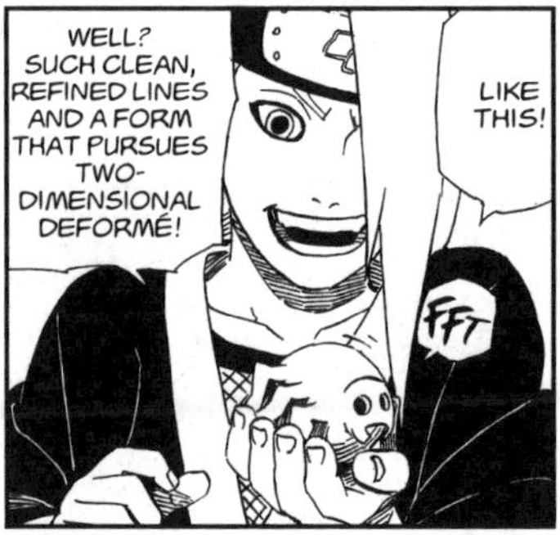
LIKE THIS!
WELL? SUCH CLEAN, REFINED LINES AND A FORM THAT PURSUES TWO-DIMENSIONAL DEFORMÉ!
FFT

The true artist lives only for the moment.

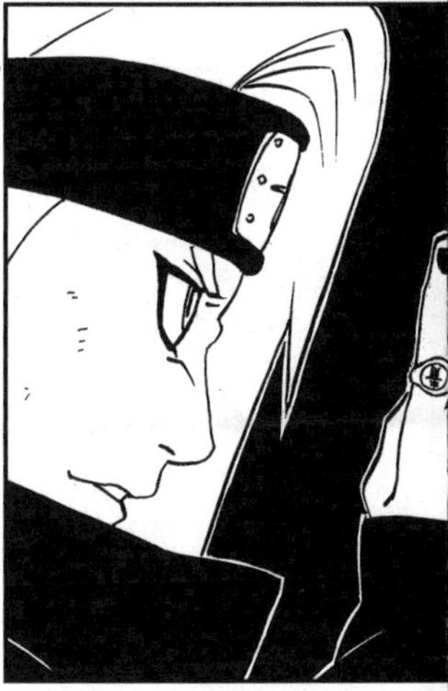

He destroys the art that he creates. The immediacy of an explosion is Deidara's definition of instantaneous art. He is a shinobi from Iwagakure and has won high praise as a clay sculptor. But his true perfection as an artist is ever elusive.

Deidara steals the village's forbidden jutsu, which allows him to fold chakra into his creations. During his escape with the jutsu, his pursuers release detonating clay. Deidara finally sees the art he has been searching for.

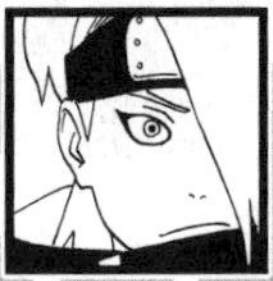

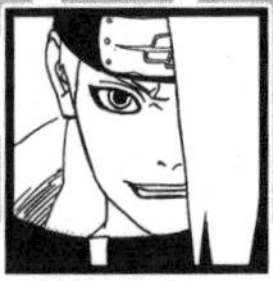

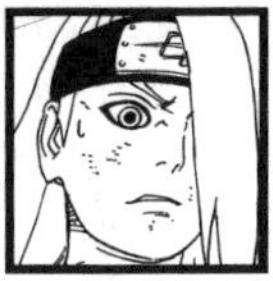

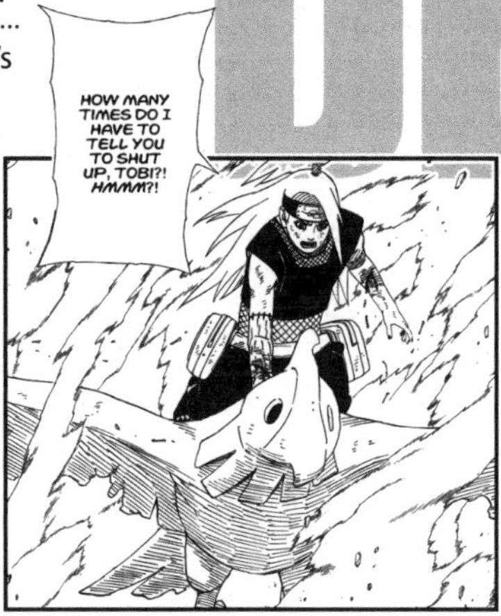
HOW MANY TIMES DO I HAVE TO TELL YOU TO SHUT UP, TOBI?! HMMM?!

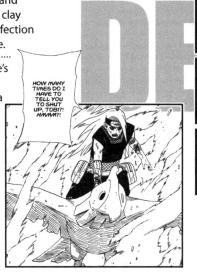

➡ Art born from the imagination of a genius and soars across the heavens.

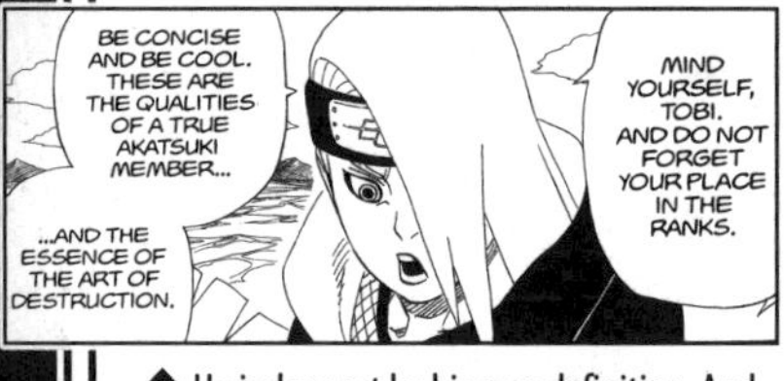
MIND YOURSELF, TOBI. AND DO NOT FORGET YOUR PLACE IN THE RANKS.
BE CONCISE AND BE COOL. THESE ARE THE QUALITIES OF A TRUE AKATSUKI MEMBER...
...AND THE ESSENCE OF THE ART OF DESTRUCTION.

⬆ He judges art by his own definition. And whatever it is that compels him be an artist defines Deidara's identity and all his actions.

Ninja Registry Number: IW-08721
Birthdate: May 5 (19 years old; Taurus)
Height: 166.0 cm (5'5") **Weight:** 50.8 kg (112 lbs.) **Blood type:** AB
Personality: Prideful, combative
Favorite food: Explosive oden
Least favorite food: Mixed rice
Would like to fight: Uchiha Itachi
Favorite word: Art is an explosion.
Interests: Creative activity (Inventing bombs)

Graduated from the Ninja Academy at age ?
Promoted to chûnin at age ?

Mission Experience	D-rank: 4	C-rank: 27
	B-rank: 35	A-rank: 13
	S-rank: 3	

He will get back his self-respect... by defeating the Sharingan.

He lost his self-respect as an artist to Itachi.

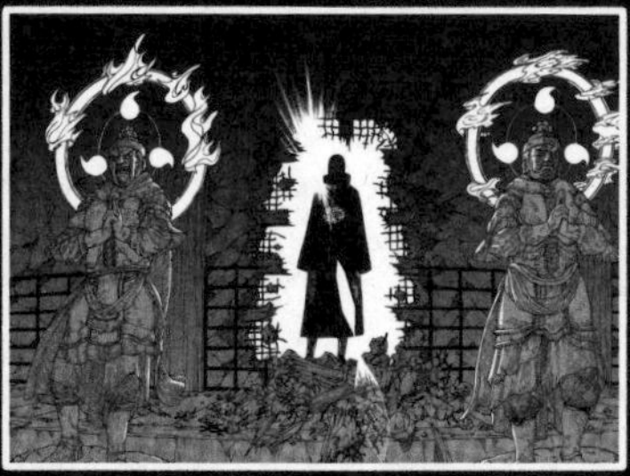
⬆ Itachi's appearance was art itself.

After obtaining detonating clay, the first opponent Deidara faces is Uchiha Itachi. Until then, every foe who saw his work cowered in fear, screamed, lost all hope or cried. His art was supposed to be...perfect. However, there was no fear in Itachi's eyes.

《The curse of the Sharingan》

Itachi's Sharingan attack teaches Deidara envy and humiliation. For that, Deidara will hate the Uchiha and the Sharingan Eye forever...

He will use his art to break the spell of the Sharingan. It is for this purpose that he hides a blade in his left eye, biding his time for the moment of revenge.

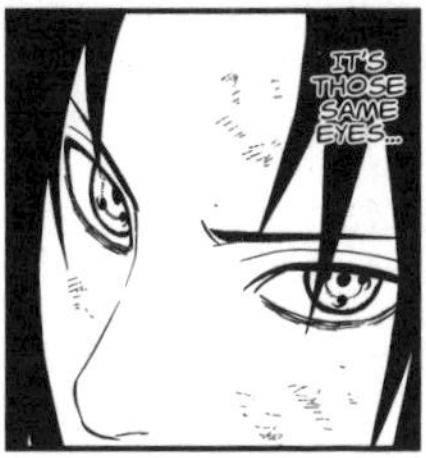
IT'S THOSE SAME EYES...

⬆⬇ Those red eyes that penetrate everything...shoot through Deidara's heart.

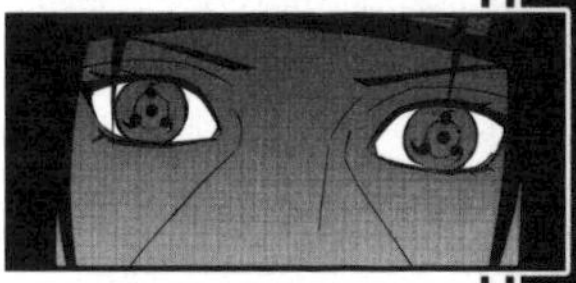

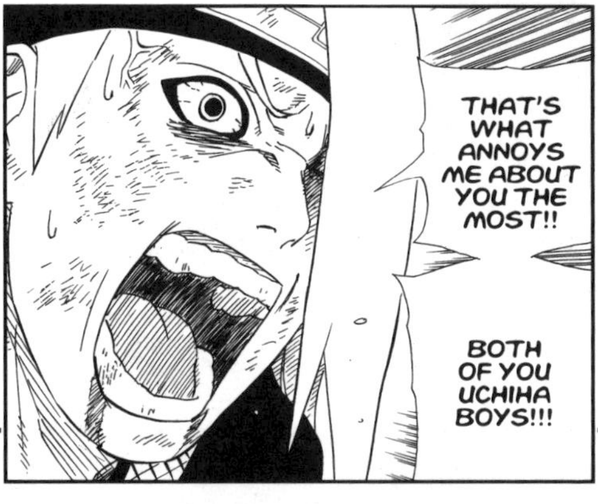
THAT'S WHAT ANNOYS ME ABOUT YOU THE MOST!!
BOTH OF YOU UCHIHA BOYS!!!

➡ Deidara seethes with anger at those eyes that disrespect his supreme art.

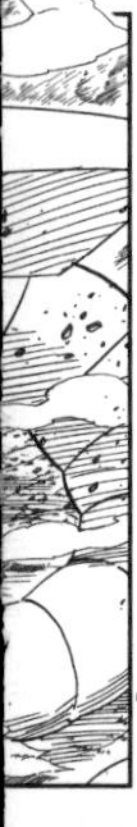

《Analytical》

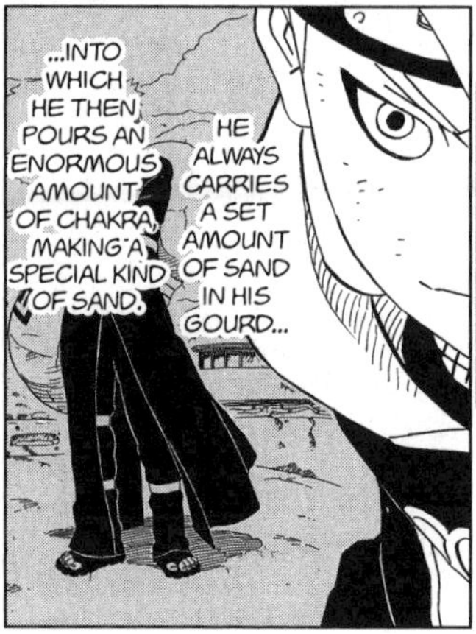
HE ALWAYS CARRIES A SET AMOUNT OF SAND IN HIS GOURD...
...INTO WHICH HE THEN POURS AN ENORMOUS AMOUNT OF CHAKRA, MAKING A SPECIAL KIND OF SAND.

Skilled in the finest artistic details

Sculpting, painting, molding… There are many methods to creating a work of art. In the same manner, Deidara's art goes through several steps before completion. The battle environment necessary for his chosen work, the opponent's method of battle… Deidara instantly analyzes these factors. The harsher the battle condition, the more determined Deidara becomes and the more elaborate his performance.

⬅ He appraises his target instantly with composure and objectivity.

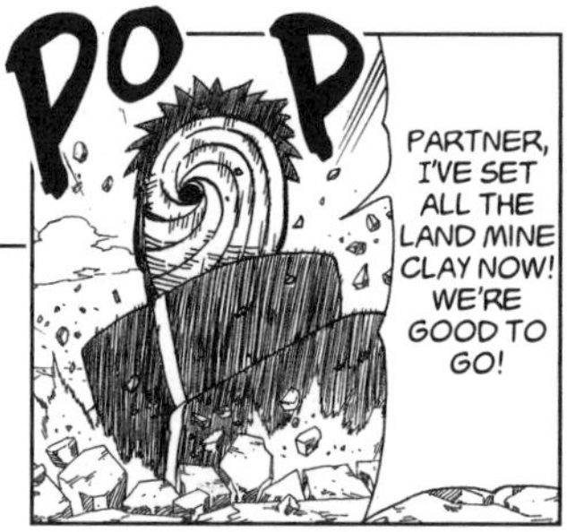
POP
PARTNER, I'VE SET ALL THE LAND MINE CLAY NOW! WE'RE GOOD TO GO!

⬆ It is his subordinate's job to set the stage. Deidara remains at high level, ready to perform his art.

《Setting》

When they must wait for a target, it is possible to further enhance the art. Deidara would never hesitate to jump at such a chance. At times, he will cower on the ground. At others, he will soar through the air or work in unison with a comrade. The setup can be extremely meticulous…

Then they corner the opponent from the air and from the ground, slowly but steadily until the moment of the explosion when his perfect work of art will be on display.

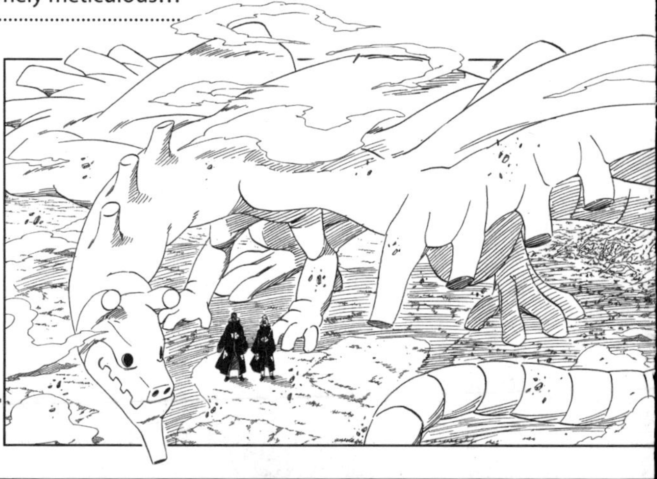

In a dazzling flash, an existence becomes sublimated.

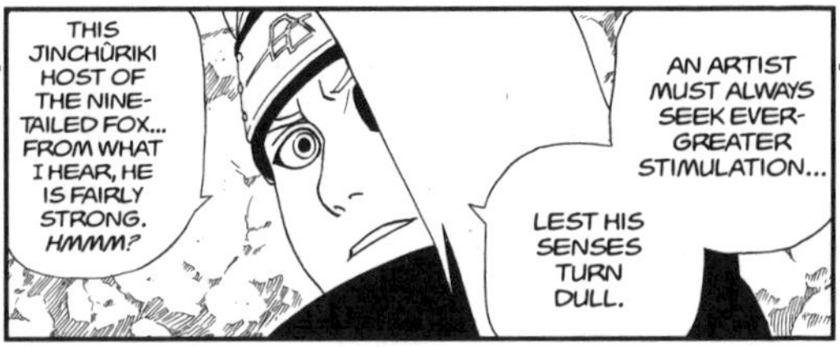
AN ARTIST MUST ALWAYS SEEK EVER-GREATER STIMULATION...
LEST HIS SENSES TURN DULL.
THIS JINCHÛRIKI HOST OF THE NINE-TAILED FOX... FROM WHAT I HEAR, HE IS FAIRLY STRONG. HMMM?

⬆ He shows respect to fellow artists. Their joint efforts remotivate Deidara.

《A view of art》

Deidara's actions all stem from his view of art. He declares that his art is the best, and it is the same with his joining the Akatsuki. Deidara sees all his fellow Akatsuki as artists. Hunting and capturing the Tailed Beasts as part of the Akatsuki artist group is a huge source of pride for Deidara.

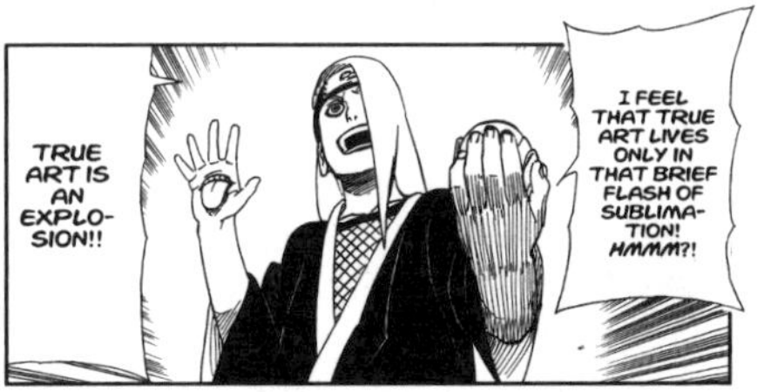
I FEEL THAT TRUE ART LIVES ONLY IN THAT BRIEF FLASH OF SUBLIMATION! HMMM?!
TRUE ART IS AN EXPLOSION!!

⬆ No one will convince Deidara that his view on art is flawed.

⬇ If anyone disagrees with his opinions as an artist, he flies into a rage.

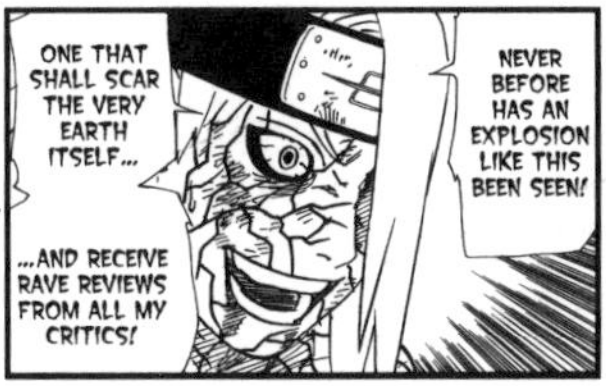
NEVER BEFORE HAS AN EXPLOSION LIKE THIS BEEN SEEN!
ONE THAT SHALL SCAR THE VERY EARTH ITSELF...
...AND RECEIVE RAVE REVIEWS FROM ALL MY CRITICS!

《Ultimate Art》

The Uchiha clan's Sharingan is completely oblivious to art. Therefore, Deidara sees it (and the clan) as disrespectful. But the Sharingan prompts him to make his final piece, his ultimate art. He turns himself into art itself. Embracing the shock and awe he is sure to generate, he transforms into a dazzling flash of light. Suddenly a light tower soars across the sky. It causes people to shudder and to remember this sight forever.

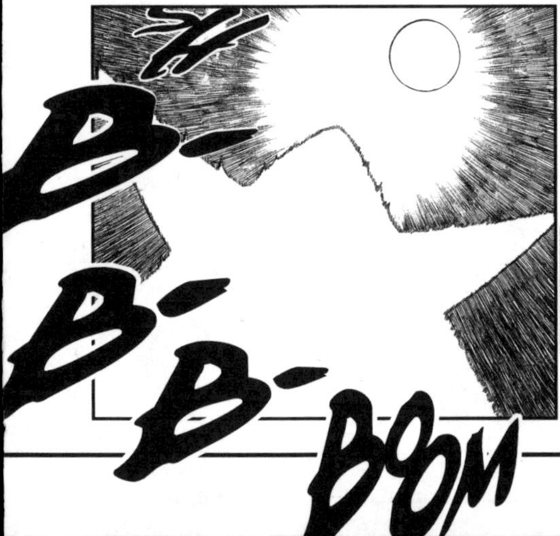
B-B-B-B-BOOM

DARA

⬅ With arms boldly outspread, he performs the Ultimate Art, sheer perfection.

He single-mindedly pursues good taste, hurling bowls with one hand and shouting orders.

In business for 34 years, Ichiraku is famous in Konohagakure. Despite its unassuming appearance, the shop is always crowded. The reason for that is the shop's adherence to taste, which reaches artistic heights. Constantly yelling at his two not-too-smart apprentices, Teuchi continues to offer the best taste experience.

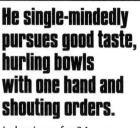

TEUCHI
テウチ

FOOL! YOU STUCK YOUR FINGER IN IT!

MATSU

NISHI

I'M MATSU!

HI, I'M NISHI!!

⬇ His shouting reverberates from the shop, helping make Ichiraku...famous?

SERVES YOU RIGHT FOR NOT MOPPING THE FLOORS PROPERLY!

YOU'RE BOTH USELESS – USELESS!

SLOSH

⬆ They mess up royally without meaning to. But these two are basically very dedicated rookies.

TEUCHI
Birthdate: August 10 (47 years old; Leo)
Height: 170.0 cm (5'6") **Weight:** 64.0 kg (141 lbs.) **Blood type:** O
Personality: Stubborn, dedicated to his craft
Favorite word: Artisan

NISHI
Birthdate: August 11 (28 years old; Leo)
Height: 180.0 cm (5'9") **Weight:** 65.0 kg (145 lbs.) **Blood type:** A
Personality: Rhetorical
Favorite word: Crewcut

MATSU
Birthdate: May 16 (28 years old; Taurus)
Height: 170.0 cm (5'6") **Weight:** 70.0 kg (154 lbs.) **Blood type:** B
Personality: Dense
Favorite word: Doodoo bi doobi dooba

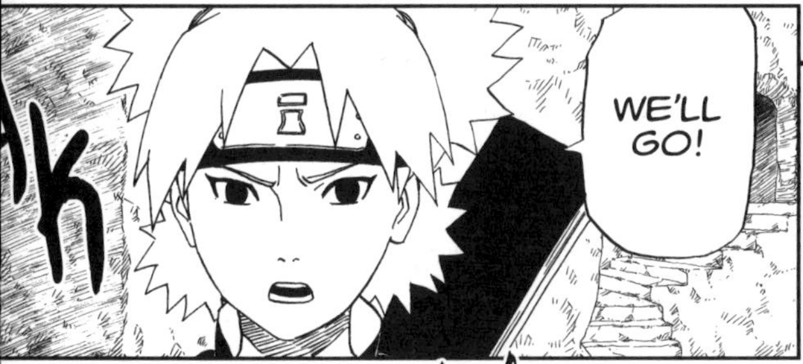
WE'LL GO!

TEMARI

テマリ

Jônin

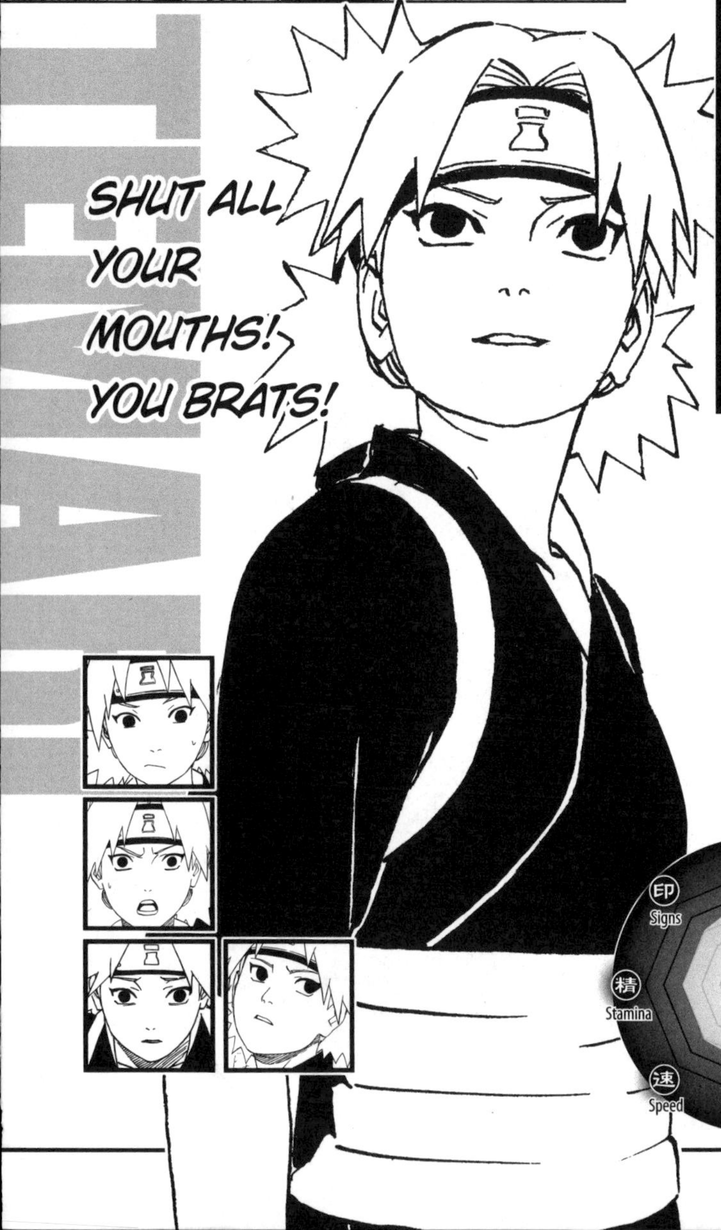
SHUT ALL YOUR MOUTHS! YOU BRATS!
TEMARI

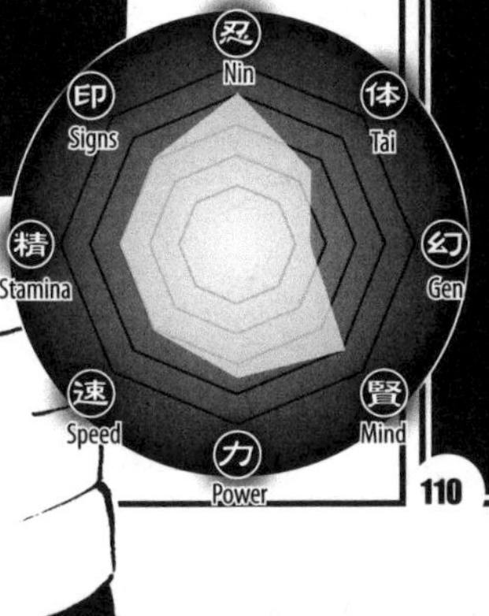
忍 Nin
体 Tai
幻 Gen
賢 Mind
力 Power
速 Speed
精 Stamina
印 Signs

With Kankuro, she assists Gaara, now the Kazekage. She's integral in the training of the young generation of recruits.

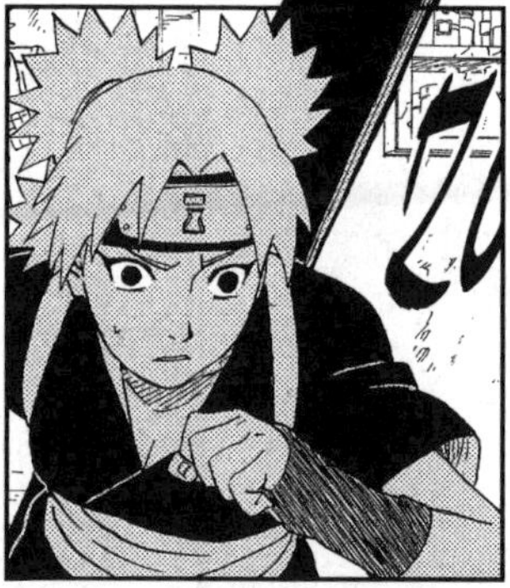

⬆ Experience has changed the way she reacts when Kankuro falters. In the past, she would have simply found fault in his failure.

This princess of the wind's budding spirit grows ever stronger.

With a sweep of her fan, she will create a sandstorm that cuts down everything in its way. Temari is the only woman among the three siblings of the Suna. In the past, she was immature and overly aggressive. But she is now a jônin. Besides having considerable skill, she is also the daughter of the previous Kazekage and opportunities for important missions have opened up for her. Hence, she is becoming more aware of her responsibilities. With Kankuro, she assists Gaara, who is now the Kazekage. And working with Konohagakure to prepare the young generation of recruits, Temari has become an indispensable part of the village.

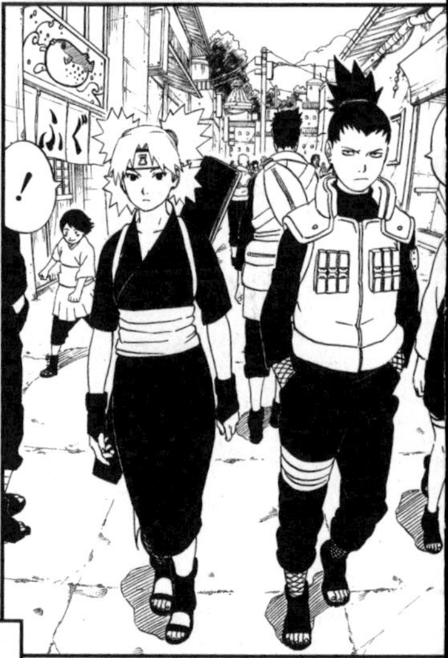
!

⬆ During the Chûnin Selection Exam, she sets out for Konohagakure as the village's messenger. In hope of adopting the Leaf's training methods, she eagerly guides the young generation.

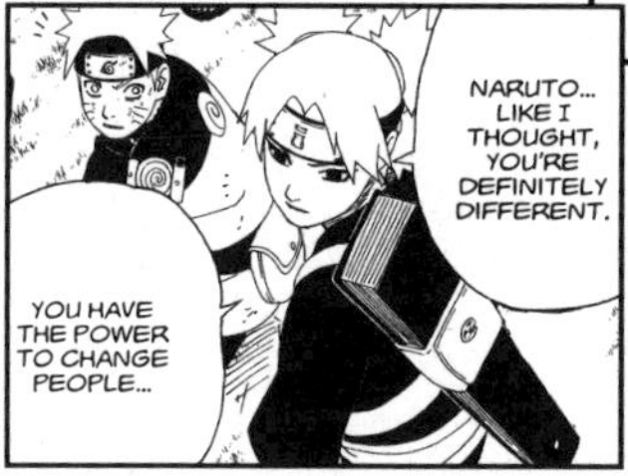
NARUTO... LIKE I THOUGHT, YOU'RE DEFINITELY DIFFERENT.
YOU HAVE THE POWER TO CHANGE PEOPLE...

➡ Temari willingly acknowledges Naruto's charisma for his part in influencing those around him and affecting change in Sunagakure. She herself has undergone a change.

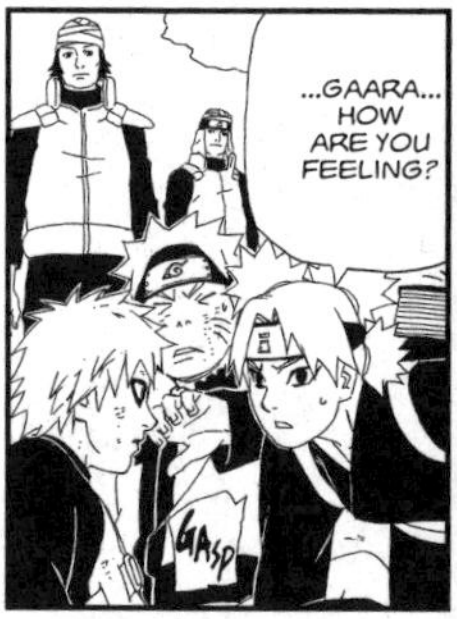
...GAARA... HOW ARE YOU FEELING?
GASP

➡ Temari has strengthened both her body and spirit. She is a caring sister to her two younger brothers, sometimes to a fault.

Ninja Registry Number: 53-004
Birthdate: August 23 (19 years old; Virgo)
Height: 165.0 cm (5'5") **Weight:** 47.9 kg (106 lbs.) **Blood type:** 0
Personality: Bold, takes every obligation seriously
Favorite food: Roasted chestnuts, kenchinjiru
Least favorite food: Squid, octopus
Would like to fight: Nara Shikamaru
Favorite word: As far as the eye can see.
Interests: plants

Graduated from the Ninja Academy at age 12
Promoted to chûnin at age 17

Mission Experience		
	D-rank: 0	C-rank: 9
	B-rank: 12	A-rank: 20
	S-rank: 1	

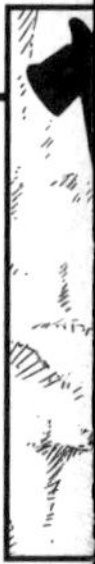

TENTEN

テンテン

Chûnin

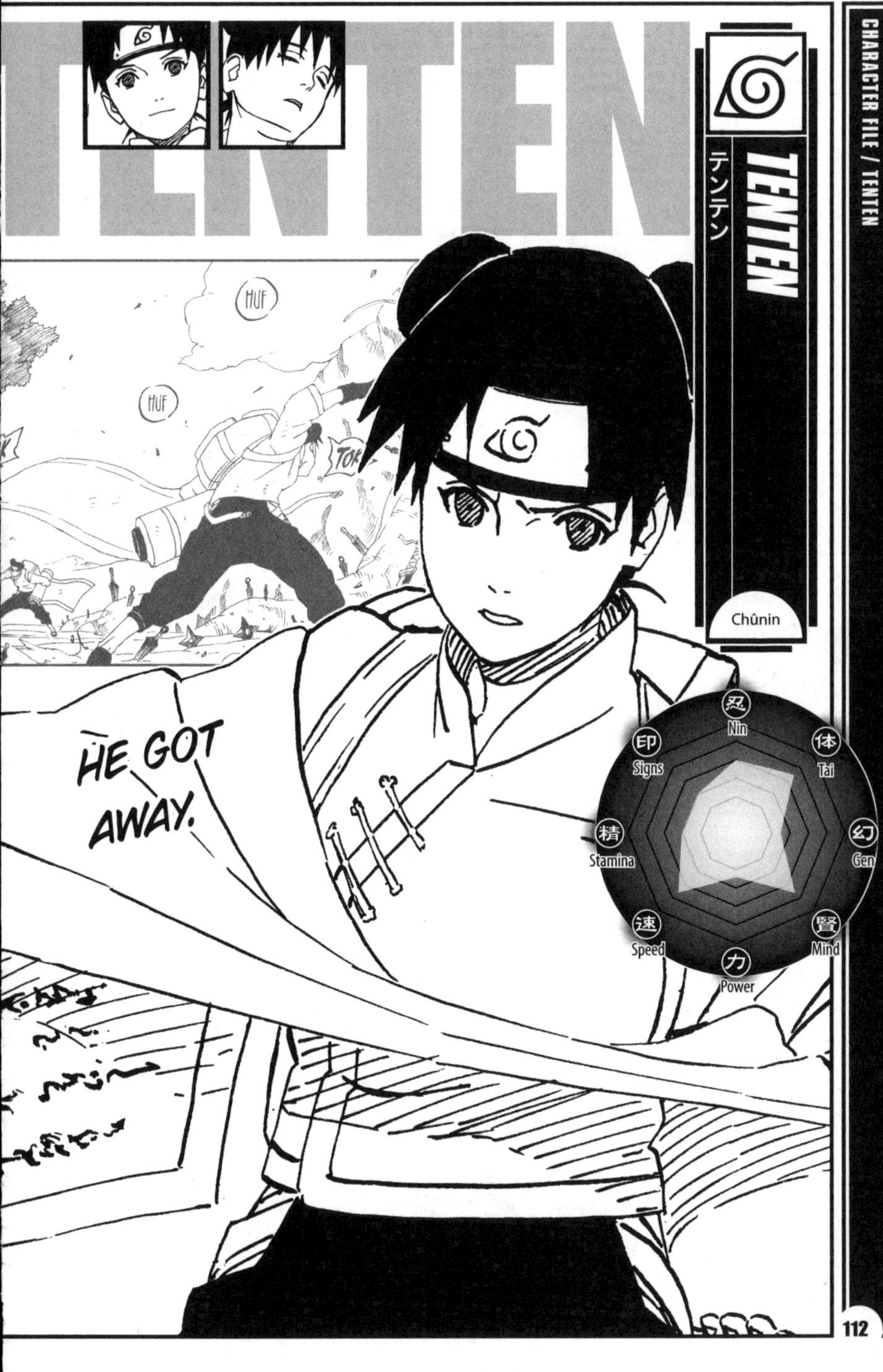
HUF
HUF
TOK
HE GOT AWAY.
忍 Nin
体 Tai
幻 Gen
賢 Mind
力 Power
速 Speed
精 Stamina
印 Signs

Infinite blades dance wildly through the air!

Through daily training, Tenten has sharpened her skills and increased the myriad of weapons she has at her disposal. Her prowess even has the Akatsuki dumbfounded. But Tenten's duties do not end here. She guides her team on missions by voicing rational opinions, and when it comes time to battle, she will take the initiative, launching long-distance attacks. Thanks to Tenten, her teammates can put their own talents to work to the fullest degree. Team Guy is made up of strong personalities, and Tenten is an absolutely essential member.

⬆ She has increased her repertoire of techniques, like this two-part attack using letter bombs.

➡ Tenten uses her weapons to stall opponents, then Lee and Neji step in to launch a coordinated attack.

IF YOU KEEP TALKING THE WHOLE TIME, IT'LL SEEM LIKE FOR-EVER... CUT IT OUT!

...I THOUGHT IT TOOK LIKE THREE DAYS...

⬆ Preventing Guy and Lee from going overboard is one of Tenten's important functions.

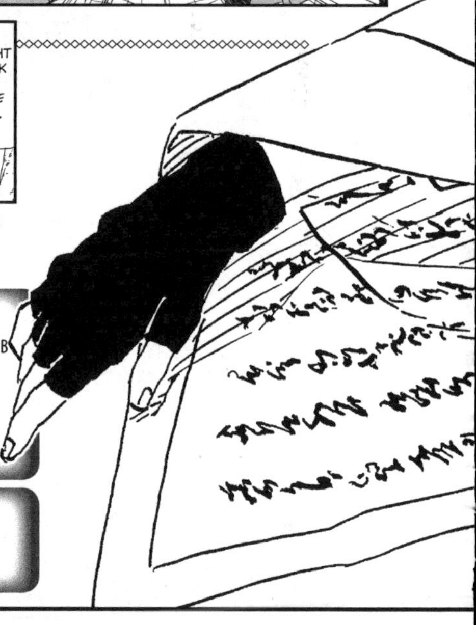

Ninja Registry Number: 012573
Birthdate: March 9 (17 years old; Pisces)
Height: 164.0 cm (5'4½") **Weight:** 47.3 kg (104 lbs.) **Blood type:** B
Personality: Loves research, meddlesome
Favorite food: Chinese meat buns, Sesame balls
Least favorite food: Pickled plums
Would like to fight: Temari, Haruno Sakura
Favorite word: Infallible
Interests: Fortune-telling

Graduated from the Ninja Academy at age 12
Promoted to chūnin at age 15

Mission Experience	D-rank: 28	C-rank: 23
	B-rank: 3	A-rank: 7
	S-rank: 1	

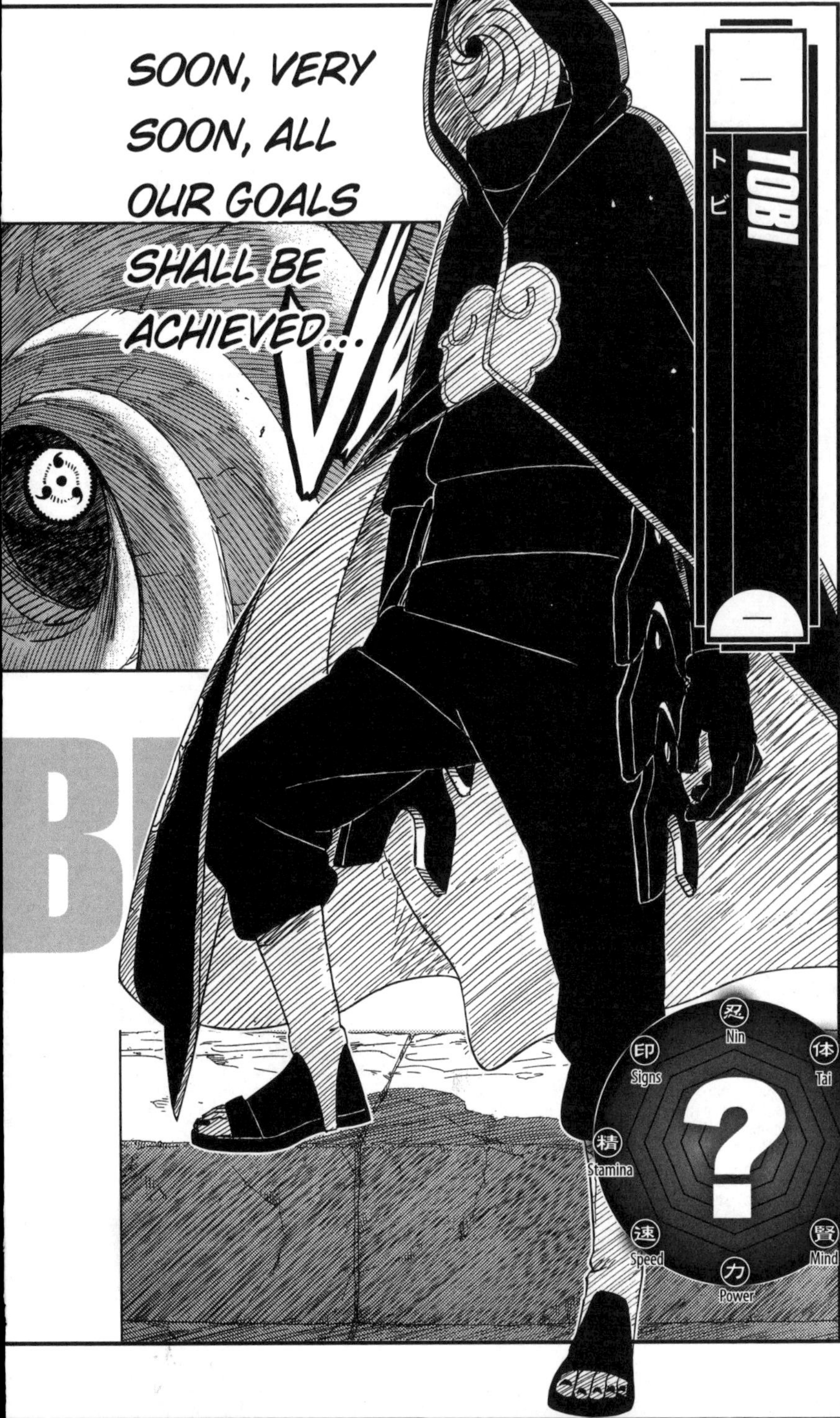
TOBI
トビ
SOON, VERY SOON, ALL OUR GOALS SHALL BE ACHIEVED...
忍
Nin
体
Tai
幻
Gen
賢
Mind
力
Power
速
Speed
精
Stamina
印
Signs
?

BY GAINING A NEW HOST, THE YOUNGER BROTHER'S EYES OBTAINED ETERNAL LIGHT...
ETERNAL MANGEKYO SHARINGAN!

⬆ The Mangekyo Sharingan in his eyes is everlasting. From the founding of Konoha to this day. . . what do these eyes reflect?

His evil eye glows from beneath the mask. The heroic figure of the Uchiha lurks in time eternal.

Tobi has done nothing remarkable since becoming Sasori's replacement in the Akatsuki. But he has an uncanny knack of showing up anywhere, anytime. Few know of his true power or the face behind the mask. Tobi is really Uchiha Madara, who was thought to have perished in the Final Valley. Why is he alive? And what does he hope to accomplish? That will become known when Tobi finally discards his mask and puts his hidden agenda into effect.

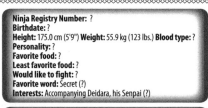

THE C4 KARURA: SUPER-TEENY, NANO-SIZED EXPLOSIVES...

⬅ Madara sees all.

REMEMBER, TRUE ART RESULTS FROM A MOMENT OF PASSION ARISING OUT OF A SEA OF CALM...
NO OFFENSE, SIR, BUT YOU SURE DO LIKE TO HEAR YOURSELF TALK...
...HA HA HA..

⬆ When he wears Tobi's mask, he is a lowly member of the Akatsuki. One unnecessary comment and Deidara will teach him a lesson.

Ninja Registry Number: ?
Birthdate: ?
Height: 175.0 cm (5'9") **Weight:** 55.9 kg (123 lbs.) **Blood type:** ?
Personality: ?
Favorite food: ?
Least favorite food: ?
Would like to fight: ?
Favorite word: Secret (?)
Interests: Accompanying Deidara, his Senpai (?)

Graduated from the Ninja Academy at age ?
Promoted to chunin at age ?

Mission Experience		
	D-rank: ?	C-rank: ?
	B-rank: ?	A-rank: ?
	S-rank: ?	

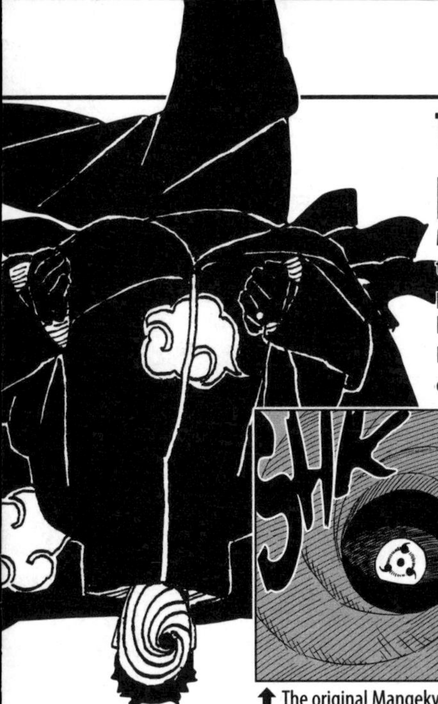

The mask hides his true power.

《Mangekyo Sharingan》

Madara's most formidable weapon is the Mangekyo Sharingan. It is an eternal power obtained through the sacrifice of his younger brother's eyes, and even the Nine Tails submits to it. However, Tobi does not use the Mangekyo Sharingan in the presence of other Akatsuki members. Is he trying to conceal his true identity or is there some other reason for it?

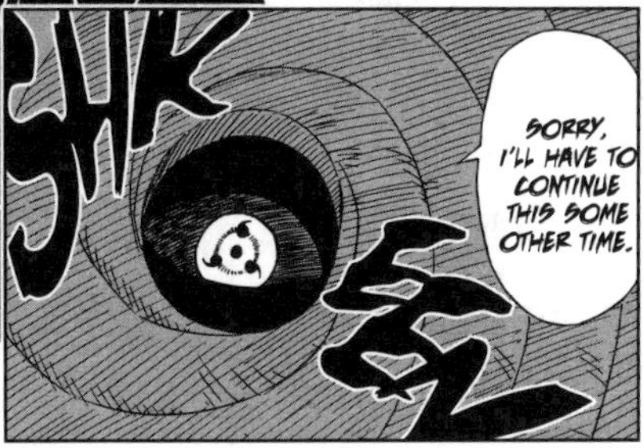
SORRY, I'LL HAVE TO CONTINUE THIS SOME OTHER TIME.

⬆ The original Mangekyo Sharingan. Anyone who carelessly looks into Tobi's eyes will be impaled by those pupils deep in the recesses.

《The mystery of his power》

No one knows the extent of Madara's true powers. No member of the Akatsuki has ever seen them. Only during a rare battle has he ever left traces of his jutsu. He has the power to deflect all offensive attacks, his body unscathed due to Itachi's Amaterasu, and vanish through the air as though transcending into space.

What is most puzzling is why Madara is still alive. This man, who should have died in the Final Valley during the era of the Hidden Leaf's founding, still exists, looking quite the same as he did then. Madara is the only one who was wily enough to deceive and outlive even the First Hokage, Hashirama.

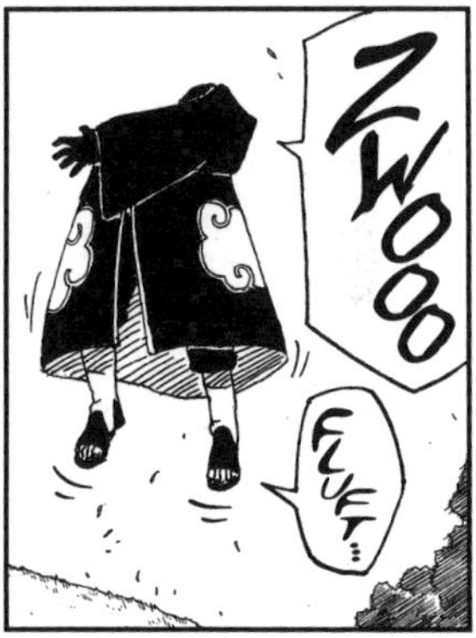
ZWOOO
FLUFT..

➡ Tobi's body disappears into nothing. Is this also one of Madara's abilities?

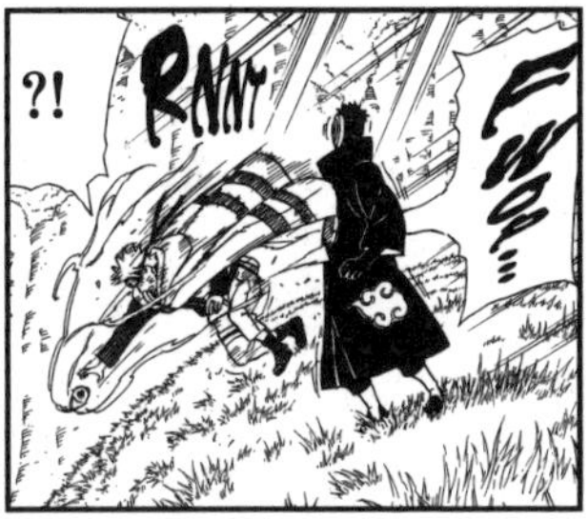
?!
RNNT
FWOA...

➡ Any attack will slip through Tobi's body, even though he doesn't seem to be using the Art of Teleportation.

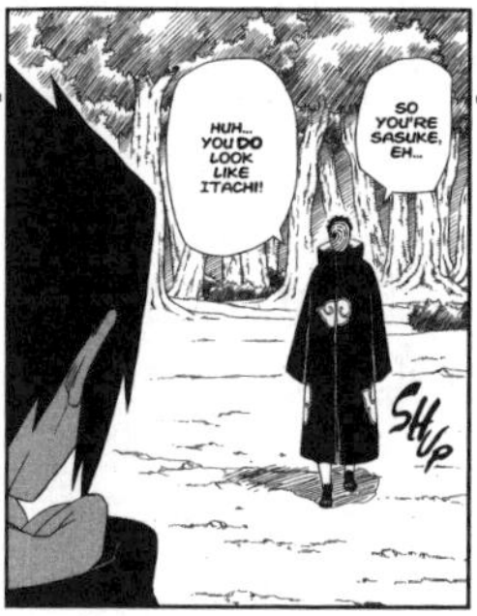
SO YOU'RE SASUKE, EH...
HUH... YOU DO LOOK LIKE ITACHI!!
SHUP

⬆ Tobi approaches Sasuke in the midst of a mission. Is it to check on his progress?

A time spent in obscurity, deceiving everyone.

《Infiltration》

Was he rushing to capture the Tailed Beast? Or was he, perhaps, just keeping an eye on Sasuke, the sole survivor of the Uchiha? There are many unknowns as to why Madara infiltrated the Akatsuki disguised as Tobi. What is the real reason for hiding his identity?

《A false face》

As Tobi, Madara acts and behaves foolishly, the complete opposite of his true self. This extreme difference in character may simply be to keep his identity hidden.

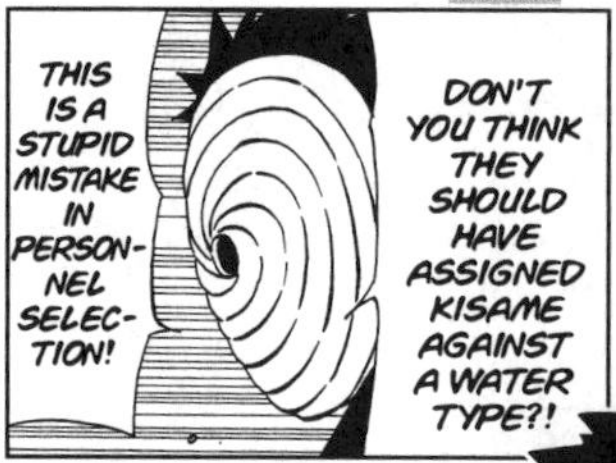
DON'T YOU THINK THEY SHOULD HAVE ASSIGNED KISAME AGAINST A WATER TYPE?!
THIS IS A STUPID MISTAKE IN PERSONNEL SELECTION!

⬅ Even in the face of danger with a Tailed Beast attacking him, Tobi conceals his true powers. Is this a demonstration of how calm and composed he is?

⬇ It seems he let Zetsu in on his secret early on.

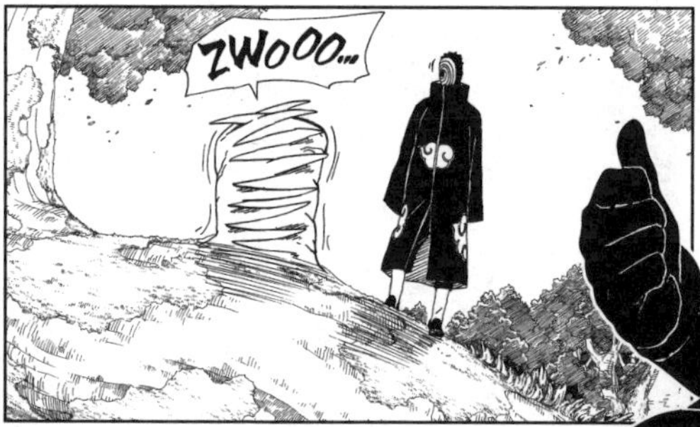
ZWOOO...

《Secret maneuvering》

Even while disguised as Tobi, Madara paves the way to realizing his goal. And always close by is Zetsu, a member of the Akatsuki, shrouded in mystery. The relationship between these two and their goals remain a mystery...

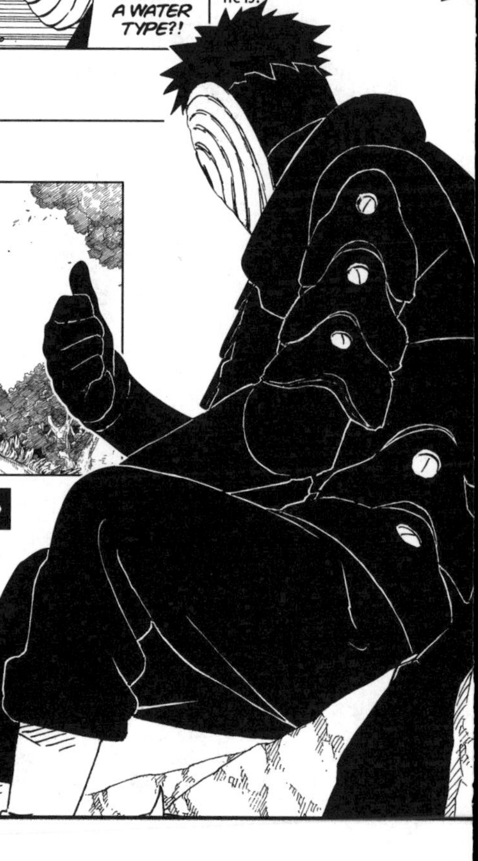

Regret and hatred amplified over time.

Isolated by pride.

I LEFT KONOHA.
HAVING BEEN BETRAYED BY ALL.

All Madara wished for was the prosperity of his clan. Battling the Senju clan, then joining with them, was solely for the sake of his clan. But what Madara did not realize was that his clan had tired of fighting.

⬅ Shunned by his clan who rejected war, Madara walks a solitary path.

Madara's way of thinking was considered dangerous and the Uchiha were left outside Konoha's nucleus of power. Soon, even his own clan turned its back to him. The anger that consumed Madara when he left the village still burns strong inside him.

BACK THEN, I SPENT EVERY DAY ON THE BATTLEFIELD.

⬆ Madara battled day and night, solely for the dignity of his clan.

Madara's crime that led to the decline of the Uchiha.

In time, Madara attacks Konohagakure using the Nine-Tailed Fox Spirit. But this leads to the worst possible outcome for the Uchiha clan. Years later, when Nine Tails attacks Konoha, the village officials believe that it was the doing of the Uchiha. They banish the Uchiha clan and curtail their movements.

⬆➡ The final battle between Madara and Senju. Madara is defeated and disappears.

THE RE-APPEARANCE OF THE NINE-TAILED FOX SPIRIT 16 YEARS AGO.

⬅ Nine Tails' attack sixteen years ago was blamed on the Uchiha clan.

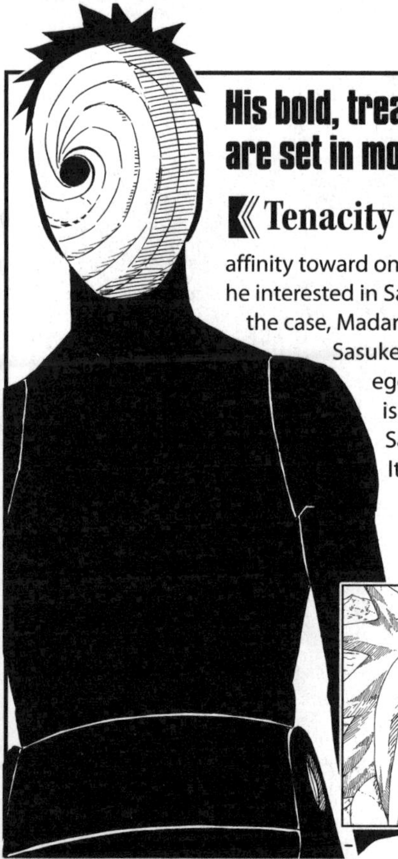

His bold, treacherous aspirations are set in motion.

《Tenacity》

Sasuke is always reflected in Madara's eyes. Does he feel an affinity toward one of the few remaining of his clan, or is he interested in Sasuke as a pawn he can use? Whichever the case, Madara waits for Sasuke to mature and eggs him on. What is it that requires Sasuke, and not Itachi?

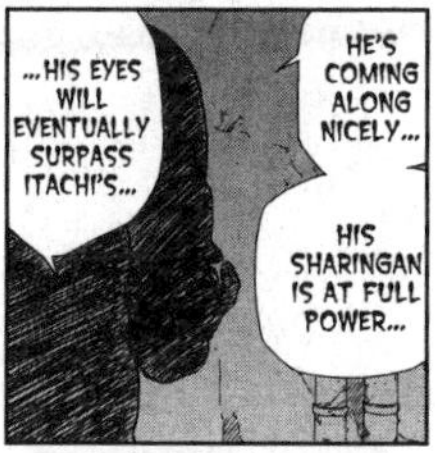
HE'S COMING ALONG NICELY...
HIS SHARINGAN IS AT FULL POWER...
...HIS EYES WILL EVENTUALLY SURPASS ITACHI'S...

⬆ Even the leader Pain defers to Madara's orders.

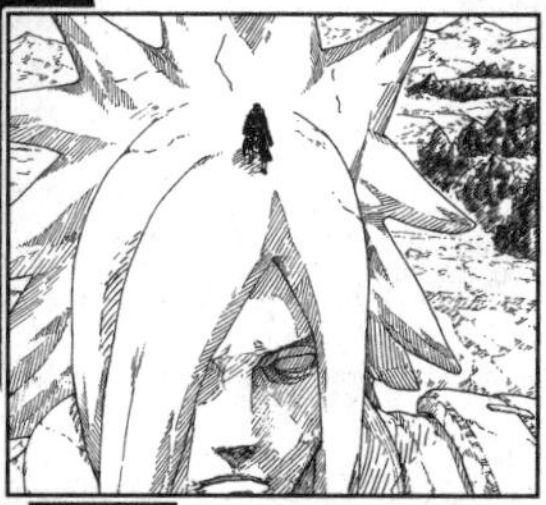

⬅ Standing on his own statue, he observes Sasuke and watches his progress.

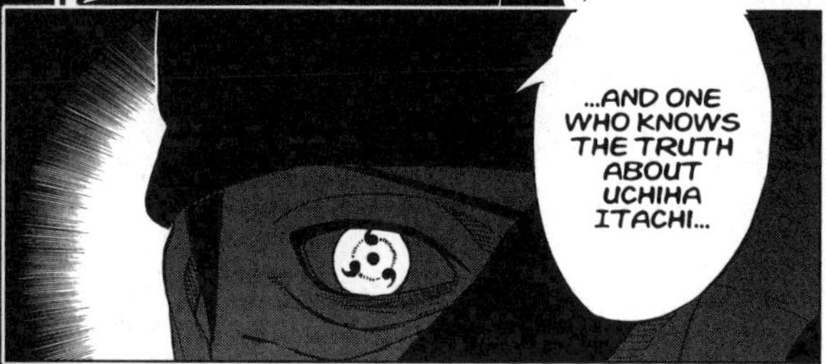
...AND ONE WHO KNOWS THE TRUTH ABOUT UCHIHA ITACHI...

⬅ In time, Madara reveals the whole truth to Sasuke. The time to put his ambition into action has come.

⬇ Taking advantage of Sasuke's feelings toward Itachi, Madara skillfully uses words to incite him.

《Encounter》

The time is ripe. Sasuke has developed just as he hoped and Itachi is dead. There are just a few more Tailed Beasts to capture and all is going exactly as planned. Madara discards Tobi's mask to face his enemy head-on. Will this enemy be Konohagakure itself?

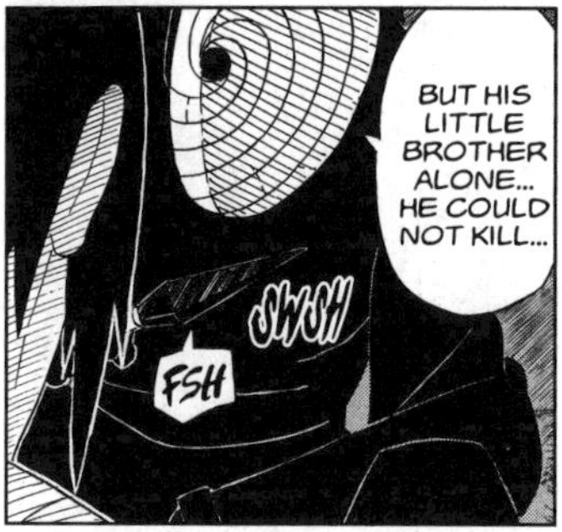
BUT HIS LITTLE BROTHER ALONE... HE COULD NOT KILL...
SWSH
FSH

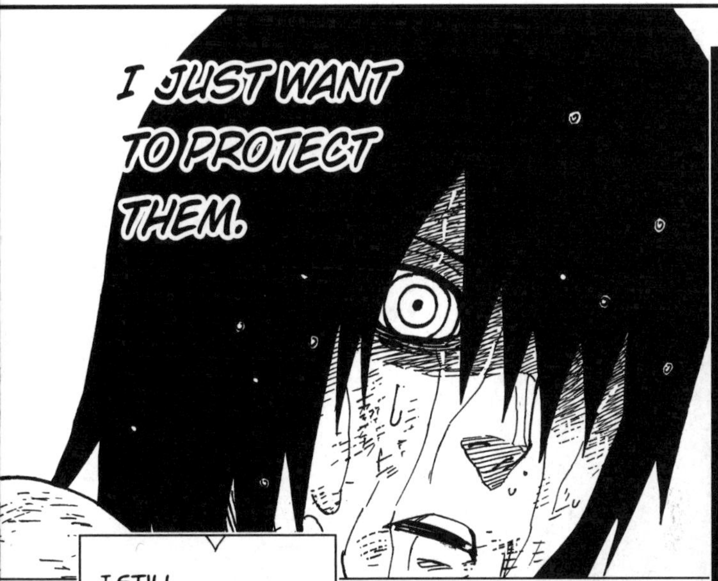
I JUST WANT TO PROTECT THEM.

NAGATO

長門

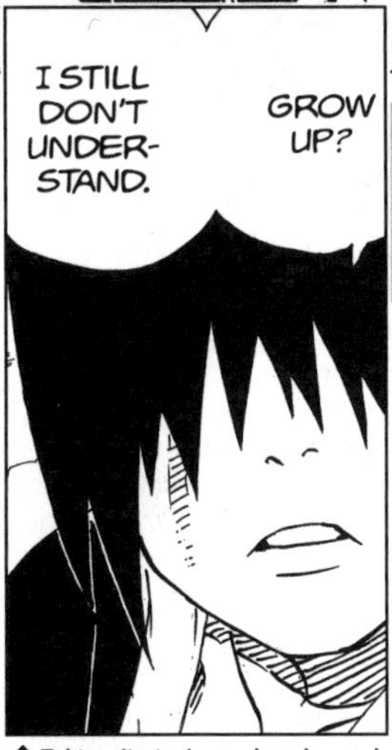
GROW UP?
I STILL DON'T UNDER-STAND.

The youth is frightened by the infinite depths of power awakened by his eyes.

The Second Great Ninja War. This fierce war that embroiled many villages turned Nagato's life upside down. This soft-hearted lad who did not want to see people hurt lost his parents. And just when he was about to lose his friends, he awakened to his miraculous eyes— Rinnegan, one of the three great ocular ninjutsu. This power would change him drastically.

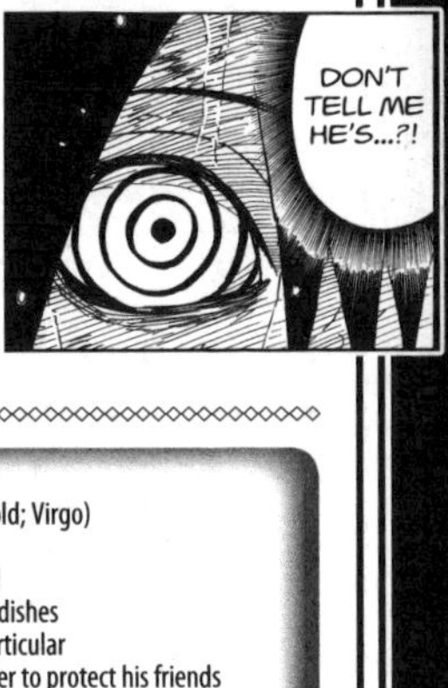
DON'T TELL ME HE'S...?!

➡ In order to protect his friends, he opts to awaken his Rinnegan.

⬆ Taking Jiraiya's words to heart, he sets out to find his purpose in life.

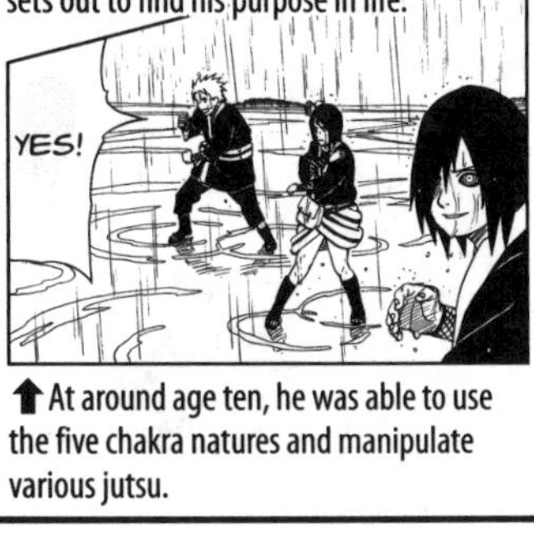
YES!

⬆ At around age ten, he was able to use the five chakra natures and manipulate various jutsu.

Ninja Registry Number: —
Birthdate: September 19 (? years old; Virgo)
Height: ? **Weight:** ? **Blood type:** A
Personality: Innocent, fainthearted
Favorite food: Grilled fish, hot-pot dishes
Least favorite food: Nothing in particular
Would like to fight: Anyone in order to protect his friends
Favorite word: Maturity
Interests: Ninjutsu training

NAMIASHI RAIDO
並足ライドウ

Special Jônin

He appears out of the dark and attacks in a flash.

His vast skill and renown in Konoha comes from his prowess in the use of Assassination Jutsu. He favors a black sword with a blade coated with lethal poison. He often teams up with Aoba, and very, very few have survived their combined attacks.

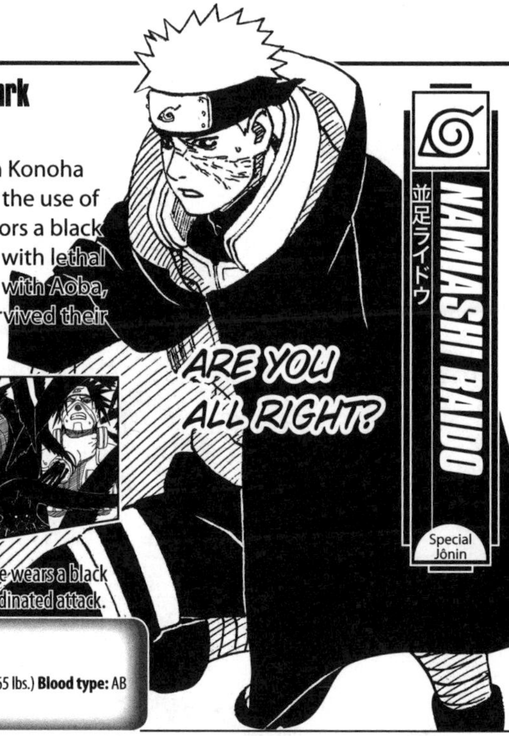
ARE YOU ALL RIGHT?

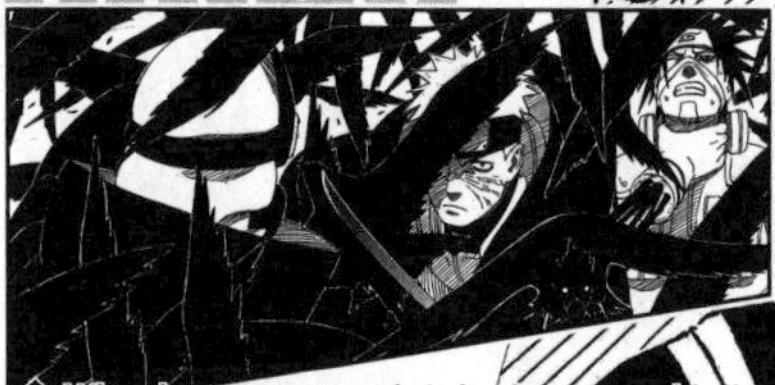

⇧When he teams up with Aoba, he wears a black cape and unleashes an original coordinated attack.

Ninja Registry Number: 009717
Birthdate: August 28 (35 years old; Virgo)
Height: 183.0 cm (6'0") **Weight:** 75.0 kg (165 lbs.) **Blood type:** AB
Personality: Austere, methodical

NARA SHIKAKU
奈良シカク

Special Jônin

A wise gentleman, he points the way without words.

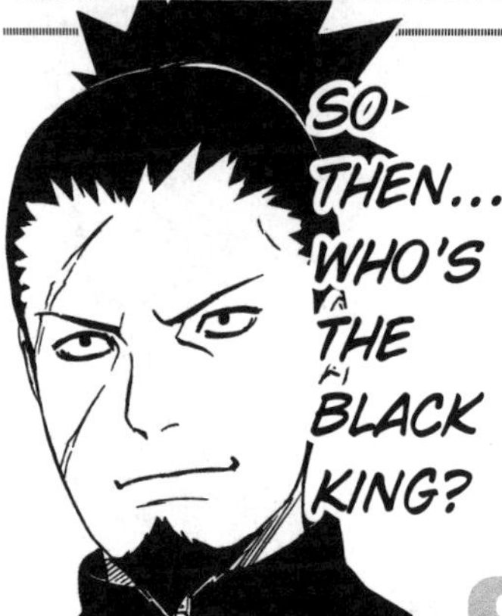
SO THEN... WHO'S THE BLACK KING?

He is the head of the Nara family, who have honed their skills in pharmacology for generations. Shikamaru inherited his judgment and prudence from his father. A man of few words, he offers valuable advice only when necessary and keeps his trustworthy eyes on his son's growth..

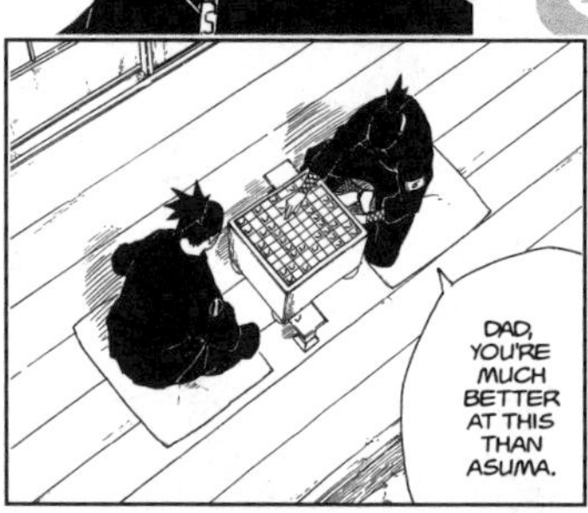
DAD, YOU'RE MUCH BETTER AT THIS THAN ASUMA.

⬅He often plays shogi with his son Shikamaru. While he sees how much Shikamaru has progressed, he shows a prowess far greater than his son.

Ninja Registry Number: 005491
Birthdate: July 15 (41 years old; Cancer)
Height: 175.2 cm (5'9") **Weight:** 59.8 kg (132 lbs.) **Blood type:** B
Personality: henpecked, intelligent
Would like to fight: Nara Shikamaru (in Shogi)

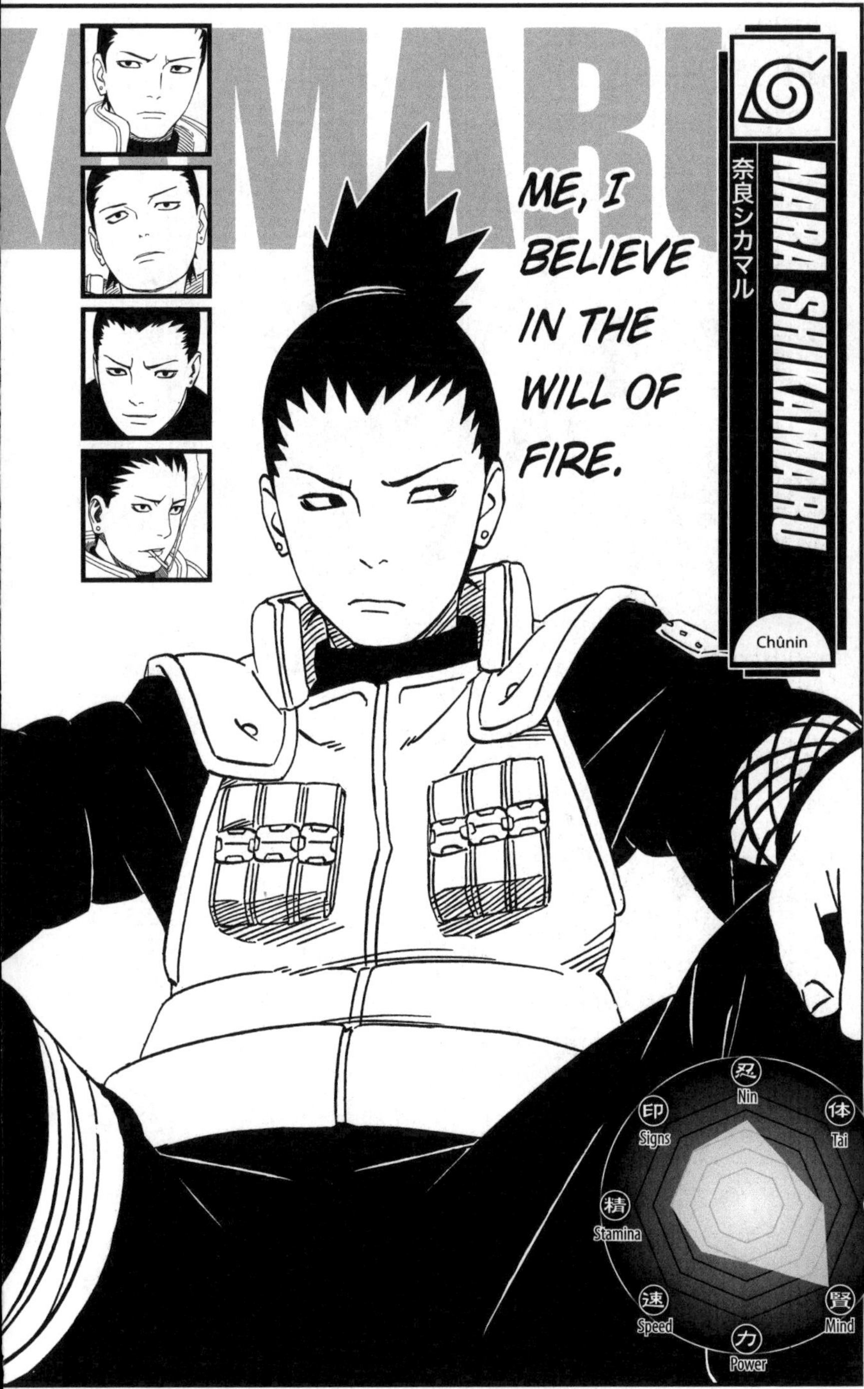
NARA SHIKAMARU
奈良シカマル
Chûnin
ME, I BELIEVE IN THE WILL OF FIRE.
忍 Nin
体 Tai
幻 Gen
賢 Mind
力 Power
速 Speed
精 Stamina
印 Signs

With the Will of Fire burning within him, he is that rare tactician who walks the shinobi path.

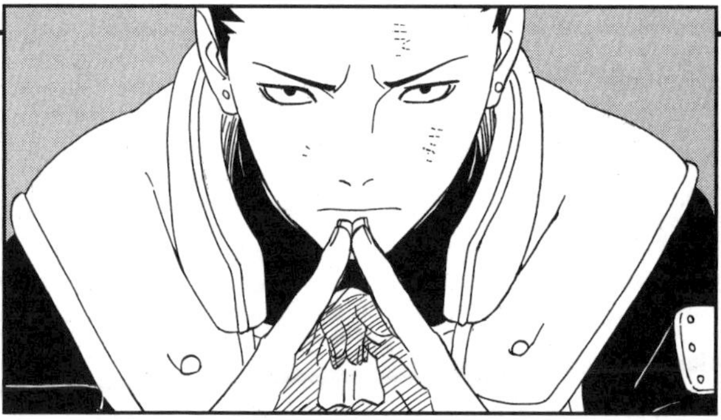

⬆ Once his strategy is complete, Shikamaru finishes with the Hiden jutsu of the Nara: the Art of Shadow Possession.

It is said that Shikamaru has an IQ that exceeds 200. He's also lazier than any other ninja around. But under that cool demeanor burns a passion passed down to him by his predecessors. He would never let down a comrade and will always complete his missions successfully. He failed the first time he was put in charge of a team and that memory has remained strong in his mind. Hence, he uses his resourcefulness to always keep his comrades from harm's way. With his tactics, Shikamaru can toy with even the Akatsuki. His ability stems from a desire to protect his friends and his village, a Will of Fire that burns stronger than anything else.

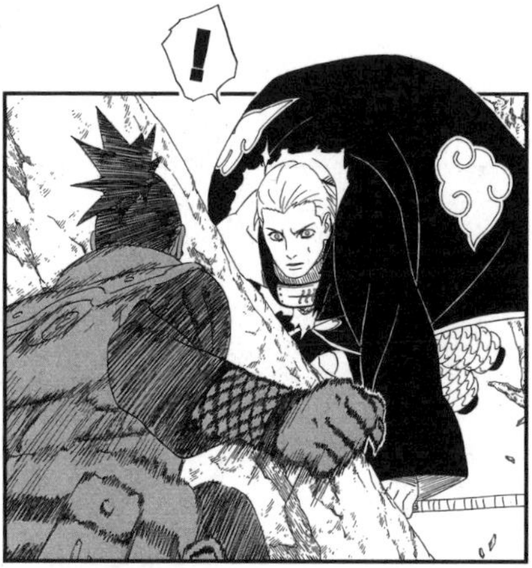
!

⬅ Although he is an intellectual, Shikamaru will not hesitate to personally engage a foe. He has faith in his strategies and is willing to put his life on the line.

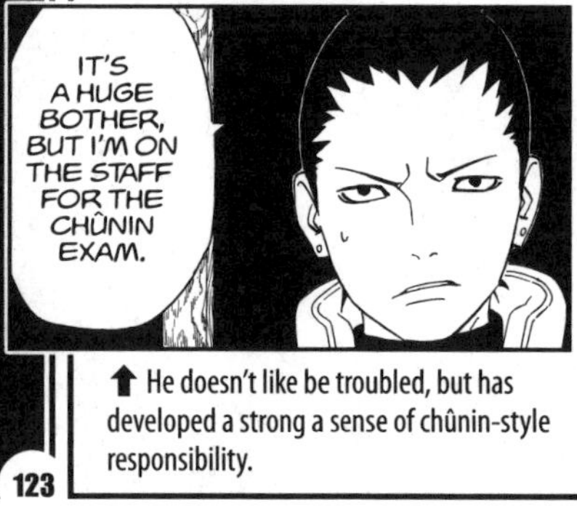
IT'S A HUGE BOTHER, BUT I'M ON THE STAFF FOR THE CHÛNIN EXAM.

⬆ He doesn't like be troubled, but has developed a strong a sense of chûnin-style responsibility.

Ninja Registry Number: 012611
Birthdate: September 22 (16 years old; Virgo)
Height: 170.0 cm (5'7") **Weight:** 53.4 kg (118 lbs.) **Blood type:** AB
Personality: Calm, hates to be bothered
Favorite food: Grilled mackerel with bean paste, sukonbu
Least favorite food: Hard-boiled eggs
Would like to fight: Wouldn't bother since it's too much of a hassle
Favorite word: Let every day be a good day.
Interests: Taking naps, shogi

Graduated from the Ninja Academy at age 12
Promoted to chûnin at age 12

Mission Experience		
	D-rank: 8	C-rank: 3
	B-rank: 9	A-rank: 19
	S-rank: 0	

Parting with his master– The fate of the shinobi thrust upon him.

《Asuma》

Shikamaru idolized Asuma, who was struck down before his very eyes. Shikamaru cannot help but think that there could have been a better strategy that would have resulted in Asuma's being saved. Asuma's final words resonate in Shikamaru's ears. He told him he was counting on him to protect the king of Konoha. The king is the most precious piece on the shogi board. Asuma meant it to be analogous to the future generations of ninja. To honor his mentor, Shikamaru presses on.

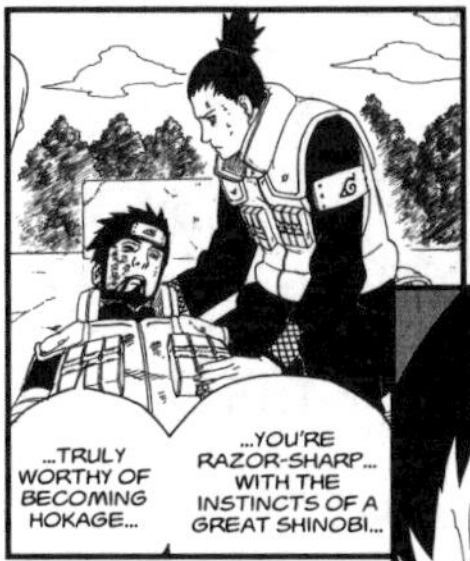
...YOU'RE RAZOR-SHARP... WITH THE INSTINCTS OF A GREAT SHINOBI...
...TRULY WORTHY OF BECOMING HOKAGE...

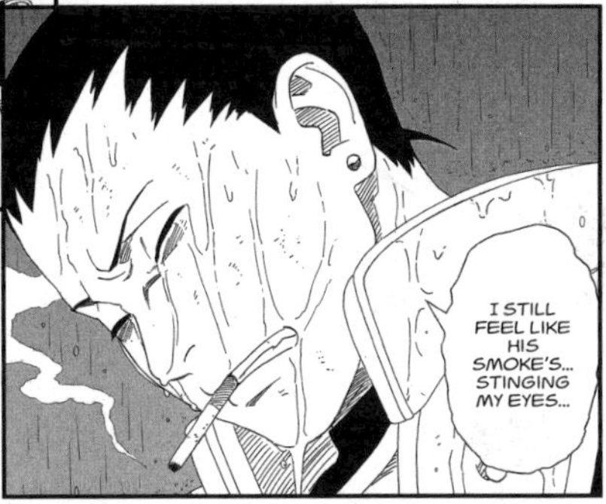
I STILL FEEL LIKE HIS SMOKE'S... STINGING MY EYES...

⬆ ➡ Ashinobi is destined to die in the line of duty. He thought he understood that. Still, Shikamaru could not stop the tears coursing down his cheeks.

《The logical thing to do》

Shikamaru, Choji and Ino leave the village in pursuit of Hidan and Kakuzu. They intend to honor their mentor, Asuma, who fell before fulfilling his mission to capture them.

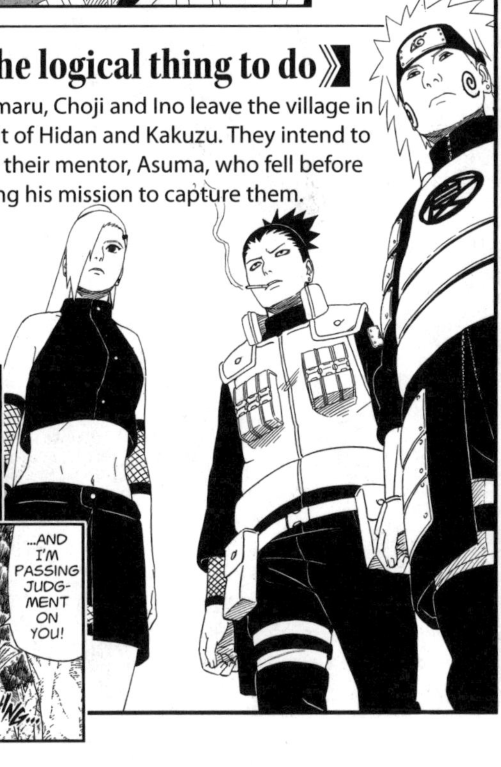

⬇ Asuma is with them in spirit through his lighter and his protégé. Even if there are only three standing, it is still a four-man cell.

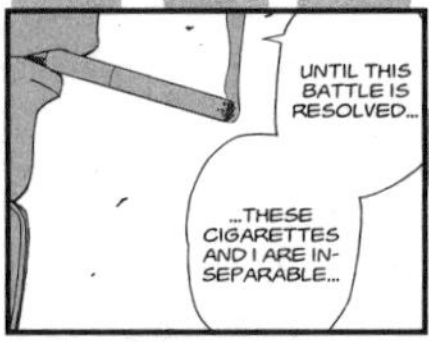
UNTIL THIS BATTLE IS RESOLVED...
...THESE CIGARETTES AND I ARE IN-SEPARABLE...

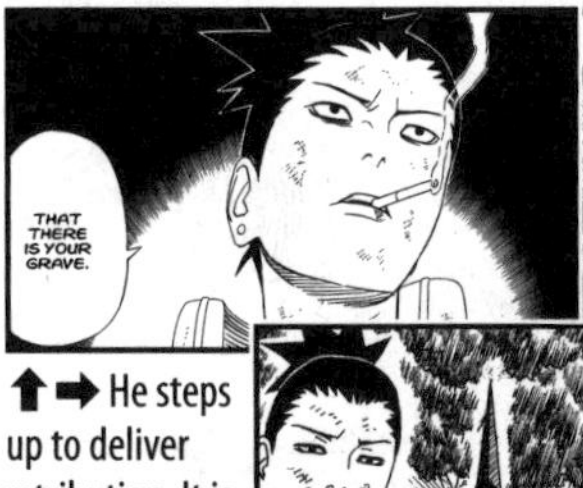
THAT THERE IS YOUR GRAVE.

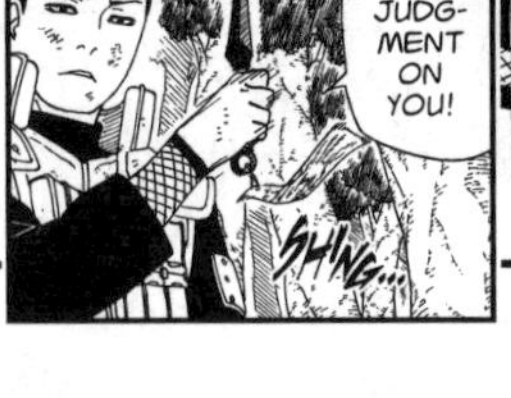
...AND I'M PASSING JUDG-MENT ON YOU!
SHING...

⬆ ➡ He steps up to deliver retribution. It is Shikamaru's way of taking responsibility.

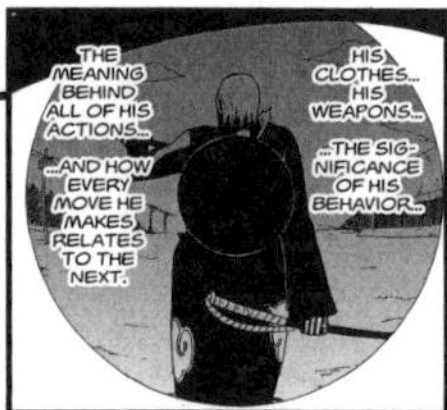
HIS CLOTHES... HIS WEAPONS... ...THE SIGNIFICANCE OF HIS BEHAVIOR...
THE MEANING BEHIND ALL OF HIS ACTIONS... ...AND HOW EVERY MOVE HE MAKES RELATES TO THE NEXT.

Bursting forth like a knight, he tears apart the evil jutsu with his Will of Fire!

《Insight》

Even during battle, Shikamaru's analytical skills are in place. He solves the puzzle piece by piece and plans a counterstrategy.

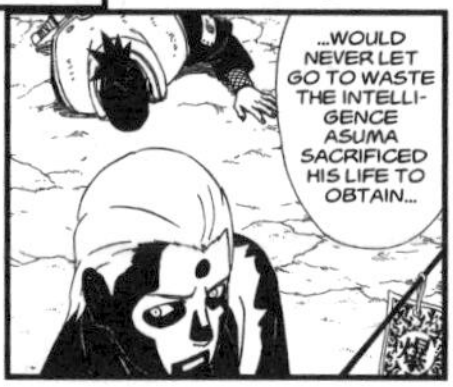
...WOULD NEVER LET GO TO WASTE THE INTELLIGENCE ASUMA SACRIFICED HIS LIFE TO OBTAIN...

⬆ The ability to see things calmly. This is a potent weapon which supports Shikamaru's resourcefulness.

⬅ He fools Hidan by pretending to throw his life away. Shikamaru's plan is to see through his foe's jutsu and lure him into lowering his guard.

《Trump card》

Full of vengeance, Shikamaru challenges Hidan to a duel. It seems a reckless move. But just when Hidan thinks his victory is imminent, Shikamaru unleashes his plan, crushing Hidan with a trap. Mission accomplished.

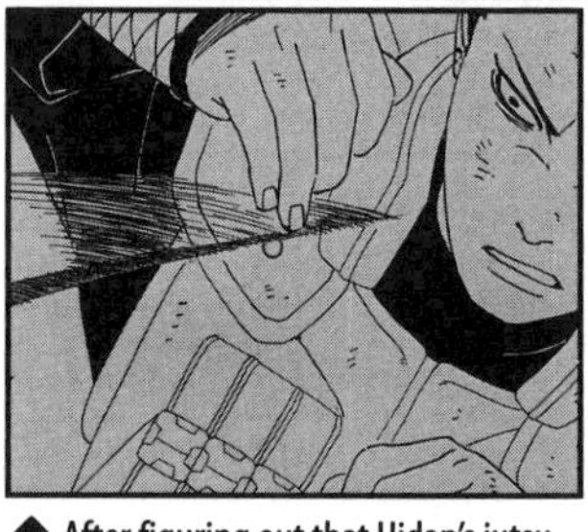

⬆ After figuring out that Hidan's jutsu relies on an opponent's blood, Shikamaru uses Kakuzu's blood.

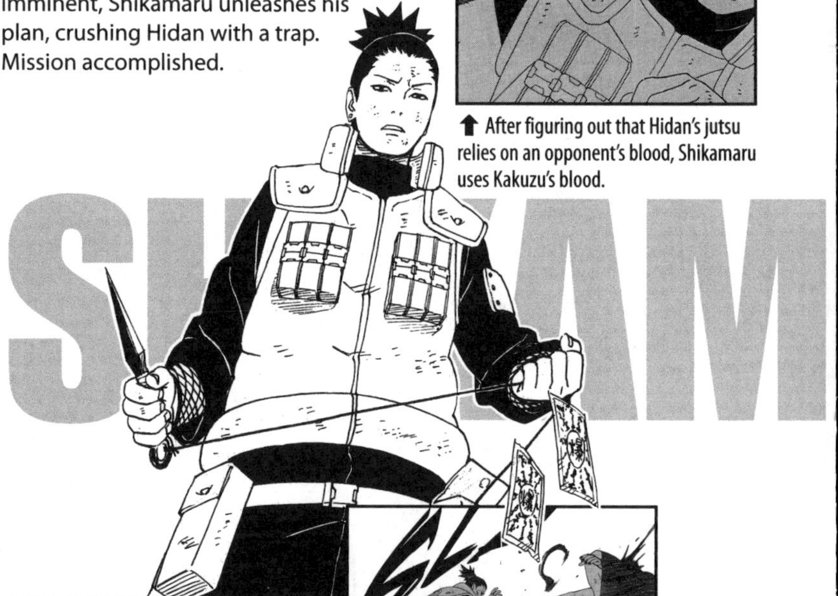
SHIKAM

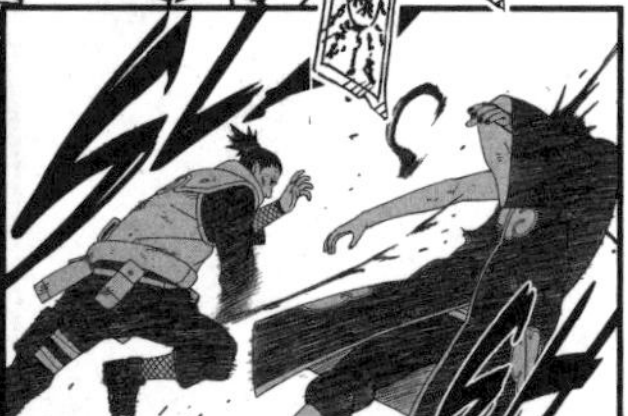

⬆ By feigning death, Shikamaru lures Hidan into a trap. He delivers the final fiery blow, a tribute to Asuma...

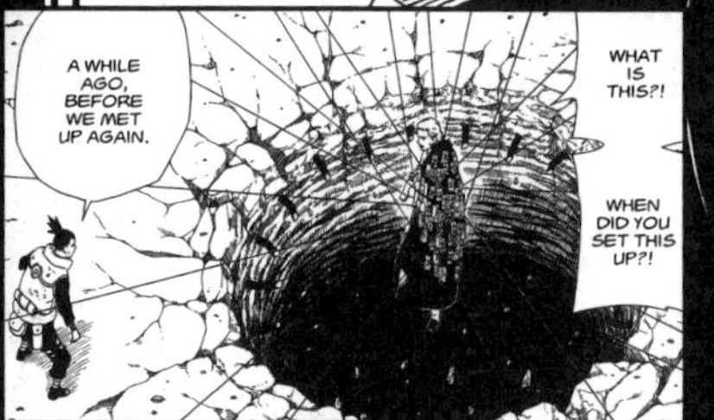
WHAT IS THIS?!
WHEN DID YOU SET THIS UP?!
A WHILE AGO, BEFORE WE MET UP AGAIN.

⬇➡ Rather than showy moves, the unexpected will confuse the enemy. That his Asuma's assessment of Shikamaru.

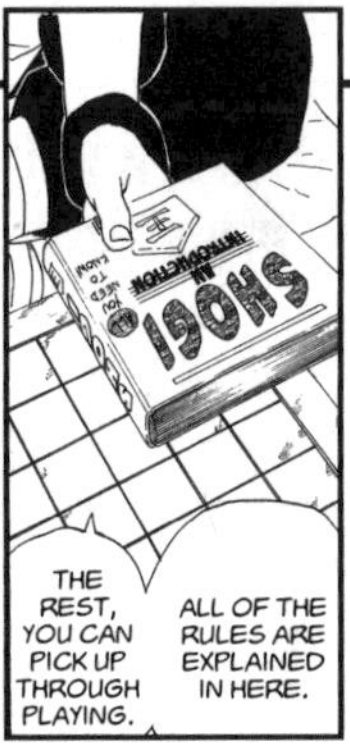
ALL OF THE RULES ARE EXPLAINED IN HERE.
THE REST, YOU CAN PICK UP THROUGH PLAYING.

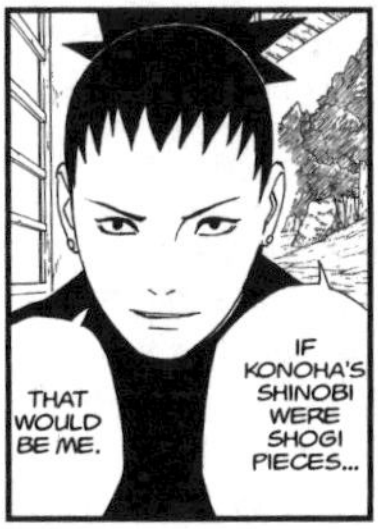
IF KONOHA'S SHINOBI WERE SHOGI PIECES...
THAT WOULD BE ME.

The light he inherits will light the path ahead.

《The Knight》

Asuma had likened Shikamaru to the knight in Shogi. At first, Shikamaru didn't quite understand what his master meant. Today, his words are a source of pride. Shikamaru now reaffirms his crucial role as the knight who clears the way for the king.

《The King》

The king—the young lives who represent the future of Konohagakure. In the same manner that grown-ups protected him, Shikamaru is now determined to protect the young. That is the true Will of Fire that has sustained the Leaf over the ages. This is what Asuma taught him during his last moments. Standing before the child growing inside Kurenai's womb, this child whom Asuma would never see, Shikamaru realizes that the time had come to become an adult. He will become a teacher whom the children can love. And he would teach these young, the future kings of the village, about the Will of Fire. And that time was just around the corner...

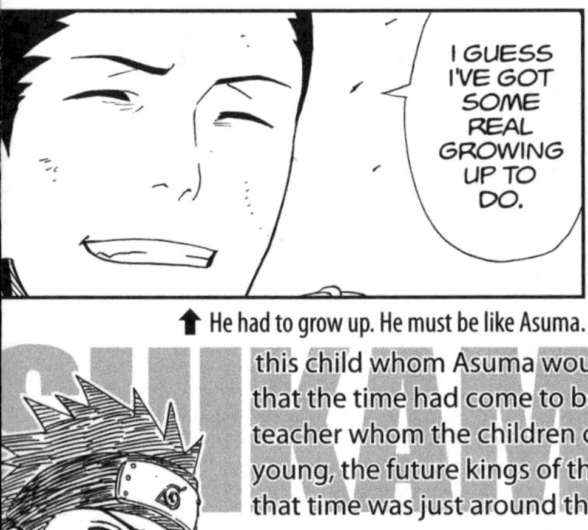
I GUESS I'VE GOT SOME REAL GROWING UP TO DO.

⬆ He had to grow up. He must be like Asuma.

I BEQUEATH MY WILL OF FIRE...TO YOU.

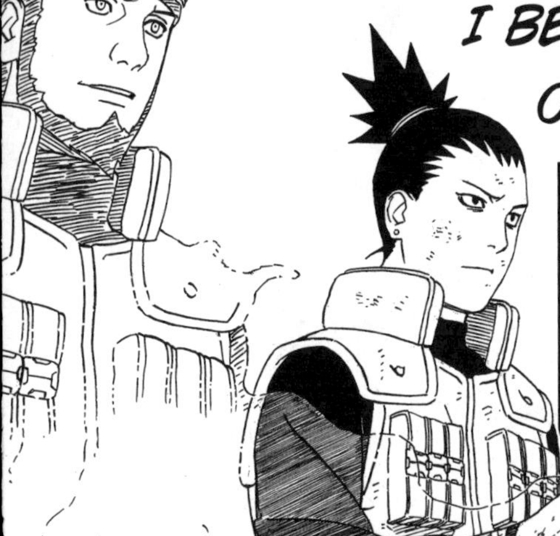

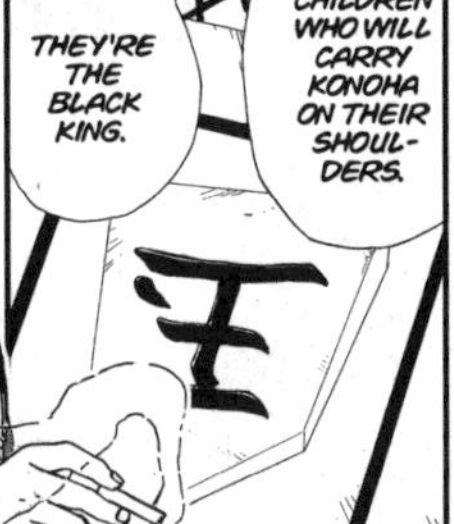
THE CHILDREN WHO WILL CARRY KONOHA ON THEIR SHOUL-DERS.
THEY'RE THE BLACK KING.

⬅ Carrying on his late master's wish, Shikamaru must be analogous to a piece on the shogi board that protects the children. In doing so, he also protects the village.

NI'I YUGITO

二位ユギト

Jônin

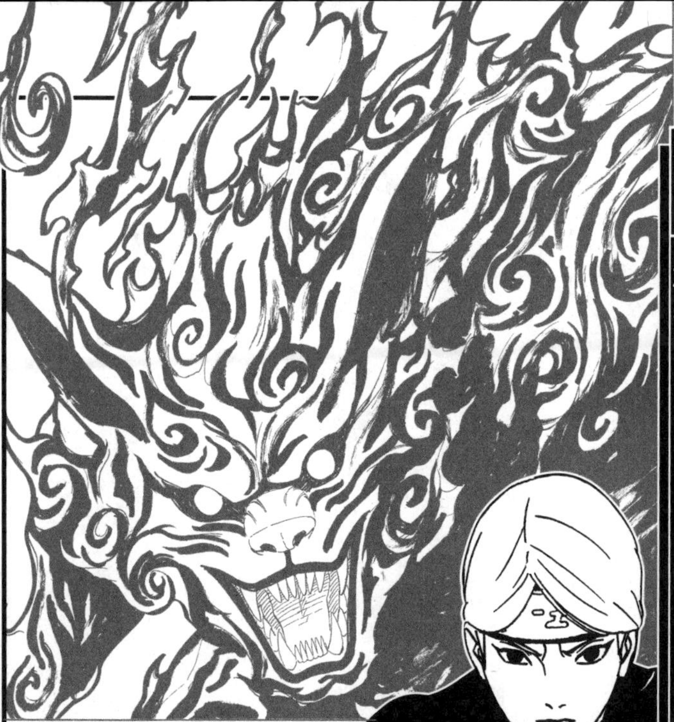

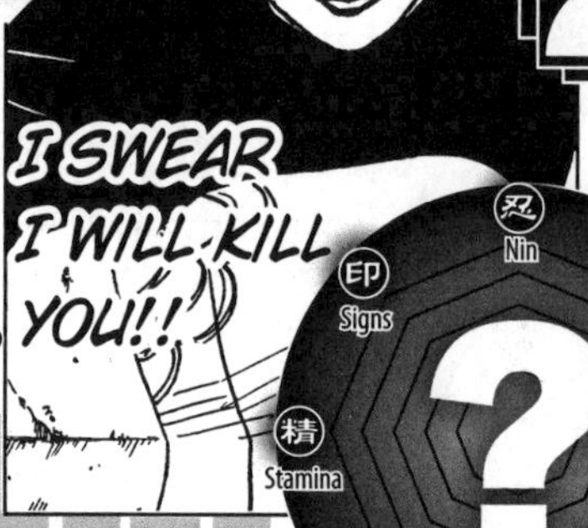
I SWEAR I WILL KILL YOU!!

The proud, sharp kunoichi who hosts the Cat Demon inside her.

Yugito became the Two Tails' jinchûriki when she was only two years old. Despite being a target of disdain, she trained hard through sheer will and gained mastery over the Tailed Beast. Earning the trust of her peers.

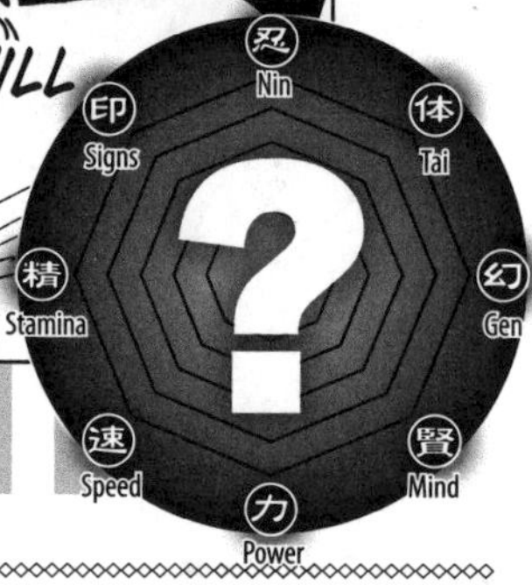
忍
Nin
体
Tai
幻
Gen
賢
Mind
力
Power
速
Speed
精
Stamina
印
Signs
?

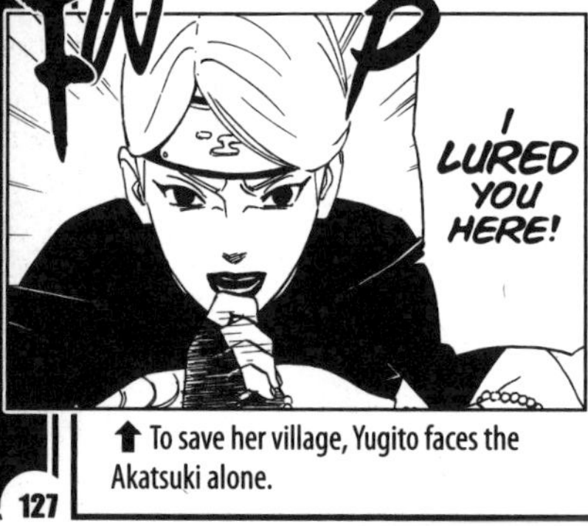
FIN
P
I LURED YOU HERE!

⬆ To save her village, Yugito faces the Akatsuki alone.

Ninja Registry Number: ?
Birthdate: July 24 (29 years old; Leo)
Height: 170.2 cm (5'7") **Weight:** 50.8 kg (112 lbs.) **Blood type:** A
Personality: Bold, proud, loyal to friends
Favorite food: Tekkadon, milk
Least favorite food: Hot foods
Would like to fight: Enemies of her village
Favorite word: A cat has nine lives.
Interests: Playing the shamisen

Graduated from the Ninja Academy at age ?
Promoted to chûnin at age ?

Mission Experience		
	D-rank: 190	C-rank: 185
	B-rank: 356	A-rank: 260
	S-rank: 34	

NINJA DOG

忍犬

FOLLOW ME.

PAKKUN

He is the leader of the eight ninja dogs. He has been summoned alone so often that there's not enough space to enumerate his achievements here.

SHIBA
BISUKE
AKINO
GURUKO
UHEI
URUSHI
BURU

Unrivaled Detective Skills! Eight of the Best Ninja Dogs!

When in a pinch, Kakashi summons these fiercely loyal ninja dogs who understand all his commands. They all have an uncanny sense of smell. Each also has a distinct personality. They are capable of employing complex ninja dog tactics and accomplishing great feats during battle. It may seem as if they each wear a funny face on their jackets, but this is really a token of courage when it comes down to battle.

OUR VOICES REACH FARTHER THAN ANY COMM UNIT.
PLUS, OUR NOSES CAN DETECT DANGER FASTER AND WE CAN ASSIST YOU IN BATTLES.
BOOF
BOOF
BOOF

⬆ Lovable and trustworthy, no one can match their investigative skills.

NINJA CAT
忍猫

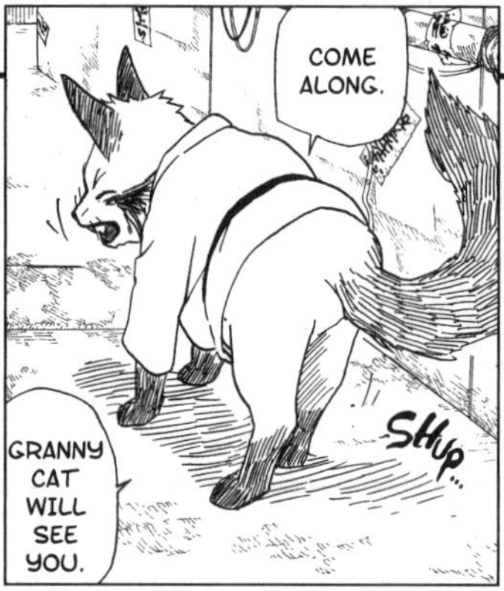
COME ALONG.
GRANNY CAT WILL SEE YOU.
SHUP...

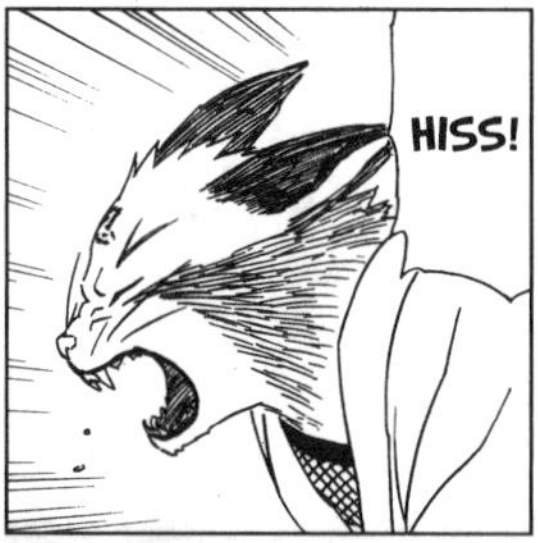
HISS!

⬆ Don't bother a ninja cat—it's disrespectful and dangerous! Only ninja cats know the whereabouts of Cat Granny.

The willful, mercenary cat guides of the Sky District.

The Sky District ruins are not affiliated with any land or village. They are home to Cat Granny's ninja cats. Although they can speak the language of humans, their behavior is strictly feline. And when they occasionally do open their mouths to talk, it is with the kind of haughtiness that was evident when they called Sasuke a boy. Their usual duties include accompanying Cat Granny, wandering through the corridors and interrogating anyone who happens by. Without winning the trust of the two cats, one can never hope to gain an audience with Cat Granny and will probably end up running away, badly bruised.

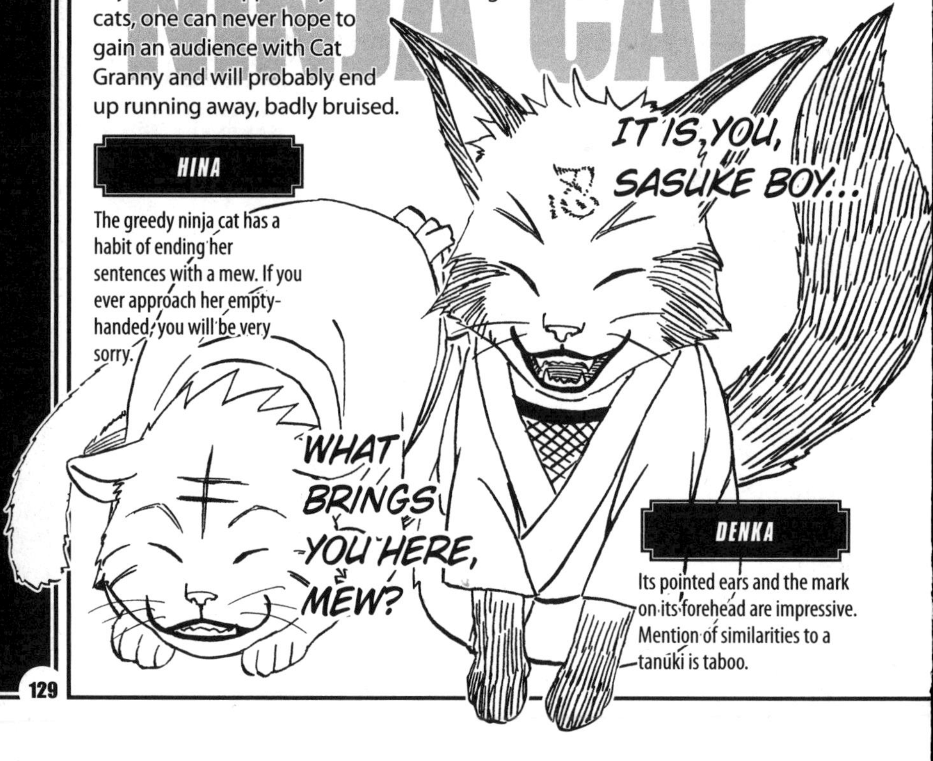
NINJA CAT
IT IS, YOU, SASUKE BOY...
WHAT BRINGS YOU HERE, MEW?

HINA

The greedy ninja cat has a habit of ending her sentences with a mew. If you ever approach her empty-handed, you will be very sorry.

DENKA

Its pointed ears and the mark on its forehead are impressive. Mention of similarities to a tanuki is taboo.

CAT GRANNY

猫バア

A black market operator with an impeccable pedigree who has known the Uchiha from ages past.

She is the old cat who leads a clan of black marketers specializing in shinobi weapons. The black cat's ear ornament signifies that she is the chief. She has absolute confidence in the quality of her goods. She chooses her customers carefully and never lowers her prices.

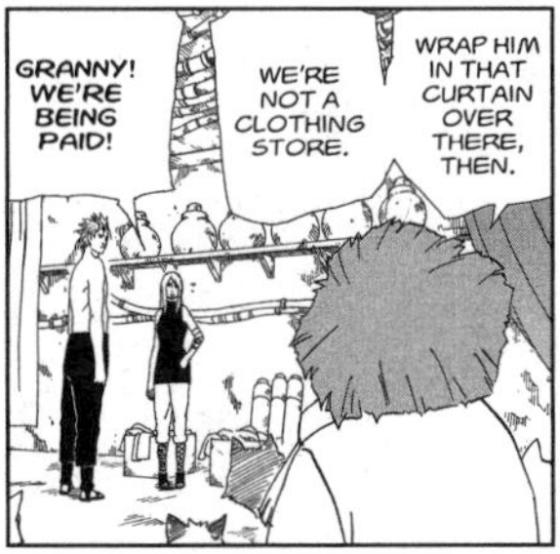
WRAP HIM IN THAT CURTAIN OVER THERE, THEN.
WE'RE NOT A CLOTHING STORE.
GRANNY! WE'RE BEING PAID!

⬆ Having done business with countless important people, she thinks nothing of dealing with a young upstart.

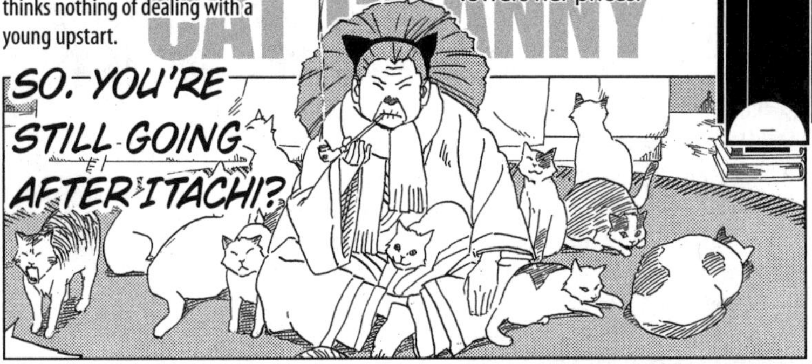
SO. YOU'RE STILL GOING AFTER ITACHI?

Collection ... Number 8

Konoha

CAT GRANNY'S OASIS FOR LOST CATS

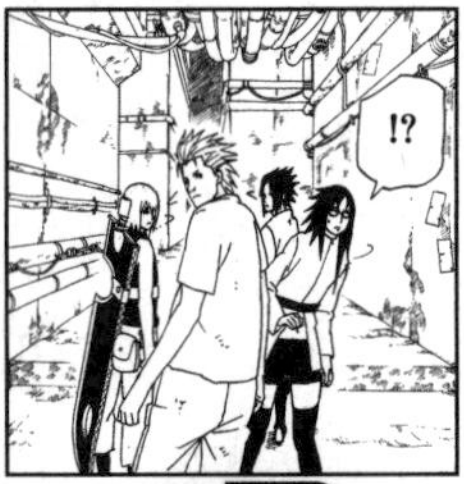
!?

⬅ The interior is a maze of corridors. Only the ninja cats know their way around.

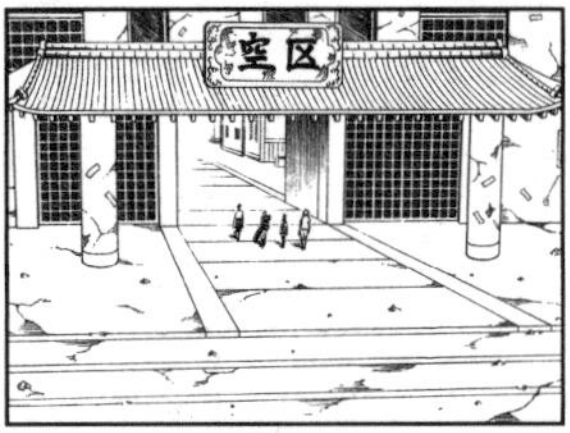
空区

➡ At first glance, this is merely a dilapidated building. But inside is a ninja tools store known throughout the Five Great Shinobi Nations.

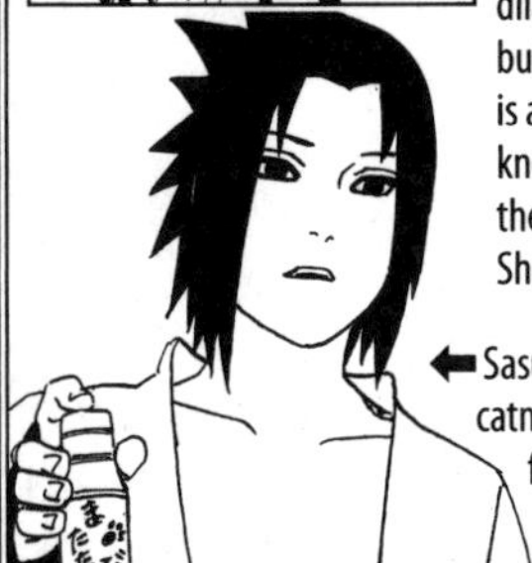

⬅ Sasuke's bottled catnip is his ticket for an audience with Cat Granny.

Ninja tools notwithstanding, the store is known for its collection of rare scrolls, which attracts many important clients. The Uchiha have been customers for a long time.

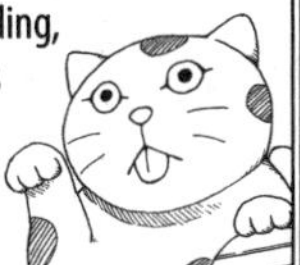

HAGANE KOTETSU

はがねコテツ

Chûnin

He swings his cudgel with ferocity.

A man of dauntless courage, Kotetsu is known in the village for his skill and experience in direct combat. He deeply respects Izumo for his many military exploits. As long-time partners with Izumo, he knows that Izumo has his back and can concentrate on the front lines, swinging his cudgel with full force.

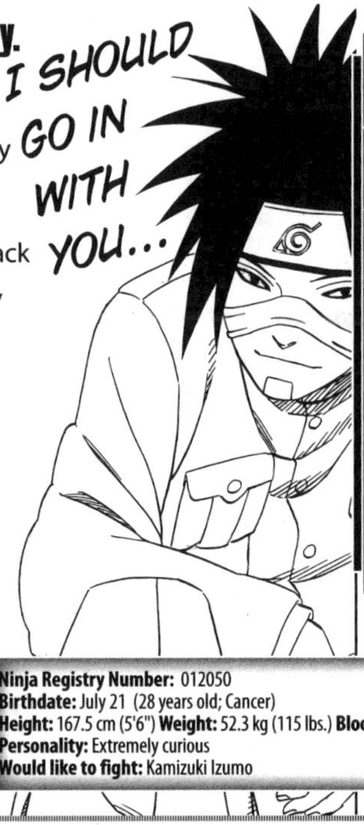
I SHOULD GO IN WITH YOU...

⬇ His combination move with Izumo works perfectly every time. It is the result of working together for a long time and the deep trust they have for each other.

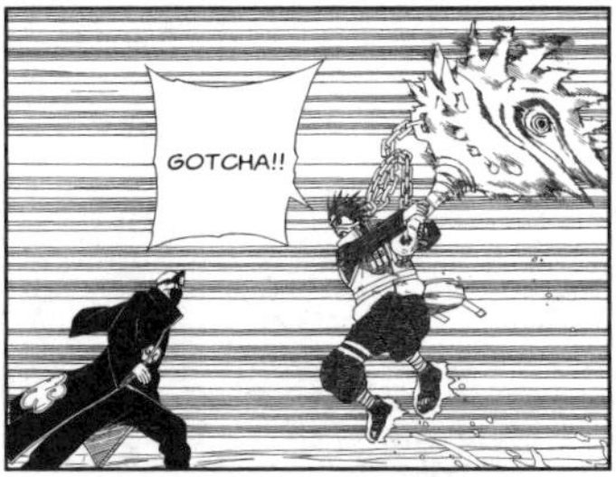
GOTCHA!!

Ninja Registry Number: 012050
Birthdate: July 21 (28 years old; Cancer)
Height: 167.5 cm (5'6") **Weight:** 52.3 kg (115 lbs.) **Blood type:** B
Personality: Extremely curious
Would like to fight: Kamizuki Izumo

BAKI

バキ

Jônin

A loyal, solid shinobi, who wishes to repair the ruins of Sunagakure.

Baki leads Sunagakure's battle regiments. His leadership skills contribute greatly to the Sand's reconstruction. When Gaara becomes the Kazekage, he quiets the voices of dissent and helps in the transition of power. He stands as the main man at the center of Sunagakure's revival.

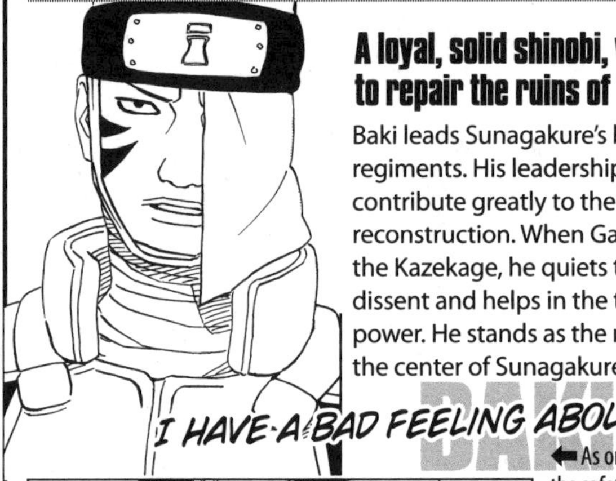
I HAVE A BAD FEELING ABOUT THIS...

⬅ As one charged with the safety of the village, he must consider worst-case scenarios and come up with contingent plans to deal with them.

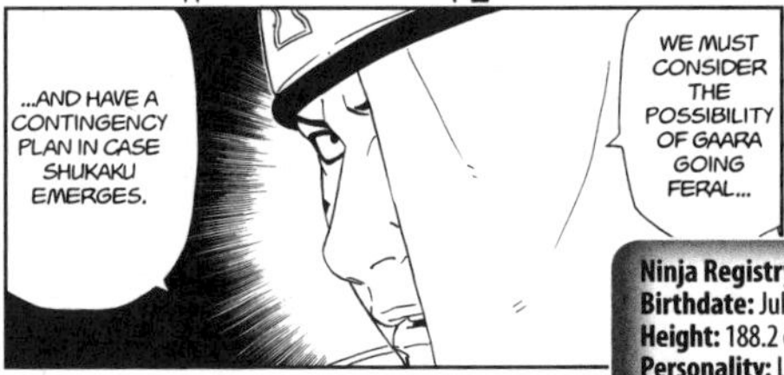
WE MUST CONSIDER THE POSSIBILITY OF GAARA GOING FERAL...
...AND HAVE A CONTINGENCY PLAN IN CASE SHUKAKU EMERGES.

Ninja Registry Number: 38-212
Birthdate: July 4 (34 years old; Cancer)
Height: 188.2 cm (6'2") **Weight:** 80.0 kg (176 lbs.) **Blood type:** A
Personality: Loyal, worrywart
Favorite food: Koyadofu

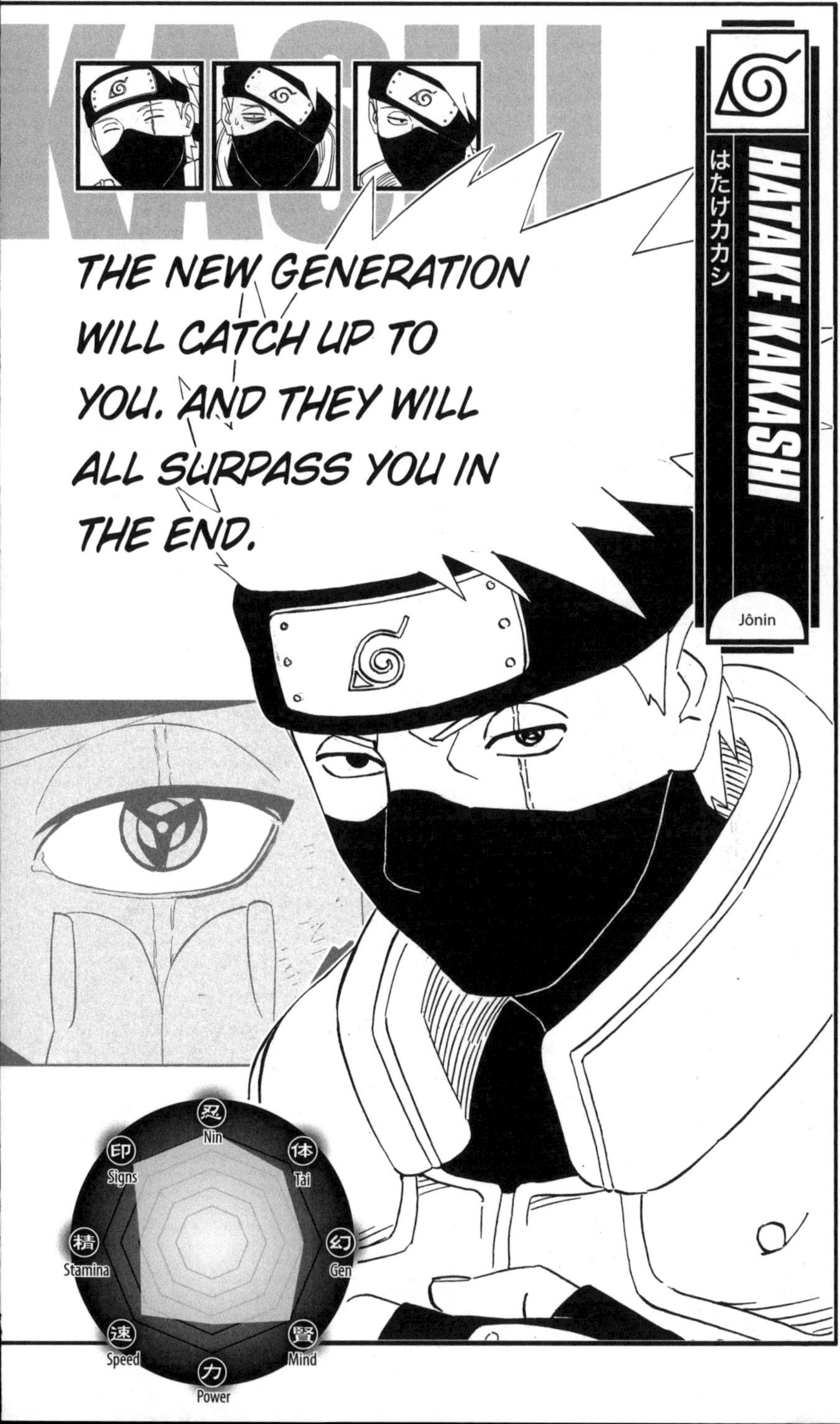
KAKASHI
HATAKE KAKASHI
はたけカカシ
Jônin
THE NEW GENERATION WILL CATCH UP TO YOU. AND THEY WILL ALL SURPASS YOU IN THE END.
忍 Nin
体 Tai
幻 Gen
賢 Mind
力 Power
速 Speed
精 Stamina
印 Signs

The hand that combines spirit and technique belongs to Konohagakure's number one ninja!

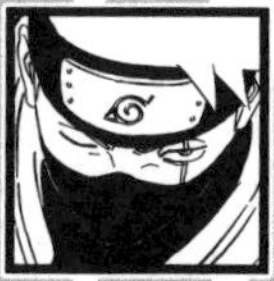

Bold and audacious, calm and collected, a master tactician… Every word that describes the ideal shinobi still doesn't seem enough to describe Hatake Kakashi. Kakashi's superiority attracts attention with every mission he completes. He is passionate on the outside and calm on the inside. The coexistence of these contrasting traits makes him a shinobi's shinobi to both friend and foe alike.

⬇ He truly understands each of the special characteristics of different ninjutsu and also knows how to use of them.

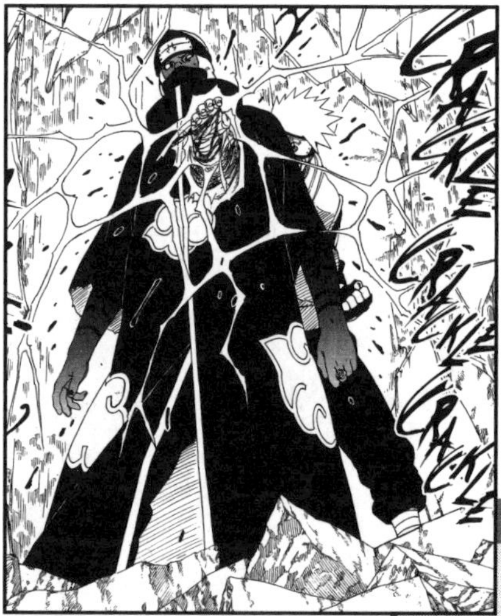
CRACKLE
CRACKLE
CRACKLE

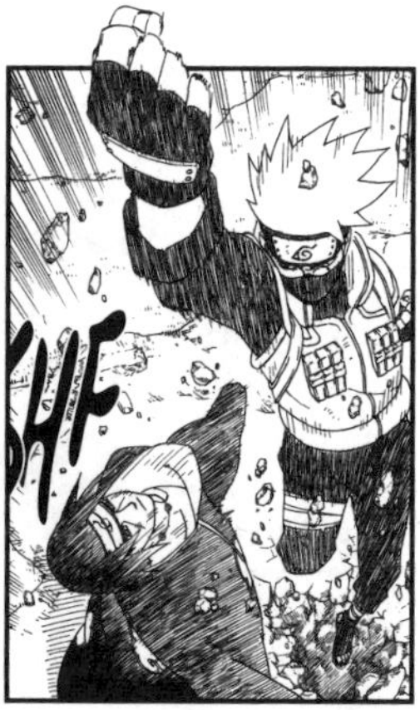

⬆ His experience, including many brushes with death on the battlefield, enables him to draw up the best strategic plans.

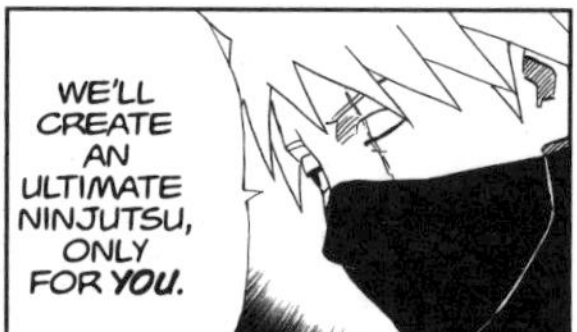
WE'LL CREATE AN ULTIMATE NINJUTSU, ONLY FOR *YOU*.

⬅ Nurturing talent requires setting aside one's ego and total devotion.

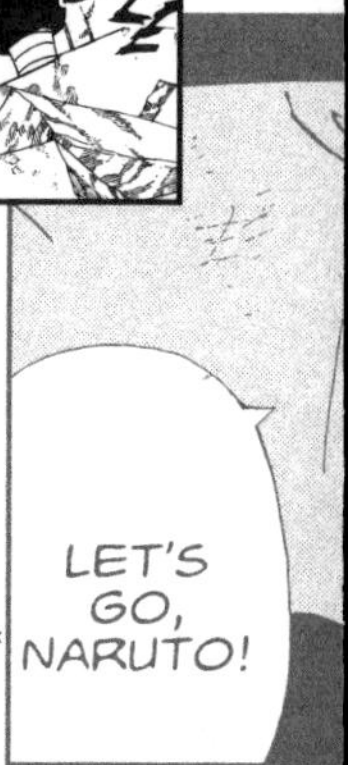
LET'S GO, NARUTO!

Ninja Registry Number: 009720
Birthdate: September 15 (30 years old; Virgo)
Height: 181.0 cm (5'11") **Weight:** 67.5 kg (149 lbs.) **Blood type:** O
Personality: Easygoing, calm and composed
Favorite food: Grilled saury, miso soup with sliced eggplant
Least favorite food: Tempura, sweets
Would like to fight: Fourth Hokage
Favorite word: Teamwork
Interests: Reading (Make-Out Paradise series)

Graduated from the Ninja Academy at age 5
Promoted to chûnin at age 6

Mission Experience	D-rank: 197	C-rank: 190
	B-rank: 414	A-rank: 298
	S-rank: 42	

⬇ His young trainees continue to grow up to become part of the village's fighting force. The gags he used to play on them when they were growing up seem to have had no ill effects…and he is unsure whether to be happy or sad.

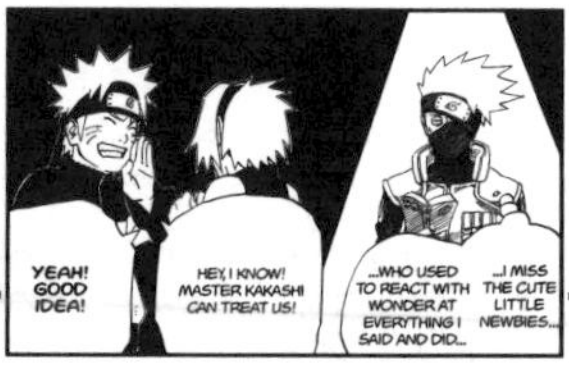
...I MISS THE CUTE LITTLE NEWBIES...
...WHO USED TO REACT WITH WONDER AT EVERYTHING I SAID AND DID...
HEY, I KNOW! MASTER KAKASHI CAN TREAT US!
YEAH! GOOD IDEA!

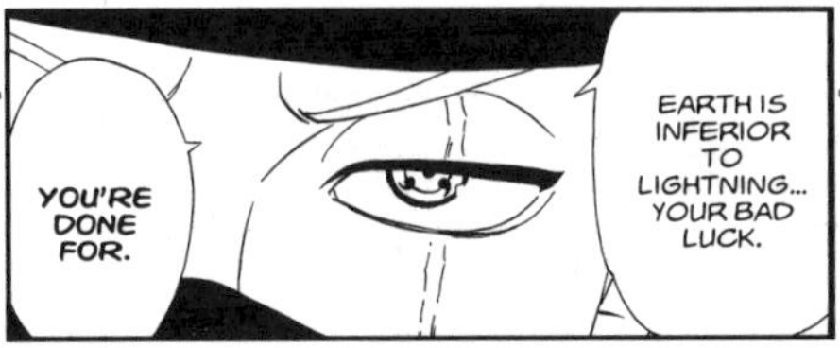
EARTH IS INFERIOR TO LIGHTNING... YOUR BAD LUCK.
YOU'RE DONE FOR.

His legend continues to evolve!

➡ How Kakashi obtained the Mangekyo Sharingan remains shrouded in mystery. The truth lies hidden in his eyes.

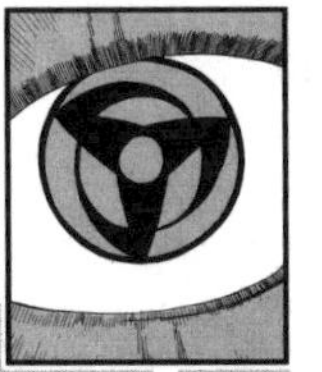

《Sharingan》

The genius Mirror Ninja hones his Sharingan still further by awakening the Mangekyo Sharingan. Even in the history of the Uchiha clan's Kekkei Genkai, only a few have managed this feat. However, he is still not able to adjust the spatial barriers and has not completely mastered his skill. However, the odds are high that Kakashi will eventually master ocular jutsu completely in his own way. This rare power has speeded up Kakashi's evolution as a shinobi a notch.

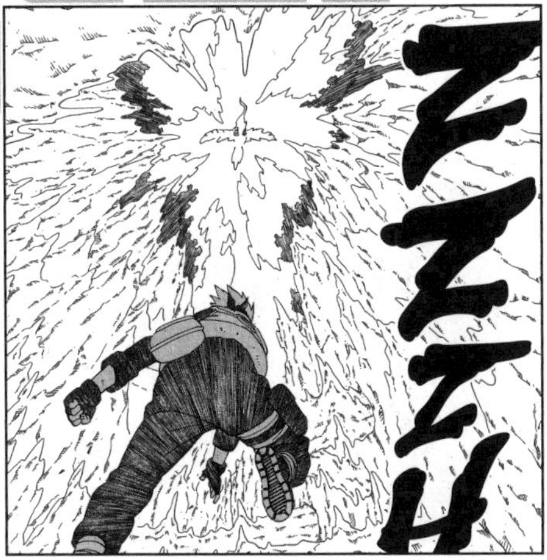

⬅ His ocular ninjutsu can bend and distort space. A target is hurled into a situation where there is no escape.

➡ Quick decision, good teamwork. He acts quickly and gives precise orders, which is essential on missions involving multiple teams.

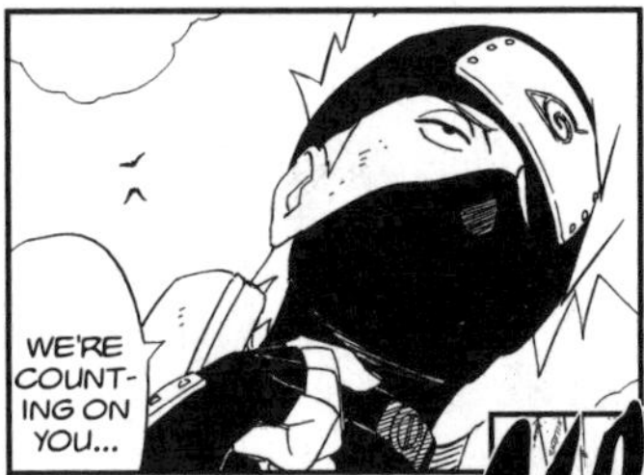
WE'RE COUNT-ING ON YOU...

⬇ With a broad outlook, he will size up one's personality and habits and offer just the right support.

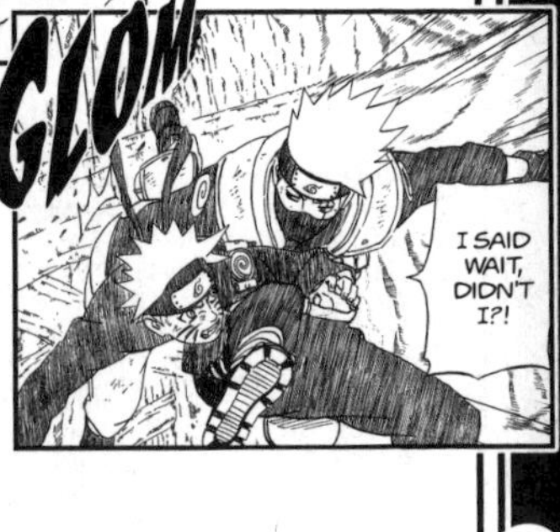
GLOM
I SAID WAIT, DIDN'T I?!

《Leadership》

His calm demeanor gives the members around him a sense of security and trust. His lucidity and intellect serve not only him, but the entire team well. Predicting battle strength, analyzing the strong and weak points, simulating every contingency—he is able to summarize them with accuracy and clarity. On the tense battlefield, Kakashi's presence resounds.

A model shinobi who accepts fate and teaches its principles.

《Nurturing》

He has acquired enormous strength and experience by risking his life. And he shares all of it without hesitation. Kakashi is well aware pride and ego are petty compared to the shinobi's important duty to protect the village. Training one's self and nurturing others are on different planes. History is passed on. Even if one loses one's life, the principles will live on forever. It is difficult to understand a shinobi's fate. But Kakashi understands and accepts his destiny. It is this trait that makes Kakashi so powerful.

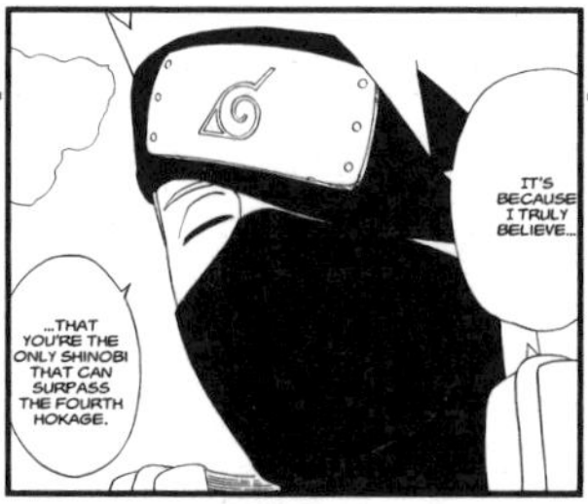
IT'S BECAUSE I TRULY BELIEVE...
...THAT YOU'RE THE ONLY SHINOBI THAT CAN SURPASS THE FOURTH HOKAGE.

⬆ His words of encouragement are never exaggerated. And he perceives things about people they themselves may not have noticed.

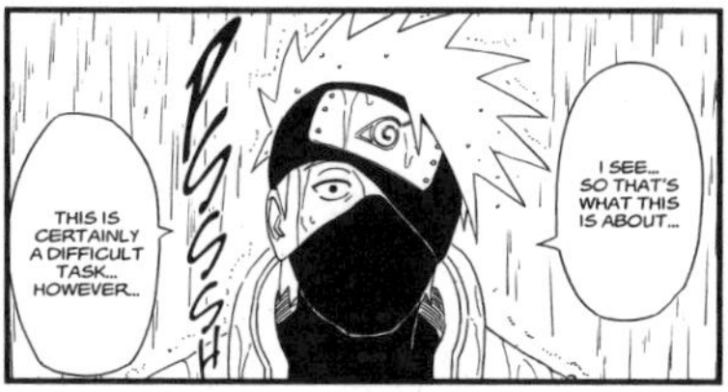
I SEE... SO THAT'S WHAT THIS IS ABOUT...
THIS IS CERTAINLY A DIFFICULT TASK... HOWEVER...

⬆ He is logical and willful. His ability to think quickly about multiple outcomes means he is always able to perceive the next road to take.

《Assisting》

A rational eye is important in order to complete a mission, but what is even more critical is the emotional state of the team. Even if they are in a losing situation, sometimes one cannot give up. That is a shinobi's fate, and Kakashi understands that.

⬇ After Asuma's death, he sensed Cell Number 10's immense sorrow and joined up with them.

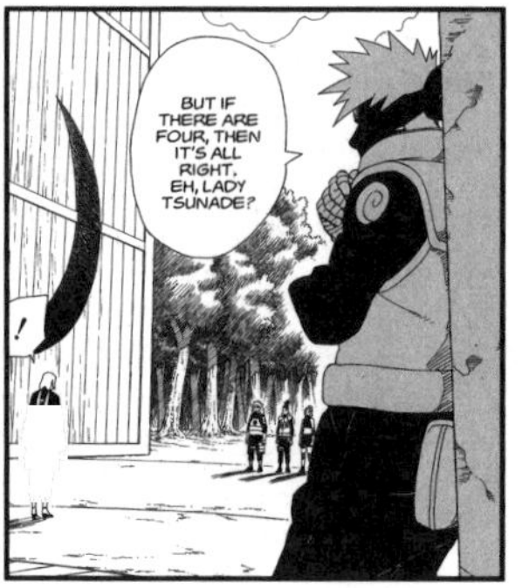
BUT IF THERE ARE FOUR, THEN IT'S ALL RIGHT. EH, LADY TSUNADE?
!

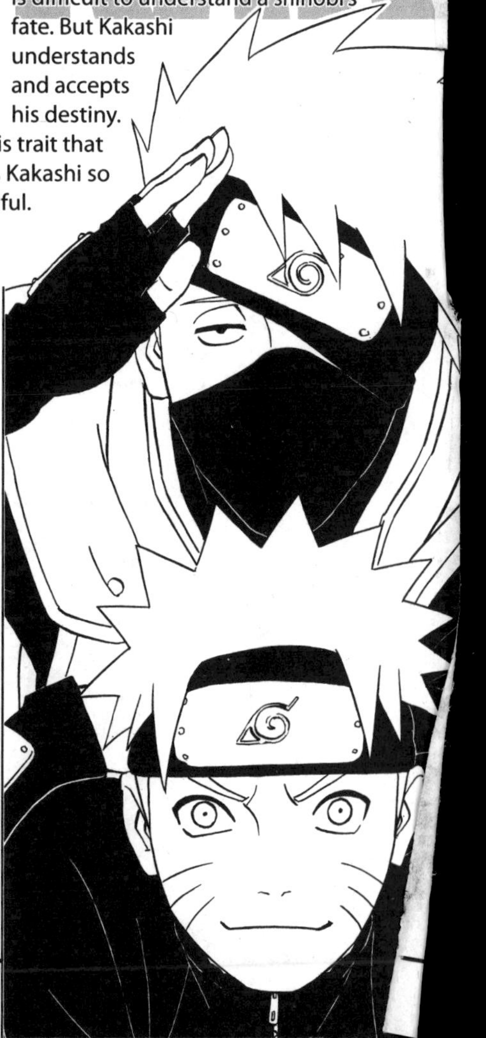

HARUNO SAKURA

春野サクラ

Chûnin

WE HAVE TO STAY STRONG. YOU AND ME, TOGETHER.

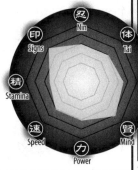

忍 Nin
体 Tai
甲 Signs
幻 Gen
精 Stamina
賢 Mind
速 Speed
力 Power

⬇ She wants to know the truth… It's this passion that turns Sakura toward investigating the Akatsuki and the Tailed Beasts.

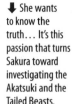

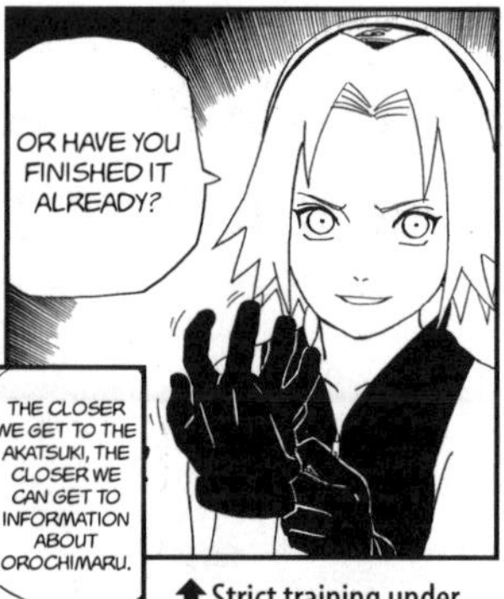
OR HAVE YOU FINISHED IT ALREADY?

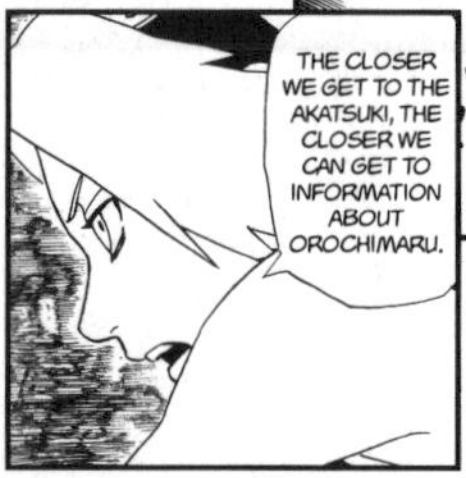
THE CLOSER WE GET TO THE AKATSUKI, THE CLOSER WE CAN GET TO INFORMATION ABOUT OROCHIMARU.

⬆ Strict training under Tsunade has given Sakura confidence.

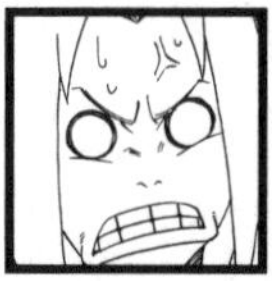

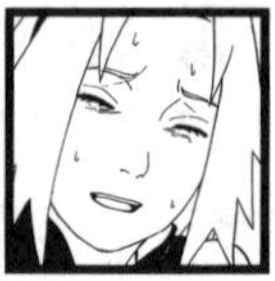

She has overcome grief many times, and now, the cherry blossom of the battlefield is in full bloom!

There is a saying that cherry blossoms are beautiful because they turn all sadness and hardship into nourishment. Without a doubt, Haruno Sakura, the kunoichi from Konohagakure, has grown up beautifully in spite of the sadness she has experienced. The deaths of people close to her, and parting with the one she loved. But with each hurt, she has faced forward and sworn through her tears to grow stronger. The sorrow carved into her heart, and the fine qualities of a shinobi she was born with, will make her even better, especially now that she has become Tsunade's apprentice. The day is near when the cherry blossoms on the battlefield will burst into bloom.

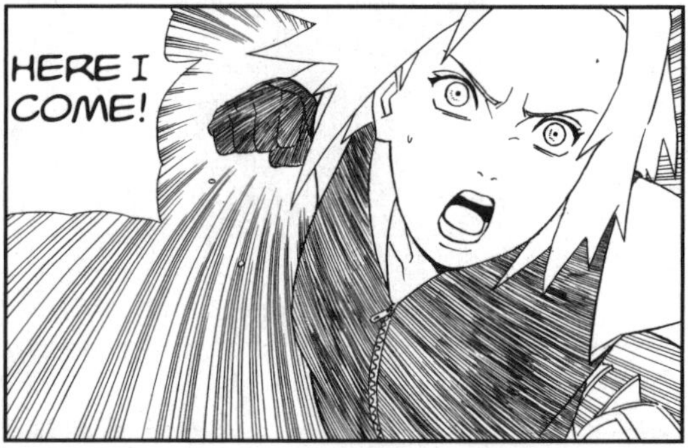
HERE I COME!

⬅ Originally, she was a support-type, but she polished her taijutsu skills and now she will even lead an attack.

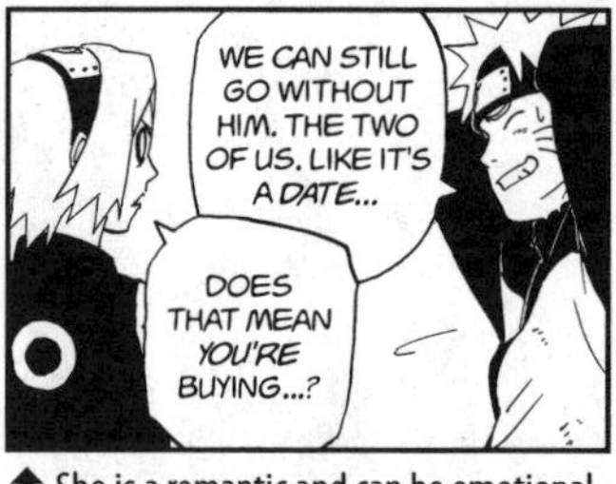
WE CAN STILL GO WITHOUT HIM. THE TWO OF US. LIKE IT'S A DATE...
DOES THAT MEAN YOU'RE BUYING...?

⬆ She is a romantic and can be emotional, but she has become very much an extreme realist.

Ninja Registry Number: 012601
Birthdate: March 28 (16 years old; Aries)
Height: 161.0 cm (5'4") **Weight:** 45.4 kg (100 lbs.) **Blood type:** 0
Personality: Honor student, willful
Favorite food: Shiratama anmitsu, pickled plums
Least favorite food: Spicy foods
Would like to fight: Yamanaka Ino
Favorite word: Courage
Interests: Quiz games, memorization

Graduated from the Ninja Academy at age 12
Promoted to chûnin at age 14

Mission Experience		
	D-rank: 12	C-rank: 9
	B-rank: 6	A-rank: 7
	S-rank: 0	

With a never-say-die attitude passed down from her mentor, the kunoichi Sakura runs to the battlefield!!

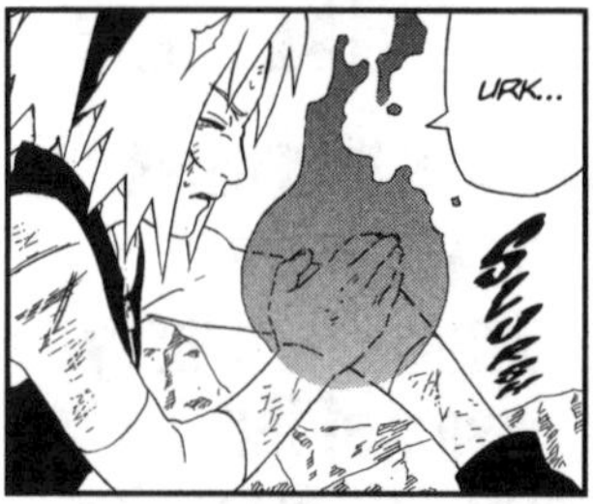
URK...

⬆ In order to apply medical ninjutsu in the midst of battle, one must have considerable skills.

《Medical ninjutsu》

Mastering medical ninjutsu is extremely difficult since one must be able to delicately control chakra as well as have extensive knowledge and perseverance. But Sakura, who has been blessed with those qualities, has amazed Tsunade with her quick learning. And she has developed into a top medical ninja even among those in the village.

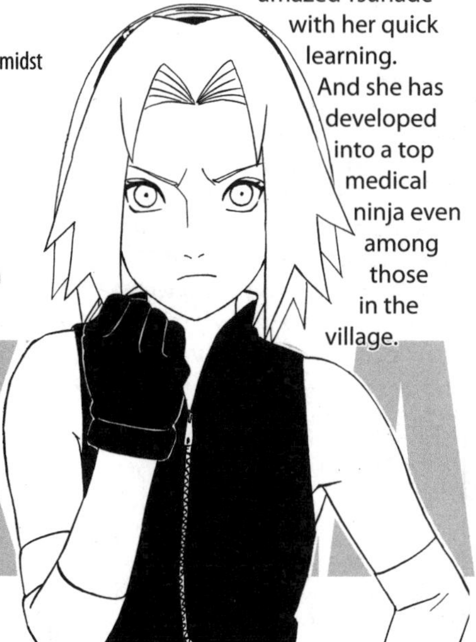

《Strength》

Having brute strength. It is not quite the description a young girl desires for herself. But contrary to how it may look, it is a ninjutsu that requires extremely precise chakra control. One must knead chakra internally, then in an instant, concentrate it all into the fist. As for super-human strength, it is more important to have courage and the ability to assess the situation. It is a jutsu that combines the qualities of femininity: sensitivity, attentiveness, and bravery.

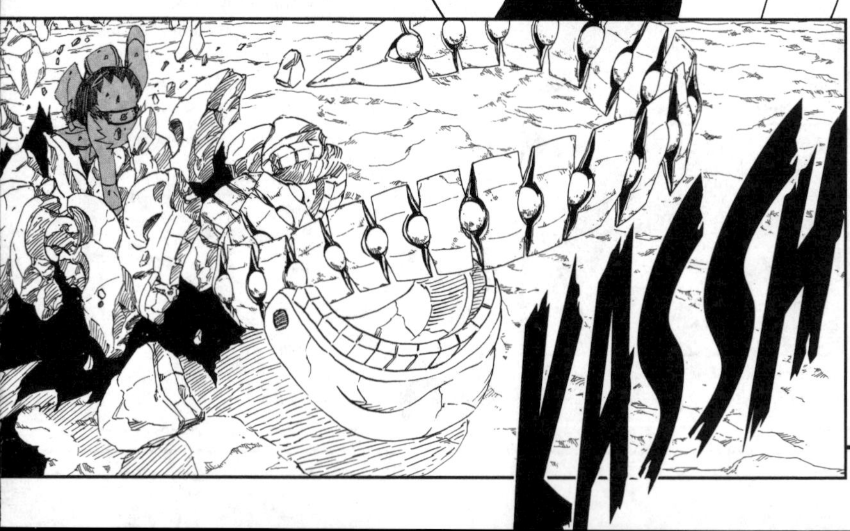

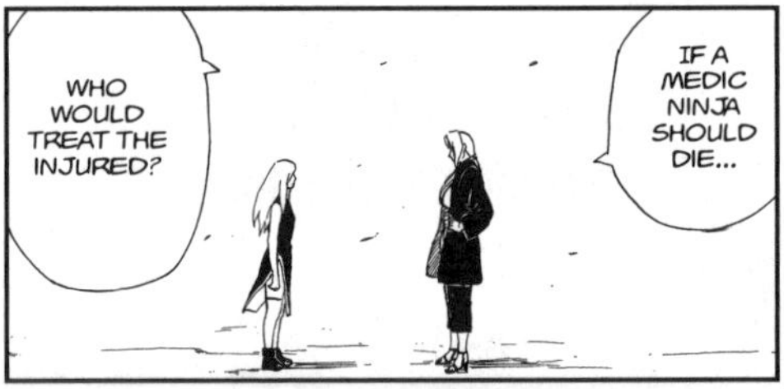
IF A MEDIC NINJA SHOULD DIE...
WHO WOULD TREAT THE INJURED?

⬆ Tsunade explains the importance of evasion skills, then gives her pupil special training.

《Evasion skills》

Tsunade stresses that a medical ninja must stay alive during battle at all costs. When death is a constant companion, sometimes the pain of surviving is often more agonizing. And Tsunade's words reverberate in her heart. Because she understands the grave responsibility she bears, Sakura trains hard to polish her evasion skills. It is not because she fears death. And certainly, it is not so she can run away.

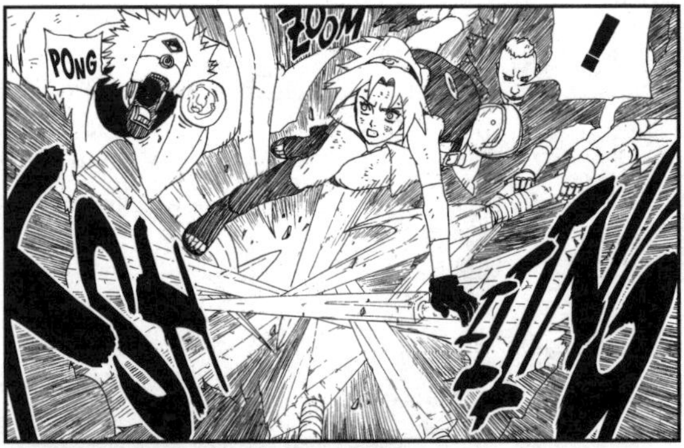
ZOOM
PONG
!

⬅ With astounding agility, she dodges an attack from a hundred puppets.

《Guts》

Medical ninjutsu can shatter stone and heal almost every injury. However, even with such amazing cards in one's hand, ultimately, whether one saves a life or not depends on one's skill.

Losing one's ability in real battle can turn into a serious burden. Sakura has what it takes to effectively use her ninjutsu. It is because she has the unshakeable spirit to see through any crisis… namely guts.

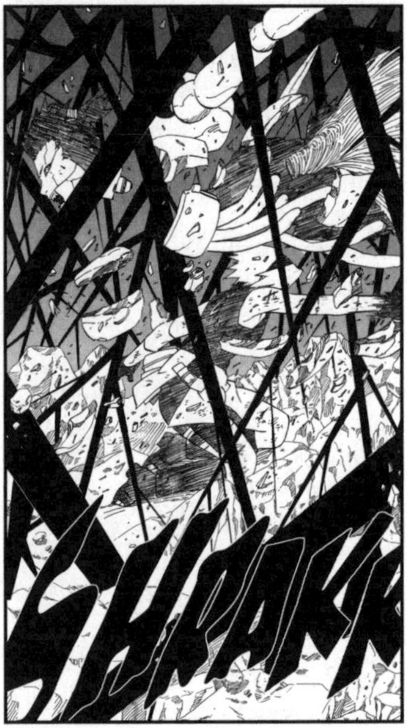

⬆ Having courage is not recklessness. It is the ability to make a rational decision, then act upon it.

⬇ Sakura destroyed even puppet-master Sasori's best puppet, Hiruko, in one blow.

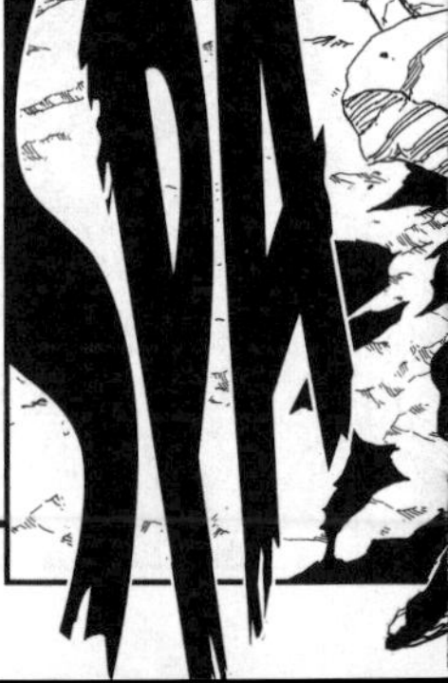

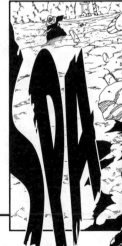

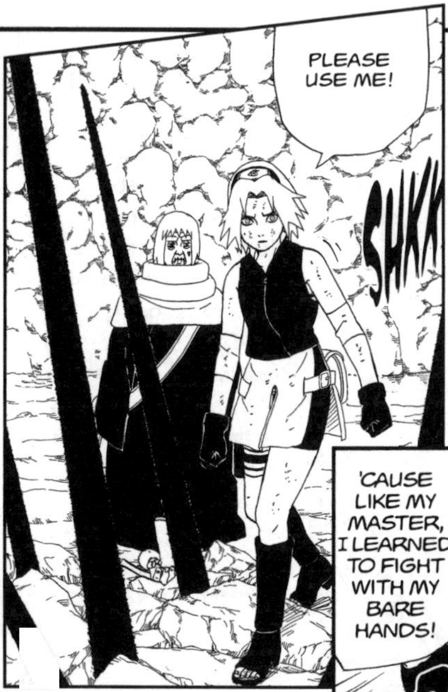
PLEASE USE ME!
SHKK

How many faces does a woman have?! As many as the feelings she hides in her heart.

《Hates to lose》

Sakura hates to lose. Tsunade's intense training has only reinforced this trait. It's evident most in her fervent desire to save Naruto and Sasuke.

As long as she continues to vow to save those two, Sakura will never waver.

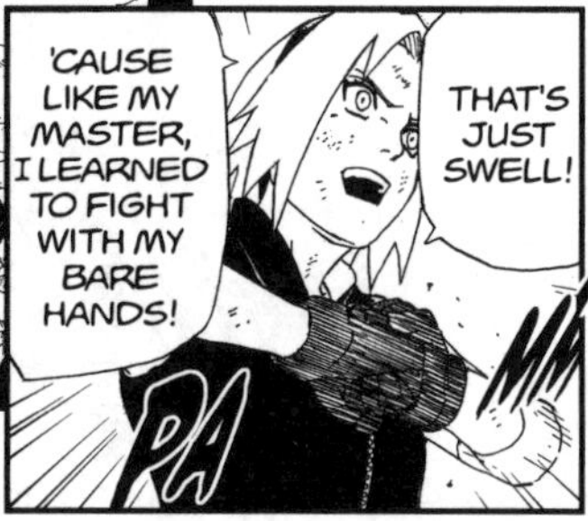
THAT'S JUST SWELL!
'CAUSE LIKE MY MASTER, I LEARNED TO FIGHT WITH MY BARE HANDS!
PA

⬅ Because of her feelings for her friends and her trust in her teacher, Sakura puts on a smile no matter how dire the situation.

《A woman's heart and her short temper》

Women are complicated creatures. Many who have come into contact with Sakura have probably thought the same thing. She is sensitive yet bold, shy yet short-tempered, affectionate yet combative. Her emotions change constantly, making her hard to predict. Naruto swears not to do anything foolish in front of Sakura, while Jiraiya sighs that she has become Tsunade Junior.

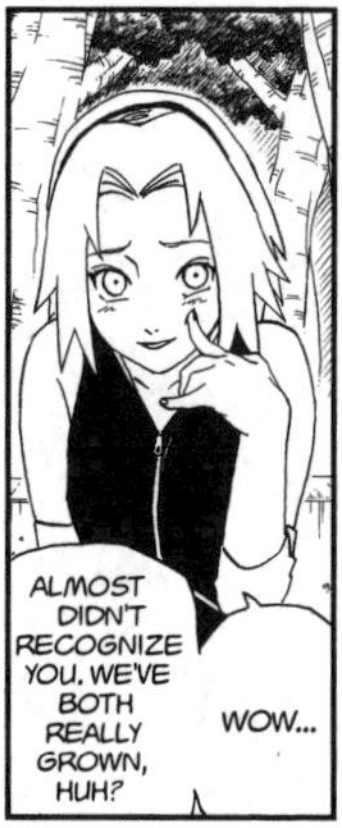
WOW...
ALMOST DIDN'T RECOGNIZE YOU. WE'VE BOTH REALLY GROWN, HUH?

➡ Her childhood friend has matured faster than she ever expected. It causes her heart to beat faster. . .

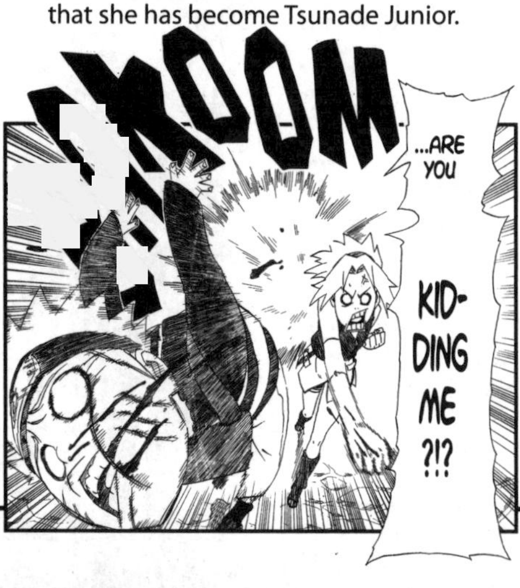
...ARE YOU KID-DING ME ?!?

⬅ In the next second, she unleashes a punch. Naruto, her victim, is caught totally unawares.

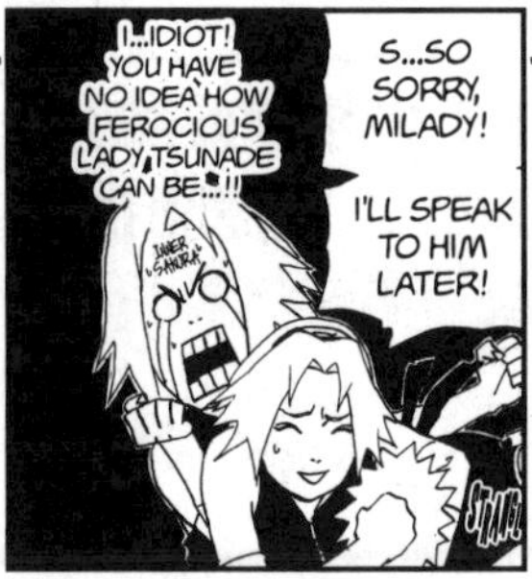
S...SO SORRY, MILADY!
I'LL SPEAK TO HIM LATER!
I...IDIOT! YOU HAVE NO IDEA HOW FEROCIOUS LADY TSUNADE CAN BE...!!

⬆ Perhaps it was beaten into her during training, but Sakura obeys Tsunade without question.

A new teacher, a new comrade... and new feelings?

《Tsunade》

Kakashi helped her to discover her ability to control chakra. Now with a new teacher like Tsunade, Sakura's talent blossoms. Tsunade is happy to have found a successor to her skills and Sakura too is coming around to respect and trust her teacher.

《Sai》

Sakura has mixed feelings about Sai who is Sasuke's replacement on Team Kakashi. Accepting Sai as a comrade means accepting that Sasuke is no longer a part of the team. But with the change that she sees in Sai, Sakura is developing a bond with him.

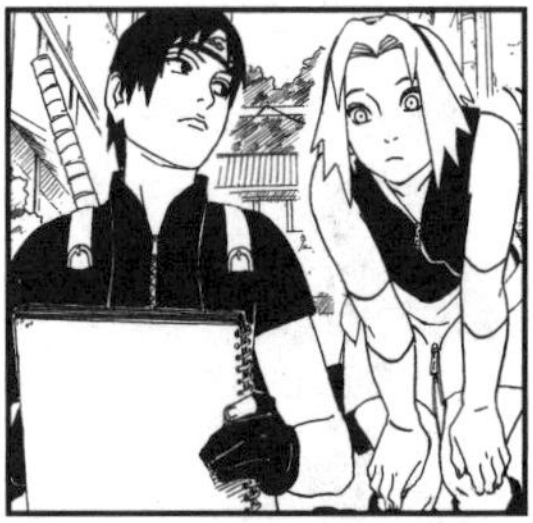

⬆ Sakura has always been attune to Sai's complexities.

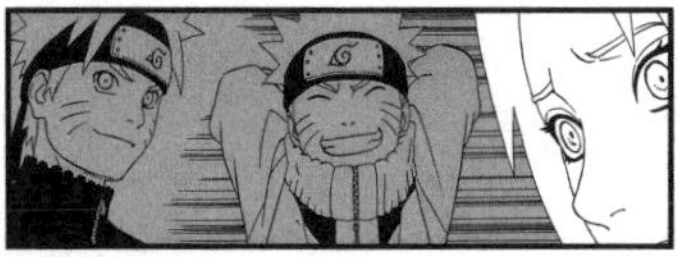

⬅ Memories of Naruto float through her mind...

《Naruto》

When she was younger, the one Sakura yearned for, then loved, was Sasuke. Naruto was merely a nuisance, the loser who always came between her and Sasuke. But as she goes over the various missions in the past, and Sakura comes to a realization. When times were hard, when she wanted to give up on life, it was always that nuisance, Naruto, who protected and encouraged her. How does she feel about Naruto? Sakura still has not found an answer.

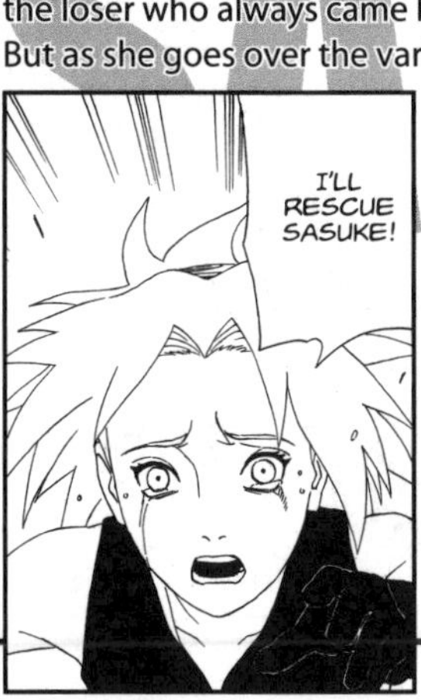
I'LL RESCUE SASUKE!

⬅ Naruto's unwavering devotion causes tears to flow down Sakura's cheeks.

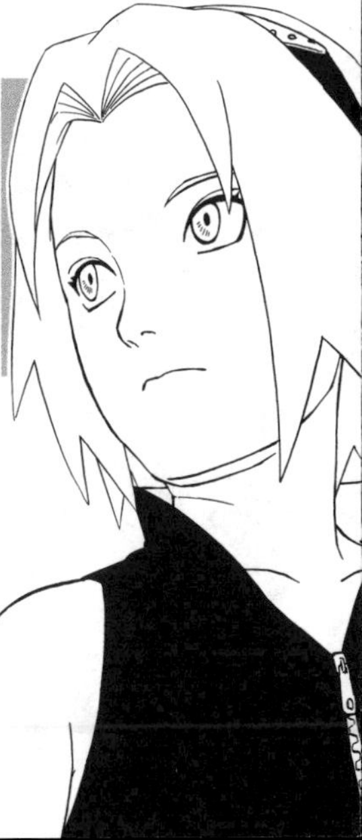

Just like before. With that hope, Sakura continues to pursue him.

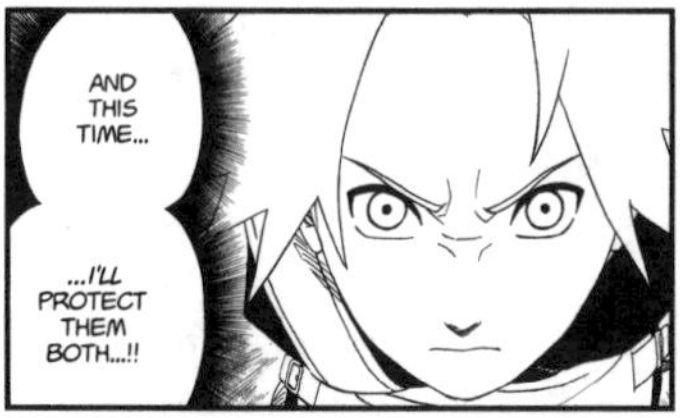
AND THIS TIME...
...I'LL PROTECT THEM BOTH...!!

⬆ The past in which she could not stop Sasuke, and hurt Naruto as a result... this is what shapes her today.

《Promise》

To bring back life as it was before Sasuke left. And to keep her friends from getting hurt. When she pounded on Tsunade's door, Sakura bid farewell to the young Sakura who could do nothing but cry on the night Sasuke left.

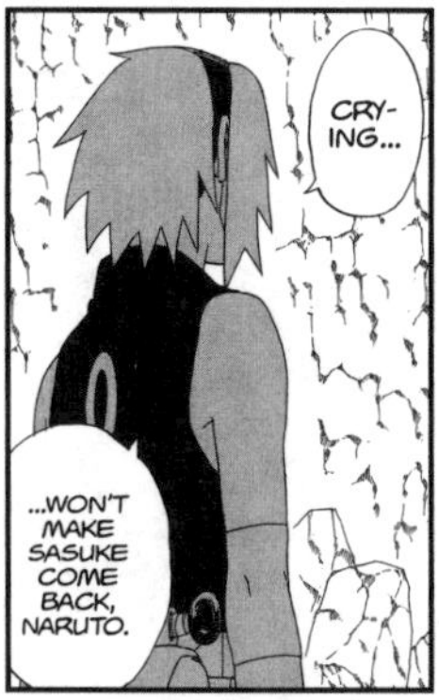
CRYING...
...WON'T MAKE SASUKE COME BACK, NARUTO.

⬆ It used to be that Naruto always encouraged Sakura. Now she is the one giving him strength...evidence of her spiritual growth.

《Resolution》

Sakura is well aware that in the shinobi world, one must pay a fair price to obtain something. If she can get Sasuke back...if those ordinary days that were lost can return again, Sakura is willing to make any sacrifice. It is this resolve that gives her the strength to forge ahead toward the future.

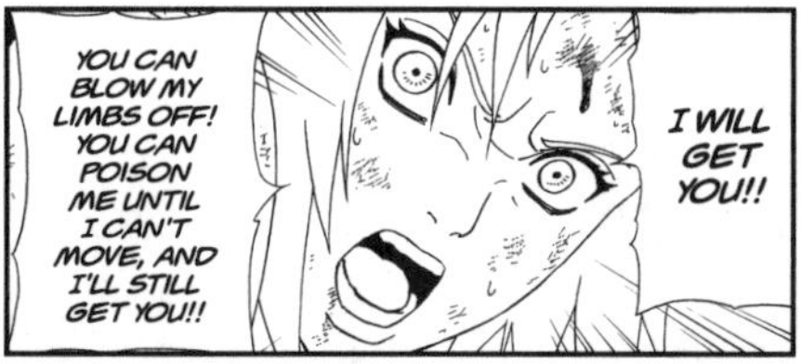
I WILL GET YOU!!
YOU CAN BLOW MY LIMBS OFF! YOU CAN POISON ME UNTIL I CAN'T MOVE, AND I'LL STILL GET YOU!!

⬆ Whenever she thinks of Sasuke, she is gripped with regret. At the same time, she feels strength welling up inside her.

SAKURA

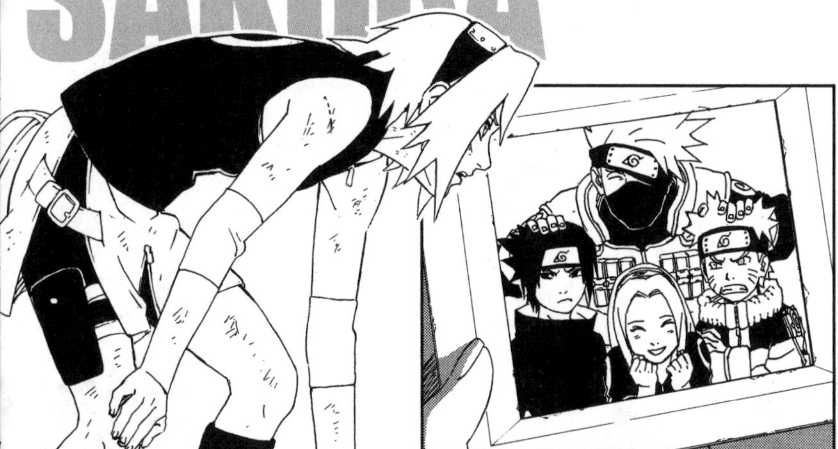

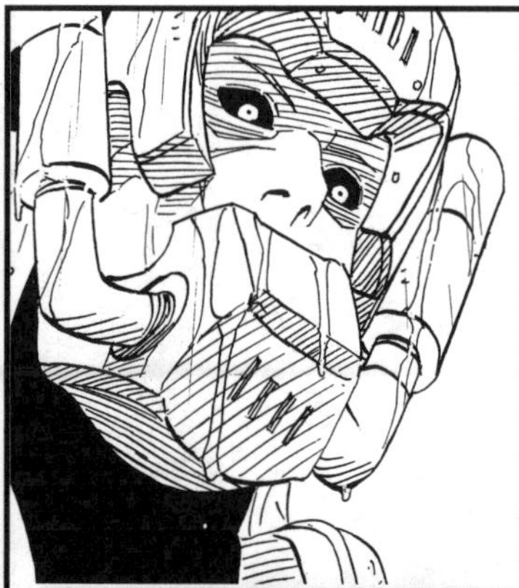

His name is legendary and he stands alone at the summit.

Hanzo, the famed ninja who raced across battlefields, riding the salamander he had summoned. During the Second Great Shinobi World War, he coined the name the Three Great Shinobi for Jiraiya, Tsunade and Orochimaru and spread their fame throughout the lands.

HANZO 半蔵

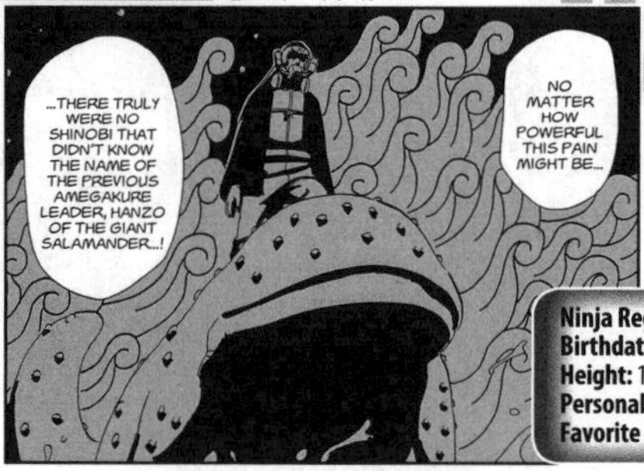
NO MATTER HOW POWERFUL THIS PAIN MIGHT BE...
...THERE TRULY WERE NO SHINOBI THAT DIDN'T KNOW THE NAME OF THE PREVIOUS AMEGAKURE LEADER, HANZO OF THE GIANT SALAMANDER...!

IN EXCHANGE FOR YOUR LIVES, I WOULD KNOW YOUR NAMES...

⬅ Wearing a special mask, he can maneuver freely underwater. No one can outdo him when submerged.

Ninja Registry Number: ?
Birthdate: February 12 (? years old; Aquarius)
Height: 177.0 cm (5'9½") **Weight:** 58.6 kg (129 lbs.) **Blood type:** A
Personality: Confident, cautious
Favorite word: Unpreparedness is the greatest enemy.

Collection ... Number 9 — Konoha

COUP D'ÉTAT IN THE SMOKING RAIN

His name is Pain. Charismatic and even more mysterious than Hanzo, Pain is revered as a god. This man, who lives behind a sealed barrier and has elevated himself to godly status... Just what is the ideal society he seeks?

⬇ To prevent a night assassination, security keeps tight watch.

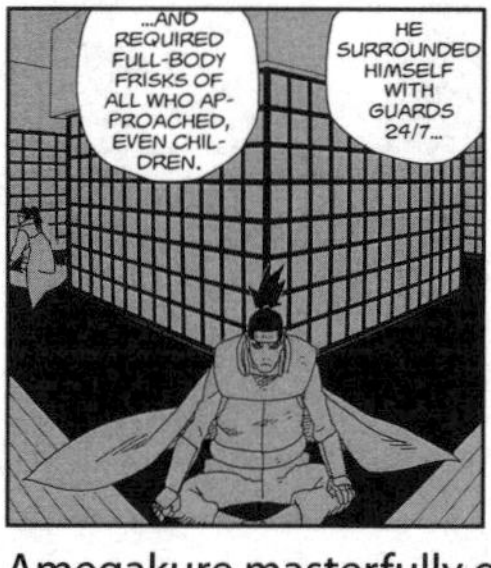
HE SURROUNDED HIMSELF WITH GUARDS 24/7...
...AND REQUIRED FULL-BODY FRISKS OF ALL WHO APPROACHED, EVEN CHILDREN.

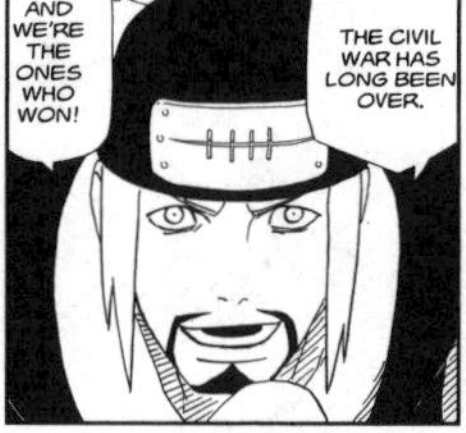
THE CIVIL WAR HAS LONG BEEN OVER.
AND WE'RE THE ONES WHO WON!

⬅ After the revolution is completed, he purges the government and cements his position.

Amegakure masterfully gathered intel in secret about its state of affairs. In this land rumored to have internal strife, a shocking thing happens. Hanzo, who ruled with an iron hand and kept himself under strict guard, is overthrown, and a new ruler takes the reins of power.

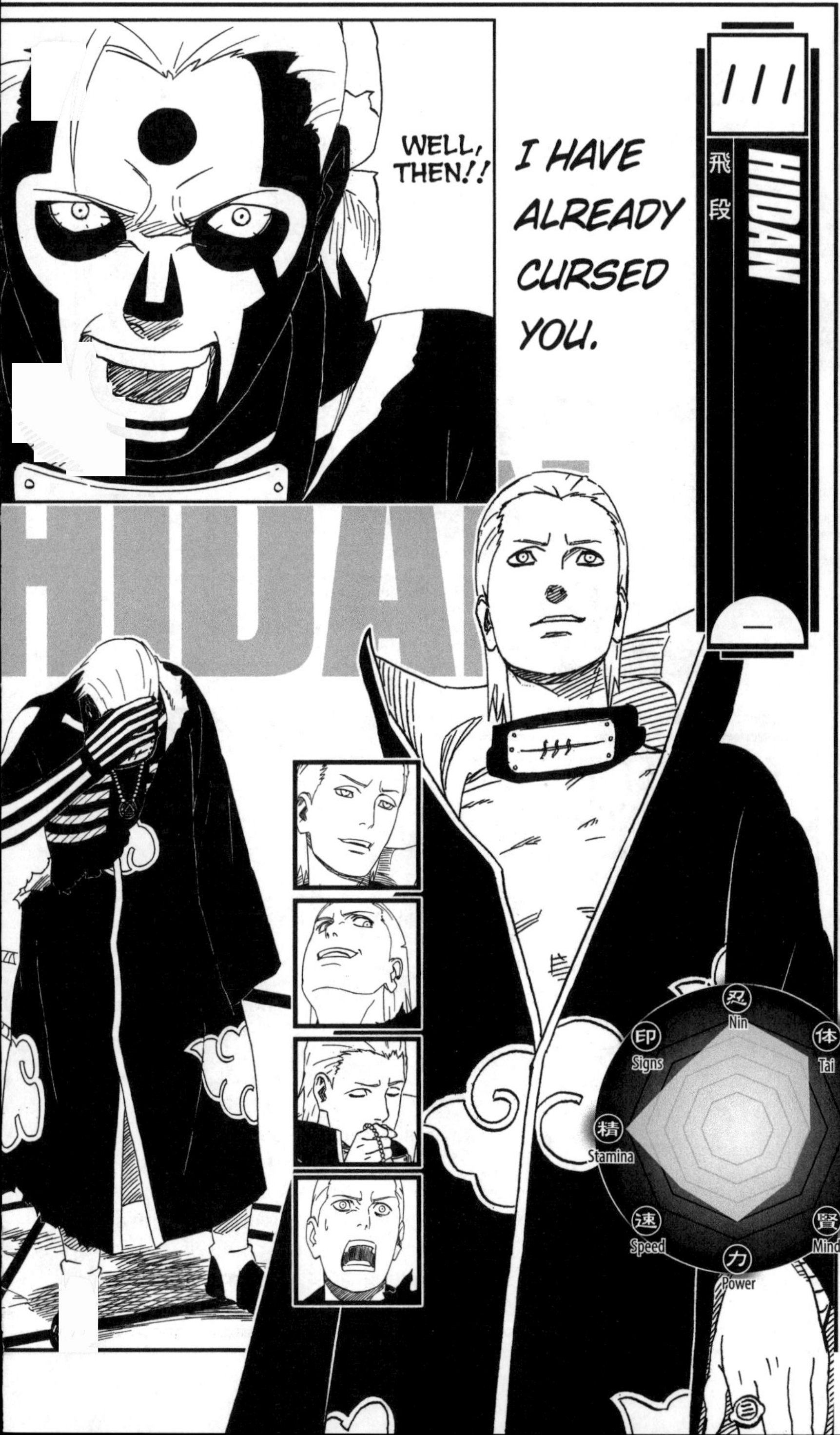
111
HIDAN
飛段
I HAVE ALREADY CURSED YOU.
WELL, THEN!!
HIDAN
忍 Nin
体 Tai
幻 Gen
賢 Mind
力 Power
速 Speed
精 Stamina
印 Signs

He follows the terrifying Way of Jashin! He is the invincible shinobi who finds pleasure in pain!!

LET'S EXPERIENCE THE ULTIMATE PAIN TOGETHER, SHALL WE!!!

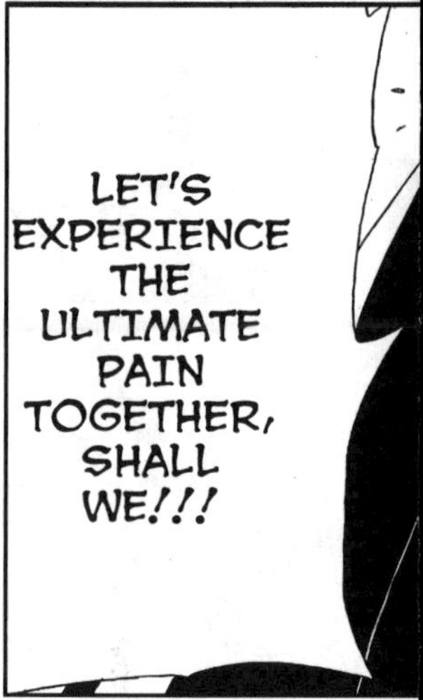

Hidan wears the black coat of the Akatsuki and wields a huge three-bladed scythe, striking fear into everyone he confronts. However, he was born in Yugakure, known as the Village That Forgot War. It was one of the hidden villages, once kept for military purposes, whose numbers dwindled when major wars disappeared from the world. Blessed with nature and resources for tourism, this village benefited from the changing of the times. But Hidan, who lived as a shinobi, was starved for battle. Sick of the village's adherence to peace, Hidan turns on the village itself. Inevitably, he finds himself attracted to a new philosophy, the Way of Jashin. Their doctrine of "Thou shalt kill thy neighbor" is one that Hidan affirms wholeheartedly.

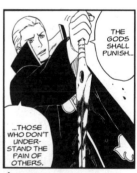

THE GODS SHALL PUNISH...
...THOSE WHO DON'T UNDER-STAND THE PAIN OF OTHERS.

⬆ He relishes causing pain. This too is part of his doctrine.

⬇ Hidan brandishes his three-bladed scythe. His aim is the blood of the sacrifice. His sinister appearance is truly one of a shinigami.

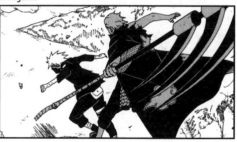

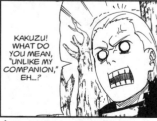

KAKUZU! WHAT DO YOU MEAN, "UNLIKE MY COMPANION," EH...?

⬆ Any criticism against him is criticism against the Way of Jashin. Hidan has a very, very short fuse.

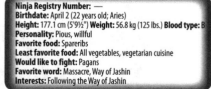

Ninja Registry Number: —
Birthdate: April 2 (22 years old; Aries)
Height: 177.1 cm (5'9½") **Weight:** 56.8 kg (125 lbs.) **Blood type:** B
Personality: Pious, willful
Favorite food: Spareribs
Least favorite food: All vegetables, vegetarian cuisine
Would like to fight: Pagans
Favorite word: Massacre, Way of Jashin
Interests: Following the Way of Jashin

Graduated from the Ninja Academy at age ?
Promoted to chûnin at age ?

Mission Experience		
	D-rank: ?	C-rank: ?
	B-rank: ?	A-rank: ?
	S-rank: ?	

YOU FOOLS HAVE NO IDEA HOW PAINFUL IT IS HAVING YOUR HEAD SLICED OFF!!!

IT REALLY, REALLY HURTS! OWWW!!!

←↓ Pain is the ultimate pleasure to Hidan. But not being able to share that pain angers him to no end…

A child of cursed flesh… sent by the gods!

《Immortal》

The Way of Jashin uses bodies of believers in forbidden jutsu rituals. Hidan was the first successful test case.

As a reward for his many massacres, Hidan acquires an immortal body via the Way of Jashin. This only helps to affirm his love for the Way.

《Immortal Combo》

Hidan made up his mind to join the Akatsuki because of a man named Kakuzu. Here was a man who would live forever, a predecessor. Kakuzu would be the ideal partner. Having no fear of death, they are a valuable fighting force for the organization.

ENOUGH, KAKUZU!

↑ The two-man cell works best, like a horse and its rider.

146

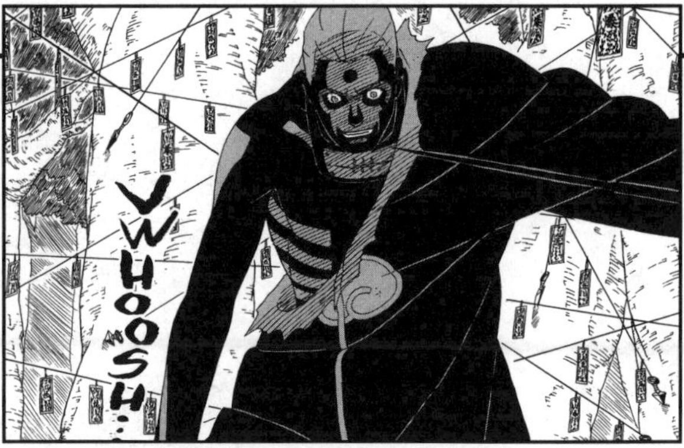
VWHOOSH...

➡ He sacrifices himself to the Way of Jashin to activate the curse. And his body fills with black power.

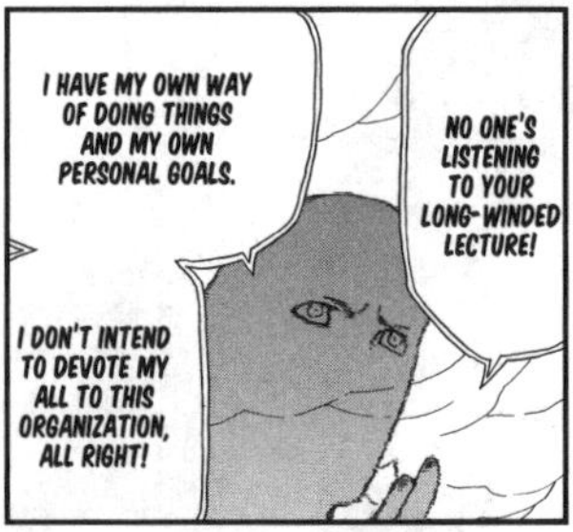
NO ONE'S LISTENING TO YOUR LONG-WINDED LECTURE!
I HAVE MY OWN WAY OF DOING THINGS AND MY OWN PERSONAL GOALS.
I DON'T INTEND TO DEVOTE MY ALL TO THIS ORGANIZATION, ALL RIGHT!

⬆ Although he is a part of the Akatsuki, Hidan's loyalty truly belongs to the Way of Jashin.

Repeated massacres in the name of the Way of Jashin.

《Supreme purpose》

The Way of Jashin is absolute for Hidan, the only thing worth believing in. He considers his supreme purpose to be to spread the Way of Jashin to nonbelievers throughout the world. It means to create a world that acknowledges mass killing. And Hidan feels that this is possible by being a part of the Akatsuki.

《Way of Jashin》

Thou shalt kill thy neighbor. This dogma is contradictory since it would allow devotees to kill each other. But to Hidan who is immortal, this is meaningless. That is why he is able to accept the doctrine and follow its teachings. Even if he ends up with just his head…

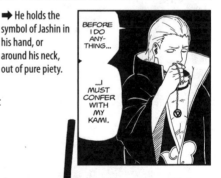

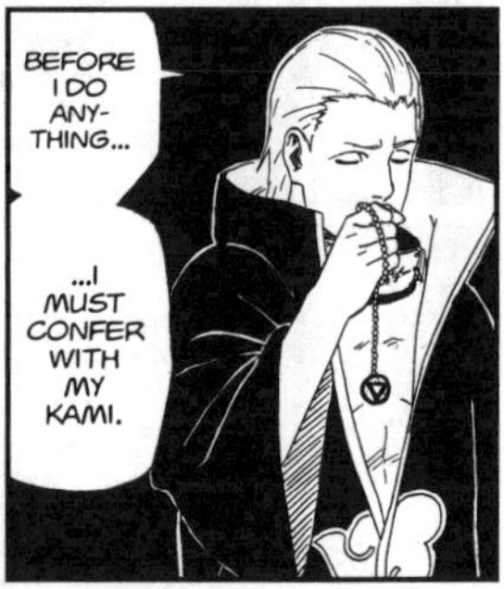
BEFORE I DO ANY-THING...
...I MUST CONFER WITH MY KAMI.

➡ He holds the symbol of Jashin in his hand, or around his neck, out of pure piety.

⬇ After a kill, he meditates for a long time. He has never skipped this ritual.

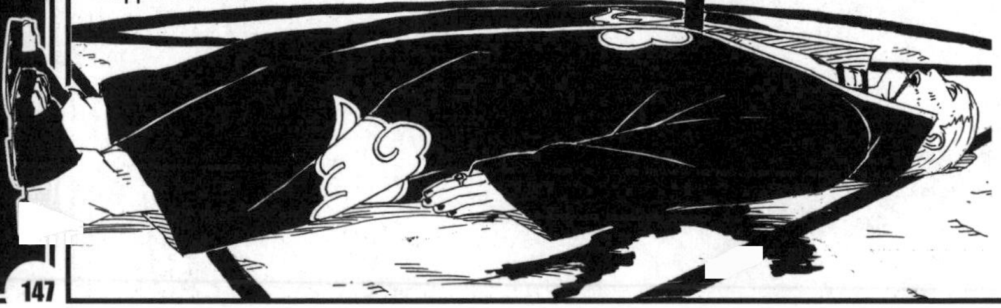

HYUGA NEJI

日向ネジ

Jônin

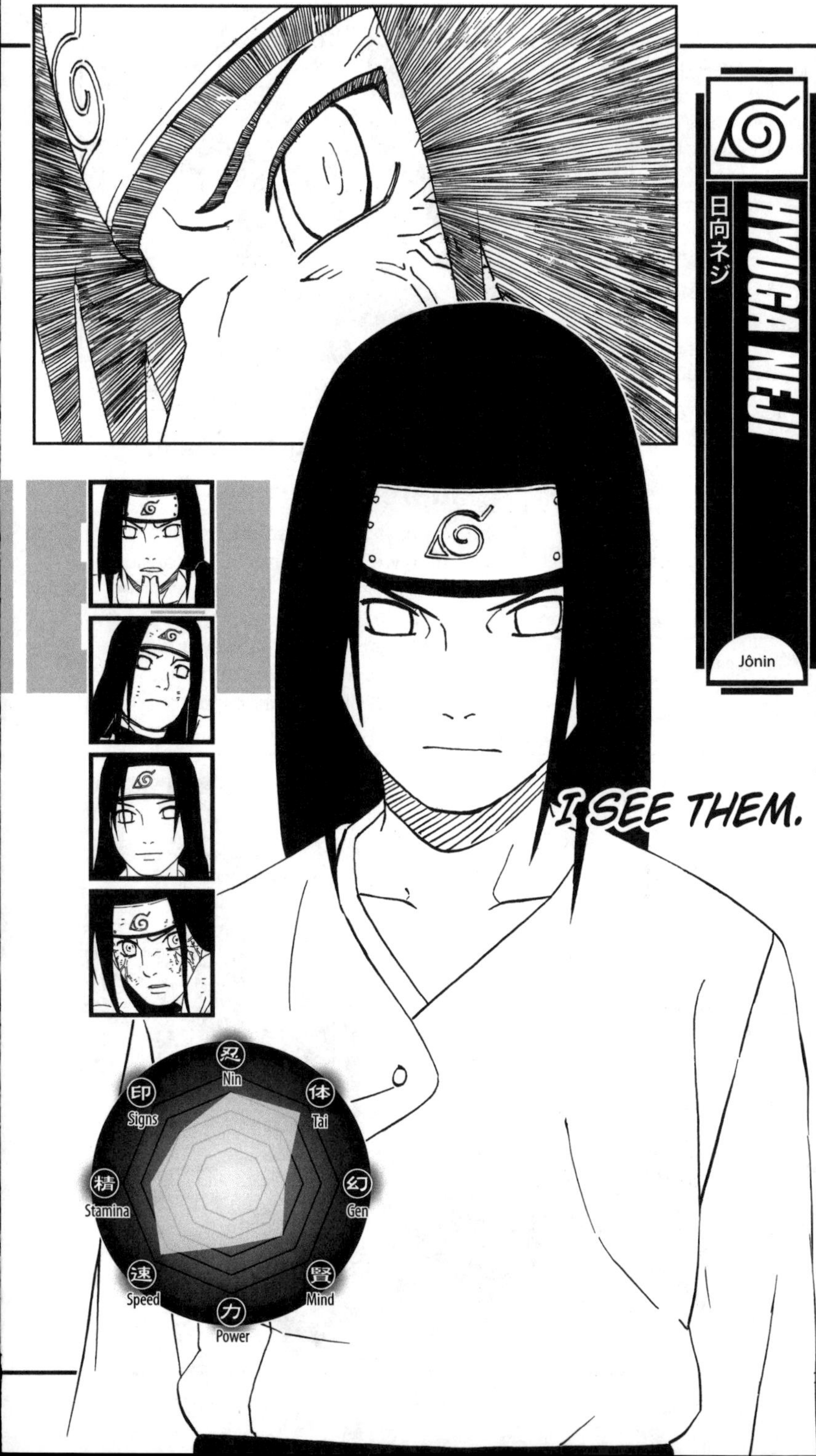
I SEE THEM.
忍
Nin
体
Tai
幻
Gen
賢
Mind
力
Power
速
Speed
精
Stamina
印
Signs

There is no doubt in his eyes.

Even among the Hyuga, exalted as the strongest in Konoha, Neji is touted and loved for his talents. There was a time in the past when he cursed himself, and even the main family and the village, for his misfortune in being born into a branch family. Interaction with his compatriots in the village has changed all that. Now, he dedicates himself to the village and to his comrades and has swiftly risen in the ranks to jônin. He sees beyond the borders of his family and serves as a shining role model for the young shinobi who adore him.

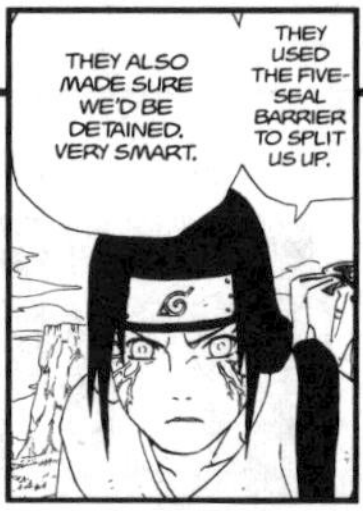
THEY USED THE FIVE-SEAL BARRIER TO SPLIT US UP.
THEY ALSO MADE SURE WE'D BE DETAINED. VERY SMART.

➡ He can use Byakugan to its full potential because he has the right judgmental and analytical skills.

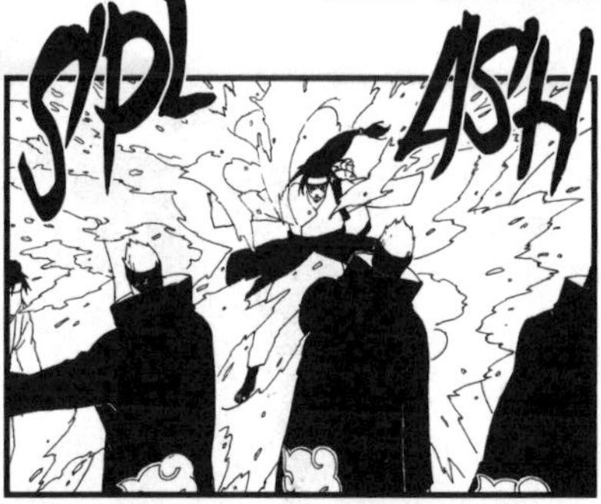
SPLASH

⬆ Byakugan holds the power to see the flow of chakra. The accuracy of taijutsu in pinpointing pressure points is the basis of its power.

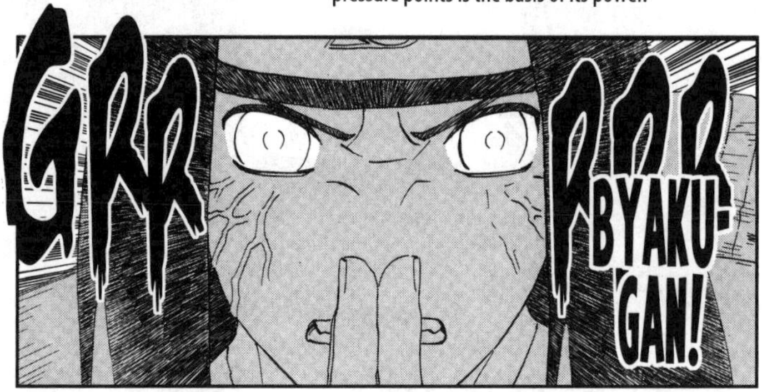
GRR
BYAKU-GAN!

⬆ He devotes himself to study with fierce determination. This gift from the heavens has limitless potential.

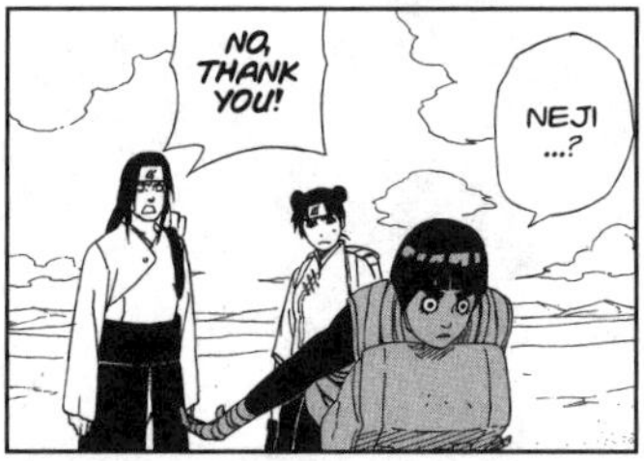
NEJI ...?
NO, THANK YOU!

⬆ Neji is intellectual, calm and composed. In a sense, he and Lee, who is always full of zeal, make the perfect duo.

Ninja Registry Number: 012587
Birthdate: July 3 (17years old; Cancer)
Height: 172.1 cm (5'7½") **Weight:** 54.2kg (119 lbs.) **Blood type:** O
Personality: Cool, pragmatic
Favorite food: Nishinsoba
Least favorite food: Pumpkin
Would like to fight: Uzumaki Naruto
Favorite word: Making great strides
Interests: Leapfrog

Graduated from the Ninja Academy at age 12
Promoted to chûnin at age 15

Mission Experience		
	D-rank: 26	C-rank: 19
	B-rank:4	A-rank: 11
	S-rank: 2	

HYUGA HINATA

日向ヒナタ

Chûnin

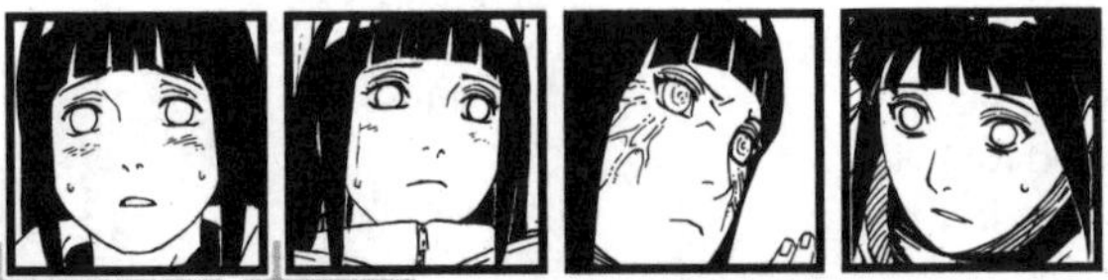

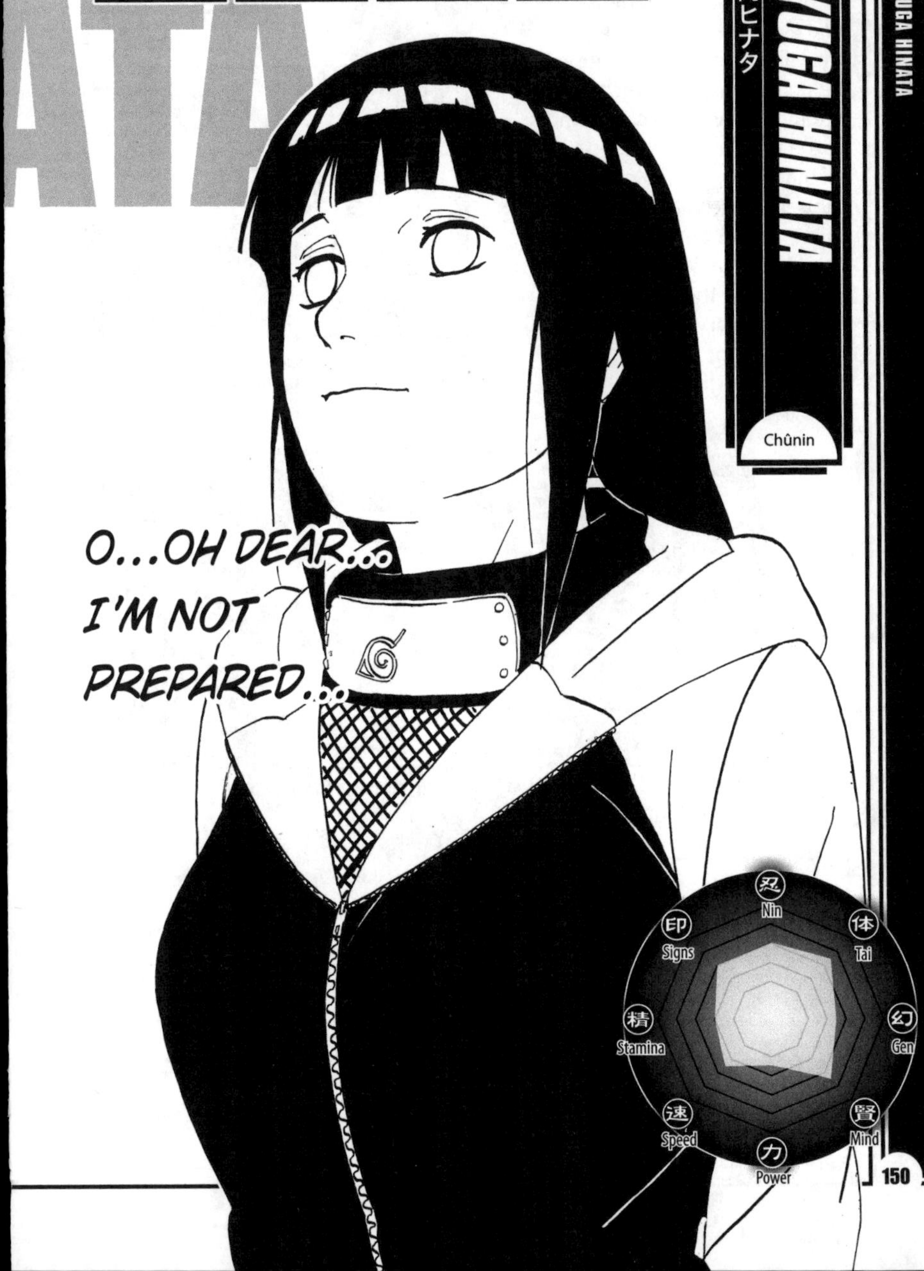
O...OH DEAR...
I'M NOT
PREPARED...
忍 Nin
体 Tai
幻 Gen
賢 Mind
力 Power
速 Speed
精 Stamina
印 Signs

Conquering her weak self, the white flower blossoms with ease.

Hinata was born into the main branch of the Hyuga clan, a renowned family in Konoha. A shy girl, who felt the weight of her family's rank on her shoulders and suppressed her own talents, she nevertheless had a carefree childhood, thanks to her friends and teachers. The person Hinata emulates is someone who is constantly growing. Even now, he is far away training hard. To Hinata, Naruto is the embodiment of potential and confidence. After a three-year absence, Naruto returns. Now Hinata is sure to display the extent of her own potential too.

HRRRM...
BYAKU-GAN!

➡ With a powerful Byakugan that rivals that of Neji, there is no doubt she has hidden potential.

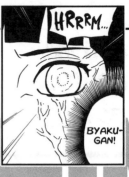

ABOUT TEN KILOMETERS AHEAD, I SEE A POWERFUL CHAKRA SPREAD OUT ACROSS A WIDE SWATH...
AND... FOR SOME REASON... THE FOREST IS ON FIRE... WITH BLACK FLAMES.

⬆ She knows exactly where her talents lie and helps the team in the best possible way.

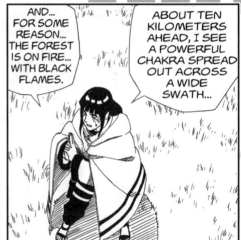

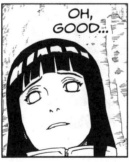

OH, GOOD...

⬅ She has become more shinobi-like, but her concern for her friends and comrades remains unchanged.

OH, IT'S YOU, HINATA!
ARE YOU HIDING OVER HERE?
POP...

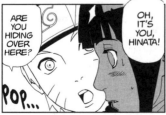

⬆ Ironically, when she is with Naruto, the one who changed her, Hinata is overcome with shyness.

Ninja Registry Number: 012612
Birthdate: December 27 (16 years old; Capricorn)
Height: 160.0 cm (5'3") **Weight:** 45.0 kg (99 lbs.) **Blood type:** A
Personality: Shy, withdrawn
Favorite food: Zenzai, cinnamon rolls
Least favorite food: Crab, shrimp
Would like to fight: Hyuga Neji, Hyuga Hiashi
Favorite word: Confidence
Interests: Pressed flowers

Graduated from the Ninja Academy at age 12
Promoted to chûnin at age 14

Mission Experience		
	D-rank: 10	C-rank: 14
	B-rank: 8	A-rank: 1
	S-rank: 0	

FUKASAKU

フカサク

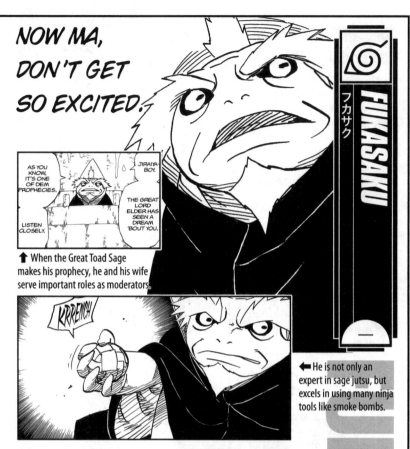

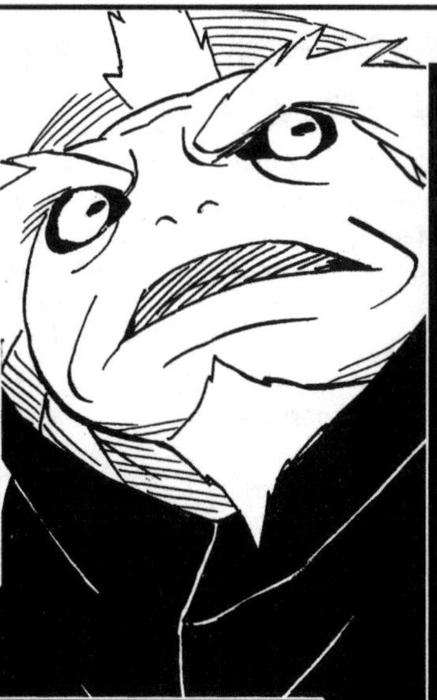
NOW MA, DON'T GET SO EXCITED.

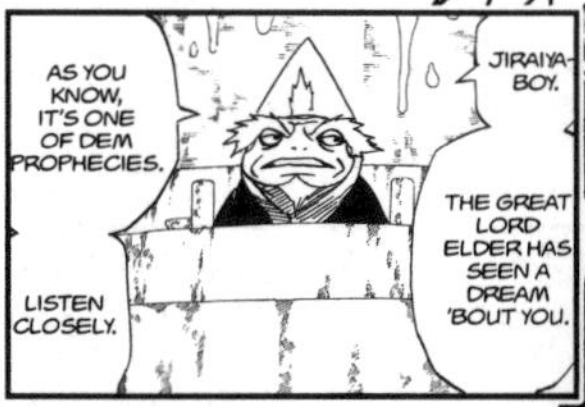
JIRAIYA-BOY.
THE GREAT LORD ELDER HAS SEEN A DREAM 'BOUT YOU.
AS YOU KNOW, IT'S ONE OF DEM PROPHECIES.
LISTEN CLOSELY.

⬆ When the Great Toad Sage makes his prophecy, he and his wife serve important roles as moderators.

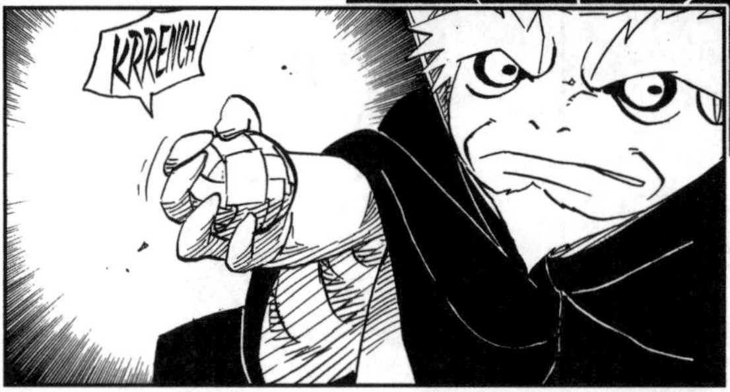
KRRENCH

⬅ He is not only an expert in sage jutsu, but excels in using many ninja tools like smoke bombs.

⬇ They exchange banter and insults like a comedy team. But deep down, their love is pure and strong.

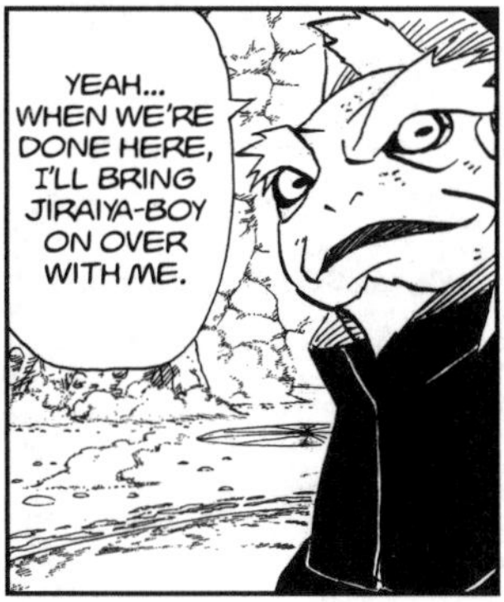
YEAH... WHEN WE'RE DONE HERE, I'LL BRING JIRAIYA-BOY ON OVER WITH ME.

The Great Toad Sage who governs the toads on Mount Myoboku.

Ruling over the many toads that live on Mount Myoboku, Fukasaku is one of two sage toads in line to succeed the Great Toad Sage. He trained Jiraiya, one of the Three Great Shinobi, in sage jutsu and toad powers. Coexisting with nature, he possesses immense chakra despite being over eight hundred years old. He has a grand demeanor, commanding respect from those under him who call him Boss. When he does step onto the battlefield, he unleashes jutsu with a skill that can only be described as worthy of the gods.

The Pupils of the Six Paths. A god created by the cycle of war.

Hunting jinchûriki and capturing Tailed Beasts, the Akatsuki work in secrecy. They are led by Pain. There is only one clue to unravel the mystery of his face—his eyes that possess the Rinnegan.

This god who declares that pain made him grow up has something for the world. Is it peace or destruction?

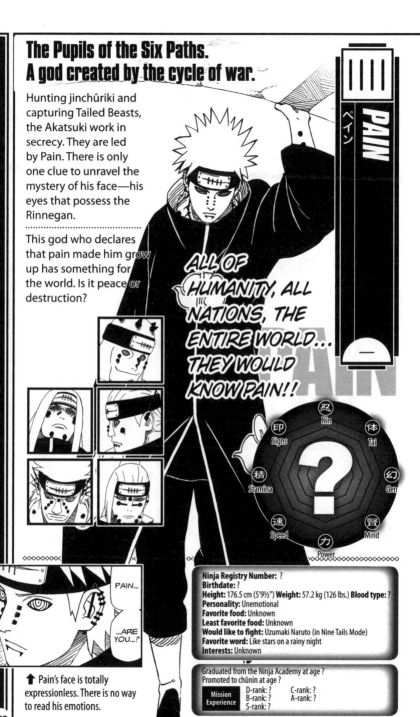

PAIN

ペイン

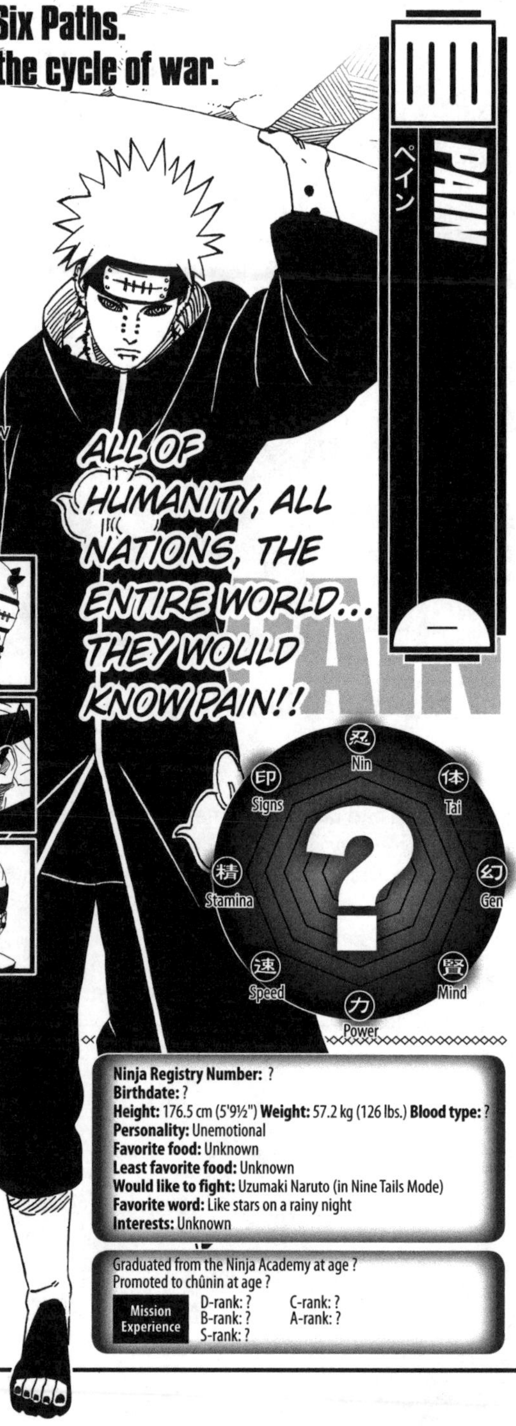
ALL OF HUMANITY, ALL NATIONS, THE ENTIRE WORLD... THEY WOULD KNOW PAIN!!
PAIN
忍
Nin
体
Tai
幻
Gen
賢
Mind
力
Power
速
Speed
精
Stamina
印
Signs
?

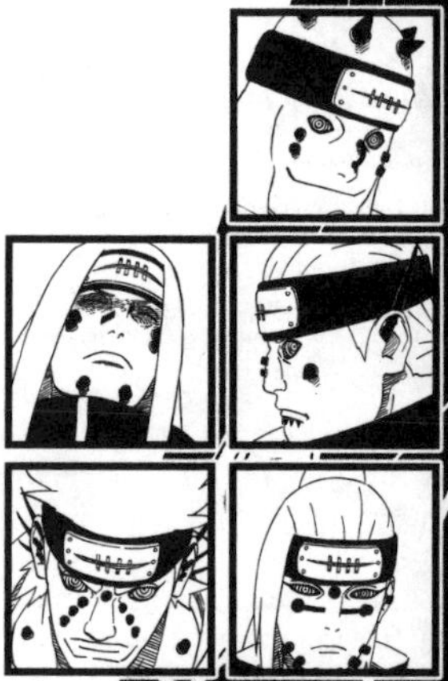

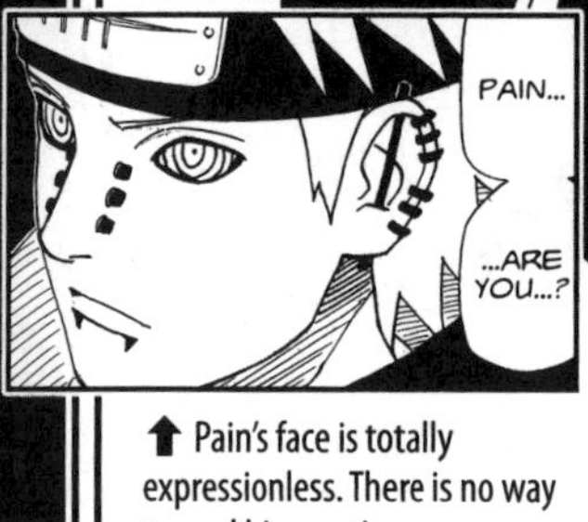
PAIN...
...ARE YOU...?

⬆ Pain's face is totally expressionless. There is no way to read his emotions.

Ninja Registry Number: ?
Birthdate: ?
Height: 176.5 cm (5'9½") **Weight:** 57.2 kg (126 lbs.) **Blood type:** ?
Personality: Unemotional
Favorite food: Unknown
Least favorite food: Unknown
Would like to fight: Uzumaki Naruto (in Nine Tails Mode)
Favorite word: Like stars on a rainy night
Interests: Unknown

Graduated from the Ninja Academy at age ?
Promoted to chûnin at age ?

Mission Experience		
	D-rank: ?	C-rank: ?
	B-rank: ?	A-rank: ?
	S-rank: ?	

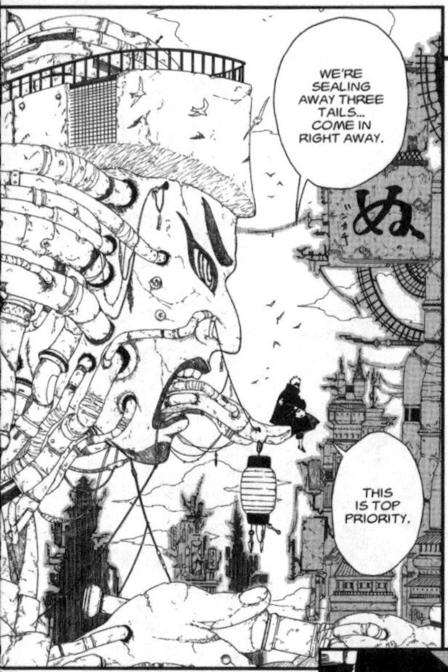
WE'RE SEALING AWAY THREE TAILS... COME IN RIGHT AWAY.
THIS IS TOP PRIORITY.

His sword represents the divine will for his bold, long-cherished hopes.

《The Akatsuki》

The shinobi of the Akatsuki each joined with his own expectations. These shinobi who have the skill and talent to battle a thousand men at once—why would they join an organization and obey Pain in capturing Tailed Beasts? The reason is Pain's charisma and his power that no one can deny. Pain boasts that he has never been defeated. And he makes plain his desire to reform the shinobi world. Furthermore, his words always reverberate in the hearts of those who hear him talk and fill them with exhilaration.

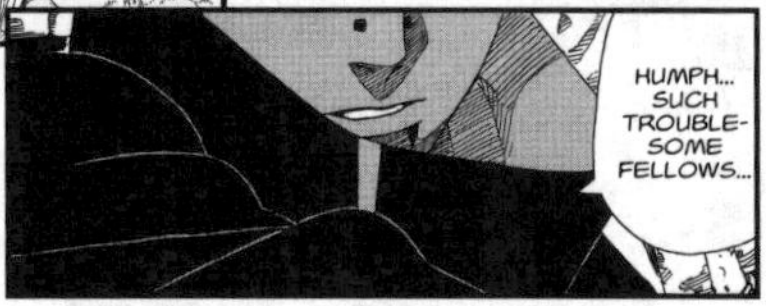
HUMPH... SUCH TROUBLE-SOME FELLOWS...

⬆ The leader's word is absolute. No one dares to question his orders, given with such majesty.

《Long-cherished desire》

The shinobi of the Akatsuki each joined with his own expectations. These shinobi who have the skill and talent to battle a thousand men at once—why would they join an organization and obey Pain in capturing Tailed Beasts? The reason is Pain's charisma and his power that no one can deny. Pain boasts that he has never been defeated. And he makes plain his desire to reform the shinobi world. Furthermore, his words always reverberate in the hearts of those who hear him talk and fill them with exhilaration.

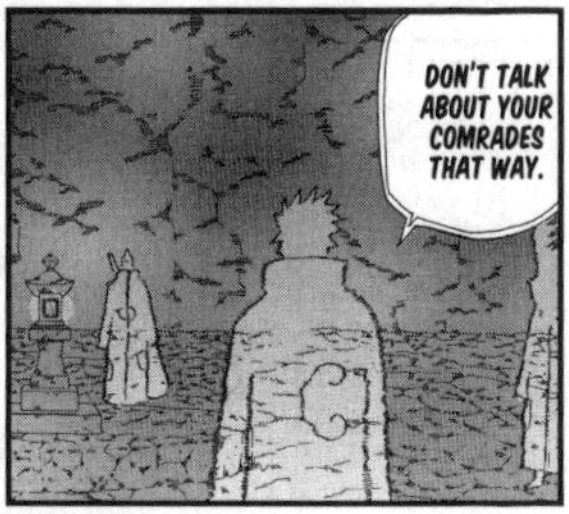
DON'T TALK ABOUT YOUR COMRADES THAT WAY.

⬆ Compatriots are given honor and respect. It is a law meant to keep the organization solid as a rock.

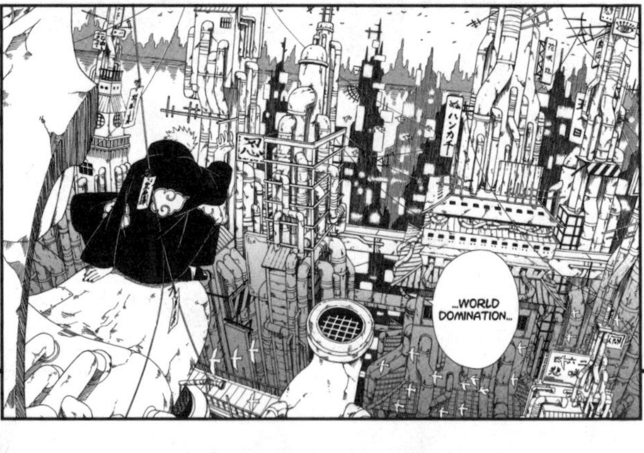
...WORLD DOMINATION...

This divine deed will paint even the blackest night a bloody red.

《The Original》

Several years earlier, there was internal conflict in Amegakure. It is not common knowledge that the reformists emerged victorious. The leader of the rebels was none other than Pain. The former leader, Hanzo, had prided himself on his iron-tight defenses.

It is rumored that Pain broke through single-handedly. But what shocked people even more was the sentence he passed. In addition to executing Hanzo, he sent the entire clan and its followers to their deaths.

Due to the veil of mystery that Pain shrouded himself in, the rebel shinobi began to revere him as a god.

PAIN

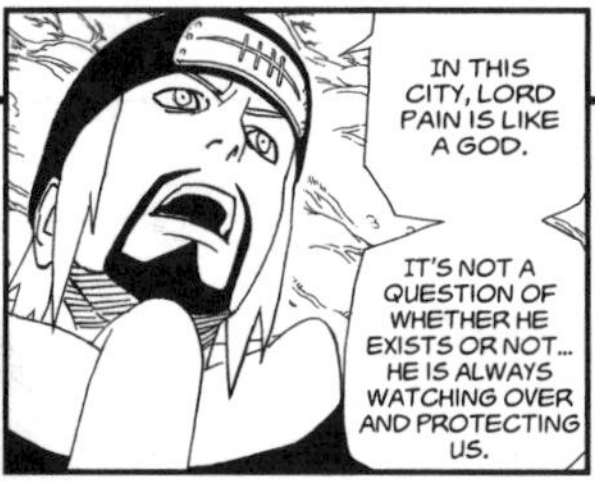
IN THIS CITY, LORD PAIN IS LIKE A GOD.
IT'S NOT A QUESTION OF WHETHER HE EXISTS OR NOT... HE IS ALWAYS WATCHING OVER AND PROTECTING US.

As a sign of loyalty to Pain, the rebel shinobi scratch out the mark on their headbands.

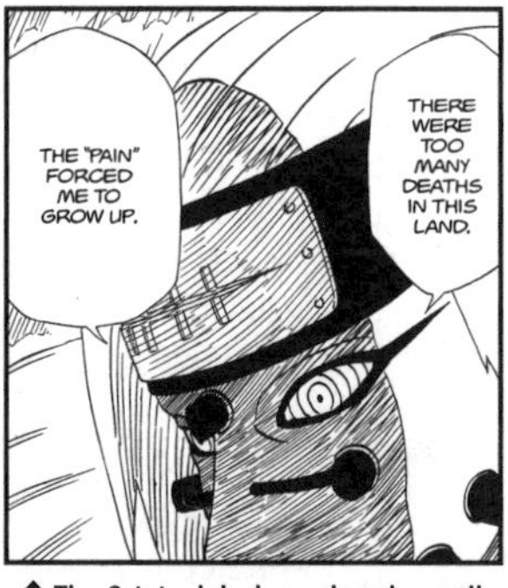
THERE WERE TOO MANY DEATHS IN THIS LAND.
THE "PAIN" FORCED ME TO GROW UP.

The Original declares that the endless cycle of war and death gave rise to him.

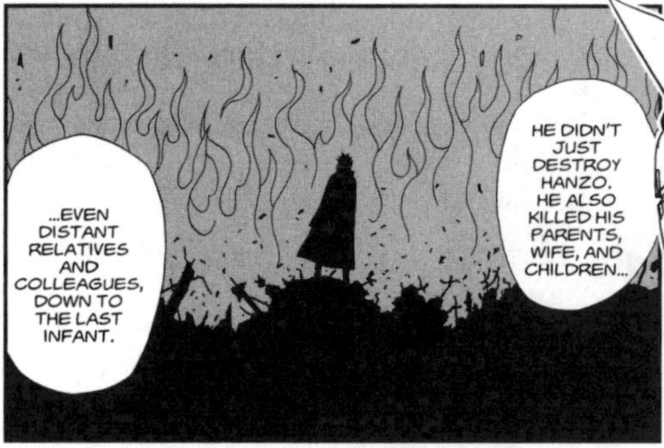
HE DIDN'T JUST DESTROY HANZO. HE ALSO KILLED HIS PARENTS, WIFE, AND CHILDREN...
...EVEN DISTANT RELATIVES AND COLLEAGUES, DOWN TO THE LAST INFANT.

During the age of civil wars, Amegakure was led by Hanzo. This highly touted clan of shinobi was exterminated by god's judgment.

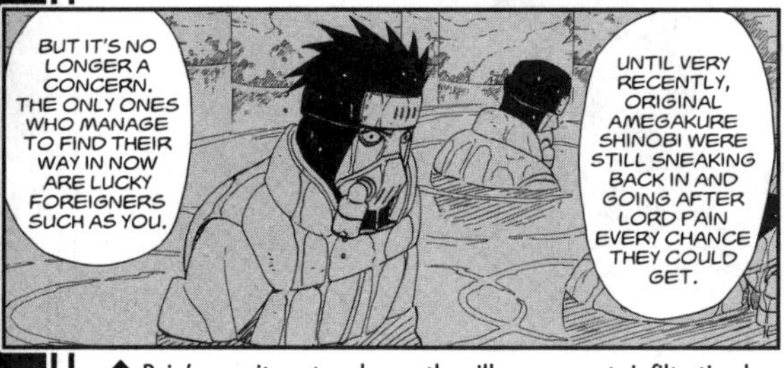
UNTIL VERY RECENTLY, ORIGINAL AMEGAKURE SHINOBI WERE STILL SNEAKING BACK IN AND GOING AFTER LORD PAIN EVERY CHANCE THEY COULD GET.
BUT IT'S NO LONGER A CONCERN. THE ONLY ONES WHO MANAGE TO FIND THEIR WAY IN NOW ARE LUCKY FOREIGNERS SUCH AS YOU.

Pain's security network over the village prevents infiltration by enemies.

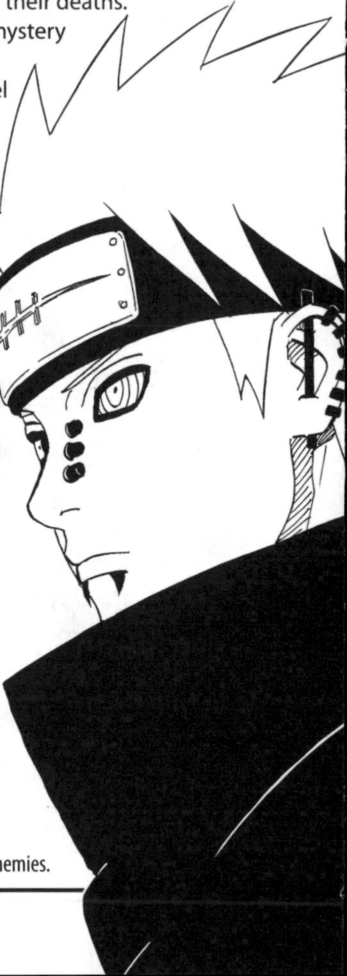

An invincible god and untold mysteries.

《Rinnegan》

It is said that the ocular jutsu Rinnegan is the wellspring of ninjutsu. It is not known whether this supreme ocular jutsu that Pain possesses has the full scope of power or just a portion of it. But without a doubt, the Rinnegan is an important clue to Pain's true identity. Long ago, one of the Three Great Shinobi, Jiraiya, had a pupil named Nagato who also possessed the Rinnegan. It cannot be said with certainty that Pain is this Nagato. But from Konan's presence at his side and through Pain's conversations with Jiraiya, one can conclude that there is a definite connection between Pain and Nagato.

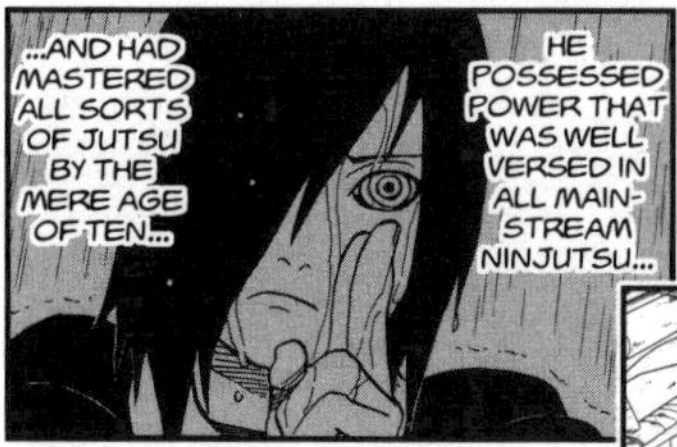
HE POSSESSED POWER THAT WAS WELL VERSED IN ALL MAIN-STREAM NINJUTSU...
...AND HAD MASTERED ALL SORTS OF JUTSU BY THE MERE AGE OF TEN...

⬆ It was said that Nagato could manipulate all the basic chakra natures. Is this the power of the Rinnegan?

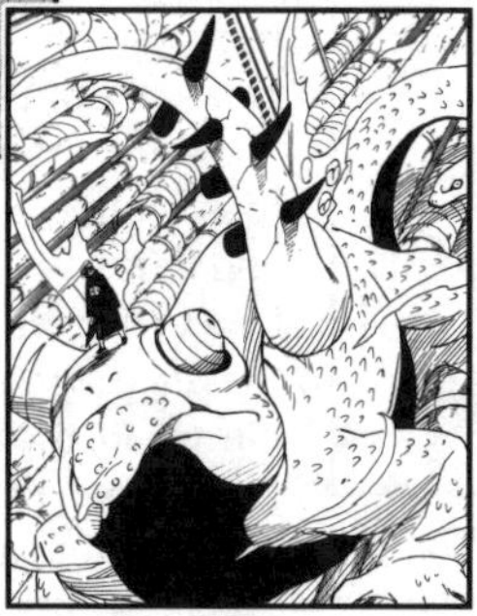

➡ The animals summoned by Pain. If one focuses on their eyes, one common trait becomes obvious. All of their eyes have ripple patterns.

《Pain of the Six Paths》

Pain summoned five shinobi, known as Pain of the Six Paths, who host the Rinnegan. They each possess frightening powers, such as rendering a jutsu ineffective and reconstructing bodies. They even share their fields of vision. It is unclear if this amazing power comes from the Rinnegan.

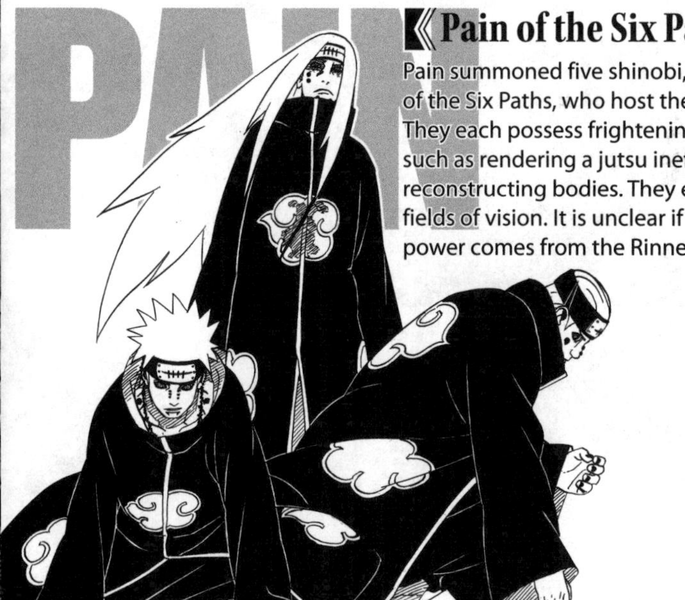
PAIN

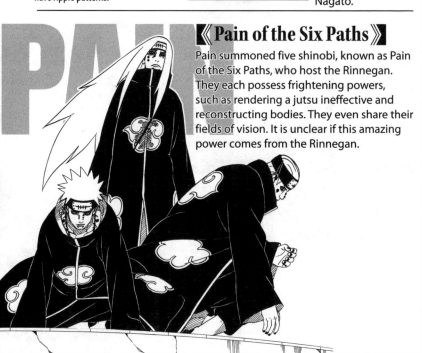

⬇ Jiraiya tries to identify the Six Paths. Among them is a shinobi rumored to be from the Fuma clan...

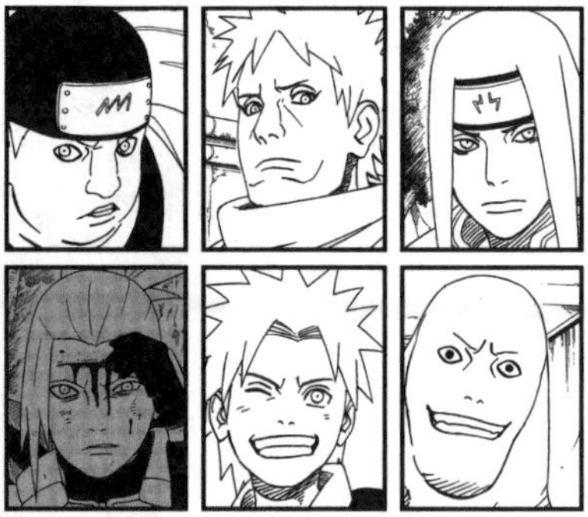

《Previous existence》

Jiraiya found one answer. All Six Paths looked like shinobi he had encountered before, including one of his pupils named Yahiko. How did they become the Six Paths? And how did they come to possess the Rinnegan?

《Weapon》

The Six Paths' weapon is a black belt-like blade. Even among the many ninja tools that exist today, there is nothing like this one, which pierces its victim, then disrupts the flow of chakra.

!!

➡ Pain's weapon stretches out from his sleeves. It pierces through Jiraiya. Feeling the cold look of Death, Jiraiya is filled with dread.

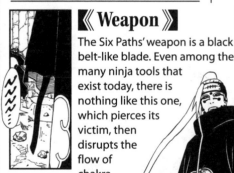

《Immortal》

Because he is immortal, he is unbeatable. One Path was dragged into the kekkei space and his activity was stopped. But it is not known whether he is dead.

YOU TAUGHT ME NOT TO LET MY GUARD DOWN...
...MASTER JIRAIYA.

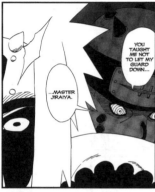

⬆ He's sure he put an end to them. But the Six Paths are resurrected and close in behind him.

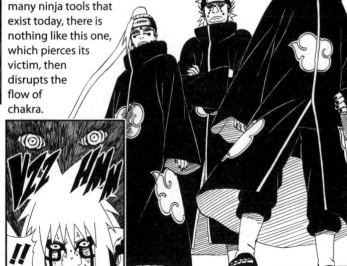

HOZUKI SUIGETSU

鬼灯水月

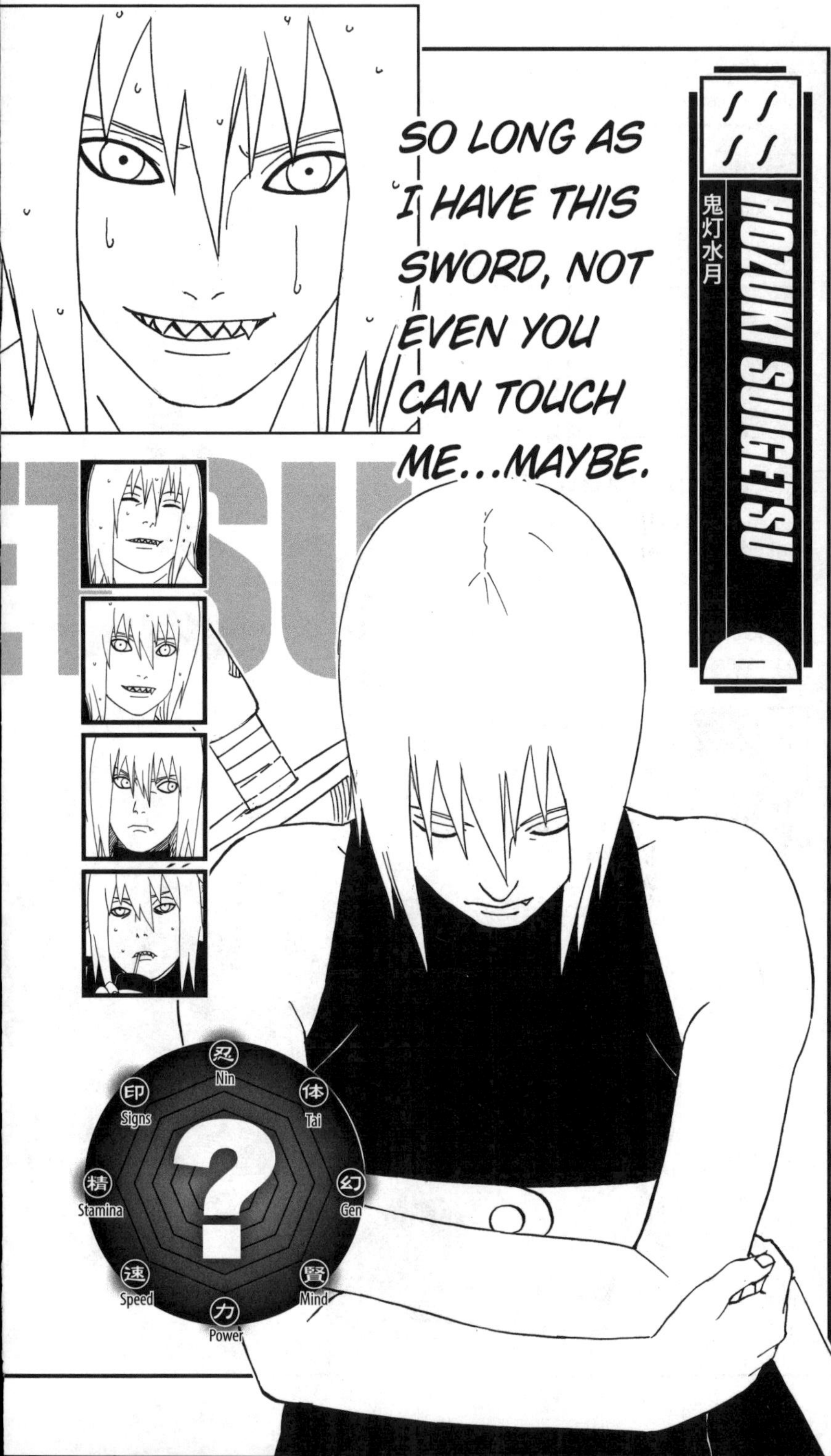
SO LONG AS I HAVE THIS SWORD, NOT EVEN YOU CAN TOUCH ME...MAYBE.
忍 Nin
体 Tai
幻 Gen
賢 Mind
力 Power
速 Speed
精 Stamina
印 Signs
?

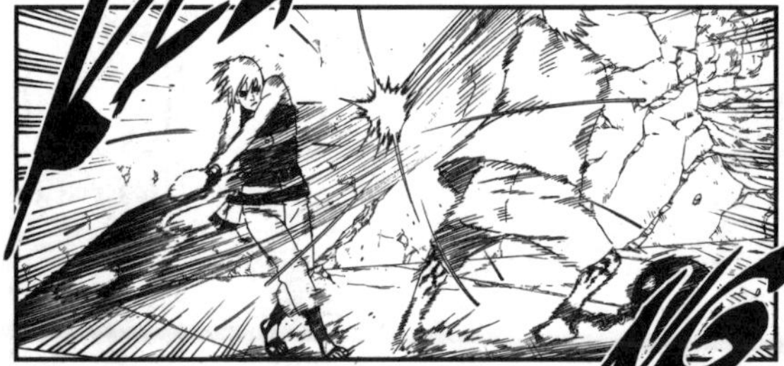

The heartless and carefree wonderboy who would wield seven swords.

⬆ Suigetsu swings in a bout with Jugo. It ends up in a draw.

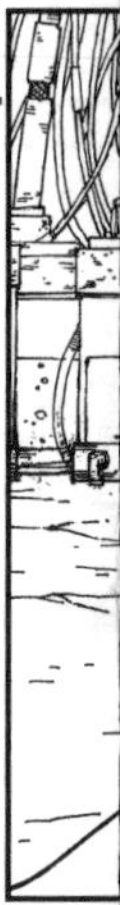

Suigetsu was born in Kirigakure, the village so dreaded for its ritual that it was nicknamed the Village of Bloody Mist. Sixteen years earlier, a boy prodigy was born there. He was the younger of the Hoshigaki brothers. Born with his family's peculiar ability and having a gruesome brother like Mangetsu, he was reputed to be the "Second Coming of the Demon." Together with his brother, Suigetsu dreams of inheriting a shinobi sword, and they set out on cruel missions day in and day out.

After his brother's death, Suigetsu's ambition becomes to collect all the swords. Not even the humiliation of being captured by Orochimaru will stop him.

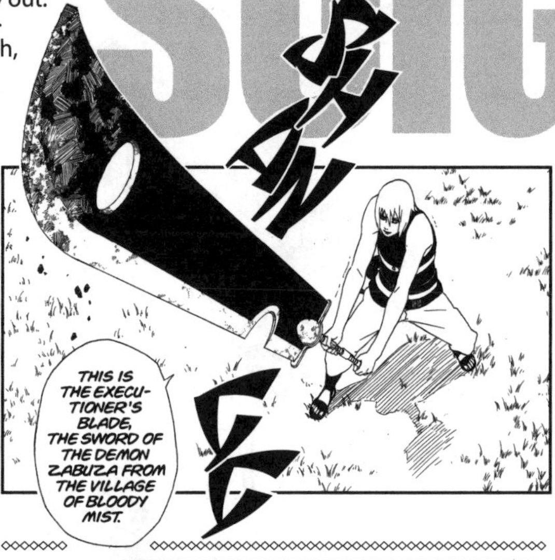
THIS IS THE EXECUTIONER'S BLADE, THE SWORD OF THE DEMON ZABUZA FROM THE VILLAGE OF BLOODY MIST.

➡ A new legend is now taking root—one that tells of the existence of the demon and the wonderboy.

⬇ Suigetsu does not like being affiliated with anyone. His intrepid attitude shows how confident he is.

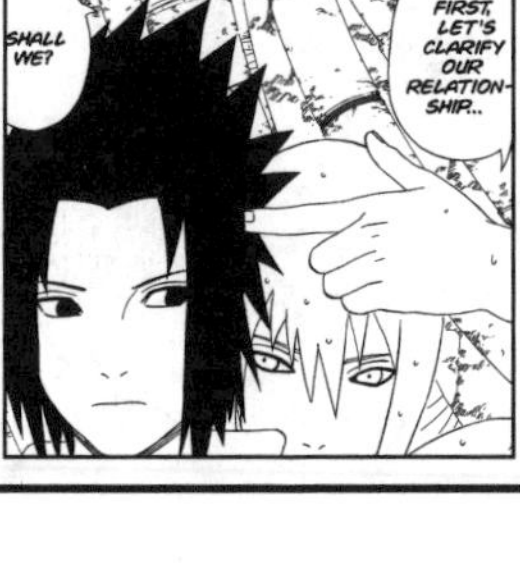
FIRST, LET'S CLARIFY OUR RELATIONSHIP...
SHALL WE?

Ninja Registry Number: —
Birthdate: February 18 (16 years old; Aquarius)
Height: 177.4 cm (5'10") **Weight:** 57.0 kg (126 lbs.) **Blood type:** B
Personality: Combative
Favorite food: Yogurt, gelatin (especially yogurt drinks)
Least favorite food: Dried cuttlefish
Would like to fight: Seven Swordsmen of the Mist
Favorite word: Juniors over seniors
Interests: Sharpening and polishing his beloved sword

Graduated from the Ninja Academy at age ?
Promoted to chûnin at age ?

Mission Experience		
	D-rank: 2	C-rank: 33
	B-rank: 40	A-rank: 13
	S-rank: 4	

FIRST HOKAGE • SENJU HASHIRAMA

火影（初代・千手柱間）

Hokage

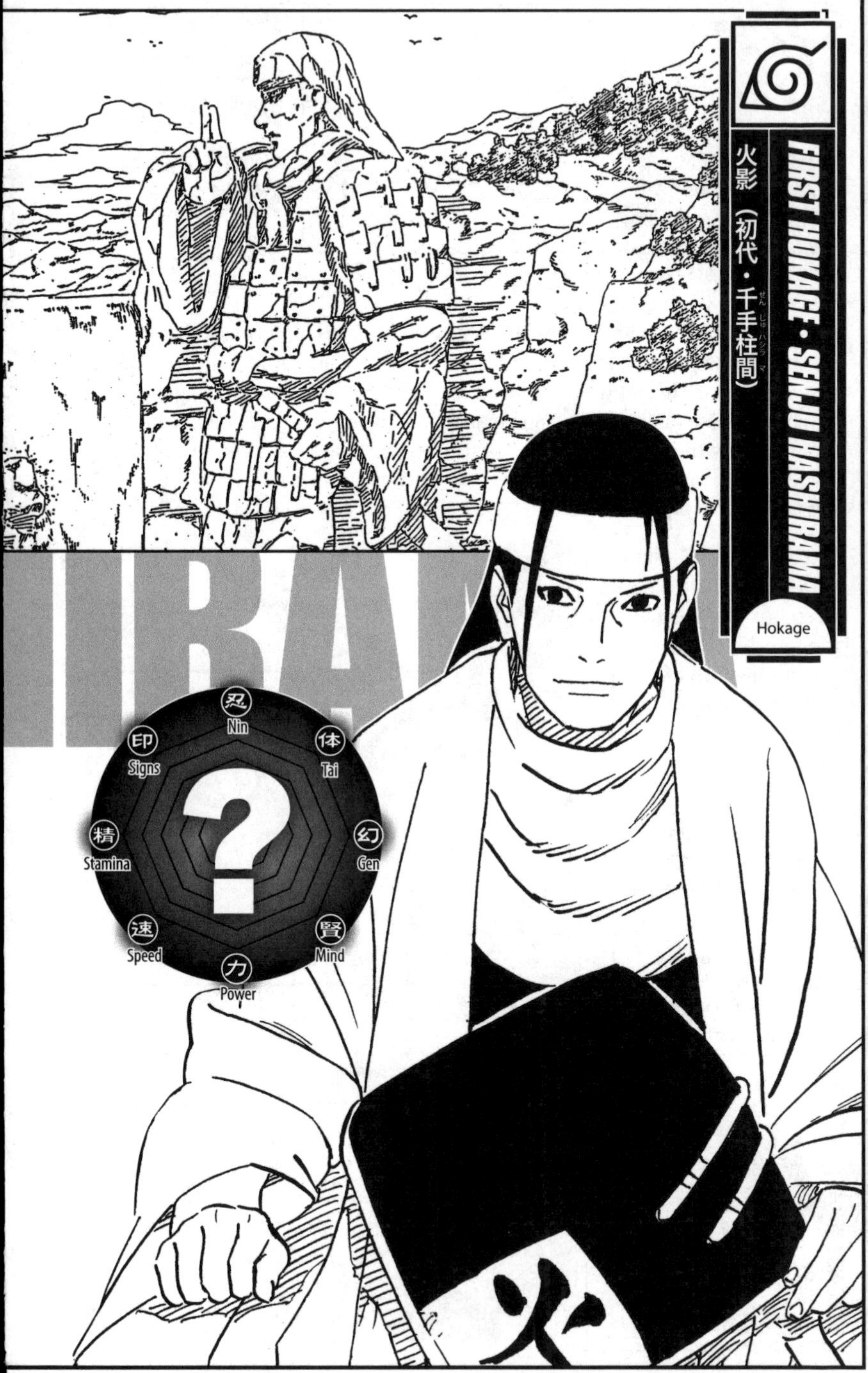
忍
Nin
体
Tai
幻
Gen
賢
Mind
力
Power
速
Speed
精
Stamina
印
Signs
?

A magnificent shinobi, lighting the way for peace on earth.

During the great age of shinobi war, one clan was known far and wide for their unrivaled strength. They were called the Mori no Senju clan, which means "the thousand hands of the forest." Their leader was Senju Hashirama. A master of Wood Style ninjutsu and highly gifted as a shinobi, he was able to unify his fractured and diverse people. Senju Hashirama was truly a hero of the age.

Once Hashirama united with long-time adversaries the Uchiha clan, he established Konohagakure in the Land of Fire. It was a hidden village system unlike any that had been before and laid the foundation for the current Five Great Shinobi Nations.

FOR OUR CLAN WAS PRETTY MUCH THE ONLY ONE WHO COULD TAKE THEM ON.
IF A NATION HIRED SENJU, THEIR OPPONENT WOULD HIRE UCHIHA... WE ENDED UP BEING LIKE RIVALS.

⬅ His skill in manipulating both Wood Style ninjutsu and Tailed Beasts made Hashirama without peer in the shinobi world.

SENJU "WOOD STYLE" HASHIRAMA, THE FUTURE FIRST HOKAGE.
THE SHINOBI WHO STOOD AT THE TOP OF THE NINJA WORLD AND THE PERSON I RESPECTED MOST.

➡ It was inevitable that someone like Hashirama, possessing the powerful charisma and ability to grasp people's hearts would build an enormous village such as Konoha.

Ninja Registry Number: —
Birthdate: October 23 (Age at death unknown; Libra)
Height: 185.1 cm (6'1") **Weight:** 74.0 kg (163 lbs.) **Blood type:** ?
Personality: Gentle, thoughtful
Favorite food: Mushroom porridge
Least favorite food: None
Would like to fight: Uchiha Madara
Favorite word: Fertility of the earth, perfect beauty
Interests: Bonsai, sculpture

⬅ On Hokage Rock in Konoha, one can see the succession of those who have carried on Hashirama's intentions. Etched into the hard rock, they signify a Will of Fire that will never be extinguished.

SECOND HOKAGE · TOBIRAMA

火影（二代目・千手扉間）

Hokage

A bold leader–assuring a prosperous future for the village.

To nurture the seedling named Konoha that his brother planted to lush green maturity was the mission of the next Hokage, Tobirama. A security force to maintain order, an academy to train the next generation, a testing system for chûnin-level shinobi; Tobirama put these systems in place one after the other. His only desire was the stability and peace of Konohagakure. The feelings the Senju brothers had for their village are passed down in Konoha to this day as the Will of Fire.

I COULDN'T HELP FEARING THAT THE UCHIHA CLAN WOULD ONE DAY...
...COME TO BE OP-PRESSED BY THE SENJU CLAN.

⬅ Due to Tobirama's efforts, the Senju clan gained influence in the village.

Ninja Registry Number: —
Birthdate: February 19 (Age at death unknown; Pisces)
Height: 182.3 cm (6'0") **Weight:** 70.5 kg (155 lbs.) **Blood type:** ?
Personality: Brave, passionate
Favorite word: Heart · technique · body

THIRD HOKAGE · HIRUZEN

火影（三代目・猿飛ヒルゼン）

Hokage

A gentle father who enveloped Konoha with his love.

In the history of Konoha, no Hokage is as beloved by the people as Hiruzen. Not only because of his abilities in ninjutsu, which earned him the nickname "Professor," but for his almost paternal love for the village. This was so even toward the Uchiha clan, which planned the revolt…

MAYBE SOMEDAY YOU'LL MEET THEM AGAIN.

I'VE NEVER SEEN ONE OF THESE BEFORE
THEY'RE EXTREMELY RARE. NOT TOO MANY GET THE OPPORTUNITY.
HEH... ME NEITHER.

⬆ The whole of the village were his children. Orochimaru was no exception.

Ninja Registry Number: 000261
Birthdate: February 8 (Age at death 69; Aquarius)
Height: 163.1 cm (5'4") **Weight:** 50.6 kg (112 lbs.) **Blood type:** A
Personality: Gentle, tolerant, loving
Favorite food: Hijiki, sardine meatballs

FOURTH HOKAGE • MINATO

火影（四代目・波風ミナト）

Hokage

As a father and a leader, he entrusts the future of the shinobi to his child.

Minato studied under Jiraiya and educated Kakashi. He is a shinobi of uncommon talent and assumed the role of Hokage at a young age. With the talent to invent many jutsu in his own style, his heart full of kindness and strong conviction, Minato's existence shone brightly as if mirroring the future of the village.
That is, until Nine Tails attacked the village. Minato died after entrusting the power of the Nine-Tailed Beast to Naruto, his son with Uzumaki Kushina. What did he see in the eyes of his child…?

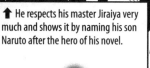

THE MAIN CHARACTER OF THIS BOOK... I THOUGHT HIS DETERMINATION TO NEVER GIVE UP WAS REALLY COOL...

⬇ What is the real reason Minato sealed Nine Tails' chakra in his son?

MINATO MUST HAVE KNOWN SOMETHING IMPORTANT...
...SO IF HE BEQUEATHED NINE TAILS' POWER TO HIS SON BASED ON THAT KNOWLEDGE...

⬆ He respects his master Jiraiya very much and shows it by naming his son Naruto after the hero of his novel.

忍
Nin
体
Tai
幻
Gen
賢
Mind
力
Power
速
Speed
精
Stamina
印
Signs
?

I'D LIKE YOUR PERMISSION TO NAME MY SON AFTER HIM.

Ninja Registry Number: ?
Birthdate: January 25 (Age at death unknown; Aquarius)
Height: 179.2 cm (5'10½") **Weight:** 66.1 kg (146 lbs.) **Blood type:** B
Personality: Generous, gentle
Favorite food: Kushina's home cooking
Least favorite food: None
Would like to fight: Jiraiya
Favorite word: The shadow of the flame lights up the village.
Interests: Reading (especially fond of Jiraiya's novels)

Graduated from the Ninja Academy at age 10
Promoted to chûnin at age ?

Mission Experience		
	D-rank: 122	C-rank: 147
	B-rank: 216	A-rank: 323
	S-rank: 39	

FIFTH HOKAGE · TSUNADE

火影（五代目・綱手(ツナデ)）

Hokage

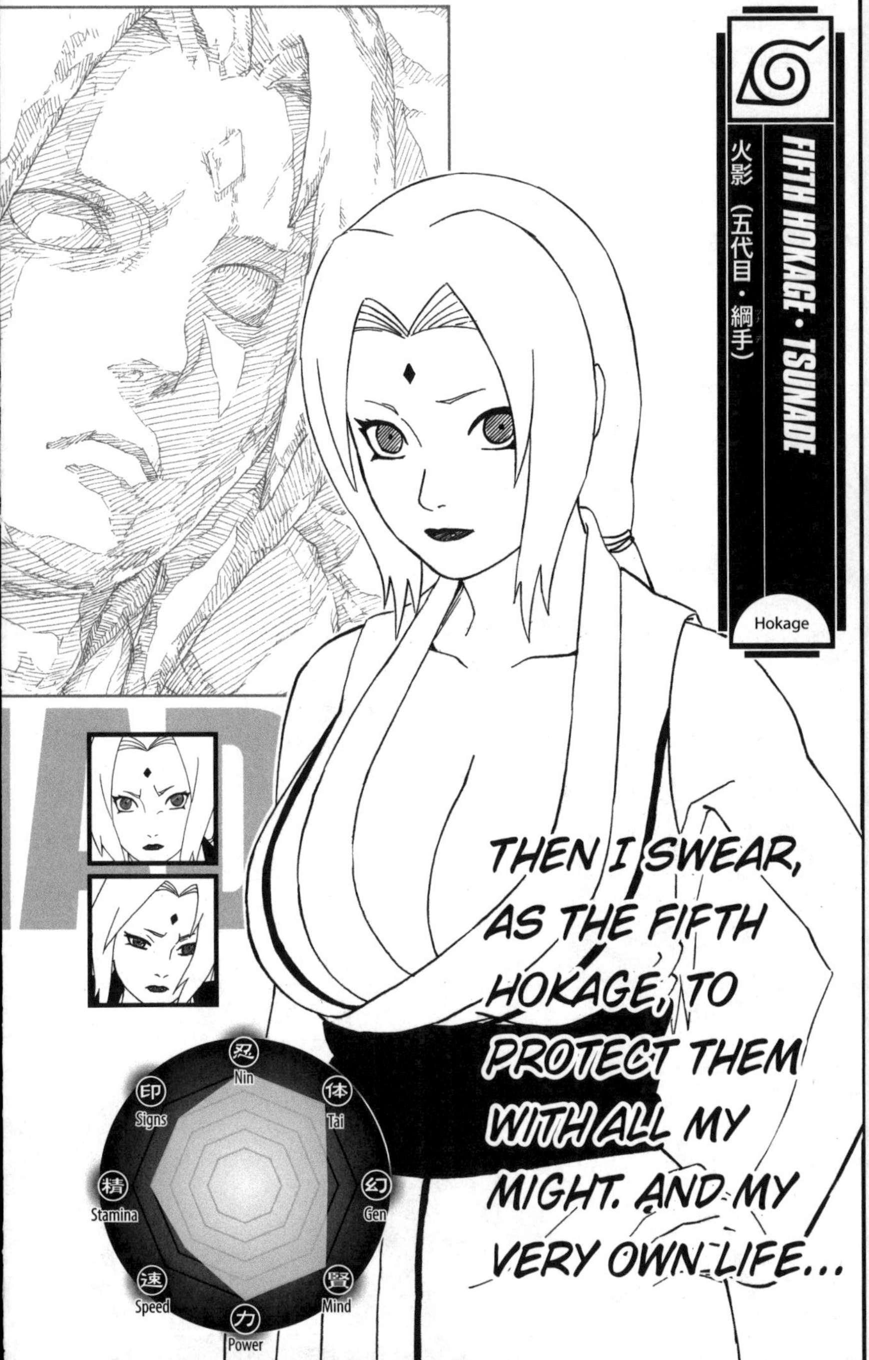
忍
Nin
体
Tai
幻
Gen
賢
Mind
力
Power
速
Speed
精
Stamina
印
Signs
THEN I SWEAR, AS THE FIFTH HOKAGE, TO PROTECT THEM WITH ALL MY MIGHT. AND MY VERY OWN LIFE...

The first woman to inherit the Will of Fire protects Konoha with unwavering devotion.

The first female Hokage in Konohagakure, Tsunade is the granddaughter of the First Hokage and is known as one of the Three Great Shinobi, along with Orochimaru and Jiraiya. She was much anticipated as the Fifth Hokage and immediately showed her talent for leadership. She put her efforts toward training skilled medical ninja and was very successful. When she discovered the secret plot of the Akatsuki, she took quick action to protect the village. But as a result, she lost long- serving shinobi such as Asuma and Jiraiya. Tsunade keeps alive the hopes of all who have been lost and continues to stoke the flames of the Will of Fire.

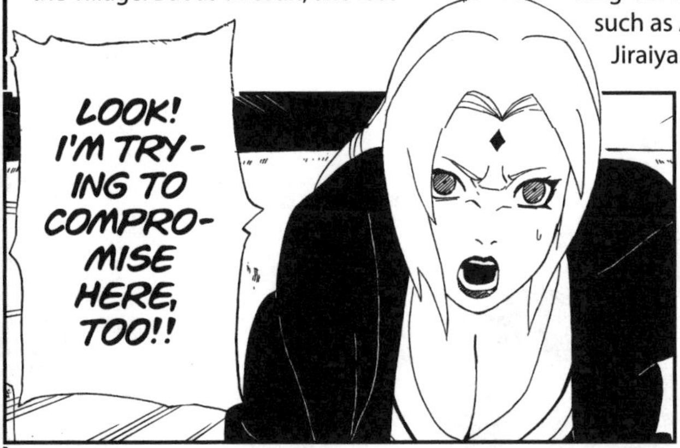
LOOK! I'M TRYING TO COMPROMISE HERE, TOO!!

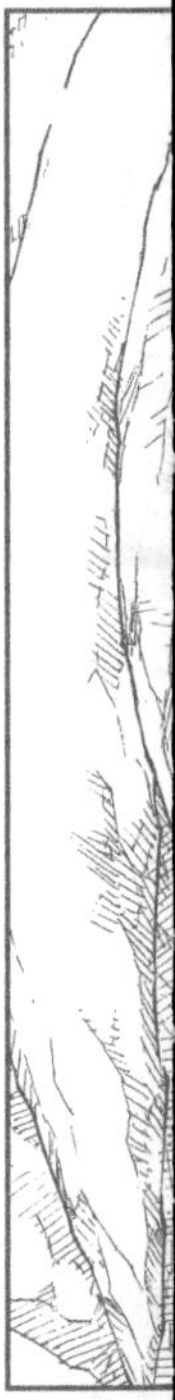

⬆ Such temper even toward an elder!! Once she is convinced, she never wavers.

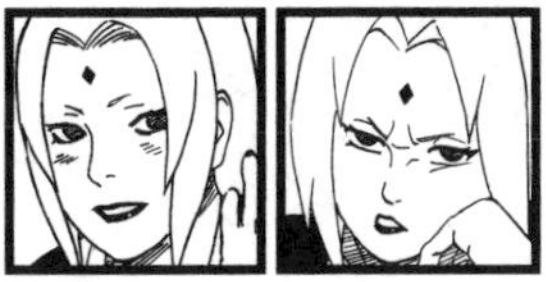

➡ Tsunade's fervent wish. . . "I do not want to lose any more people dear to me."

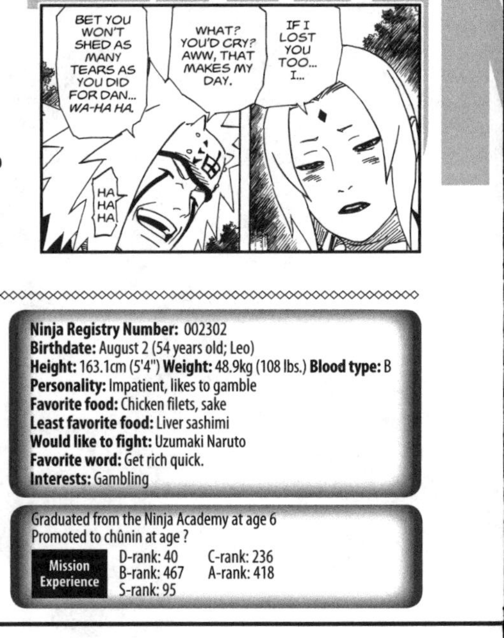
IF I LOST YOU TOO... I...
WHAT? YOU'D CRY? AWW, THAT MAKES MY DAY.
BET YOU WON'T SHED AS MANY TEARS AS YOU DID FOR DAN... WA-HA HA.
HA HA HA

⬇ The larger-than-life persona hasn't changed since she became a Hokage. If anything, it's become stronger. . . ?!

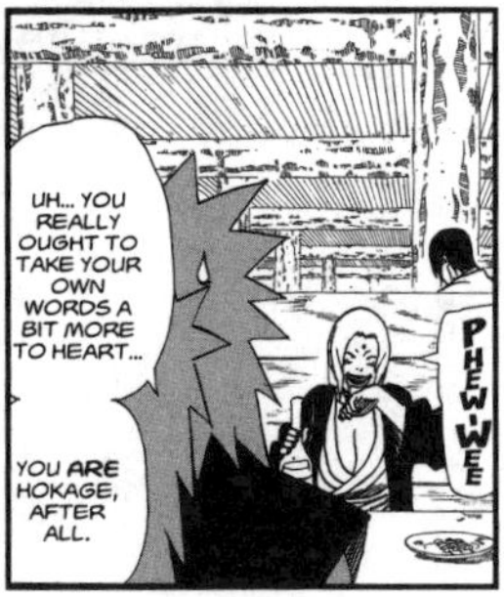
PHEW-WEE
UH... YOU REALLY OUGHT TO TAKE YOUR OWN WORDS A BIT MORE TO HEART...
YOU ARE HOKAGE, AFTER ALL.

Ninja Registry Number: 002302
Birthdate: August 2 (54 years old; Leo)
Height: 163.1cm (5'4") **Weight:** 48.9kg (108 lbs.) **Blood type:** B
Personality: Impatient, likes to gamble
Favorite food: Chicken filets, sake
Least favorite food: Liver sashimi
Would like to fight: Uzumaki Naruto
Favorite word: Get rich quick.
Interests: Gambling

Graduated from the Ninja Academy at age 6
Promoted to chûnin at age ?

Mission Experience		
	D-rank: 40	C-rank: 236
	B-rank: 467	A-rank: 418
	S-rank: 95	

HOSHIGAKI KISAME

干柿鬼鮫

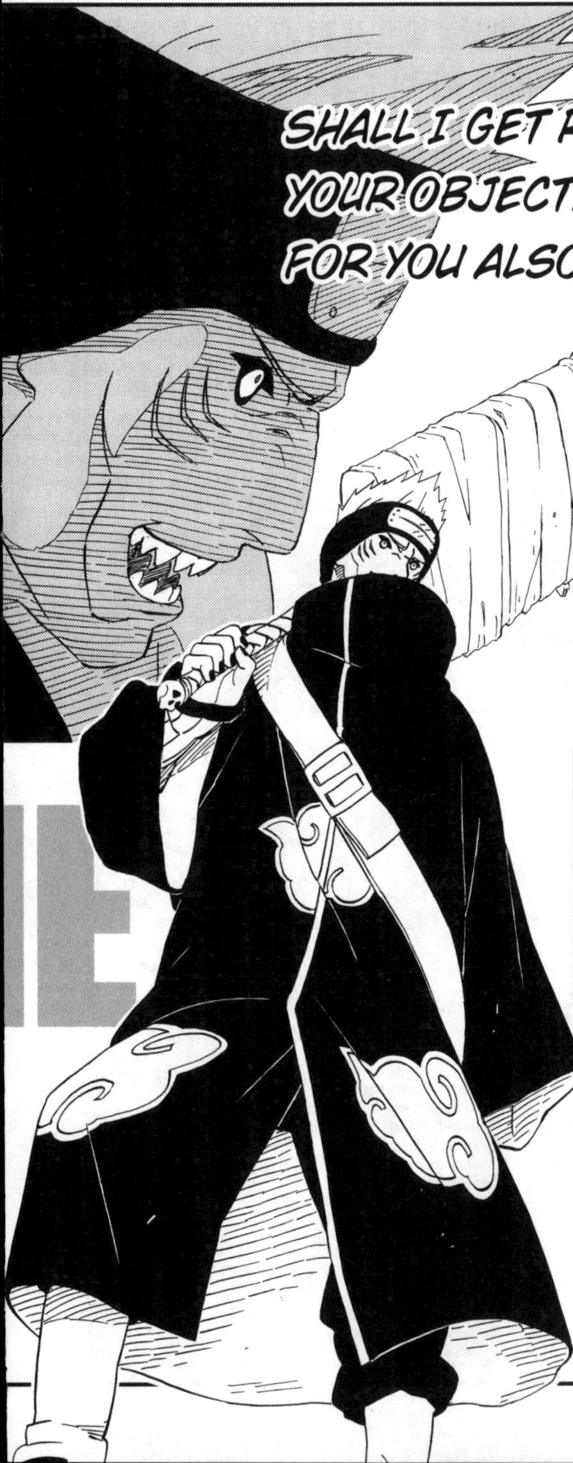
SHALL I GET RID OF
YOUR OBJECTIVE
FOR YOU ALSO?

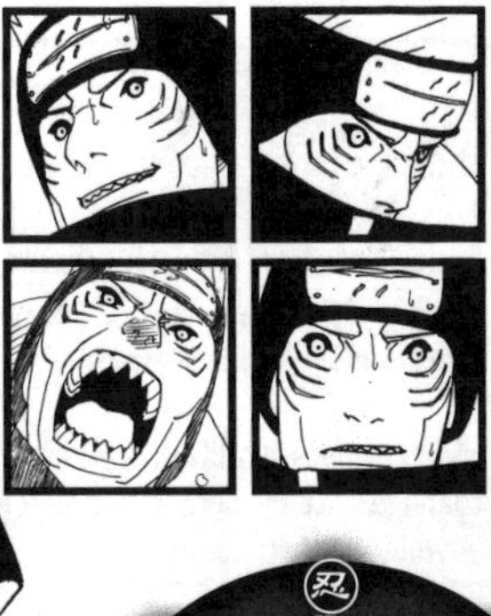

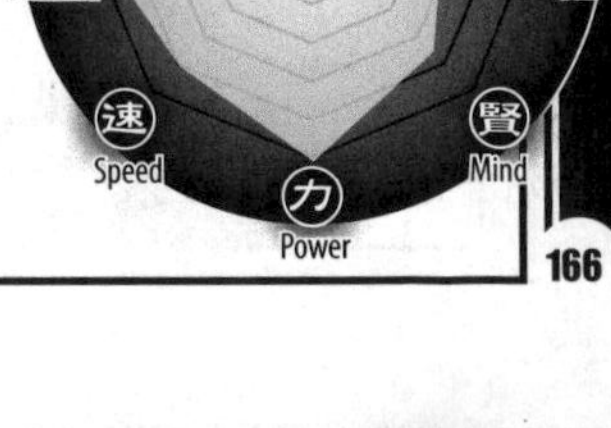
忍
Nin
体
Tai
幻
Gen
賢
Mind
力
Power
速
Speed
精
Stamina
印
Signs

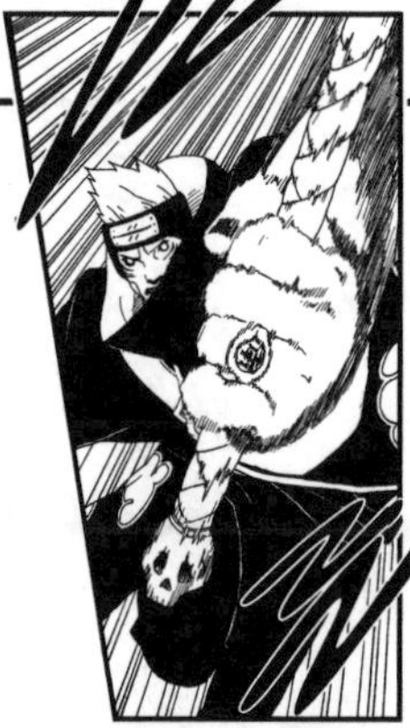

An enigma who hides the truth behind his blank eyes.

Ambition, revenge, belief—the reasons for joining the Akatsuki are varied, but Kisame's motives are the hardest to read. He usually never discusses his beliefs or goes against the Akatsuki. One can catch glimpses of his nature in the violence during fighting and the occasional conversation. Why does Kisame serve the Akatsuki? Even that answer is hidden by the darkness of his eyes.

⬅ The long sword Samehada recognizes only Kisame as its master.

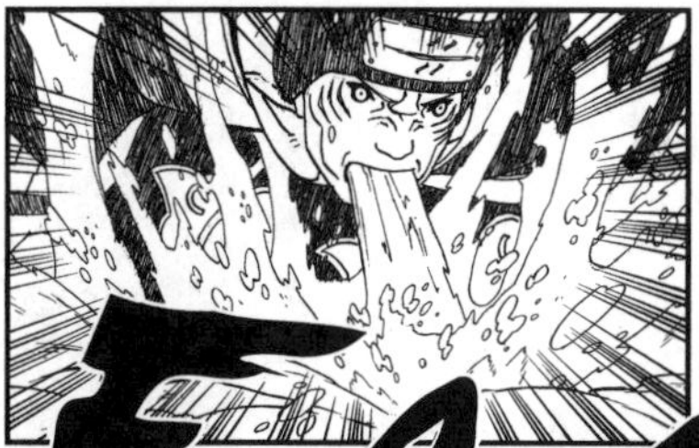

⬅ A native of Kirigakure, his specialty is Water Style ninjutsu.

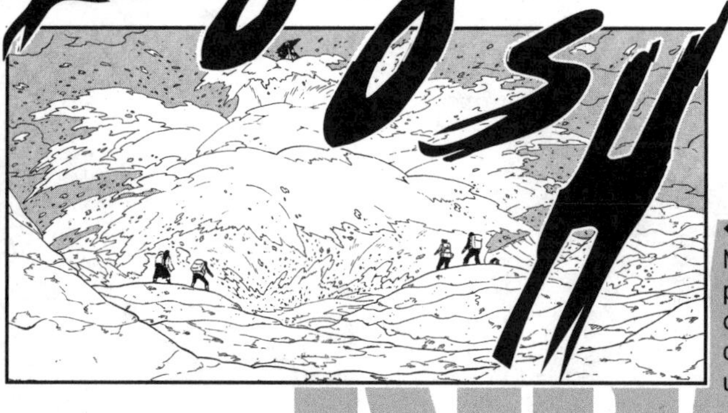
FOOSH

⬅ As with Naruto, Kisame possesses a huge chakra! The scale of his ninjutsu is unreal!!

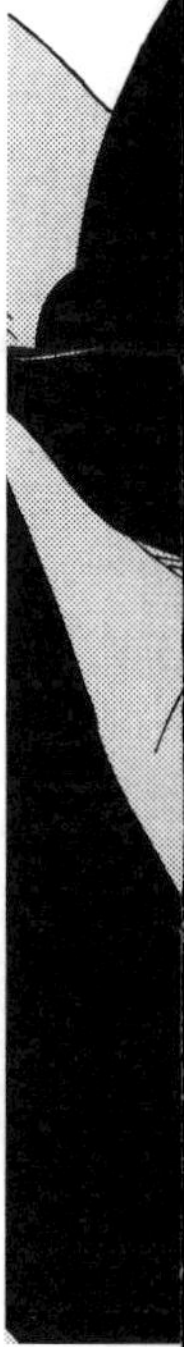

⬇ His usual delivery is extremely polite. He is submissive toward Itachi and is sometimes even considerate. . .

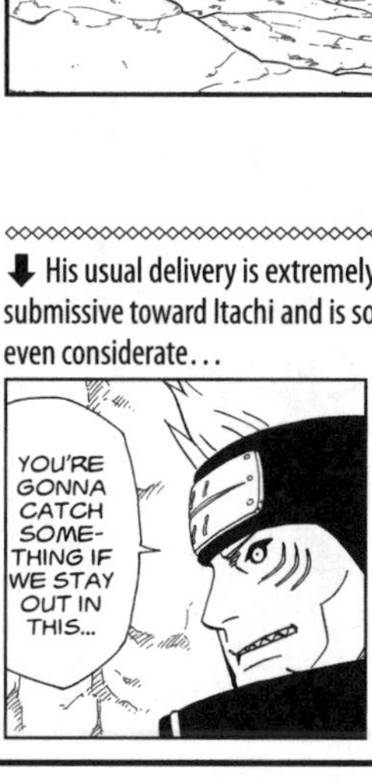
YOU'RE GONNA CATCH SOME-THING IF WE STAY OUT IN THIS...

Ninja Registry Number: —
Birthdate: March 18 (32 years old; Pisces)
Height: 195.0 cm (6'4½") **Weight:** 83.1 kg (183 lbs.) **Blood type:** AB
Personality: Cruel, loves to fight
Favorite food: Shrimp, crab
Least favorite food: Shark's fin
Would like to fight: Anyone
Favorite word: Survival of the fittest
Interests: Grooming sharkskin

Graduated from the Ninja Academy at age 10
Promoted to chûnin at age ?

Mission Experience		
	D-rank: 3	C-rank: 68
	B-rank: 154	A-rank: 78
	S-rank: 29	

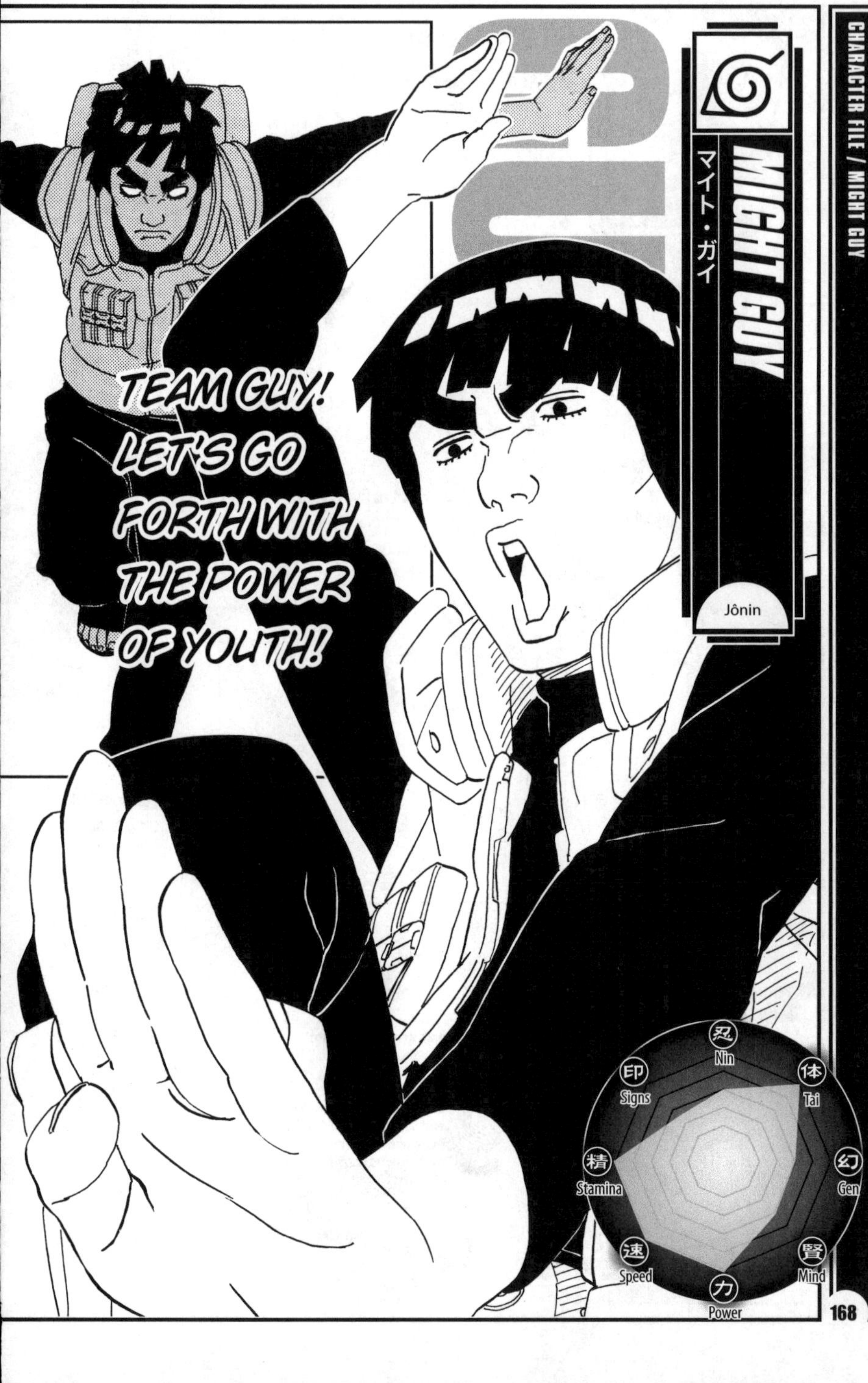
MIGHT GUY
マイト・ガイ
Jônin
TEAM GUY! LET'S GO FORTH WITH THE POWER OF YOUTH!
忍 Nin
体 Tai
幻 Gen
賢 Mind
力 Power
速 Speed
精 Stamina
印 Signs

Hot-blooded with fists as fast as lightning!!

He has a steel-like body honed through training, taijutsu polished to shatter rock… But these are not what support Guy's strength. It's his straightforward nature, devotion to study and aspiration to achieve greater goals. These are what allow him to be more than equal to anyone in the Akatsuki. Guy gives his all to becoming more excellent, he is capable of staking his life on it!! Regardless of what he thinks, Guy's nindo has taken root in his three disciples. Increasing one's fighting skills, vastly improving teamwork and greater combat skills at the platoon level—you can see the hot-blooded, youthful style of instruction that Guy advocates in full bloom!!

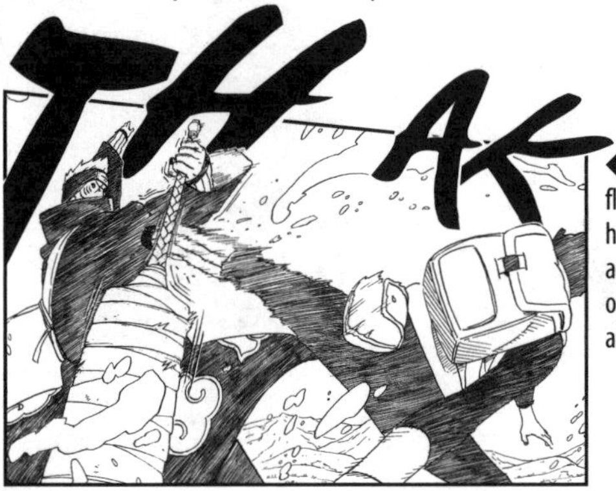
THAK

⬅ His quick-as-a-flash reflexes mean he can go unarmed against an opponent who is armed!!

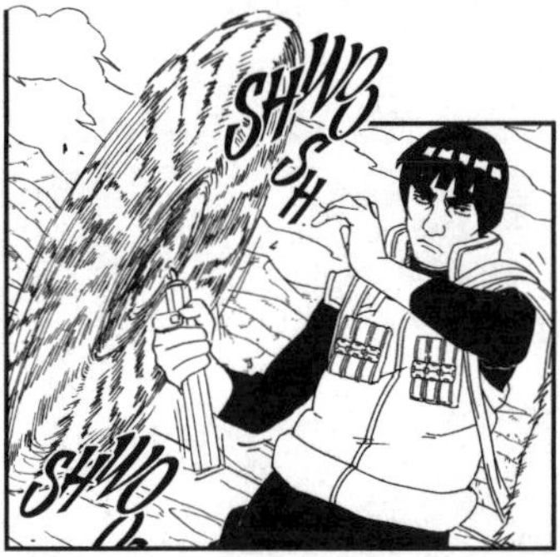

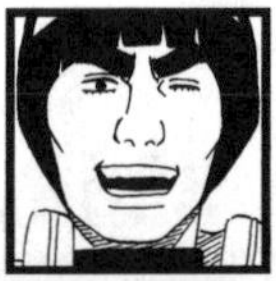

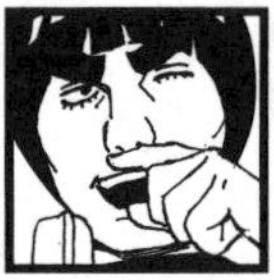

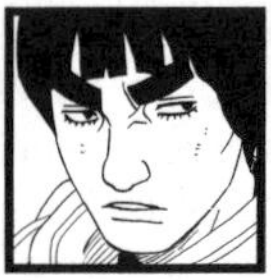

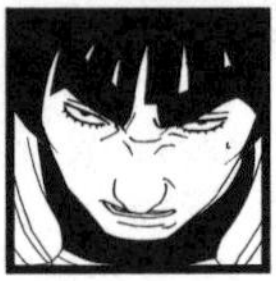

⬅ He is skilled in the use of many physical weapons. However he prefers weapons without blades.

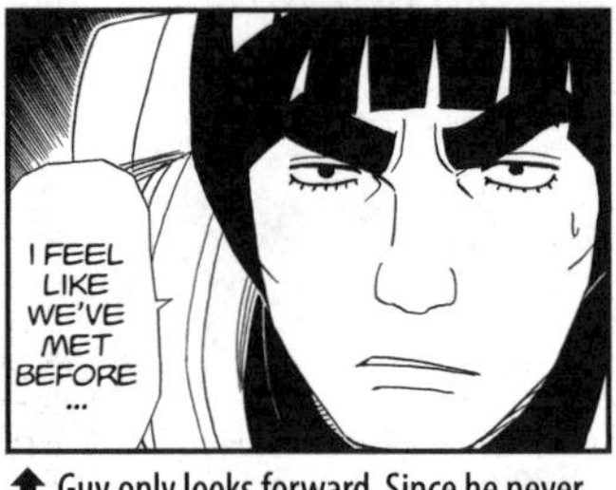
I FEEL LIKE WE'VE MET BEFORE ...

⬆ Guy only looks forward. Since he never looks back, he has a poor memory?

Ninja Registry Number: 010252
Birthdate: January 1 (30 years old; Aries)
Height: 184.0 cm (6'0½") **Weight:** 76.0 kg (167 lbs.) **Blood type:** B
Personality: Excitable, quick to tears
Favorite food: Extremely spicy curry, curry udon
Least favorite food: Nothing!
Would like to fight: Hatake Kakashi!
Favorite word: Jump out, youth!!
Interests: Side jump repetitions, hitting pads

Graduated from the Ninja Academy at age 7
Promoted to chûnin at age 11

Mission Experience		
	D-rank: 86	C-rank: 270
	B-rank: 210	A-rank: 199
	S-rank: 23	

MORINO IBIKI

森乃イビキ

Special Jônin

Knows unparalleled hardship, Konohagakure's righthand man.

An expert at questioning prisoners and suspicious characters and extracting information. From threats as a psychological weapon to physical torture, he has much varied expertise in all areas. He uses them very effectively. His scarred physical appearance belies the fact that he is an intellectual and honest man.

I WILL GET YOU TO CONFESS

AND WHEN YOU GET THERE, GO STRAIGHT TO IBIKI.
HE ALREADY KNOWS YOU'RE COMING.
RIBBIT!

⬆ One of the most experienced and skilled among the Leaf, Jiraiya and many other shinobi rely on him.

Ninja Registry Number: 010913
Birthdate: March 20 (31 years old - Pisces)
Height: 193.5 cm (6'4") **Weight:** 88.0 kg (194 lbs.) **Blood type:** A
Personality: Very patient, sadist
Favorite word: Truth

Collection ... Number 10

Konoha

SPECIALIST TEAMS
BEHIND THE SCENES!

At Konohagakure, in addition to the shinobi who carry out their duties, there are many who remain in the village in specialized roles. In areas such as medicine, interrogation, code deciphering, specialists work at a high level to support the missions.

⬆ The Cipher Corps quickly deciphers encoded secret messages.

CLAMP!!
THAT'S SUNAGAKURE'S HAWK, TAKAMARU!

⬆ The communications team manages all forms of communication from other villages and shinobi on duty.

⬆ The military police that keep the peace in the village are entrusted to the Uchiha clan.

YAKUSHI KABUTO

薬師カブト

Serving evil, entranced by a snake, he is a manipulating shadow.

Growing up without a country, without parents, as a spy… for Kabuto, the concept of good and evil has no meaning. Work for a power or struggle against power. He can only get a sense of himself through confronting overwhelming power. His path is tainted with the smell of darkness and death.

…TO BECOME A BETTER, STRONGER YAKUSHI KABUTO.

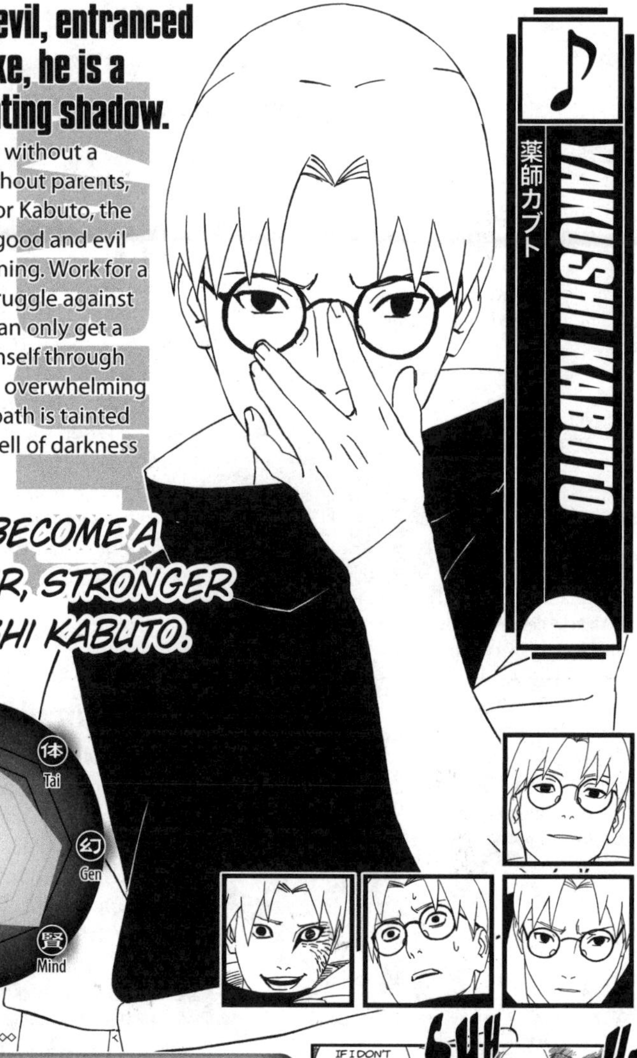

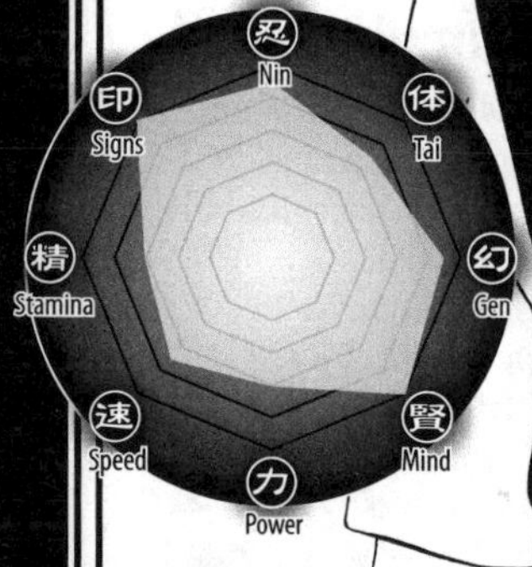
忍
Nin
体
Tai
幻
Gen
賢
Mind
力
Power
速
Speed
精
Stamina
印
Signs

Ninja Registry Number: 012140
Birthdate: February 29 (23 years old; Pisces)
Height: 177.0 cm (5'9½") **Weight:** 65.0 kg (143 lbs.) **Blood type:** AB
Personality: Calculating, cold-blooded
Favorite food: Grilled salted mackerel, grilled salted sea bream
Least favorite food: raw meat
Would like to fight: Orochimaru, Uzumaki Naruto
Favorite word: Immeasurable changes
Interests: Maintaining scalpels

Graduated from the Ninja Academy at age 10
Promoted to chûnin at age —

Mission Experience		
	D-rank: 163	C-rank: 28
	B-rank: 0	A-rank: 0
	S-rank: 0 (during Konohagakure era)	

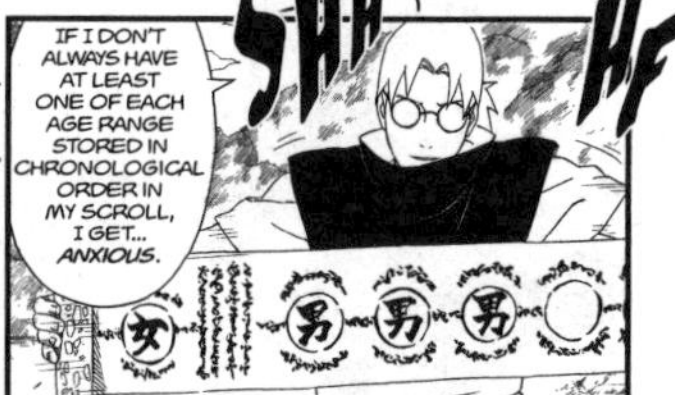
SHH
HF
IF I DON'T ALWAYS HAVE AT LEAST ONE OF EACH AGE RANGE STORED IN CHRONOLOGICAL ORDER IN MY SCROLL, I GET... ANXIOUS.
女
男
男
男

⬆ The fastidiousness of Kabuto's personality is an important quality when serving others. Perhaps that is why Orochimaru wanted him close by?

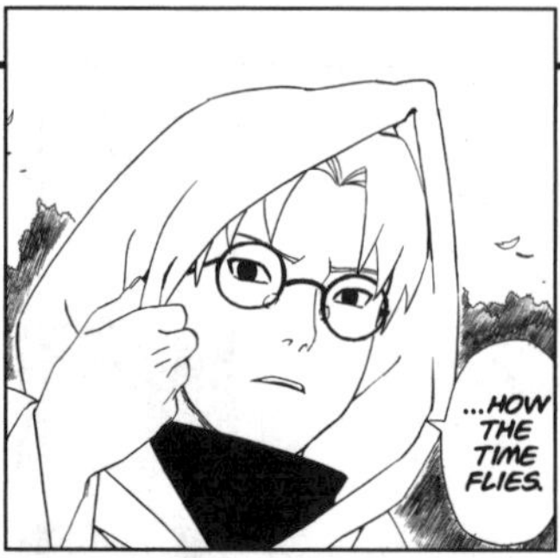
...HOW THE TIME FLIES.

⬆ For a spy who deceives others, an attachment to one's identity is a useless luxury.

At the end of his wanderings, he drifts into a reptile world, turning his back on humanity.

《Double spy》

Kabuto is known as a loyal follower of Orochimaru, but originally, he was sent in by Sasori of the Akatsuki to spy on Orochimaru's activities. Kabuto had survived by erasing himself, but he saw an evil light in Orochimaru's efforts to obtain eternal life…!! When that light was shone on him and he saw his shadow, Kabuto discovered who he was. It was Kabuto's moment of self-realization.

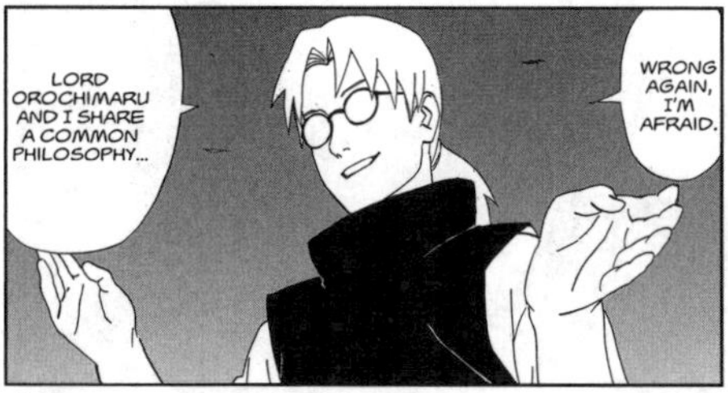
WRONG AGAIN, I'M AFRAID.
LORD OROCHIMARU AND I SHARE A COMMON PHILOSOPHY...

⬆ When he decided to serve Orochimaru of his own accord, something changed within Kabuto.

《Orochimaru》

By serving Orochimaru and gaining his trust, Kabuto defined who he is. For him, the defeat of Orochimaru also signified his own disappearance. That is why Kabuto absorbed Orochimaru, the symbol of rebirth, into his own body. The evil waves that pound from within give him physical stimulation and the realistic feeling of being alive…!!

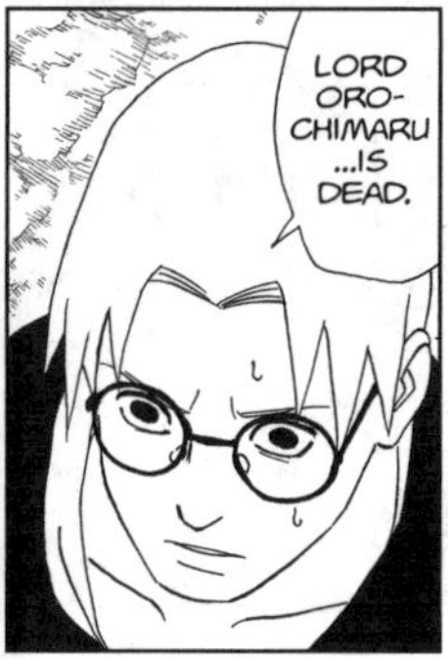
LORD OROCHIMARU ...IS DEAD.

⬇➡ The cells of Orochimaru that he absorbed are trying to take over Kabuto! Will the day come when Kabuto can control the power of the great snake?

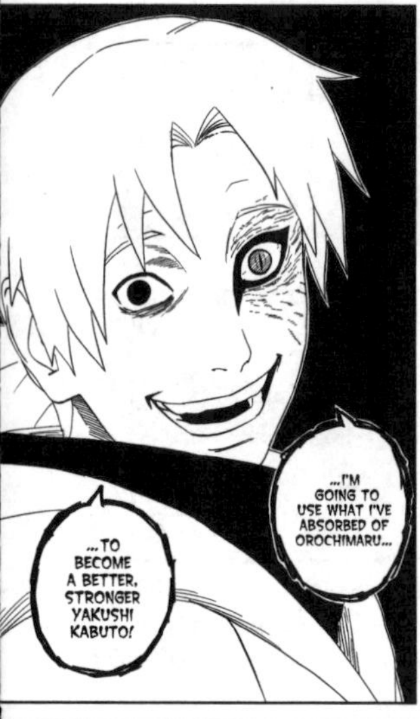
...I'M GOING TO USE WHAT I'VE ABSORBED OF OROCHIMARU...
...TO BECOME A BETTER, STRONGER YAKUSHI KABUTO!

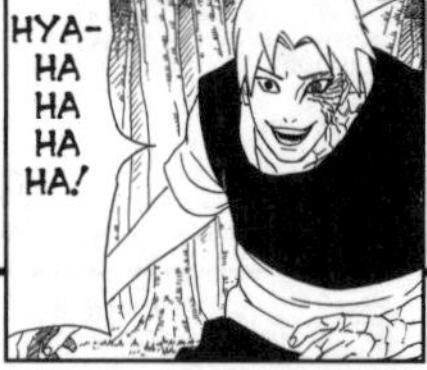
HYA-HA HA HA HA!

➡ Over 30 percent of Kabuto's body is already controlled by the cells of Orochimaru.

Seeking strength to protect his friends, an orphaned child of the sun.

YAHIKO 弥彦

A boy who lost his parents in the Second Great Ninja War. Together with fellow orphans Konan and Nagato, they meet the Three Great Shinobi and plead with Jiraiya for ninjutsu training. He has a happy and outgoing nature and is something of a leader amongst the orphans, always offering them encouragement. He works hard at his training every day in order to protect himself and those he loves.

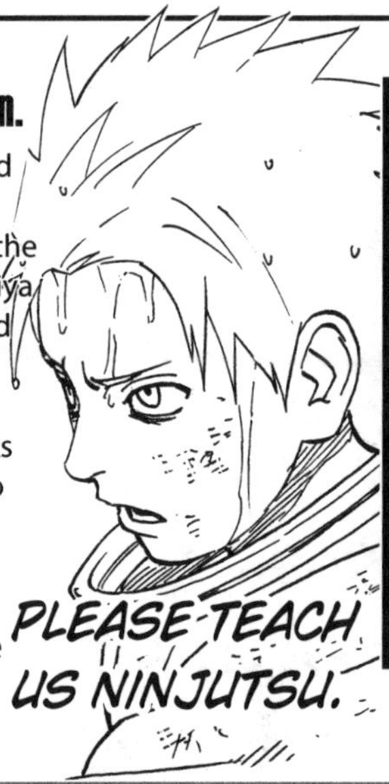
PLEASE TEACH US NINJUTSU.

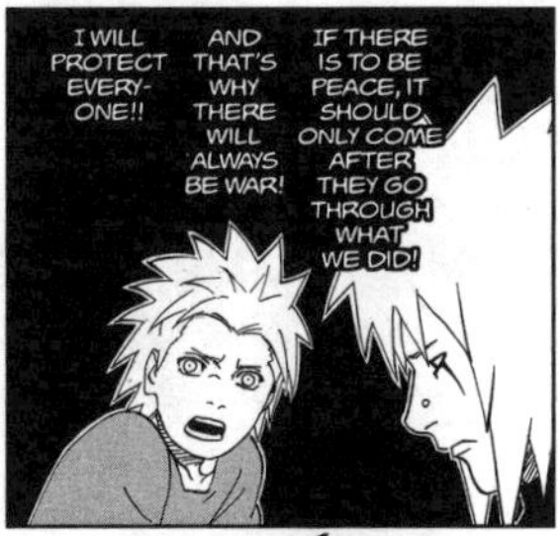
IF THERE IS TO BE PEACE, IT SHOULD ONLY COME AFTER THEY GO THROUGH WHAT WE DID!
AND THAT'S WHY THERE WILL ALWAYS BE WAR!
I WILL PROTECT EVERY-ONE!!

⬅ He detests war and loves his friends. The purity of his feelings struck Jiraiya.

Ninja Registry Number: —
Birthdate: February 20 (? years old; Pisces)
Height: ? **Weight:** ? **Blood type:** 0
Personality: Loyal to his friends, outgoing
Interest: fishing

He hides the fire that burns in his eyes and completes his mission.

YAMASHIRO AOBA 山城アオバ

Special Jônin

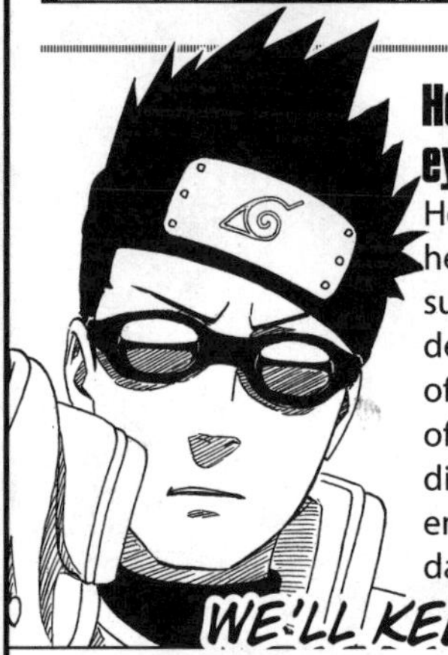
WE'LL KEEP THESE TWO BUSY.

He is a special jônin who came to help rescue Asuma. He always has his sunglasses on and maintains his cool demeanor. He can manipulate a flock of crows and utilizes them for a variety of missions including reconnaissance, diversion and attack. He never shows his emotions but is willing to put himself in danger for his comrades.

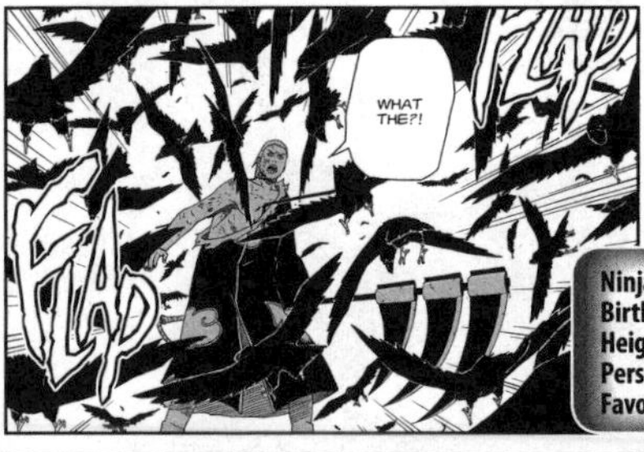
FLAP
WHAT THE?!
FLAP

⬅ Innumerable black wings blocking all sight! Depending on the platoon formation and strategy, there are seven different ways to deploy the crows.

Ninja Registry Number: 009744
Birthdate: September 3 (34 years old; Virgo)
Height: 178.0 cm (6'10") **Weight:** 66.0 kg (145 lbs.) **Blood type:** 0
Personality: Does the right thing, shy
Favorite word: According to plan.

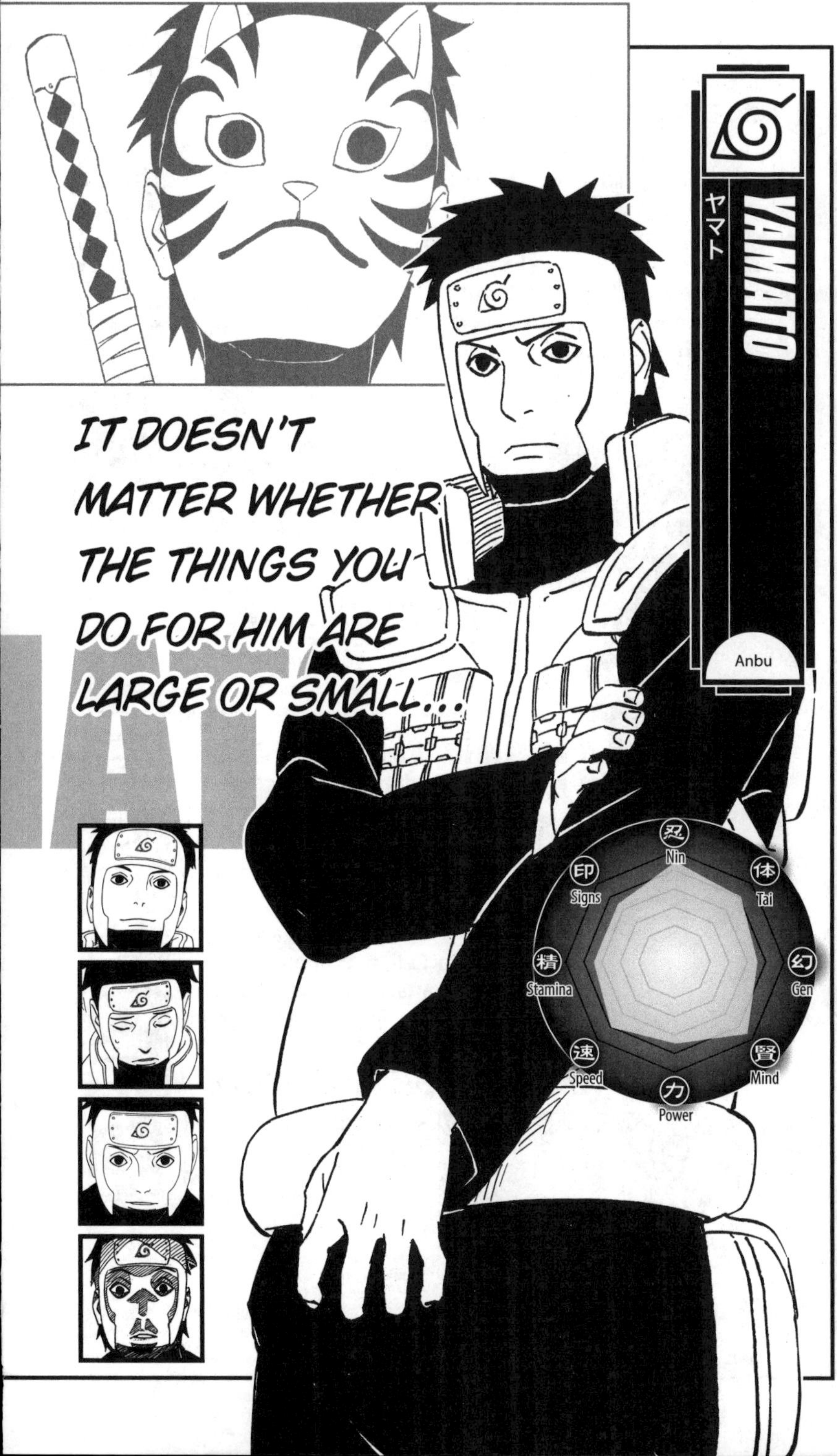
YAMATO
ヤマト
Anbu
IT DOESN'T MATTER WHETHER THE THINGS YOU DO FOR HIM ARE LARGE OR SMALL...
忍 Nin
体 Tai
幻 Gen
賢 Mind
力 Power
速 Speed
精 Stamina
印 Signs

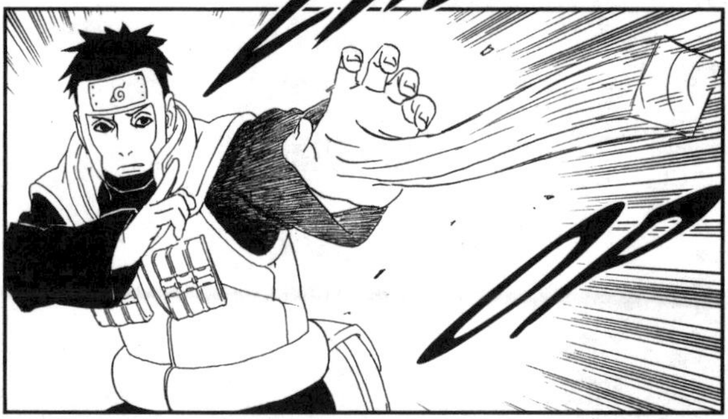

⬅ Only Yamato is capable of the Wood Style Secret Technique!! It is a jutsu that is suitable for offense, defense and backup

A ghostly stillness behind the mask, Secret Technique unparalleled within!!

In order to cover Kakashi's duties while Hatake Kakashi was absent, the Fifth Hokage Tsunade considered forming a new Kakashi team. Yamato, with his direct line to the Hokage, was selected to be the leader. As the only one since the first Hokage to use trees and Secret Technique, Yamato is a clear stand-out within the Anbu. He was known far and wide as Wood Style Tenzo. A heavy fate is etched into his DNA. But he embraces it fully and wields his power to fight with his new subordinates.

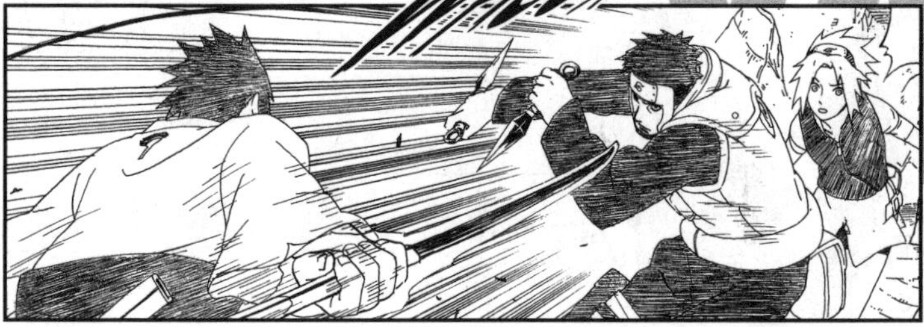

⬆ His enhanced instincts sense danger. . .!! He risked his life to save his subordinates!!

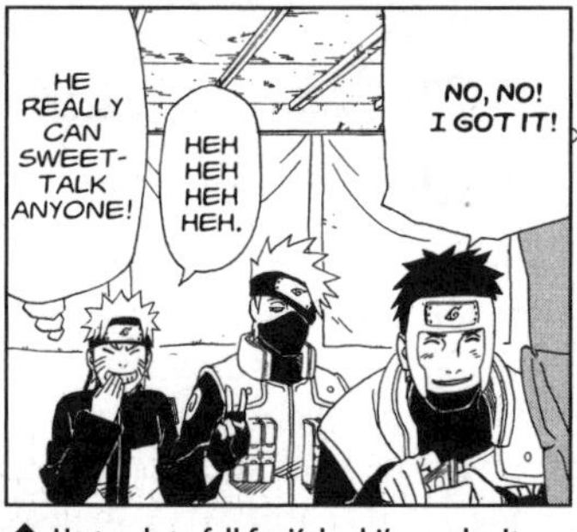
NO, NO! I GOT IT!
HEH HEH HEH HEH.
HE REALLY CAN SWEET-TALK ANYONE!

⬆ He tends to fall for Kakashi's pranks. It goes beyond aspiration and borders on adoration.

Ninja Registry Number: 010992
Birthdate: August 10 (26 years old; Leo)
Height: 178 cm (5'11") **Weight:** 58.4 kg (129 lbs.) **Blood type:** A
Personality: Cautious, well-prepared
Favorite food: Walnuts
Least favorite food: Greasy food
Would like to fight: Hatake Kakashi
Favorite word: You cannot be too careful.
Interests: Reading books on architecture

Graduated from the Ninja Academy at age 6
Promoted to chûnin at age 6

Mission Experience		
	D-rank: 80	C-rank: 176
	B-rank: 400	A-rank: 305
	S-rank: 35	

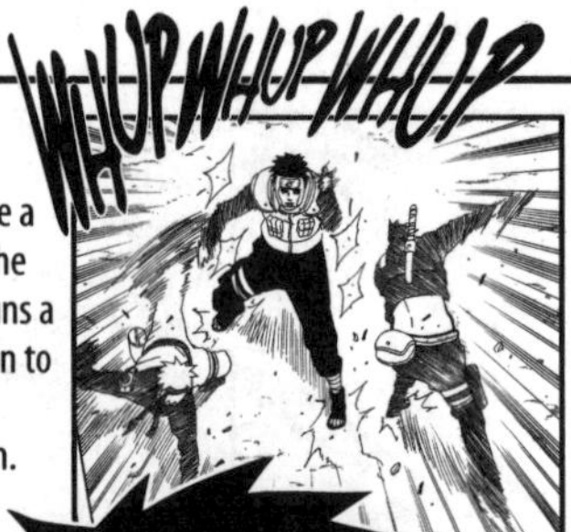
WHUP WHUP WHUP

➡ Before a mission, he always runs a simulation to confirm formation.

Composed thinking leads to a young shinobi's independence.

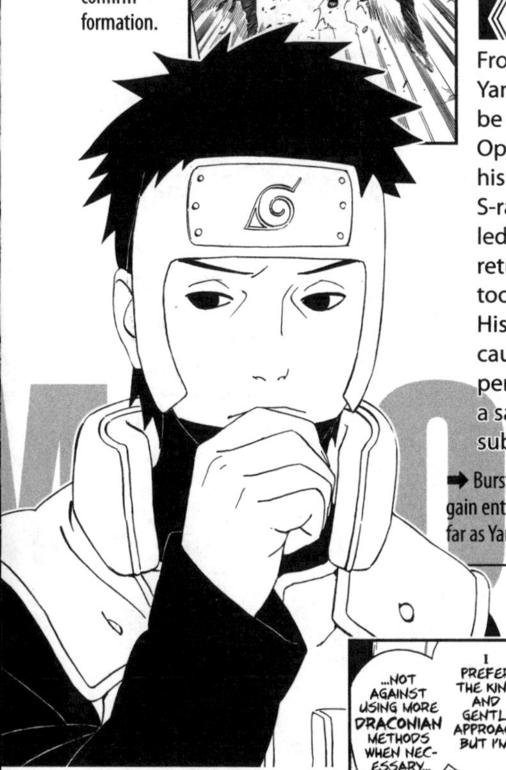

《Cautious》

From the Third Hokage's reign, Yamato was acknowledged to be at the top of the Anbu Black Ops. The available data back up his considerable skills. D-rank to S-rank—in all the missions that he led, his troops have a remarkable return rate. "You can never be too careful."

His excessively cautious personality acts as a safety net for his subordinates.

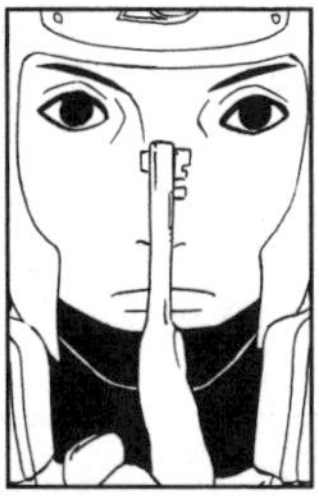

➡ Bursting through doors to gain entry makes no sense as far as Yamato is concerned…

⬇ In order to unify the team, he will sometimes resort to scare tactics.

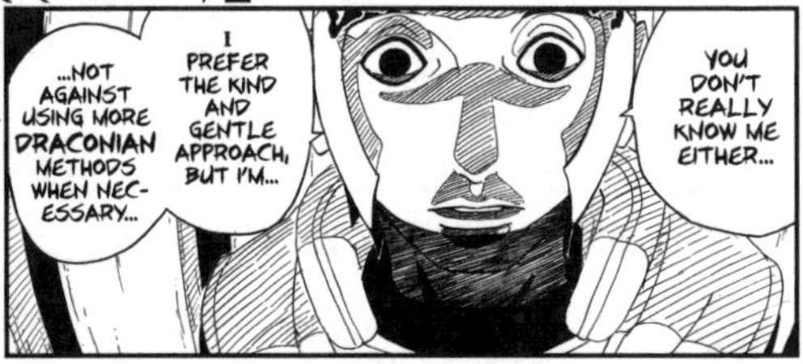
YOU DON'T REALLY KNOW ME EITHER...
I PREFER THE KIND AND GENTLE APPROACH, BUT I'M...
...NOT AGAINST USING MORE DRACONIAN METHODS WHEN NECESSARY...

⬇ Rather than stand above, Yamato prefers to bring others up to his level.

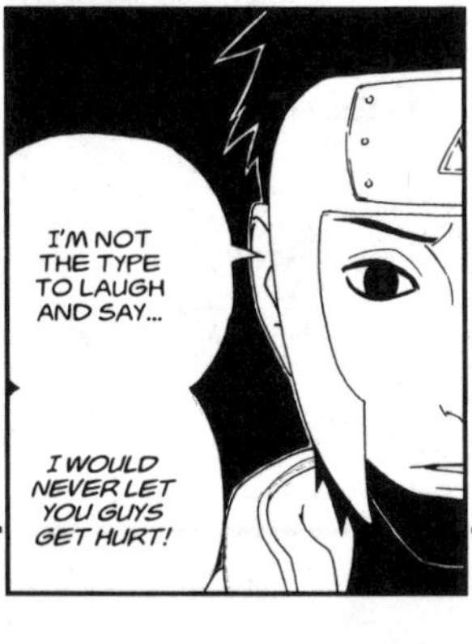
I'M NOT THE TYPE TO LAUGH AND SAY...
I WOULD NEVER LET YOU GUYS GET HURT!

《Acting leader》

While he respects Kakashi, Yamato's philosophy of leadership is different. Yamato does not hesitate to criticize a novice. He goes beyond the rank of higher, middle or lower and acknowledges each subordinate as a shinobi. He knows that will lead to a unified team and a successful mission.

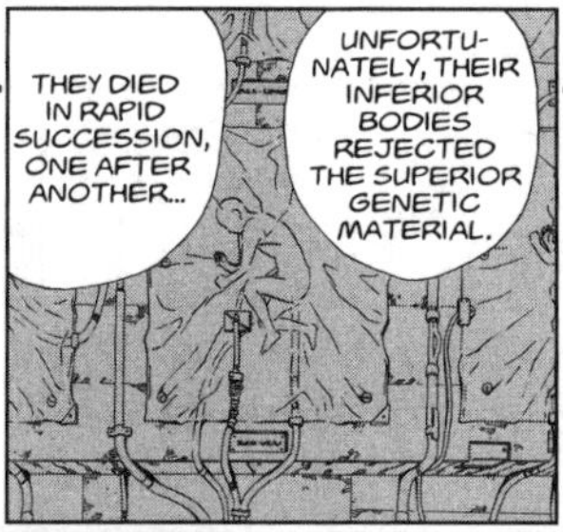
UNFORTU-
NATELY, THEIR
INFERIOR
BODIES
REJECTED
THE SUPERIOR
GENETIC
MATERIAL.
THEY DIED
IN RAPID
SUCCESSION,
ONE AFTER
ANOTHER...

⬆ The heinous live human experiments of Orochimaru. . . Yamato is the only survivor out of sixty.

With the passage of time, a sad past can become a key to the future.

《Genetics of the First Hokage》

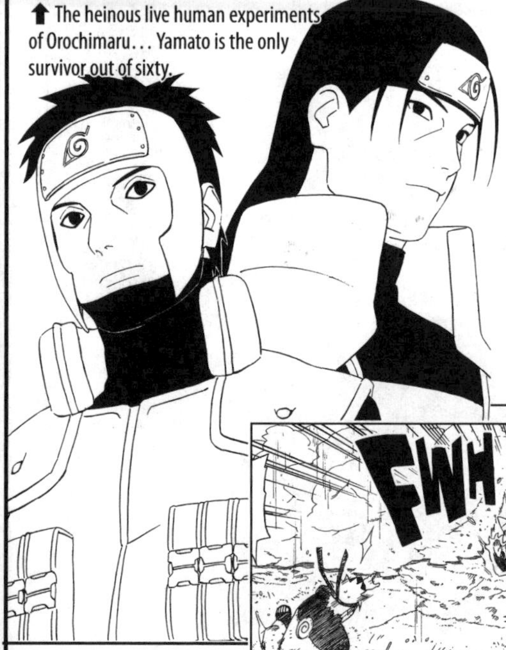

Yamato's Wood Style hijutsu—its origin lies in the DNA transplanted in him from the First Hokage. A live human experiment produced by Orochimaru. It is a past that could easily have traumatized him, but Yamato embraces it. The reason is that the Wood Style ninjutsu is his greatest weapon for protecting his comrades and a point of pride for Yamato.

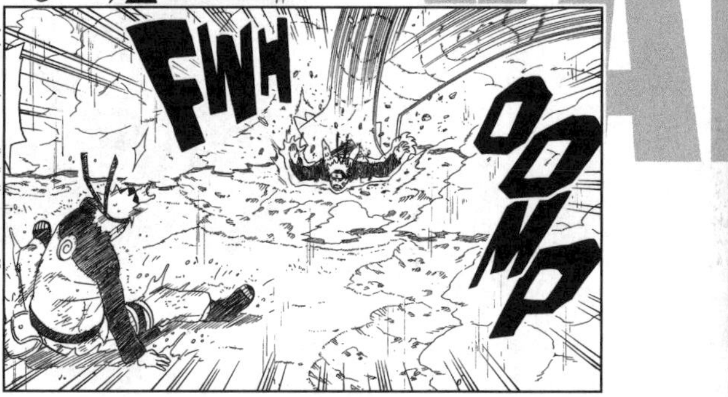
FWH
OOMP

⬆ A technique possible only for one who can manipulate Wood Style!! It silences even Tailed Beasts!!

《The cornerstone of training》

Use your power to give strength to Naruto. The biggest reason why Yamato was selected to be the leader is because his hidden jutsu is the only thing that will keep the Tailed Beast inside Naruto under control. The man who was born as a live human experiment would become the driving force behind Naruto's new power. . .!!

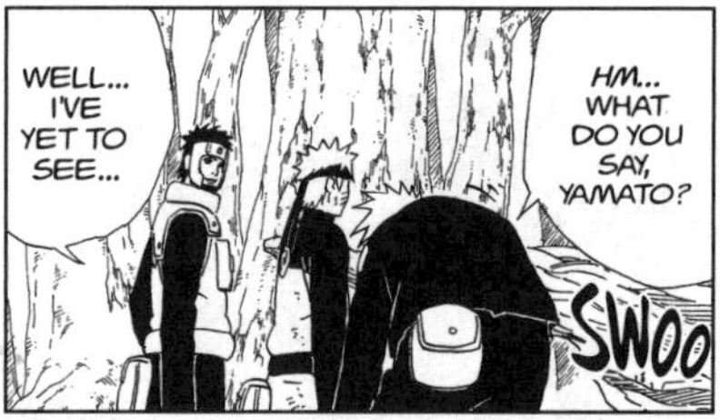
HM...
WHAT
DO YOU
SAY,
YAMATO?
WELL...
I'VE
YET TO
SEE...
SWOO

⬆ He sees a bright future for subordinates who have successfully completed their training by fighting Tailed Beast chakra.

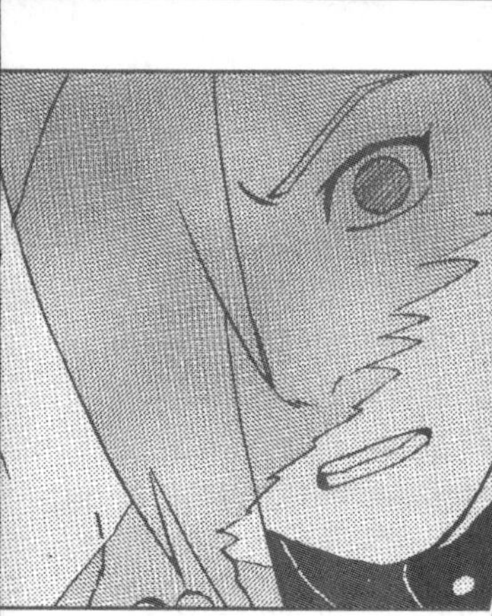

YAMANAKA INO

山中いの

Chûnin

MASTER ASUMA'S LOOKING FOR YOU!

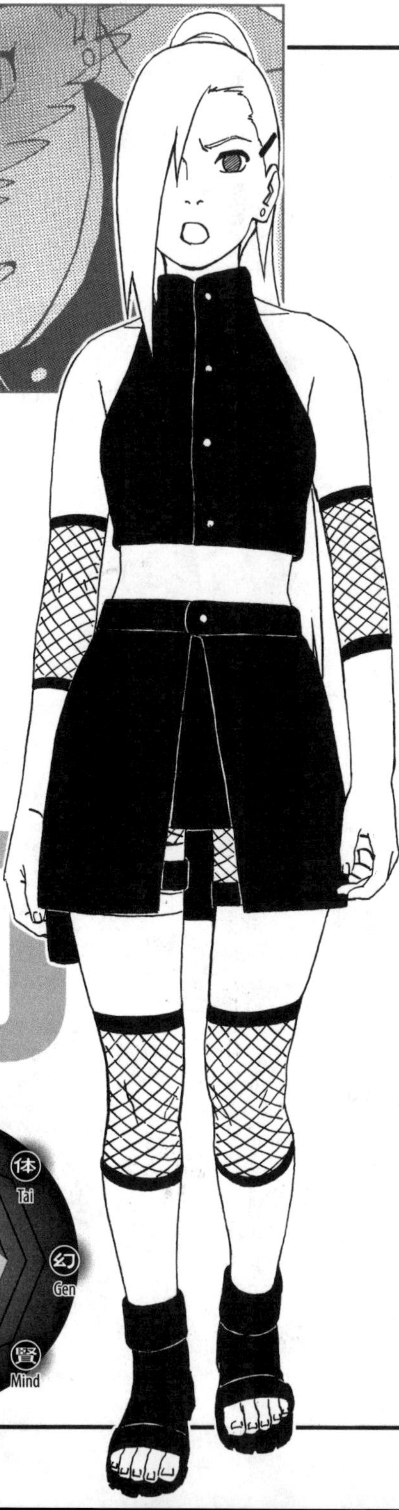

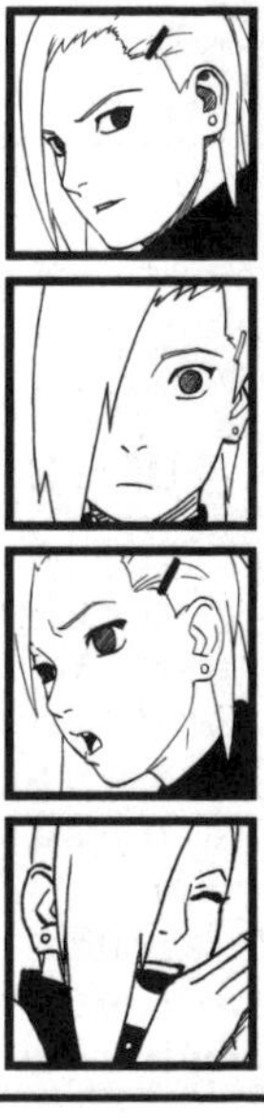

INO

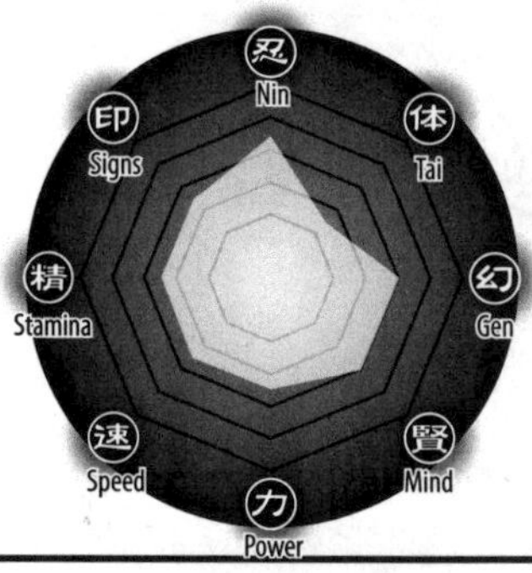
忍
Nin
体
Tai
幻
Gen
賢
Mind
力
Power
速
Speed
精
Stamina
印
Signs

I'VE GOT THE MOST CHAKRA IN RESERVE RIGHT NOW, PLUS I'M NOT USEFUL IN SIMPLE BATTLES, SO...
...I CAN USE MY MIND TRANSFER TECH-NIQUE...

➡ Lead a successful mission, even if it means endangering oneself. . .!! She possesses the courage and nerve to disregard the risk!!

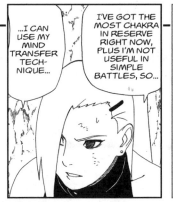

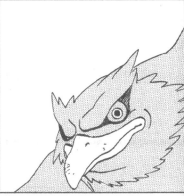

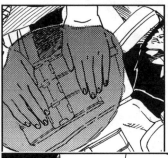

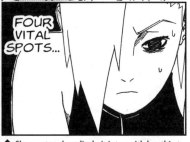

FOUR VITAL SPOTS...

⬆ She mastered medical ninjutsu with her thirst for knowledge and good instincts. Her skill level is high enough that she can make an immediate judgment about the condition of a patient.

A proud, gorgeous young woman who blossoms through training.

"At the academy, I wanted to get top grades amongst the female ninja. My classmate Sakura and I are well-matched rivals. But ever since Sakura started an apprenticeship with Tsunade, she's grown by leaps and bounds." Ino is very motivated by this. But she's not in a rush. She faithfully performs her training lessons every day. Ino knows, no matter how large the flower, it still grows by daily increments as it stretches toward the sun. . . The flower of effort blooms after a winter spent persevering and will no doubt produce beautiful fruit. . .!!

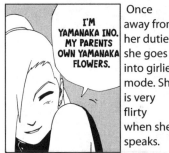

I'M YAMANAKA INO. MY PARENTS OWN YAMANAKA FLOWERS.

Once away from her duties, she goes into girlie mode. She is very flirty when she speaks.

Ninja Registry Number: 012604
Birthdate: September 23 (16 years old; Libra)
Height: 162.2 cm (5'4") **Weight:** 46.0 kg (101 lbs.) **Blood type:** B
Personality: Selfish, lively
Favorite food: Cherry tomato, crème caramel
Least favorite food: Sashimi
Would like to fight: Haruno Sakura
Favorite word: Language of flowers
Interests: Shopping

Graduated from the Ninja Academy at age 12
Promoted to chûnin at age 14

Mission Experience		
	D-rank: 23	C-rank: 9
	B-rank: 6	A-rank: 2
	S-rank: 0	

YUHI KURENAI

夕日紅

Jônin

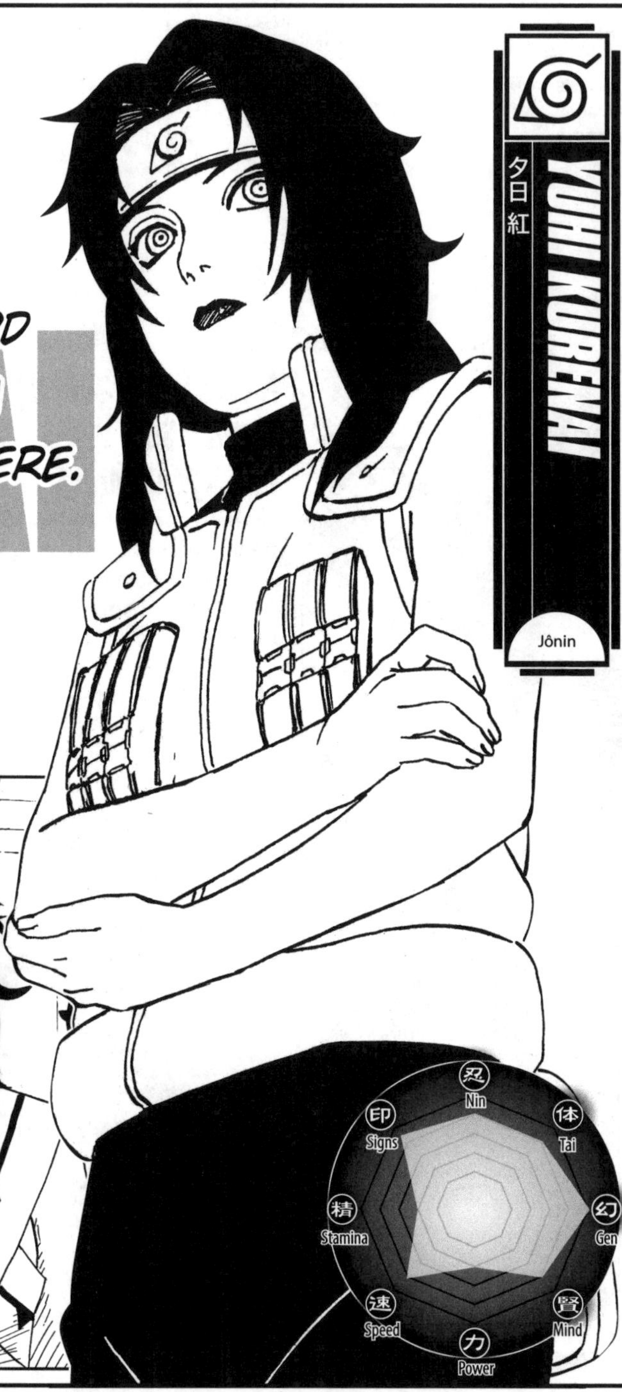
I HEARD
ASUMA
WAS HERE.
忍
Nin
体
Tai
幻
Gen
賢
Mind
力
Power
速
Speed
精
Stamina
印
Signs

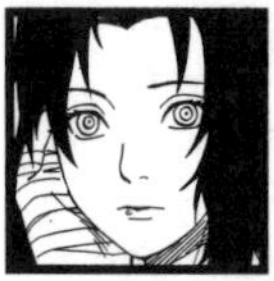

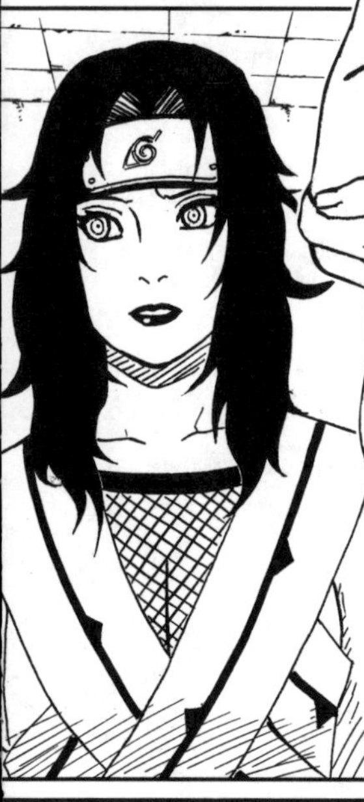

Hidden inside are eternal memories and light of the future.

Her red eyes are able to discern the truth in an instant, and she lures enemies to a place far beyond illusion as a graceful genjutsu practitioner. With many successes and results behind her, she trains younger ninja as a platoon leader. In between her busy days, she became friendly with Asuma, who appears relaxed but keeps a watchful eye on his students. Born of mutual respect, they nurtured their love until fate dealt them a cruel farewell. Asuma died protecting the village and those he loved… Knowing his feelings, Kurenai shakes free her sorrow and continues moving forward so that the bright future she and Asuma envisioned for Konoha does not become an illusion.

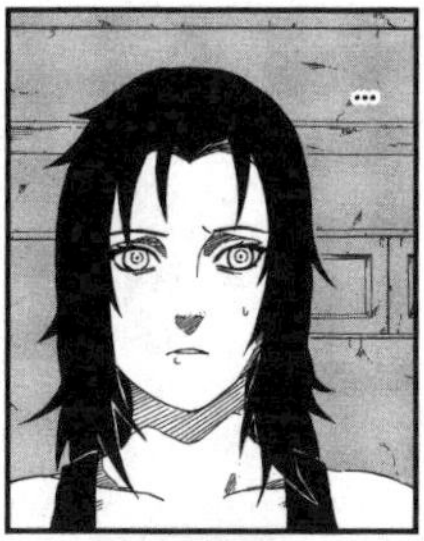
...

⬅ An ominous thought crosses her mind… The anxiety mounts as she knows how harsh the missions are.

⬇ The two rays of hope that Asuma left behind, their child and their favorite student. Her expression is full of love at the sight of the two of them.

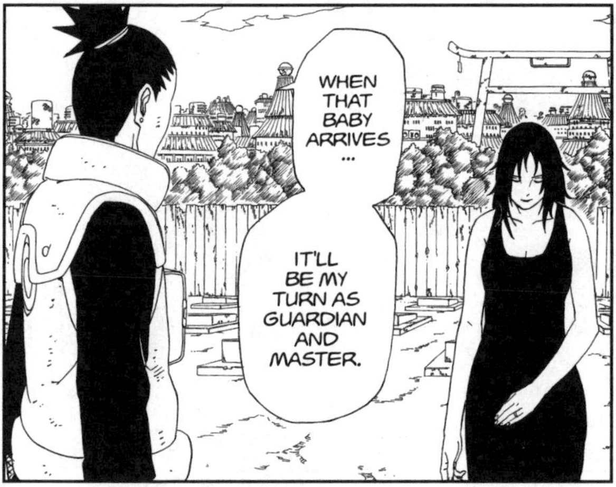
WHEN THAT BABY ARRIVES...
IT'LL BE MY TURN AS GUARDIAN AND MASTER.

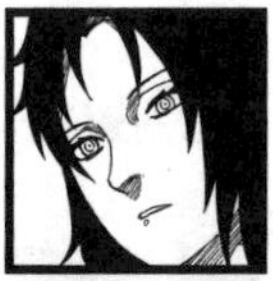

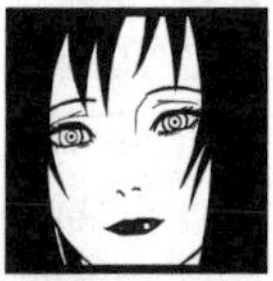

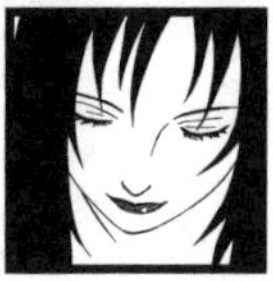

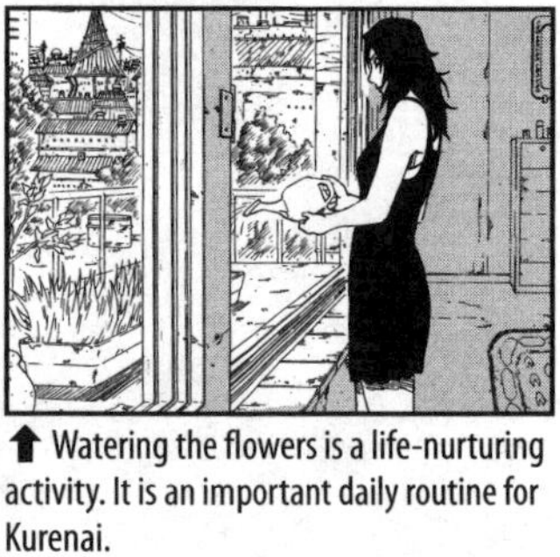

⬆ Watering the flowers is a life-nurturing activity. It is an important daily routine for Kurenai.

Ninja Registry Number: 010881
Birthdate: June 11 (31 years old; Gemini)
Height: 169.1 cm (5'6½") **Weight:** 54.4 kg (120 lbs.) **Blood type:** AB
Personality: Macho, fastidious
Favorite food: Shochu, vodka, octopus with wasabi
Least favorite food: Pastry
Would like to fight: None
Favorite word: The glory of the rose of Sharon lasts but a day.
Interests: A tipple before dinner

Graduated from the Ninja Academy at age 9
Promoted to chûnin at age 13

Mission Experience		
	D-rank: 152	C-rank: 158
	B-rank: 235	A-rank: 138
	S-rank: 14	

YURA 由良

Jônin

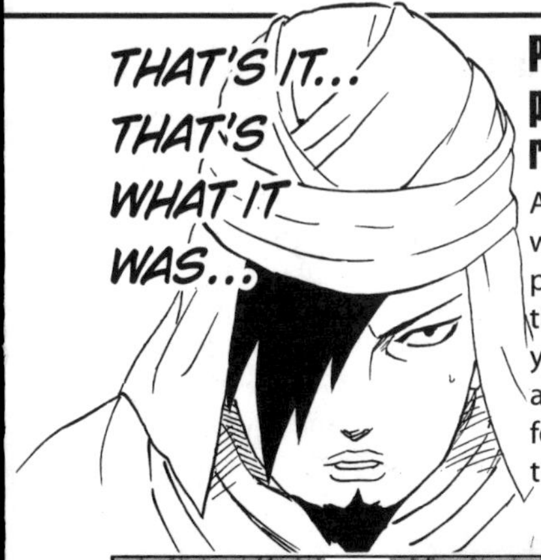
THAT'S IT... THAT'S WHAT IT WAS...

Participant in the Akatsuki plot, the brilliant spy of the red sands.

After many heroic deeds, he was promoted to a senior position. Yura had the trust of the governing body for his fair yet stern outlook. But when he awakened to his real role as a spy for Sasori, the sharp blade was turned toward the Sand...

YURA

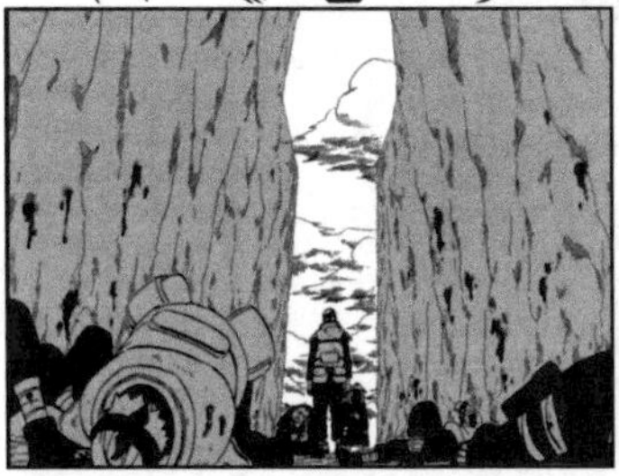

⬅ Once he regains his memory as a subordinate for Sasori, he is able to destroy many of the Sand in an instant... A power to be feared.

Ninja Registry Number: 44-005
Birthdate: October 31 (28 years old; Scorpio)
Height: 173.0 cm (5'8") **Weight:** 53.4 kg (118 lbs.) **Blood type:** AB
Personality: Studious, loyal
Favorite food: Dried abalone

SAGE OF THE SIX PATHS 六道仙人

—

He explains the principles of chakra and weaving seals and is the originator of shinobi!!

RIKUDO SENNIN

Sage of the Six Paths: he is the creator of all jutsu and the originator of shinobi. He has the Rinnegan Eye and is said to be sent from heaven in times of turmoil. Is he a creator or a destroyer? It is not certain whether he even existed, and his name only appears in legends.

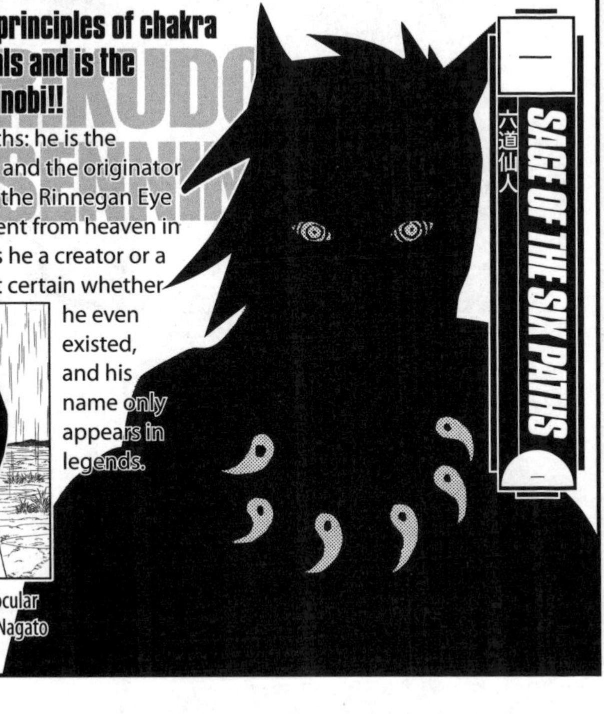

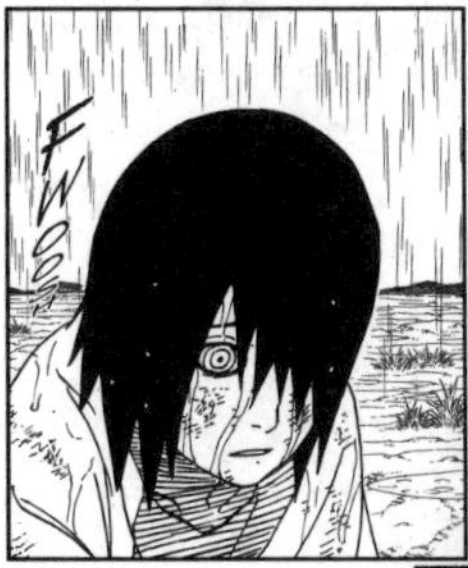

⬆ The highest form of ocular ninjutsu, Rinnegan Eye. Nagato has the same eye...

ROSHI 老紫

He turned his back on his village to acquire this jutsu which induces searing heat!!

From an early age, Roshi harbored Four Tails within him and traveled extensively to try and control the excess energy. At the end of his wanderings and with the help of Four Tails, he acquired Lava Style ninjutsu, which combines the characteristics of fire and earth. The flowing lava melts anything in its path.

ROSHI

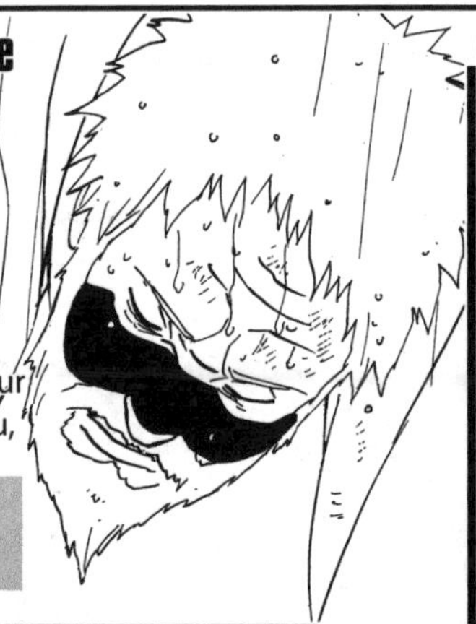

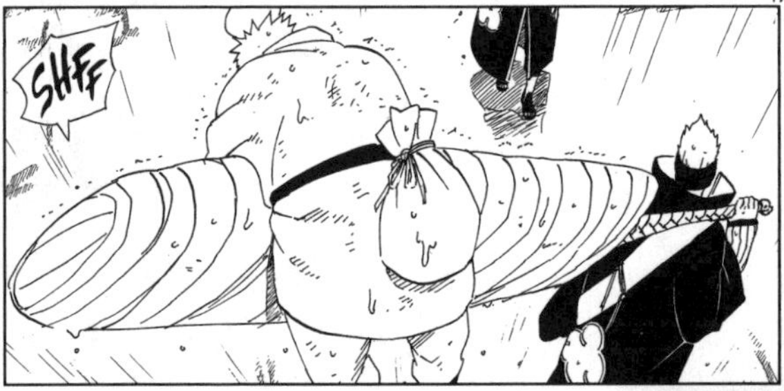
SHFF

⬅ Even using the tremendous chakra of the Tailed Beast he has within him, he lost to Kisame's Samehada and Water Style Ninjutsu.

Collection ... Number 11

Konoha

JINCHÛRIKI: DESTINED TO HARBOR TAILED BEASTS

During the Era of the Great Ninja Wars, the First Hokage distributed the Tailed Beasts to various lands. Jinchûriki were born to harness the power of the Tailed Beasts for military purposes. By sealing the mass of chakra—Tailed Beast—within a human, the host acquires superhuman powers.

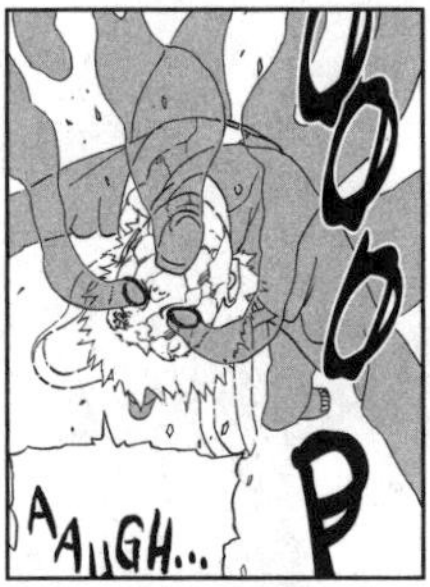
AAUGH...

⬆ Gaara, who had the Tailed Beast Shukaku extracted from him, lost his life.

The jinchûriki acquires tremendous powers, but it comes at a great risk. If the host becomes unstable and runs amok, it could bring untold damage to the village.

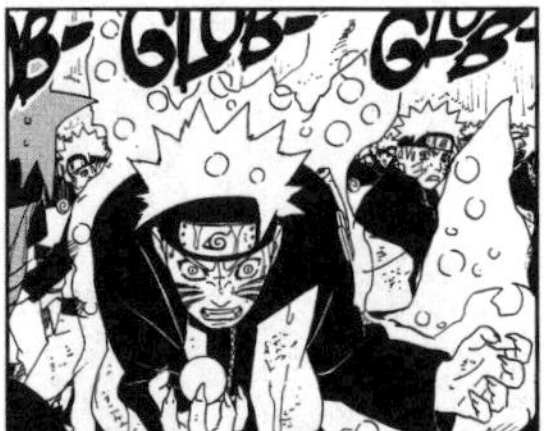
GLOB-
GLOB-

⬆ Jinchûriki, with their tremendous powers, were often feared and shunned by people.

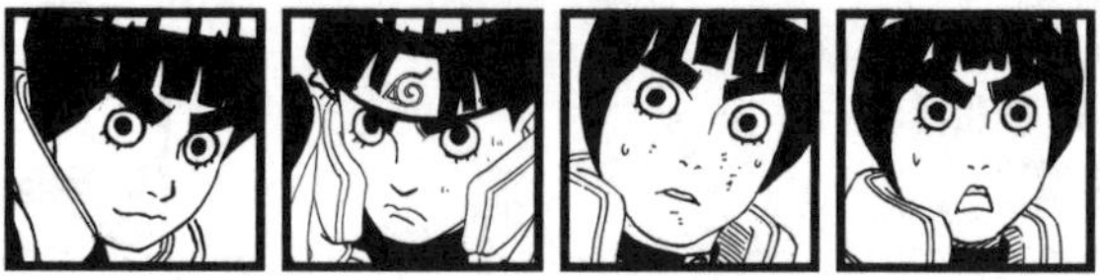

ROCK LEE

ロック・リー

Chûnin

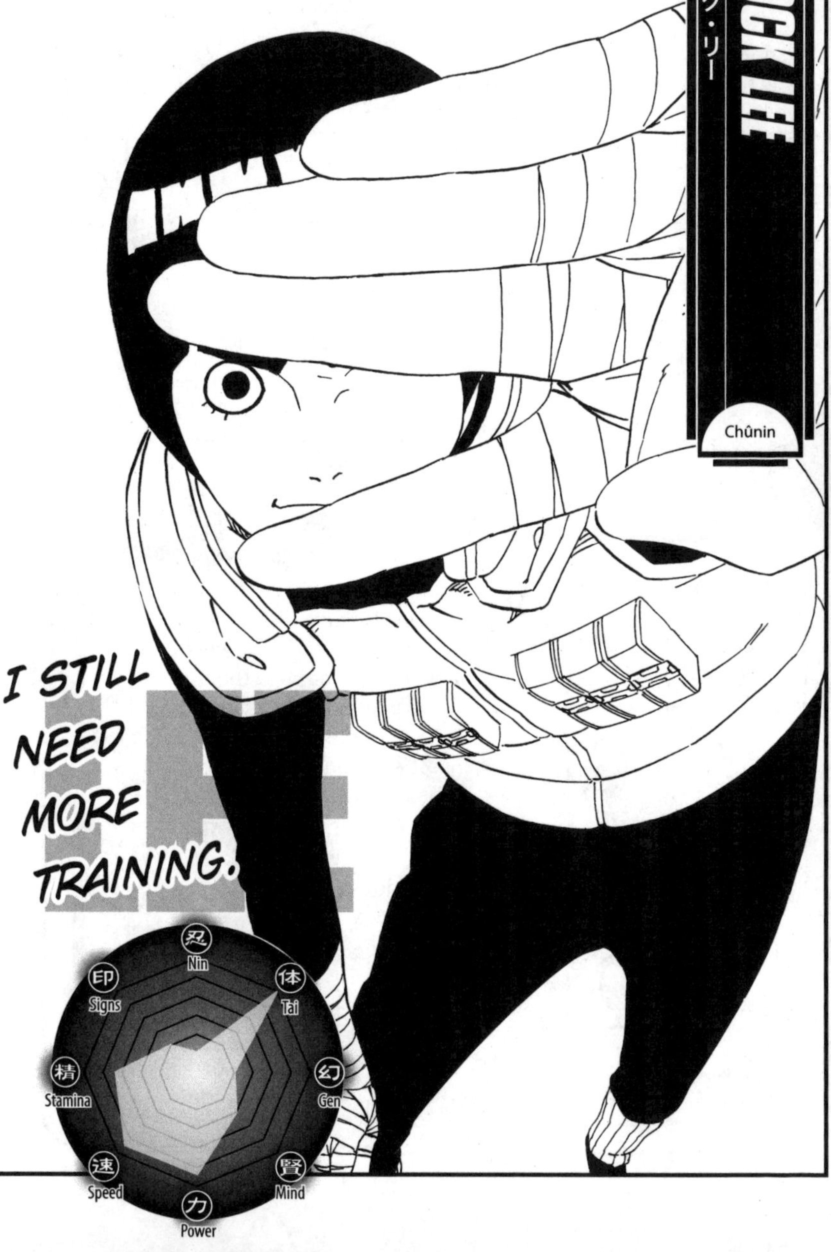
I STILL NEED MORE TRAINING.
忍
Nin
体
Tai
幻
Gen
賢
Mind
力
Power
速
Speed
精
Stamina
印
Signs

With a heart and fist inherited from his master, the blue beast climbs ever higher.

Taijutsu—it was the only bright spot for Lee who was told unequivocally that he had no talent for being a shinobi. Guy showed Lee the path he should follow. Lee took Guy's teachings, and armed only with the determination to improve, he kept training. Just like his master Guy, Lee's efforts bore fruit, and his improved taijutsu manifested fully in a surprise attack on Hoshigaki Kisame. Having surmounted the rigorous training, at times losing the will to continue, Lee has achieved master status. But his training does not end here. He remains stoic and focused on training and growing.

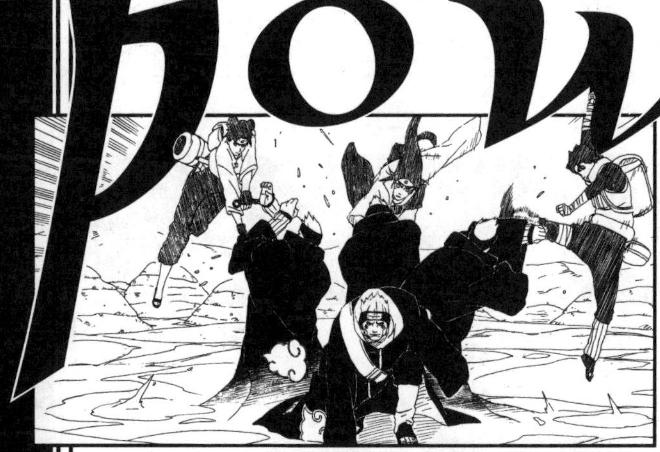
POW

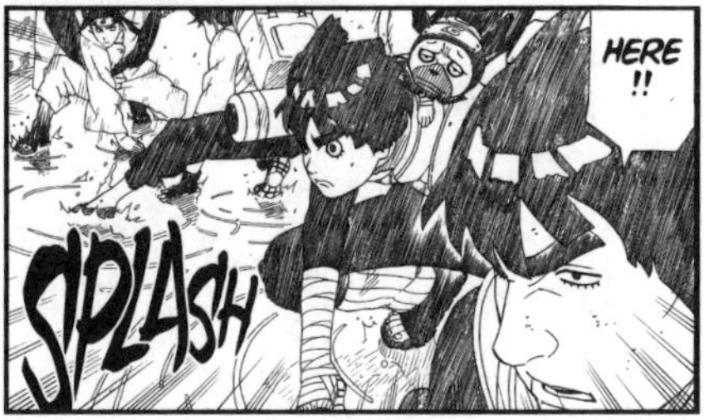
HERE !!
SPLASH

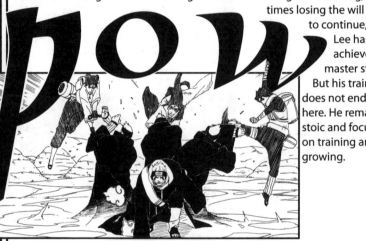

⬆ Taijutsu is the trademark of Guy's cell. In perfect unison, various coordinated attacks rain down on Kisame.

⬅ Lee tries to absorb all of Guy's techniques. Even on a mission, the training continues.

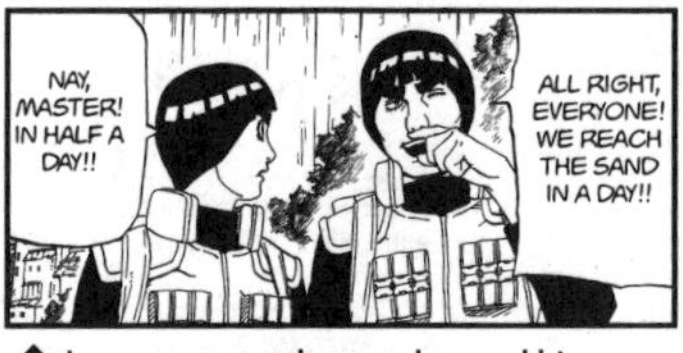
ALL RIGHT, EVERYONE! WE REACH THE SAND IN A DAY!!
NAY, MASTER! IN HALF A DAY!!

⬆ Lee races to catch up and exceed his master. For sheer momentum and high spirits, he surpasses even Guy!! When the two get together, the word "impossible" disappears from the dictionary. . .!!

Ninja Registry Number: 012561
Birthdate: November 27 (17 years old; Sagittarius)
Height: 172.0 cm (5'7½") **Weight:** 54.7 kg (121 lbs.) **Blood type:** A
Personality: Passionate, loves to train
Favorite food: Medium hot curry, curry pilaf
Least favorite food: None!
Would like to fight: Sasuke, Neji, Gaara, Naruto
Favorite word: Effort, guts, love
Interests: Effort

Graduated from the Ninja Academy at age 12
Promoted to chûnin at age 15

Mission Experience		
	D-rank: 25	C-rank: 21
	B-rank: 4	A-rank: 10
	S-rank: 1	

Character Detail List

Data for 52 inhabitants of the ninja world!

How to Read This Chart

❶ Face
❷ Name
❸ Sex
❹ Age (At appearance)
❺ Occupation or affiliation
❻ Volume and page of appearance
❼ Profile

Inomatsu

M 23 Genin v37 p17

A Konoha genin who used to study under Asuma. Like Shikamaru and his friends, he is deeply saddened by Asuma's death.

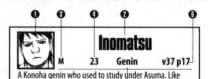

The Village Hidden in the Leaves

The most powerful village in the Five Great Shinobi Nations. Many shinobi live here under the rule of the Hokage.

Tora
M 30 Anbu v43 p183

A member of the Anbu with the speed and strength of a tiger. His targets never get away.

Inomatsu
M 23 Genin v37 p17

A Konoha genin who used to study under Asuma. Like Shikamaru and his friends, he is deeply saddened by Asuma's death.

Natori
M 24 Chûnin v28 p122

He receives daily reports on neighboring countries and makes announcements about them. The speed and accuracy of his announcements is top notch!

Ushi
M 32 Anbu v43 p183

An Anbu under the direct command of Senju Tobirama. He keeps constant watch over the Uchiha clan to make sure there aren't any traitors among them.

Baku
M 31 Anbu v43 p183

One of the Anbu members who is keeping watch over the Uchiha clan. He can see everything from behind his mask.

Uchiha Setsuna
M 26 Police Force v43 p183

An Uchiha clan shinobi who had doubts about the Second Hokage. He planned to reclaim power from the Senju clan.

Hyo
M 21 Anbu The Foundation v32 p96

A former member of the Foundation. Sai's superior. Before Sai goes on his top-secret mission, Hyo reminds him of what the Foundation stands for.

Uchiha Yakumi
M 28 Police Force v43 p187

He aided Fugaku as a member of the police force. He is very loyal and has strong feelings for the Uchiha clan.

Minakura Tomaru
M 8 Ninja Academy Student v28 p52

A Konoha boy. He admires ninja and works hard every day to become the Sixth Hokage.

Kage
M 22 Anbu v34 p36

A member of the Anbu who directly reports to the Hokage. He carries out his missions by approaching his targets by hiding in the darkness like a shadow.

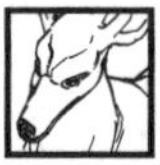

Rikumaru

M | 6 | pet deer | v38 p47

A deer owned by the Nara clan. A special drug that works on all diseases can be made from his majestic antlers.

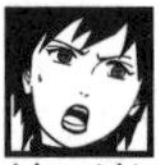

Yurika

F | 24 | Cipher Corps | v28 p123

A kunoichi who works for Konoha's Cipher Corps. She is the village's top specialist on code analysis.

The Village Hidden in the Sand

Village surrounded by a desert full of sandstorms. They are currently in an alliance with Konoha.

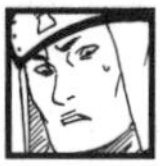

Sekka

M | 36 | Medical Corps | v28 p144

A ninja with exceptional medical abilities. He has saved many shinobi with his excellent medical ninjutsu.

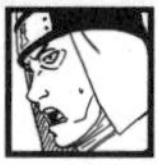

Isago

M | 38 | Jônin | v28 p112

A Sunagakure jônin who acts as Baki's right arm. He forms and commands a tracking party to retrieve the Kazekage.

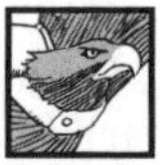

Takamaru

M | 3 | pet hawk | v28 p122

The fastest hawk in Sunagakure. He is sent to Konoha to let them know that the Kazekage has been abducted.

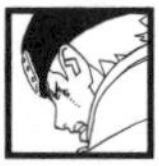

Ittetsu

M | 16 | Genin | v31 p169

A Sunagakure genin who deeply admires the Kazekage. When the Kazekage is brought back to life, he is relieved and sheds tears of joy.

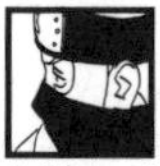

Tsubusa

M | 25 | Chûnin | v28 p62

A chûnin who keeps watch at the entrance of the Village Hidden in the Sand. No one can match his ability to see distant things.

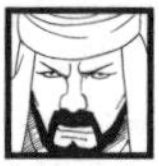

Goza

M | 44 | Senior Officer | v30 p72

A Sunagakure senior officer. The village's dignity is his top priority. When the Kazekage is kidnapped, he fears for the stability of the village.

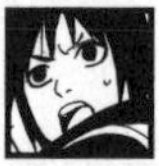

Matsuri

F | 17 | Genin | v31 p169

A Sunagakure kunoichi who is close friends with Sari. She likes elites and admires the Kazekage. She has no interest in other men.

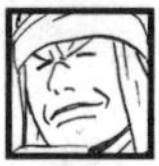

Sajo

M | 50 | Senior Officer | v28 p57

He has been working hard for the prosperity of the Village Hidden in the Sand for a long time. He is looking forward to the results of the International Joint Chûnin Exam.

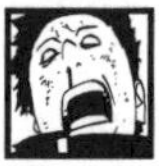

Mukade

M | 28 | Jônin | v29 p145

A Sand shinobi under the control of Pain's Art of Impersonation. He is chosen for his talents to become a vessel for Kisame.

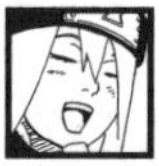

Sari

F | 15 | Genin | v31 p170

A Sunagakure kunoichi. She admires the Kazekage more than anyone and would give her life to save him.

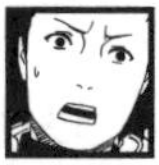

Yakku

M | 18 | Genin | v28 p178

The guide who waits for the Konoha shinobi. He leads Naruto and the others to the medical room where Kankuro lies.

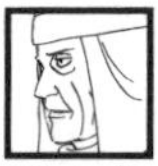

Joseki

M | 51 | Senior Officer | v30 p72

A Sunagakure senior officer who makes keeping the peace in the village his top priority. He does not like the idea of Gaara becoming Kazekage.

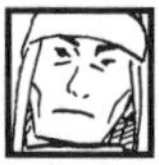

Ryusa

M | 41 | Senior Officer | v28 p57

A senior officer who has been supporting the Village Hidden in the Sand for a long time. He is very careful about what he does and says. He only takes action after careful consideration.

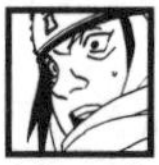

Suname

M | 36 | Chûnin | v28 p72

A Sunagakure chûnin who guards the village. He's on watch day and night to keep the peace in the village.

Reki

M   27   Jônin   v31 p172

A young Sunagakure jônin who has seen many battles. He is deeply saddened by the death of Chiyo when she uses her transference ninjutsu.

Ryokan

M   25   Medical Corps   v28 p176

An apprentice medical ninja who is Sekka's subordinate. He is frustrated that he doesn't have the skill to detoxify Kankuro.

Other Villages

People who belong to villages other than Konoha or the Sand. People who follow their beliefs are listed here.

Funari

M   30   Lookout   v39 p110

One of Kakuzu's subordinates. While standing guard at a pawnshop, he is killed in an attack by Suigetsu.

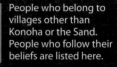

Ugatsu

M 28 Survivor of the Old Amagakure v40 p180

At Hanzo's bidding, he snuck into the Village Hidden in the Rain to kill Pain. He is very skilled in the art of infiltration.

Yudachi

M   27   Genin   v40 p160

An Amegakure shinobi who worships Pain. He is captured by Jiraiya in Club Frog and is turned into a frog.

Kyoya

M   23   Bookkeeper   v39 p110

One of the bookkeepers who works for Kakuzu. He is absolutely loyal to his superiors and would never defy an order.

Ryusui

M   33   Genin   v40 p160

An Amagakure shinobi who accompanies Yudachi. Even after being captured by Jiraiya, he resists by following his beliefs.

Ginji

M   23   Bookkeeper   v39 p110

The leader of the bookkeepers. In front of his subordinates, he is confident and doesn't show any weakness, but he is actually a coward.

Orochimaru's Hideout

A place to hold captives. Human experimentation and development of forbidden jutsu are done here.

Tsukushi

M   23   Prisoner   v39 p19

He has absolute confidence in his powers and is very daring. He will take on any person, no matter how powerful.

Ahiko

M   25   Prisoner   v39 p17

A prisoner in the northern hideout who has had curse mark experiments done on him. He has a ferocious look and is extremely aggressive.

Tetsuru

M   35   Prisoner   v38 p158

He fears Orochimaru to the depths of his heart and has given up on escaping. He is pessimistic about the future and has no hope in his eyes.

Glen

M   25   Prisoner   v38 p182

He kills several prisoners before he escapes. He is extremely violent and cruel, and is unable to control his lust for battle.

Bakuto

M   36   Prisoner   v38 p158

He has imprisoned longer than any other prisoner. He is very close to the prisoners around him and is open with them.

Takishi

M   29   Prisoner   v39 p30

An arrogant man who hates to lose. Despite being fatally injured, he persistently defies Suigetsu until the end.

Fire Temple

A temple in the Land of Fire where priests live. It is surrounded by verdant forest and overflowing with flora and fauna.

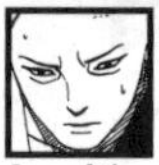

Sentoki

M 25 Ninja Priest v35 p99

One of the priests in training who returned to the Fire Temple immediately after Hidan and Kakuzu's assault. He informs Konoha of the emergency at hand.

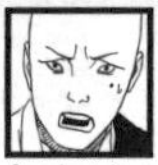

Ichigen

M 22 Ninja Priest v35 p87

A priest in training at the Fire Temple who still has much to learn. He respects and admires Chiriku more than anyone.

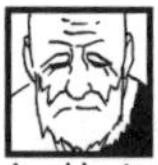

Bansai

M 64 Ninja Priest v36 p8

An old priest at the Fire Temple who is currently retired. He prays for the safety of Asuma and his comrades when they go into battle.

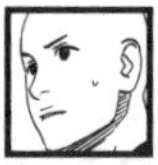

Zenza

M 20 Ninja Priest v36 p8

The young priest in training who was patrolling the temple. He is shocked by the death of Chiriku and many of his friends.

Hot Spring Lodge

A lodge where travelers come to rest. It is bustling with customers every day.

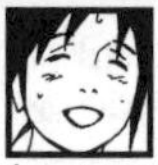

Nae

F 19 Traveler v32 p123

A woman who has traveled from the Village of Sunagakure. She absolutely loves hot springs and travels around the world to visit them.

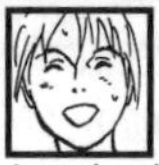

Emiru

F 17 Traveler v32 p123

A traveler who loves to take sojourns and hot springs. She bathes in the hot spring upon discovering its skin moisturizing properties.

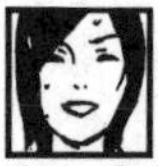

Yui

F 28 Traveler v32 p123

She is refreshing her mind and body at the hot spring in order to relieve the tension in her neck and shoulders. She is satisfied by her short break.

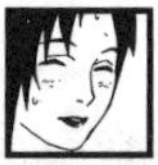

Sumire

F 20 Traveler v32 p123

A married woman with two children. She visits the hot spring lodge to take a break from raising children.

Others

A bunch of people from the feudal age to the modern age. They have many different values.

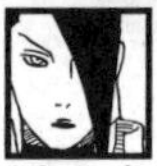

Senju Toka

F 27 Senju Clan Shinobi v43 p176

A Senju clan kunoichi. One of Hashirama's aides. She is skilled in genjutsu and her powers are well known in other countries.

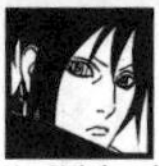

Uchiha Hikaku

M 25 Uchiha Clan Shinobi v43 p168

An Uchiha clan shinobi. Despite his youth, he is the most talented in his clan and is very adept at being a leader.

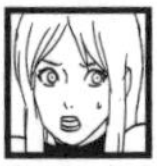

Tamaki

F 16 Daughter of Arms Dealer v39 p90

Cat Granny's granddaughter who is the poster girl at the restaurant she works at. She treats the customers who come by with sincerity.

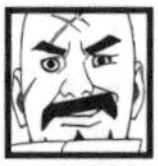

Zangei

M 36 Collection Office Staff v36 p20

An evil black-market dealer who buys the bodies of famous people from Kakuzu for high prices. He is later interrogated by Ibiki.

IMPROMPTU
PROFILE RANKING!

Exciting! Heart-stopping!

I'm looking forward to the results!

Reasonable comparisons of anything! The four great rankings are revealed! Which shinobi will prevail?!

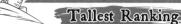

I like this curtain quite a bit.

Tallest Ranking

1. **Jugo** 202.1 cm (6'7¼")
2. **Hoshigaki Kisame** 195 cm (6'4½")
3. **Morino Ibiki** 193.5 cm (6'4")
4. **Jiraiya** 191.2 cm (6'3¼")
5. **Sarutobi Asuma** 190.8 cm (6'3")

⬅ The only one who is over two meters tall and who stands seven centimeters taller than the person in second place, Jugo is clearly in first place! Because of his exceptional height, all of his clothes are specially made.

... CHUB—
GRRR

Weight Ranking

1. **Morino Ibiki** 88 kg (194 lbs.)
2. **Akimichi Choji** 87.5 kg (193 lbs.)
3. **Jiraiya** 87.5 kg (193 lbs.)
4. **Hoshigaki Kisame** 83.1 kg (183 lbs.)
5. **Sarutobi Asuma** 81.6 kg (180 lbs.)

⬅ Ibiki gets first place by just a one-pound (500 grams) difference. But it makes sense for someone who is tall to weigh a lot. If you take that into consideration, Choji is definitely the fa—

Shinobi with Extreme Interests Ranking

Let's do this, Lee!
Okay, Guy Sensei!

1. **Might Guy** (repetitive sidestepping, mitt training)
2. **Rock Lee** (hard work)
3. **The Hokage** (second, Senju Tobirama) (perfecting himself)

⬆ The extremely spirited, extremely eye-browed, extremely intense teacher and student team who are all about youth are in the top two spots! They are always training and a good example of what shinobi should aspire to be.

Shinobi I Want to Fight Ranking

I knew it!
I'm the one closest to becoming the Hokage.
NUH-UH
ERNT! WRONG ANSWER! PLEASE TRY AGAIN!

1. **Uzumaki Naruto** (8 votes)
2. **Haruno Sakura** (3 votes)
3. **Hatake Kakashi** (3 votes)

⬆ Following his nindo in his goal to become Hokage, Naruto takes first place. As he becomes more powerful through his training, Naruto is receiving attention from shinobi who want to be his rival.

Shinobi Facts

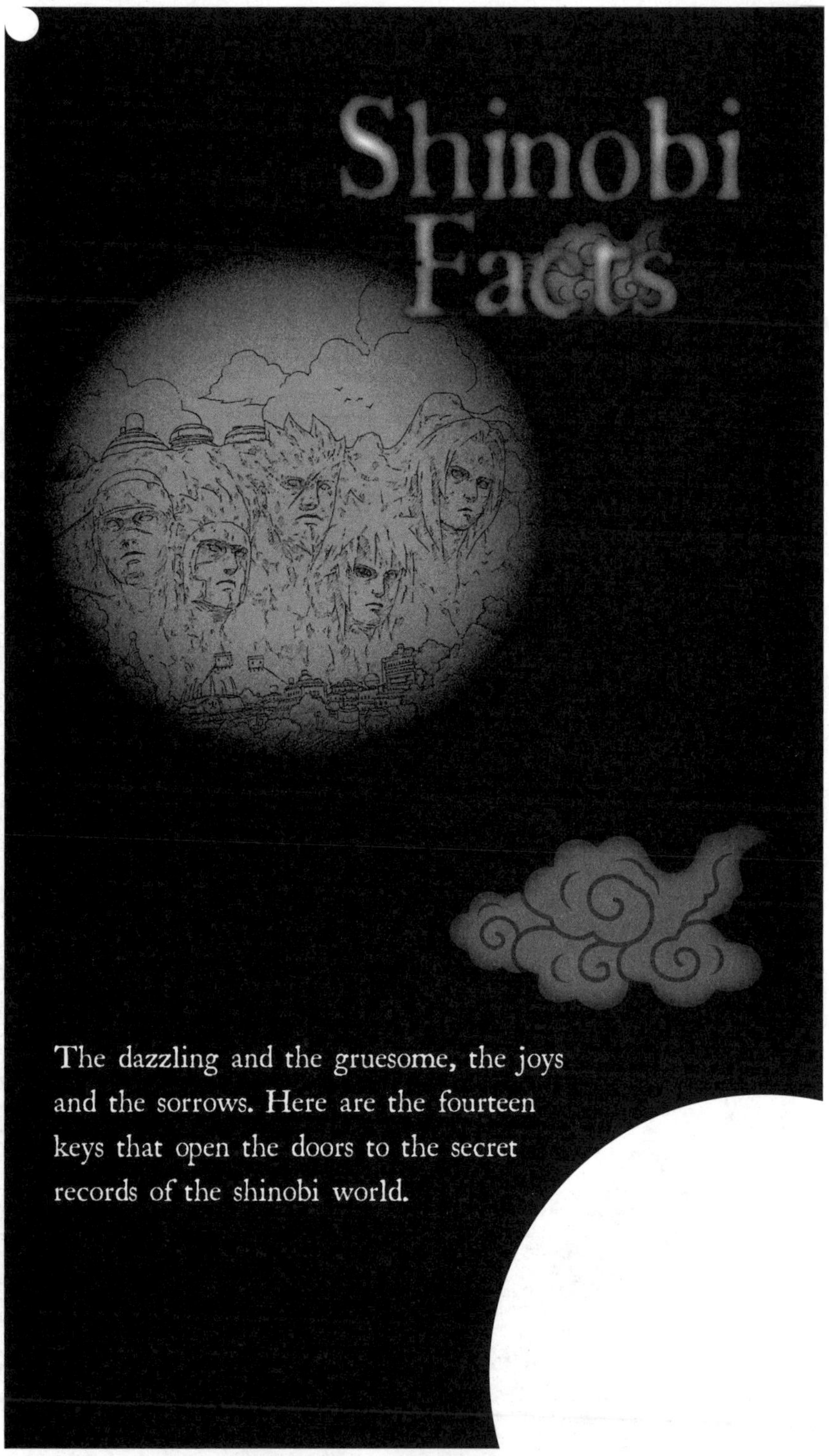

The dazzling and the gruesome, the joys and the sorrows. Here are the fourteen keys that open the doors to the secret records of the shinobi world.

Shinobi Facts

The founding of Konoha

Konohagakure, the largest hidden village of the Five Great Nations. Against the harsh flow of time, they rose and established themselves in the annals of history.

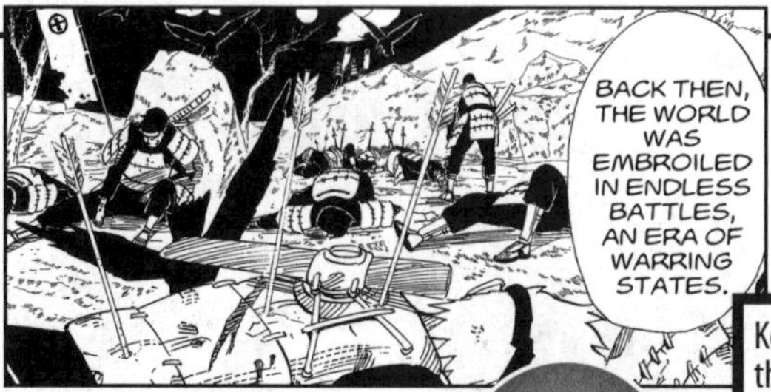
BACK THEN, THE WORLD WAS EMBROILED IN ENDLESS BATTLES, AN ERA OF WARRING STATES.

ERA OF WARRING STATES

A world of unrest where blood was washed with blood.

Over eighty years ago, nations seeking power and territory were constantly at war. These nations had weapons, hired fighters known as shinobi. At that time, hidden villages were not yet in existence and the shinobi operated as mercenaries grouped together by family ties.

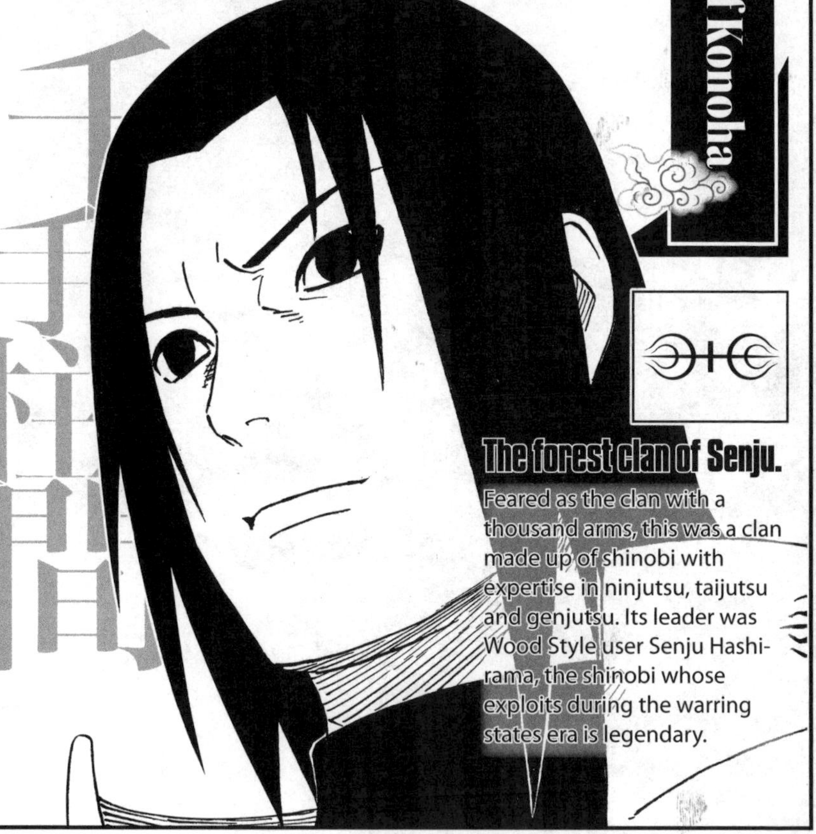

The forest clan of Senju.

Feared as the clan with a thousand arms, this was a clan made up of shinobi with expertise in ninjutsu, taijutsu and genjutsu. Its leader was Wood Style user Senju Hashirama, the shinobi whose exploits during the warring states era is legendary.

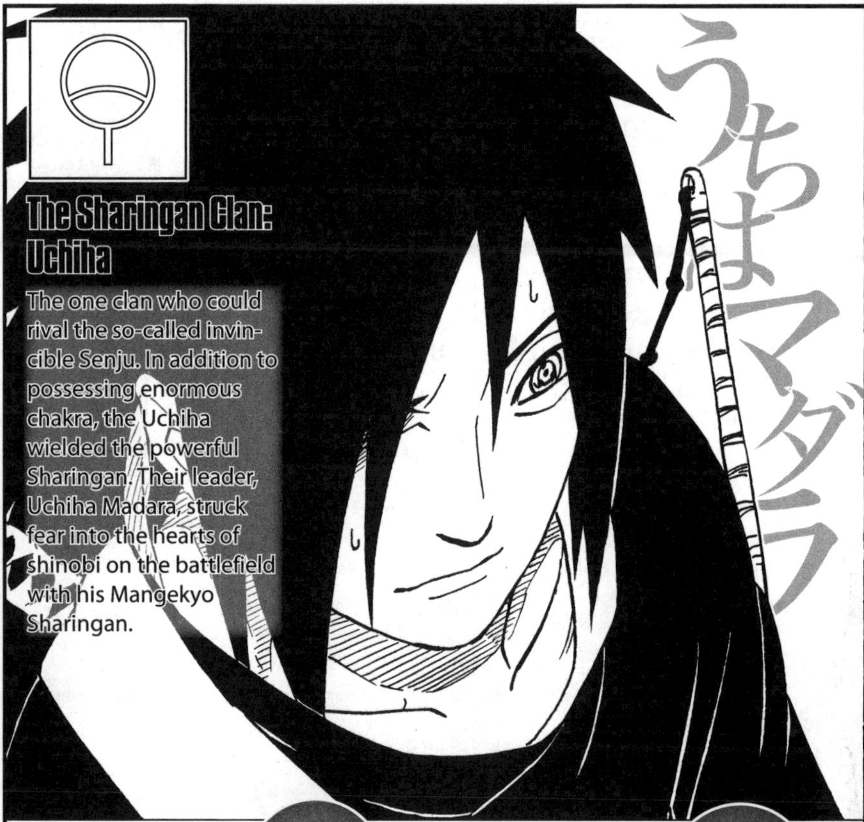
うちはマダラ

The Sharingan Clan: Uchiha

The one clan who could rival the so-called invincible Senju. In addition to possessing enormous chakra, the Uchiha wielded the powerful Sharingan. Their leader, Uchiha Madara, struck fear into the hearts of shinobi on the battlefield with his Mangekyo Sharingan.

The end of a long war is finally in sight.

POST-WAR

When the fighting ended, peace was established between the Senji and Uchiha clans. They formed an alliance and signed a pact with the Land of Fire, and Konohagakure was founded. The creation of this most powerful organization served as a deterrent to war and fighting in the regions, which steadily came to a halt.

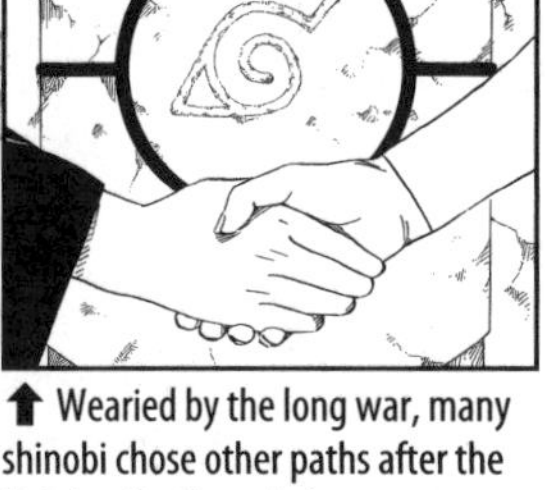

⬆ Wearied by the long war, many shinobi chose other paths after the fighting finally ended.

The two most feared clans.

TWO POWER CLANS

Among the many shinobi groups in existence, two groups were always in demand by the warring nations. They were the Senji and Uchiha clans. So great was their power that if one nation hired the Senju, their rival was sure to hire the Uchiha. The end of the age of warring nations marked the beginning of the rivalry between the two men.

Shinobi Facts

Uchiha Clan

As if to mirror the Japanese proverb, **The prosperous must decay**, the Uchiha clan descended into the darkness of history. Here is a look into the path of their decline.

They distinguished themselves in war with the power of their Sharingan.
With their overwhelming ocular ninjutsu, they subdued shinobi groups one after another.

⬅ With their overwhelming ocular ninjutsu, they subdued shinobi groups one after another.

THE GLORY

They distinguished themselves in war with the power of their Sharingan.

Their Sharingan could see through everything, and their Fire Style dyed the battlefield crimson with flames. The Uchiha clan became known as the fighting clan with their prowess in combat. After the alliance with the Senju was formed and Konohagakure was established, they should have lived in glory. But it was only the prologue of their tragic saga.

⬇ Those loyal to Madara formed a faction which rebelled against the higher-ups.

THERE WERE FINALLY SOME UCHIHA WHO DISCERNED THAT MOTIVE.
AND AN ANTI-ESTABLISHMENT FACTION THAT HAD INHERITED MY WILL.

REBELLION

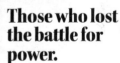

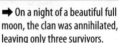

Those who lost the battle for power.

Hashirama or Madara. Regarding who would lead Konohagakure, the Land of Fire along with the members of the village chose Hashirama. From this day on, the fate of the Uchiha clan took a twisted turn. After losing the fight for power, Madara went rogue. And his threat of revenge bred fear among the higher-ups over the existence of the Uchiha. Furthermore, the suspicion and dread toward this clan was cemented with the attack of Nine Tails.

➡ On a night of a beautiful full moon, the clan was annihilated, leaving only three survivors.

DESTRUCTION

The fateful night of the full moon

The Konoha leaders learned of the Uchiha coup d'état plot from Itachi. Declaring "An eye for an eye," they ordered the eradication of the clan.

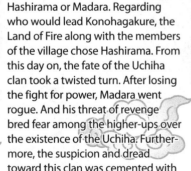

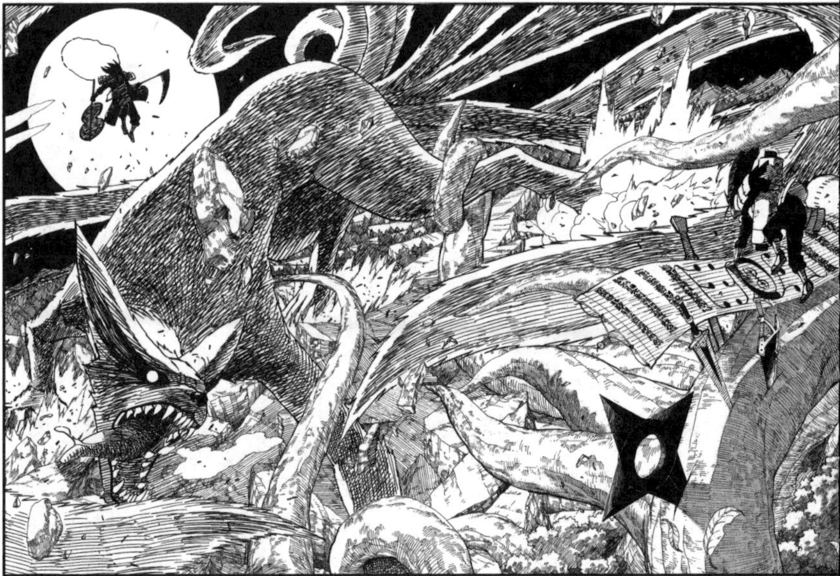

⬆ Ocular ninjutsu capable of subduing even Nine Tails. This also contributed to the suspicions raised towards the clan during the Nine Tails attack.

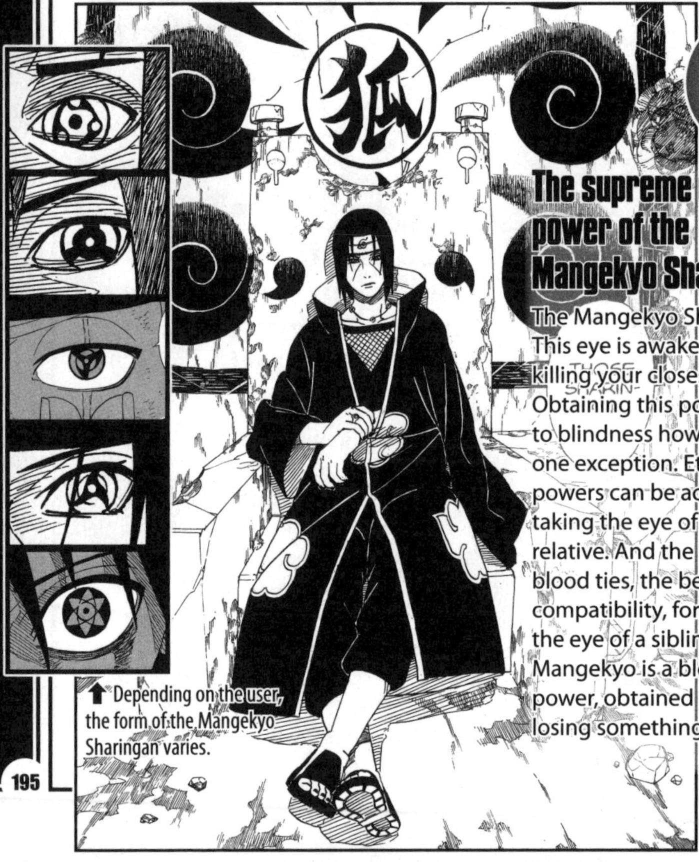
狐

⬆ Depending on the user, the form of the Mangekyo Sharingan varies.

OCULAR NINJUTSU

The supreme eye: The power of the Mangekyo Sharingan

The Mangekyo Sharingan. This eye is awakened by killing your closest friend. Obtaining this power leads to blindness however, with one exception. Eternal ocular powers can be achieved by taking the eye of a blood relative. And the closer the blood ties, the better the compatibility, for example, the eye of a sibling. The Mangekyo is a blood-soaked power, obtained only after losing something precious.

Shinobi Facts

The Akatsuki

The Akatsuki. Its members, enveloped in black cloaks with red cloud patterns, boast unusual talents. Revealed here are their hidden powers and ambitions.

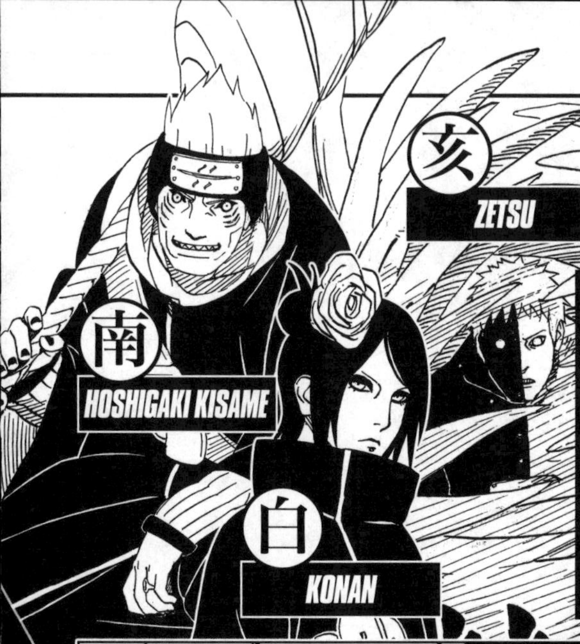

亥
ZETSU
南
HOSHIGAKI KISAME
白
KONAN

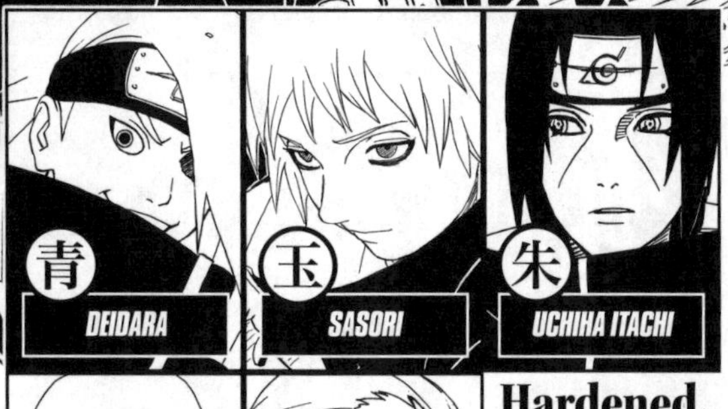

青
DEIDARA
玉
SASORI
朱
UCHIHA ITACHI
北
KAKUZU
三
HIDAN

MEMBERS

Hardened, skillful masters, even stronger than a jinchûriki.

The Akatsuki organization is made up of rogue shinobi from various lands. But they are not run-of-the-mill rogue shinobi. They are wanted for heinous crimes including a daimyo killing, bomb terrorism, and the slaughter of a clan. They always operate in two-man cells, and each member has a quota of one Tailed Beast to capture. It is their leader's belief that when two members team up, even a Tailed Beast or jinchûriki will have no chance against them. So he has recruited members with unique specialties such as human puppetry and clay bombs. The insignia ring each member wears is proof that they are part of the Akatsuki. When a newcomer is accepted by the old-timers and given a ring, then he can truly call himself an Akatsuki. At one time, Orochimaru belonged to the Akatsuki and wore a ring with Sky engraved on it.

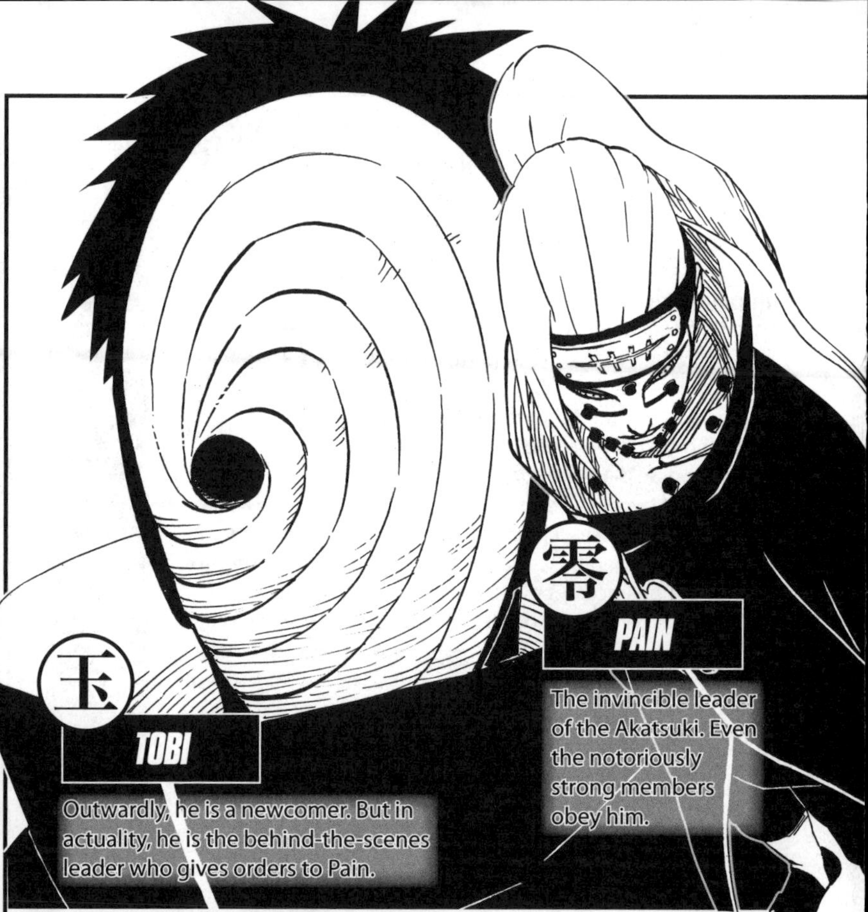
零
PAIN
The invincible leader of the Akatsuki. Even the notoriously strong members obey him.
玉
TOBI
Outwardly, he is a newcomer. But in actuality, he is the behind-the-scenes leader who gives orders to Pain.

The take-over of the shinobi world to start a reformation.

AMBITION

The ultimate goal of the Akatsuki is world domination. Putting "a stop to this war-riddled ludicrous world" and starting a reformation is its true aim. That is the reason for accumulating money, for creating an organization that will accept money for contracts of war. By crushing the hidden villages in each nation, they hope to gain a monopoly and control all wars.

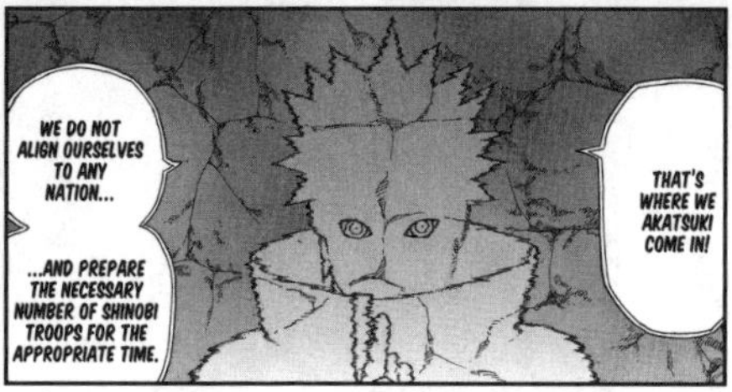
THAT'S WHERE WE AKATSUKI COME IN!
WE DO NOT ALIGN OURSELVES TO ANY NATION...
...AND PREPARE THE NECESSARY NUMBER OF SHINOBI TROOPS FOR THE APPROPRIATE TIME.

⬆ The present plan to gather all the Tailed Beasts is just part of the picture.

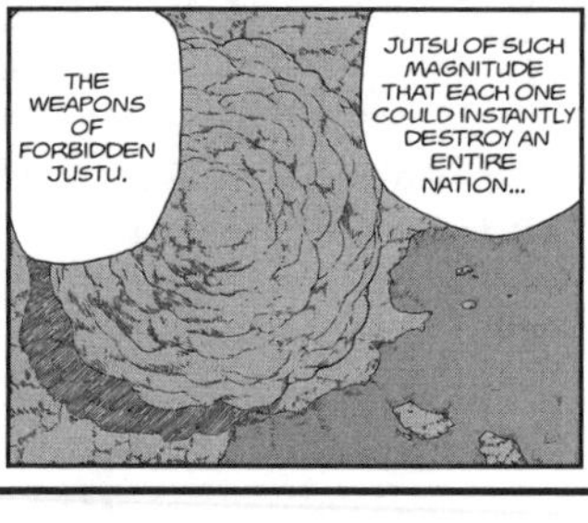
JUTSU OF SUCH MAGNITUDE THAT EACH ONE COULD INSTANTLY DESTROY AN ENTIRE NATION...
THE WEAPONS OF FORBIDDEN JUSTU.

➡ Starting a war by using weapons of forbidden jutsu and conquering the world is their aim.

Shinobi Facts

Tailed Beasts

MENACE

A power beyond the imagination of humans threatens the world.

Did Heaven's ire or human malice create them? The mysteries of the Tailed Beasts unfold here.

Tailed Beasts, including the Nine-Tailed Fox Spirit sealed inside Naruto, are basically demonic beasts that suddenly appear at the critical juncture of an era. Like earthquakes and lightning, they are natural calamities. Formed from huge concentrations of chakra, they are brutal and ferocious. When they run rampant, they are uncontrollable; the epitome of the word menace. It has been confirmed that there are nine Tailed Beasts and they are named by the number of tails they possess. Hence, One Tail has one tail, Two Tails has two, etc. Long ago, the First Hokage captured several Tailed Beasts and distributed them to each nation as guarantees of security agreements in order to equalize the balance of power. In recent years, Tailed Beasts have been dispersed throughout the regions of the world and their whereabouts are known only to a select few.

NINE TAILS

The Tailed Beast with immense power which once attacked Konohagakure. It is presently sealed inside Naruto, placed there by the jutsu of the Fourth Hokage.

➡ The Akatsuki travel far and often in their hunt for the Tailed Beasts.

⬇ Captured Tailed Beasts are sealed in a giant statue.

SEAL

Two Tailed Beasts remain to be captured.

The Akatsuki continues to hunt the Tailed Beasts in order to use them as weapons of forbidden jutsu. Only two, Eight Tails and Nine Tails, remain free. What will happen when the Akatsuki has them all under their control?

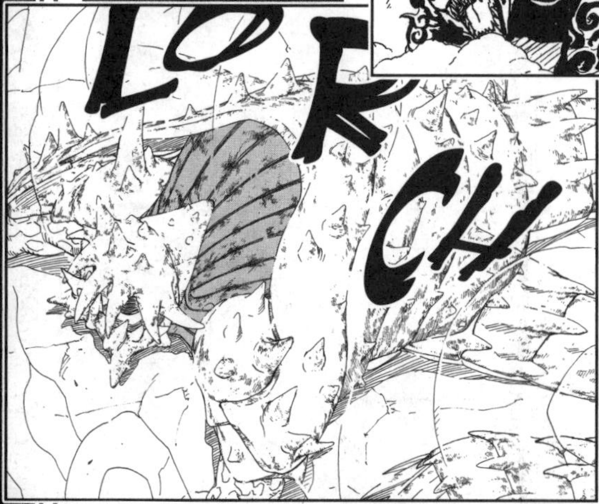

THREE TAILS

It is a giant turtle with a hard shell. Instead of a jinchûriki host, it inhabited the bottom of a lake. Deidara uses a clay bomb and successfully captures it.

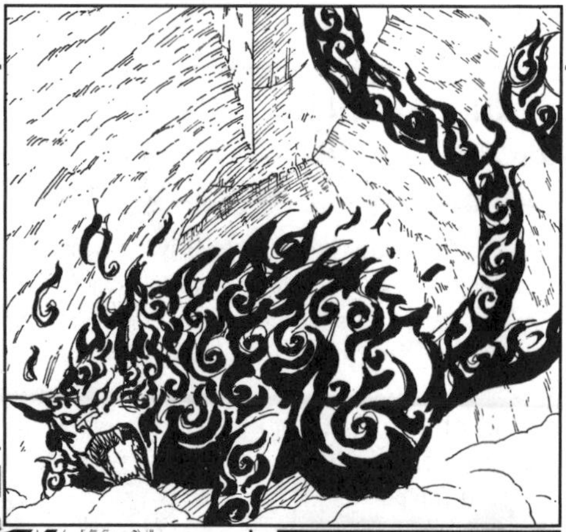

TWO TAILS

A demon cat said to have been spawned from a vengeful spirit. Its muscles are soft and pliant and despite its huge size, it moves swiftly.

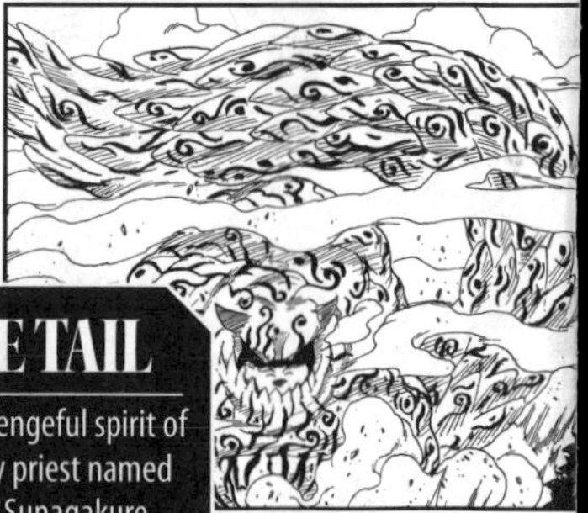

ONE TAIL

It is the vengeful spirit of an elderly priest named Shukaku. Sunagakure obtained the One Tail and used it for research on jinchûriki.

Where is this other Tailed Beast...?!

One Tail through Seven Tails have been captured by the Akatsuki. Nine Tails is sealed inside Naruto. Just where is the remaining Eight Tails…?

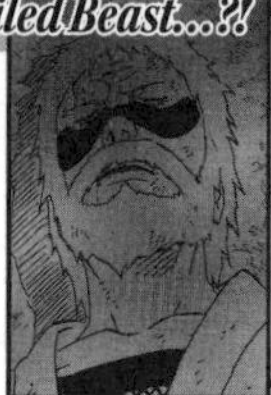

WEAPONS

Their powers are sought during the chaos of war

During the Great Ninja Wars, the overwhelming power possessed by the Tailed Beasts was coveted as a military weapon. However, controlling that power was no easy task. So Tailed Beasts were sealed into the bodies of hosts in order to make them more manageable. Thus was born the jinchûriki, and the way to control their power.

⬇ Each nation tried to take advantage of the jinchûriki as a military weapon.

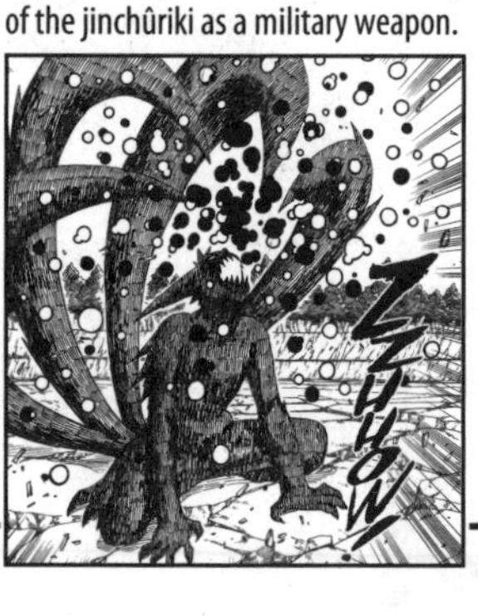

Shinobi 忍 Facts

The Hebi

The Hebi: the troop organized by Uchiha Sasuke. Made up of four shinobi, here is the story of their path of carnage.

FORMATION

Crawling out of the snake pit, an elite group of only the best.

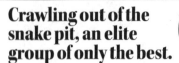

Find Itachi and settle the score swiftly. For this sole purpose, Uchiha Sasuke selects three shinobi. Hoshigaki Kisame, the child prodigy of Kirigakure. Karin, the female member, with her prominent sensory skills. And bipolar Jugo from whom the curse mark originated. Because all four of them have been involved with Orochimaru, Sasuke decides to name his troop the Hebi.

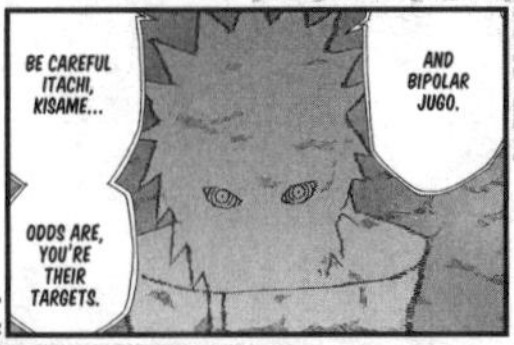

BE CAREFUL ITACHI, KISAME...
AND BIPOLAR JUGO.
ODDS ARE, YOU'RE THEIR TARGETS.

⬆ The Akatsuki is also very cautious about the Hebi's movements.

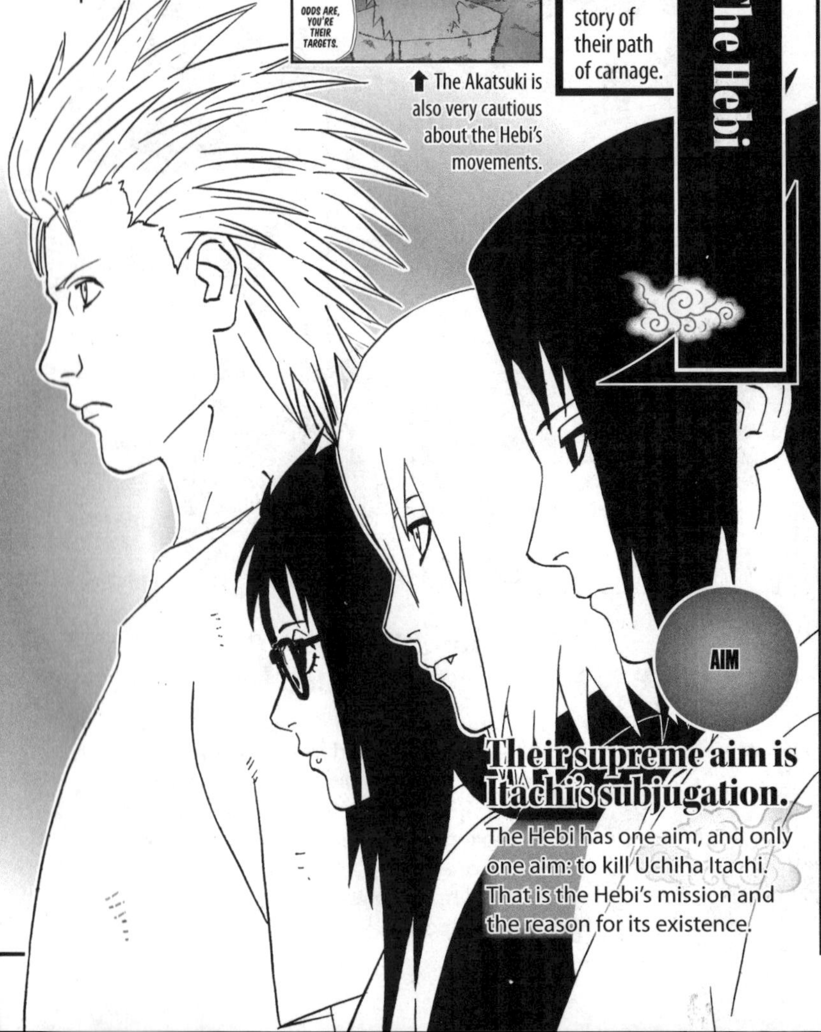

AIM

Their supreme aim is Itachi's subjugation.

The Hebi has one aim, and only one aim: to kill Uchiha Itachi. That is the Hebi's mission and the reason for its existence.

➡ The nightmare has continued since he was a child. A new power awakens in Sasuke.

SPLOOSH

TURNING POINT

From the Hebi to Team Taka - A new purpose.

With Uchiha Itachi's death, the Hebi accomplishes its mission. But upon learning Itachi's real intention and the bitterness he felt, Sasuke is consumed with anger toward the machinations of the Konoha leaders that led to the tragic fate of his brother and family. And he renames his troop Team Taka. This time, the sole mission and absolute aim is the destruction of Konohagakure.

⬅ Is it all part of Madara's plan?

Eastern Hideout

The Eastern Hideout is packed with huge research apparatuses. This is where Hozuki Suigetsu was imprisoned.

SH SHOOSH

Southern Hideout

A tiny island completely surrounded by the sea. Captives who will serve as test subjects are kept here under the supervision of their jailer, Karin.

Northern Hideout

Wedged between two high cliffs, this facility is a test station for live human experiments. Test subjects implanted with the curse mark of Jugo are confined here.

Orochimaru's many hideouts.

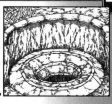

Although he is the leader of the Village Hidden in Sound, Orochimaru establishes hideouts in many lands and regions, starting with the small island in the lake north of Tenchi Bridge. These hideouts have various uses; some are research facilities, some are prisons, etc. Only Orochimaru's trusted subordinates know their locations.

Shinobi 忍 Facts

Anbu Black ops

The shinobi who support the giant tree known as Konoha. We move on to the Anbu whose shinobi stay even deeper in the shadows.

Pursuit

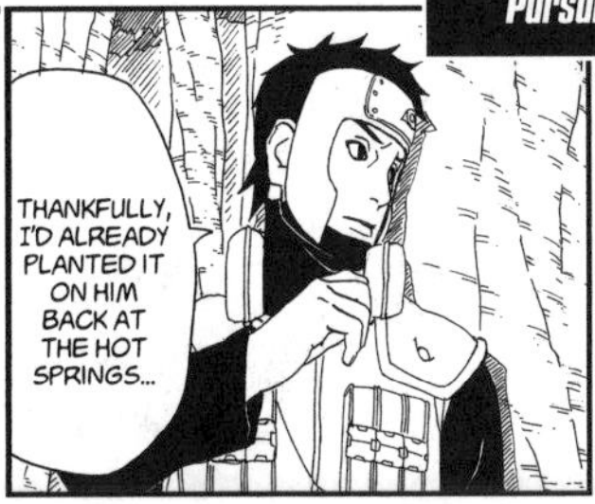
THANKFULLY, I'D ALREADY PLANTED IT ON HIM BACK AT THE HOT SPRINGS...

← They track persons of interest to check on their movements and if necessary search their hideouts.

UNDER THE HOKAGE'S DIRECT CONTROL

This elite battalion acts solely on the orders of the Hokage.

If duty and one's nindo are the reasons for a shinobi's existence, then the Anbu exist solely for the village. With their faces hidden behind masks, they obey only the orders of their leader, the Hokage. Since the missions are conducted in secret under harsh conditions, only the elite are chosen to become Anbu. They live out of sight in Konoha, lurk in the shadows and rule over the darkness. The Anbu can truly be called shinobi among shinobi.

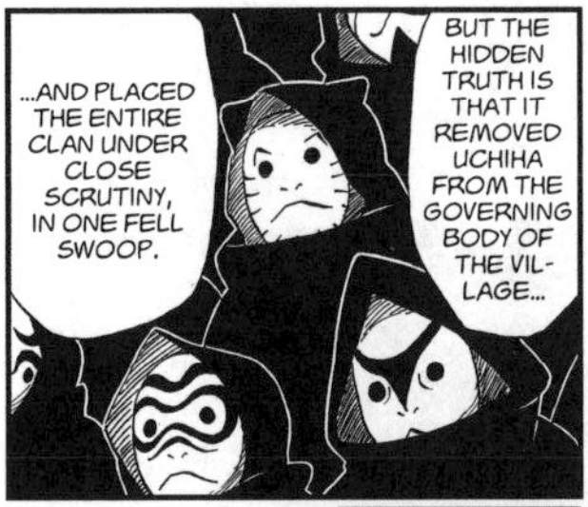
BUT THE HIDDEN TRUTH IS THAT IT REMOVED UCHIHA FROM THE GOVERNING BODY OF THE VIL-LAGE...
...AND PLACED THE ENTIRE CLAN UNDER CLOSE SCRUTINY, IN ONE FELL SWOOP.

← Risk factors are observed and changes are recorded, often for years.

Assassination

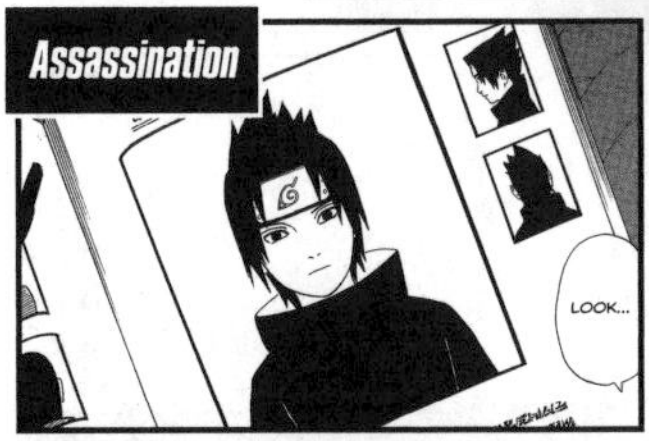
LOOK...

Observation

← The Bingo Book of the Anbu Black Ops contains detailed intel about each mark.

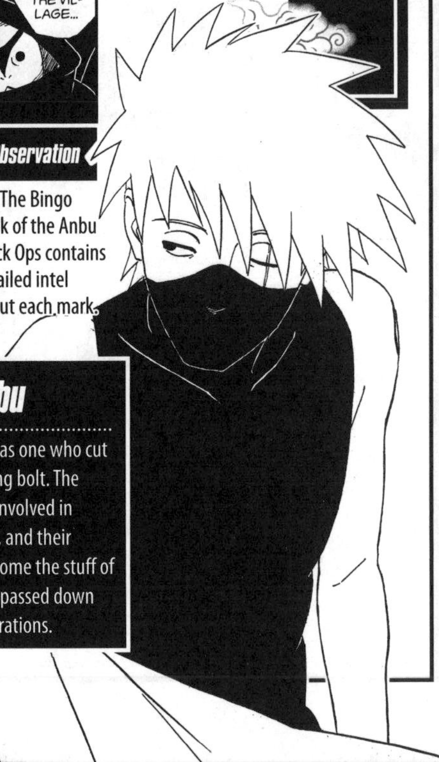

A legend born from the Anbu

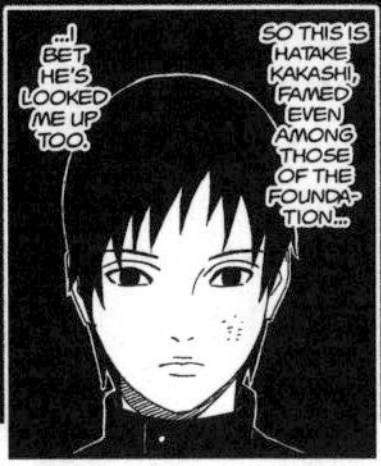
SO THIS IS HATAKE KAKASHI, FAMED EVEN AMONG THOSE OF THE FOUNDA-TION...
...I BET HE'S LOOKED ME UP TOO.

Kakashi is known as one who cut through a lightning bolt. The Anbu are always involved in rigorous missions, and their exploits often become the stuff of legend which are passed down through the generations.

THE FOUNDATION

Operating in the shadows, this is the unique Anbu division under Danzo's direct supervision.

Danzo vied with Sarutobi Hiruzen for the role of Third Hokage. It is Danzo who formed a separate training division of the Anbu known as the Foundation. Although it was officially disbanded after Hiruzen became the Hokage, the Foundation continues, most definitely, to operate in secret.

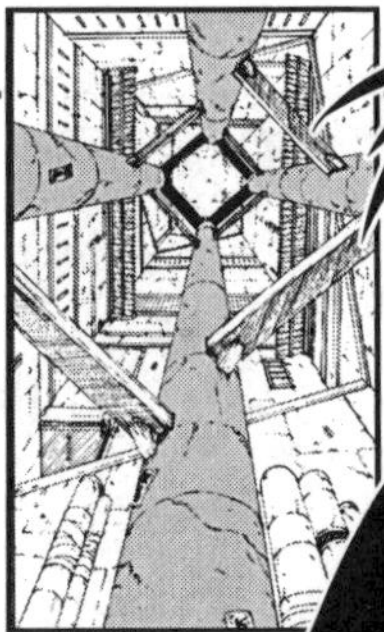

⬆ The Foundation is headquartered in and operates out of the deepest recesses of Konoha.

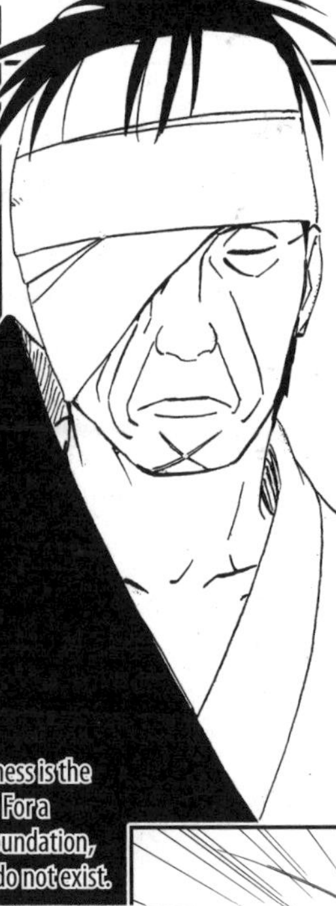

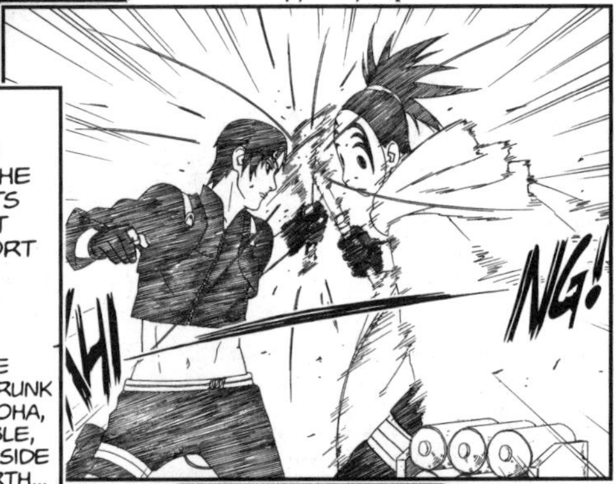
NG!

⇨ Unpreparedness is the greatest enemy. For a shinobi of the Foundation, rest and repose do not exist.

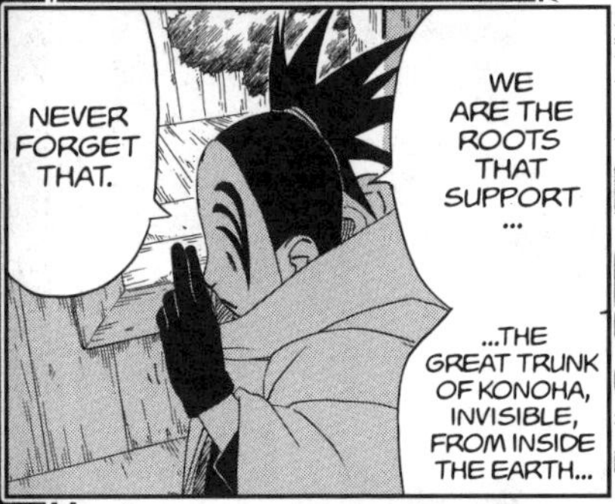
WE ARE THE ROOTS THAT SUPPORT ...
...THE GREAT TRUNK OF KONOHA, INVISIBLE, FROM INSIDE THE EARTH...
NEVER FORGET THAT.

⬆ The shinobi of the Foundation swear loyalty to Danzo, abandoning their names, feelings and future to serve as his vessels of the dark.

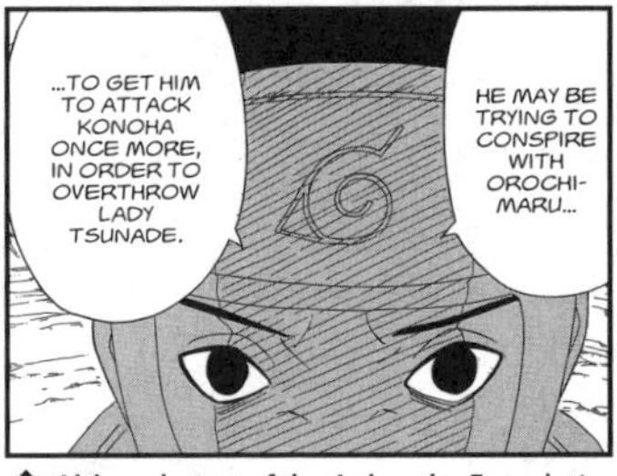
HE MAY BE TRYING TO CONSPIRE WITH OROCHIMARU...
...TO GET HIM TO ATTACK KONOHA ONCE MORE, IN ORDER TO OVERTHROW LADY TSUNADE.

⬆ Although part of the Anbu, the Foundation is seen as a possible risk and is under surveillance.

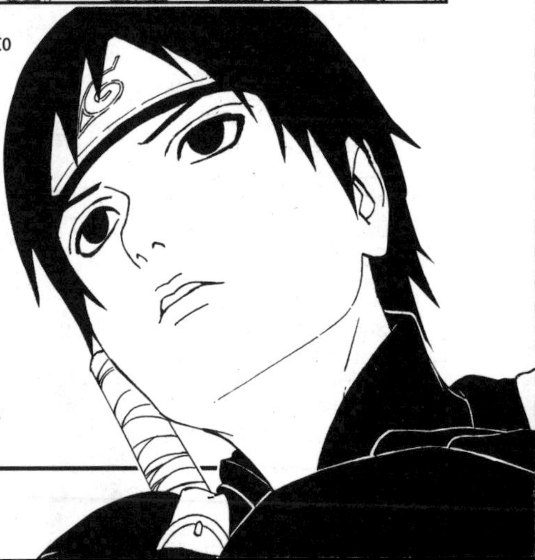

Shinobi Facts
Mount Myoboku

The toad mountain where Jiraiya underwent his training. Here are recorded the secrets of Mount Myoboku.

SECLUDED REGION

A sacred mountain where toads with strange powers gather.

This is the sacred land of toads. It's about a month's journey on foot from Konohagakure. Also known as the Mountain of Doubt, there are only two ways to get here. Via a secret path or through the Art of Reverse Summoning cast by one who has entered into a contract with a toad. However, it is said that once in a while, a traveler who has lost his way inadvertently gets on the secret path.

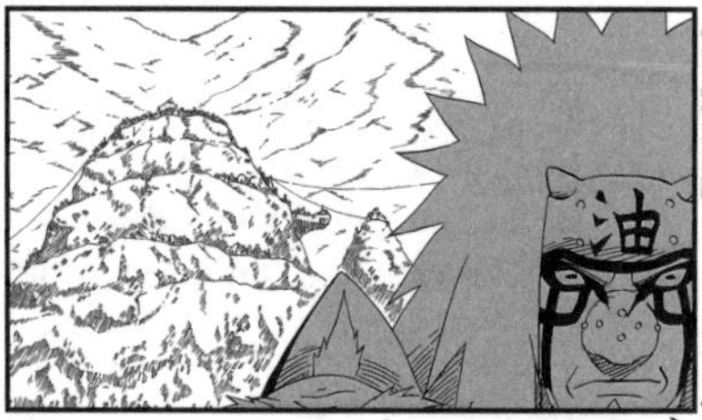

⬅ Jiraiya and others are led by fate into this mountain.

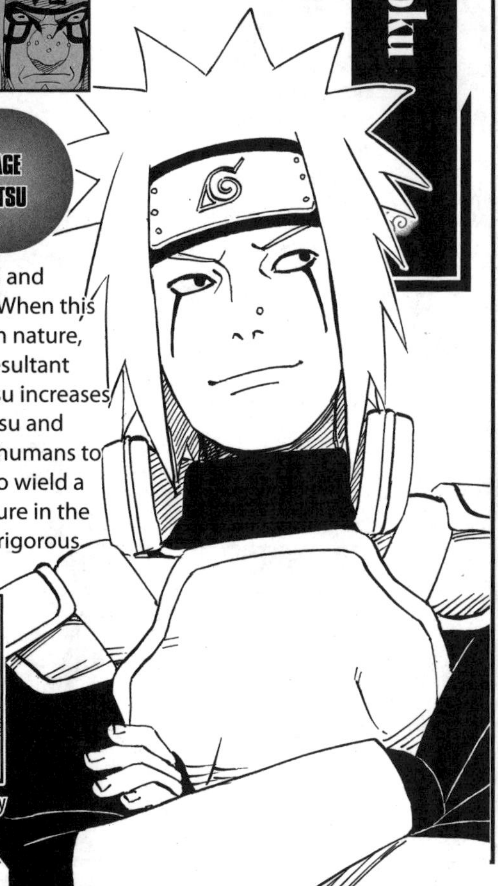

SAGE JUTSU

The power of the toads who turn nature into chakra.

All living things have spiritual and physical energy inside them. When this is combined with energy from nature, the jutsu released from the resultant chakra is sage jutsu. Sage jutsu increases the power of ninjutsu, genjutsu and taijutsu, and it is possible for humans to master it too. But to be able to wield a jutsu by synergizing with nature in the same way as the toads, long, rigorous training is essential.

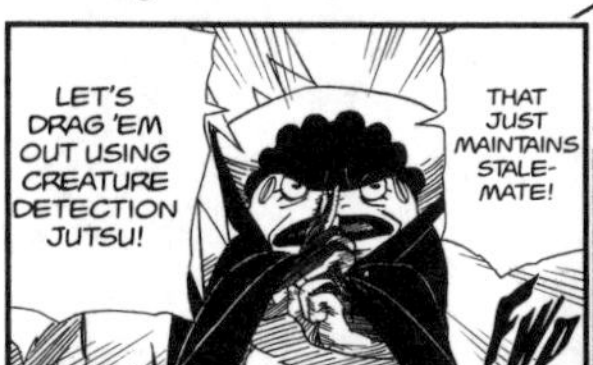
LET'S DRAG 'EM OUT USING CREATURE DETECTION JUTSU!
THAT JUST MAINTAINS STALE-MATE!

⬆ Toads of higher rank possess mastery over sage jutsu of tremendous force.

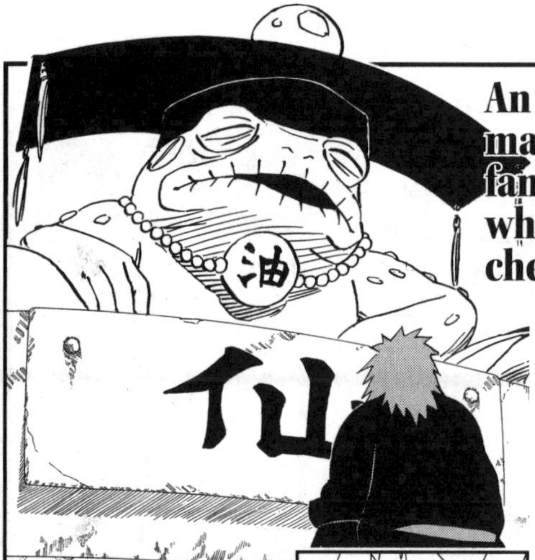

FAMILY ORGANIZATION

An organization made up of family members who share a cherished bond.

The toads of Mount Myoboku are led by the Great Toad Sage, the oldest among them. While they are a giant family, they have risen above bloodlines to become an organization. Even single toads have family and are considered households that fall under the jurisdiction of the organization. Hence, when one enters into a contract with a toad, one contracts with all toads of Mount Myoboku. However, the toads one is able to summon will depend on his/her abilities.

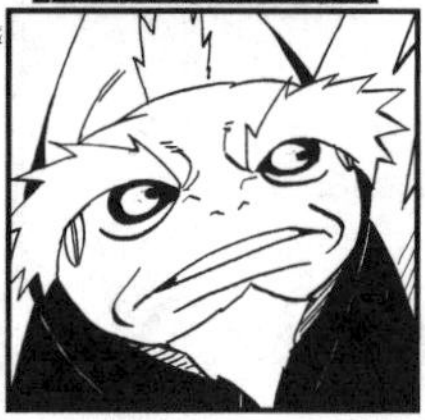

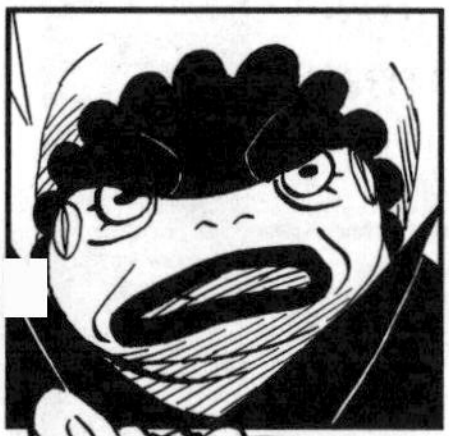

← ↑ The toads are guided by Fukasaku the patriarch, and Shima, the matriarch.

← ↓ The great family of Mount Myoboku.

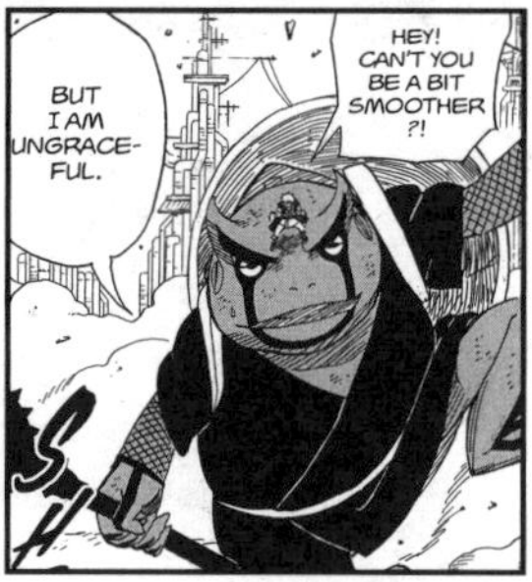
HEY! CAN'T YOU BE A BIT SMOOTHER ?!
BUT I AM UNGRACE-FUL.

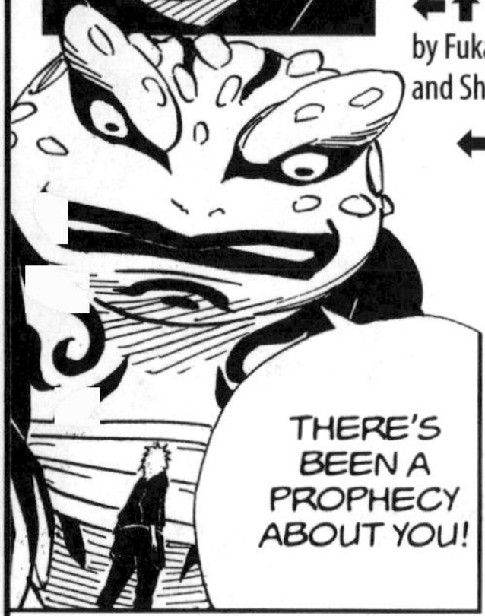
THERE'S BEEN A PROPHECY ABOUT YOU!

THE FAMILY

A household of toads with a myriad of powers.

From average toads to Sage Toads who transcend humans, Mount Myoboku is home to many species. While living in harmony with nature, they have each evolved their powers in unique ways.

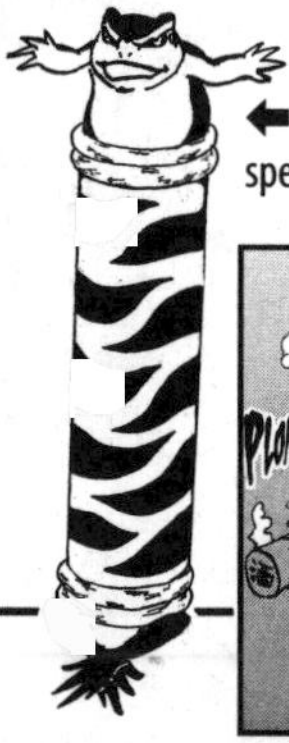

← Gerotora is a scroll toad, a rare species even on Mount Myoboku.

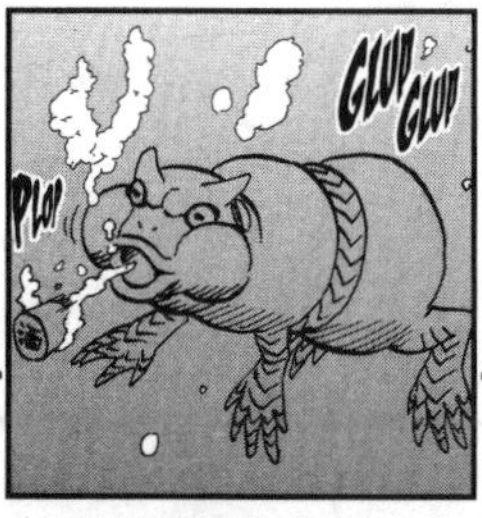
GLUP GLUP
PLOP

← Gamahyotan possesses a space barrier inside his body.

Shinobi Facts: Kazekage Rescue Mission

Shortly after Naruto's return to his homeland, he is given an A-rank mission upon which depends Konoha's tie with an ally.

MISSION

Rescue the Kazekage who has been captured by the Akatsuki.

The Kazekage of Sunagakure has been kidnapped by the Akatsuki whose aim is to collect all the Tailed Beasts. Konoha, an ally of the Suna, forms a rescue team immediately upon receiving an urgent message.

SNARING YOU ALIVE WAS THE HARD PART...
...AND A MOST SATISFYING END TO THIS MASTER-PIECE...

⬆ Deidara infiltrates Sunagakure alone. He defeats the Kazekage in a fierce aerial battle.

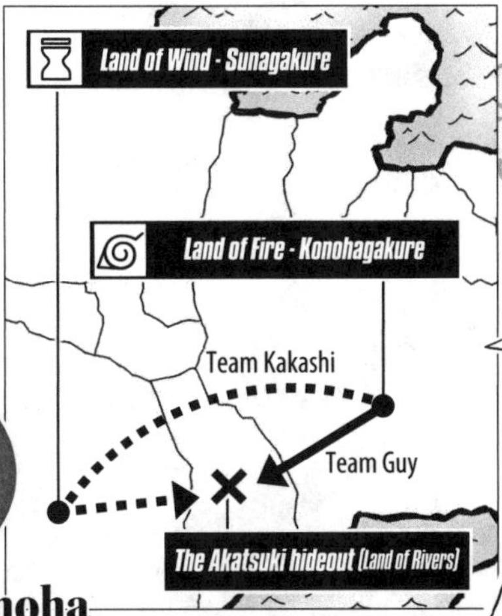
Land of Wind - Sunagakure
Land of Fire - Konohagakure
Team Kakashi
Team Guy
The Akatsuki hideout (Land of Rivers)

➡ Team A heads straight for Sunagakure. Team B gets intel en route and proceeds to the Akatsuki hideout.

IN PURSUIT

Both Konoha and Sunagakure dispatch teams.

Konoha's Cell Number 7, led by Hatake Kakashi, is Team A, and they rush to Sunagakure. After tending to the injured and gathering intel, the team (now a four-man cell which includes Chiyo, an elder of the Suna) heads for the Land of Rivers. The following day, Team B, made up of members of Team Guy, set out to merge with Team A at the Akatsuki hideout in the Land of Rivers.

Assassins and traps obstruct their path.

CONFINED

The Akatsuki aims to extract One Tail from its jinchûriki, the Kazekage. In order to delay the rescue teams, it sets traps all along the routes. Both teams overcome the hindrances, but they arrive a moment too late…

One Tail is extracted and the Kazekage dies. Because of a Five Seal Barrier, the teams are once again separated. But Team A manages to infiltrate the hideout and confronts the Akatsuki.

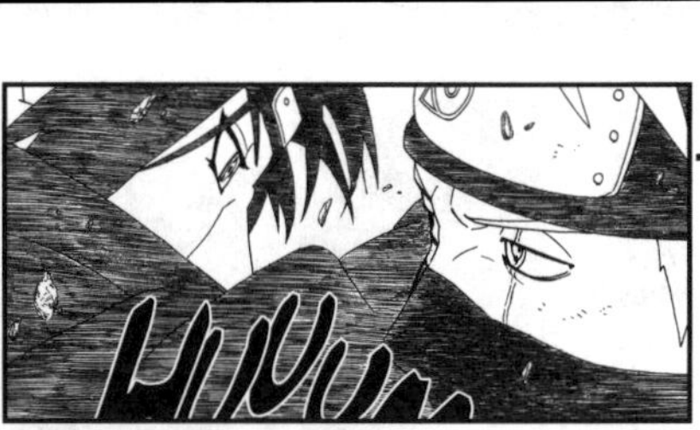

⬆ The strategy is to make the teams each battle two members of the Akatsuki.

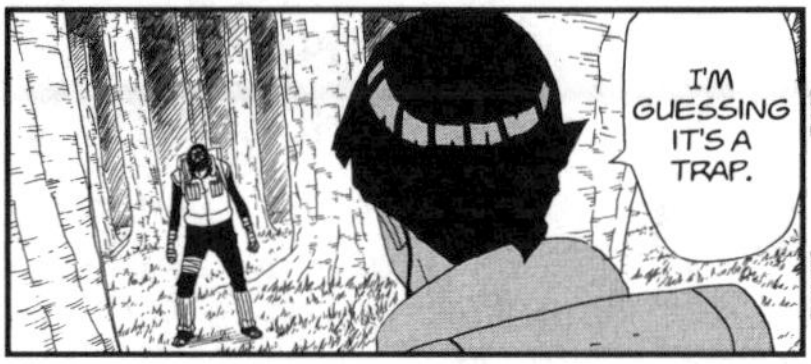
I'M GUESSING IT'S A TRAP.

⬆ Team B's progress comes to a stop due to a trap.

⬇ The young Kazekage and his rescuers from Konohagakure forge a strong bond of friendship.

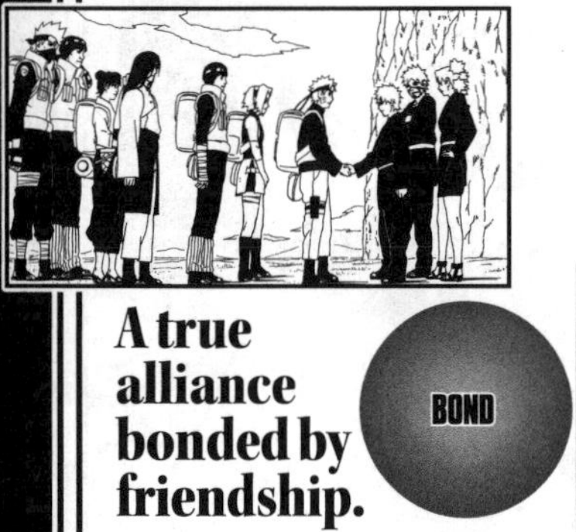

A true alliance bonded by friendship.

BOND

The Akatsuki are beaten in battle. But the Kazekage has not survived. However, Chiyo uses her Transference Technique and resurrects Gaara. She entrusts the future to this renewed life.

⬇ Inside the hideout, a battle between two puppet masters rages.

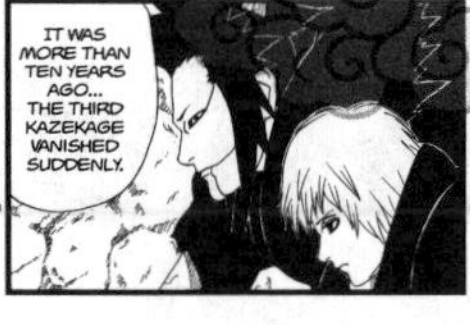
IT WAS MORE THAN TEN YEARS AGO... THE THIRD KAZEKAGE VANISHED SUDDENLY.

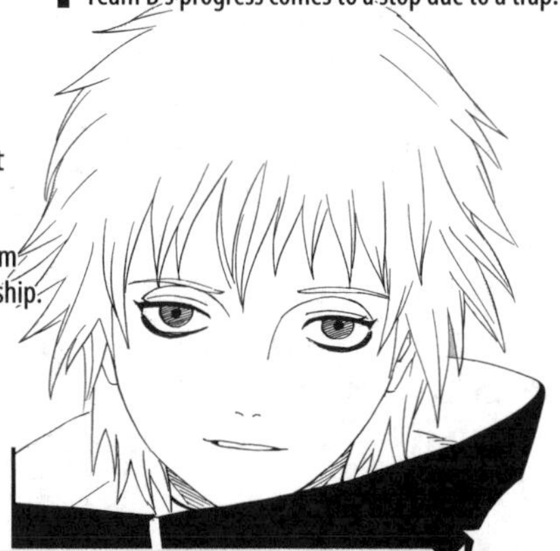

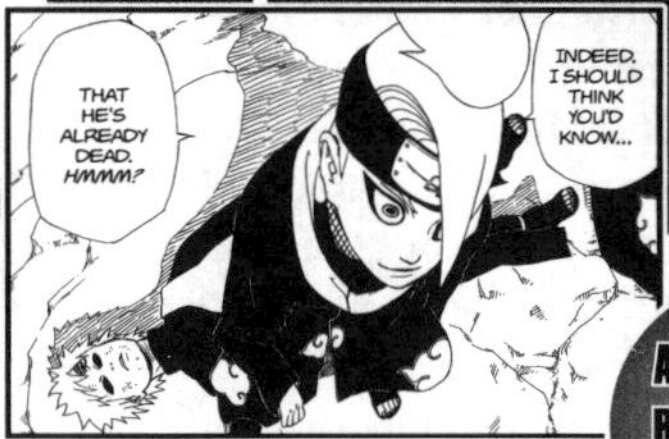
INDEED. I SHOULD THINK YOU'D KNOW...
THAT HE'S ALREADY DEAD. HMMM?

⬅ Deidara takes the Kazekage and flees the hideout.

AT THE POINT BETWEEN LIFE AND DEATH.

What will be the outcome of the battle as a life hovers near death?

The Akatsuki cannot prevent Team A from breaking through, but manages to split up the four-man cell. Sakura and Chiyo take on Sasori. The battle between two experienced puppet masters reaches gruesome heights, but in the end, Sakura and Chiyo's coordinated effort and their faith in each other win out.

Shinobi Facts

Tenchi Bridge Reconnaissance Mission

Here is a look at the new Team Kakashi, formed just days after the Kazekage rescue mission was completed.

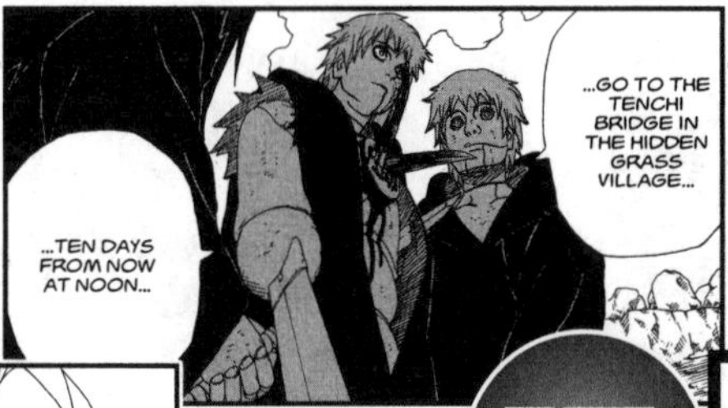
...GO TO THE TENCHI BRIDGE IN THE HIDDEN GRASS VILLAGE...
...TEN DAYS FROM NOW AT NOON...

➡ Sasori's dying words lead to this mission.

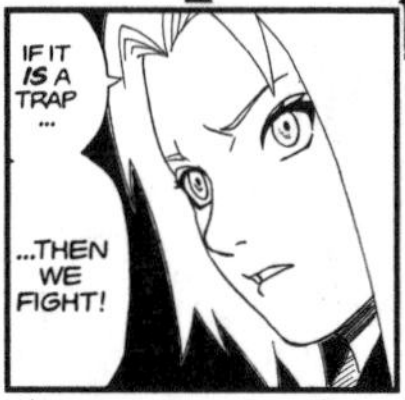
IF IT IS A TRAP ...
...THEN WE FIGHT!

⬆ Sakura volunteers for this reconnaissance mission.

TOP SECRET INFORMATION

Sasori's last words.

The intel brought back by Kakashi's Cell Number 7 rocks Konoha. Capturing the Akatsuki spy who infiltrated the Sound would produce information about Orochimaru and Sasuke. However, there is a high probability that this is a trap. The day of the meeting is just around the corner, and the Hokage must make a decision.

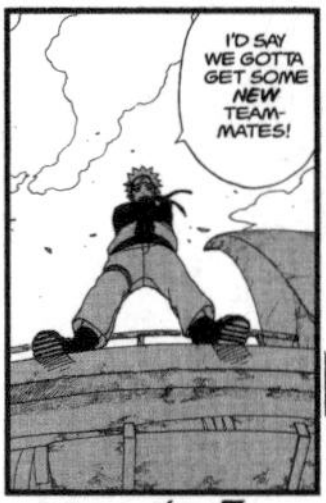
I'D SAY WE GOTTA GET SOME NEW TEAM-MATES!

⬅ Tsunade is advised that sending Naruto as part of the mission is dangerous. . .

NEW FORMATION

The new Team Kakashi goes on its first mission.

Konoha's Cell Number 7 takes on a new formation for its reconnaissance mission to Tenchi Bridge. Tsunade wagers that the desire to save a comrade will lead to a successful mission, but the village advisors counter that jinchûriki participation poses great risks. The interference by Konoha's high-ranking elders, including Danzo of the Foundation, leads to complications.

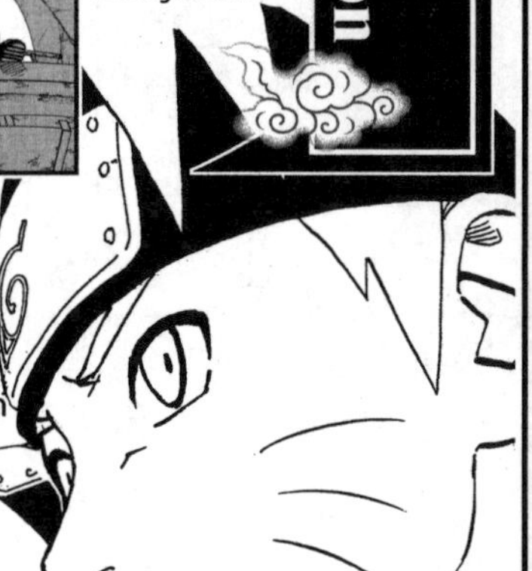

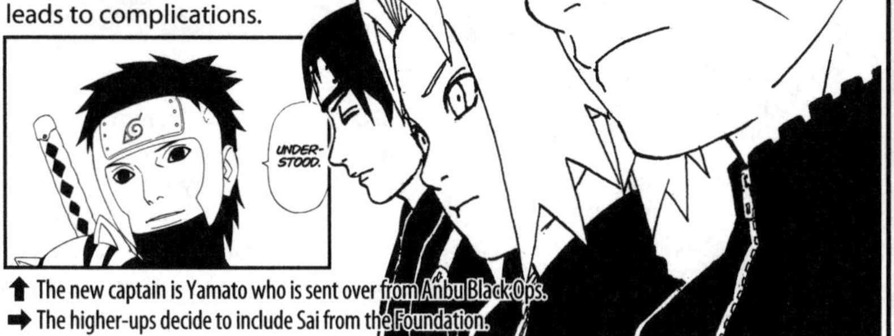
UNDER-STOOD.

⬆ The new captain is Yamato who is sent over from Anbu Black Ops.

➡ The higher-ups decide to include Sai from the Foundation.

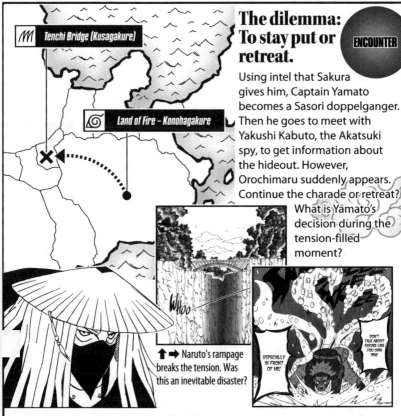

Tenchi Bridge (Kusagakure)
Land of Fire - Konohagakure

ENCOUNTER

The dilemma: To stay put or retreat.

Using intel that Sakura gives him, Captain Yamato becomes a Sasori doppelganger. Then he goes to meet with Yakushi Kabuto, the Akatsuki spy, to get information about the hideout. However, Orochimaru suddenly appears. Continue the charade or retreat? What is Yamato's decision during the tension-filled moment?

WHOO

DON'T TALK ABOUT SASUKE LIKE YOU OWN HIM!
ESPECIALLY IN FRONT OF ME!

↑ → Naruto's rampage breaks the tension. Was this an inevitable disaster?

ALL CLEAR... KEEP MOVING...

← Captain Yamato's Wood Style hijutsu guides Sakura and Naruto swiftly into the hideout.

INFILTRATION

Orochimaru's hideout confirmed.

The team enters the hideout in pursuit of Orochimaru and Kabuto, and Sai, who has suddenly become a turncoat. They pass through mazelike corridors and get to the innermost chamber, where they confront Sasuke. With cold, steely eyes, Sasuke points his sword at his former comrades without a moment's hesitation. The team launches a coordinated attack, but the fight is interrupted by Orochimaru and Kabuto's entrance. Maintaining superiority, the trio fades into the darkness. But just what is their true aim?

BOOF

Shinobi Facts

The Akatsuki Subjugation Mission

The Akatsuki enter the Land of Fire, targeting the Tailed Beasts. Konohagakure makes its move to subjugate them.

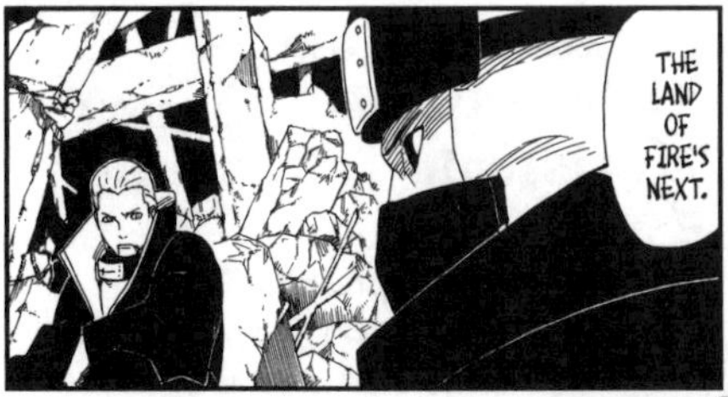
THE LAND OF FIRE'S NEXT.

⬅ Two of the Akatsuki attack indiscriminately.

The shadow of the Akatsuki falls upon the Land of Fire.

DANGER

The famed Fire Temple protected by an impregnable Iron Wall Barrier comes under attack by a two-man cell from the Akatsuki. The shinobi monks led by Chiriku, once a member of the Guardian Shinobi Twelve, are pushed to their limits.

⬇ Even monks wielding the power known as the Gift of the Sages seem to be no match for the Akatsuki.

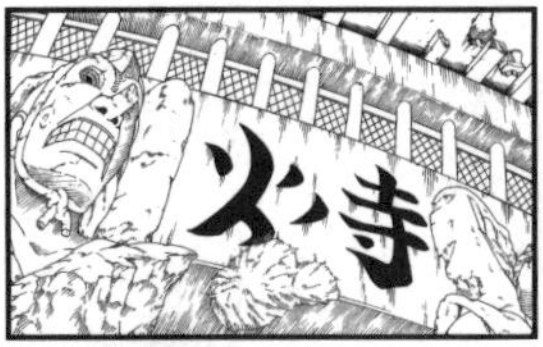
火寺

Twenty newly formed platoons begin the hunt for the Akatsuki.

CONVENED

The Akatsuki infiltrate the Land of Fire. After learning of the destruction of the Fire Temple, the Hokage dispatches twenty newly formed platoons made up of elite shinobi. They travel to every corner of the land.

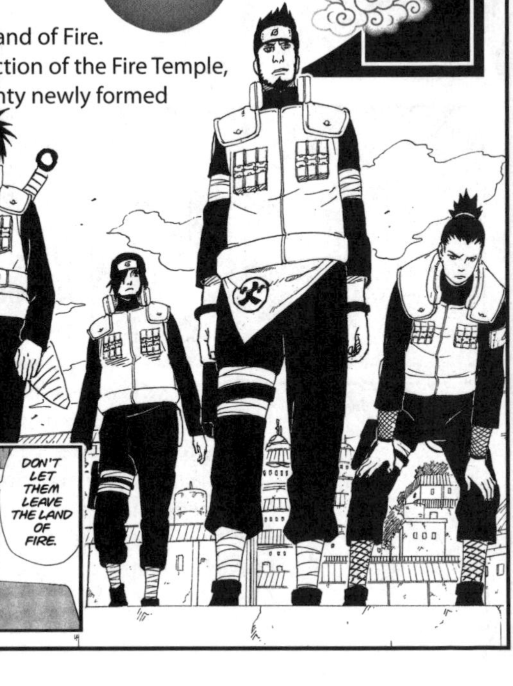

⬇ As the leader of the hidden villages of the Land of Fire, Tsunade lays a security net of a massive scale in every region.

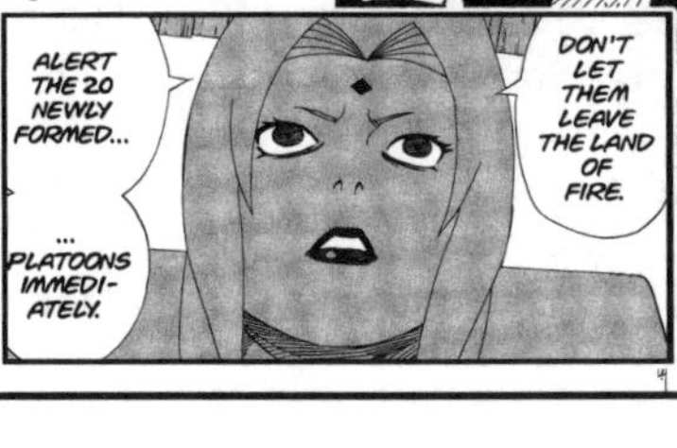
DON'T LET THEM LEAVE THE LAND OF FIRE.
ALERT THE 20 NEWLY FORMED...
...PLATOONS IMMEDIATELY.

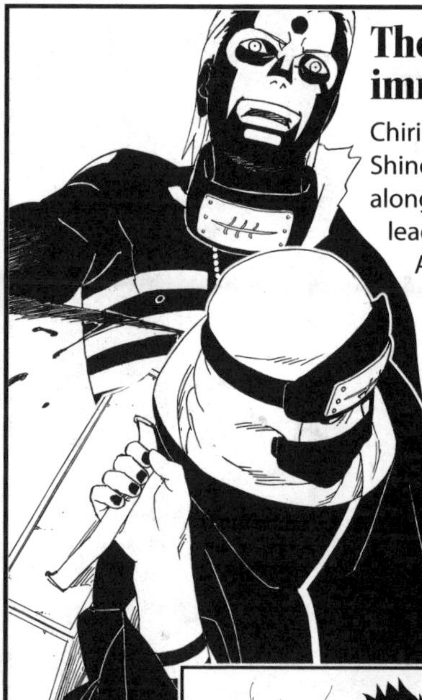

Those possessing immortal bodies.

THE UNKNOWN

Chiriku was a former Guardian Shinobi Twelve who had fought alongside him on the battlefield. His death leads Sarutobi Asuma and his platoon to the Akatsuki. The confrontation takes place in front of the bounty collection office near the Fire Temple. Thanks to Shikamaru's brilliant analytical prowess, they win the battle. However, the Akatsuki possess a unique power—immortality. With bodies that transcend the boundaries of human knowledge and the power to lay curses, they steadily push the platoon into a corner.

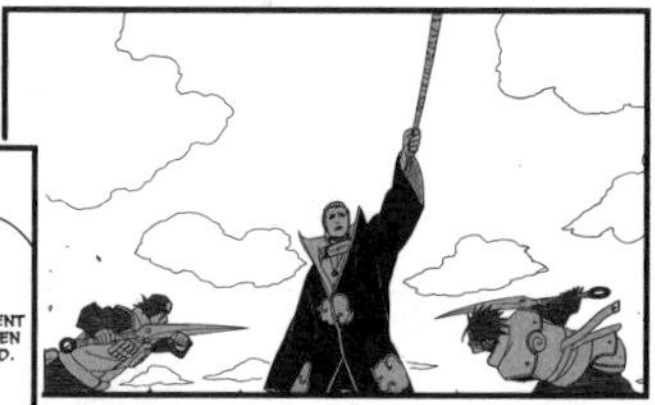

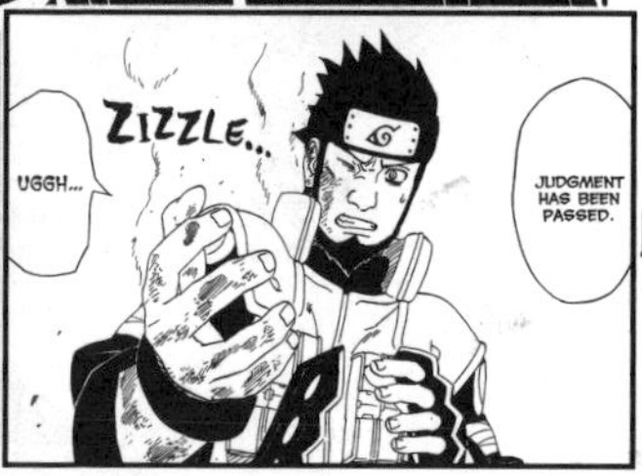
JUDGMENT HAS BEEN PASSED.
ZIZZLE...
UGGH...

⬅⬆ He can place a curse that transfers his own injuries to a foe. Even if his head is cut off, he will not die. Hidan's unusual powers makes one shudder in horror.

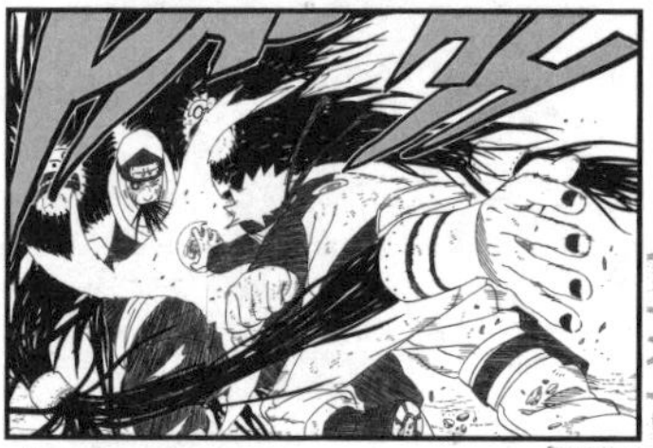

⬆ Naruto's powerful new jutsu explodes.

The Konoha youth get their revenge.

CONCLUSION

Meanwhile, Naruto is undergoing intense training to master a new jutsu. He is dispatched as a back-up just in time to debut his Wind Style! Rasen-Shuriken!! With his comrades watching in awe, Naruto brings down Kakuzu who possesses five hearts in one blow.

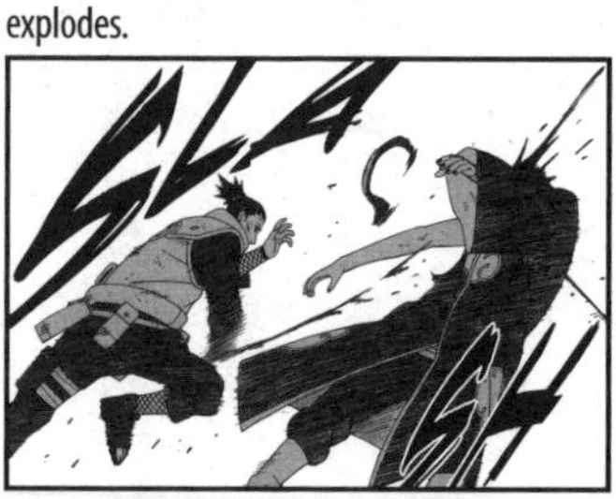

⬅ Hidan is easily outdone by a brilliant battle strategy.

Shinobi Facts

The Hunt for Itachi

Konoha and the Hebi begin their pursuit simultaneously. Will it be capture or death? Here are the facts.

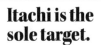

TARGET

Itachi is the sole target.

With the death of Orochimaru, Sasuke forms a new platoon, the Hebi. Its sole purpose is revenge. Upon learning of this, Konoha sends a newly formed team in pursuit of the Akatsuki member Uchiha Itachi, the focus of Sasuke's revenge.

UCHIHA
ITACHI!

⬆ On the same day, at the same hour. Although the location differs, unbeknownst to the other, Sasuke's and Naruto's destinies cross.

木ノ葉小隊 Konoha platoon

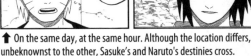

Konoha's strategy is to use two cells, both of which encounter Sasuke and Itachi. But their plans to stop them are thwarted by Tobi of the Akatsuki. Sasuke disappears and many are left uneasy at the appearance of the mysterious Tobi and what threat he may represent.

The hunt for Itachi.

ME.
OH DEAR... MOCKING ME?

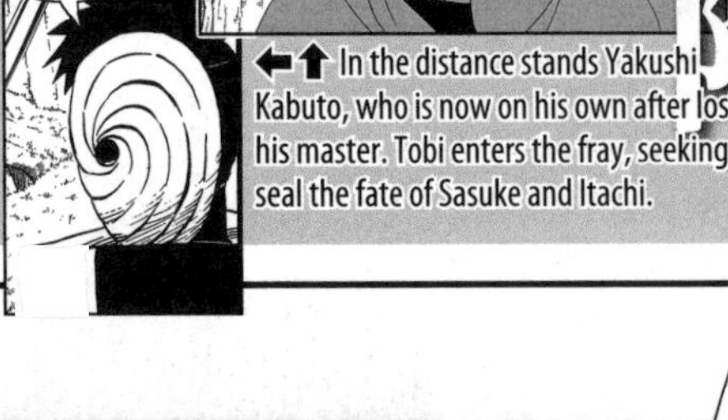

⬅⬆ In the distance stands Yakushi Kabuto, who is now on his own after losing his master. Tobi enters the fray, seeking to seal the fate of Sasuke and Itachi.

SEARCH TACTICS

Tracking Sasuke's whereabouts with unique jutsu.

Team Kakashi with its new and old members join up with the master trackers in the Kurenai cell. Taking their ninja dogs, the Leaf ninja embark on a wide-scale search for Sasuke, tracking him by his scent. Meanwhile, Sasuke, who has been using Karin's and Jugo's skills to find the Akatsuki, is already onto Konoha's strategy and has secured an alternate route to evade them. This round goes to the Hebi.

SNIFF SNIFF

⬆ Konoha uses ninja dogs and their highly sensitive sense of smell to track Sasuke.

SWISH

⬅ The Hebi gets intel from Jugo's bird and produces a map pinpointing the Akatsuki hideout. With this data and Karin's sensory skills, they go after Itachi.

I SENSE AN ENORMOUS AMOUNT OF THE SAME CHAKRA!
WHAT'S GOING ON?!

⬆ Karin is familiar with sensory-type jutsu of all the hidden villages. Her knowledge and quick wit keeps the Konoha platoons constantly one step behind.

The Hebi 蛇

The plan to kill Itachi.

The Hebi, led by Sasuke, search for the Akatsuki, intent on encountering Itachi. Despite interference by the Leaf and the Akatsuki, they catch up to Itachi. And at the Uchiha hideout, the enmity between the two brothers finally comes to a head.

⬇ Deidara, who abhors the Sharingan, runs interference against Sasuke with his partner Tobi.

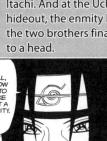

WELL, ALLOW ME TO MAKE THAT A REALITY.

➡ Waiting at the Akatsuki hideout is Itachi himself. And he challenges Sasuke to a one-on-one fight.

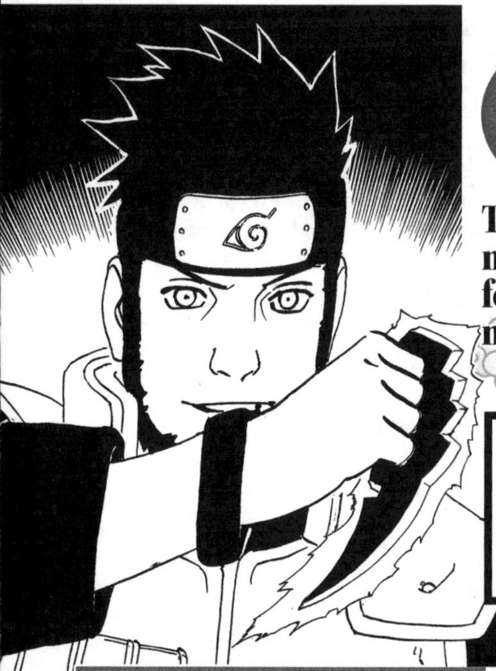

THE FIVE GREAT CHANGES

Shinobi Facts

Change in Chakra Nature

The five chakra natures are the foundation of ninjutsu.

Change in chakra nature is at the foundation of ninjutsu and is essential in the development of new jutsu. The particulars are recorded here.

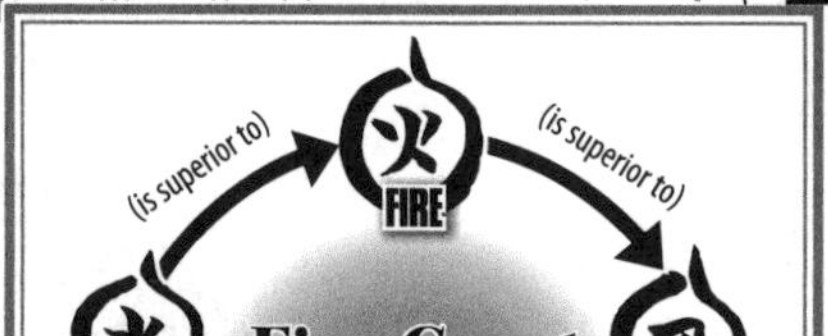
Five Great Changes in Nature
火 FIRE
風 WIND
雷 LIGHTENING
土 EARTH
水 WATER
(is superior to)
(is superior to)
(is superior to)
(is superior to)
(is superior to)

⬅ In the way that Earth is weaker than Lightning, each of the five natures is stronger than one and weaker than another.

In the course of using ninjutsu, when one adds Fire and Wind elements to chakra to increase effectiveness, that is known as change in chakra nature. While it depends on the person, most individuals can tap into one chakra nature easily. At the jônin level, most can use two or more.

The characteristics of the Five Great Changes in Nature.

火 **FIRE:** Chakra as hot as fire, with the power to burn anything it touches. It can turn its target into flames and, like Wind, is especially suited to offensive attacks.

風 **WIND:** Chakra as sharp as a blade which can cut and tear anything in its path. It is used for specialty ninja weapons and jutsu and is most effective in short to mid-range distances.

雷 **LIGHTNING:** It diffuses easily and is compatible with mid to long distance jutsu. Adding it to metal weapons makes them more lethal and increases the electrical shock.

土 **EARTH:** It increases the solidity and composition of all things. A master can make steel unbreakable and clay more pliable. It can be applied to jutsu and other things.

水 **WATER:** It is compatible with the multi-faceted change in chakra form. As in creating fog to camouflage oneself, or a tsunami wave to obstruct something, it is effective for defensive purposes.

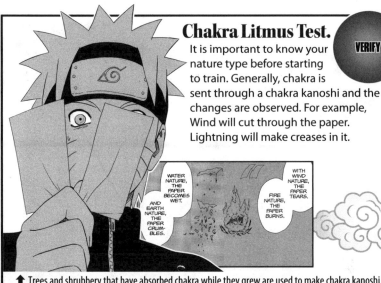

Chakra Litmus Test.

VERIFY

It is important to know your nature type before starting to train. Generally, chakra is sent through a chakra kanoshi and the changes are observed. For example, Wind will cut through the paper. Lightning will make creases in it.

WITH WIND NATURE, THE PAPER TEARS.
FIRE NATURE, THE PAPER BURNS.
WATER NATURE, THE PAPER BECOMES WET.
AND EARTH NATURE, THE PAPER CRUMBLES.

⬆ Trees and shrubbery that have absorbed chakra while they grew are used to make chakra kanoshi.

Each nature requires special training.

TRAINING METHODS

In order to master change in chakra nature, one must undergo special training in each elemental nature. For Wind change in chakra nature, there are three levels. One: to strengthen the nature. Two: to increase the amount of change. Three: to merge it with a jutsu. Mastery of all natures can take years of training.

Training for Wind change of chakra nature

HEH HEH HEH ...

First level

Strengthening change of chakra nature!

⬆ Sustain Wind chakra until a leaf is cut in two.

Second level

Increase change instantaneously

⬆ Cutting through a waterfall is special training to magnify the ability to release large amounts of chakra in an instant.

Third level

Merge change in chakra nature with a jutsu!

⬆ The most difficult level is the third one of incorporating the elemental nature into a jutsu.

Shinobi Facts

Change in Chakra Form

Like change in chakra nature, this is another method of increasing the power of ninjutsu.

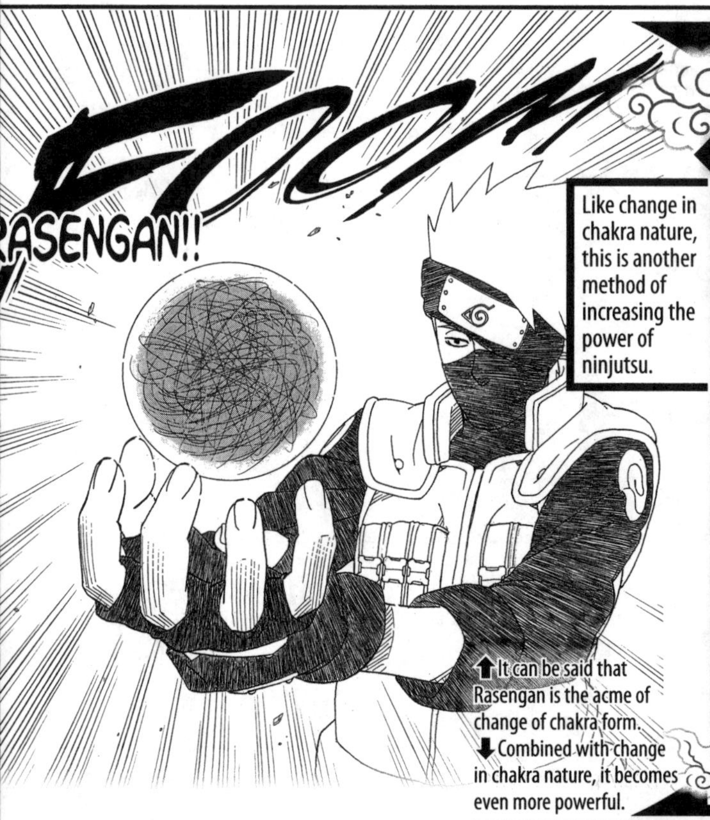
RASENGAN!!

⬆ It can be said that Rasengan is the acme of change of chakra form.
⬇ Combined with change in chakra nature, it becomes even more powerful.

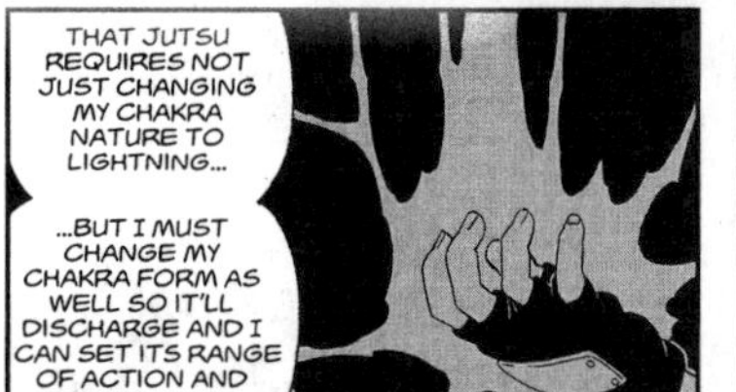
THAT JUTSU REQUIRES NOT JUST CHANGING MY CHAKRA NATURE TO LIGHTNING...
...BUT I MUST CHANGE MY CHAKRA FORM AS WELL SO IT'LL DISCHARGE AND I CAN SET ITS RANGE OF ACTION AND POWER LEVEL.

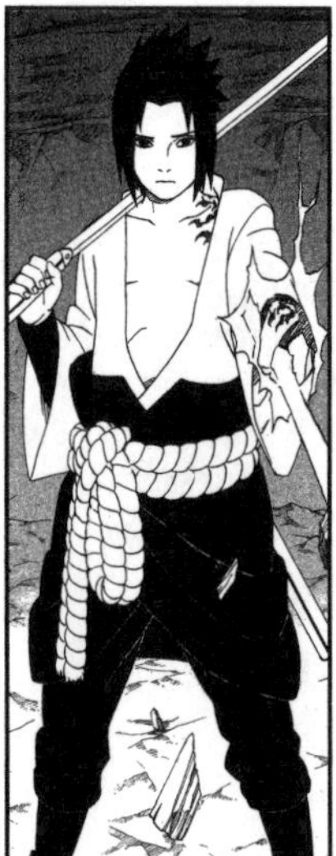

⬅ Sasuke can change Chidori into the shape of a spear. A jutsu will manifest itself according to the user's conception of it.

Depending on the user's skill and how he manifests it, ninjutsu can change shapes.

CHANGE IN CHAKRA FORM

Change in chakra form transforms chakra in ninjutsu and allows one to control its power and range of effectiveness. It individualizes one's jutsu even more than change in chakra nature. However, much of its use depends on the jutsu, the method of training, and the individual's own innovation and conception of the jutsu.

The world of ninjutsu is diverse and goes to the extreme.

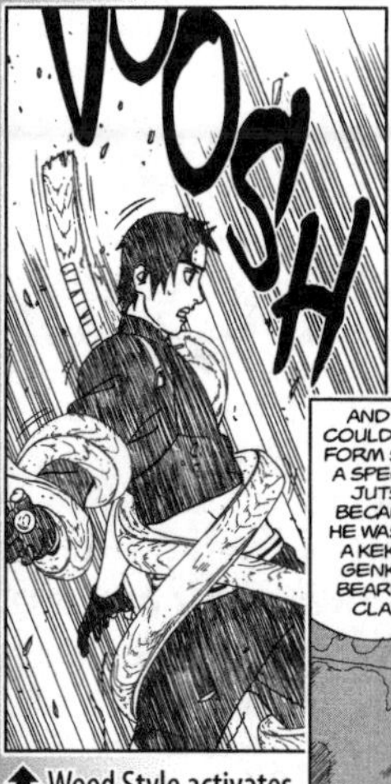
VOOSH

↑ Wood Style activates the change in chakra nature in Earth and Water simultaneously.

A new nature is born from two.

Kekkei Genkai

Even jônin-class ninja find it difficult to use two change in chakra natures simultaneously. In essence, it means combining change in nature to create something new. This is called Kekkei Genkai and it requires special strength.

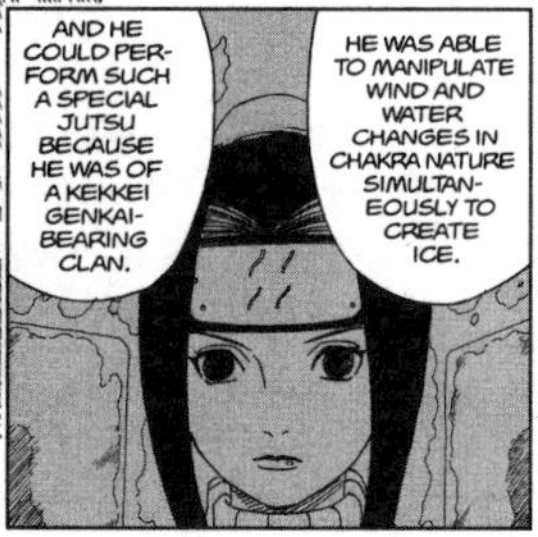
HE WAS ABLE TO MANIPULATE WIND AND WATER CHANGES IN CHAKRA NATURE SIMULTANEOUSLY TO CREATE ICE.
AND HE COULD PERFORM SUCH A SPECIAL JUTSU BECAUSE HE WAS OF A KEKKEI GENKAI-BEARING CLAN.

← Haku was one of those rare shinobi who possessed the Ice Style Kekkei Genkai.

Depending on the user, even basic ninjutsu can be extremely powerful.

Creativity

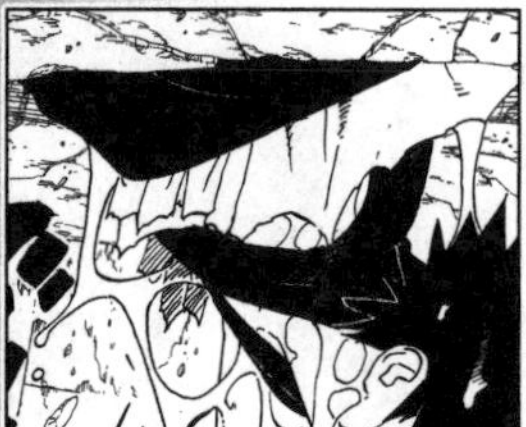

↑ When Orochimaru uses his Art of Substitution, he leaves behind his cast-off skin to delay detection.

Change in nature and change in form are not the only methods to power up one's ninjutsu. The effectiveness of ninjutsu is greatly enhanced by how an individual uses it and by one's own innovation. The world of ninjutsu is vast and deep. That is why the possibilities are infinite. This next generation of shinobi is sure to forge a new future with continued training and the creation of new types of jutsu.

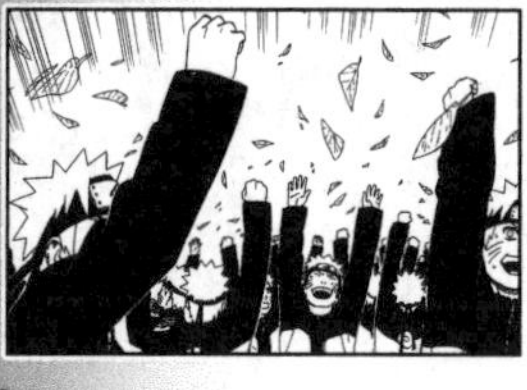

← Kakashi uses his Art of the Shadow Doppelganger during training. This has played an influential role in Naruto's progress.

How much... have Naruto and the others progressed?!

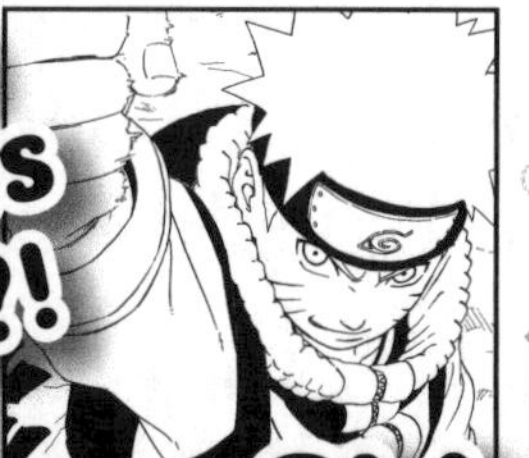

SPECIAL FEATURE

Facts

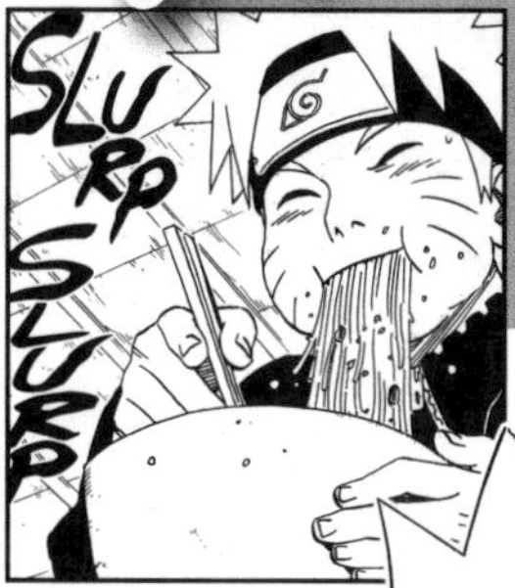
SLURP
SLURP

Growth isn't just about getting taller!

Shinobi Progress Chart

Shinobi train hard. Take a look at their amazing progress over the past few volumes!

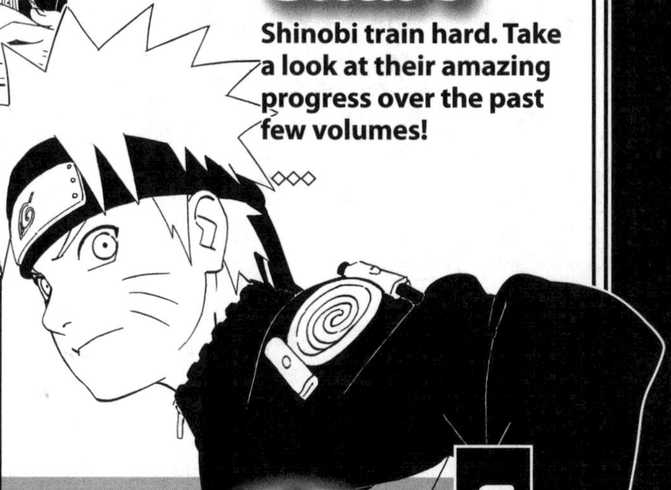

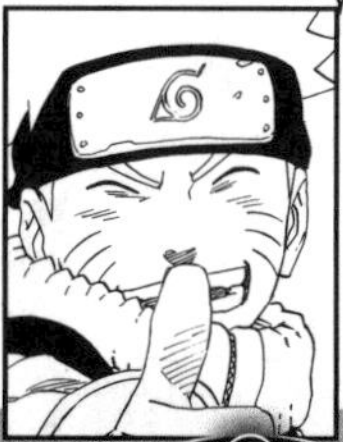

Uzumaki Naruto

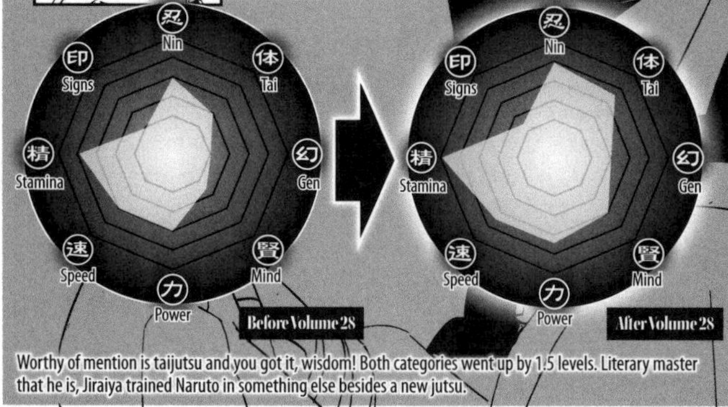
忍 Nin
体 Tai
幻 Gen
賢 Mind
力 Power
速 Speed
精 Stamina
印 Signs
Before Volume 28
忍 Nin
体 Tai
幻 Gen
賢 Mind
力 Power
速 Speed
精 Stamina
印 Signs
After Volume 28

Worthy of mention is taijutsu and you got it, wisdom! Both categories went up by 1.5 levels. Literary master that he is, Jiraiya trained Naruto in something else besides a new jutsu.

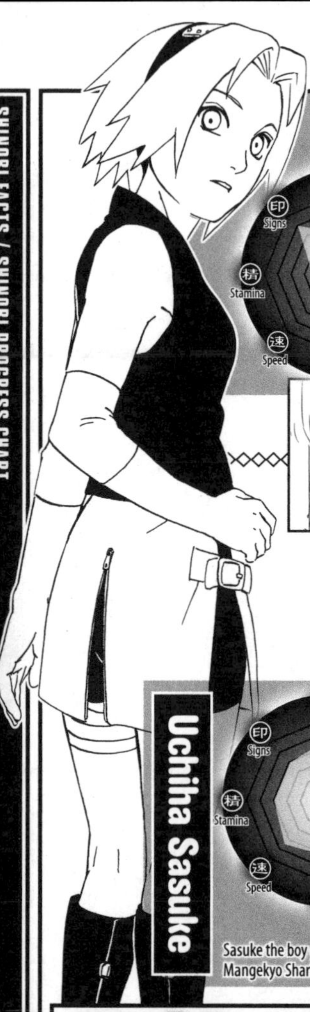

Haruno Sakura

In this third data book, she has advanced two levels. With her drastic improvement in taijutsu and strength, she has truly earned her nickname Tsunade Junior.

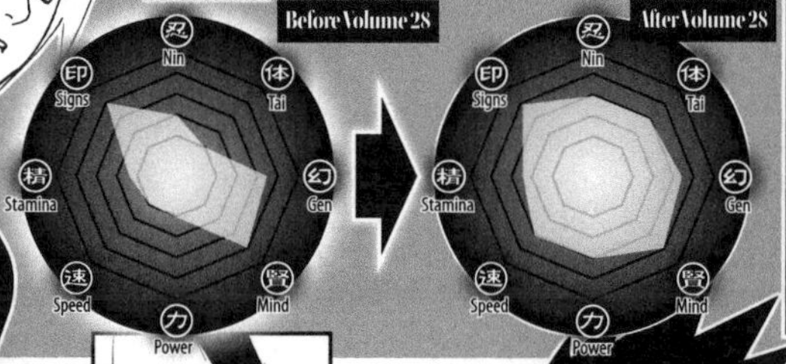
Before Volume 28
After Volume 28
Nin
Tai
Gen
Mind
Power
Speed
Stamina
Signs

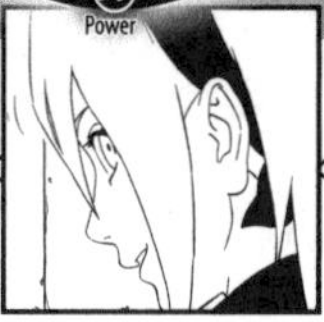

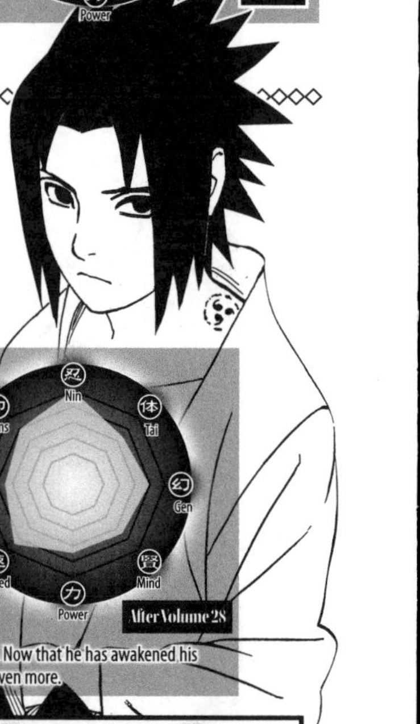

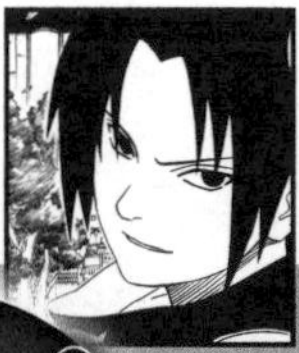

Uchiha Sasuke

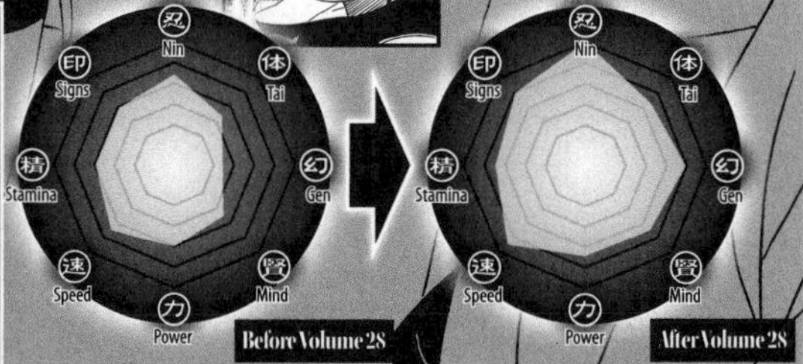
Nin
Tai
Gen
Mind
Power
Speed
Stamina
Signs
Before Volume 28
After Volume 28

Sasuke the boy genius continues to show improvement. Now that he has awakened his Mangekyo Sharingan, his numbers are bound to grow even more.

Hyuga Neji

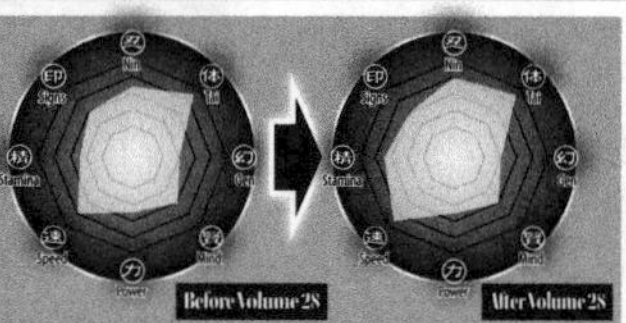
Before Volume 28
After Volume 28

You will be amazed at Neji's increased stamina, absolutely essential to one who uses the strength-sapping Byakugan.

Nara Shikamaru

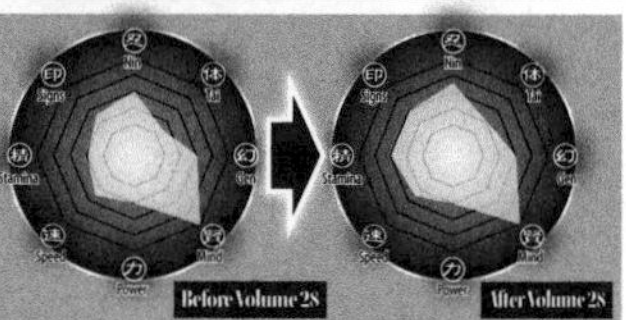
Before Volume 28
After Volume 28

He was born with amazing intellect. He is sure to make further strides with his improved stamina.

Gaara

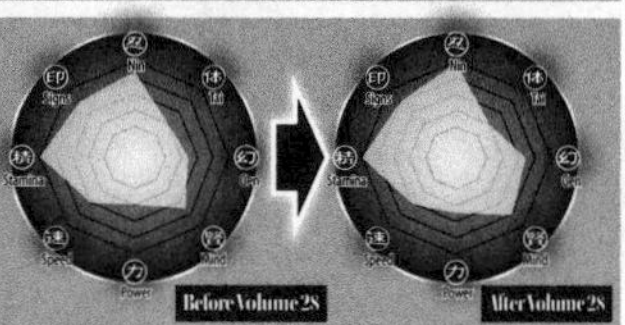
Before Volume 28
After Volume 28

His progress is probably due to increased training to fulfill his role as the Kazekage. His levels in wisdom and genjutsu keep rising.

Rock Lee

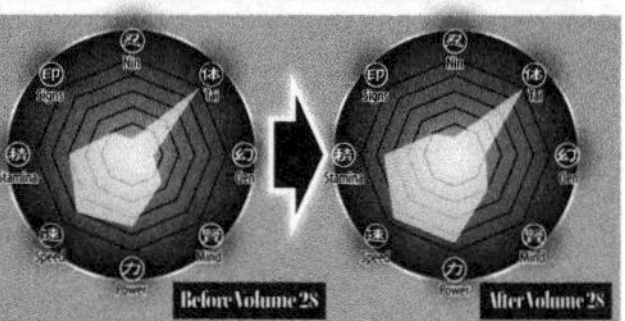
Before Volume 28
After Volume 28

The boy wonder who never gives up has honed his skills even more. Is there no limit to Lee's physical strength?

NARUTO OFFICIAL HEIGHT COMPARISON CHART

Naruto and his friends have all grown!
You can see the difference in heights with one glance.

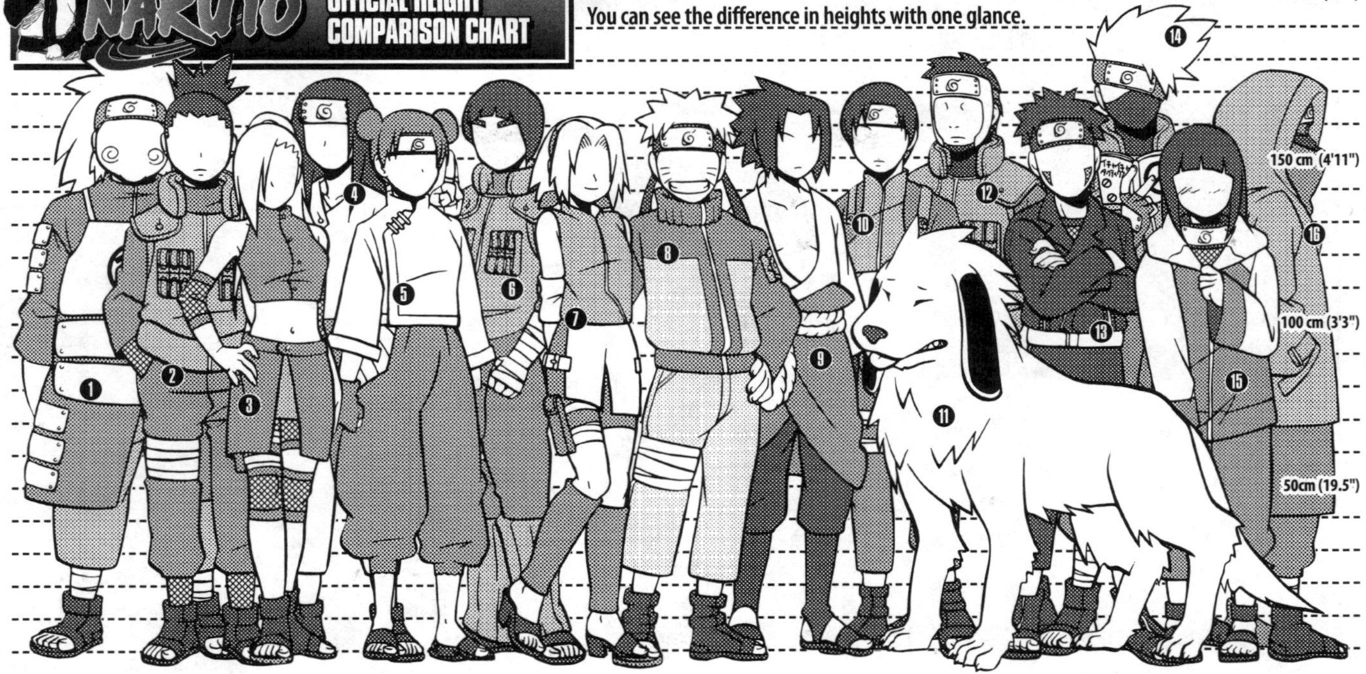
200 cm (6' 6")
150 cm (4'11")
100 cm (3'3")
50cm (19.5")
1
2
3
4
5
6
7
8
9
10
11
12
13
14
15
16

1 Akimichi Choji 2 Nara Shikamaru 3 Yamanaka Ino 4 Hyuga Neji 5 Tenten 6 Rock Lee 7 Haruno Sakura 8 Uzumaki Naruto
9 Uchiha Sasuke 10 Sai 11 Akamaru 12 Yamato 13 Inuzuka Kiba 14 Hatake Kakashi 15 Hyuga Hinata 16 Aburame Shino

Jutsu Data

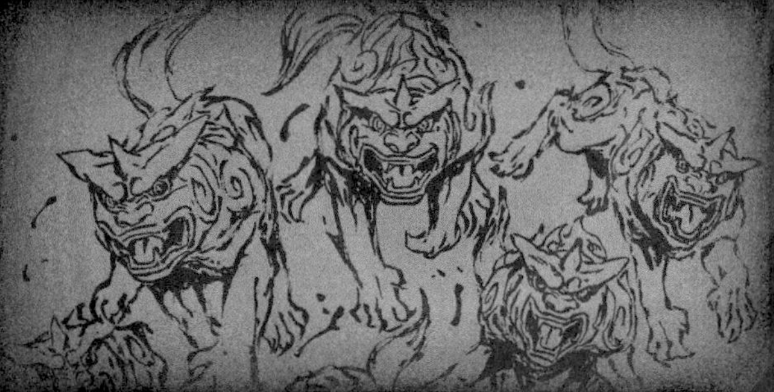

Here, you will be initiated in minute detail to the principles of 115 closely guarded amazing secret jutsu.

【JUTSU】 —How to read these pages—

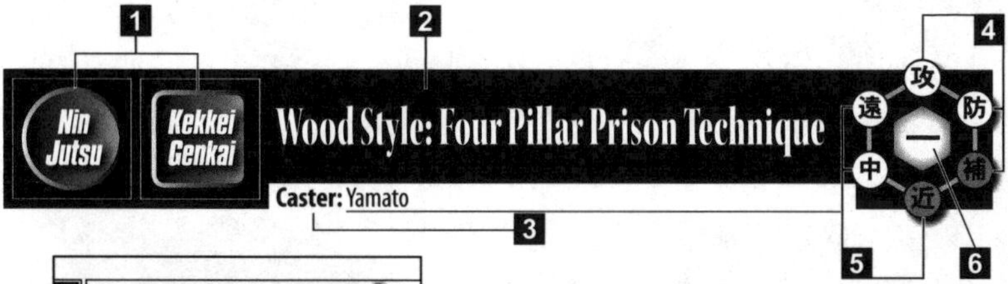

1
2
4
Nin Jutsu
Kekkei Genkai
Wood Style: Four Pillar Prison Technique
攻
遠
防
—
中
補
近
Caster: Yamato
3
5
6

Wood Style
Tearing open the earth to give birth to life—a hidden jutsu like no other.

1 Jutsu Line

Line 1) Every jutsu falls into one of the three lines of jutsu, depending on its effect on a target.

Line 2) A jutsu is further broken down into four categories, depending on special conditions required to master it.

Line 1

Nin Jutsu | Tai Jutsu | Gen Jutsu

Line 2

Kekkei Genkai | Sealing Jutsu | Hiden | Sage Jutsu

2 Name of jutsu

3 Primary caster/user of the jutsu

4 Type of jutsu

There are three types of jutsu and they are used for different results: an offensive attack, a defensive move, or to provide assistance. Sometimes jutsu may fit into more than one type at once.

攻 **OFFENSIVE:** A jutsu used for a direct attack to inflict damage upon a target.

防 **DEFENSIVE:** A jutsu used to counter or defend against an attack from others.

補 **ASSIST:** Jutsu used to improve or take advantage of a battle situation; for example, using genjutsu or doppelgangers.

5 Effective Range

The range of a jutsu is divided into three categories: short, middle and long distance. (Depending on the user's skill, this range often varies.)

近 **SHORT:** Short-distance jutsu.
The range is about 0 m to 5 m (0 ft. to 16.4 ft.)

中 **MIDDLE:** Mid-distance jutsu.
The range is about 5 m to 10 m (16.4 ft. to 32.81 ft.)

遠 **LONG:** Long-distance jutsu.
The range is greater than 10 m (32.81 ft.)

6 Degree of difficulty

There are six levels of difficulty. (However, Kekkei Genkai, Hiden (also known as birthright jutsu) and Sage Jutsu require unique conditions for mastery, so they are marked with a "—".)

S **SECRET JUTSU:** Ultimate level

A **FORBIDDEN JUTSU:** Extremely high-level ninjutsu

B **JÔNIN LEVEL**

C **CHÛNIN LEVEL**

D **GENIN LEVEL**

E **NINJA ACADEMY LEVEL**

— **SECRET JUTSU:** Jutsu requiring the unique skills of the user (such as Kekkei Genkai, Hiden, and Sage Jutsu). Jutsu utilized by the summoned animals.

Nin Jutsu — Secret Red Technique: Performance of a Hundred Puppets

攻 防 補 近 中 遠 — S

Caster: Sasori

A sea of morbid puppets capable of destroying a nation.

The true ability of a puppet master is measured by the number of puppets he is able to control. The number of fingers—i.e., ten—was previously considered the maximum, but his jutsu defied conventional wisdom. By directly connecting the nucleus of his body with the puppets, the caster's will is reflected in the movements of the puppets without having to manipulate them with his fingers. He succeeded in manipulating one hundred puppets as though they were his own hands and feet.

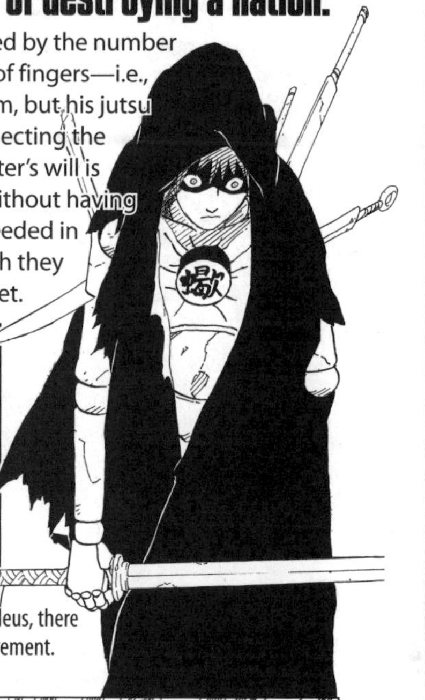

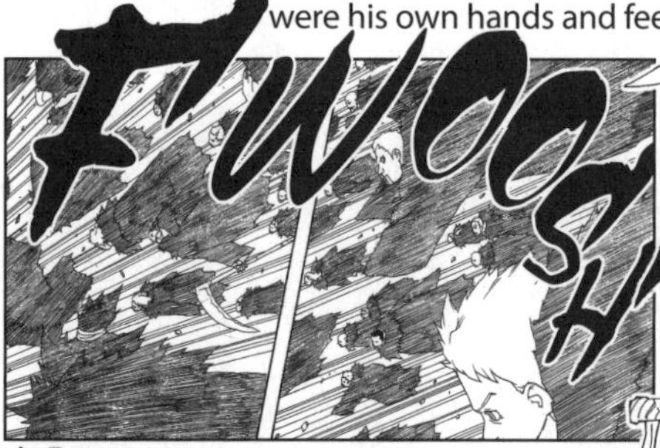
FWOOSH

⬆⬇ Because the puppets are directly connected to his nucleus, there is no time lag between the caster's will and the puppets' movement. That fighting power is mighty enough to take down a nation.

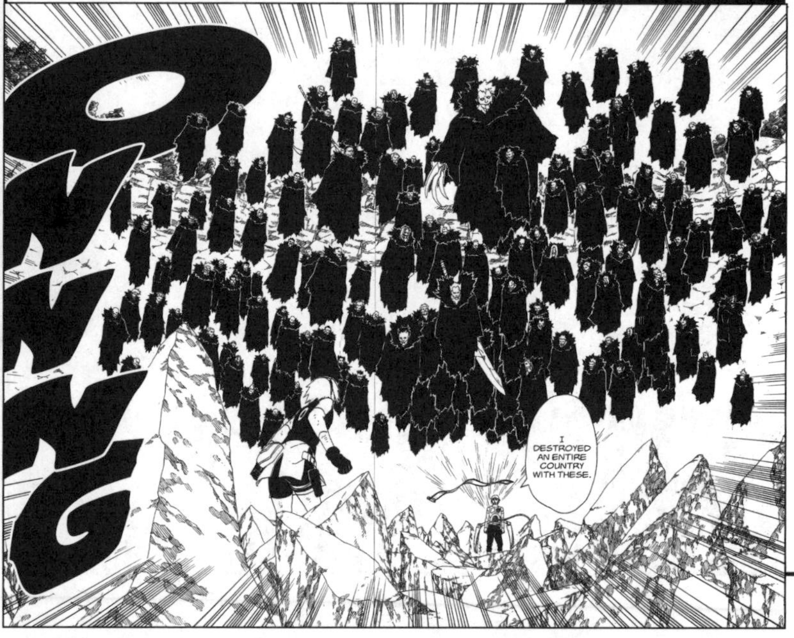
I DESTROYED AN ENTIRE COUNTRY WITH THESE.

Tai Jutsu

Asakujaku

Caster: Might Guy

A powerful yet feathery barrage!

Asakujaku is a deadly technique. In principle, it works by opening up to six of the Eight Gates and exponentially increasing Guy's abilities, allowing him to punch out the opponent with an infinite number of fists. The speedy fists create a friction resulting in flames. When Guy expects certain victory, the flames that fly out from his fists paint the sky in brilliant colors like the tail feathers of a peacock.

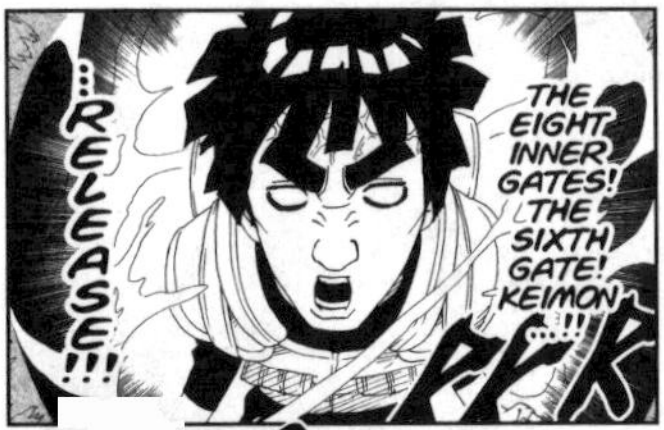
THE EIGHT INNER GATES! THE SIXTH GATE! KEIMON...!!!
...RELEASE!!!

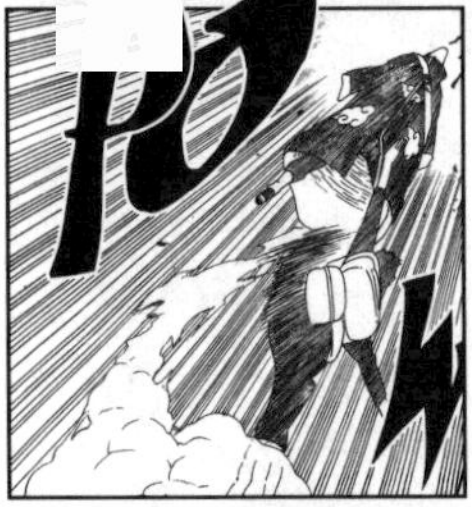

⬆ Only Guy could withstand opening up to six gates!

⬅ He initiates the technique after kicking his enemy into the air. An ordinary man would be killed by this single blow.

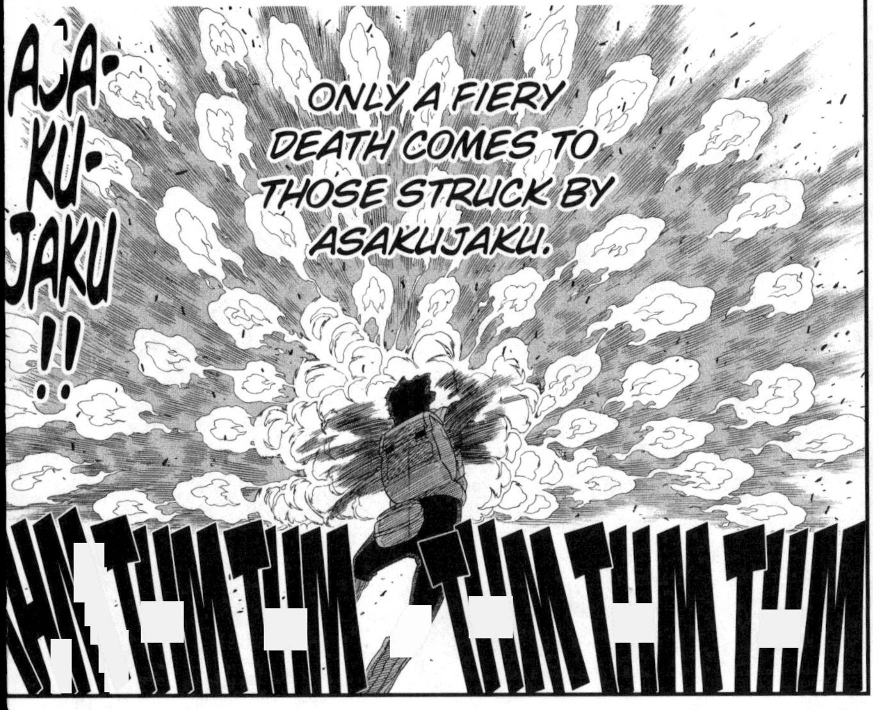
ONLY A FIERY DEATH COMES TO THOSE STRUCK BY ASAKUJAKU.
THUM THUM THUM THUM

Rainmaker Jutsu

Caster: Pain

LET'S DO THIS.

Are the rains that surround us the tears of a shinobi crying for his village?

A sensory ninjutsu Pain can manipulate at will, essentially Rainmaker Jutsu is rain imbued with his chakra. In Amegakure, it rains every Sunday. Pain creates this rainfall from rain clouds that he forms with his own chakra. Each and every raindrop is intimately linked with his senses. Because the chakra of those who are not of Amegakure will block the rain, Pain is able to sense the presence of intruders. Pain always applies this jutsu when he leaves the village, maintaining watch over Amegakure.

A TIGHT SECURITY NET SURROUNDING THE VILLAGE.

⬆ Rain provides a lucky opportunity for invaders. But therein lies the trap.

Jutsu Art of Otokonoko Tachi

遠 防 D 中 補 近

Caster: Konohamaru

BONNG

A jarring mental assault.

This jutsu is an adaptation of Art of Onnanoko Tachi. It shocks by putting someone the target knows well in a compromising position.

⬅ The shock of seeing someone they know in such a position gives maximum impact.

Nin Jutsu Art of Onnanoko Tachi

攻 遠 防 D 中 補 近

Caster: Konohamaru

An even further-developed pervy ninjutsu.

This is Konohamaru's version of Naruto's Ninja Harem. It is cast by applying the Art of the Shadow Doppelganger and the Art of Transformation in succession, but it achieves the revolutionary advance of transforming the caster and his doppelganger into different people.

Okasho: Sakura Strike

Tai Jutsu

Caster: Haruno Sakura

C

A fist attack imbued with resolve and chakra. One punch can easily pulverize even a boulder.

Though generally considered to be superhuman strength, Okasho: Sakura Strike is an adaptation of medical ninjutsu that requires delicate chakra control and concentration. Chakra of the greatest intensity developed instantaneously in the body is concentrated in its entirety in the right fist.

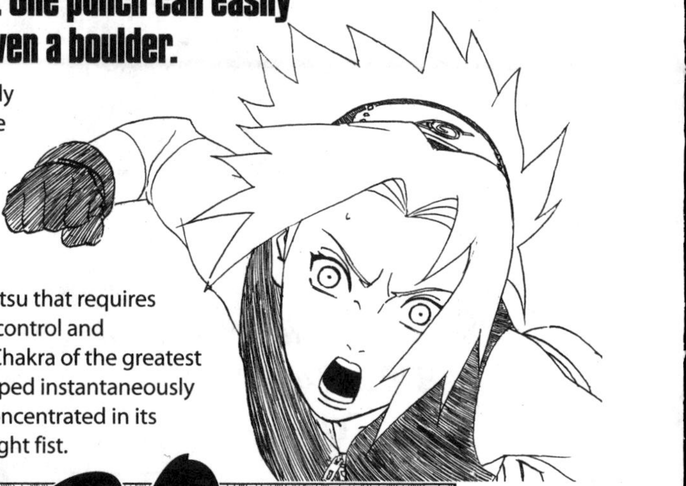

⬇ With a deafening yell, Sakura unleashes a powerful punch.

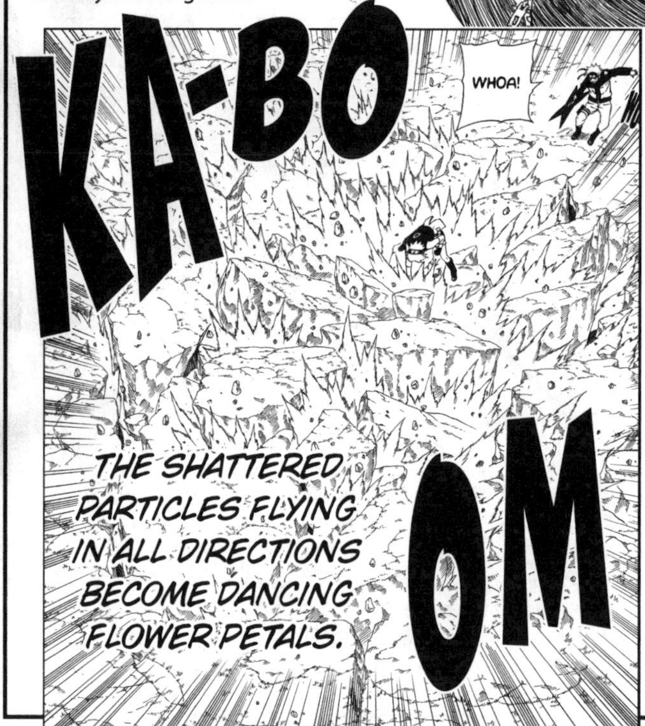
KA-BOOM
WHOA!
THE SHATTERED PARTICLES FLYING IN ALL DIRECTIONS BECOME DANCING FLOWER PETALS.

⬅ Ground struck by the fist is pulverized by the immense impact, sending minute particles scattering through the air like flower petals.

Nin Jutsu — Ôdama Rasengan

攻 防 補 近 中 遠 **A**

Caster: Uzumaki Naruto

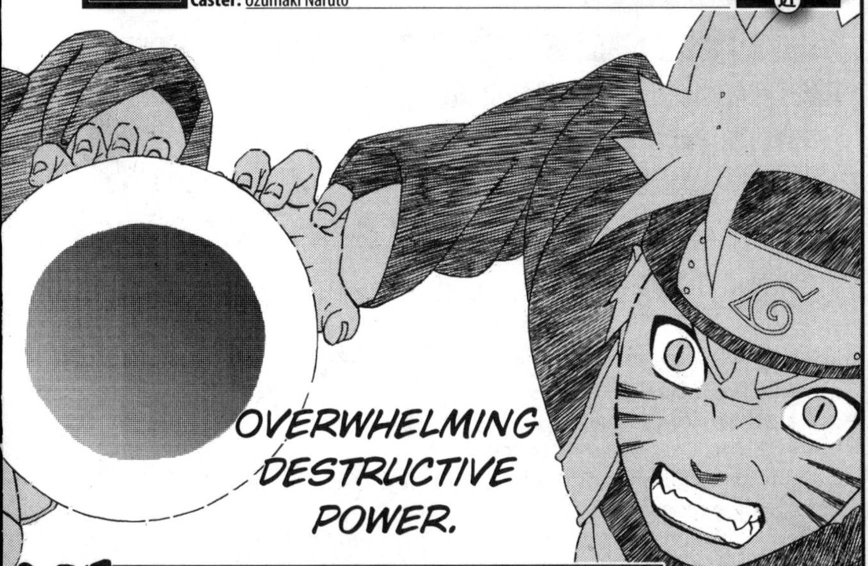
OVERWHELMING DESTRUCTIVE POWER.

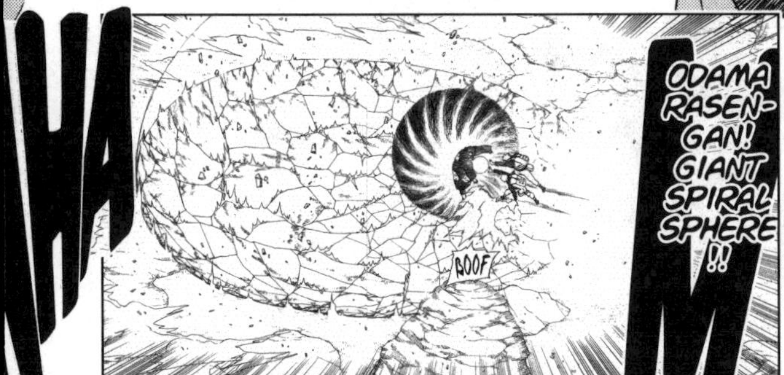
ÔDAMA RASENGAN! GIANT SPIRAL SPHERE!!
BOOF

A maelstrom of immense chakra becomes a huge projectile to take out the enemy.

↑ Destructive power so incredible that it blasts right through its target and gouges the ground. The impact created from compressed Nine-Tails' chakra is equivalent to the impact of a small meteor.

Rasengan is a ninjutsu of immense destructive force created by firing high-density chakra. It's formed by the caster spinning chakra in his hand to compress it. At the moment this chakra, which is of much higher density, impacts the target, it is released for maximum destructive effect. Chakra consumption, proportional to the force generated, is off the charts. It is a jutsu that only Naruto, with nearly inexhaustible Nine-Tails' chakra, can command.

Nin Jutsu — Bazooka Arm

Caster: Pain

This jutsu modifies his body to allow his severed arm to shoot forth like a projectile. Chakra concentrated in the wound creates a small-scale explosion that provides propulsion to the arm which then flies out along a straight line with tremendous force. Although the destructive power is enough to easily destroy thick rock, the chakra-protected arm is not even scratched and is attracted back like a magnet to the chakra in the wound, where it once again reattaches to the body.

A heavy-fisted destructive attack of that shoots forth like arrows.

← The wrist to be fired gains its propulsive force from a chakra-created explosion at the break point.

Nin Jutsu — Ninja Art of Transformation: Toad

Caster: Jiraiya

The silence is broken, but it is too late; the toad croaks in vain.

Using this jutsu, the caster places his hand on the target's forehead, and using an image in his mind, instantly turns the target into a toad. This jutsu is used when intimidating a number of captives. When captives see their fellows being turned into toads, they become like a chorus of toads themselves, freely croaking out all the information they hold secret! It is a frightening jutsu that truly develops "information leaks."

↑→ From toads to tree frogs... Frightened by what their fellows have become, captives spill their guts before they even know it.

Nin Jutsu | Hiden

Kagura Shingan: The Mind's Eye

Caster: Karin

The Mind's Eye sees what lies ahead... and beyond

A jutsu for finding enemies over a wide area, only made possible by the superior sensory capabilities of Karin. By closing her eyes and opening her mind's eye, she is able to detect the chakra of unusual activities within a radius of several dozen kilometers. In addition, if it is a specific chakra, she is able to perceive its location and activities in even greater detail.

...SO THEY'RE TRACKING US BY SCENT, HUH...
EITHER AKATSUKI... OR KONOHA...

⬅ She is able to pin down in detail the number, characteristics and movements of the target.

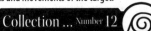

Collection ... Number 12

Konoha

INVESTIGATIVE JUTSU

LOCATING A TARGET

Among the methods ninja use to track and pursue their targets, many involve borrowing the help of animals with superior eyesight and sense of smell. There are also methods that search for the chakra given off by the target, but this is a skill only superior sensory-type ninja can attain.

SASUKE'S SCENT IS SCAT-TERING!
IT'S ALL OVER THE PLACE NOW! GOING IN ALL DIFFERENT DIRECTIONS AT ONCE?!

⬆ In Kiba's case, he uses his sense of smell, superior to even a ninja dog's, to find his target.

⬅ It is also possible to transfer one's senses to birds or other animals to search a wider area.

➡ By determining the adversary's search methods, it is possible to use it against him as an obstruction.

SENSORY-TYPE SHINOBI HAVE DIFFERENT SPECIALTIES DEPENDING ON THEIR VILLAGE OF ORIGIN.
KONOHA TENDS TO USE NINJA HOUNDS FOR TRACKING.

Nin Jutsu | Hiden

Art of Shadow-Stitching

攻 防 補 近 中 遠 —

Caster: Nara Shikamaru

Sharp shadows pierce the enemy!!

A Nara clan hidden jutsu. Shikamaru transforms his own shadow into multiple sharp, needlelike forms and controls each of them separately. He can attack multiple targets at once. And he can string the shadows together to create a barrier to impede the movement of the enemy. The move causes great harm to the victim, and therefore is to be used only in extreme situations.

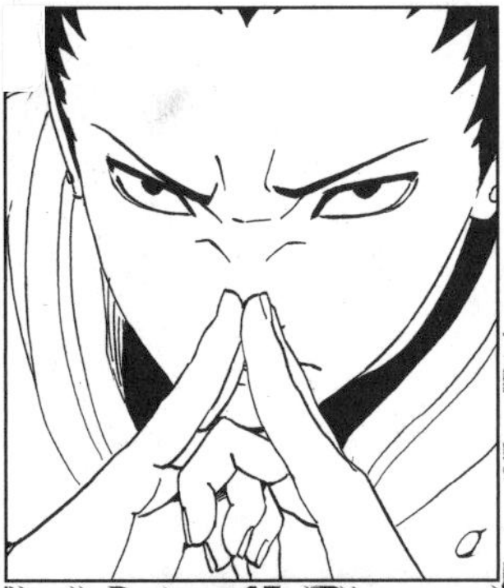

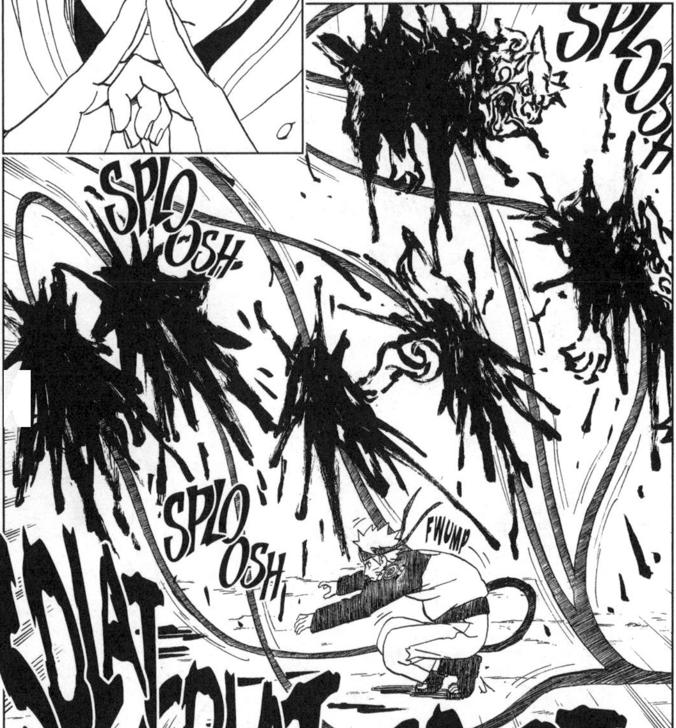
SPLOOSH
SPLOOSH
SPLOOSH
FWUMP
SPLAT
SPLAT
SPURT

⬅⬇ Although basically a jutsu for capturing one's target, depending on the adversary, this jutsu can be used to kill with a single blow. These attributes display their greatest effectiveness in behind-the-lines support.

Nin Jutsu | Hiden

Art of Shadow Possession Shuriken

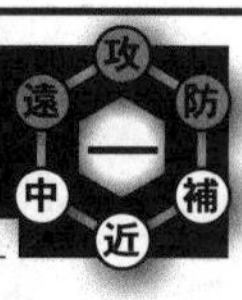
攻
防
補
近
中
遠
—

Caster: Nara Shikamaru

Piercing Power

An intellectual ninjutsu unique to Shikamaru that merges ninjutsu and ninja tools peculiar to the Nara clan. He prepares by allowing a chakra blade to absorb his chakra, imbuing it with the effects of shadow jutsu. Piercing his enemy's shadow with that weapon forces his adversary to mimic the movements of the caster, thus invoking the Art of Shadow Possession. It is not only difficult for an enemy to detect, but it compensates for the downside of having a limited effective range.

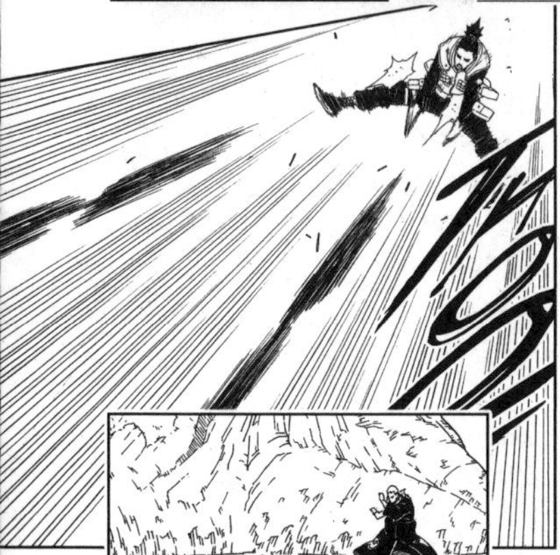

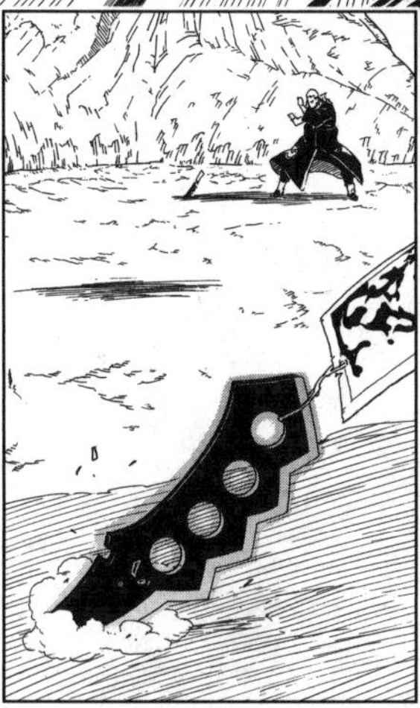

←↑ In order to pierce a shadow, the caster must miss his target by a hairsbreadth. Shikamaru overcame this difficult challenge by attaching a false detonating tag to his blade.

AN INTELLECTUAL NINJUTSU USING A CHAKRA BLADE AND RESOURCEFULNESS

↓ By merging his intellect with a chakra blade, the jutsu shows infinitely great possibilities.

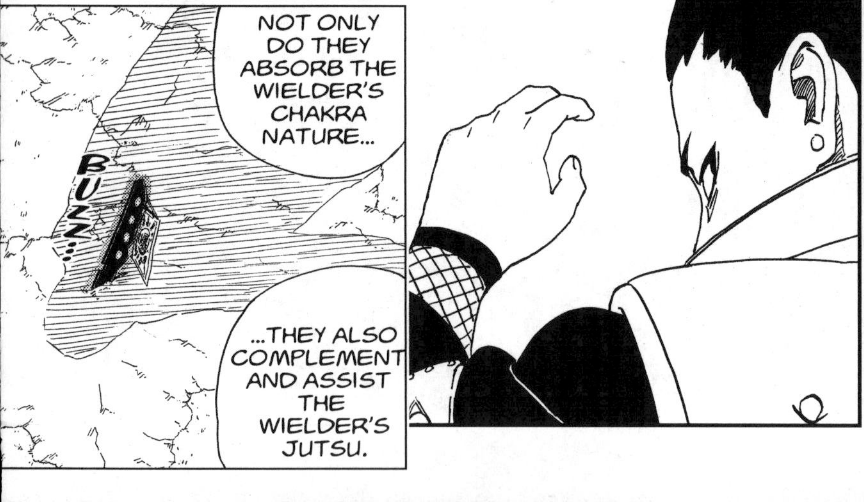
NOT ONLY DO THEY ABSORB THE WIELDER'S CHAKRA NATURE...
...THEY ALSO COMPLEMENT AND ASSIST THE WIELDER'S JUTSU.
BUZZ...

Nin Jutsu | Hiden

Art of the Shadow Pull

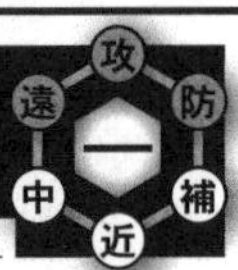
攻
防
補
近
中
遠
—

Caster: Nara Shikamaru

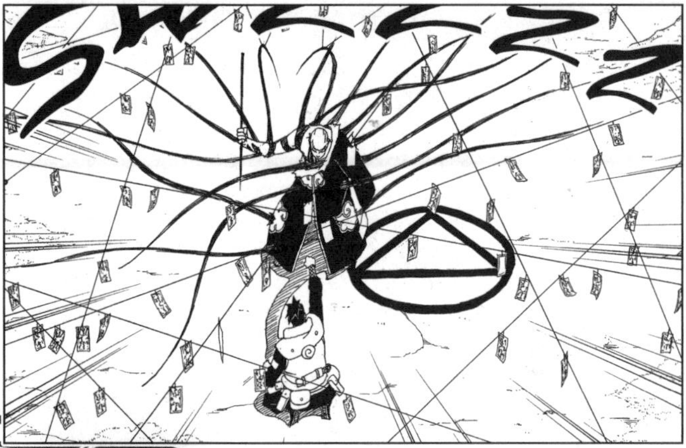

⬅ The number of shadow tentacles and even their direction can be controlled at will.

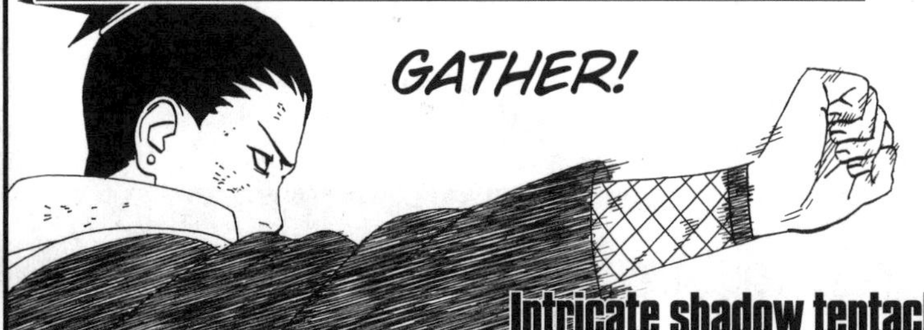
GATHER!

Intricate shadow tentacles wiggling at their caster's will.

Compared to the Art of Shadow-Stitching, which is of the same type, this jutsu places emphasis on the precision movements of the shadows. This jutsu basically involves transforming one's shadow into countless thin tentacles, which are then extended to grab and pull objects toward the caster. In addition, because of the dexterity of the tentacle-shaped shadows, it is possible to throw weapons such as kunai knives. There are numerous ways this jutsu can be used.

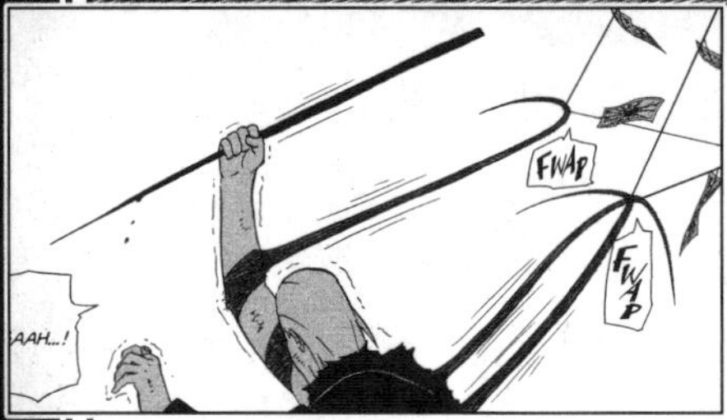
FWAP
FWAP
AAH...!

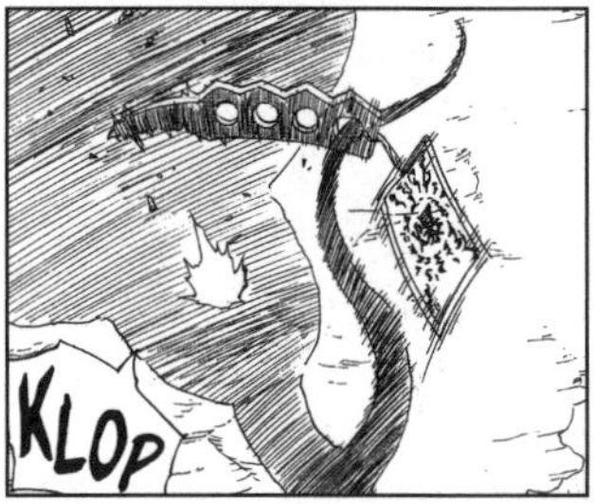
KLOP

⬆ The tentacles can be controlled so precisely that they can even thread themselves through tiny holes.

⬅ The jutsu shows maximum effectiveness when used in conjunction with ninja tools.

Nin Jutsu — Kagero: Transitory Jutsu

攻 防 補 近 中 遠 —

Caster: Zetsu

Gliding along the ground at root level.

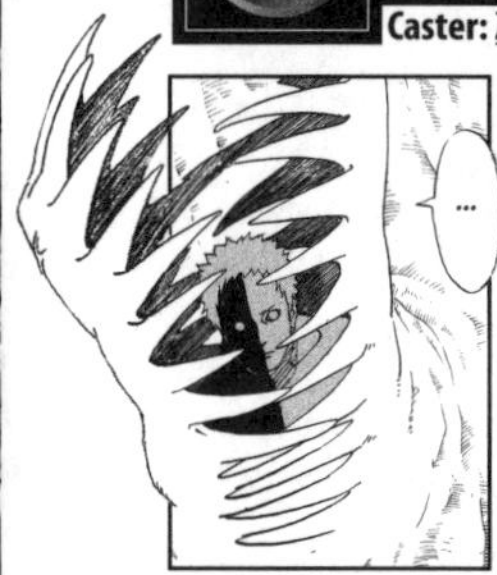
...

Unique to Zetsu, this jutsu allows him to merge his body with plants and the ground to travel at high speed. By charging his insectivorous plantlike outer shell with chakra, it becomes possible to merge with the ground. This makes it possible for him to travel anywhere at high speed using the organic network of plant roots and water veins that exist in the ground. While the jutsu is in effect, his presence is completely concealed, and no one, no matter who it is, is able to detect Zetsu's presence.

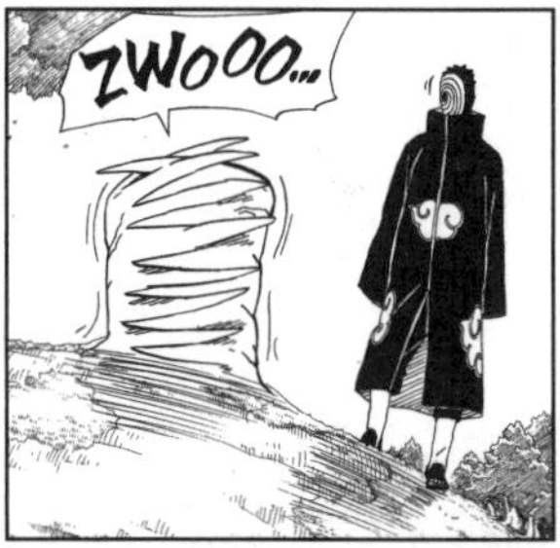
ZWOOO...

⬅ Zetsu hides under the trees and sand. He uses this jutsu to conceal his presence when watching battles between ninja.

Nin Jutsu — Fire Style: Flame Bombs

攻 防 補 近 中 遠 C

Caster: Jiraiya

A sneak attack using mysterious flames that catches the enemy off guard and brings a message of death.

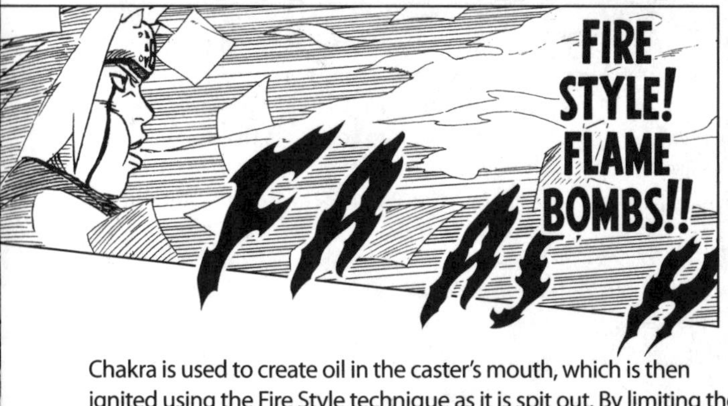
FIRE STYLE! FLAME BOMBS!!

⬅ If the fireballs are shot after the enemy is first smeared with Toad Oil Bombs, the jutsu is fully capable of killing. And, because it keeps chakra consumption down, it is like killing two birds with one stone.

Chakra is used to create oil in the caster's mouth, which is then ignited using the Fire Style technique as it is spit out. By limiting the amount of oil created, the interval between fireballs is decreased. If the enemy is caught unawares, the oil-filled fireball will combust the enemy completely.

Nin Jutsu

Fire Style: Art of the Magnificent Dragon Flame

攻 防 補 近 中 遠 B

Caster: Uchiha Sasuke

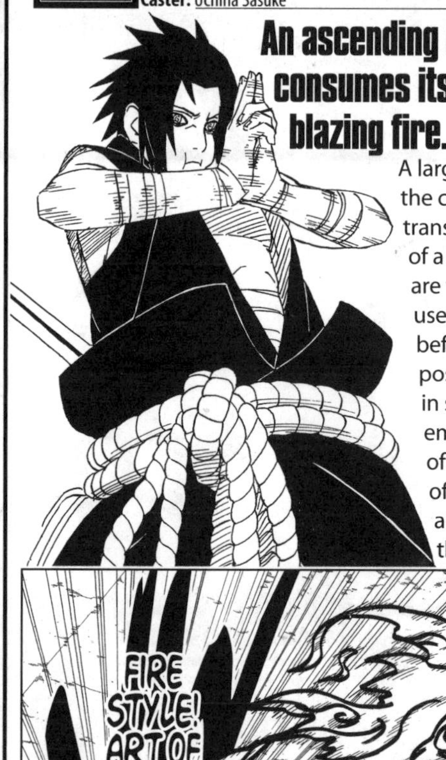

An ascending dragon of flame that consumes its enemy with fangs of blazing fire.

A large quantity of chakra created in the caster's body is compressed and transformed into flames in the form of a dragon. The powerful flames are then skillfully manipulated and used to attack the enemy standing before him. With mastery, it becomes possible to fire multiple flames in succession. This jutsu places emphasis on power and certainty of the attack rather than the range of attack. The flames create a rising air current that is so hot it creates thunderheads.

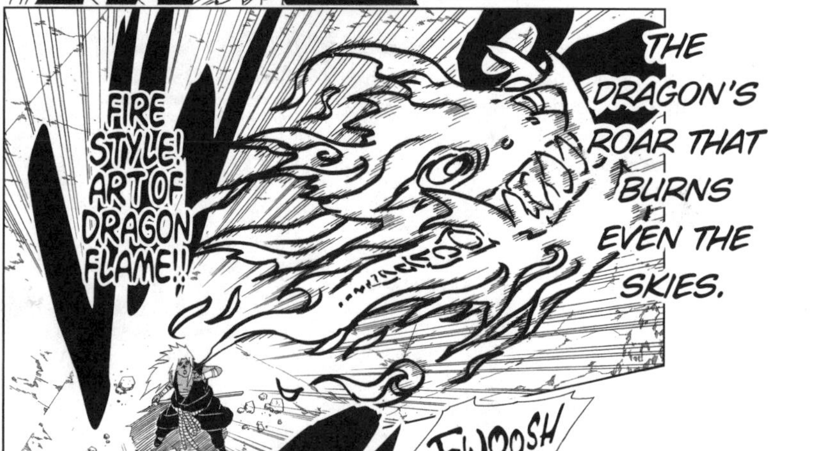
THE DRAGON'S ROAR THAT BURNS EVEN THE SKIES.
FIRE STYLE! ART OF DRAGON FLAME!!

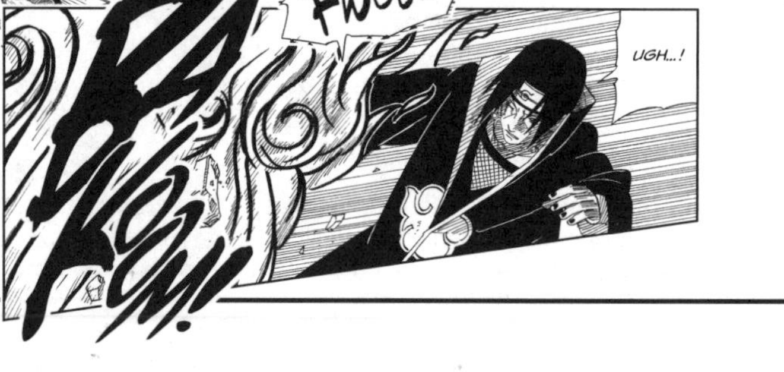
FWOOSH
UGH...!

⬆➡The released flames take the shape of a dragon. It will not stop until its prey is completely consumed.

Nin Jutsu

Fire Style: Searing Migraine

攻 防 補 近 中 遠 B

Caster: Kakuzu

Reduces to Ash.

A tiny fireball is dropped to the ground. Upon contact, it erupts into a raging firestorm that burns everything to the ground. When combined with the properties of wind, the flames increase in intensity. These flames have sufficient explosive combustive force to turn the surrounding areas into a charred wasteland.

BOM
FWOOSH

➡ The raging flames take away the enemy's footing. This jutsu's wide range makes escape difficult.

Collection ... Number 13

Kono

THE LOGIC OF CHANGE IN CHAKRA NATURE

The five basic elements are mutually exclusive of each other, so what happens when two jutsu of the same element clash? The answer depends on how much chakra is put into the jutsu, but if the amount is the same, the two jutsu cancel each other out.

FWOOO

⬅ Sasuke and Itachi clash using Fire Style: Fireball Technique. Sasuke displays the strength of second state to overwhelm Itachi.

However, where the amount of chakra is greater, it is sometimes possible to push back the opposing jutsu. In that event, because the loser is also hit with his own jutsu, the loser of the pushing contest suffers immeasurable damage.

LIGHTNING BLADE!!

➡ Kakuzu's Lightning Style: False Darkness cancels out Lightning Style: Lightning Blade.

Nin Jutsu · Sage Jutsu — Fire Style: Giant Flame Bombs

Caster: Jiraiya

Huge bombs of flame consume all!

➡ Just a single shot is enough for a huge flame bomb that fills a hallway.

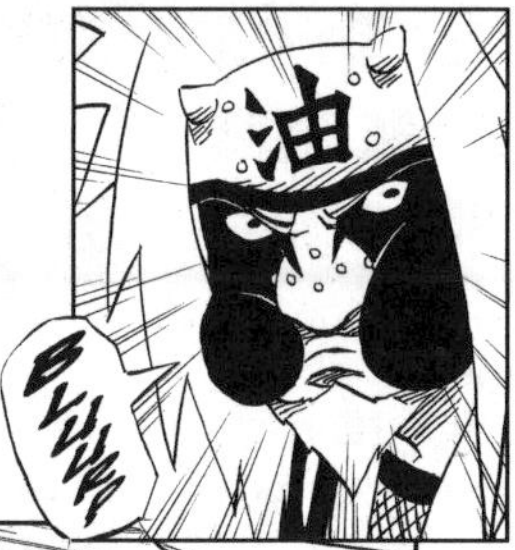
B-LUUU

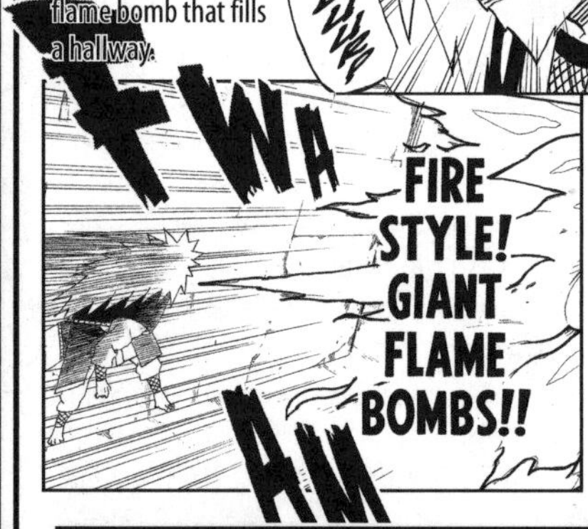
FWA
FIRE STYLE! GIANT FLAME BOMBS!!
AM

After filling his mouth with oil created inside his own body from sage jutsu chakra, the caster sprays the oil out as he ignites it with a Fire Style technique. The flames are more than ten times as large as Flame Bombs. The jutsu is used to completely seal off the escape route to the outside after an enemy has been cornered in a hall or room. Or, it can completely burn down the enemy, escape route and all.

⬅ In sage mode, the inside of Jiraiya's mouth swells as it fills with toad oil he created.

Nin Jutsu — Fire Style: Burning Ash

Caster: Sarutobi Asuma

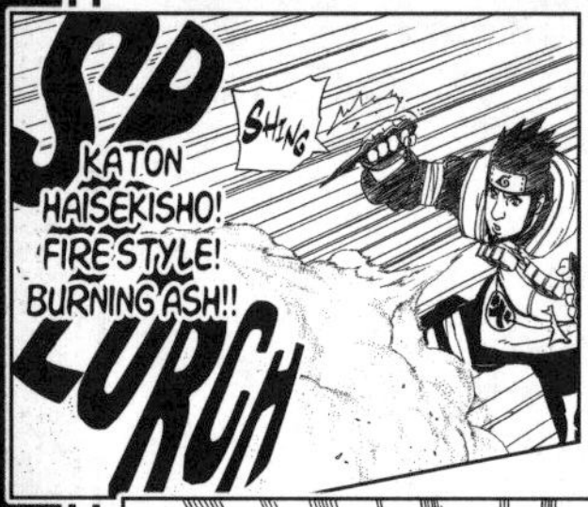
SP
SHING
KATON HAISEKISHO! FIRE STYLE! BURNING ASH!!
LURCH

A gray formation obstructs the view—a spark turns it into an explosive flame.

Explosive powder created by altering chakra is sprayed around the area, then ignited with a flint previously placed in the caster's molars, enveloping the area where the cloud of explosive powder hangs in a huge explosion. This jutsu demands keen senses to read the air currents, insight to read the enemy's movements, and an eye for battle tactics to ensure that one's allies are not caught in the blast.

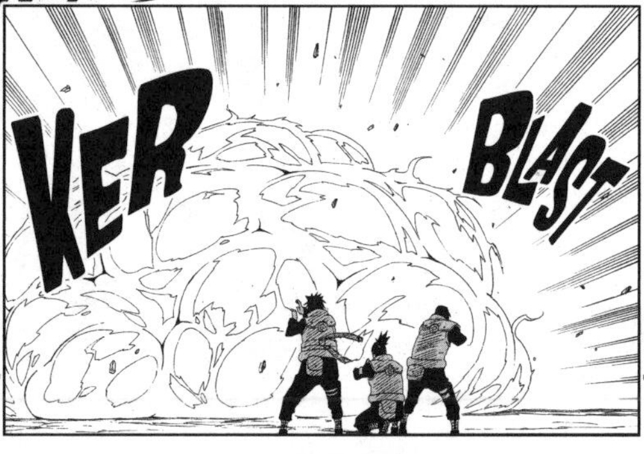
KER
BLAST

⬅ The explosion consumes everything in the area in an instant. It demands extreme care in timing the ignition.

Nin Jutsu

Gamagakure Jutsu

Caster: Jiraiya

GLOP
ZWOO...

An infiltration jutsu where one invades from the water, hiding inside a toad's mouth.

An infiltration jutsu whereby the caster summons a Diving Toad from Mount Myoboku and conceals himself inside it. In fresh water, the toad can dive to depths of up to 328 ft., making this a particularly effective means for infiltrating enemy camps surrounded by lakes and rivers. The inside of the toad is a barrier space that blocks chakra, and thus it can protect the caster from being detected by sensory-type ninjutsu.

⬆⬅ Jiraiya crawling out from the barrier space inside the belly of the Gamamoguri. It is at this moment that he must be the most wary of sensory-type ninjutsu.

Nin Jutsu

Toad Subjugation: Art of the Manipulated Shadow

Caster: Jiraiya

A body as thin as paper controlling at will via a shadow.

⬇ While the jutsu is in effect, the target becomes paralyzed and can be used as the caster's shield.

PWIF

After first casting his chakra onto the target's shadow, the caster then makes his body as thin as possible to merge with the subject's shadow jutsu and temporarily take away the target's ability to control his mind and body. While the jutsu is in use, the caster must hold his breath. The caster is still able to speak through the target. When the caster resumes breathing, the jutsu is canceled and the caster's body regains its shape.

PLMP PLMP
PLMP
PLISH

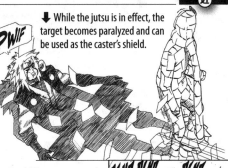

➡ When the caster takes a big breath, his once paper-thin body expands, and the target is released from his paralysis.

Nin Jutsu — Toad Oil Bombs

Caster: Jiraiya

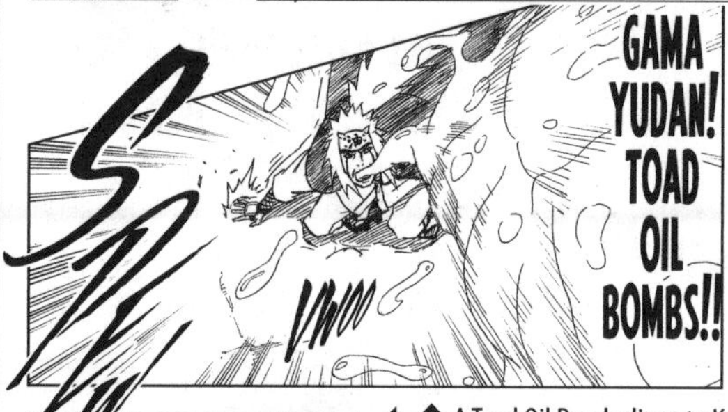
GAMA YUDAN! TOAD OIL BOMBS!!

Never let your guard down! This sticky oil will immobilize you completely!

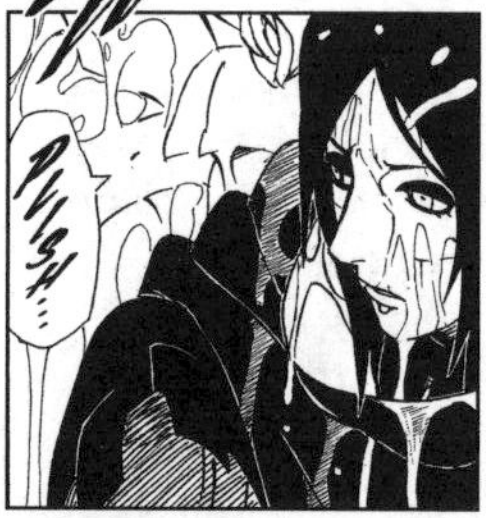

⬅⬆ A Toad Oil Bomb clings to Konan's limbs. Because it is oil, it does not wash off easily with water.

Chakra created in the body is converted to oil and expelled all at once as a huge mass. Because this oil is extremely sticky, it not only adheres to the target, but also completely covers the target with a film of oil, which prevents it from moving. In addition, if a Fire Style technique is unleashed, the target would instantly be engulfed in flames.

Nin Jutsu — Paper Shuriken

Caster: Konan

Pieces of paper whose edges are sharpened with chakra become blades sharp enough to split the air.

Chakra is instantaneously infused into scraps of paper, which then harden and sharpen, and are used as shuriken. The sharpness is equal to shuriken made of metal. It is possible to further increase their power by changing the shape of the finished paper weapon.

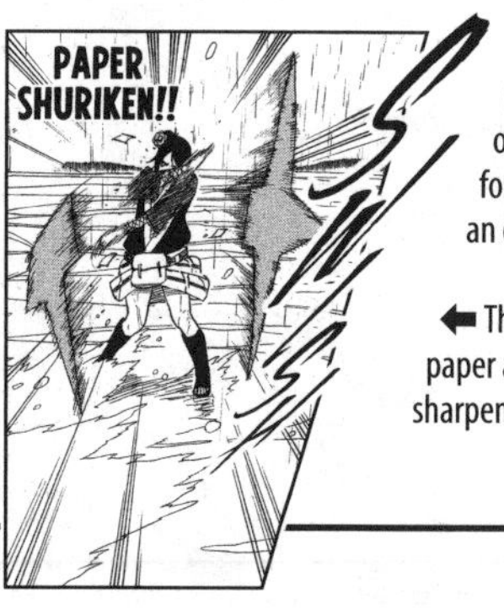
PAPER SHURIKEN!!

➡ Although it's an emergency measure to be used when one runs out of ninja tools, it can be a formidable weapon in the hands of an experienced caster.

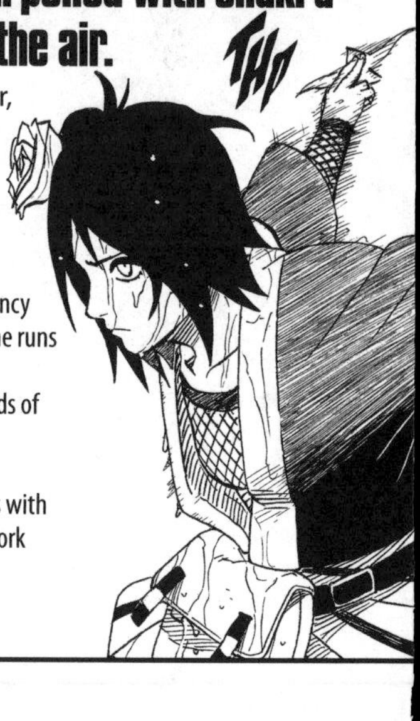

⬅ The amount of time one works with paper and the accumulated hard work sharpen the edge to the extreme.

Nin Jutsu | Kekkei Genkai

Kamui

Caster: Hatake Kakashi

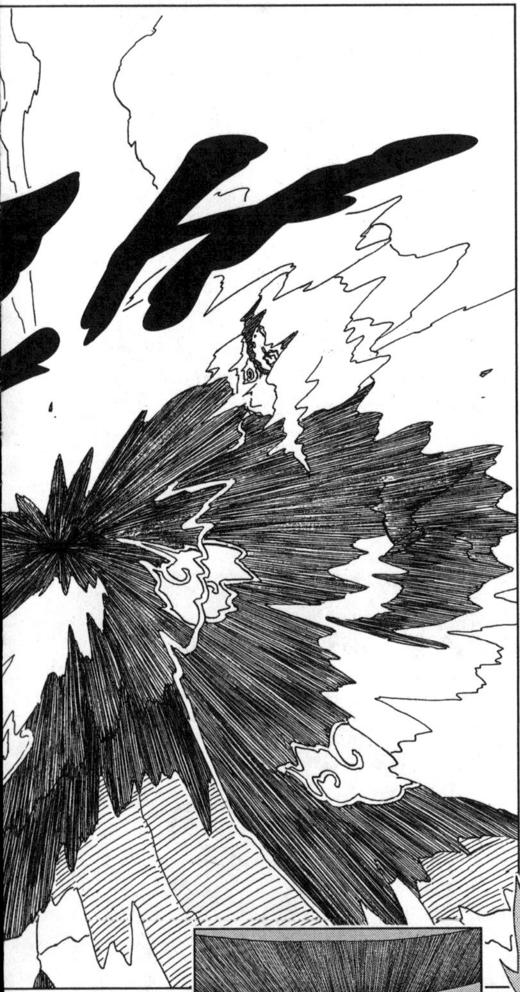

An unmatched jutsu that changes the dimension of the visible world.

An original ocular jutsu of Kakashi's unleashed from Mangekyo Sharingan. It makes possible the transference of any object to another world. This technique can be used only after taking time to create as much chakra as he can. Kakashi captures his target in the sealed dimension and concentrates his mind on a point beyond his line of sight… The target will struggle, but there is no defense against this jutsu. All the target can do is be drawn into the wrinkle in space.

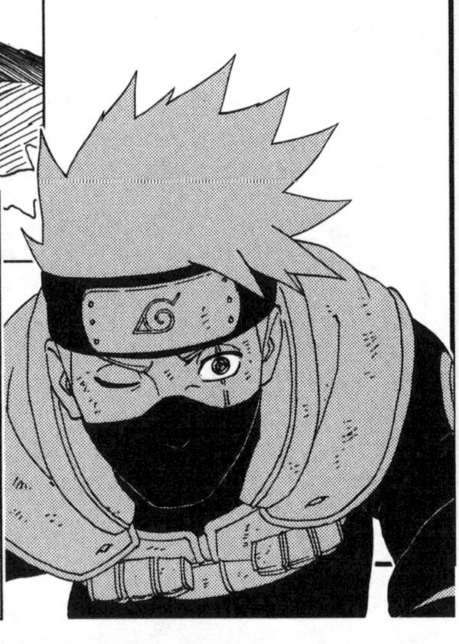

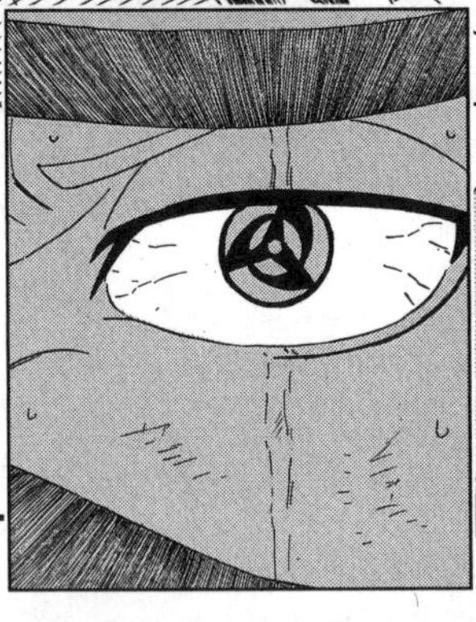

➡ Kakashi stares with Mangekyo Sharingan. He is able to specify the barrier's location and size at will.

⬇ A very slight miss strikes the arm... Instantaneously a portion of the arm is ripped off and sent to another world.

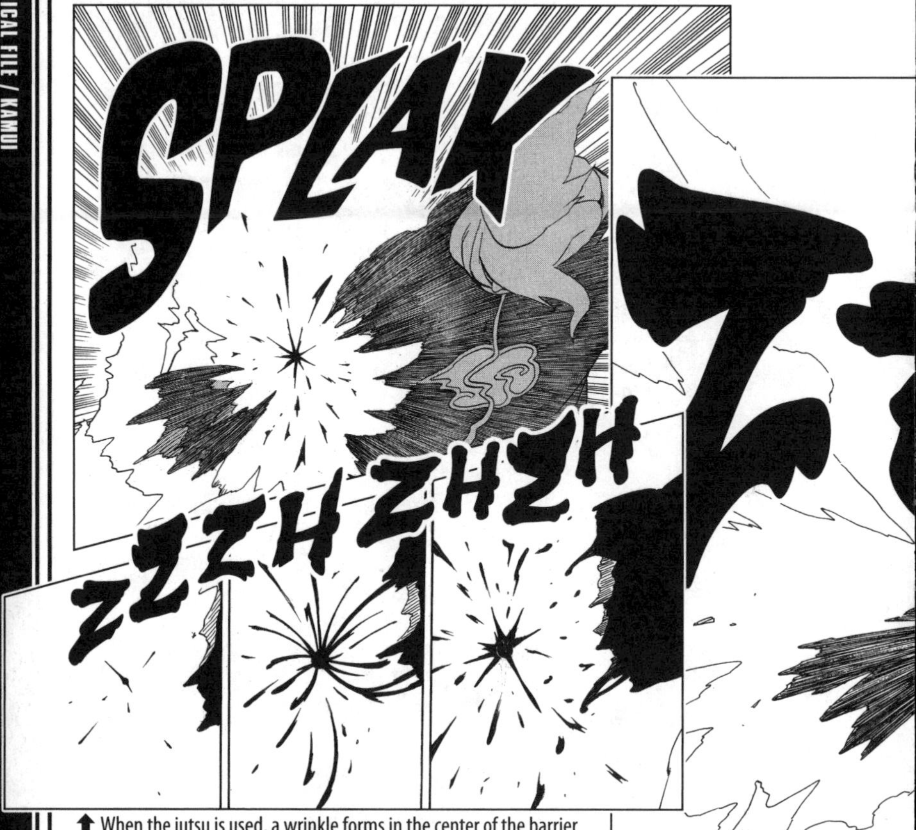
SPLAK
ZZZHZHZH

⬆ When the jutsu is used, a wrinkle forms in the center of the barrier and every target inside the barrier is sucked in. There is no jutsu to fight this. With proficiency, it becomes a frightening jutsu that can suck a person whole into another world.

Beyond the wrinkle in the landscape

A PITFALL IN THE POWER.

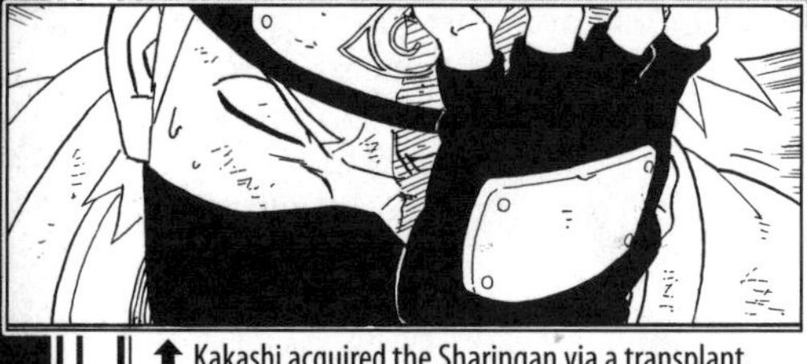

⬆ Kakashi acquired the Sharingan via a transplant. The physical strain it causes may be far greater than the effect it has on members of the Uchiha clan.

Mangekyo Sharingan is an ocular jutsu that can cause blindness if used continuously. Using Kamui, which is based on Mangekyo Sharingan, in rapid succession could endanger Kakashi's life.

Nin Jutsu

Crow Doppelgangers

C

Caster: Uchiha Itachi

FLAP
FLAP
FLAP
FLAP

Servants gather to create human form and receive power from their master.

SWOOSH...
A SHADOW DOPPEL-GANGER...!

⬅⬆ Several dozen crows form a single doppelganger. When the caster's chakra is cut off, the crows scatter.

The caster creates a doppelganger of himself by casting his own chakra upon several dozen crows. By using crows as the medium, it is possible to use less chakra than the Art of the Shadow Doppelganger normally requires.

Nin Jutsu

Kiko Junpu

B

Caster: Chiyo

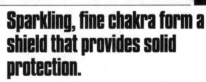

Sparkling, fine chakra form a shield that provides solid protection.

A chakra shield using puppet technology. By opening a puppet mechanism installed in the arms, it radiates the caster's chakra. The chakra, spread out like a thin film, becomes a curtain of defense against all types of physical attacks, thus protecting the caster.

SSSSSS

⬅ By passing chakra threads, it becomes possible to deploy the chakra infused into the puppets.

Nin Jutsu — Kishotensei: Self-Destruct Technique

攻 防 補 近 中 遠 — S

Caster: Chiyo

A forbidden jutsu that transcends death by using one's own life as a medium.

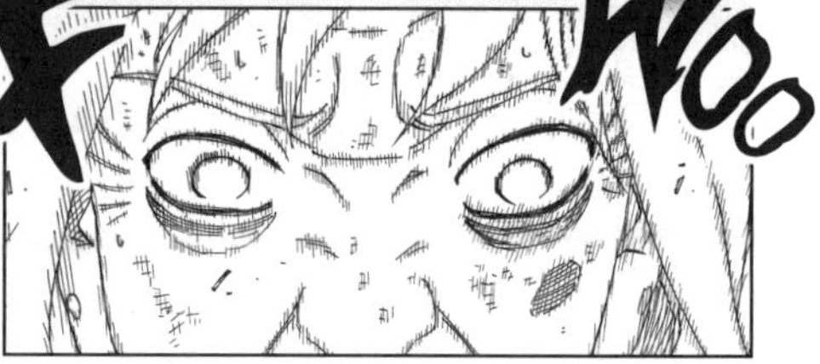
FWOO

⬆ While the jutsu is in use, radiating chakra glows a pale blue color.

A transference technique developed in Sunagakure. By using the entirety of one's chakra as a medium, the caster shares their own life force with the target. While the target can be either living or dead, when the jutsu is applied to one who is dead, the caster's chakra is converted to the deceased's soul and the caster will meet certain death. For moral reasons, Sunagakure deemed this a forbidden jutsu immediately after it was developed. Now, only its developer, Chiyo, can use it.

A TECHNIQUE THAT CONSIGNS ONE'S LIFE TO ANOTHER IN HOPES FOR THE FUTURE.

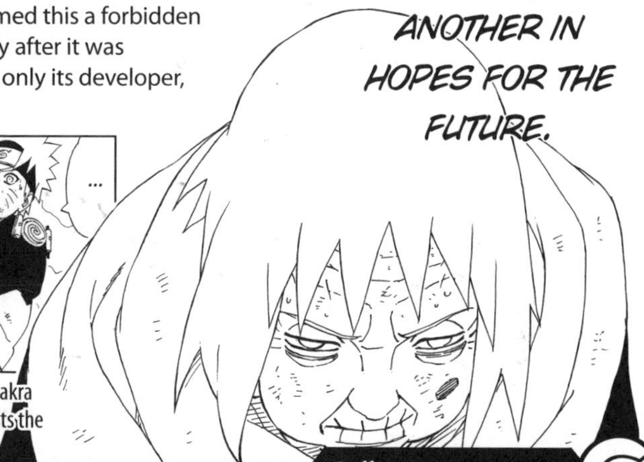

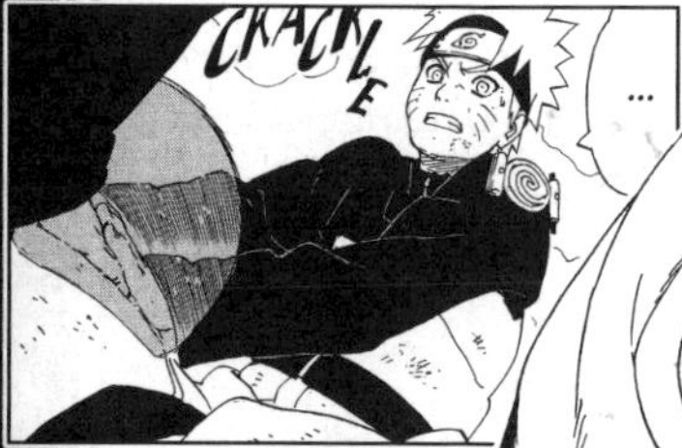
CRACKLE
...

⬆ When one's own chakra is insufficient, she enlists the assistance of another.

THE CREATION OF A FORBIDDEN JUTSU

Collection ... Number 14 — Konoha

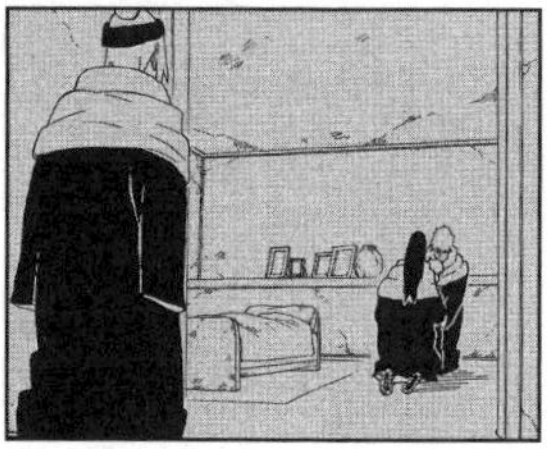

⬆ Chiyo intended to give her grandson, Sasori, the warmth of his parents in exchange for her own life.

Kishotensei: Self-Destruct Technique was created to imbue a soul into puppets of Sasori's parents. Part of it was due to a feeling of remorse for having involved the children, who bore the hopes of the future, in battle.

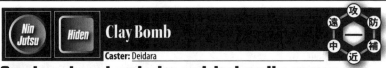

| Nin Jutsu | Hiden | **Clay Bomb** |

Caster: Deidara

Create a shaped explosion and destroy the enemy. The ultimate art form—a tapestry of clay art and destruction.

Art: Objects with form losing their shape in an instant, vaporizing… Art is an explosion. Clay Bomb is a ninjutsu unique to Deidara which fuses his views of art with the practical. He kneads clay with explosive properties using the multiple "mouths" on his body and infuses the clay with chakra. Using that clay, he creates various objects, which he then triggers with the scream "Yeeaagh!!" to cause huge explosions. Because he can control the objects from a distance with chakra, he can attack from land, sea and air. Also, depending on the type of chakra that is infused, he can create a wide variety of Clay Bombs with differing explosive power or destructive effects.

← Deidara has mouths on both hands, but he uses his left more often.

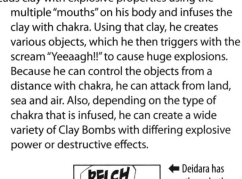

TRUE ART IS REVOLUTIONARY... INCENDIARY...

...AN EXPLOSION!

↑ The caster can detonate the bombs at any time of his choosing.

Creating different Clay Bombs by kneading in chakra

C1

Tiny Clay Bombs whose explosive force is toned down to the maximum possible extent. Used mainly for covert operations or sneak attacks. They are often molded into shapes resembling deformed beetles.

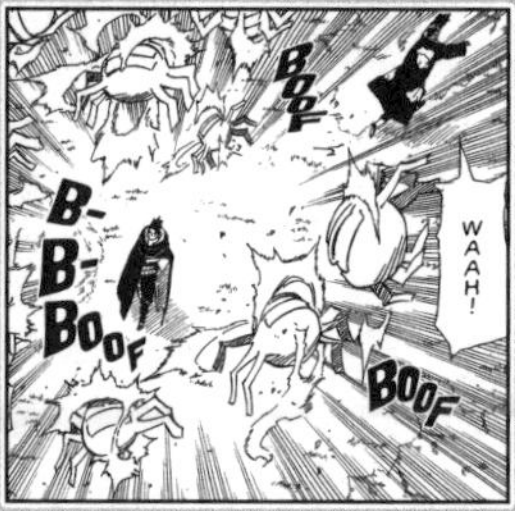
BOOF
WAAH!
B-B-BOOF
BOOF

C2

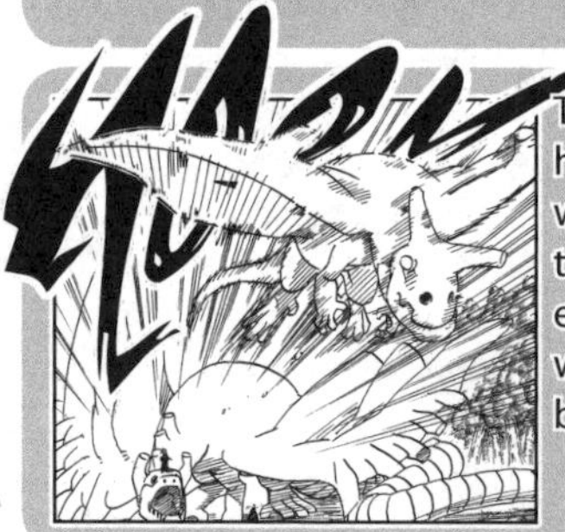

The caster rides on the back of a huge dragon-shaped Clay Bomb which spits out guided smart bombs that pursue the target. It is most effective when used in conjunction with land mines that had previously been set.

C4

When a giant doll in the form of Deidara bursts, microscopic bombs inside its body are dispersed over a wide area. These nano-size bombs cannot be seen by ordinary eyes. The target unknowingly inhales them, setting bombs off throughout his body. The countless tiny explosions that occur within the target's body destroy the target at the cellular level.

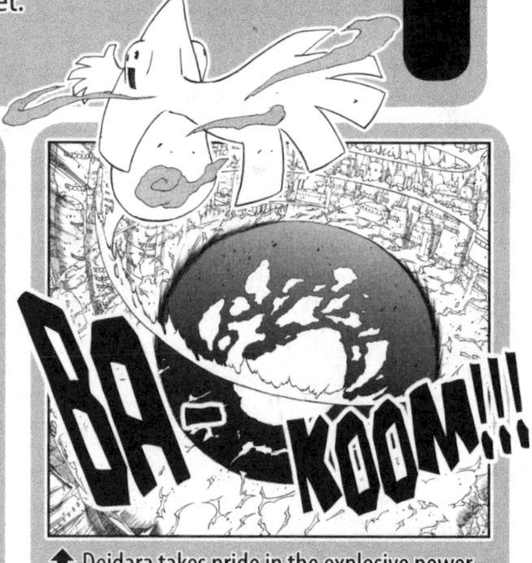
BA-KOOM!!!

⬆ Deidara takes pride in the explosive power of his bombs. Their exceptional power can destroy an entire village.

C3

Although a simple type dropped from the sky, in terms of explosive power alone, its explosion is at the highest level of scale and beauty. It is a Clay Bomb designed to the extreme with nothing extraneous. Deidara takes pride in its doll design.

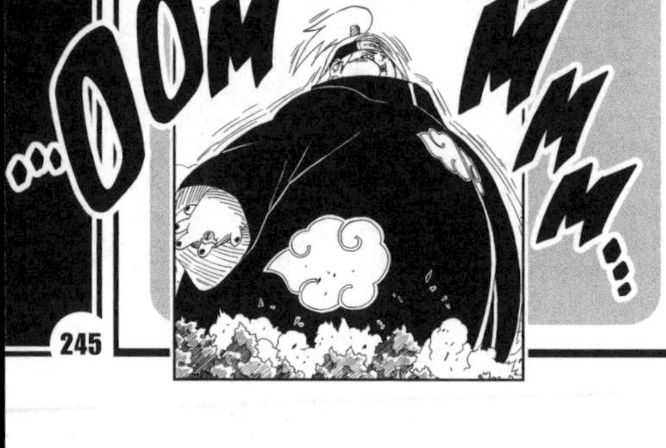
...OOM
MMM...

Nin Jutsu

Mirror Attacker

攻 防 補 近 中 遠 A

Caster: Pain

A Mirror Image Enemy!

A double trap set in the Five Seal Barrier. The jutsu is activated when any of the tags labeled 禁, which means "forbidden," are removed. A tireless, and therefore deadly, clone of the person who removed the tag attacks the original. Only powering up to maximum strength can save the original ninja who removed the tags and created the clone. In essence, they must defeat their more powerful self!

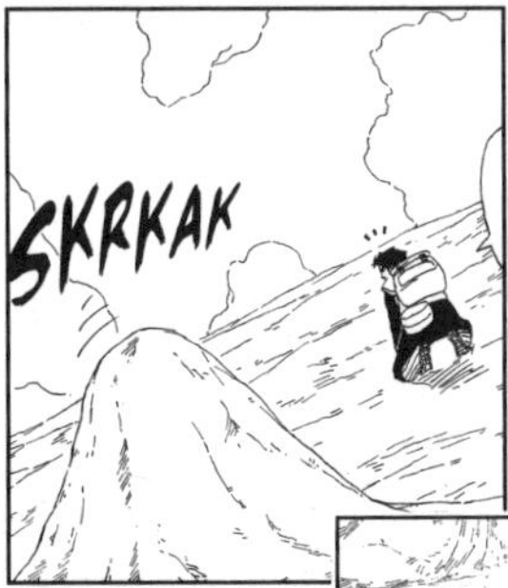
SKRKAK

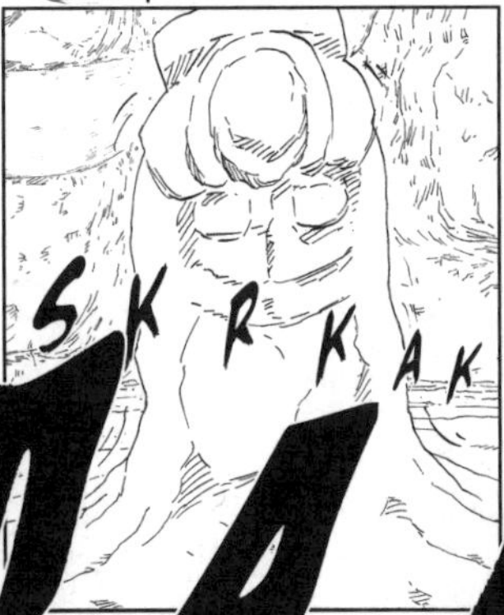
SKRKAK

⬆➡When the tags are removed, the ground moves to become the more powerful clone.

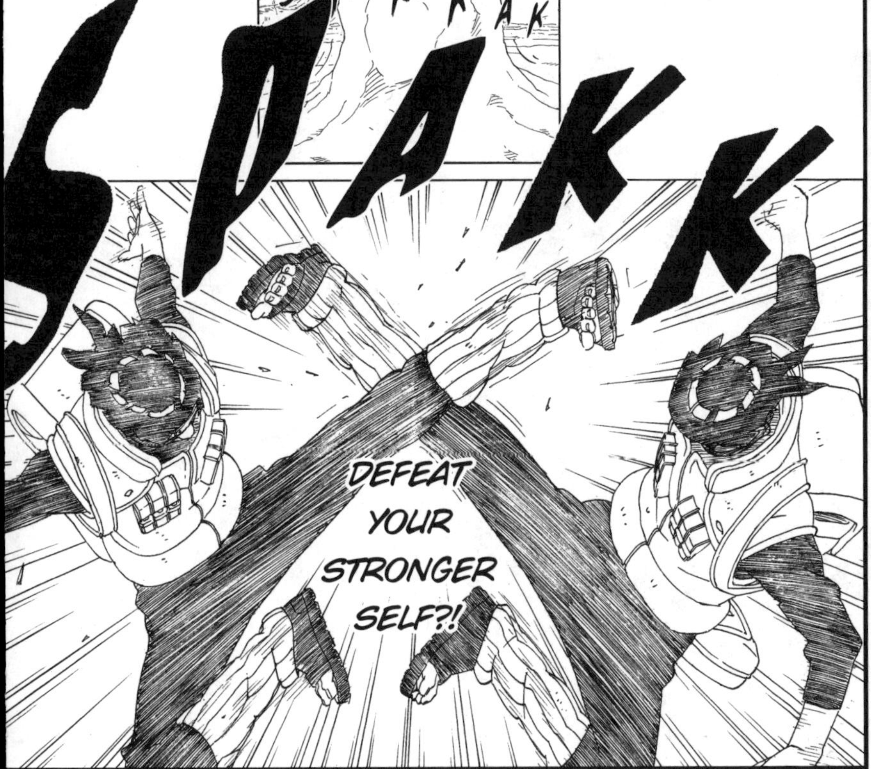
SPAKK
DEFEAT YOUR STRONGER SELF?!

Nin Jutsu

Kirin

Caster: Uchiha Sasuke

攻 遠 防 S 中 補 近

The cry of a mythical beast rocks the world.

Sasuke created this to be the ultimate lightning jutsu. He uses a Fire Style jutsu such as the Dragon Flame Technique to quickly heat the air and create a violent rising current of air. The rising current creates thunderheads, which in turn create lightning, which is guidable toward a specific target. It is a relatively low-impact chakra on the user. In essence, Sasuke has tamed lightning!

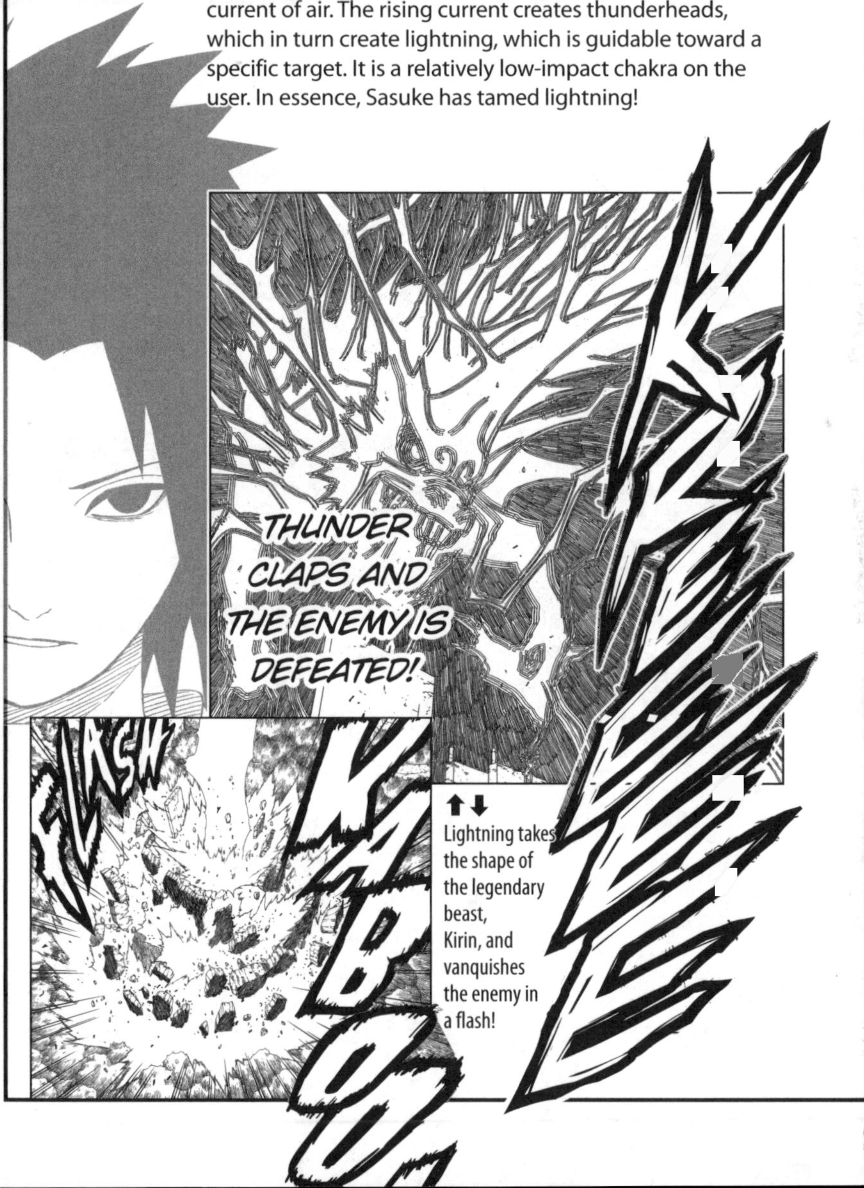
THUNDER CLAPS AND THE ENEMY IS DEFEATED!
FLASH

⬆⬇ Lightning takes the shape of the legendary beast, Kirin, and vanquishes the enemy in a flash!

Nin Jutsu

Aerial Sand Bulwark

Caster: Gaara

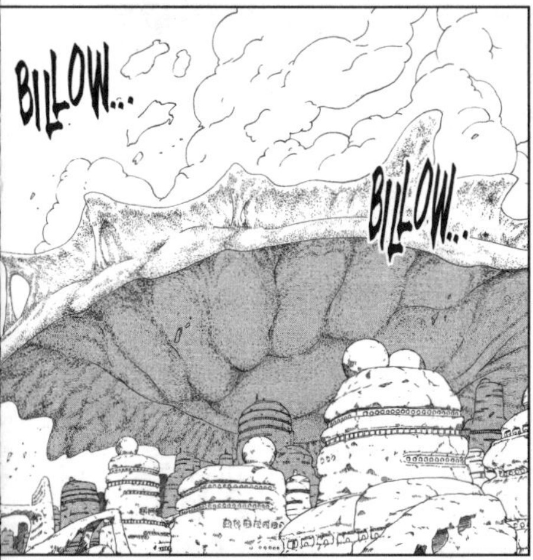
BILLOW...
BILLOW...

⬆ Even Deidara's signature C3 attack could not scratch the strong defense.

Limitless sand comes together to form a defense against an air attack.

A defense against attack from above created by lifting up a large amount of sand from the ground to create a huge shield floating in the air. Gaara not only increases the defensive capabilities of the shield by infusing it with chakra, he chooses hard sand that contains minerals to the greatest extent possible. Gaara's strong sense of duty as the Kazekage is what prompts him to use this to protect the village.

Nin Jutsu

The Kusanagi Chidori Blade

Caster: Uchiha Sasuke

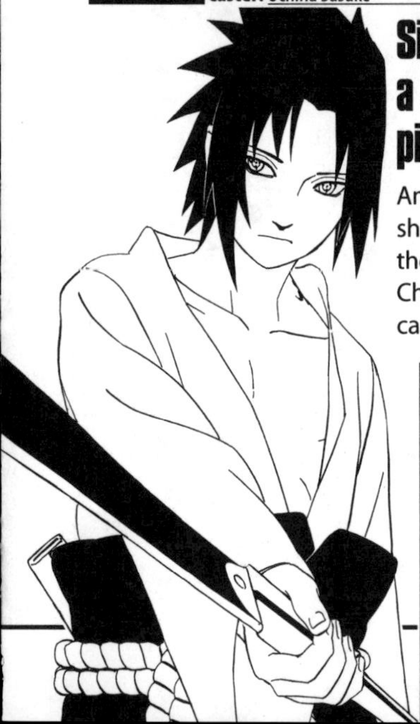

Singing the song of lightning–a sharp pale-blue blade that can pierce anything.

Among the chakra streams which are made sharper by pouring lightning-type chakra into the sword, those jutsu using Chidori are called Chidori Katana. The glistening, whistling blade can easily cut through steel. In addition, it leaves its victim paralyzed and unable to move.

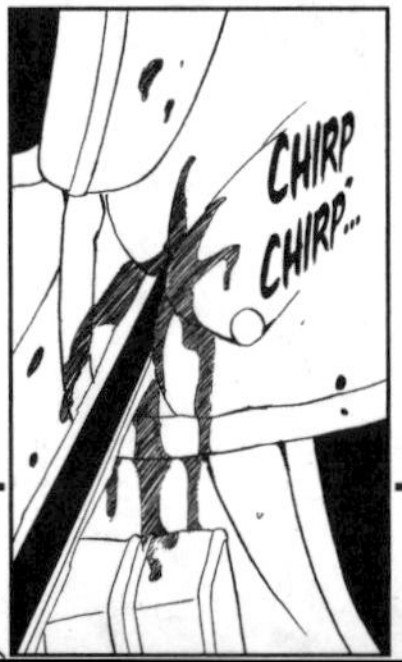
CHIRP CHIRP...

⬅ Chidori flows into the enemy's body through the blade. The electric shock locks the muscles, rendering the enemy unable to move.

Nin Jutsu

Kuchiyose Summoning: Toad Shop Jutsu

攻 防 補 近 中 遠 B

Caster: Jiraiya

Trapped in the stomach of a toad!

A jutsu where one summons a Shop Toad from Mount Myoboku and seals an enemy inside of it. The Shop Toad can transform itself into an architectural structure, and the caster uses chakra to mold it to the design and specs of his choosing. The target, who is lured in with the bait of "all you can drink for 500 ryo" is swallowed whole instead...!!

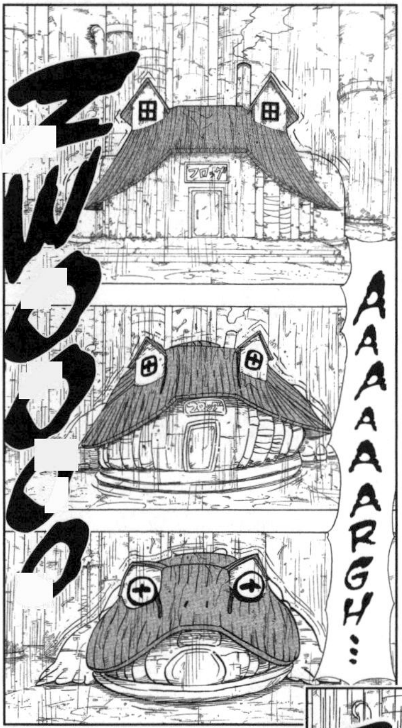
AAAAAAAARGH!!

⬆When the sign is woven, Club Frog turns back into a toad, trapping the target inside.

⬇Once the release sign is woven, it only takes a few seconds for the Shop Toad to shrink back to its original size.

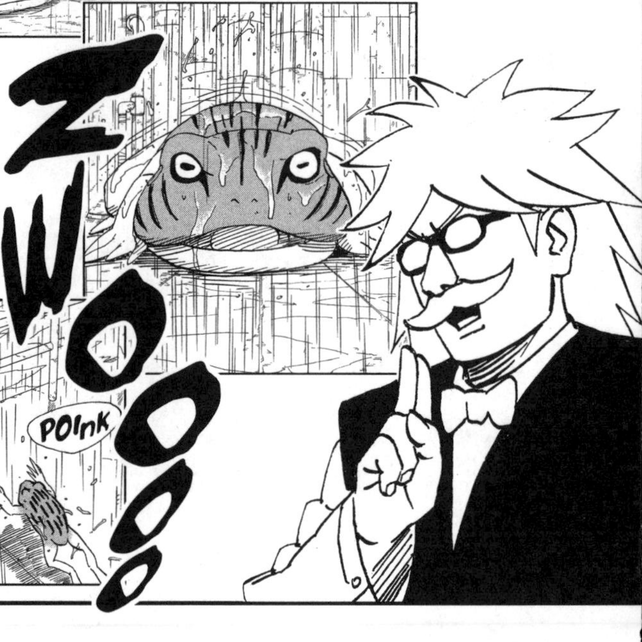
ZWOOOOOOO

⬇Once the enemy is trapped, the shop becomes a toad and hops away!

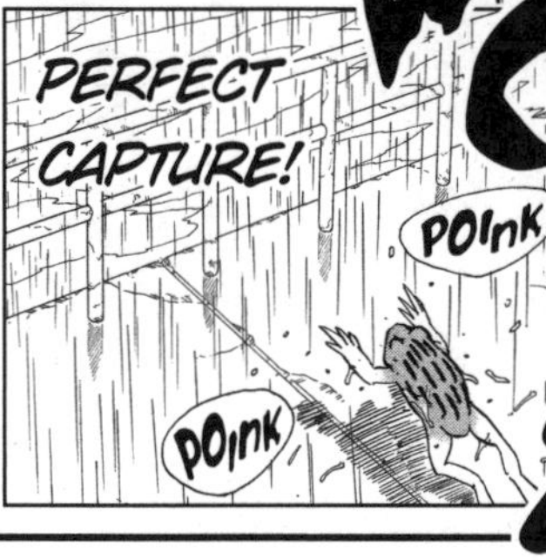
PERFECT CAPTURE!
POINK
POINK

Nin Jutsu

Kuchiyose Summoning: Triple Rashomon

攻 防 補 近 中 遠 A

Caster: Orochimaru

Receive, diminish, disperse! The three-level absolute defense.

A physical defense jutsu by Orochimaru that summons three Rashomon gates. The first gate bears the brunt of any powerful attack. The second gate reduces the attack's power. The third gate disperses the pressure. By the time the attacker reaches the caster, his attack is completely diminished. It takes a huge amount of chakra to summon even a single gate. To summon three Rashomon at once is a feat only possible to a few, including Orochimaru, one of the Three Great Shinobi.

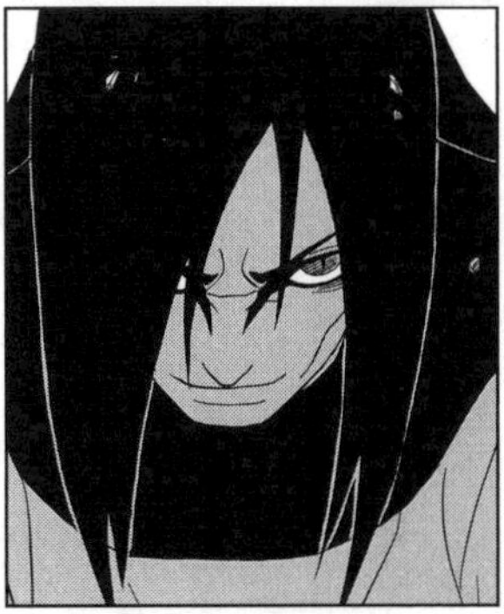

⬆ Rising from the earth, the gates give Orochimaru great power.

⬇ The towering triple gates are immense. They oppress and intimidate all who must face them.

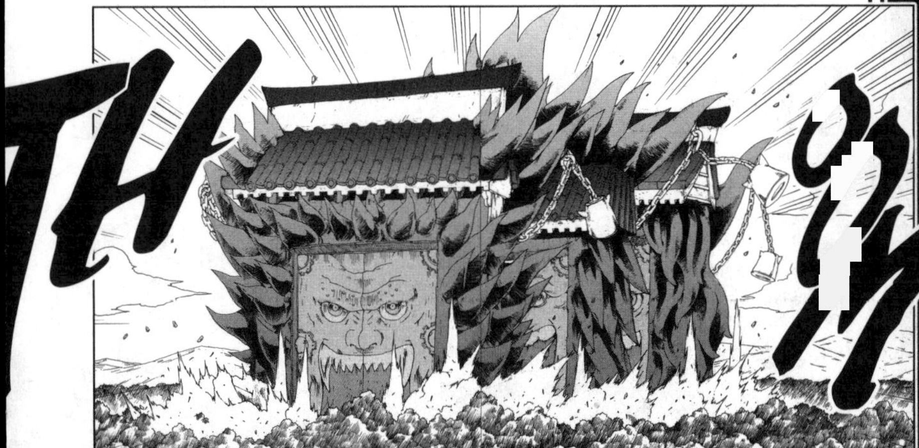
TWIN SEALS SUMMON THE DOOR THAT NEVER OPENS.

Nin Jutsu

Kuchiyose Summoning: Lightning Speed Weapons Retrieval

Caster: Uchiha Sasuke

A multitude of ninja tools appear at their master's desire.

A ninja tool summoning jutsu where ninja tools such as swords and kunai knives are sealed away beforehand in a scroll or in one's clothing and recalled as needed. The greatest benefit of this jutsu is that the process of taking out a ninja tool, taking a stance and putting it into action is sped up to the extreme. Ninja tools are deployed at truly lightning speeds that literally take the air out of an adversary's sails and allow the caster to take the initiative in battle. Also, because the summoned ninja tools can be kept hidden until the moment they are unleashed regardless of how large they are, this jutsu, once mastered, dramatically increases the range of fight strategies that can be employed.

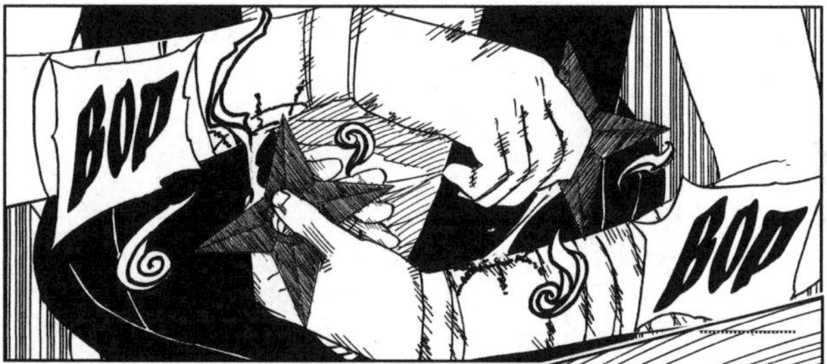
BOP
BOP

⬆ Touch the signs, summon the tools.

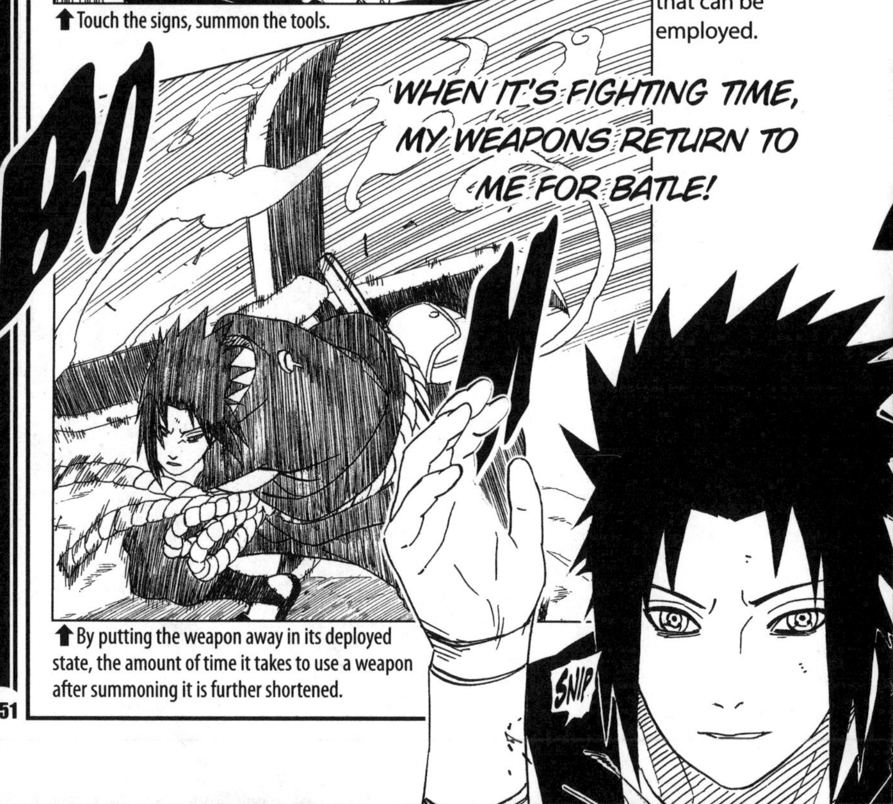
WHEN IT'S FIGHTING TIME, MY WEAPONS RETURN TO ME FOR BATLE!
SNIP

⬆ By putting the weapon away in its deployed state, the amount of time it takes to use a weapon after summoning it is further shortened.

Jutsu

Art of the Hurricane Vortex

遠 攻 防 B 中 近 補

Caster: Uzumaki Naruto / Yamato

Gales and rushing waters create a protective curtain of white fog.

A compound jutsu created by combining the water currents of Water Style: Ripping Torrent!! with the wild rotations of Rasengan to form a huge amount of water vapor. Once invoked, a powerful whirlwind forms inside an extremely thick fog, becoming an impregnable barrier that repels jutsu and attacks. Furthermore, the fog created by the powerful rotation of Rasengan has the added benefit of instantly taking away an enemy's field of vision. It can be used as a distraction when making one's escape or as a means of conducting a sneak attack by hiding in the fog. This jutsu has many applications.

➡ Naruto's Wind Style merged with Yamato's Water Style. If one is capable of handling several elements, a singe individual can invoke this jutsu.

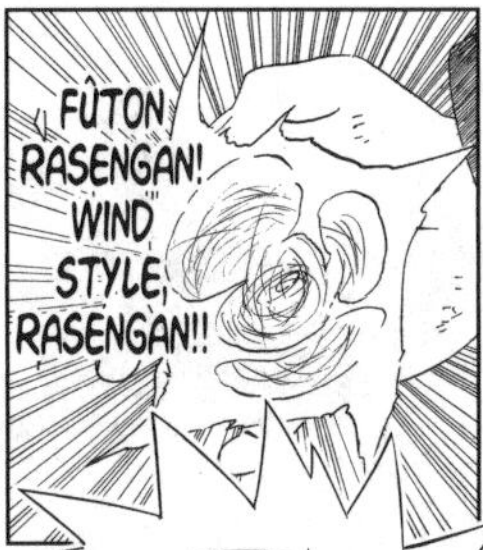
FÛTON RASENGAN! WIND STYLE, RASENGAN!!

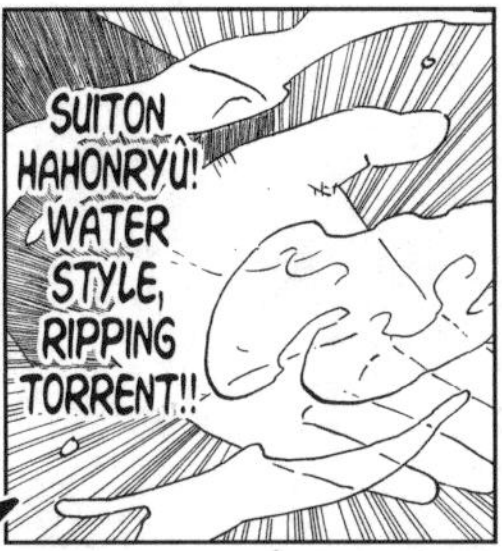
SUITON HAHONRYÛ! WATER STYLE, RIPPING TORRENT!!

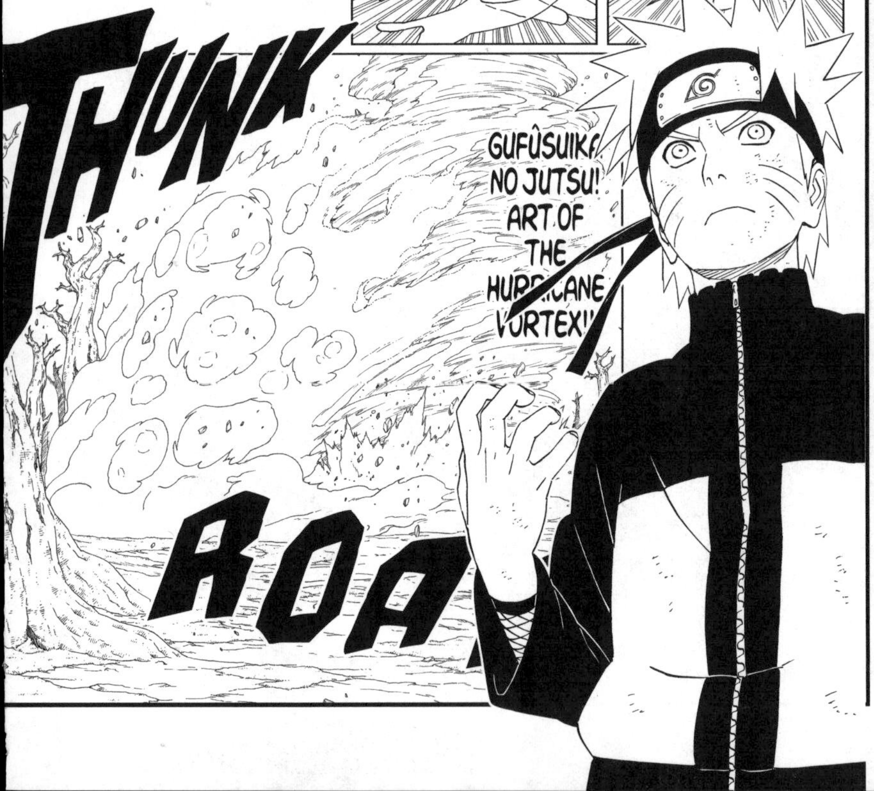
THUNK
GUFÛSUIKA NO JUTSU! ART OF THE HURRICANE VORTEX!!
ROA

Nin Jutsu — Kekkai Barrier: Gamahyoro

遠 防 中 補 近 B

Caster: Jiraiya

Inside a gourd filled with silence and fear—a sealed dimension from which there is no escape.

⬇ The caster himself can enter and exit the toad at a moment's notice by giving an order.

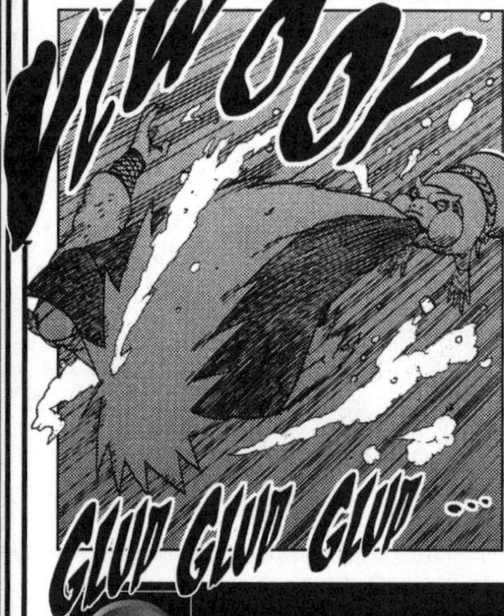
VWOOP
GLUP GLUP GLUP ...

The caster summons the Gourd Toad, Gamahyotan, who lives on Mount Myoboku, then drags the target into the toad's stomach, where a sealed dimension isolated from the outside world exists. It is also possible to melt one's adversary by shoving him into a lake of acid.

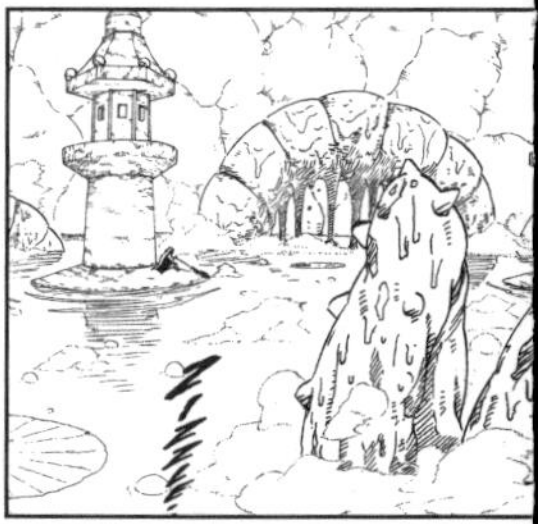

⬆ The inside of a toad's stomach is dominated by silence. The lake, however, is filled with a powerful acid.

Nin Jutsu — Tengai Perimeter Barrier

遠 防 中 補 近 B

Caster: Jiraiya

Wide-ranging battle tactic that detects anyone who enters.

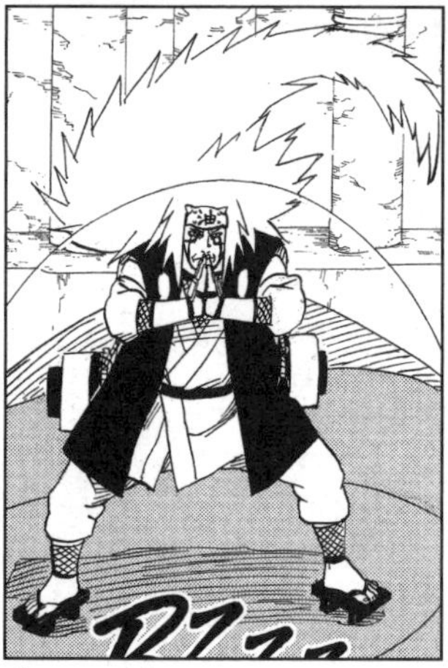

A jutsu that sets a sphere-shaped detection barrier with the caster at its center. At the caster's will, the barrier can be expanded to seize an entire space. The caster is then able to feel the activities of those existing inside the barrier through his senses.

⬆ ➡ Jiraiya's detection barrier far surpasses even Gamaken's giant body, completely filling up the space needed for battle.

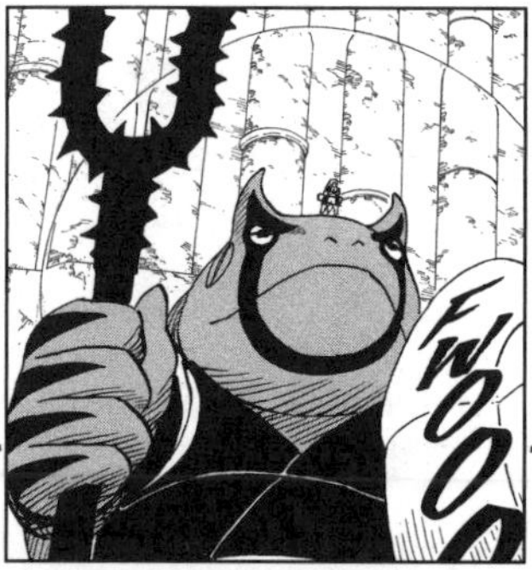

Nin Jutsu

Art of Astral Projection

Caster: Pain

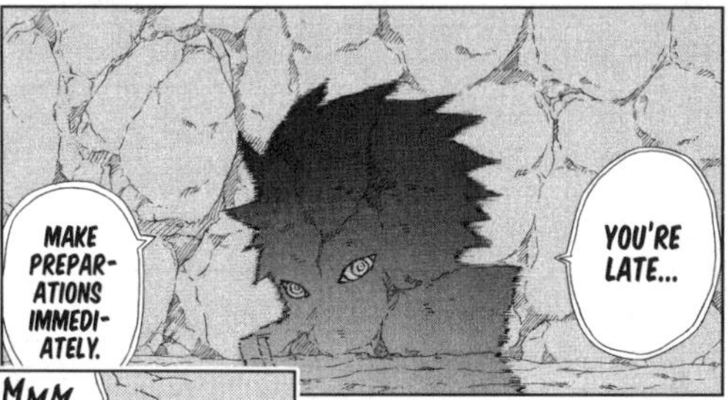
YOU'RE LATE...
MAKE PREPAR-ATIONS IMMEDI-ATELY.

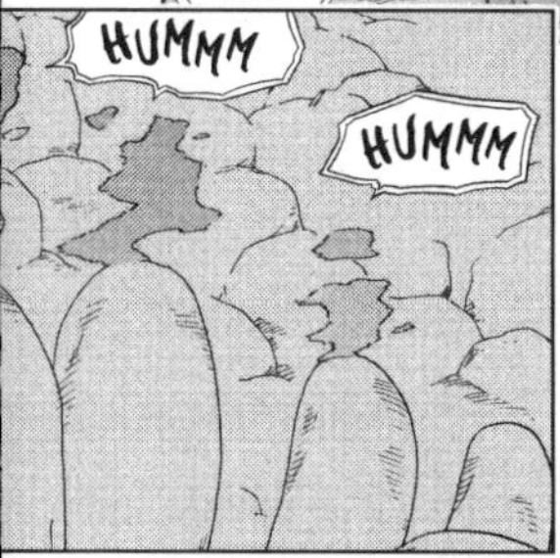
HUMMM
HUMMM

Akatsuki virtual images appear in the darkness.

⬅ Pain is able to perceive the chakra of Akatsuki members. Their amplified thought waves appear as a phantom body image.

When members of the Akatsuki sit down and release thought waves from converted chakra, Pain, acting as the "control tower" receives these waves, amplifies them, and uses them to create a phantom body image in a specific location. Unlike a simple projected image, the phantom body image can, with Pain relaying commands, invoke a range of jutsu.

Tai Jutsu

Konoha Rising Wind

Caster: Rock Lee

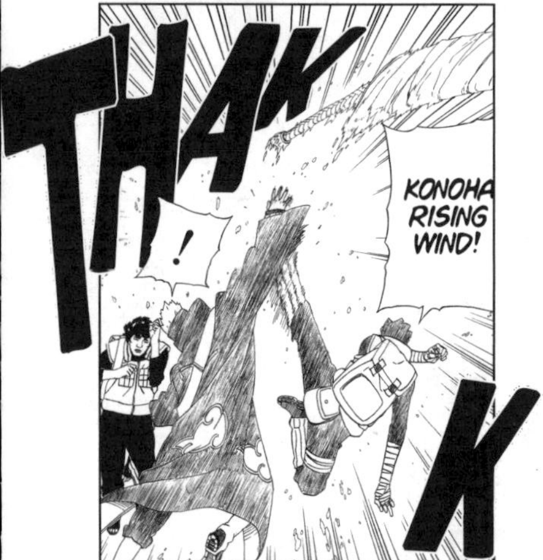
THAK
!
KONOHA RISING WIND!

⬆ The attack is difficult to see because it comes from directly below. It has the power to easily kick away the Sharkskin Blade, Samehada, from Kisame's hands.

Wind becomes a dragon, dancing toward the sky with a powerful force!

This jutsu is somewhat similar to Guy's Dynamic Entry. A powerful straight-up kick propels the caster high into the sky.

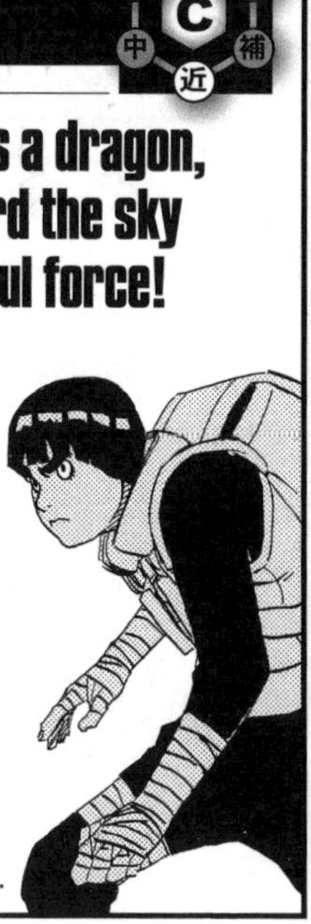

Nin Jutsu

Five Seal Barrier

Caster: Pain

攻 防 補 近 中 遠 C

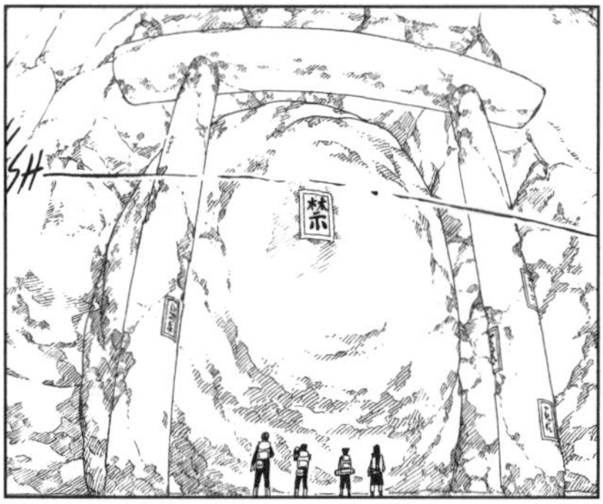

The firm connection between five tags prevents the opening of any doors.

Five forbidden tags connected by the caster's chakra are placed in various locations, including on the stronghold to be defended at the center, turning the area surrounded by the tags into a sealed dimension. Because destruction of objects within the sealed dimension is forbidden, it is necessary to find and remove all five tags to cancel this jutsu.

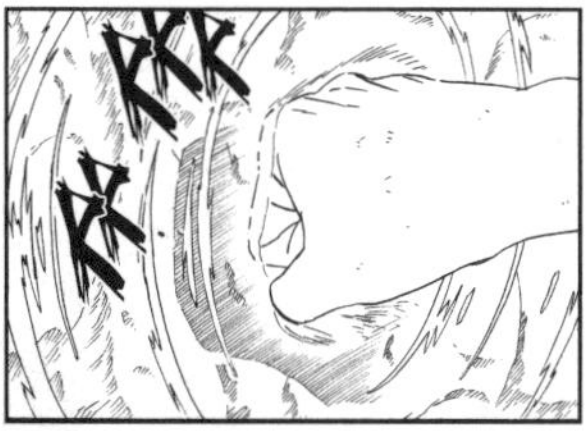

⬅⬆ Inside the sealed dimension, it is impossible to even scratch, much less destroy, anything using any sort of physical attack.

Collection ... Number 15

Konoha

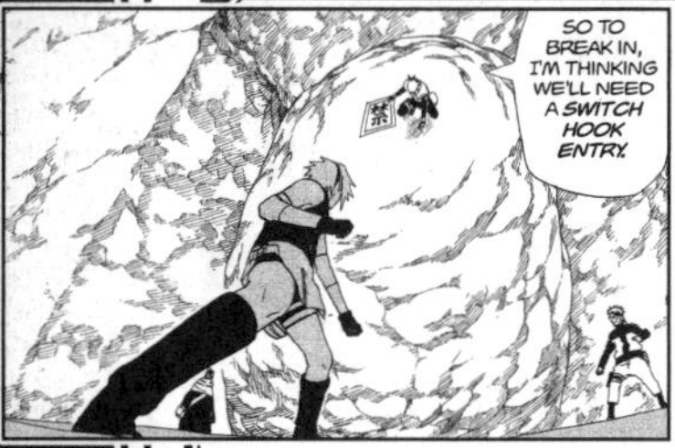
SO TO BREAK IN, I'M THINKING WE'LL NEED A *SWITCH HOOK ENTRY.*

⬆ Attackers must be wary of being met with an attack immediately upon making entry.

CAPTURING THE BARRIER IN TWO-MAN CELLS

It is said that a group of four, in two smaller groups of two, are the preferred means of attacking an enemy stronghold protected by a Five Seal Barrier. One group removes four of the tags while the other group removes the final tag on the stronghold itself, before attacking simultaneously. This is done so that the attackers can break in while retaining their fighting ability. A sensory-type shinobi among the group allows them to react even more quickly.

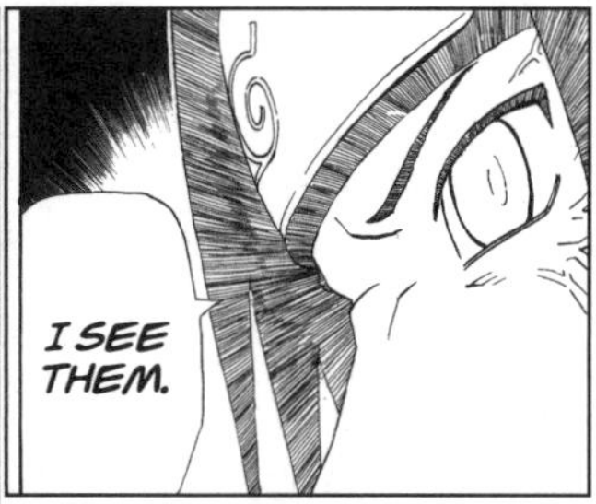
I SEE THEM.

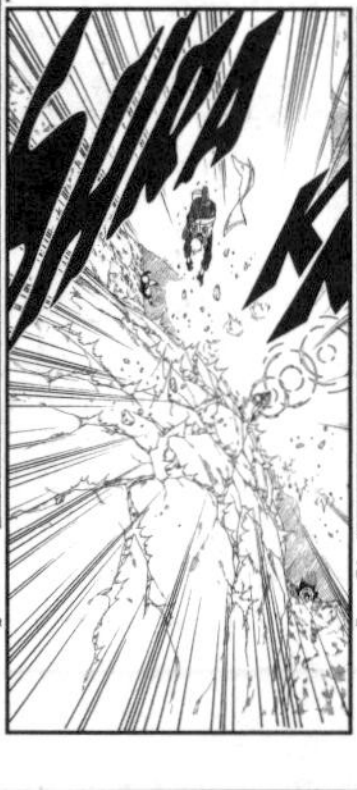

Nin Jutsu

Cellular Extraction Healing Jutsu

B

Caster: Haruno Sakura

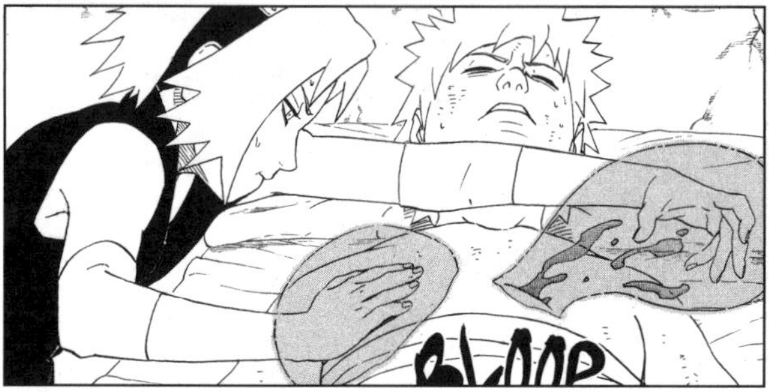
BLOOP

Ascertains damaging poisons in the body and removes them all.

⬆ This jutsu demands diagnostic abilities to spot the afflicted area, the skill to make an incision, and incredibly precise control of chakra.

By sensing disturbances in the chakra inside the body, this jutsu can detect the cause of damage to the body such as toxins and pathogens. Using a chakra scalpel, the afflicted area is cut open and the toxic elements sucked out. At the same time, the wound is healed from the outside. It is categorized as among the most difficult of medical ninjutsu. Most commonly, after this jutsu is used to heal the afflicted person, an antidote or other medicine is used to complete the healing process.

Collection ... Number 16

Konoha

MEDICAL NINJUTSU: WHAT'S POSSIBLE?

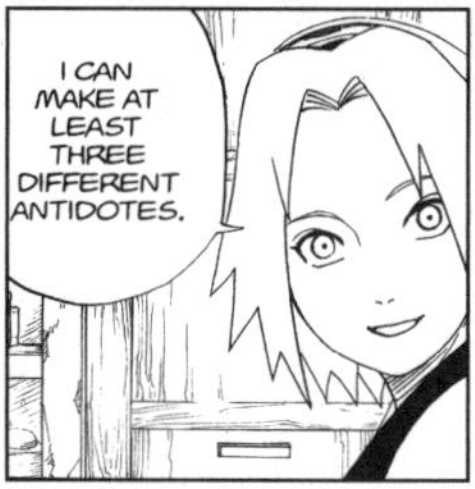
I CAN MAKE AT LEAST THREE DIFFERENT ANTIDOTES.

⬆ Medic ninja must also possess the knowledge and skill to prepare medicines.

At the time of the Great Ninja War, Tsunade advocated the assignment of a medic ninja to every platoon. However, this recommendation was rejected on the basis that it would require an enormous amount of time to train such personnel. Medic ninja are required to possess many skills including delicate control of chakra and knowledge of the human body and medicines.

Presently, there is a system to train them and the number of medic ninja has increased, but there remains a shortage of people who are capable of using this jutsu with complete command. It remains a difficult to achieve, but invaluable, jutsu.

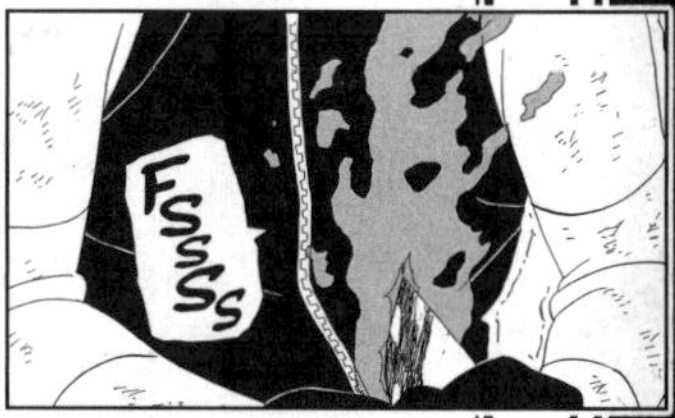
FSSSS

⬆ The ability to heal oneself even while being attacked is the pinnacle of external injury treatment.

Nin Jutsu | Kekkei Genkai

Iron Sand World Order

攻 防 補 近 中 遠 —

Caster: Sasori / Third Kazekage

Poison Needles!

This jutsu uses high-density iron sand particles fused into two masses of opposite magnetic polarities. By suddenly increasing the magnetism of the particles and using the repelling force of like magnetic fields, the iron sand is scattered over a wide area. Each sand particle contains a poison that can kill with the slightest scratch.

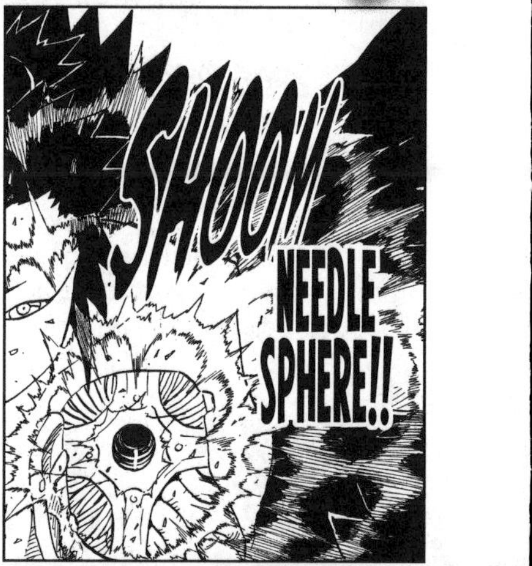
SHOOM
NEEDLE SPHERE!!

⬇ Jet black and full of poison!

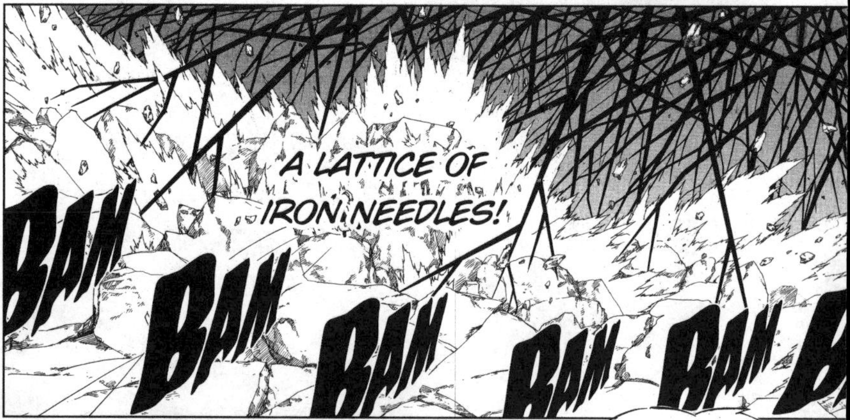
A LATTICE OF IRON NEEDLES!
BAM
BAM
BAM
BAM
BAM

➡ Even if an enemy is able to avoid the needles and their poison, an attack by the Third Kazekage awaits. Pinned down, all an enemy can do is await his death.

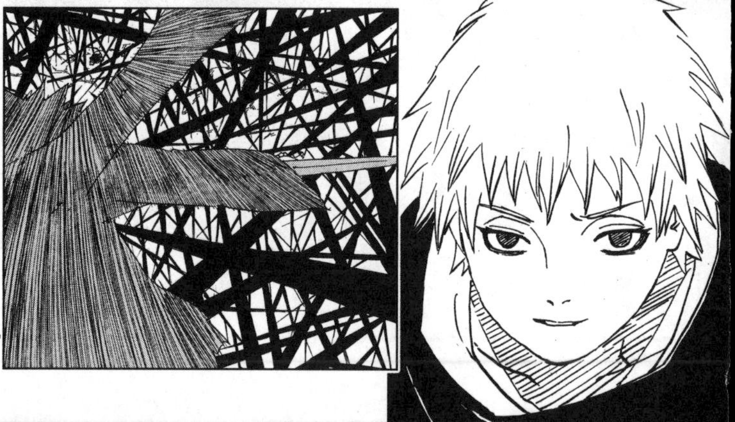

Nin Jutsu | Kekkei Genkai

Iron Sand Block Attack

攻 防 補 近 中 遠 —

Caster: Sasori / Third Kazekage

Vengeful quantities of iron sand create a powerfully piercing concerto.

Huge quantities of iron sand are amassed and compressed into a high-density shape, instantaneously creating a large, iron weapon that is harder and heavier than the sand from which it was formed. Because the original material is iron sand, it can be formed into any shape the caster desires. A conical shape with a sharp point becomes a giant spear. A rectangular block shape with an enlarged contact face becomes a giant iron hammer. The caster is able to choose the appropriate method of attack depending on the target type and the terrain of the battlefield. Of course, iron sand possesses powerful magnetic properties that render weapons and ninja tools made of iron useless.

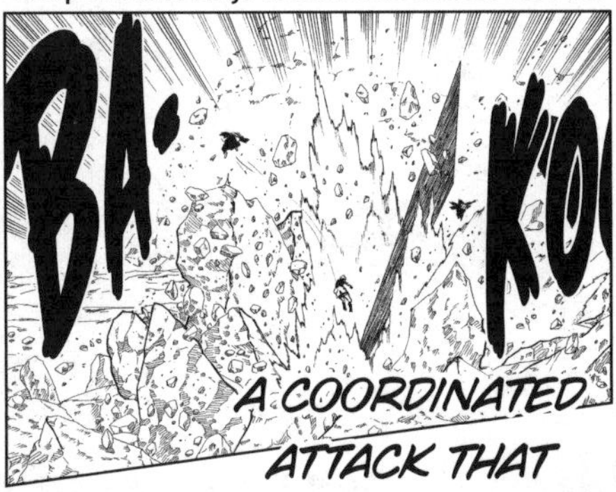
BA-KOO

⬅ Its weight allows it to easily go through even bedrock, pulverizing it.

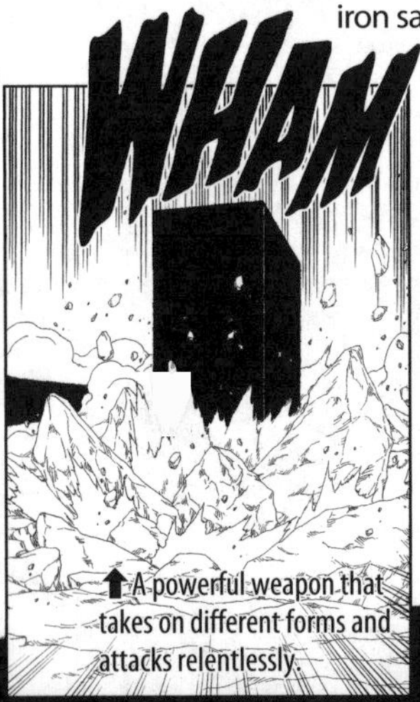
WHAM

⬆ A powerful weapon that takes on different forms and attacks relentlessly.

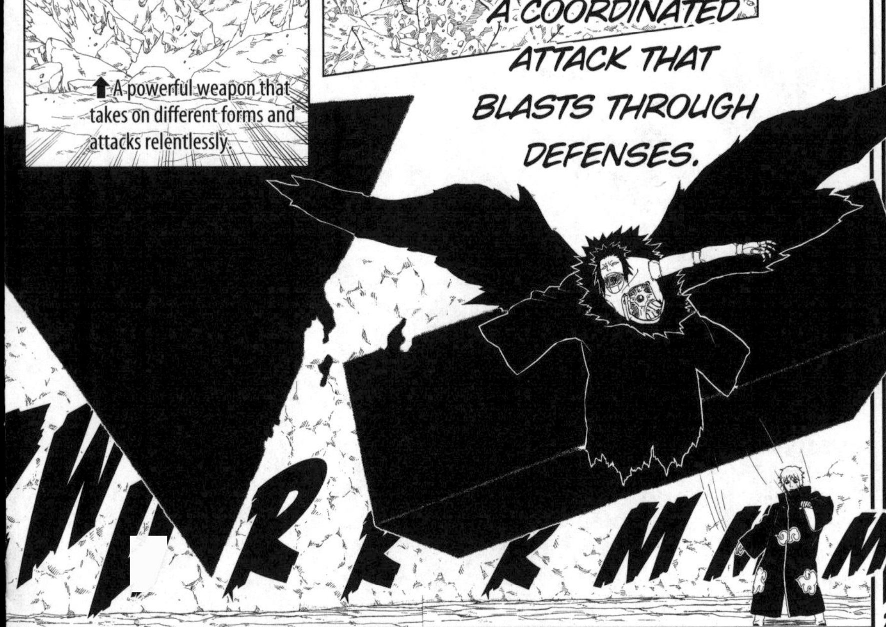
A COORDINATED ATTACK THAT BLASTS THROUGH DEFENSES.

Nin Jutsu | Kekkei Genkai

Iron Sand Shower

Caster: Sasori / Third Kazekage

Dark rain is a prologue to life and death.

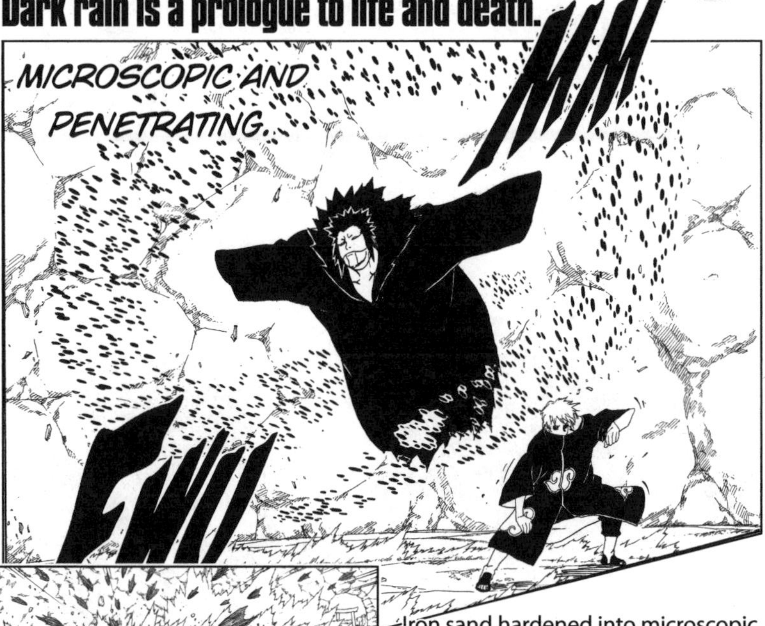
MICROSCOPIC AND PENETRATING.

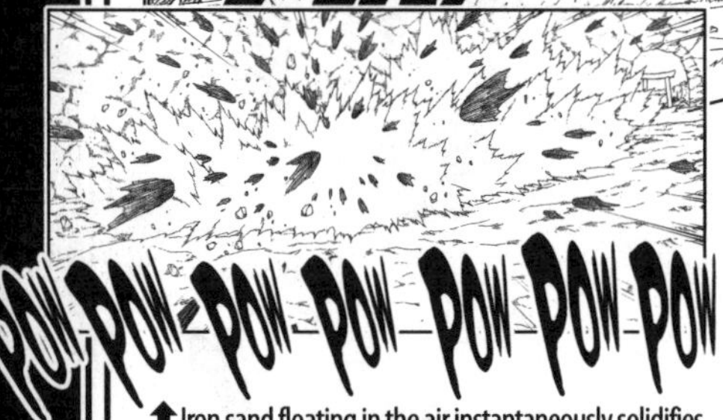
POW POW POW POW POW POW POW

⬆ Iron sand floating in the air instantaneously solidifies. If an enemy is a split second late in making a decision, he will already be unable to avoid the attack.

Iron sand hardened into microscopic grains is launched out to attack a large area. The speed of the particles is so fast that it is difficult to see them coming with the naked eye, making them very difficult to avoid once the caster has assumed a firing position. There are also other attack patterns where the pellets are transformed into sharp needle shapes to increase their killing capability. And, because iron sand possesses magnetic properties and contains poison, it is impossible to defend against. In particular, this is a powerful jutsu against puppet users because it renders their puppets unable to fight.

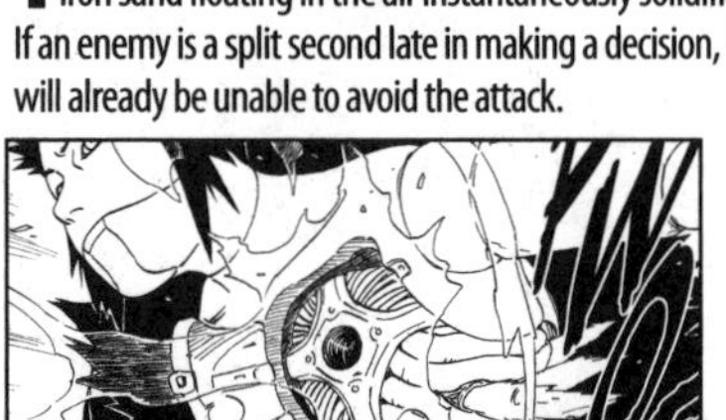

⬆➡ It is possible to use the repellent properties of magnetism to greatly increase the speed of the pellets or to change their flight after they are launched.

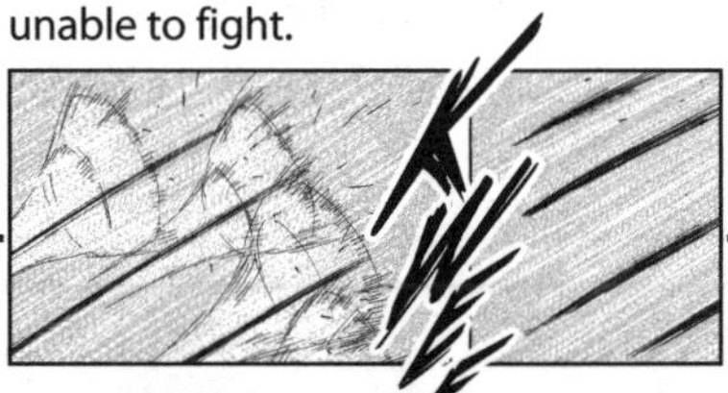

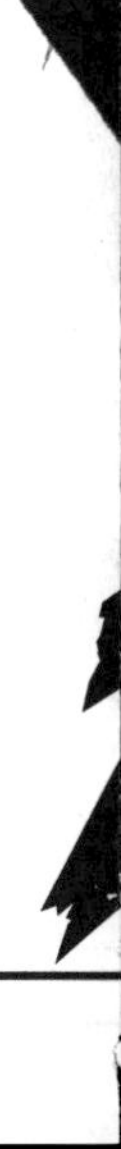

Nin jutsu

Sand Prison

攻 防 補 近 中 遠 **B**

Caster: Gaara

Vast, raging waves of sand bind and capture.

This ninjutsu for capturing one's enemy is unique to Gaara. The speed, hardness and scale of the sand depends on the amount of chakra applied and can be adjusted according to the quarry's size and characteristics. Regardless of whether they run along the ground or fly up into the sky, anyone hostile toward Gaara is fated to certain capture. Furthermore, even if one is able to escape from the sand prison, this jutsu can be part of a two-pronged attack that leads to such techniques as the Coffin of Crushing Sand.

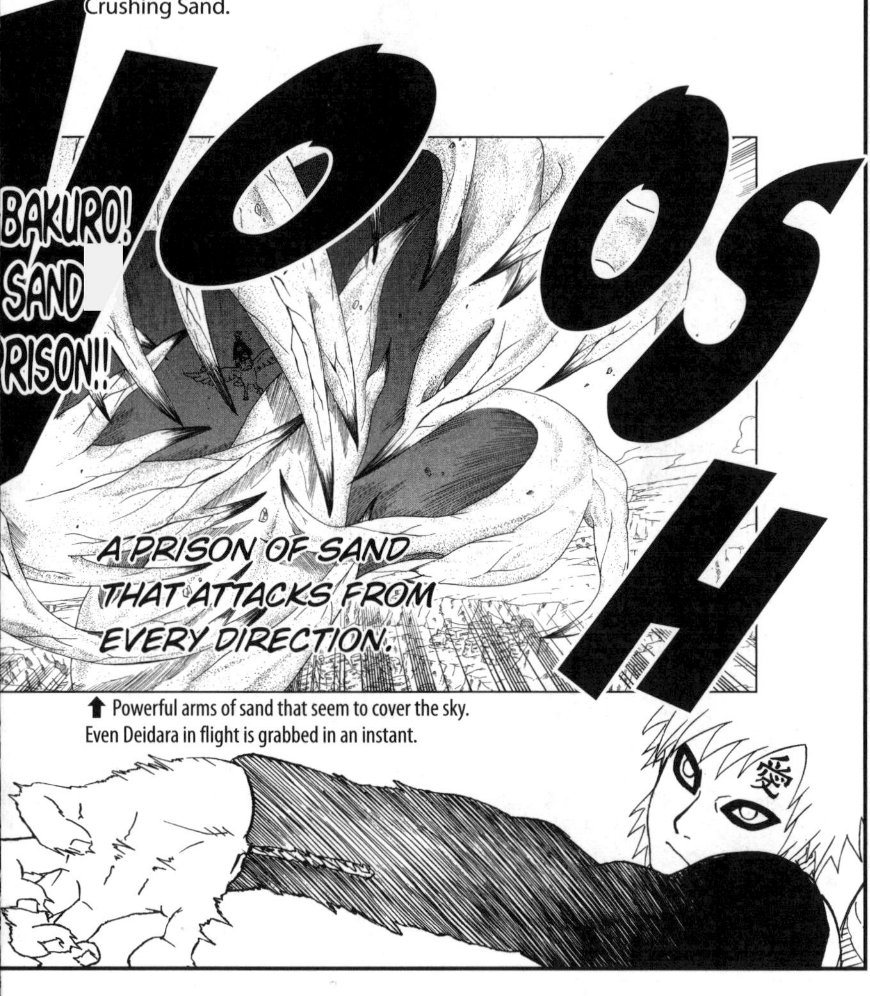
BAKURO! SAND
RISON!!
WOOSH
A PRISON OF SAND THAT ATTACKS FROM EVERY DIRECTION.

⬆ Powerful arms of sand that seem to cover the sky. Even Deidara in flight is grabbed in an instant.

Nin Jutsu — 1,000 Crows

Caster: Yamashiro Aoba

攻 防 補 遠 C 中 近

The black flutter of wings that cover the field of vision confuses an enemy by enveloping him in darkness.

A PITIFUL ATTEMPT AT OBFUS-CATION.

A supplementary ninjutsu used to temporarily confuse an enemy by summoning countless crows. Chakra flowing from the caster's fingertips is converted into high-frequency waves that control the birds at will. The birds repeatedly clone themselves as they wrap themselves around the target, completely rendering the target unable to see. While this jutsu can be used for attack, it is basically invoked as a starting point for a collaborative attack.

HUP

The crows color the area around the target black. Scattering 1,000 Crows can also be used to aid one's friends. ⬆

Nin Jutsu | Fūin Jutsu — Sealing Spell: Three Treasures Vacuum

Caster: Chiyo

攻 防 補 遠 B 中 近

SANPO KYUKAI!! THREE TREA-SURES VACUUM!!

Three puppets in prayer create a whirlwind that sucks in and crushes all things.

A mechanical performance by three of Chikamatsu's puppets. Three puppets create a triangular formation. The jutsu is invoked by opening the Buddha, Dharma, and Sangha mechanisms. This creates a fierce tornado that sucks the target into the center of the formation. Everything that is sucked in is crushed before being discharged out the back of the formation.

⬅⬆ The tornado destroys many puppets at once.

Nin Jutsu

Hiden

CO

Caster: Deidara

The caster dies as his life is vaporized; as compensation, a sublime explosion is born.

CO, which Deidara takes pride in calling the ultimate art, boasts the largest-scale explosion among ninjutsu that use detonating clay. Unlike similar jutsu that use the mouths in the palms of his hands, this jutsu uses the mouth on his chest to knead the clay. He kneads chakra that comes directly from the meridians of his heart and continues to do so without interruption until the moment of the explosion. In other words, the explosion occurs inside his body, vaporizing everything in the vicinity including the caster's soul as it releases the light of life.

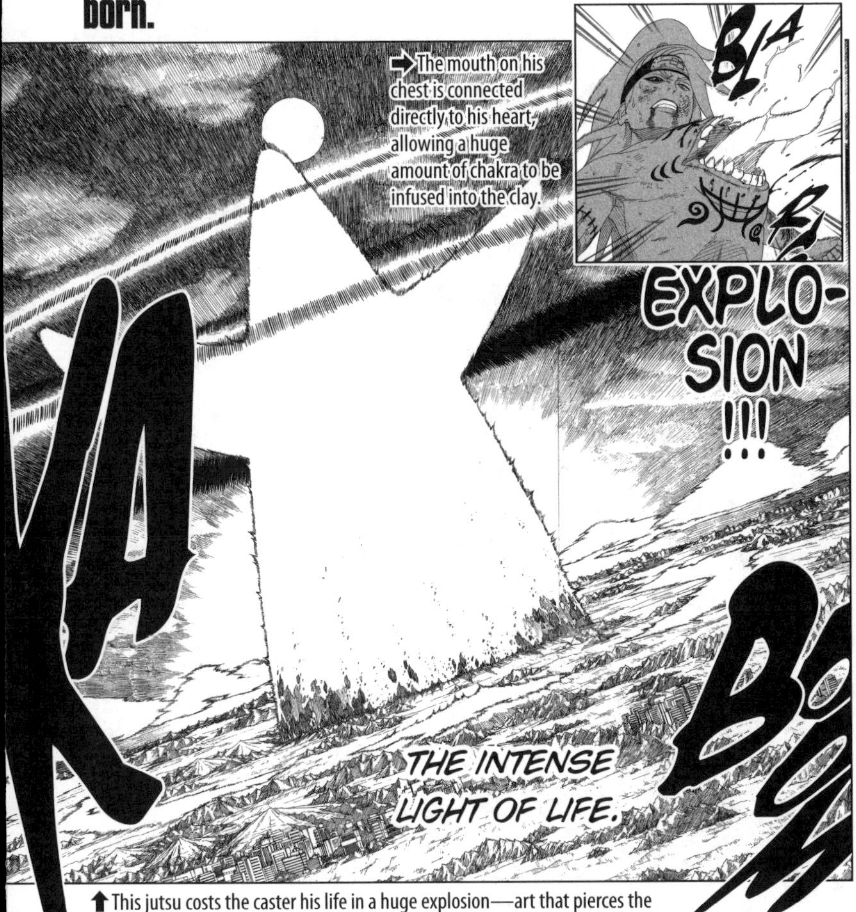
EXPLO-
SION
!!!
THE INTENSE LIGHT OF LIFE.

➡ The mouth on his chest is connected directly to his heart, allowing a huge amount of chakra to be infused into the clay.

⬆ This jutsu costs the caster his life in a huge explosion—art that pierces the heavens and leaves its mark on the earth.

Nin Jutsu | Hiden | **Jiongu**

Caster: Kakuzu

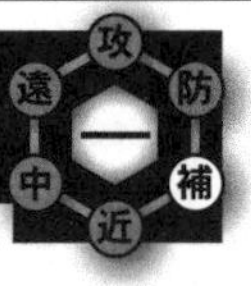
攻
防
補
近
中
遠
—

Wriggling, jet-black tentacles.

An unusual jutsu that makes it possible to attack from a distance by using chakra to manipulate black tentacles that emerge from the body. This allows the caster to use a fighting method where the distance from his opponent does not matter. Also, by using these tentacles to steal the hearts of his adversaries and placing that heat and chakra into his own body, Kakuzu became able to control all of the five basic elements and live a nearly immortal life.

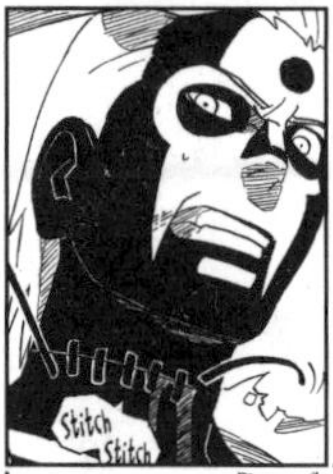
Stitch
Stitch

⬅The sharply pointed tentacles are also used to stitch his body together.

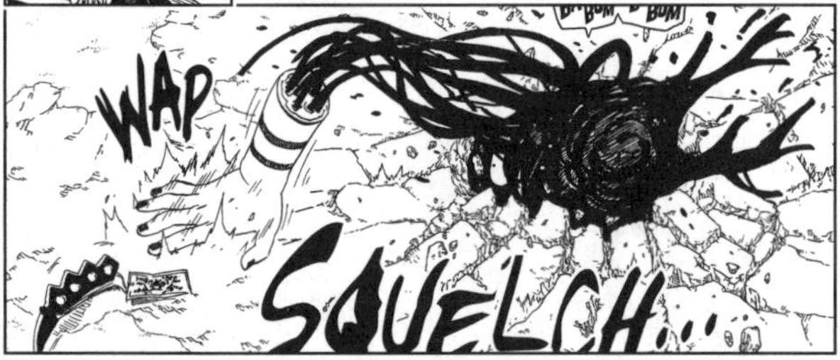
WAP
SQUELCH...

⬆Even if an arm is severed from his body, it moves about at will like a separate living organism.

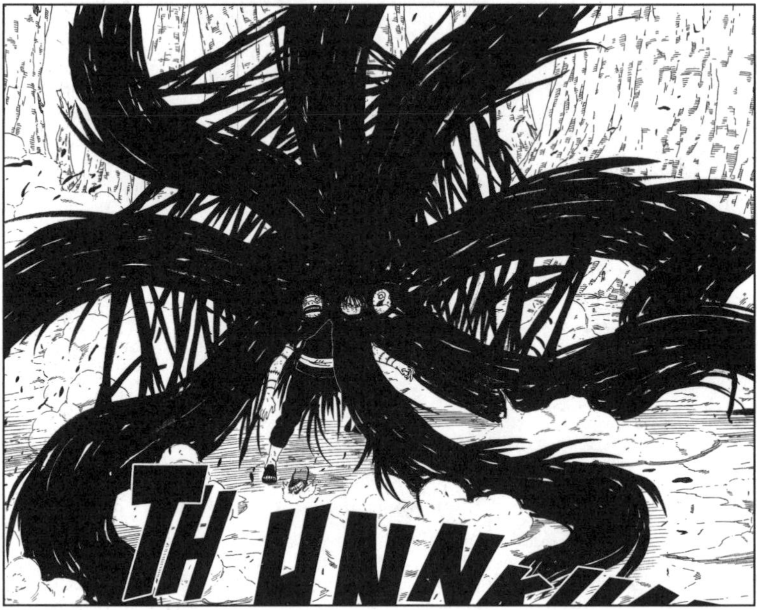
THUNN...

⬆By changing the length and form of the tentacles at will, Kakuzu is able to control many different situations. Once Earth, Grudge, and Fear are invoked, Kakuzu has no blind spots.

Nin Jutsu

Shikigami Dance

Caster: Konan

攻 防 補 近 中 遠 **B**

A lovely, ever-changing paper technique performed by an alluring, dancing butterfly.

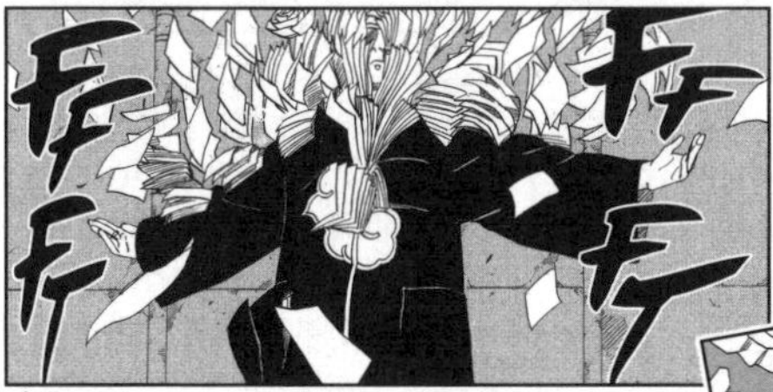
FF
FT
FF
FT

⬆Countless pieces of paper fly in all directions as Konan's form disappears like a phantom.

⬇Every part of Konan's body begins to peel away when the jutsu is invoked.

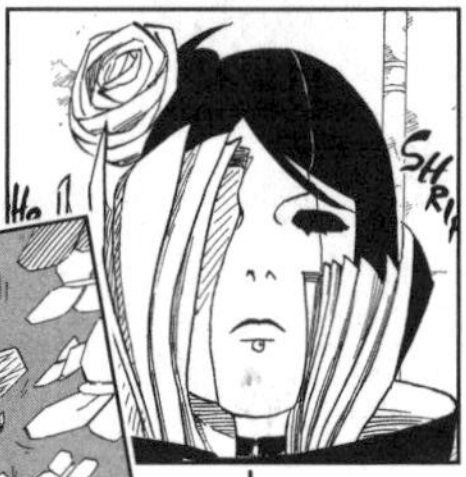

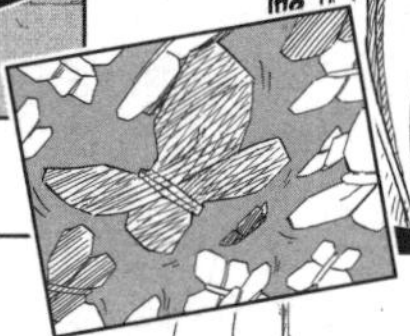

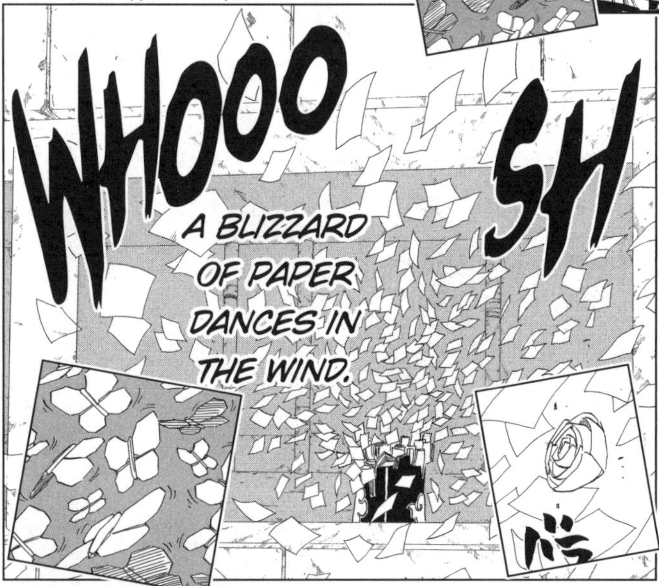
WHOOOSH
A BLIZZARD OF PAPER DANCES IN THE WIND.

⬅Like origami, each and every piece of scattered paper takes the form of a butterfly, leaving behind only a lingering scent.

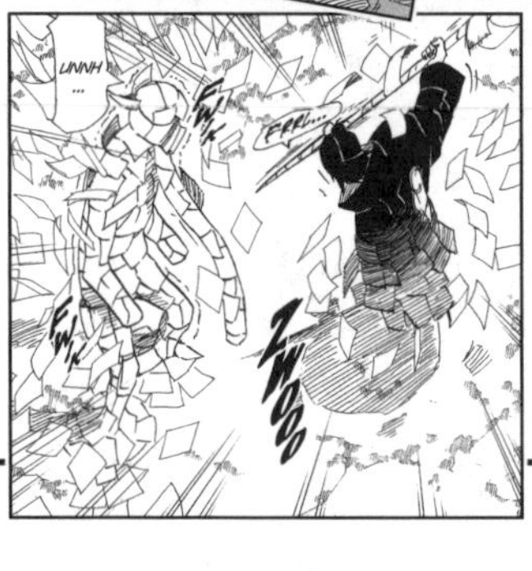
UNNH ...
FWIK
FRRL...
FWIK
ZWOOO

A ninjutsu that allows Konan to move about and change her shape at will by turning her body into countless tiny shreds of paper. The jutsu has many applications, from surveillance to sneak attacks. In addition, the magical appearance of countless pieces of paper flying through the air has the ability to mesmerize an adversary.

⬅The enemy is enveloped in paper, then attacked with weapons shaped from the paper.

Nin Jutsu | Fûin Jutsu

Sealing Spell: Finger-Carved Seal

Caster: Jiraiya

BZZZ

The flame of life lit on the fingertips engraves words before turning dark again.

⬅ The fire lit on the index finger is the flame of life, entrusting the future to the Child of Prophecy.

⬇ Jiraiya engraves a code onto Fukasaku's back.

UGH...
ZIZZLE...

This is the jutsu used by Jiraiya—with wounds all over his body—during his battle to the death with Pain. Chakra is concentrated in the caster's fingertips to create heat that is used to engrave characters on the target. It can be used to engrave many objects, from skin to sheet iron, and demands delicate chakra control.

Nin Jutsu | Hiden

Self-Destruct Doppelganger

Caster: Deidara

The Ultimate Forgery

A jutsu for making one's escape using a diversion created by having a shadow doppelganger ingest detonating clay and then making it explode. Deidara uses that moment to swap himself with the shadow doppelganger. This is a jutsu that requires skill at verbal deception, and only works because it is built on a foundation of being able to toy with an opponent using many arts.

⬆ "Behold my ultimate art!" With these words and eerie body movements, Deidara makes his enemy wary.

YEEAAGH

Nin Jutsu

Twin Snakes Curse

攻 防 補 近 中 遠 C

Caster: Orochimaru / Uchiha Sasuke

Two giant snakes appear from the sleeves, wrapping themselves ominously around their prey to capture it.

Two large snakes are summoned that slither out from the caster's sleeves to wrap themselves around the enemy before them. The snakes can capture the enemy alive, squeeze them to inflict damage, or if the need warrants, make the prey the victims of their poisonous fangs.

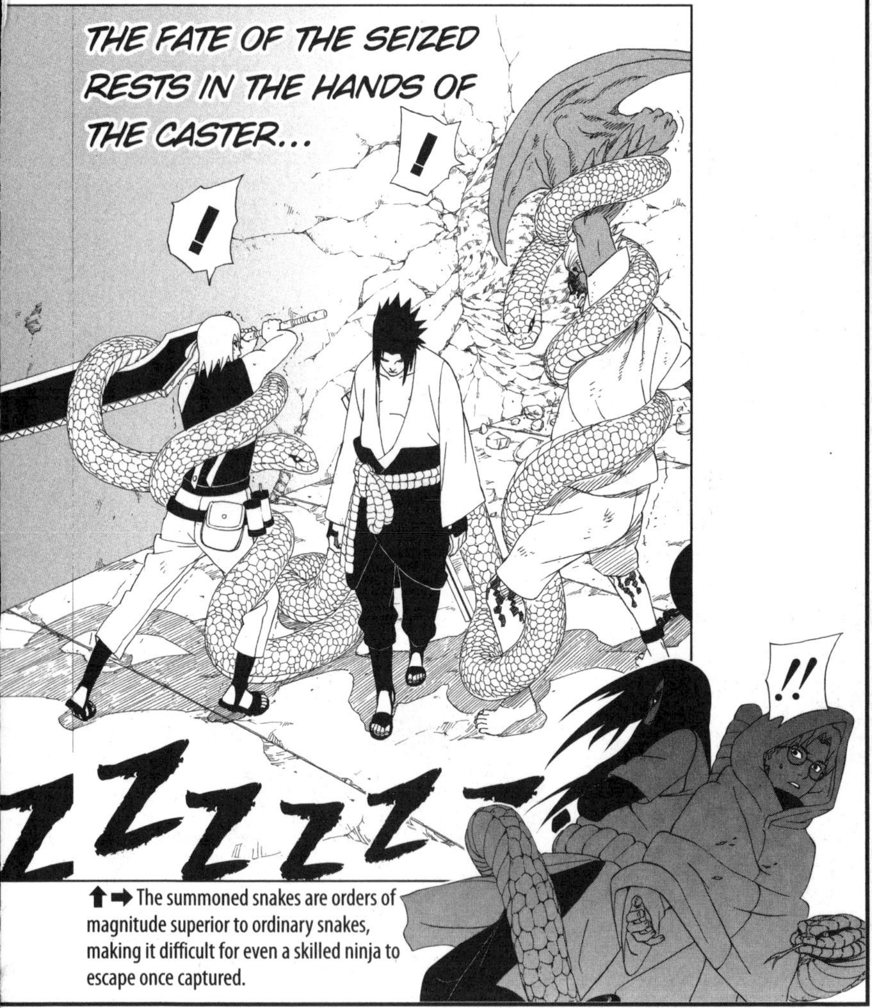
THE FATE OF THE SEIZED RESTS IN THE HANDS OF THE CASTER...
!
!
!!
ZZZZZ

⬆ ➡ The summoned snakes are orders of magnitude superior to ordinary snakes, making it difficult for even a skilled ninja to escape once captured.

Nin Jutsu | Hiden

Cursed Art: Blood Rite Death

Caster: Hidan

The only curse of its kind!

A curse acquired by Hidan through the Way of Jashin. The target's blood is used as the medium through which to invoke the jutsu. The target is inflicted with the exact wounds that the caster inflicts upon himself. It's a devious curse. And there's no escape from it. Because this jutsu cannot be invoked unless the caster himself is injured, the only one who can use this jutsu repeatedly is Hidan with his immortal body.

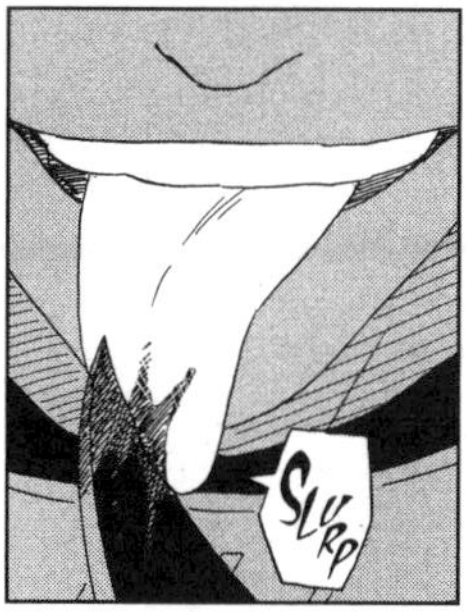
SLURP

⬆ The first stage of this jutsu is to drink the target's blood.

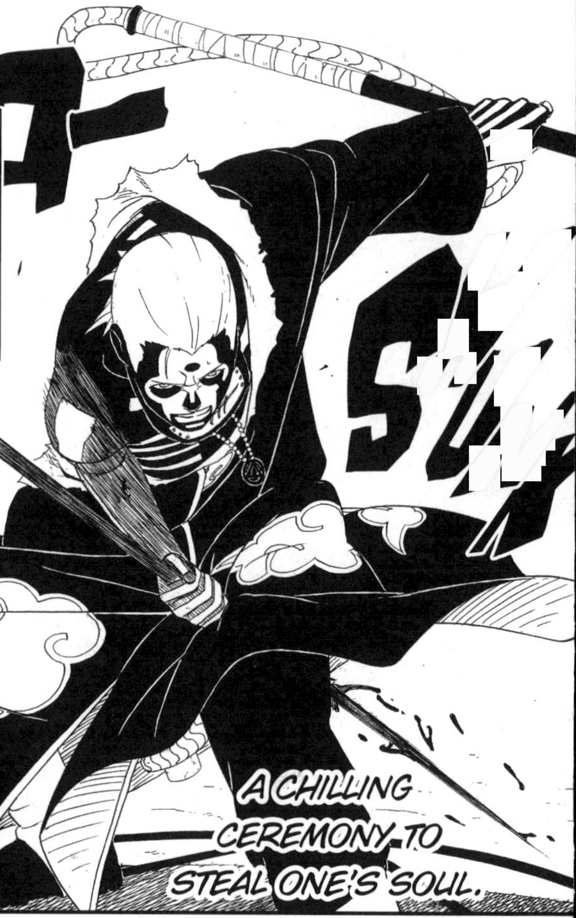
A CHILLING CEREMONY TO STEAL ONE'S SOUL.

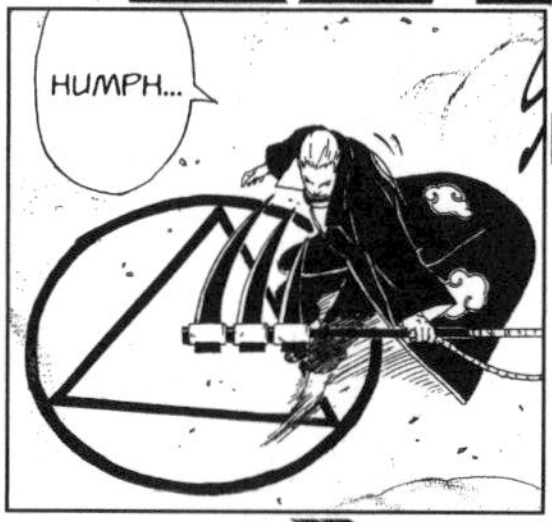
HUMPH...

⬆ The second stage is to step into a symbol drawn with the caster's own blood. If he steps outside the symbol, the effect disappears.

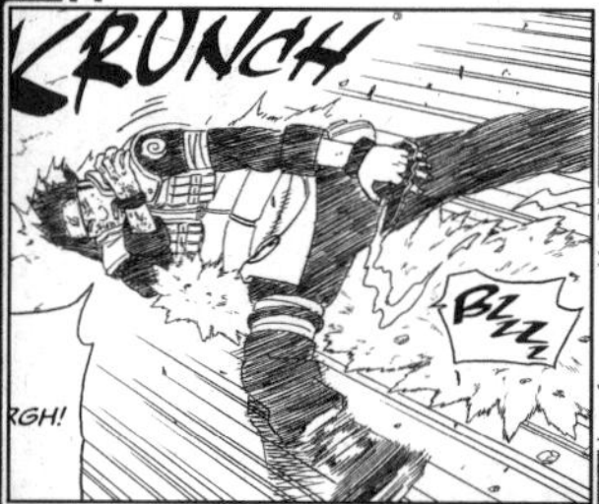
KRUNCH
BZZZ

⬆ If the caster is injured inside the symbol, the target is equally injured.

Nin Jutsu

Art of Impersonation

Caster: Pain

Chakra makes a sacrifice play out one's life as a powerful ninja.

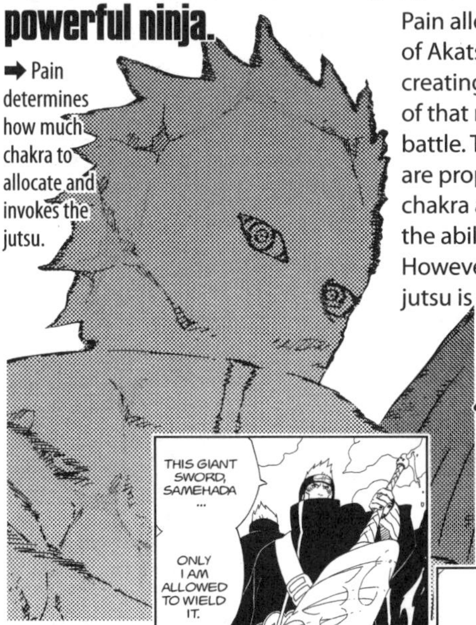

➡ Pain determines how much chakra to allocate and invokes the jutsu.

Pain allocates a portion of the chakra of Akatsuki members to his target, creating an ingenious duplicate of that member with which to do battle. The abilities of the duplicate are proportional to the amount of chakra allocated to it, and it can use the abilities of the original person. However, when the chakra runs out, the jutsu is canceled, and the target dies.

AN AKATSUKI FOR A MOMENT.

⬇ When the Art of Impersonation is applied, the target is 100 percent identical in appearance to the original.

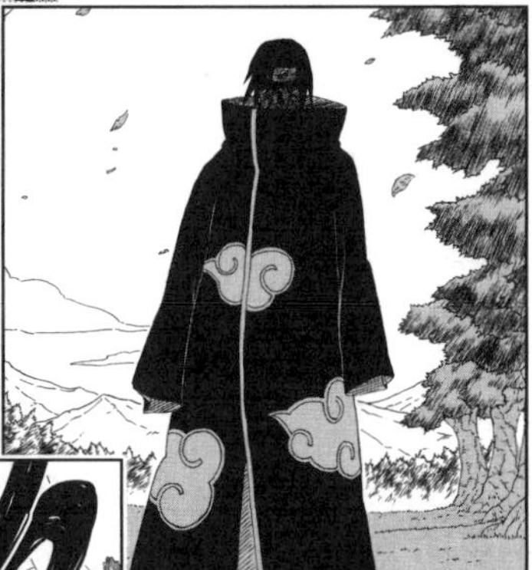

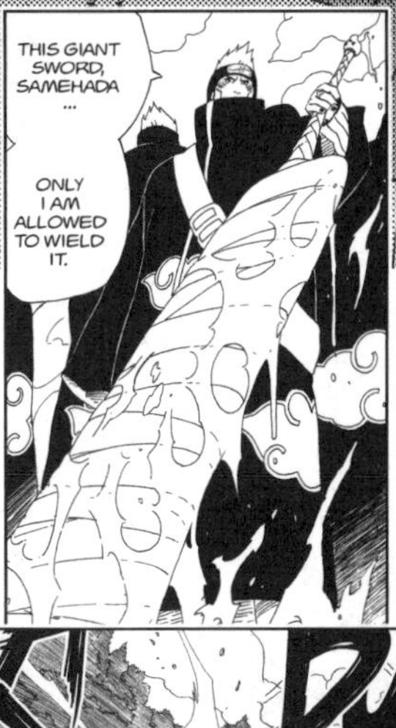
THIS GIANT SWORD, SAMEHADA ...
ONLY I AM ALLOWED TO WIELD IT.

➡ The Art of Impersonation imitates even the weapons and ninja tools of the original to battle alongside the original himself.

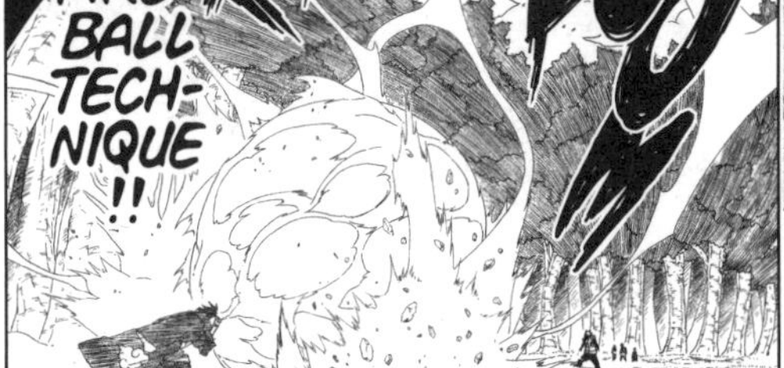
FIRE-BALL TECH-NIQUE !!

⬅ Of course, the target's ninjutsu is identical to that of the original person's. Even the Fire Style: Fireball Technique!! of the Uchiha clan is perfectly replicated.

Nin Jutsu

Secret White Move: Chikamatsu's Ten Puppets

攻 防 補 近 中 遠 S

Caster: Chiyo

The original puppet master's Ten Masterpieces—each a proud, mighty warrior.

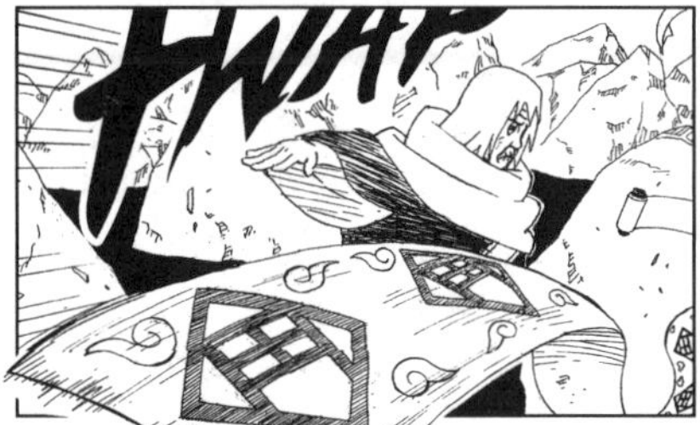
FWAP

The Ten Puppets, the masterpiece of the first-generation puppeteer Monzaemon are summoned and manipulated at will in this ultimate expression of the Art of the Puppet Master. As their name suggests, these puppets can be controlled one puppet per finger. Each of the puppets is a mighty warrior in its own right. However, to release the entirety of the powers in the mechanism requires expert, ultra-high level technique.

⬆⬇ Chiyo unrolls her scroll. Chikamatsu's Ten Puppets appear from the mon crest.

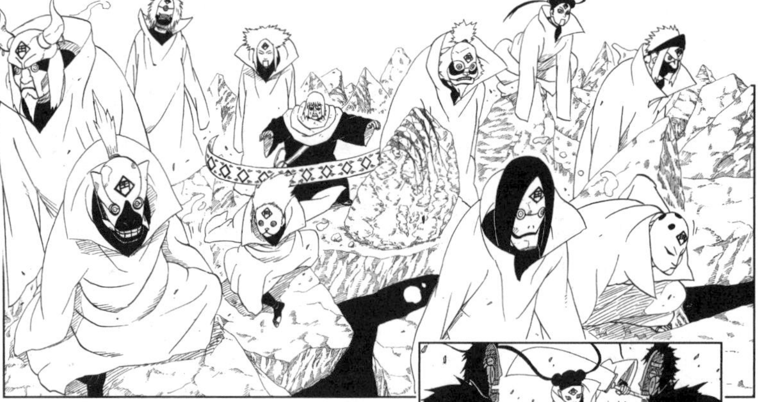

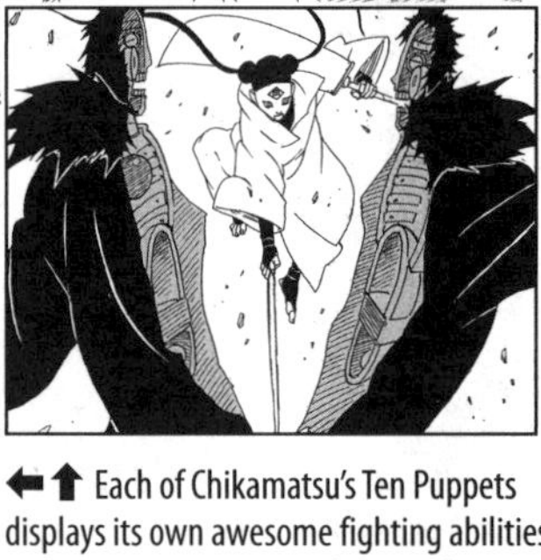

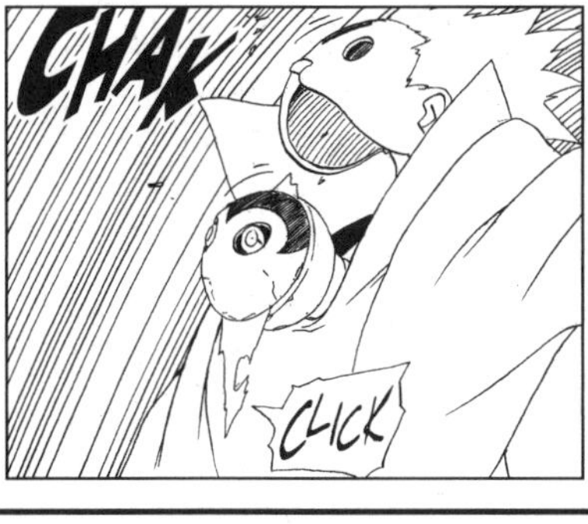
CHAK
CLICK

⬅⬆ Each of Chikamatsu's Ten Puppets displays its own awesome fighting abilities with taijutsu, ninjutsu and projectile weapons. Furthermore, by combining them together, they display even greater abilities.

Nin Jutsu | Hiden

Liquefy Jutsu

攻 防 補 近 中 遠 —

Caster: Hozuki Suigetsu

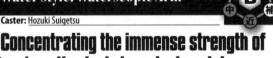

Melting one's body at will

A jutsu that renders physical attacks ineffective by liquefying one's body at will. This jutsu boasts high strategic effectiveness because in addition to allowing one to avoid an enemy's attack during a close-range battle, it allows one to infiltrate buildings and launch surprise attacks from a liquefied state.

⬇ The caster is able to liquefy and harden everything, from a single hair to skin and muscles, at will.

I'M FREE... AT LAST...
SLURR
MY EGARDS, ASUKE.

⬆ If the caster is trapped in a sealed container, he is unable to move.

Nin Jutsu | Hiden

Water Style: Waterscopic Arm

攻 防 補 近 中 遠 B

Caster: Hozuki Suigetsu

Concentrating the immense strength of one's entire body in a single point.

A variation of Water Style whereby the muscles of the arm are temporarily expanded and strengthened by compressing water collected from the entire body into the length of the arm. However, this is a very difficult jutsu necessitating balanced control of water levels in the body.

SHR
AK

⬅ Water collected from the entire body is forced into the left arm, giving it the incredible strength to tear apart iron doors and rock walls.

Nin Jutsu

Water Style: Five Hungry Sharks

Caster: Hoshigaki Kisame

B

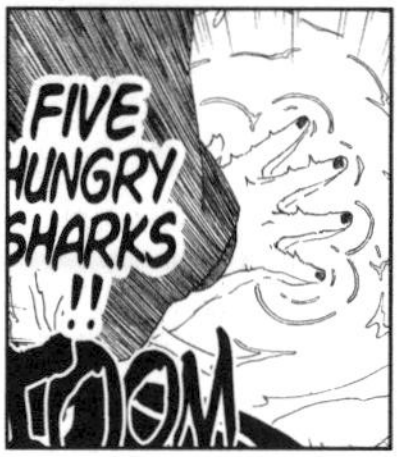
FIVE HUNGRY SHARKS!!
DOOM

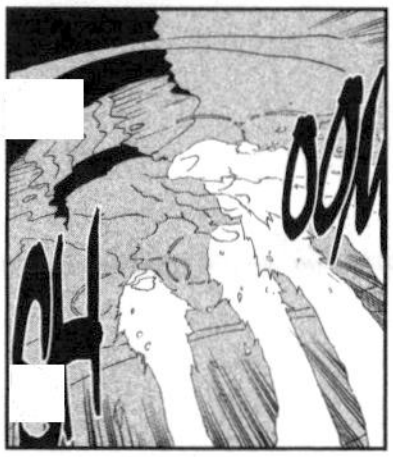
OOM

⬇⬆ The sharks' huge bodies undulate, creating a large vortex in the water.

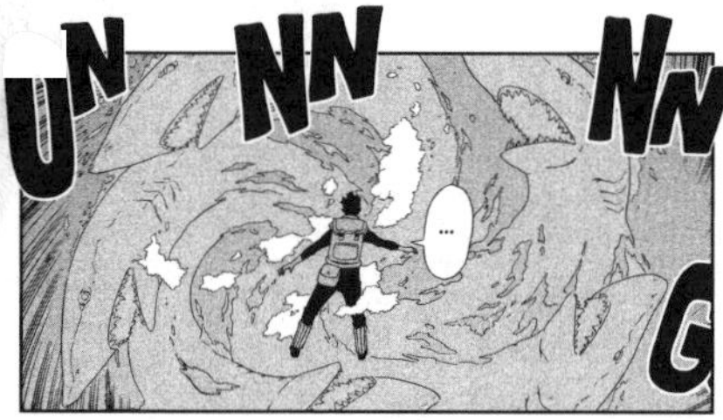
UN
NN
NN
G
...

Five fingers guide ferocious toothed swords.

Chakra released underwater from the five fingertips becomes ferocious sharks that attack their prey. The five sharks swim in circles around the target, creating a wicked current that takes away their prey's freedom of movement before tearing apart their defenseless prey with their sharp teeth. It is a jutsu that epitomizes the quintessential savagery of Kisame.

Nin Jutsu

Water Style: Art of the Waterfall Basin

Caster: Yamato

C

A lovely waterfall with multiple uses.

⬇ The water source, waterfall, and waterfall basin can be expanded as long as the caster's chakra lasts.

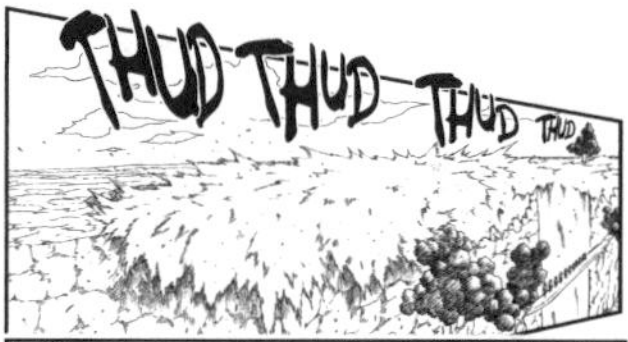
THUD THUD THUD THUD

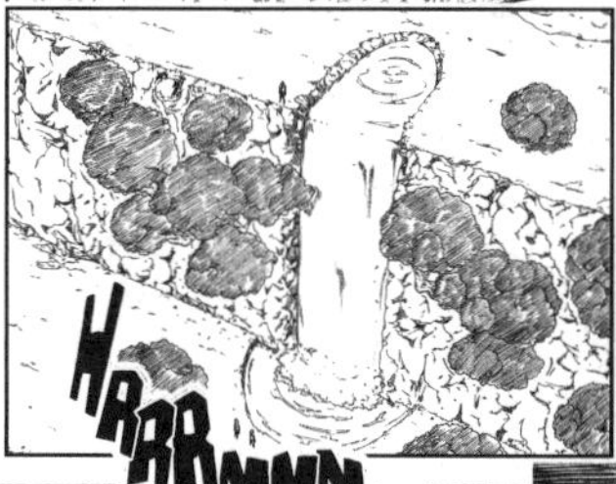
HRRRMMM...

Water is made to well up from ground that has no water and turned into a waterfall by manipulating its flow. It is a very convenient jutsu that can have the effect of causing an enemy to have a false sense of his location by greatly changing the scenery, or it can be used for training or relaxation.

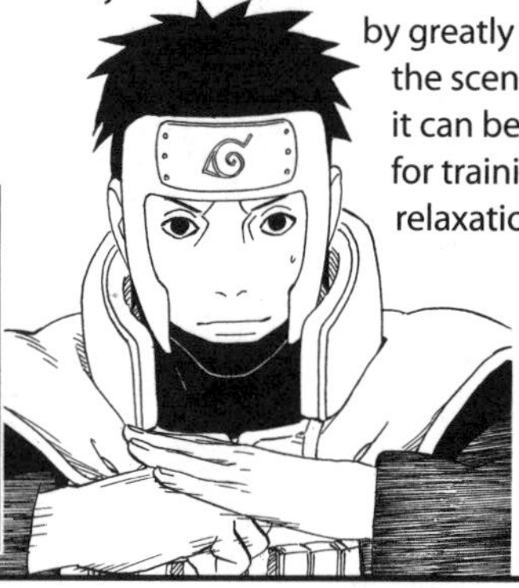

Nin Jutsu

Water Style: Exploding Water Shock Wave

攻 防 補 近 中 遠 B

Caster: Hoshigaki Kisame

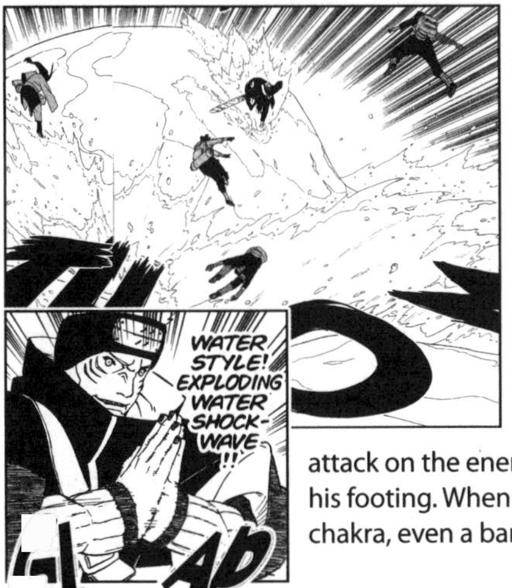
WATER STYLE! EXPLODING WATER SHOCK-WAVE!!

Trapped by a violent tsunami in an unprecedented water calamity.

A flood of water is expelled from the mouth that swallows up and crushes an enemy with a huge oncoming wave. Moving at high speed by riding the wave, the caster is able to stage a one-sided attack on the enemy after the wave washes away his footing. When invoked by Kisame's immense chakra, even a barren plain turns into a raging sea.

⬆ Kisame practically owns the water element. He changes the battlefield the moment this jutsu is invoked, allowing him to fight in his most comfortable arena.

Nin Jutsu

Water Style: Raging Froth

攻 防 補 近 中 遠 C

Caster: Pain's summoning

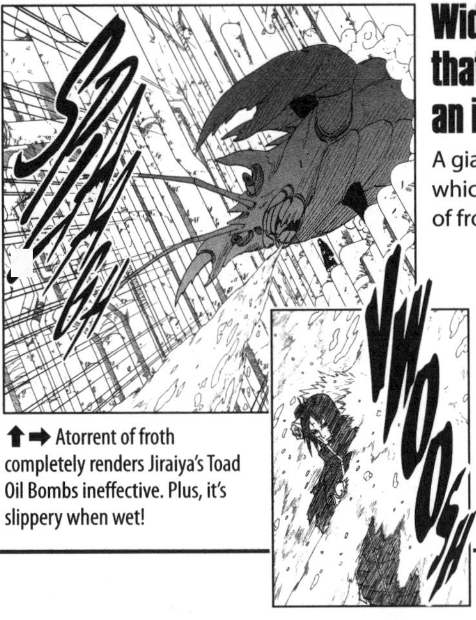
WHOOSH

Wide-dispersion froth that buries an enemy in an instant.

A giant crab is summoned, which spews out a huge amount of froth, covering an entire area in white within moments. Not only is the enemy blinded, but all other jutsu is washed away. Even the most well conceived plan disappears, like bursting bubbles, against this jutsu.

⬆➡ Atorrent of froth completely renders Jiraiya's Toad Oil Bombs ineffective. Plus, it's slippery when wet!

Nin Jutsu — Water Style: Syrup Trap

攻 防 補 近 中 遠 C

Caster: Kamizuki Izumo

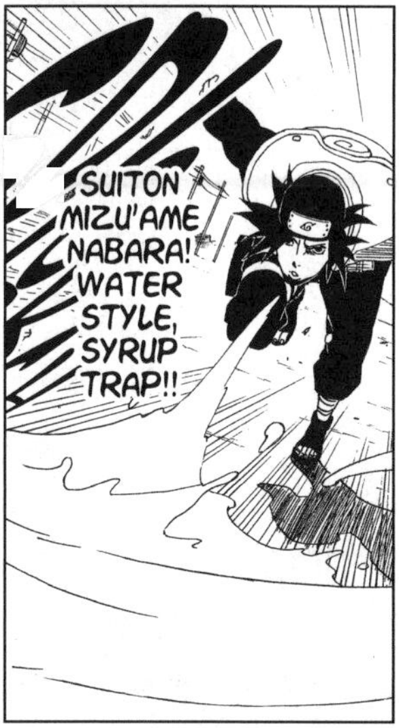
SUITON MIZU'AME NABARA! WATER STYLE, SYRUP TRAP!!

A pond that ensnares and binds all who touch it.

Water made more viscous by infusing it with chakra is sprayed out over a wide area of the ground. If an enemy carelessly steps into the water, he becomes unable to move. However, by sending chakra to the soles of the feet, one can move freely, making it an effective way to limit the range of an enemy.

⬇ This jutsu is effective for securing control of a space on the battlefield. While it ordinarily has a range of several feet, a pond of syrup can be created if there is time to prepare.

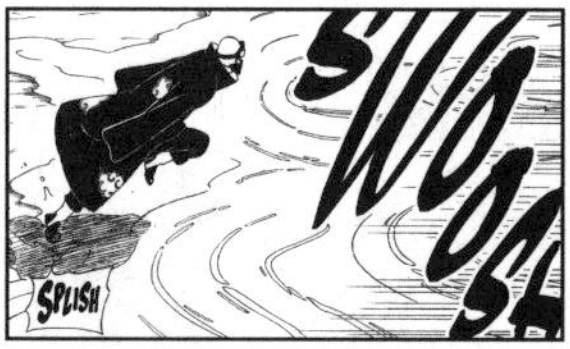
SWOOSH
SPLISH

Nin Jutsu — Water Style: Raging Waves

攻 防 補 近 中 遠 C

Caster: Yahiko

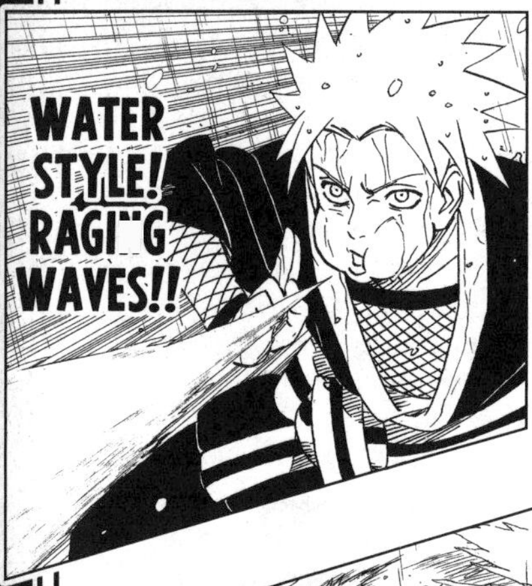
WATER STYLE! RAGING WAVES!!

A water gun fired from the lips.

Water is sprayed out from the mouth like a waterfall, washing away the enemy. The power can be controlled at will by the amount of chakra released. This is basic Water Style jutsu and there are many variations.

⬅ This jutsu can be performed if one is able to weave signs and control chakra. It is a simple jutsu, but it has many uses.

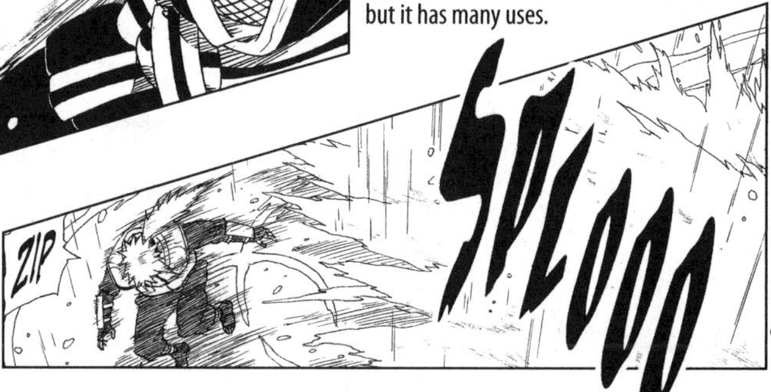
ZIP
SPLOOO

Nin Jutsu

Kekkei Genkai

Susano'o

攻 防 補 近 中 遠 一

Caster: Uchiha Itachi

➡⬇ A godlike technique used only by those who have achieved mastery beyond Mangekyo Sharingan, a jutsu feared by those around them as the most powerful of the ocular jutsu. It is the caster's guardian deity and at the same time can consume the caster as well.

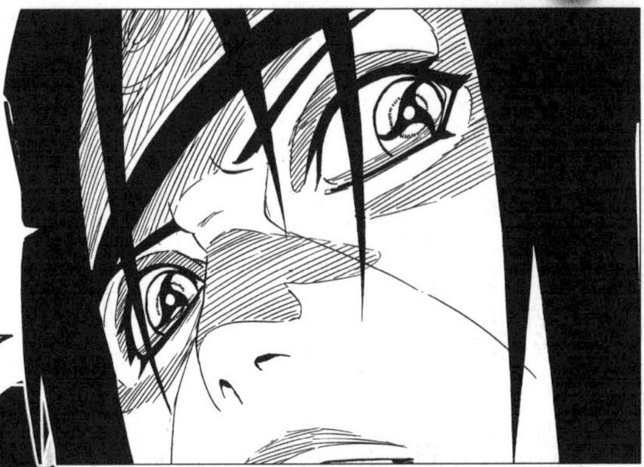

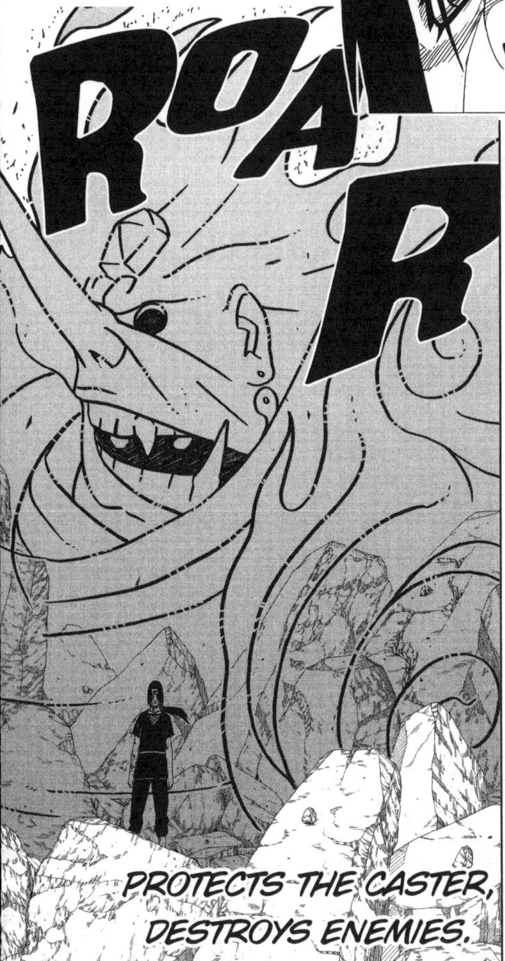
ROAR
PROTECTS THE CASTER, DESTROYS ENEMIES.

Residing in the eyes of those who grasp the workings of Heaven and Earth is a tempestuous warrior wielding a sword and shield.

Two jutsu allowed to be used only by those whose eyes have opened to Mangekyo Sharingan, the heavenly eyes that see all things in the universe: Amaterasu, representing the light of the material world; and Tsukuyomi, the nightmare realm, representing the world of the mind and darkness. Susano'o is the strength of the tempestuous force that resides only within those who have mastered both of these techniques. Chakra takes the physical form of a formidable-looking warrior whose rampaging soul will not settle down until it has destroyed all enemies before him.

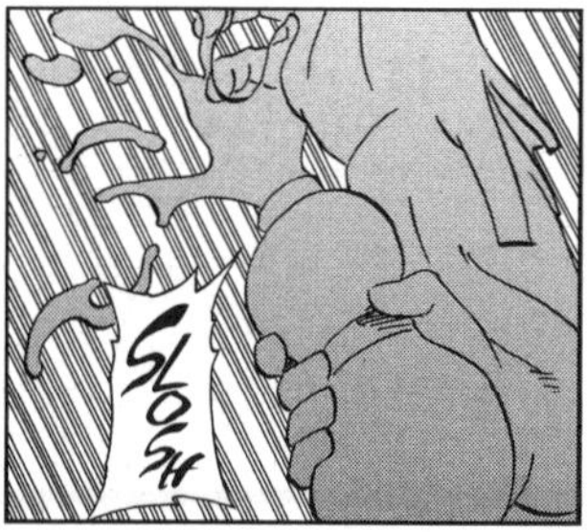
SLOSH

⬆ Liquid spilling from its gourd bottle turns into the Kusanagi Blade. Souls sucked out by the sword are sealed inside.

Its hands wield magical, matchless sacred weapons.

Susano'o boasts an absolutely perfect attack and defense because of the Spirit Weapon it wields in both hands: The Ten-Handed Sword that can cut down any enemy in its right, and the Yata Mirror, a shield that can repel any attack. In the face of a god's powers, all attacks, whether from a material or astral body, ninjutsu or physical, lose their meaning.

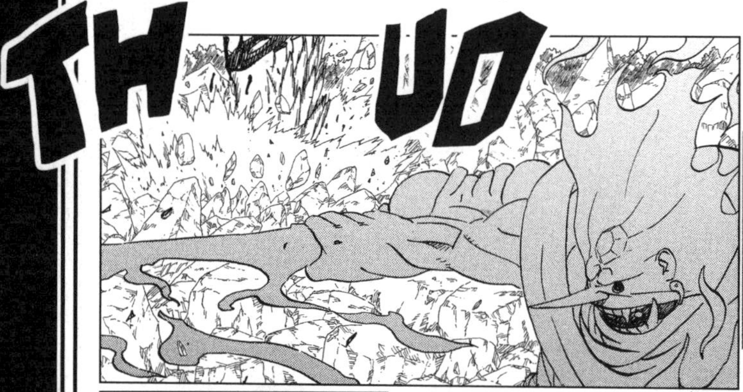
THUD

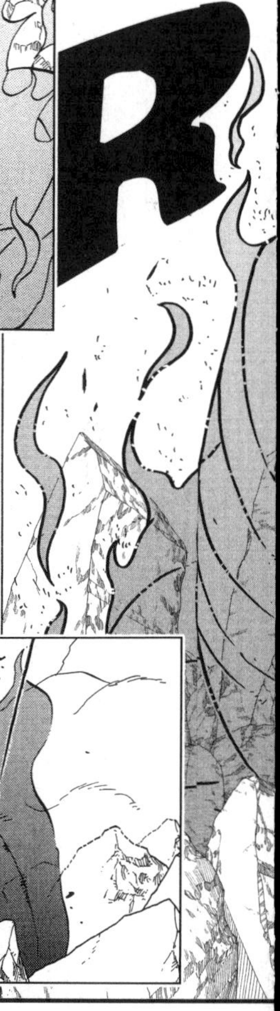
R

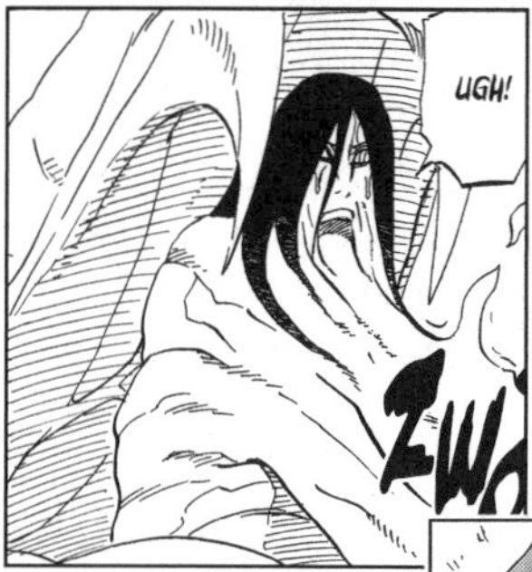
UGH!
ZWA

TOTSUKA BLADE

⬅ A variant of the Kusanagi Blade that is endowed with the power to plunge those it pierces into a genjutsu world of drunken dreams and seal them away for all time. The blade itself is imbued with sealing jutsu.

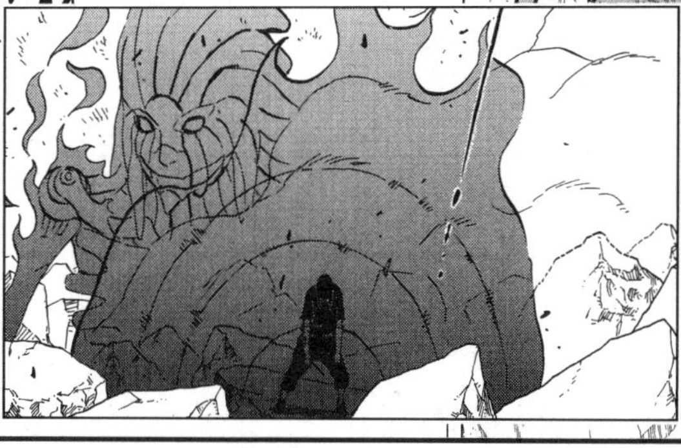

YATA MIRROR

➡ A spirit weapon without a physical form with the power to change every one of its properties, allowing it to alter its attributes in accordance with the attributes of the attack, rendering the attack ineffective.

Nin Jutsu

Art of Ink Mist

C

Caster: Sai

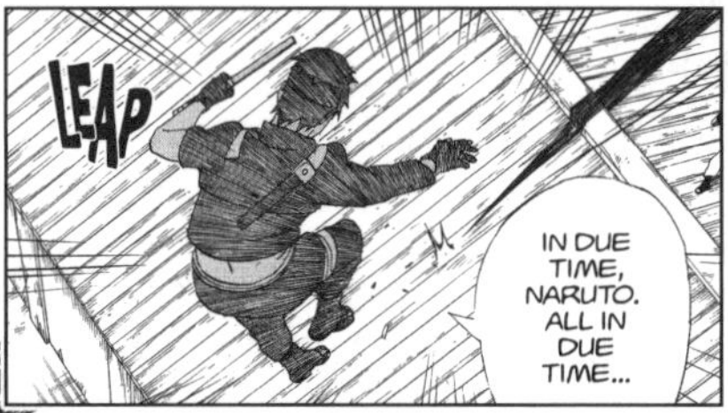
LEAP
IN DUE TIME, NARUTO. ALL IN DUE TIME...

⬅ With Sai's agility, this jutsu becomes an even more effective diversion.

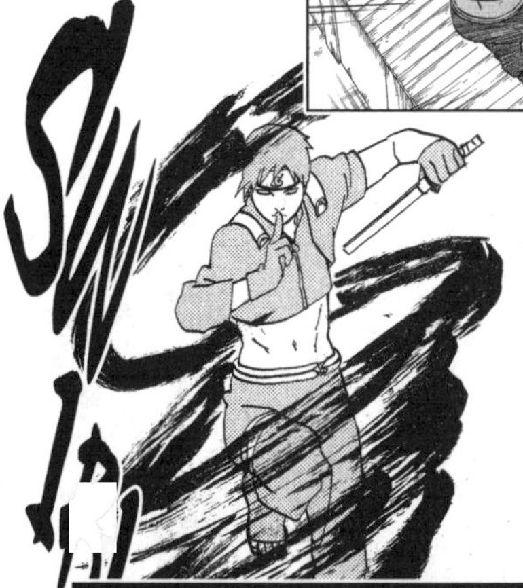

Hiding, as though blotted out in an inky mist.

Chakra is used to envelop the caster's body and confuse his pursuers. It is the best jutsu for Foundation tasks where stealth is required. Used together with the Art of Teleportation to move from one location to another, it allows the caster to quickly and safely leave the battlefield.

Nin Jutsu

Art of Ink Doppelganger

C

Caster: Sai

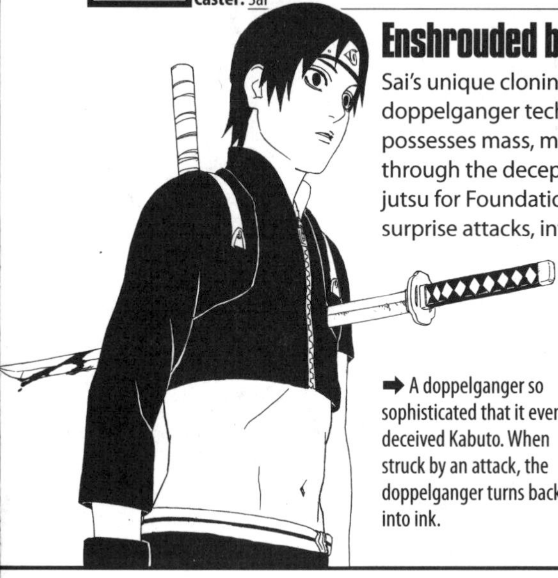

Enshrouded by darkness.

Sai's unique cloning technique. Unlike a regular doppelganger technique, the ink doppelganger possesses mass, making it difficult to see through the deception. It is an extremely useful jutsu for Foundation missions that often involve surprise attacks, infiltration and assassinations.

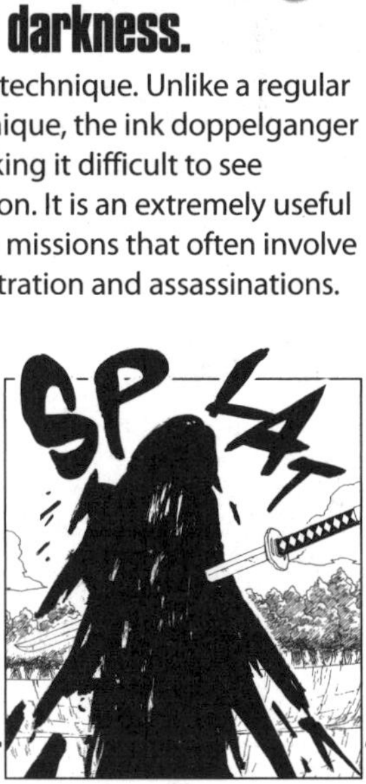
SPLAT

➡ A doppelganger so sophisticated that it even deceived Kabuto. When struck by an attack, the doppelganger turns back into ink.

Nin Jutsu | Sage Jutsu

Tongue Knife

攻 防 補 近 中 遠 —

Caster: Fukasaku

A shake of the tongue and the enemy is cut in two with the precision of a battle-axe.

➡ Fukasaku's tongue flies at its prey with tremendous force.

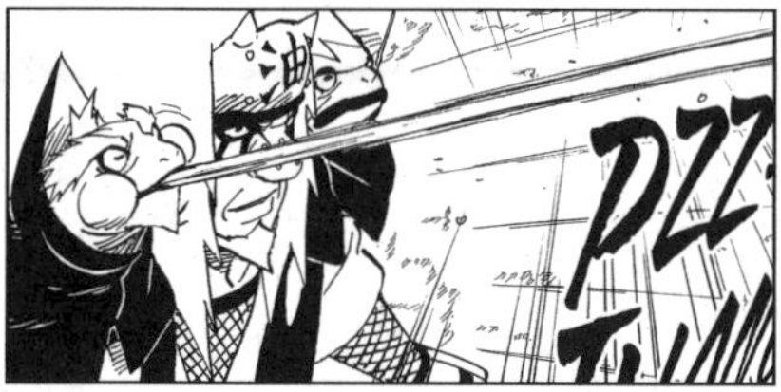

By manipulating sage jutsu chakra, Fukasaku's long tongue gains extreme hardness and the cutting edge of a fine sword.

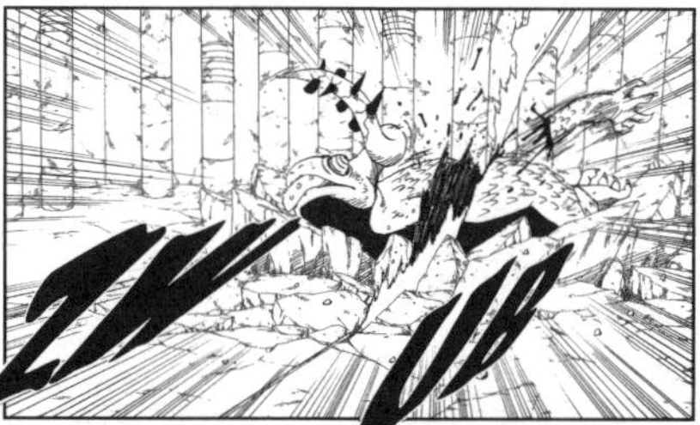

His tongue leaps from his mouth cavity, slicing his target in half with power that can pierce bedrock with its tip and crack the ground.

⬅ The way it slices through both the ground and the enemy conjures images of a large sword.

Nin Jutsu | Sage Jutsu

Tongue Trap

攻 防 補 近 中 遠 —

Caster: Shima

Bound and rendered unable to move by a tongue that detects living creatures and melts them with acid slime.

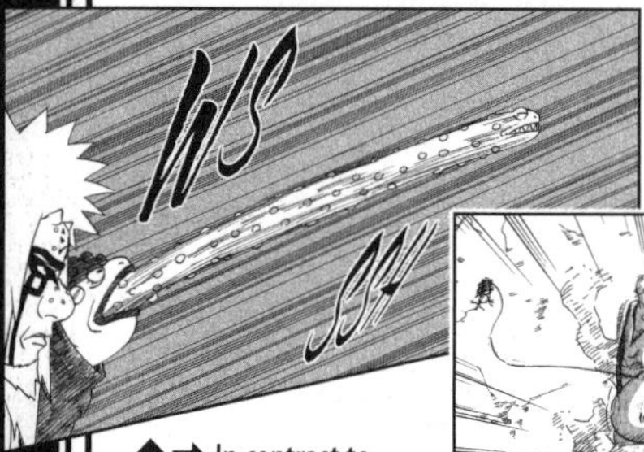

Shima's incredibly developed tongue takes the form of a face through the skillful use of sage jutsu chakra. It has the capability of discerning between the unique scents given off by living creatures. Once she has ascertained the prey's location, her tongue extends at incredible speed, flexibly wrapping it around the prey like a whip before dissolving it with a powerful acidic slime exuded by the bumps on her tongue.

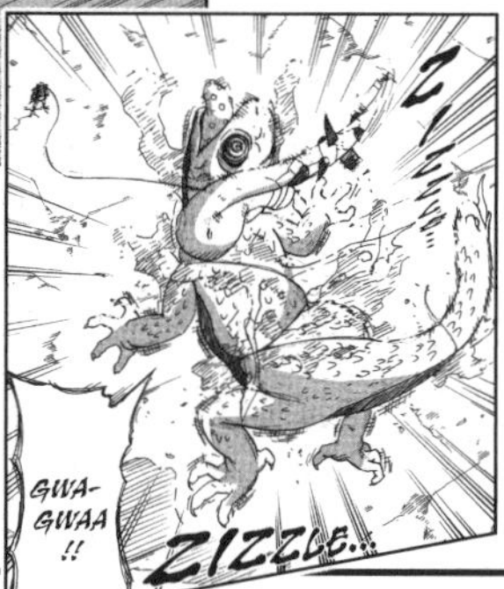
GWA-GWAA !!
ZIZZLE...

⬆ ➡ In contrast to Fukasaku's Tongue Knife, Shima's tongue is very flexible. The captured prey is dissolved alive by the powerful acid slime.

Nin Jutsu — Multiple Striking Shadow Snakes Technique

B

Caster: Orochimaru

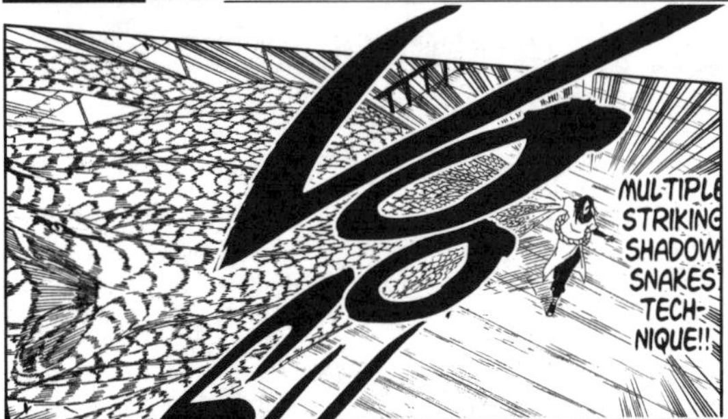
MULTIPLE STRIKING SHADOW SNAKES TECH-NIQUE!!

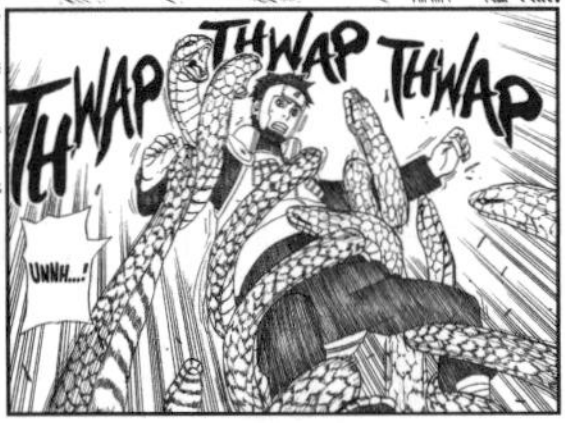
THWAP THWAP THWAP
UNNH...!

⬆➡ The snakes wrap around all four limbs and sink their fangs into vital spots. As their numbers increase, the snakes move with greater control. If there are multiple enemies, the snakes possess the intelligence to divide up their attack.

The undulations of a snake that devours and binds.

A ninjutsu made more diverse by increasing the number of snakes summoned by the Striking Snake Technique. Each of the spontaneous giant snakes take turns intimidating, delaying and capturing an enemy as they work as a team to attack.

Nin Jutsu — 1,000 Puppet Arms

C

Caster: Sasori

A thousand arms rip enemies asunder.

The key to stopping this jutsu are the seals placed in the puppet shooting out the arms. By the time an enemy realizes that, he is already at Sasori's mercy, to be captured or tortured to death.

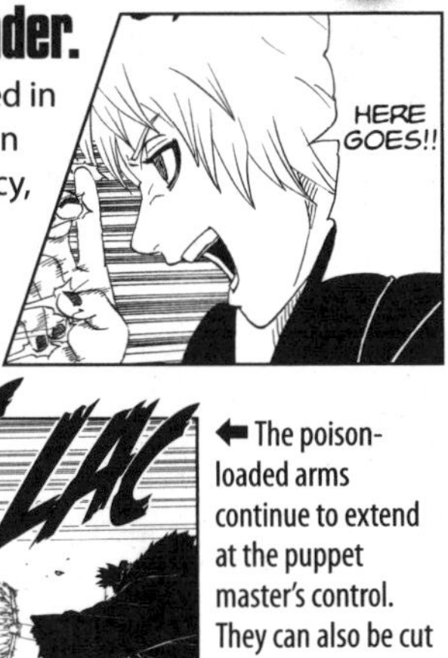
HERE GOES!!

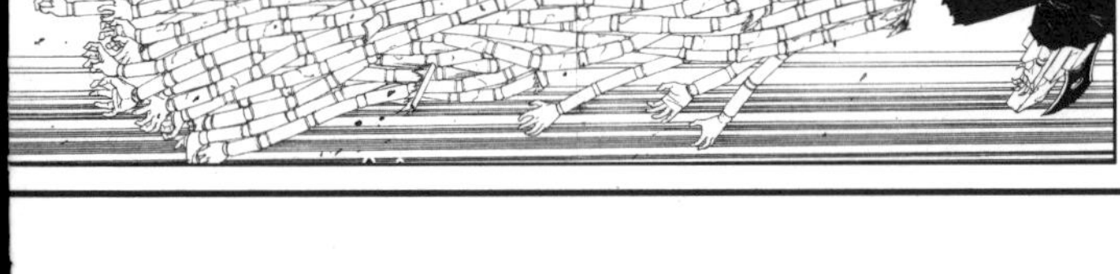
KLAC LAC LAC LAC LAC

⬅ The poison-loaded arms continue to extend at the puppet master's control. They can also be cut loose if needed.

Sage Jutsu

Sage Mode

Caster: Jiraiya

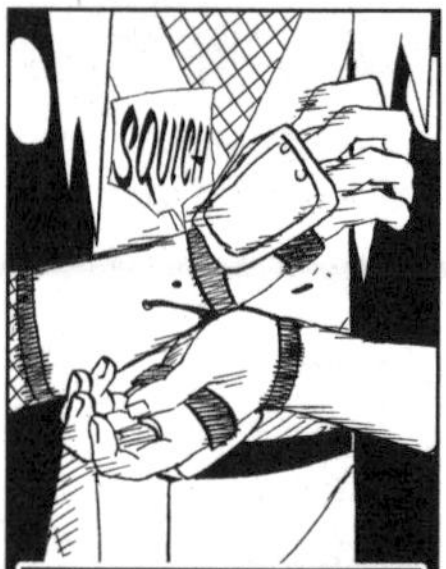
SQUICH

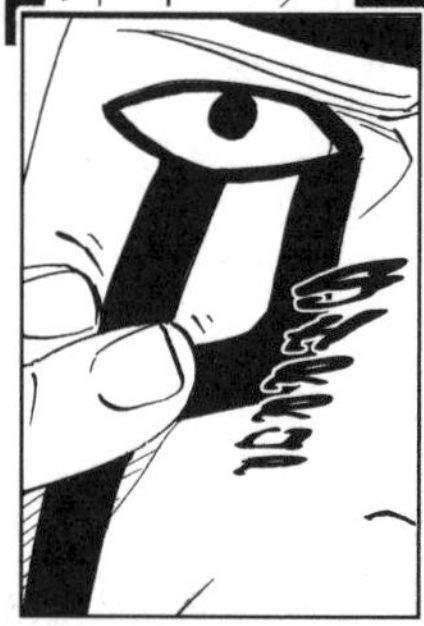

A toad-lion warrior brimming with divinity who wields senjutsu that surpasses ninjutsu.

The style for senjutsu displayed by Jiraiya during his decisive battle with Pain. Jiraiya summons the two great Sage Toads of Mt. Myoboku, and by borrowing their powers, absorbs a huge amount of nature's energy in his body. By blending it with his chakra, he is able to dramatically increase the level of ninjutsu, taijutsu and genjutsu. Sage Mode makes the use of senjutsu possible. Combining with the two great Sage Toads in body makes it possible for all three to work as a team, bringing him truly to the realm of a sage.

←↓ Using his own blood, Jiraiya shades the undersides of both eyes. This takes the place of a blood contract, allowing him to summon the legendary two great Sage Toads to his own body.

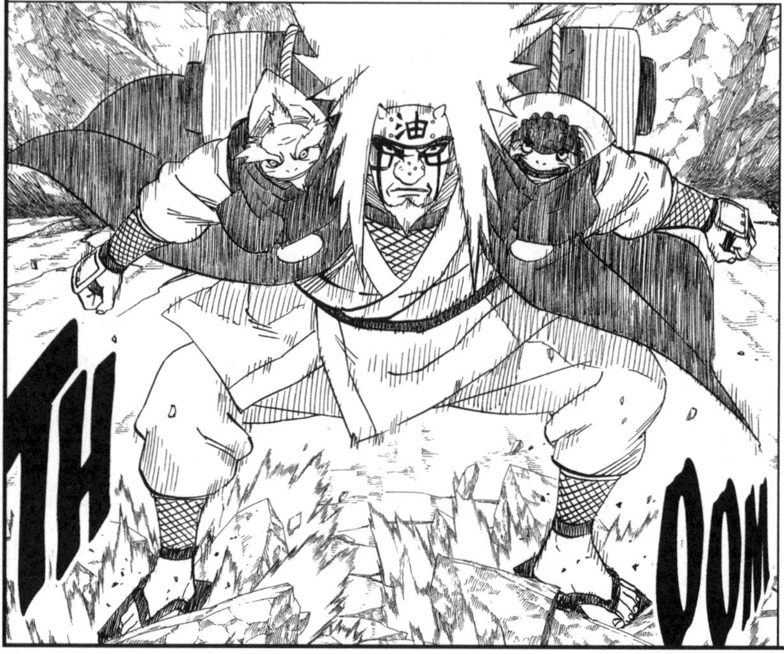
TH
OOM

Jutsu

Sand Brainwash

Caster: Sasori

Needles attack memories!

ZAP
I SEE...
...SO THAT'S THAT'S...

A jutsu that seals the target's memories by piercing the memory center of the brain with ultra-tiny needles. Releasing the jutsu causes the needles to disintegrate and restores the target's memories. Applying this jutsu to the brains of one's subordinates and sending them to infiltrate an enemy camp allows them to perform their spy activities over a long period of time with greater safety.

⬅⬆ When the caster releases the jutsu, the target awakens to his mission.

Nin Jutsu | Sage Jutsu

Sage Art: Kebari Senbon

Caster: Jiraiya

SAGE ART! KEBARI SENBON!!

Like a raging storm, a mountain of needle-like hairs rain down at super speed.

Hairs from one's head are hardened and fired at the target one after another. The speed of this attack is the fastest among attacks in Sage Mode. With Fukasaku and Shima invigorating the roots of Jiraiya's hair even as he fires his chakra-infused kebari, he can fire a nearly infinite number of shots.

⬅⬆ Kebari Senbon rains salvos on its target. The super-sharp points turn the target's entire body into a pincushion.

Nin Jutsu · Sage Jutsu — Sage Art: Bath of Boiling Oil

攻 防 補 近 中 遠 —

Caster: Jiraiya / Fukasaku / Shima

Fire and wind poured in to fill a boiling cauldron of the netherworld.

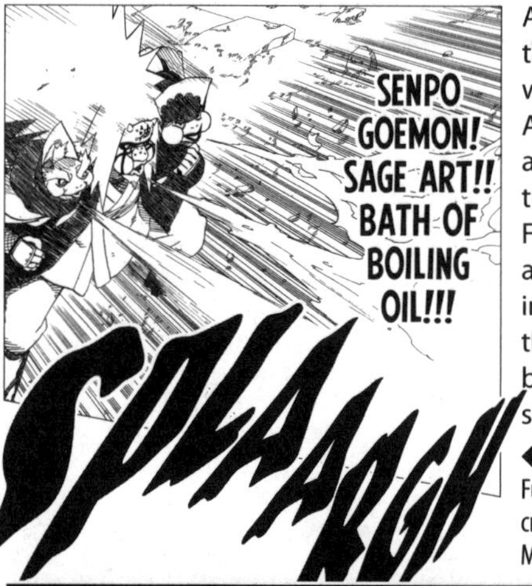
SENPO GOEMON! SAGE ART!! BATH OF BOILING OIL!!!
SPLAARGH

A collaborative fighting technique that Jiraiya uses in Sage Mode with the two great Sage Toads. After cornering an enemy inside a building or in a depression in the ground, Jiraiya releases oil, Fukasaku unleashes Wind Style, and Shima unleashes Water Style in huge quantities. Sometimes, the three are able to fill the area with bubbling oil at a temperature of several thousand degrees.

⬅ With Shima's voice giving the commands, Fukasaku and Jiraiya follow her orders to create superb teamwork only possible in Sage Mode.

Nin Jutsu — Puppet Performance: Human Puppet

攻 防 補 近 中 遠 A

Caster: Chiyo

An incredibly intricate puppet performance that makes even a living person dance.

A jutsu to control a human being like a puppet by connecting chakra threads to the head, body, both arms and both legs. The person being controlled is able to use both the techniques of the puppet master and his own jutsu.

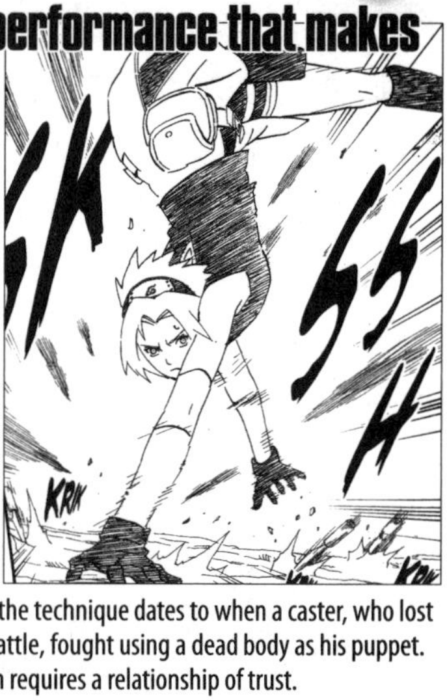
KRIK

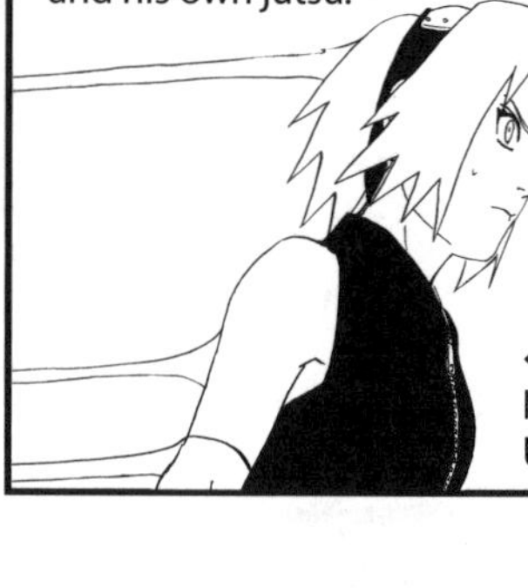

⬅⬆ The origin of the technique dates to when a caster, who lost his own puppet in battle, fought using a dead body as his puppet. Using a living person requires a relationship of trust.

Jutsu

Art of Tripwire Shuriken

D

Caster: Uchiha Sasuke

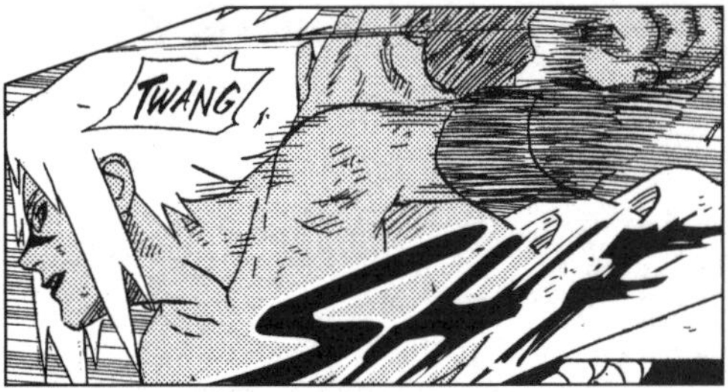
TWANG

A delicate concealed blade controlled by a single thread.

A jutsu that allows the trajectory of a shuriken to be altered after it is thrown by tying on a translucent, highly durable and flexible string. A skilled caster can make the shuriken move up and down, left and right with just a single flick of his finger.

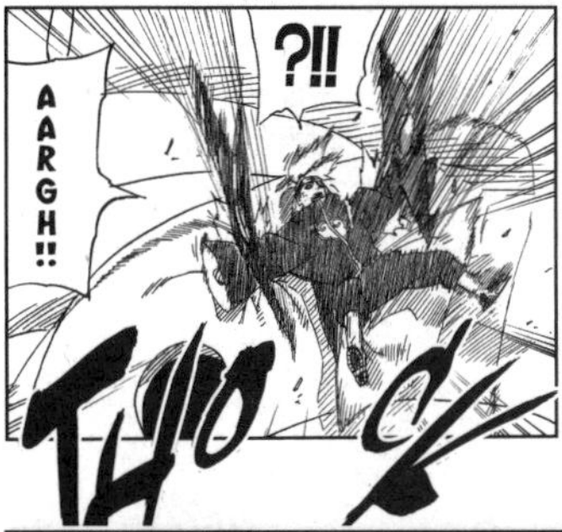
?!!
AARGH!!

⬅⬆ The strategic possibilities become limitless depending on how the shuriken are controlled. The caster might make the first shuriken miss on purpose, only to follow it several seconds later with another right behind it.

Nin Jutsu

Endless Summoning Jutsu

B

Caster: Pain

With each blow, another head. An endless cycle of attacks.

A summoning jutsu to which special conditions have been added. The summoned entity is given a certain condition, such as multiply when attacked. When that condition is met, a jutsu that causes the entity to multiply is invoked.

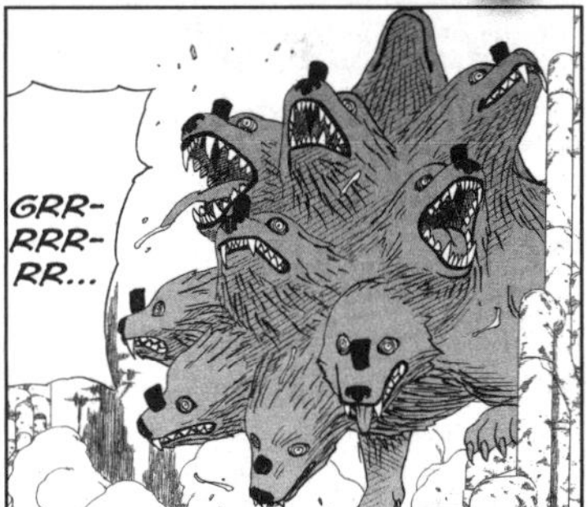
GRR-RRR-RR...

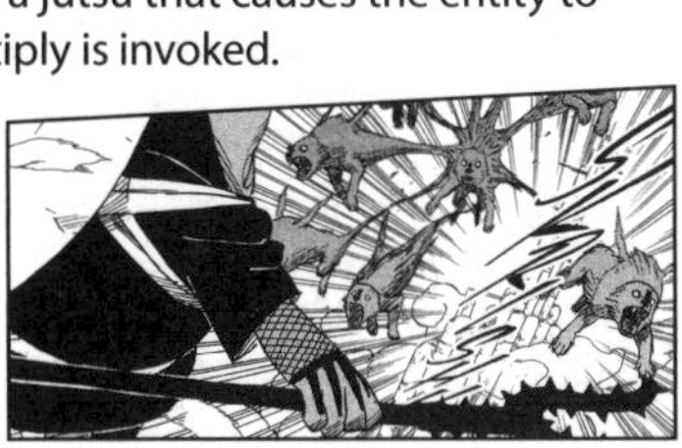

⬆ The large dogs Pain summoned multiplied each time they were struck. The endlessly multiplying heads made it look like the guard dog of the underworld.

⬅ Of course, they can separate and attack the enemy as well.

Nin Jutsu

Chidori Spear

攻 防 補 近 中 遠 A

Caster: Uchiha Sasuke

A lightning bolt spear that sings a song of death.

This jutsu, which is suited to electrical discharges, becomes effective when used in conjunction with Sasuke's thrust. Chidori is shape-shifted into a spear form, making it effective as a medium-range attack weapon. While a single attack is inferior in power to Chidori, there is less risk to the caster because of its longer range. It also has the benefit of being usable for sneak attacks and capture.

ZAP-ZAP-ZAP-ZAP-ZAP-ZAP

⬆ Chidori Spear pierces an enemy. Further damage is inflicted if the spear expands in a radial pattern.

Nin Jutsu

Chidori Senbon

攻 防 補 近 中 遠 A

Caster: Uchiha Sasuke

A flock of Chidori turned into a thousand needles attack an enemy.

This is another variation of Chidori. In order to specialize this ultimate Lightning Style jutsu with greater speed, the lightning is shape-shifted into countless sharp needles called Senbon that are launched at an enemy. Needles that fly with a chirping sound in the guise of a thousand birds. Using this jutsu in conjunction with Sharingan makes it possible to aim for the target's vital spots, increasing its effectiveness.

⬅ Increasing the quantity of chakra expended increases the number of Senbon that can be launched.

Nin Jutsu

Chidori Stream

攻 防 補 近 中 遠 A

Caster: Uchiha Sasuke

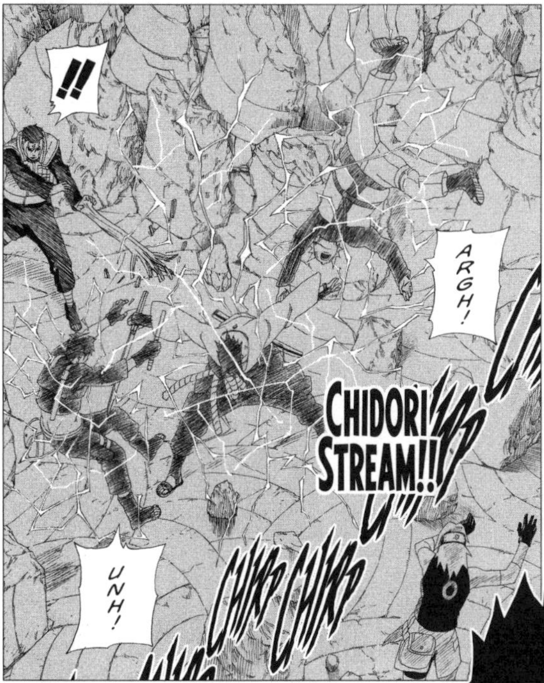
ARGH!
!!
CHIDORI STREAM!!
CHIRP CHIRP
UNH!

Chidori flying in all directions– attack and defense in one wild flash.

⬅ Anyone who comes in contact with Chidori suffers muscle contractions as their body mistakes Chidori lightning properties for its own nerve signals. Their body becomes rigid and sustains damage at the same time.

ANYONE WHO APPROACHES WILL BE MET WITH A BROAD ATTACK!

This jutsu takes advantage of the lightning element's unique ability to make anyone who comes in contact with it become temporarily rigid, and is an adaptation of Chidori with an expanded range of attack designed to engulf more enemies at once. Because Chidori is discharged from the entire body in all directions, it is possible to attack anyone within a certain range. It is also an effective defense tactic when attacked by a multitude of enemies at once.

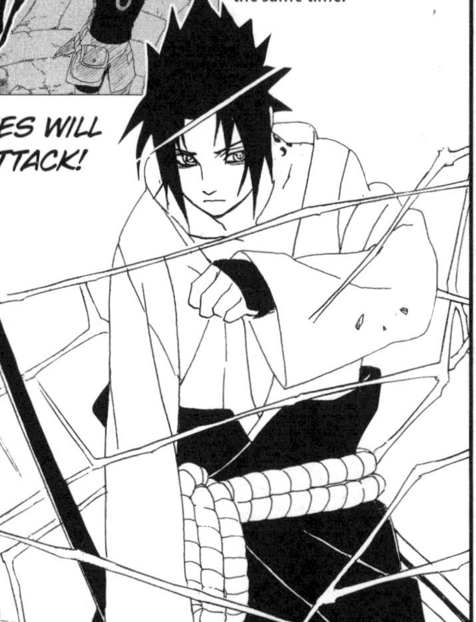

Nin Jutsu | Sage Jutsu

Massive Rasengan

Caster: Jiraiya

攻 防 補 近 中 遠 —

A storm rages in the palm of the hand, slicing through the air, swallowing everything in its path.

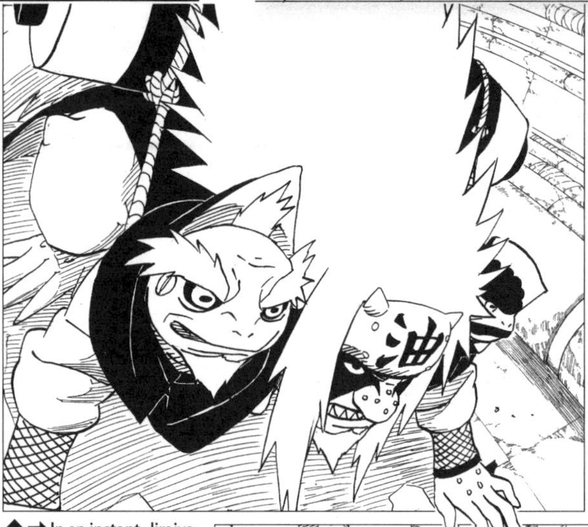

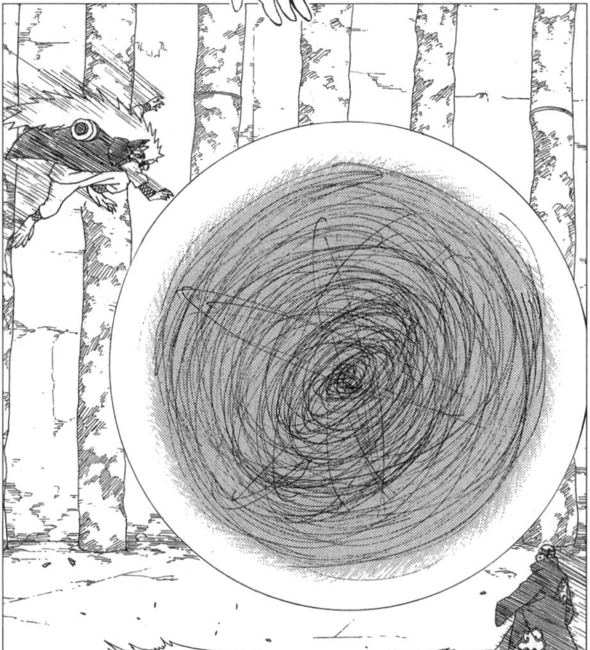
A WHIRLWIND OF MAXIMUM CHAKRA.

⬆ ➡ In an instant, Jiraiya creates an extra-large storm that can easily swallow a human being.

Rasengan chakra in the hand made to spin fiercely and formed into a sphere. Massive Rasengan is Rasengan with chakra increased via the caster and shadow doppelgangers. Jiraiya in Sage Mode is able to dramatically increase their size by adding energy from nature. The ball of light thus formed creates a huge whirlwind storm that, when unleashed, can easily carve away a mountain.

Nin Jutsu

Art of Cartoon Beast Mimicry

攻 防 補 近 中 遠 B

Caster: Sai

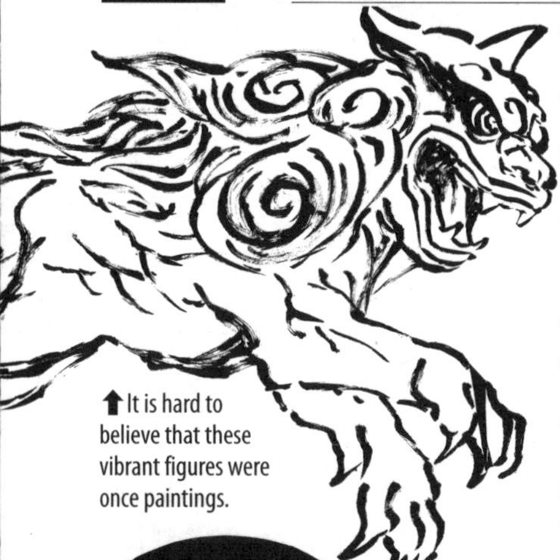

⬆ It is hard to believe that these vibrant figures were once paintings.

The artist's wishes pass through his brush as beasts dance with false life.

As images are drawn with brush strokes infused with chakra, the pictures jump off the paper and move at the caster's will. Among existing jutsu, few are as versatile as this one. Many of the Foundation assignments are of a special nature, meaning Sai must often work alone. Peculiar to Sai, this jutsu, which can adapt to any situation, could be called his lifeline.

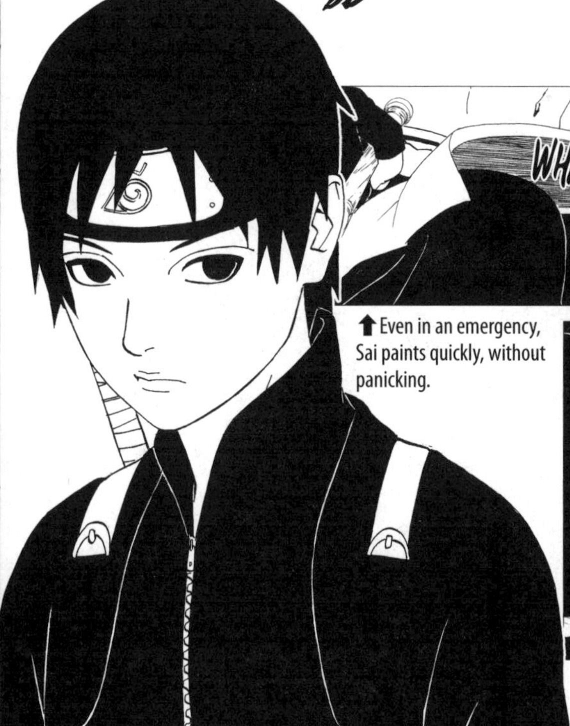

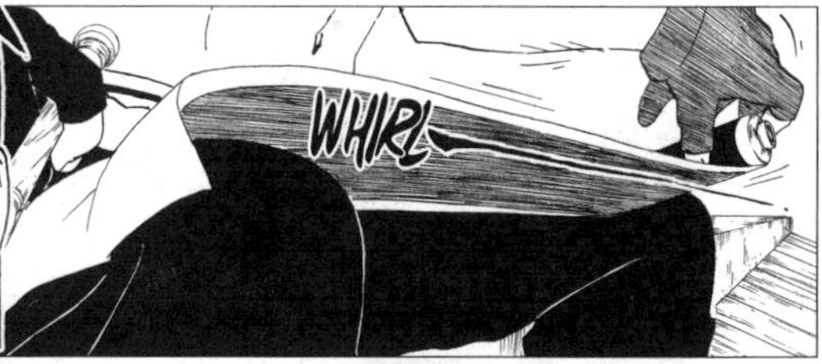
WHIRL

⬆ Even in an emergency, Sai paints quickly, without panicking.

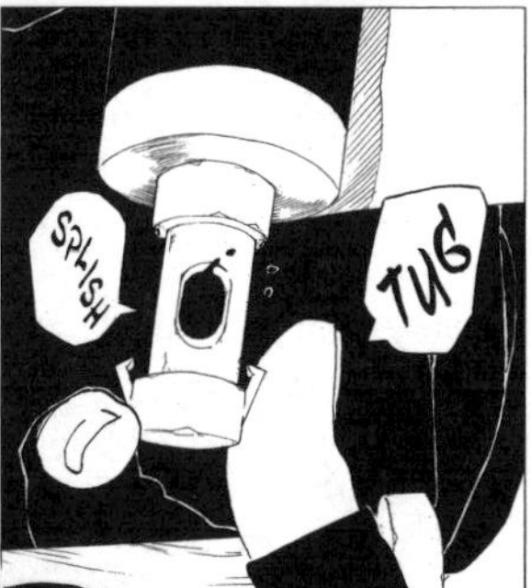
TUG
SPLISH

⬆ An ink well and small brush are built into the scroll rod. Sai is all set to use the jutsu at any time.

⬇➡ By painting multiple images, the number of animals that come to life increases.

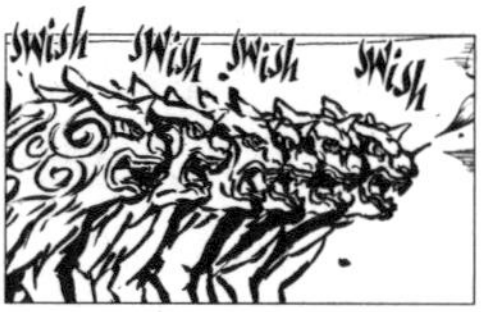
SWISH
SWISH
SWISH
SWISH

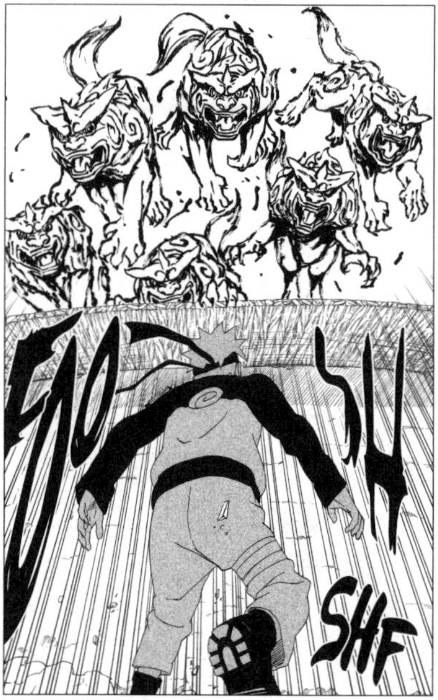
SHF

➡ Sai flying through the sky on a bird he painted. The bird has a wide range of uses including surveillance and moving from one place to another at high speed.

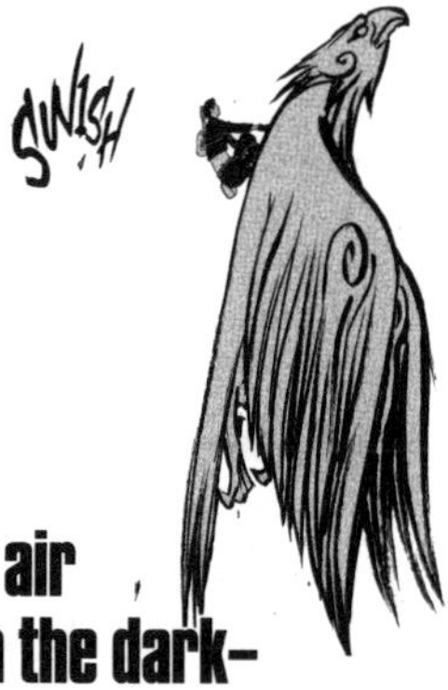
SWISH

Flying through the air or lurking in the dark– changing at will for the mission at hand.

The biggest feature of Art of Cartoon Mimicry is that many different effects can be had depending on the animals that are painted. If surveillance from the sky is needed, paint a bird. Painting ferocious beasts allows attacks to be made from a distance. In addition, by painting countless mice, the caster can conduct investigative activities without even moving himself by using their sheer numbers. It is a jutsu that exhibits a truly all-encompassing ability according to the ingenuity of the caster.

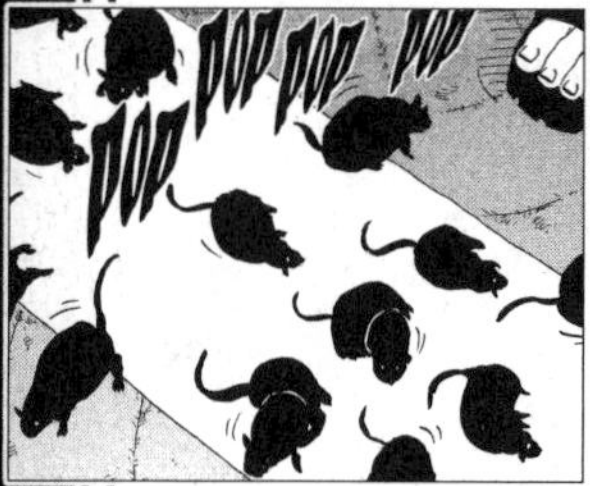
POP POP POP POP POP

⬅ Mice use any path available and go unnoticed—they are the best choice not only for searches, but also for relaying information collected inside an enemy camp to Konoha.

➡ Snakes are also used for assassinations because they can enter silently through tiny openings.

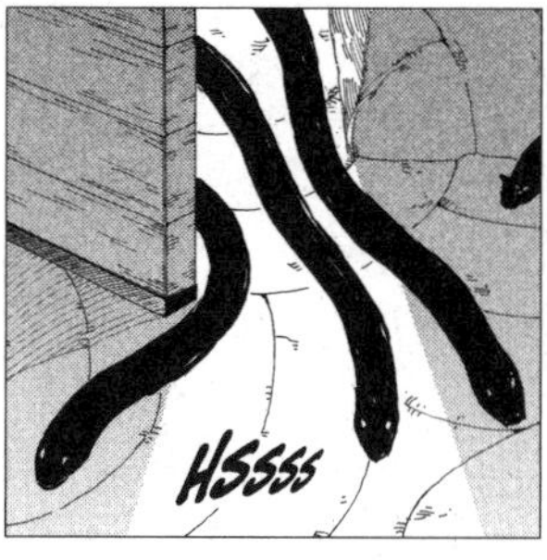
HSSSS

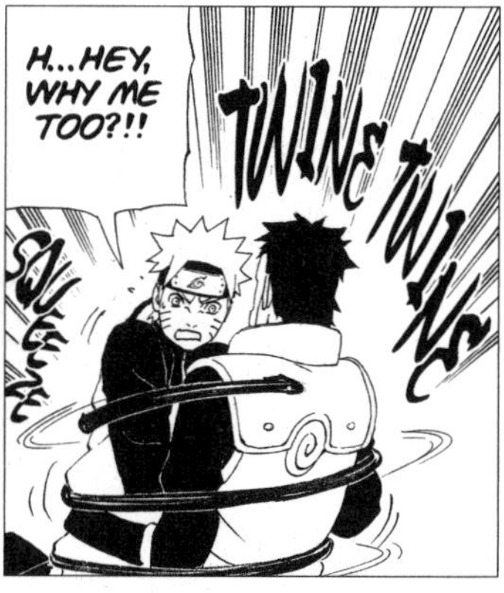
H...HEY, WHY ME TOO?!!
TWINE TWINE

Tai Jutsu

Super-Slap

攻 防 補 近 中 遠 B

Caster: Akimichi Choji

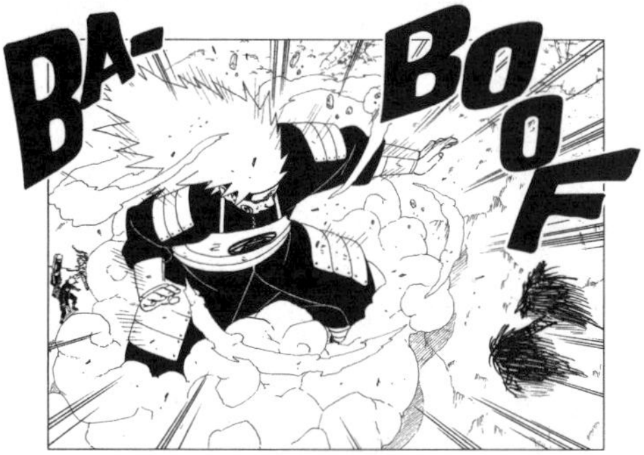
BA-BOOF

Two palms make the ground quake.

Performed by Choji after making himself a giant using The Art of Expansion. The increase in weight and power gained by expanding his body coupled with the increased thickness of his hands through the concentration of chakra to vitalize his muscles creates a blow that can cause the ground to cave in.

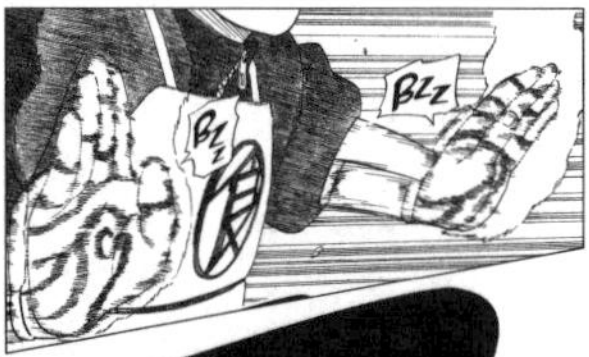
BZZ
BZZ

➡ Chakra in quantities large enough to be visible turn Choji's palms into iron sledgehammers.

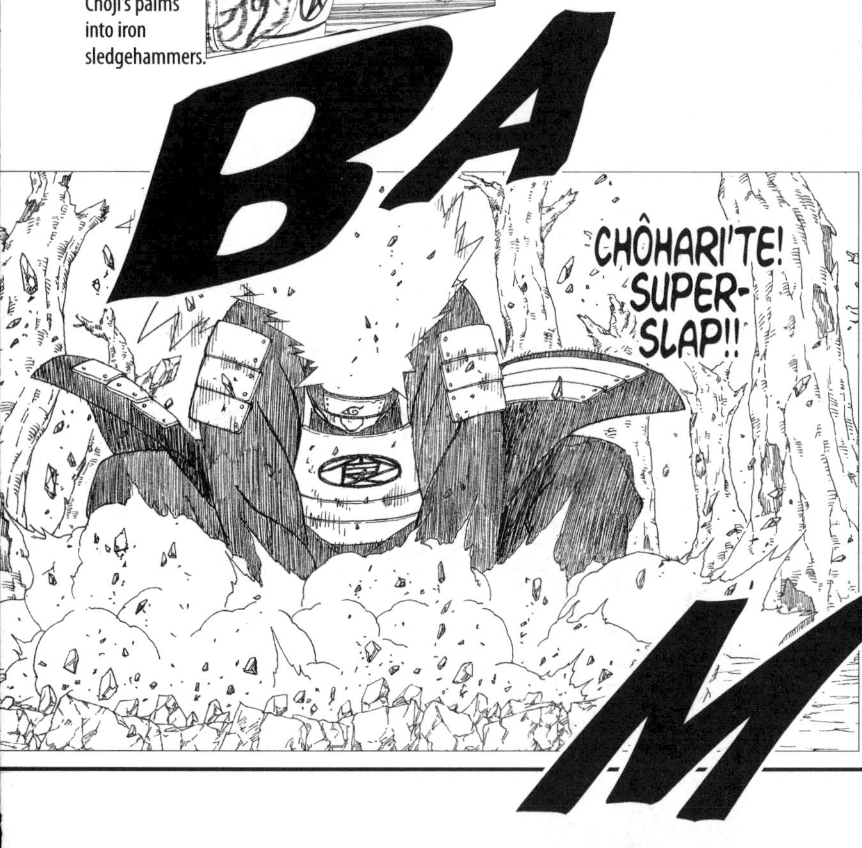
BA
CHÔHARI'TE! SUPER-SLAP!!
M

Nin Jutsu | Sealing Jutsu

Transfer Seal: Amaterasu

攻 防 補 近 中 遠 —

Caster: Uchiha Itachi

Sharing the black inferno using Sharingan as a medium

The highest Fire Style jutsu Amaterasu can only be used by those whose eyes have opened to Mangekyo Sharingan. Transfer Seal: Amaterasu is the sealing of the effects of Amaterasu in a third person's Sharingan. When the eye in which the jutsu is sealed sees a previously specified target, the seal is undone and black flames that can devour even fire are unleashed on the target.

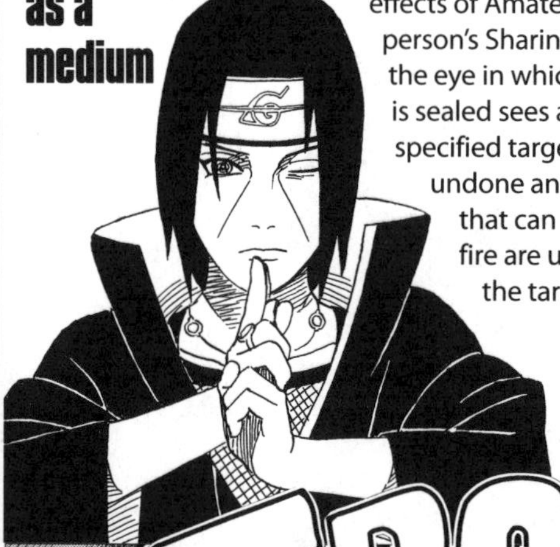

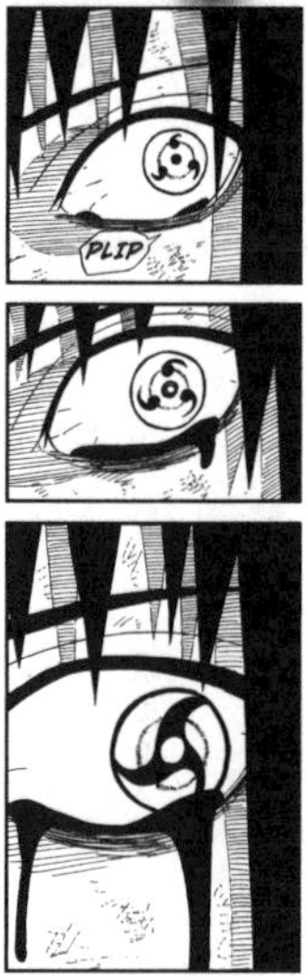
PLIP

➡ A Sharingan in which Amaterasu had been sealed acquires the image of its predetermined target…

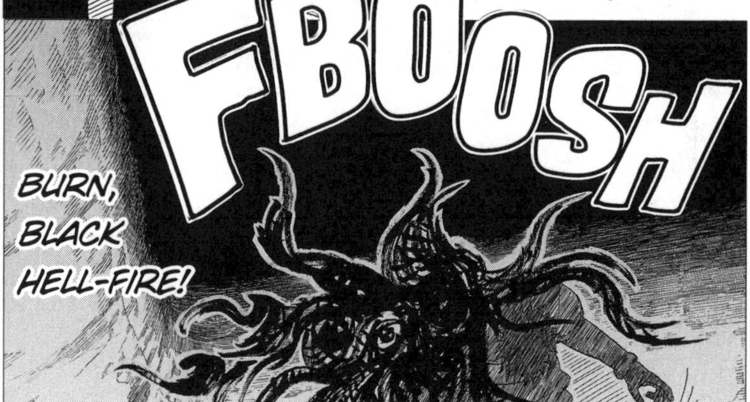
FBOOSH
BURN, BLACK HELL-FIRE!
ARGH !!

➡ Raging black fire spews from the eye, attacking its target. There is no jutsu to escape its fury.

Jutsu

Earth Style: Underground Swim

攻 防 補 近 中 遠 C

Caster: Hoshigaki Kisame

Shark teeth swimming through the earth.

A jutsu that uses chakra to transform the earth around the caster into a fluid state. It allows the caster to move at high speed, as though swimming through the earth to approach an enemy.

When Kisame thrust Samehada through the ground, he provedthat this jutsu works well as an assault art when combined with a weapon.

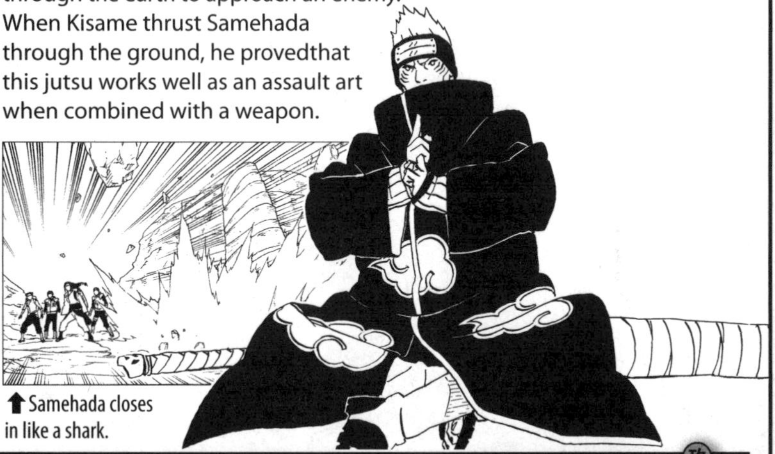

⬆ Samehada closes in like a shark.

Nin Jutsu

Earth Style: Diamond Morph

攻 防 補 近 中 遠 B

Caster: Kakuzu

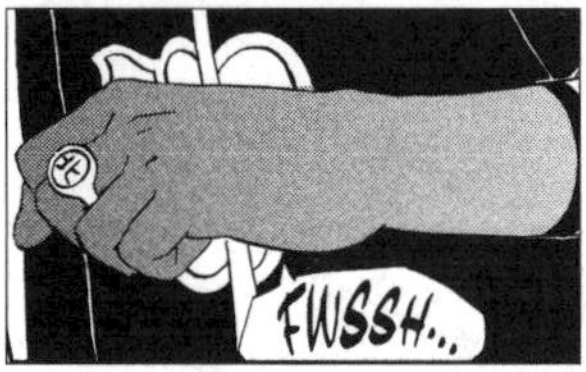
FWSSH...

⬅ Kakuzu obliterated the Fire Temple gate with a single blow.

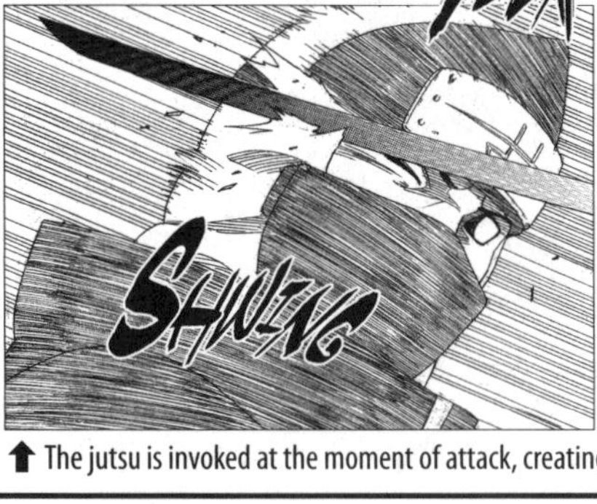
DUK
SHWING

⬆ The jutsu is invoked at the moment of attack, creating an immortal body.

Nothing can land a hit!

A highly versatile jutsu that increases the destructive force of unarmed attacks and increases defensive capability to its maximum by sending chakra throughout the body to harden the skin. Although it has an Achilles' heel in that the hardened body part cannot be moved, there are nearly no jutsu other than Lightning Style ninjutsu that can defeat Diamond Morph.

Nin Jutsu

Earth Style: Planet Splitter

Caster: Yamato

Splitting the earth at will by making the underground ryumaku comply.

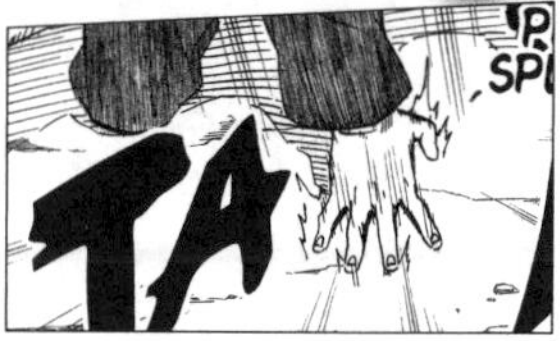
TA

By concentrating chakra in the palms of his hands, the caster rips open the ground by using the ryumaku, the veins in the earth in which chakra flows. Although it requires delicate control of chakra to manipulate the ryumaku, a skilled caster can use it as a defense by separating the enemy's camp from one's own, and as an attack by destroying an enemy camp.

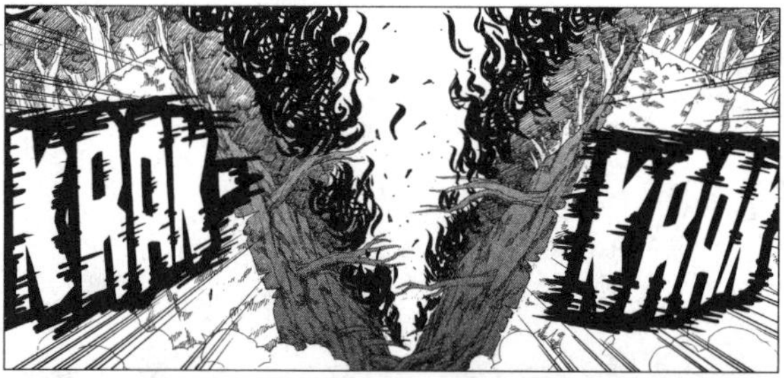
KRAK

⬅The caster has complete control—up, down, left and right. The earth will remain split as long as Yamato maintains his flow of chakra.

Nin Jutsu

Earth Style: Rampart of Flowing Soil

Caster: Yamato

Earth rising up becomes a robust rampart.

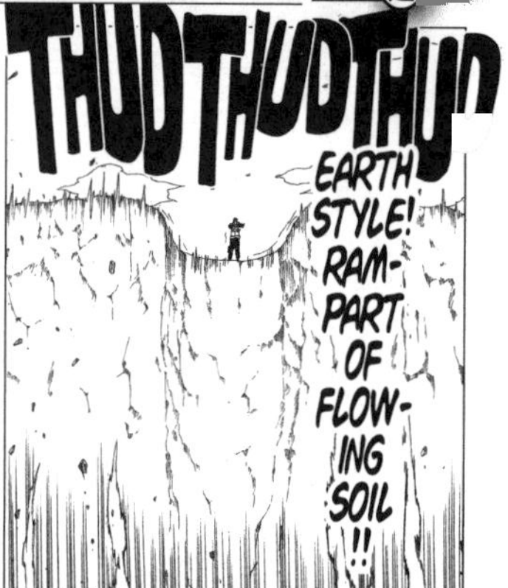
THUD THUD
EARTH STYLE! RAMPART OF FLOWING SOIL!!

A jutsu that uses chakra to increase the amount of earth, making the earth rise up to form a huge soil rampart at the caster's feet. The caster can change the form of the soil rampart based on his own imagination, from a rather flat one to a mountain of needle-like spikes.

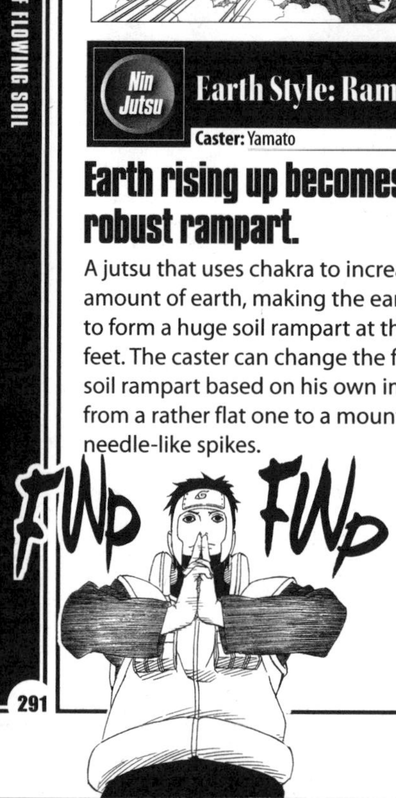
FWP FWP

➡By increasing the quantity of earth rather than creating it, chakra consumption can be kept down.

Nin Jutsu — Earth Style: Hiding Mole

攻 防 補 近 中 遠 C

Caster: Deidara / Tobi

The Ultimate Escape

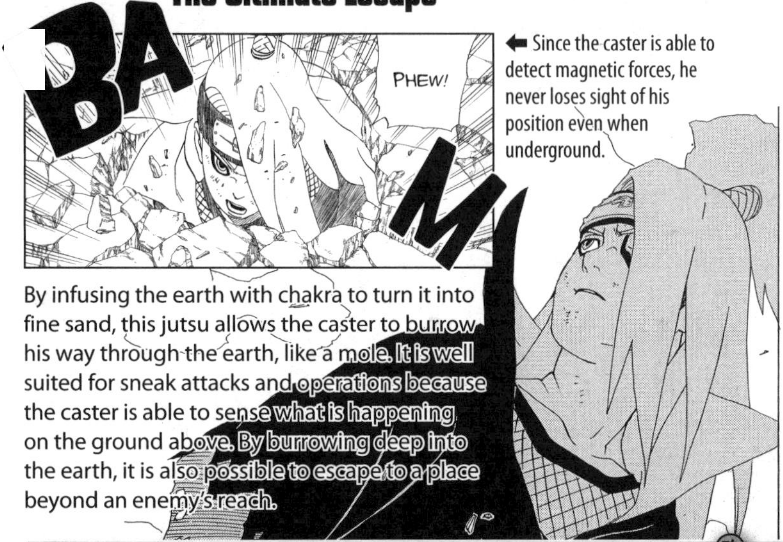
BAM
PHEW!

⬅ Since the caster is able to detect magnetic forces, he never loses sight of his position even when underground.

By infusing the earth with chakra to turn it into fine sand, this jutsu allows the caster to burrow his way through the earth, like a mole. It is well suited for sneak attacks and operations because the caster is able to sense what is happening on the ground above. By burrowing deep into the earth, it is also possible to escape to a place beyond an enemy's reach.

Nin Jutsu — Hiden — Clay Doppelganger

攻 防 補 近 中 遠 —

Caster: Deidara

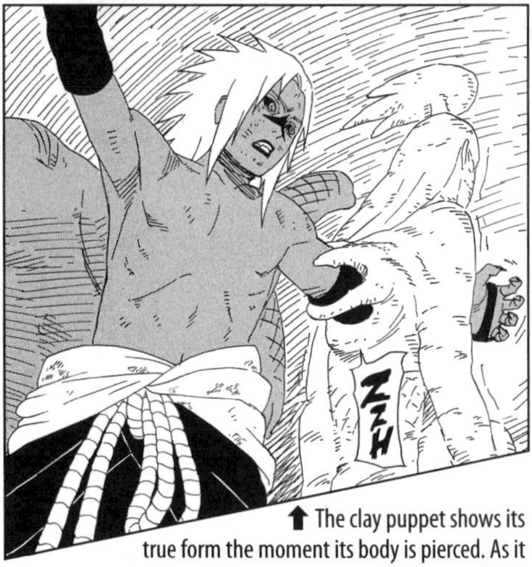
ZZZH

⬆ The clay puppet shows its true form the moment its body is pierced. As it hardens, the clay skillfully wraps around the enemy's arm.

A puppet that deceives in order to capture. No jutsu can rescue the victim.

Jutsu unique to Deidara. It's a doppelganger technique that can be used both to substitute himself and to capture an enemy. When attacked, the clay doppelganger absorbs attacks with its body to capture an enemy. If detonating clay is mixed in, the doppelganger can be exploded, taking the enemy with it.

TECHNICAL FILE / 8 TRIGRAMS AIR PALM / SECRET ART: BEETLE SPHERE

Tai Jutsu · **Kekkei Genkai**

8 Trigrams Air Palm

Caster: Hyuga Neji

Compressing air = high-speed palm attack!

An extremely fast strike with the palm is unleashed after pinpointing an enemy's vital spot. The compressed "vacuum shell" with aspects of Gentle Fist thrusts through an enemy's vital spot with tremendous force. It is a short to mid-range attack that more than compensates for weaknesses in taijutsu.

←↑ Using the All-Seeing Eye as a scope, Neji detects the enemy's vital spot with precision. The enemy is blown away before even realizing he's been struck.

Nin Jutsu · **Hiden**

Secret Art: Beetle Sphere

Caster: Aburame Shino

Dispersed kikaichu gather around chakra to form a sphere

A jutsu using kikaichu that inhabit the body to envelop the body of an enemy. Kikaichu, which detect chakra, are spread over a large area. The moment they detect an enemy, the caster issues a command that instantly consolidates the kikaichu. They restrain the enemy and gradually eat away his chakra, ultimately causing death...

←↑ Those who end up as a Beetle Sphere must endure the fear of having their chakra eaten away.

Nin Jutsu

Sealing Jutsu

Sealing Jutsu:
Nine Phantom Dragons Seal

Caster: Pain

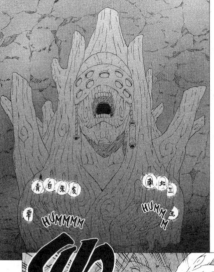

Sealing all captured jinchûriki in a giant statue.

A maximum of ten shinobi concentrate their aggregate consciousness to activate the sealing statue and use the absorption chakra that flows from its mouth to extract the chakra of tailed beasts and seal them away. It takes Akatsuki-class casters several days of keeping the statue active. It is impossible for ordinary shinobi to even activate the statue.

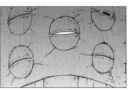

←↑ Absorption chakra takes the form of a dragon with nine bodies that completely seals the chakra of tailed beasts. Once the sealing is completed, the eyes of the statue open.

294

Nin Jutsu	Sealing Jutsu	**Sealing Jutsu: Lion Roar**

Caster: Chiyo

Light becomes lion!

⬆ Another method is to throw a ninja tool into where a seal spell formula has been placed.

➡ The Lion Cannon ninja tool transforms from a sphere into a massive lion head.

⬆➡ The seal spell formula is invoked the moment the lion opens its huge mouth, pinning the target against a wall.

Writing a seal spell formula on the ground or on a wall completely suppresses those nearby. At the center of the seal spell formula is the character for hei, which means "to close." Anyone who comes in contact with its center has all their Tenketsu closed. However, because it is difficult to lure in a target with pinpoint accuracy, many different techniques, such as placing the seal spell formula in puppets or ninja tools, are used to deploy the jutsu.

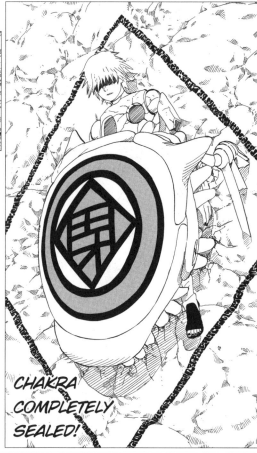

CHAKRA COMPLETELY SEALED!

Nin Jutsu | Sealing Jutsu

Iron Wall Seal

Caster: Chiriku

攻 防 補 近 中 遠 — **B**

A TEMPLE? YOU SURE THIS IS THE PLACE?
WE'LL SEE.

A strong and robust jutsu to ensure the gates do not open for the unholy.

The seal invoked on the gateway to the Fire Temple in order to keep out intruders from the outside world. The two stone statues on each side of the gate form a barrier. The seal can be undone by channeling the unique chakra of the sages known as the Gift of the Sages.

⬆ Ordinarily, only ninja monks can enter and exit the gate. The Akatsuki, however, destroyed the stone statues and entered the temple by destroying the seal itself.

Nin Jutsu | Sealing Jutsu

Jutsu Absorption

Caster: Pain

攻 防 補 近 中 遠 — **—**

An endless whirlpool that sucks away every jutsu.

This jutsu causes the body's chakra circulation to flow in reverse, sucking away the jutsu of the target. The absorbed chakra disperses inside the body, and the power is sucked away as if into a bottomless swamp.

⬆ Every jutsu, regardless of its chakra properties, is sucked away and rendered ineffective.

Nin Jutsu

Wind Style: Pressure Damage

攻 防 補 近 中 遠 B

Caster: Kakuzu

Wind blasts!

A powerful Wind Style ninjutsu unleashed by one of Kakuzu's five hearts. A very densely compacted tornado mass is launched at the target. When it impacts, the air pressure, raised to the extreme, knocks down everything in its path. In the hands of a master of wind nature transformation, the fierce whirlwind explodes over a wide area, inflicting severe damage to the target and his surroundings.

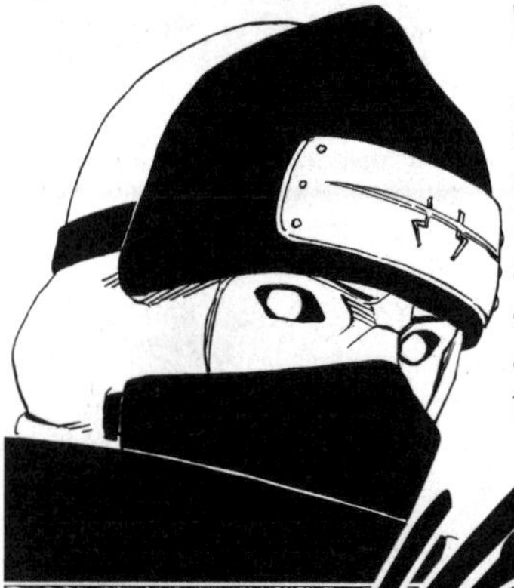

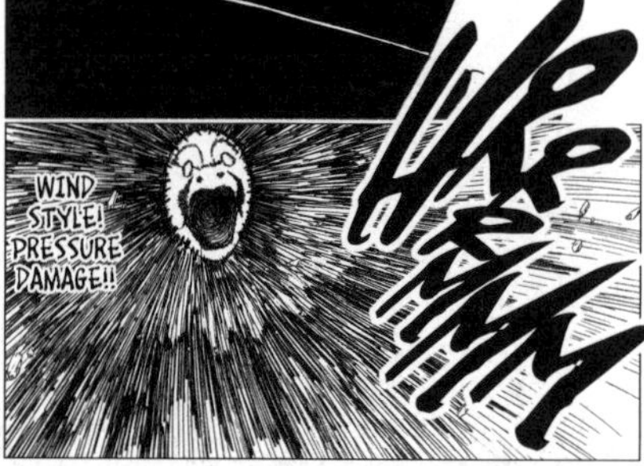
WIND STYLE! PRESSURE DAMAGE!!

⬆ Because it is expelled suddenly from behind a mask, it is an extremely difficult jutsu to anticipate.

⬇ With a thunderous roar, winds of overwhelming power and quantity bear down at the target. The wild, raging winds knock down trees and gouge the earth.

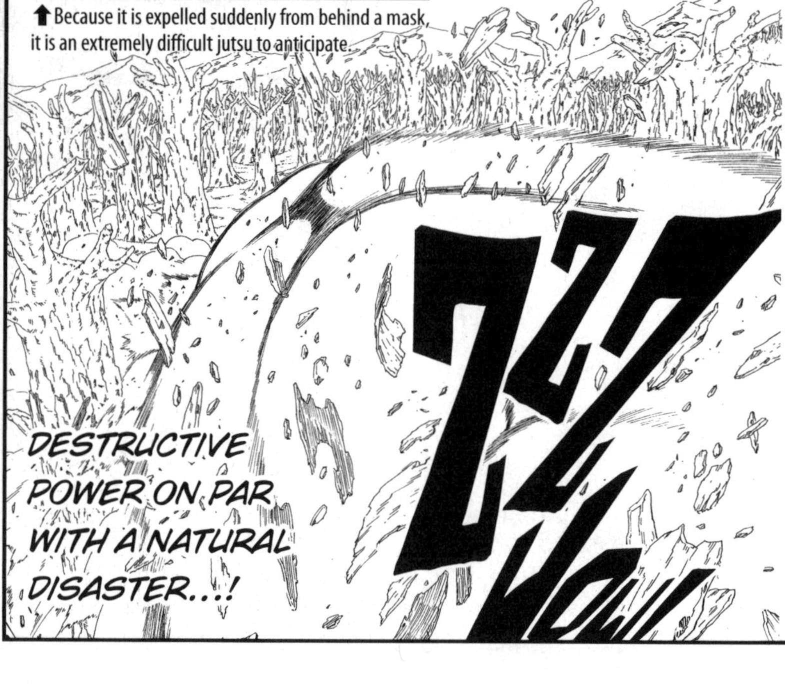
DESTRUCTIVE POWER ON PAR WITH A NATURAL DISASTER...!

Nin Jutsu

Wind Style: Rasen-Shuriken

Caster: Uzumaki Naruto

攻 防 補 近 中 遠 S

Wind adds polish to Rasen, creating a striking blade of certain death.

This is shape-shifting to the highest degree, adding the nature transformation of wind to the enormous destructive power of Rasengan. A sharp wind blade greatly increases killing power. Although the jutsu has a weakness in that the caster must be in close range to hit the target, no one can withstand its impact when it strikes. Even so, it is currently only fifty-percent perfect. Its destructive power once perfected staggers the imagination.

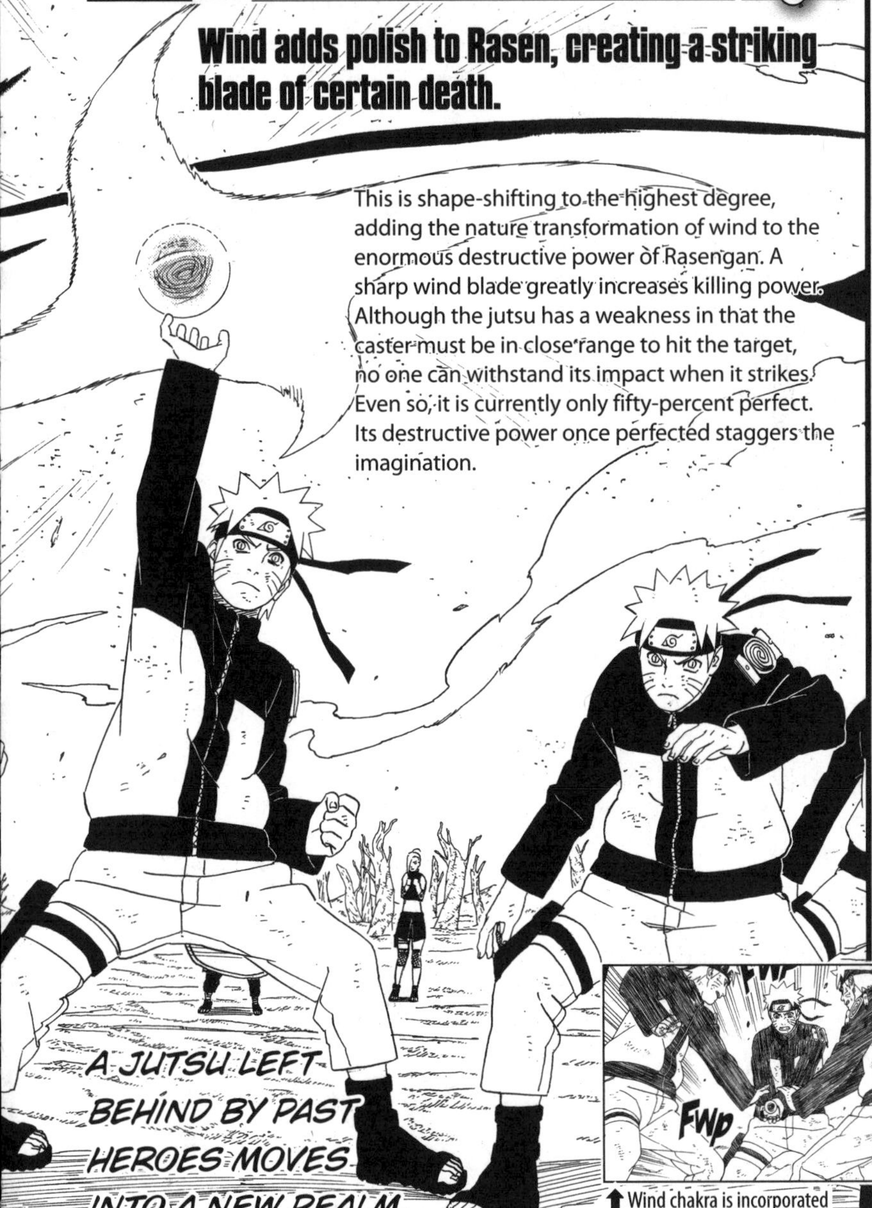
A JUTSU LEFT BEHIND BY PAST HEROES MOVES INTO A NEW REALM.
FWP
FWP

⬆ Wind chakra is incorporated into a perfected Rasengan.

Winds of destruction blow needles of danger!

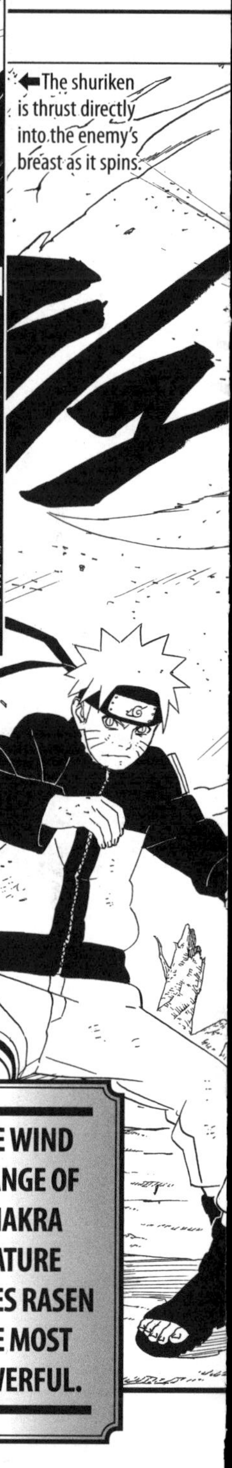

⬅The shuriken is thrust directly into the enemy's breast as it spins.

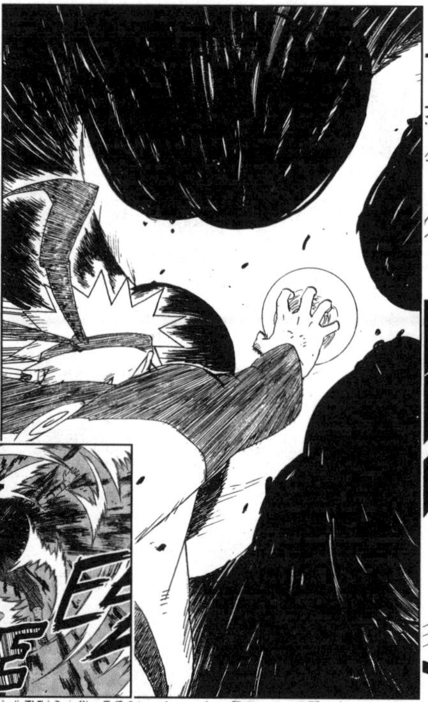

⬇Countless blades cut apart the target. It is impossible to see how many times it attacks.

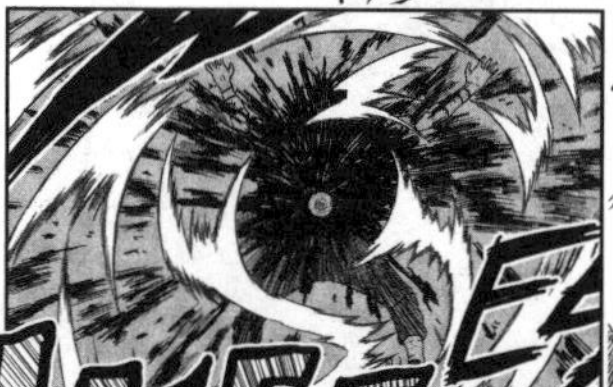

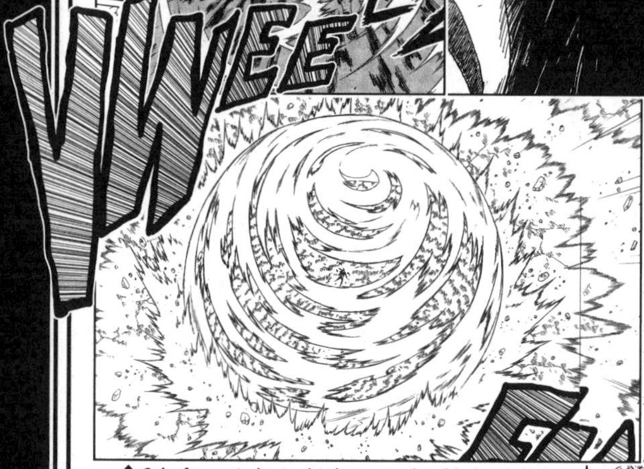
VWEEE

⬆Gale-force winds give birth to countless blades that pierce and pulverize everything.

THE WIND CHANGE OF CHAKRA NATURE MAKES RASEN THE MOST POWERFUL.

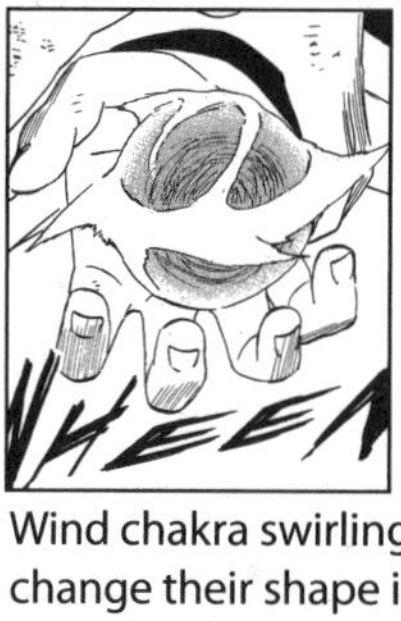

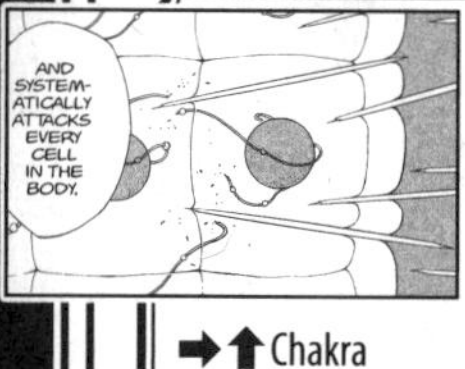
AND SYSTEM-ATICALLY ATTACKS EVERY CELL IN THE BODY.

➡⬆Chakra shaped like small swords directly sever the meridians connecting the body's cells.

As its name implies, it looks like a giant shuriken, but in actuality, it is a collective entity made up of microscopic little swords. Wind chakra swirling around the Rasen change their shape into blades and attack the enemy all at once…

Nin Jutsu

Wind Style: Gale Palm

C

Caster: Nagato

A violent, supersonic gale unleashed with a prayer.

A jutsu where chakra is transformed to create wind, which is then compressed via Kashiwade to develop it into a fierce gale. An attack by Gale Palm alone is enough to send a man flying, but the true worth of the jutsu is in attacks used in conjunction with projectile weapons such as shuriken and kunai knives. It increases velocity, impact and killing power.

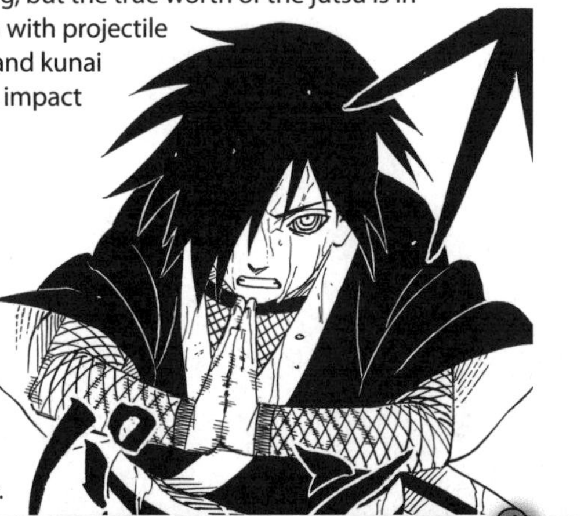

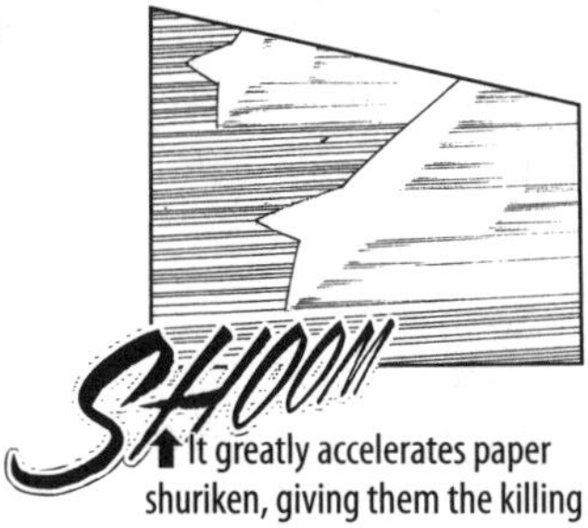
SHOOM

⬆ It greatly accelerates paper shuriken, giving them the killing power to go right through an enemy.

Nin Jutsu / Kekkei Genkai

Hokage Style Elder Jutsu: Kakuan's Tenth Edict on Enlightenment

—

Caster: Yamato / First Hokage

Laid out on the ground, ten pillars that silence even disasters.

A jutsu to forcibly control the chakra of tailed beasts using the power of Wood Style for the jutsu to be invoked, it is necessary for either the tailed beast or jinchûriki to be in possession of the chakra crystal. Ten pillars that restrain the beast appear when the caster's palm comes in contact with the tailed beast's chakra.

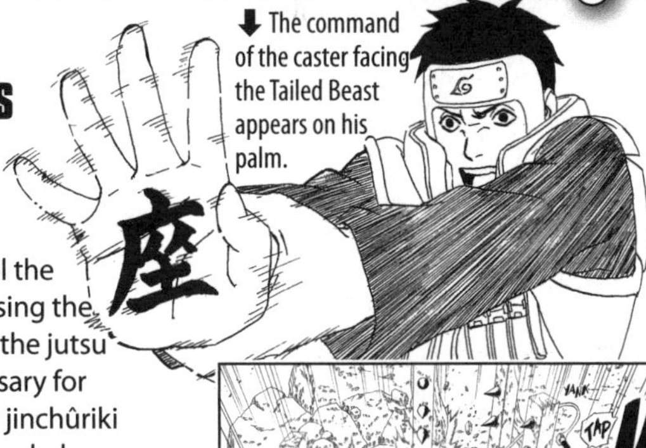
座

⬇ The command of the caster facing the Tailed Beast appears on his palm.

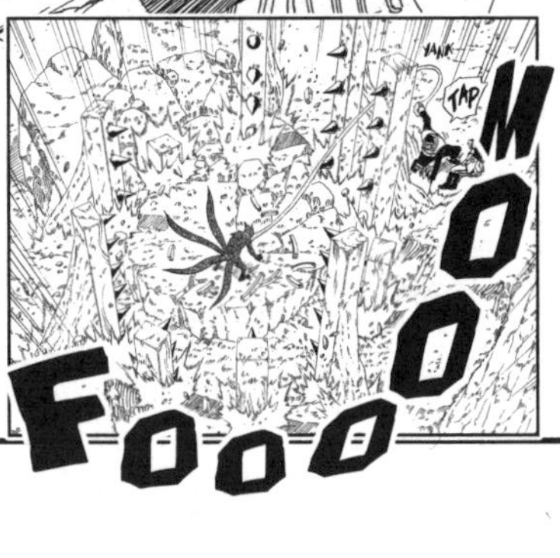
YANK
TAP
FOOOOOOM

Gen Jutsu | Kekkei Genkei

Demonic Illusion: Shackle Stakes

Caster: Uchiha Itachi / Uchiha Sasuke

Loss of Movement

A genjutsu enabled by the Saimingan, or Hypnotic Eye ability of the Sharingan. Anyone caught in the world of the mind created by the caster finds himself tormented by a feeling of having stakes driven into each of his four limbs and becomes completely unable to move freely. Since the victim experiences the illusion of physical pain at the same time, this jutsu is very effective for torture.

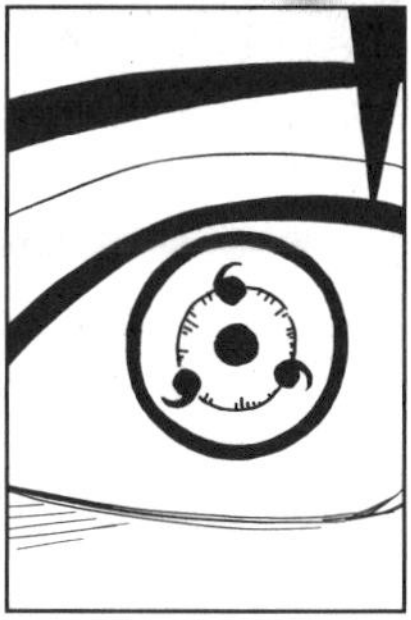

⬆ The jutsu can be invoked by simply looking eye-to-eye with the target, without the need for a blood seal.

⬇ Even Orochimaru became paralyzed against this jutsu.

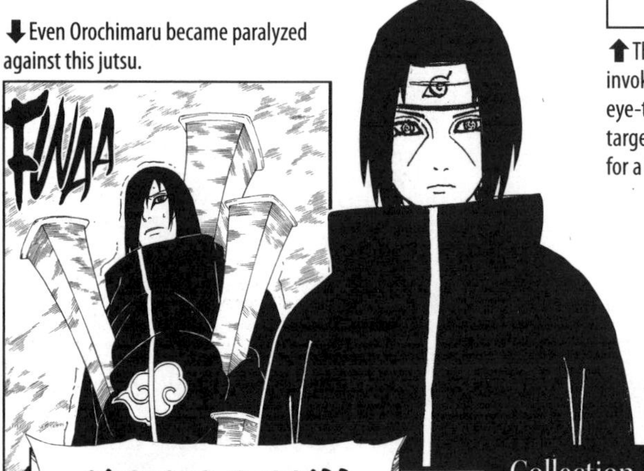
FWAA

Collection ... Number 17

Konoha

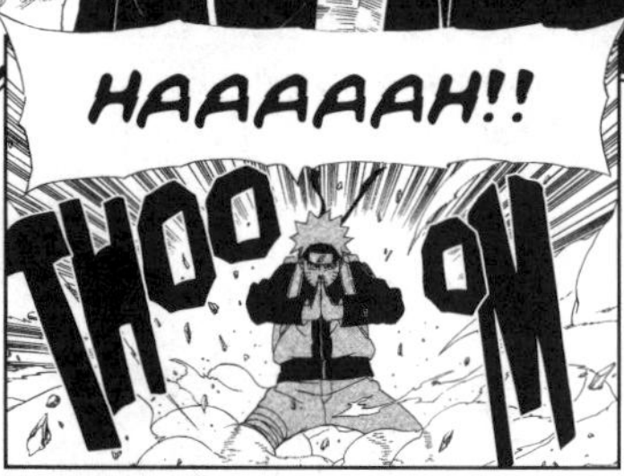
HAAAAAH!!
THOOOM

⬅ Breaking a genjutsu can be learned with training. It behooves even those who do not use genjutsu themselves to learn these methods.

GENJUTSU TYPES AND COUNTERS

Genjutsu come in two types—those invoked via a seal and those that are invoked through an ocular jutsu such as Sharingan. The ways of dealing with these jutsu differ accordingly.

Anti-ocular jutsu

Two against one is the rule. If the first person falls victim to the jutsu, the other attacks the caster to release the jutsu.

Anti-genjutsu

(other than ocular jutsu)
By intentionally disrupting the chakra within one's body, it becomes possible to block an interference from another.

Gen Jutsu | Sage Jutsu

Demonic Illusion: Gamarinsho

攻 防 補 近 中 遠 一

Caster: Shima / Fukasaku

Once you hear it, you become captive to an illusion—a duet of death.

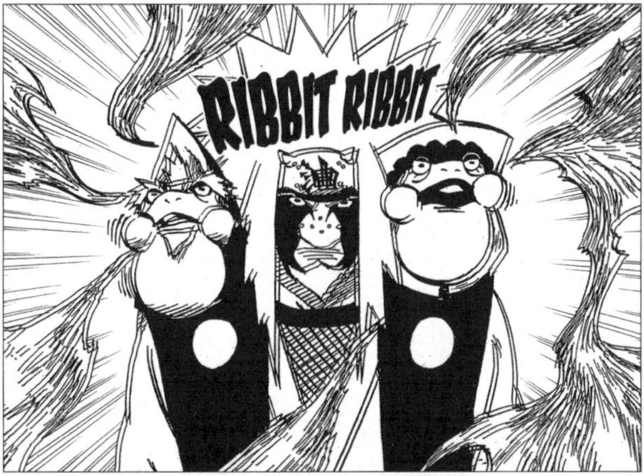
RIBBIT RIBBIT

⬅ After invoking Sage Mode, the husband and wife toads sing Genjutsu from Jiraiya's shoulders. The exquisite harmony of the two great Sage Toads married for several hundred years can warp even space.

Two or more toads sing in harmony to a musical scale passed down secretly on Mount Myoboku. Those who hear it are drawn into a genjutsu world where their minds are paralyzed. Because it takes many long years of training to acquire, presently only the two great Sage Toads couple can perform this jutsu.

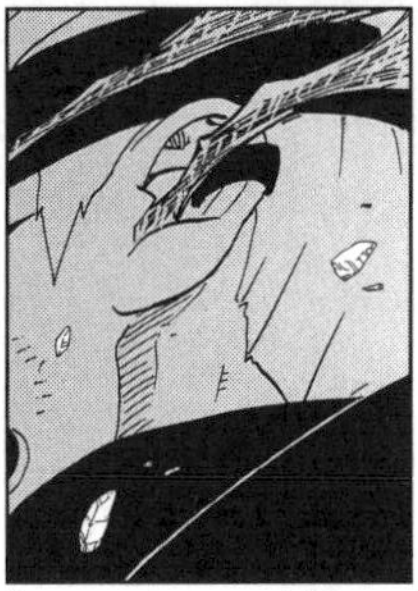

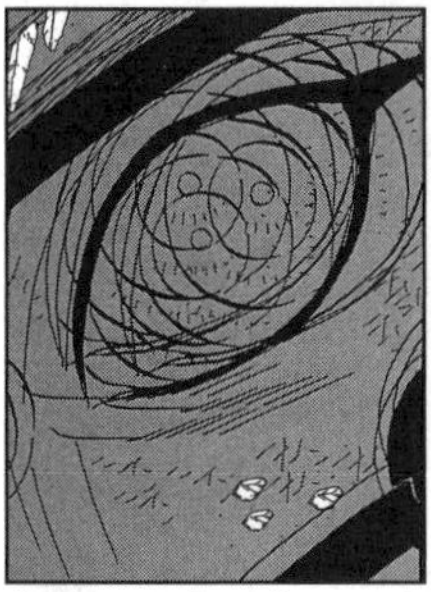

⬆ Gamarinsho will succeed if the target is even within earshot. Conversely, it also comes with the vulnerability of the sound giving their location away.

Collection ... Number 18

Konoha

A MELODY PASSED DOWN ON MOUNT MYOBOKU

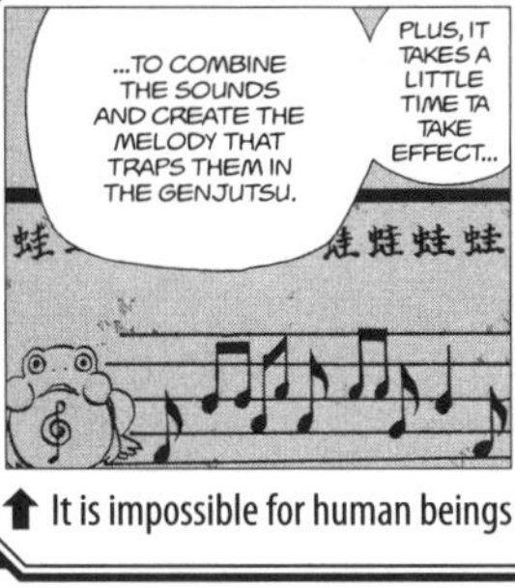
PLUS, IT TAKES A LITTLE TIME TA TAKE EFFECT...
...TO COMBINE THE SOUNDS AND CREATE THE MELODY THAT TRAPS THEM IN THE GENJUTSU.

At Mount Myoboku, there is sheet music for genjutsu recognized since ancient times. Combining lyrics and a melody that only toads can produce invokes the most powerful genjutsu.

⬆ It is impossible for human beings to sing this song written for the vocal range of toads.

GLUP GLUP...

⬅⬆ Even if the targets number in the hundreds, it makes no difference. Each and every one who hears the Gamarinsho of their minds and bodies are sealed in the clutches of a giant Gamafuda.

Four toads on all sides, stand bound in both dream and reality.

MASTER JIRAIYA... YOU HAVE THAT JUTSU...

⬇ A stone sword passed down secretly from Mount Myoboku is driven through the captive's heart. Only then is he released, at last, to the other world.

This jutsu surrounds the opponent in all four directions with massive toads and seals them behind a barrier. The toads will not release their grasp until the caster gives the order. All that is left is for the caster is to finish off his captives in the real world.

Nin Jutsu

Mandala of Endless Snakes Formation

攻 防 補 近 中 遠 **B**

Caster: Orochimaru

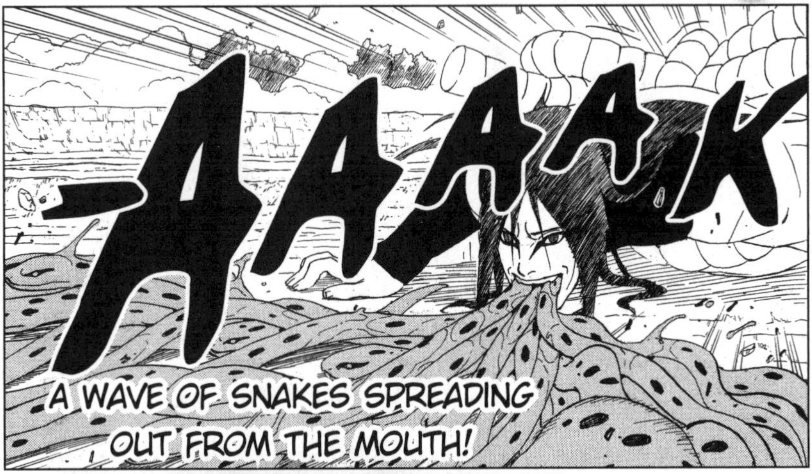
AAAAK
A WAVE OF SNAKES SPREADING OUT FROM THE MOUTH!

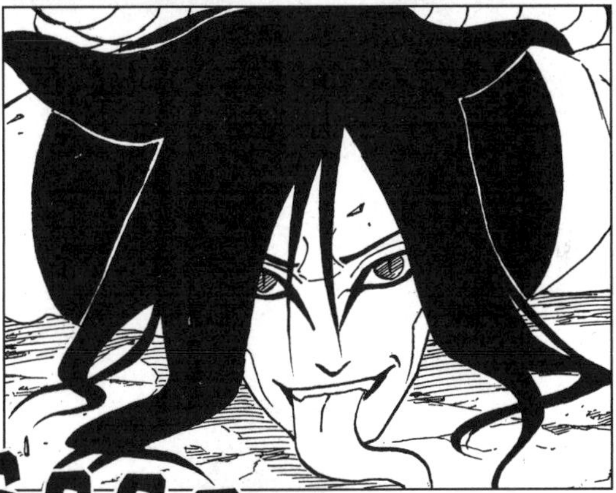

⬆ Snakes as far as the eye can see wrap around an enemy, rendering him powerless. Then, they dig their poisonous fangs into their immobilized prey.

The wonder of infinite snake blades slithering over the ground.

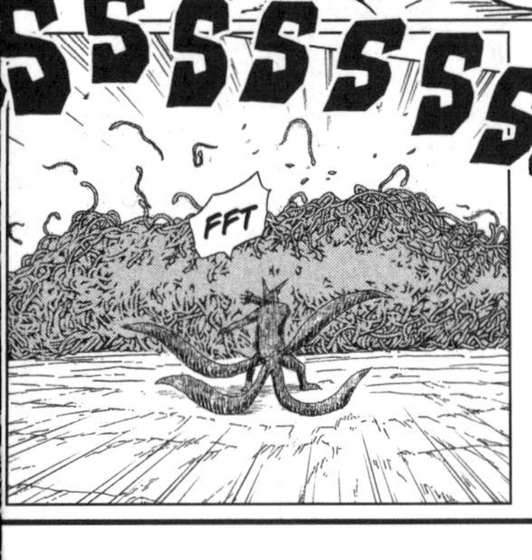
SSSSSSS...
FFT

Countless numbers of summoned snakes slither out from Orochimaru's mouth and attack their enemy. In the face of overwhelming numbers of snakes—a veritable wall of snakes—defense or avoidance lose their meaning as all the target can do is be buried in snakes. Also, when the endless number of snakes that come slithering from out gather together, they become a defense that can block any sort of attack.

Nin Jutsu | Kekkei Genkai

Wood Style: Four-Pillar House Technique

Caster: Yamato

攻 防 補 近 中 遠 —

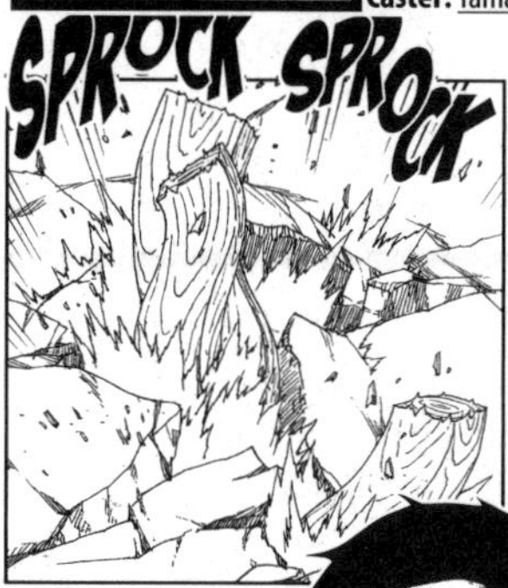
SPROCK
SPROCK

➡⬆ At the signal, trees come bursting through already prepared to serve as timber to build the structure.

Rising up out of the ground for a short period is an intricate Wood Style cottage.

Plant roots in the ground are transformed into building materials by channeling chakra into the ground. This jutsu spurs rapid growth and builds structures. In a manner identical to Four-Pillar Prison Technique, the size and design of the structure is left up to the memories and imagination of Yamato, the caster. By setting a barrier around the Four-Pillar House via the use of tags, a safe place to camp out can be built without being detected by an enemy.

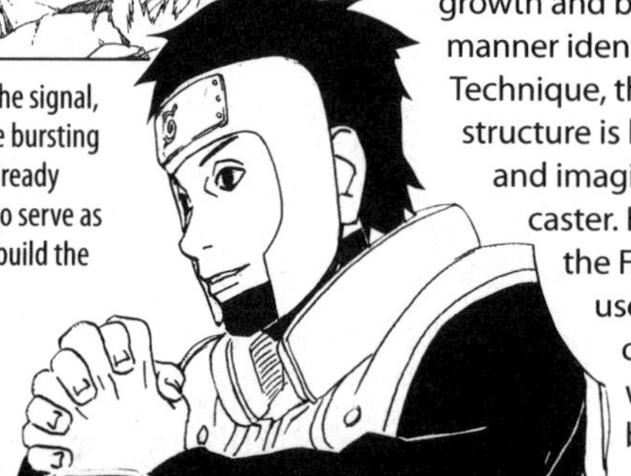

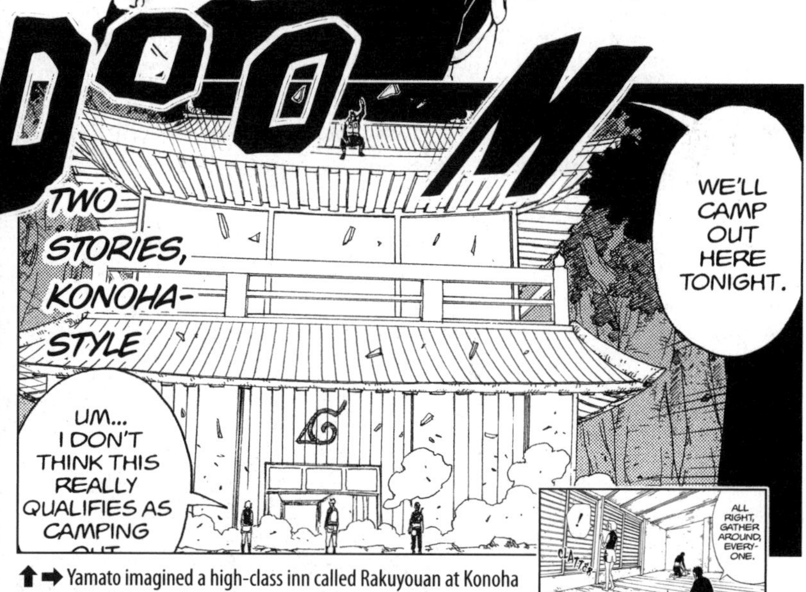
WE'LL CAMP OUT HERE TONIGHT.
DOOM
TWO STORIES, KONOHA-STYLE
UM... I DON'T THINK THIS REALLY QUALIFIES AS CAMPING

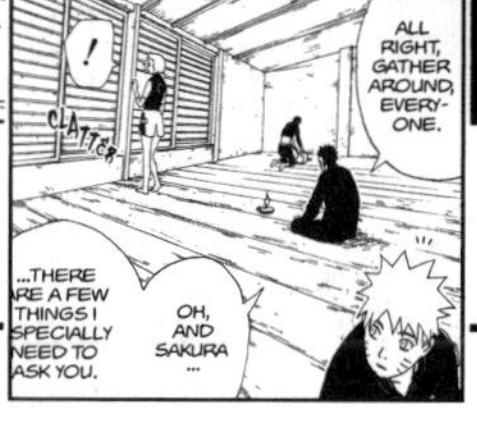
ALL RIGHT, GATHER AROUND, EVERY-ONE.
!
CLATTER
OH, AND SAKURA ...
...THERE RE A FEW THINGS I SPECIALLY NEED TO ASK YOU.

⬆➡ Yamato imagined a high-class inn called Rakuyouan at Konoha hot spa. He did it out of consideration to allow his subordinates to rest. . . but it's not good to go overboard.

Nin Jutsu | Kekkei Genkai

Wood Style: Four-Pillar Prison Technique

Caster: Yamato

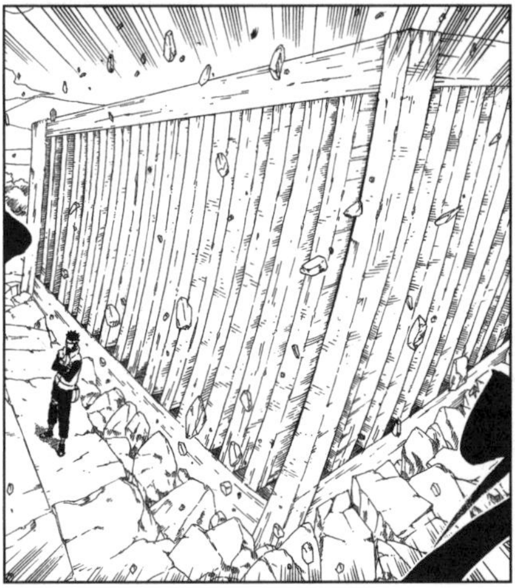

An inescapable wooden prison, thrusting up through the ground and built in an instant.

Chakra is transformed in the earth into timber, forming a wooden prison as the wood grows rapidly. The size of the prison is based on Yamato's imagination and can be freely changed from bug cage size to a huge penitentiary. The timber is coated with chakra, making it extremely difficult to break out of the prison.

⬆ A prison appears in an instant from Yamato's imagination. During battle, it shows its effectiveness as a place to keep prisoners; it can also be used as a place to punish subordinates who don't get along.

Nin Jutsu | Kekkei Genkai

Wood Style: Art of the Giant Forest

Caster: Yamato

A large tree trunk grows from his arm, becoming a stake for capturing or piercing an enemy.

A jutsu where Yamato turns his arm into a huge tree. By using chakra to transform his cells into a tree and stimulating and encouraging rapid growth, the tree grows rapidly and branches out. The branches can be used to capture an enemy. At the same time, if he changes the branch tips into a stake shape, they can become countless sharp spears with which to run an enemy through.

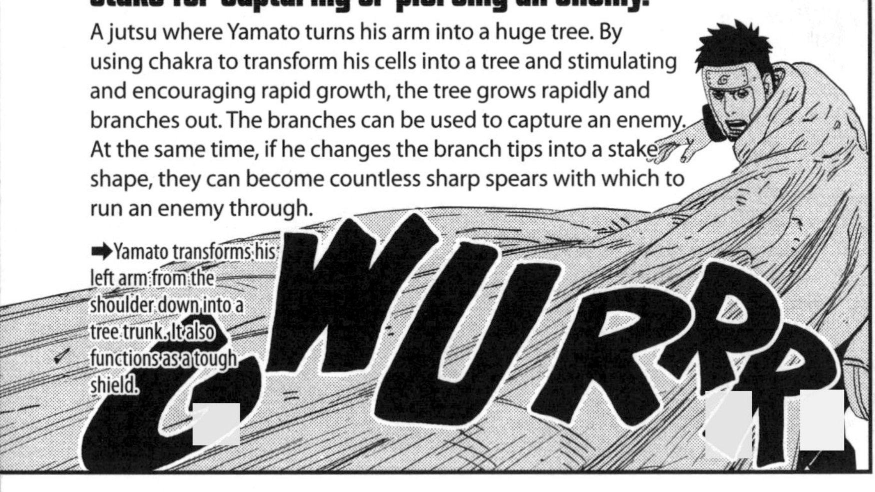
WURP

➡ Yamato transforms his left arm from the shoulder down into a tree trunk. It also functions as a tough shield.

Nin Jutsu **Kekkei Genkai** # Wood Style

Caster: Yamato / First Hokage

➡ When Yamato forms the sign for Wood Style, trees appear on a sheer rock wall. If he wishes, he can even turn a desert into a forest.

BOOM
BOOM
BOOM

Tearing open the earth to give birth to life–a hidden jutsu like no other.

A legendary jutsu that turns chakra into the origin of life and a hidden jutsu that presently only Yamato can handle. It is a genetically inherited skill whereby the basic Earth Style and Water Style chakra elements are invoked simultaneously to make plants and trees appear. By transforming the plants and trees, this jutsu shows tremendous effectiveness both for attack and defense.

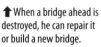

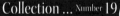

Collection ... Number 19

COPING WITH EVERY SITUATION: WOOD STYLE SURVIVAL

No jutsu boasts a wider variety of uses that Yamato's Wood Style. The jutsu displays outstanding effectiveness in every situation during the performance of his duties. It is a reason for his rising mission success rate.

Konoha

PBOM

PBOM

⬆ When a bridge ahead is destroyed, he can repair it or build a new bridge.

⬅ In an instant, he can create a wooden doll version of himself to use in a substitution jutsu.

➡ Changing the shape into rings creates a restraint stronger than rope.

Nin Jutsu | Kekkei Genkai

Wood Style: Domed Wall

攻 防 補 近 中 遠 一

Caster: Yamato

A robust barrier wall that closes together from both sides.

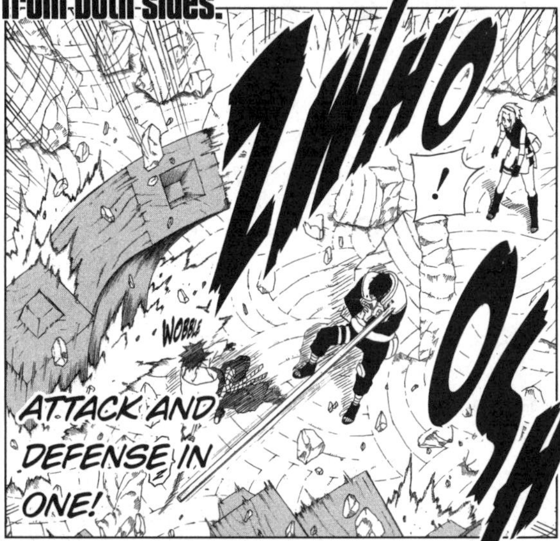

ZWHOOSH
!
WOBBLE
ATTACK AND DEFENSE IN ONE!

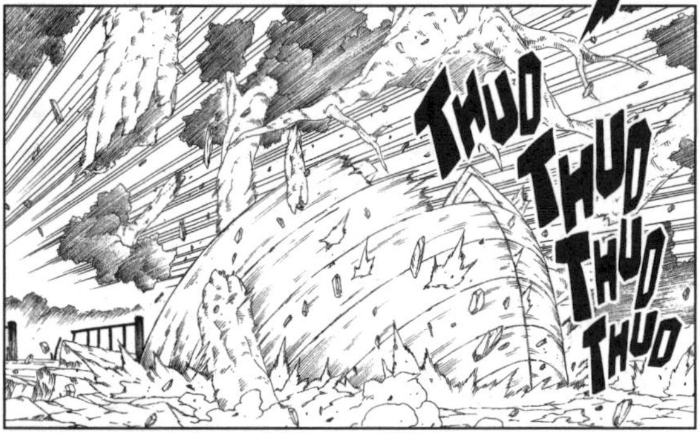

THUD
THUD
THUD
THUD

This jutsu makes wood pillars appear from both sides of Yamato, the central point, by activating roots in the ground. In the process of forming its dome shape, the wood pillars can be used as a pincer attack against an enemy. It is also possible to seal an enemy inside the dome for close combat or to create a one-on-one situation. Furthermore, it functions as a simple shelter against an enemy's attack from a distance using shuriken and kunai knives. It is a truly versatile barrier wall.

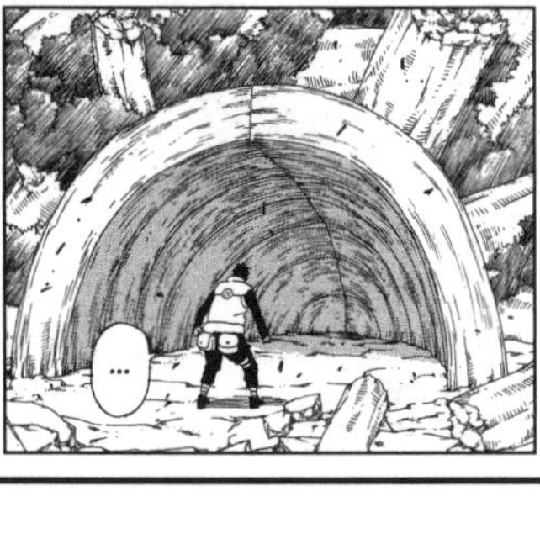

...

⬆ While conceived for the purpose of confining an enemy, it serves as a defensive wall, as well. Because its size can be adjusted at will, it can save a great many people.

Nin Jutsu | Kekkei Genkai

Art of the Wood Doppelganger

Caster: Yamato

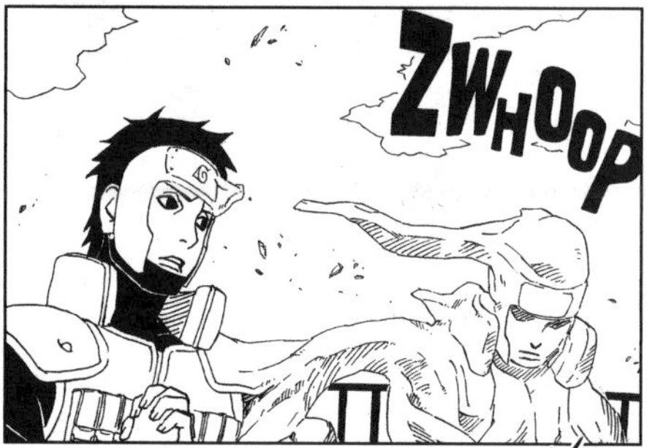
ZWHOOP

A protean wood doppelganger onto which one's heart and soul is projected.

By using chakra to change the nature of one's own cells, a doppelganger is created that is more durable than the usual shadow doppelganger—one that will not vanish with a single blow. In addition, because it has the ability to merge with plants, it works well in reconnaissance missions.

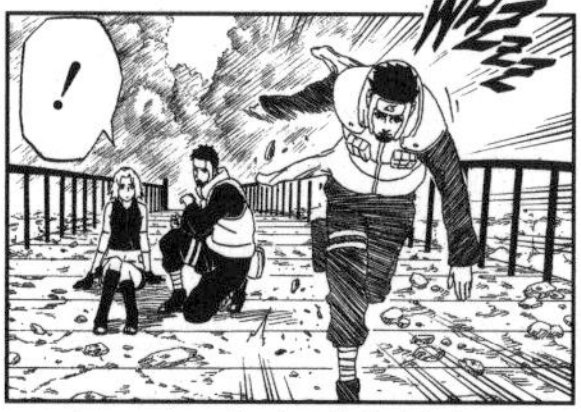
!

⬆ A doppelganger created using chakra and one's own cells.

➡A wood doppelganger, equipped with sufficient attack and defense abilities, can be sent to the battlefield alone.

Collection ... Number 20

Konoha

A COUNTERFEIT KAGEBUNSHIN

⬇ When turned into the shape of seed, it becomes a transmitter that resonates with Yamato's chakra.

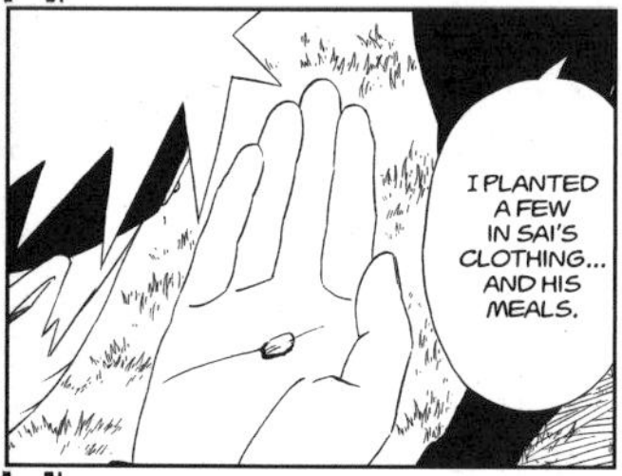
I PLANTED A FEW IN SAI'S CLOTHING... AND HIS MEALS.

The fundamental shadow doppelganger concept that information held by the doppelganger will be accumulated in the real body applies to the wood doppelganger as well. However, the shadow doppelganger, which is comprised of chakra, and the wood doppelganger based on cells are completely different jutsu. Wood doppelgangers change the nature of Yamato's own cells into plants. By transforming a doppelganger into the shape of a seed, it can serve as a transmitter once the intended target swallows it. Capabilities like this make it an extremely convenient jutsu.

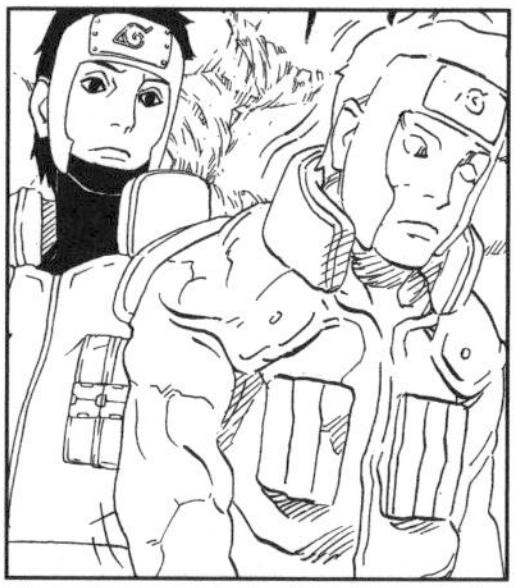

➡ Yamato placing his hand directly on a wood doppelganger to change its shape as he absorbs the information it gathered.

Nin Jutsu

Art of the Eight-Headed Serpent

攻 防 補 近 中 遠 S

Caster: Orochimaru

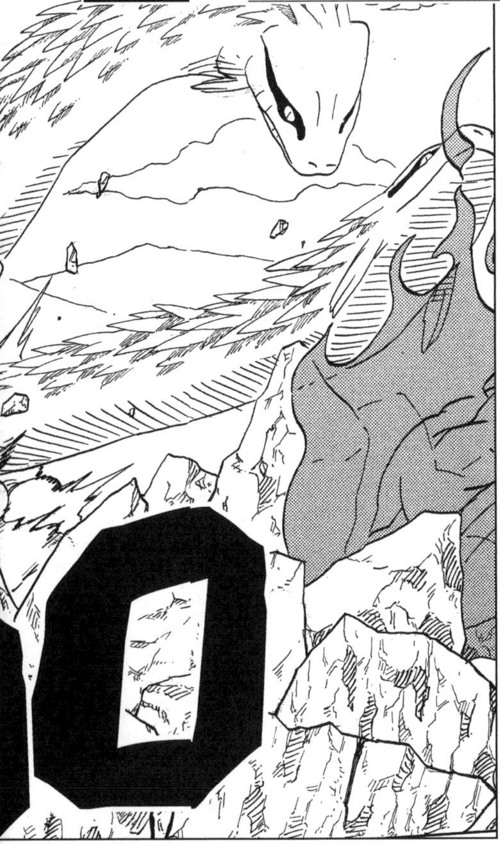

Eight peaks, eight giant serpents–wicked masterpieces incarnate of long-standing resentment

After being taken down by Sasuke, Orochimaru unleashes this hidden jutsu with the last of his strength at the moment Sasuke's "control chakra" is about to run out. Using the regenerative powers of the white snake as his vehicle, Orochimaru transforms it into an eight-headed, eight-tailed white serpent that appears from Sasuke's curse mark. The serpent crushes the Uchiha hideout by simply slithering over it with the scales on its belly. This is Orochimaru's greatest and most powerful jutsu, and the embodiment of Orochimaru's long years of vengefulness.

➡ Boasting a body even larger than Manda, feared as the most powerful giant serpent, it has a sinister appearance as it bares its ferocious fangs. It is almost like a dragon god, having surpassed even Orochimaru...

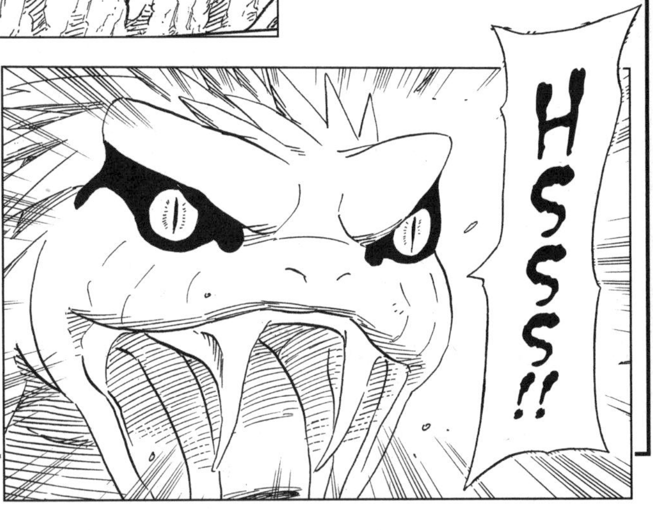
HSSS!!

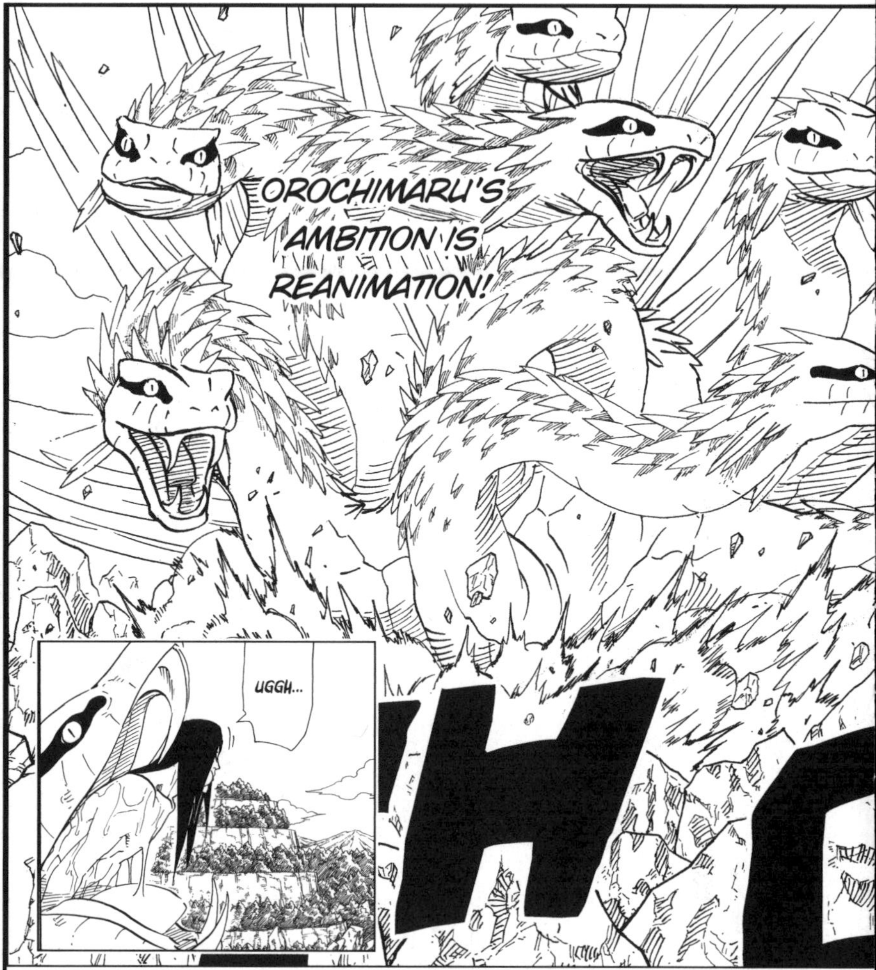
OROCHIMARU'S AMBITION IS REANIMATION!
UGGH...

➡ Young Orochimaru's obsession with immortality drove him insane.

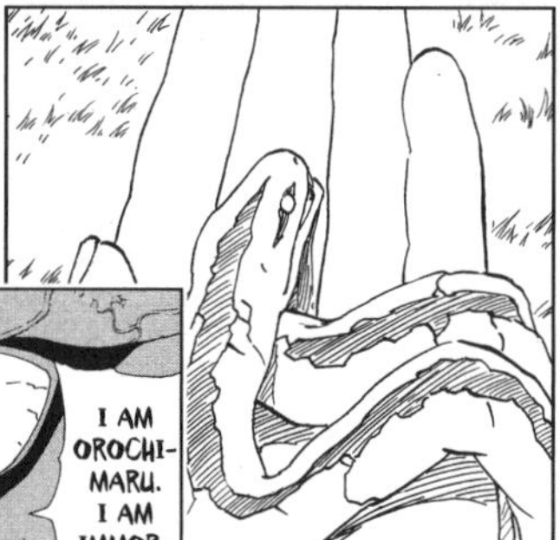

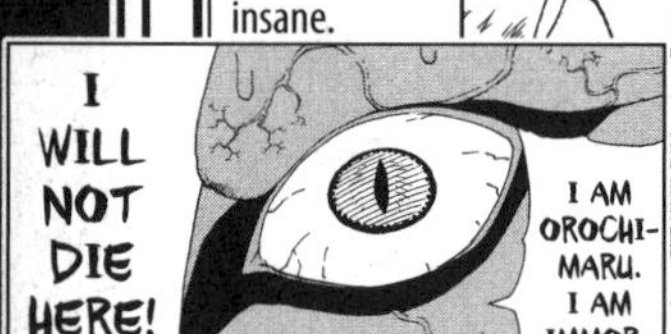
I WILL NOT DIE HERE!
I AM OROCHI-MARU. I AM IMMOR-TAL!

HIS AMBITION IS NOT YET CRUSHED.

No matter what line of death he crosses, Orochimaru has always regenerated himself. At the root of his tenacity is the power of the white snake that controls good fortune and regeneration. Through long years of research, Orochimaru acquired the ability to regenerate himself.

Nin Jutsu — Lightning Style: False Darkness

攻 防 補 近 中 遠 **B**

Caster: Kakuzu

A sharp, giant spear of lightning unleashed from a bizarre mask.

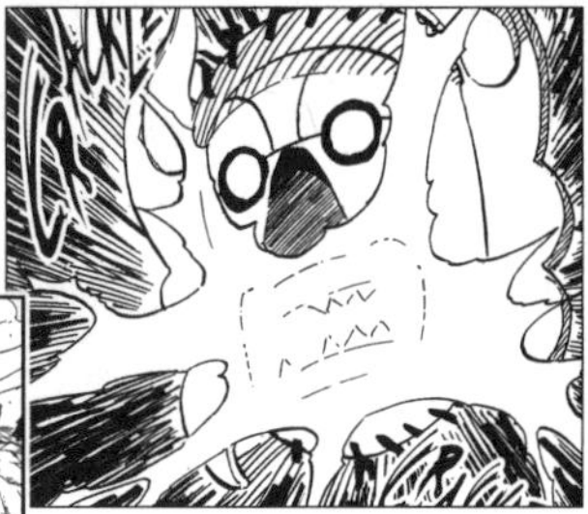

⬅ Increasing the number of lightning bolts makes it possible to slay multiple enemies in an instant. It is exceedingly difficult to dodge a lightning bolt flying at high speed.

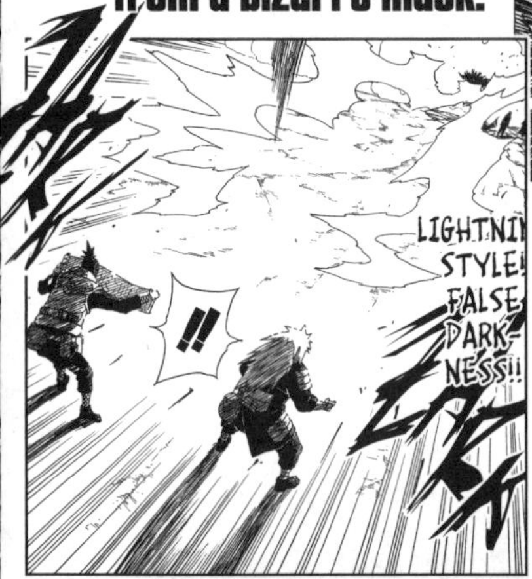
LIGHTNI STYLE! FALSE DARK-NESS!!
!!

A Lightning Style jutsu unleashed from the odd form inside Kakuzu's body. Converged lightning is transformed into a sharp, spearlike form that pierces through an enemy. It is a jutsu with extremely great killing power that possesses an astounding sharpness that can gouge through even rock.

Nin Jutsu — Art of the Raging Lion's Mane

攻 防 補 近 中 遠 **B**

Caster: Jiraiya

The white king of beasts runs across the battlefield wasteland.

⬇ In an instant, hair covers the entire area.

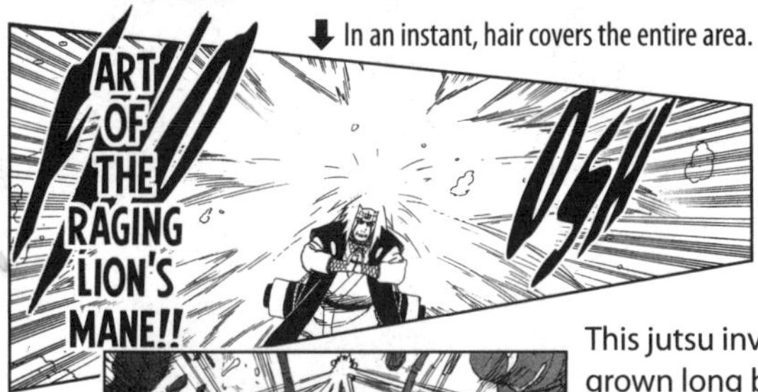
ART OF THE RAGING LION'S MANE!!

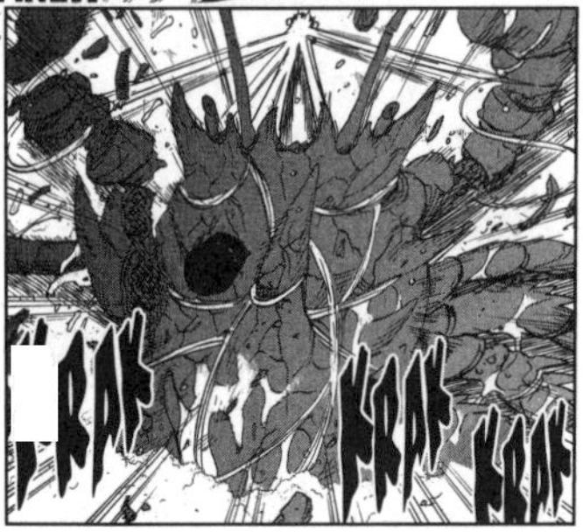

This jutsu involves manipulating hair grown long by temporarily increasing the metabolism of the scalp with chakra. Because chakra flows through the hair, its hardness is comparable to steel wire. Thickly bundling the hair further increases its hardness and improves its destructive power.

⬅ An attack where he captures, then strangles, the enemy with his hair. Its strength is extraordinary—even capable of pulverizing the shell of a giant crab.

Nin Jutsu
Kekkei Genkai

Rinnegan

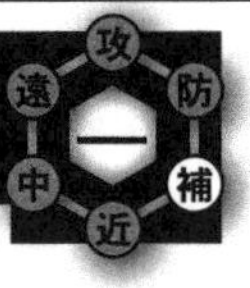

Caster: Nagato

SPREADING LIKE RIPPLES ON WATER— THE SECRET ORIGIN OF NINJUTSU.

...THE RINNE-GAN...!!

The supreme eye that appears in chaotic times–will it bring creation or destruction?

The ocular jutsu said to have been possessed by the founder of shinobi, the Sage of the Six Paths. Rinnegan, characterized most noticeably by the ripple pattern that spreads in the eye, is considered the most sublime of the three great ocular jutsu, which includes Sharingan and Byakugan. The possessor of this eye, said to be the creator of all ninjutsu, mastered every one of the Five Great Changes in Nature. He is either a god of creation who subjugates the world, or a god of destruction who reduces everything to nothing.

⬇ The Six Paths of Pain, which shares the vision, boasts a coordination that leaves nothing unguarded.

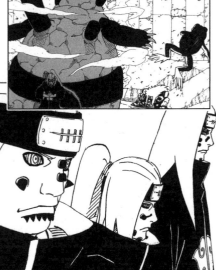

⬅⬆ In addition to a shared vision, Pain, whose eyes have opened to Rinnegan, possesses a common weapon that disrupts chakra and an immortal body. But it remains a mystery whether these powers are from Rinnegan.

NARUTO INDEX

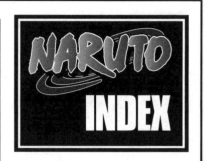

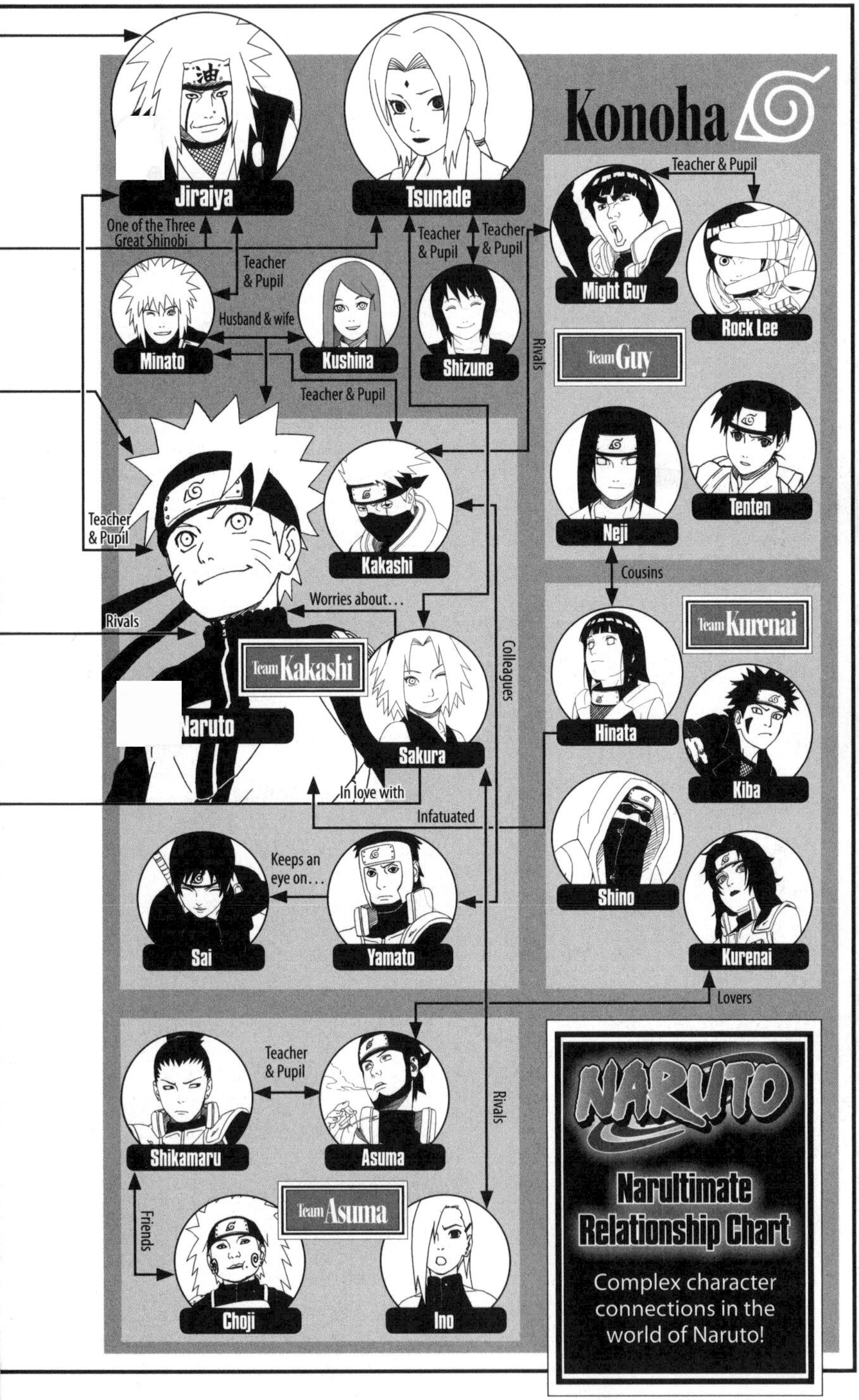
Konoha
Jiraiya
Tsunade
One of the Three Great Shinobi
Teacher & Pupil
Teacher & Pupil
Teacher & Pupil
Minato
Husband & wife
Kushina
Shizune
Teacher & Pupil
Rivals
Teacher & Pupil
Might Guy
Rock Lee
Team Guy
Neji
Tenten
Cousins
Team Kurenai
Hinata
Kiba
Shino
Kurenai
Teacher & Pupil
Kakashi
Worries about…
Rivals
Team Kakashi
Colleagues
Naruto
Sakura
In love with
Infatuated
Keeps an eye on…
Sai
Yamato
Lovers
Teacher & Pupil
Shikamaru
Asuma
Rivals
Friends
Team Asuma
Choji
Ino
NARUTO
Narultimate Relationship Chart
Complex character connections in the world of Naruto!

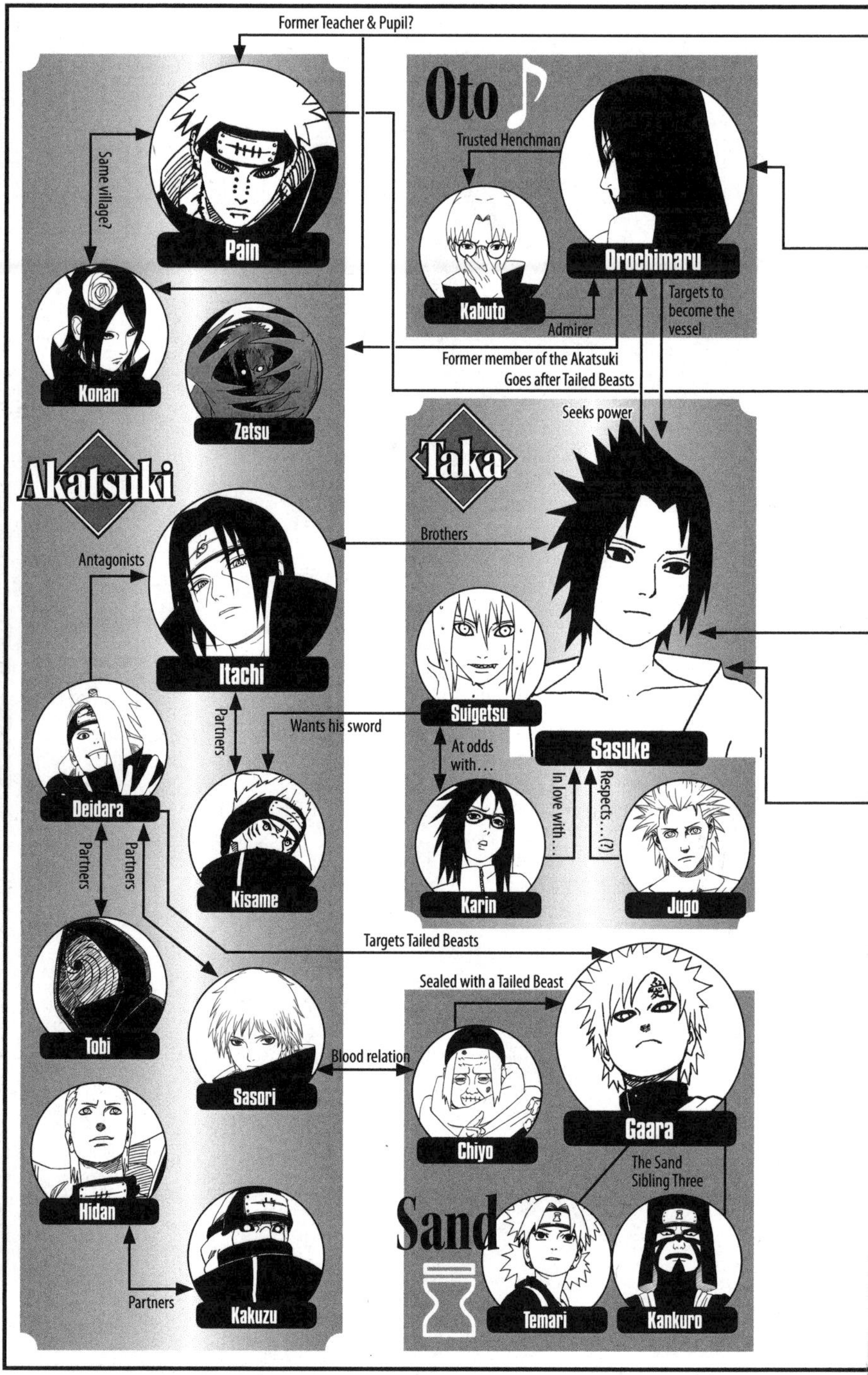
Former Teacher & Pupil?
Oto
Trusted Henchman
Same village?
Pain
Kabuto
Orochimaru
Admirer
Targets to become the vessel
Konan
Zetsu
Former member of the Akatsuki
Goes after Tailed Beasts
Seeks power
Akatsuki
Taka
Brothers
Antagonists
Itachi
Suigetsu
Partners
Wants his sword
Sasuke
At odds with...
In love with...
Respects...(?)
Deidara
Kisame
Karin
Jugo
Partners
Partners
Targets Tailed Beasts
Sealed with a Tailed Beast
Tobi
Blood relation
Sasori
Chiyo
Gaara
The Sand Sibling Three
Hidan
Sand
Partners
Kakuzu
Temari
Kankuro

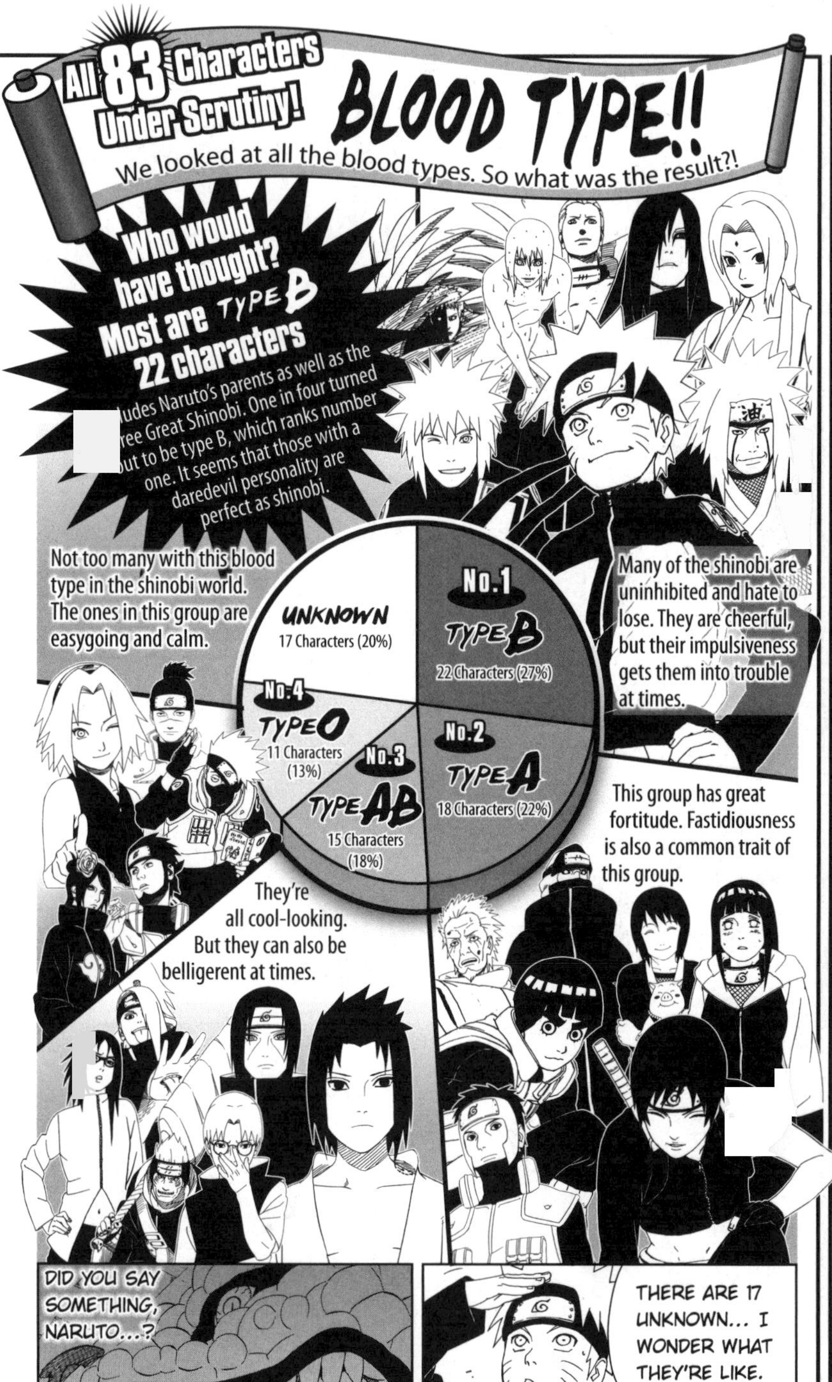
All 83 Characters Under Scrutiny!
BLOOD TYPE!!
We looked at all the blood types. So what was the result?!
Who would have thought? Most are TYPE B 22 characters
ludes Naruto's parents as well as the
ree Great Shinobi. One in four turned
out to be type B, which ranks number
one. It seems that those with a
daredevil personality are
perfect as shinobi.
No.1 TYPE B 22 Characters (27%)
No.2 TYPE A 18 Characters (22%)
No.3 TYPE AB 15 Characters (18%)
No.4 TYPE O 11 Characters (13%)
UNKNOWN 17 Characters (20%)
Many of the shinobi are uninhibited and hate to lose. They are cheerful, but their impulsiveness gets them into trouble at times.
This group has great fortitude. Fastidiousness is also a common trait of this group.
They're all cool-looking. But they can also be belligerent at times.
Not too many with this blood type in the shinobi world. The ones in this group are easygoing and calm.
THERE ARE 17 UNKNOWN... I WONDER WHAT THEY'RE LIKE.
DID YOU SAY SOMETHING, NARUTO...?

Reader Survey Results

Hidden Jutsu!
Postcard-style!!

To the left, you'll see the six categories of the Survey.

Cha!!

Who you'd want as your sibling.

King of frontispieces

Who you'd want as your teacher.

Favorite battles

Favorite lines

Favorite scenes

The voices of the fans have been transformed into chakra, filling up each one of the six categories!

Please keep up your support, everyone!

The Top Twenty!
Favorite Scenes
The Ultimate!
That tugged at your heart

What touches us most about the life of a shinobi?

1st	From No.	
161 votes	306	**Naruto and Sasuke Reunite**

Their first meeting since the Final Valley. No words really can do this moment justice. It is the first time a grown-up Sasuke appears, and readers were as anxious about it as Naruto was.

Reader Comments

It's a memorable scene where passion collides with composure. (Y.H., Kagawa Prefecture)

I had been waiting for this moment for so long, my heart was pounding. (N.T., Chiba Prefecture)

2nd — 132 votes

From No. 279 Gaara's Resurrection

Reader Comments

It was a validation of his existence, that he was needed!! (T.O., Tokyo)

...GAARA...

Freed at last from the pain of loneliness, Gaara comes back to life to see his fellow members of Suna at his side in a truly heartwarming moment.

3rd — 122 votes

From No. 393 Itachi's Final Moments

Even as he breathed his last, Itachi was the big brother, tapping Sasuke's forehead like he used to long ago. With that tap, he was, in fact, passing on the ocular ninjutsu, Amaterasu, to Sasuke in order to protect him.

Reader Comments

I thought this was the moment he would lose his eye... Then tap! Right on the forehead. What a tearjerker. (K.Y., Yamanashi Prefecture)

Published in color.

TOK

4th — 87 votes

From No. 281 A Handshake with Gaara

Reader Comments

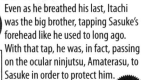

This is the bond that Gaara wants to cherish. (H.K., Mie Prefecture)

Heartfelt gratitude from the one who changed him. One can't help but smile at Gaara's words that he will guide Naruto with his sand.

5th — 63 votes

From No. 383 Sasuke vs. Itachi Ignites

Reader Comments

In light of what is yet to come, this was a crucial scene. (H.H., Tokyo)

...LET'S GET TO IT.

Sasuke confronts the brother he despises. Itachi takes pride in his little brother's growth. Emotions and blade clash at the Uchiha hideout. The long-awaited battle begins.

6th — 56 votes

From No. 362 The Ultimate Work of Art

Driven into a corner, Deidara detonates himself. This was not only to surpass the Uchiha as a shinobi, but an artist's final work.

Reader Comments

His ultimate work of art is also the personification of death. At that moment, I spontaneously began to cry. (M.K., Osaka)

...IS AN EXPLOSION!!!

7th — 49 votes

From No. 310 Friends

Emotions begin to stir within Sai and he learns the true meaning of the word *friend*. And later, beyond the window, is a piece of work with the four of them. What kind of picture will it make?

Reader Comments

At this instant, Team 7 becomes a real team of true comrades. It doesn't get better than this. (M.N., Mie Prefecture)

仲間

Published in color.

10th
38 votes

🐾 From No. **339**

Strong Enough

He is the only one who can surpass the Fourth Hokage... And so it is with high hopes that Kakashi continues to watch over Naruto. This protégé with his amazing progress has the strength to carry on the will of his beloved Fourth Hokage...

9th
40 votes

The Painful Cry

🐾 From No. **278**

Published in color.

Gaara dies after One Tail is taken out of him. As a jinchûriki himself and as a friend, Naruto is consumed with rage at this cruel, tragic loss. And he lets out a heart-wrenching cry.

8th
45 votes

Shikamaru's Tears

🐾 From No. **328**

Shikamaru must face the sudden reality that his mentor has died in battle. He is overcome with sadness and gives way to tears. The tearstains on his cheeks make his stout-hearted words even more poignant.

Here are numbers 11 through 20!!

20th	19th	18th	17th	16th	15th	14th	13th	12th	11th
12 votes	15 votes	19 votes	20 votes	24 votes	29 votes	30 votes	32 votes	35 votes	37 votes
From No. 351	From No. 339	From No. 304	From No. 338	From No. 245	From No. 391	From No. 382	From No. 347	From No. 275	From No. 383
Sasuke's Intent to Kill	Wind Style! Rasen-Shuriken! Activated	Sai's Smile	From Asuma to Shikamaru: The Passing of the Will of Fire	Naruto's Homecoming	Kirin Is Activated	Jiraiya's Real Choice	Sasuke's Thought	Sasori's Death	Jiraiya's Death

Published in color.

Published in color.

HO HO... JUST BARELY GLORIOUS, BUT GLORIOUS INDEED....

Thanks to all 1,142 of you for voting!!

I BEQUEATH MY WILL OF FIRE... TO YOU.

SURVEY RESULTS

Ratio of male to female: **3:7**
Average age: **18.8** years old
Total votes cast: **1,142**

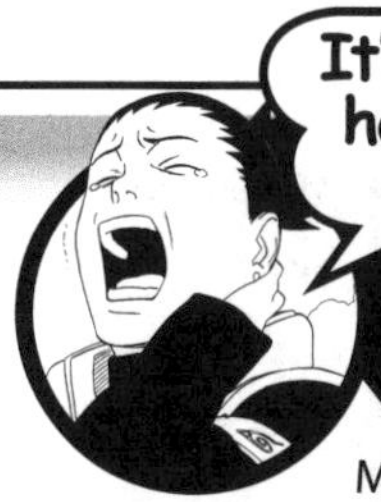
It's tiresome, so how about just 15...?

Gives you goose bumps!

Favorite Lines
That moved you to tears

Making your point with words is the mark of a good shinobi.

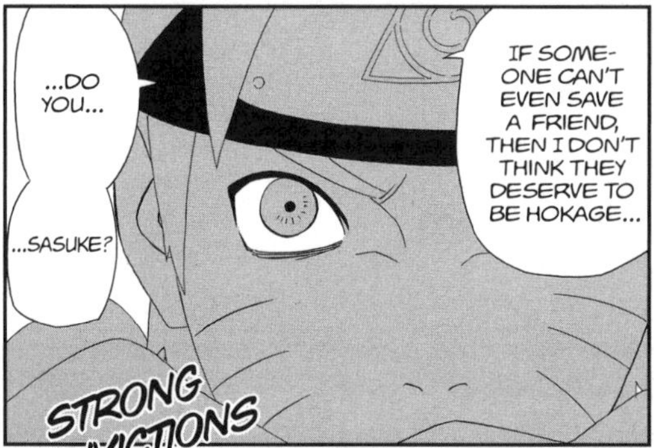
IF SOMEONE CAN'T EVEN SAVE A FRIEND, THEN I DON'T THINK THEY DESERVE TO BE HOKAGE...
...DO YOU...
...SASUKE?

1st — Naruto

131 votes · From No. 307

Hokage is simply the name of the leader of the village. Still, even though shinobi may exist in the dark, he will bring a comrade back into the light. That is the path Naruto will walk to become the Hokage.

STRONG CONVICTIONS AND FRIENDSHIP

Reader Comments
I can feel Naruto's strength and it warms my heart. (A.S., Saitama Prefecture) I'm so inspired by Naruto's steadfastness and honesty. (M.N., Saitama Prefecture)

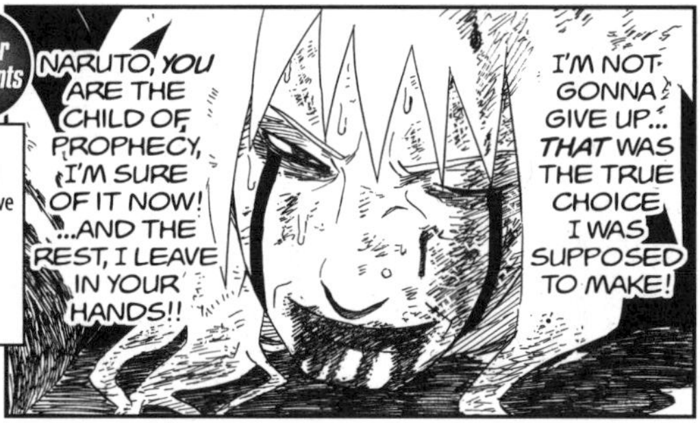
I'M NOT GONNA GIVE UP... *THAT* WAS THE TRUE CHOICE I WAS SUPPOSED TO MAKE!
NARUTO, *YOU* ARE THE CHILD OF PROPHECY, I'M SURE OF IT NOW! ...AND THE REST, I LEAVE IN YOUR HANDS!!

Reader Comments
I'm so touched by his love for his pupil. (T.N., Tokyo)

2nd — Jiraiya

97 votes · From No. 382

With certain death just moments away, he discovers the truth. He sends intel to Konoha, and leaves his hopes for Naruto. . . ending his life with guts and gallantry.

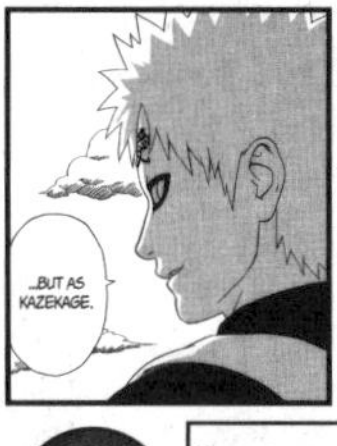
...BUT AS KAZEKAGE.

3rd — Gaara

90 votes · From No. 249

He will love and protect the village. Gaara has grown up and his words overflow with feeling.

Reader Comments
Gaara is so refreshing, and I love that about him. (A.S., Miyazaki Prefecture)

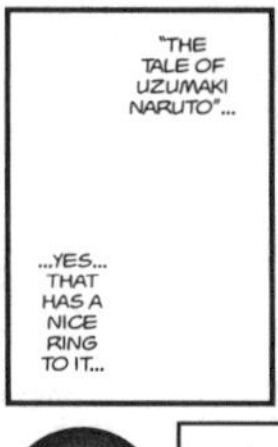
"THE TALE OF UZUMAKI NARUTO"...
...YES... THAT HAS A NICE RING TO IT...

4th — Jiraiya

75 votes · From No. 383

His beloved pupil is the hero of the sequel, although Naruto has yet to see it. And thus, *The Tale of Jiraiya the Gallant* comes to a brilliant close.

Reader Comments
What a super-splendid ending. (M.M., Miyazaki Prefecture)

5th Kakashi

63 votes

From No. 321

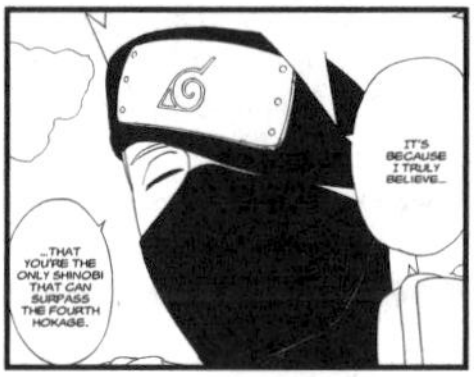
IT'S BECAUSE I TRULY BELIEVE...
...THAT YOU'RE THE ONLY SHINOBI THAT CAN SURPASS THE FOURTH HOKAGE.

His heartfelt words give Naruto a push.

6th Naruto

61 votes

From No. 333

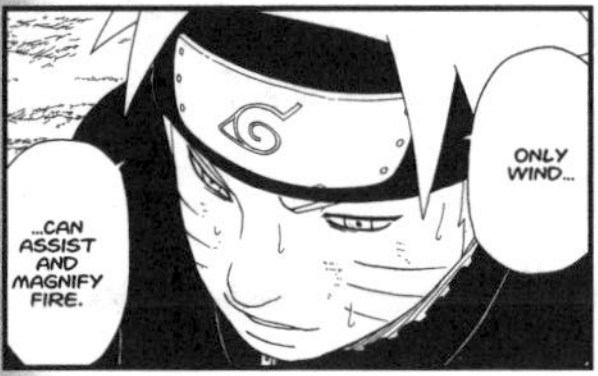
ONLY WIND...
...CAN ASSIST AND MAGNIFY FIRE.

He can save Sasuke. The concept of change in chakra nature gives Naruto hope.

7th Deidara

57 votes

From No. 362

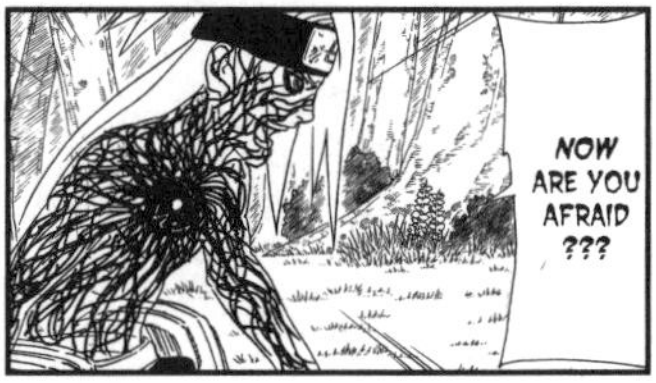
NOW ARE YOU AFRAID ???

The power of the Uchiha is overwhelming and the only way to defeat them is by self-detonation. His baleful last stand reverberates deep into the forest.

8th Naruto

47 votes

From No. 303

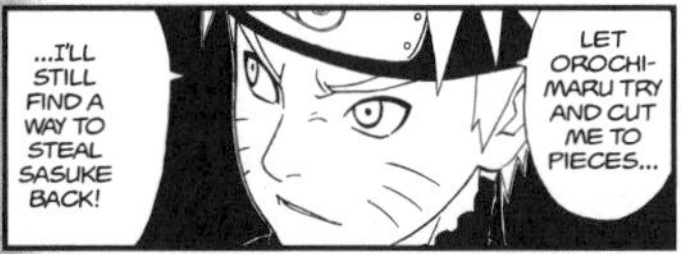
LET OROCHI-MARU TRY AND CUT ME TO PIECES...
...I'LL STILL FIND A WAY TO STEAL SASUKE BACK!

He'd gladly give his life to save a friend. Then or now, Naruto's will is always strong.

9th Naruto

40 votes

From No. 278

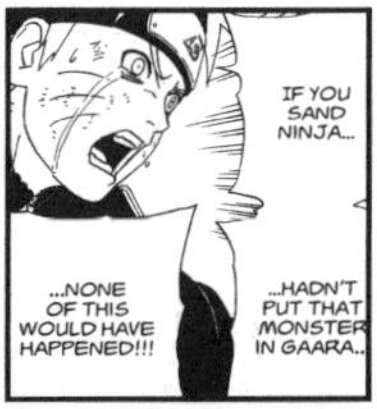
IF YOU SAND NINJA...
...HADN'T PUT THAT MONSTER IN GAARA...
...NONE OF THIS WOULD HAVE HAPPENED!!!

An unforgivable practice... His voice shaking with emotion, he rails against the injustice done to Gaara! This wrong must never, ever be repeated.

10th Sai

38 votes

From No. 304

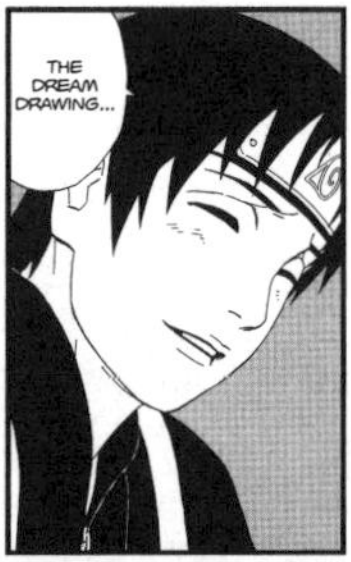
THE DREAM DRAWING...

Naruto pierces his shell and Sai begins to open up his heart. These feelings and expressions which he had wanted to forget... They're not pretense. They're real.

See number 11 through 15 below!

The top THREE favorite line makers!!

We totaled the votes from the postcards we received!

1) Naruto
2) Jiraiya
3) Kakashi and Sakura

.... 8) Shikamaru

SURVEY RESULTS

Ratio of male to female: **4:6**
Average age: **17.6** years old
Total votes cast: **1,055**

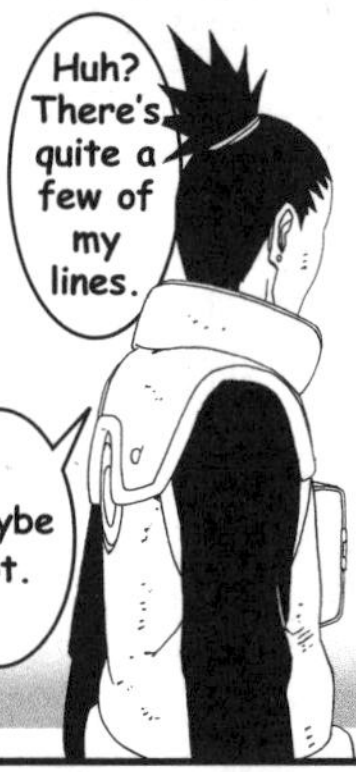
Huh? There's quite a few of my lines.
Maybe not.

Shikamaru From No. 342
"When that baby arrives... It'll be my turn as guardian and master. I guess I've got some real growing up to do."

Madara From No. 397
"It was to protect you."

Itachi From No. 402
"Sorry...Sasuke... This is it."

Shikamaru From No. 328
"I still feel like his smoke's...stinging my eyes..."

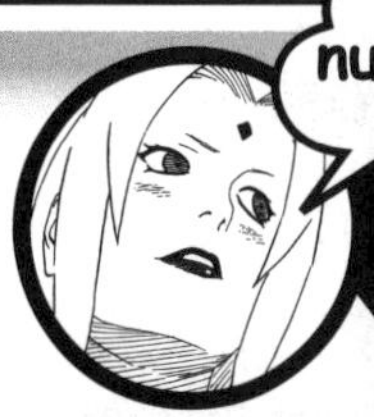

The total number of votes was 1,004.

Heart Pounding Action

Favorite Battles

That had you screaming

The Ultimate Ninja Battles!

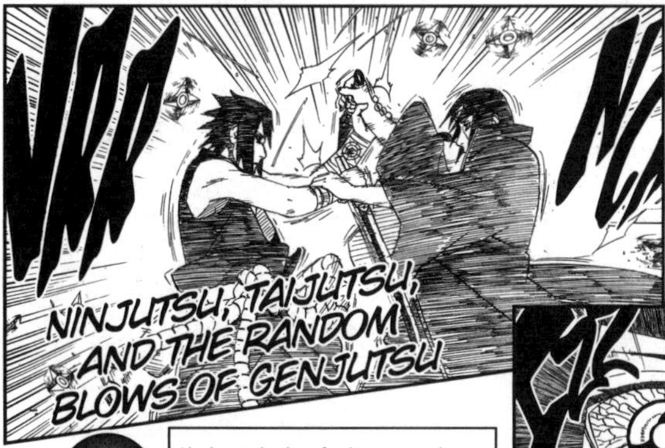
NINJUTSU, TAIJUTSU, AND THE RANDOM BLOWS OF GENJUTSU

1st Sasuke vs. Itachi

361 votes

Finally, the brothers face each other. Putting their lives on the line, they release one brilliant jutsu after another. It is indeed the most exciting battle the shinobi world has ever scene.

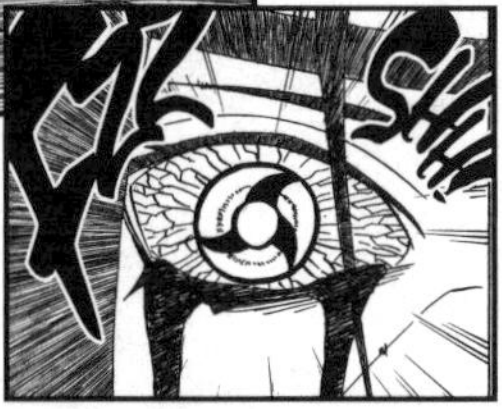

Reader Comments

I had waited so long for this moment, but then it was so nerve-wracking, and sad, scary. (M.H., Osaka)

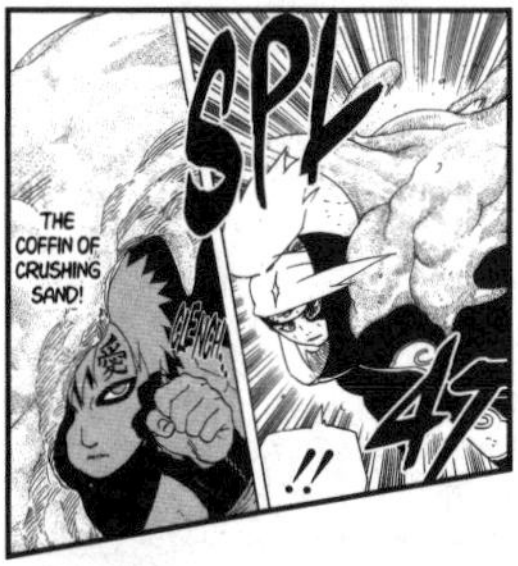
THE COFFIN OF CRUSHING SAND!
!!

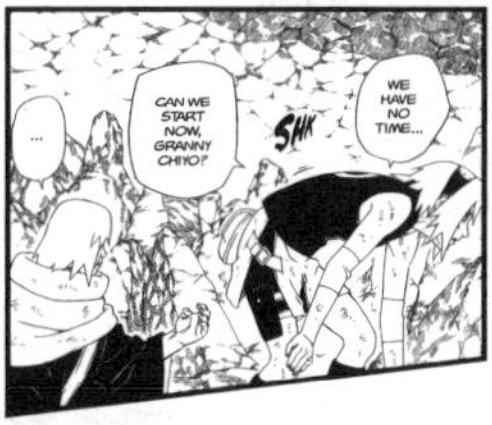
WE HAVE NO TIME...
CAN WE START NOW, GRANNY CHIYO?
...
SHK

2nd Sasuke vs. Deidara

130 votes

Two very different ninja use contrasting styles in a heated battle: long-distance versus close-range. Sasuke shines, showing off the power of his Sharingan.

Reader Comments

I witnessed Deidara's tenacity. (K.N., Yamaguchi Prefecture)

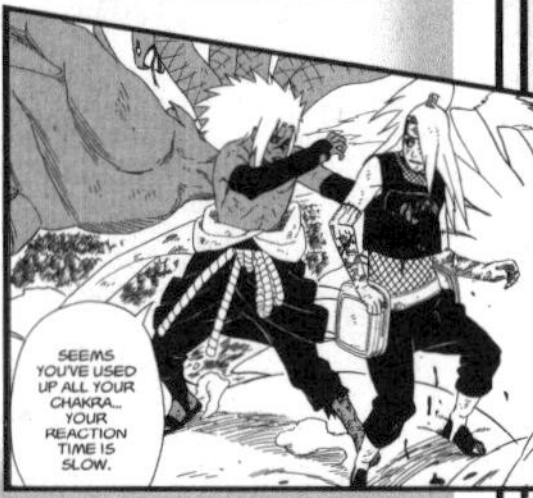
SEEMS YOU'VE USED UP ALL YOUR CHAKRA... YOUR REACTION TIME IS SLOW.

3rd Sakura & Chiyo vs. Sasori

107 votes

Aided by Granny Chiyo, Sakura's prowess shows when she holds her own against the rogue puppet master.

Reader Comments

I am amazed at Sakura's growth. (Y.Y., Osaka)

4th Gaara vs. Deidara

94 votes

Sand versus clay in aerial combat. Although he has a slight advantage in the beginning, Gaara, who must protect his village single-handedly, suffers a defeat.

Reader Comments

I was deeply moved by Kazekage Gaara. (A.T., Ibaragi Prefecture)

7th 46 votes Naruto vs. Kakuzu

Surpass the Fourth Hokage! Here is the milestone battle in which Naruto debuts his new jutsu, Wind Style! Rasen-Shuriken.

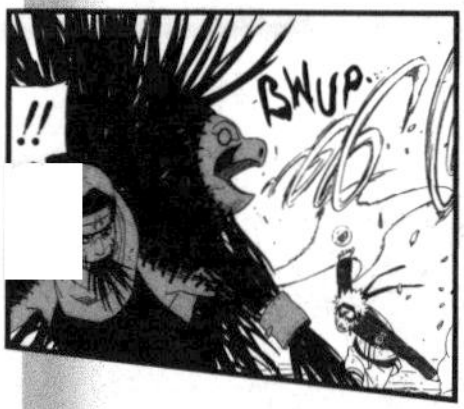
!!
BWUP

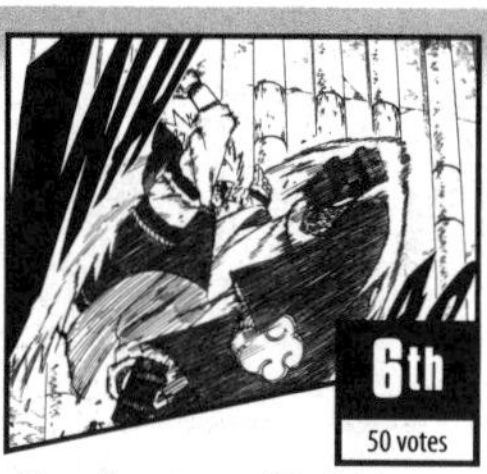

6th 50 votes Jiraiya vs. Pain

The leader of the Akatsuki who has concealed himself in the Village of Amegakure . . . It turns out to be his former student. Jiraiya fights his last battle against the one who possesses the Rinnegan Eye.

5th 56 votes Shikamaru vs. Hidan

A strong and capable challenger confronts Hidan whose body is invulnerable. It is Shikamaru, out to avenge his master. His precision planning to take out his foe is nothing short of amazing.

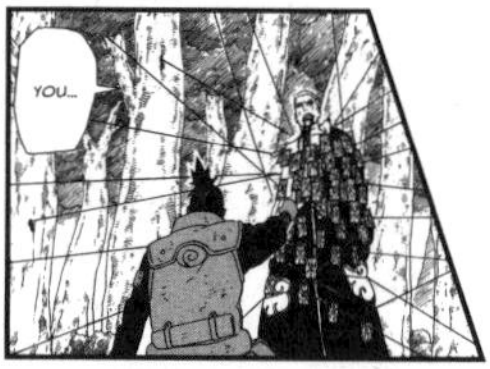
YOU...

10th 43 votes Hashirama vs. Madara

It is Wood Style ninjutsu versus the Mangekyo Sharingan in a crucial battle fought before the founding of Konohagakure. It left long-lasting scars, festering ill will that continues to this day.

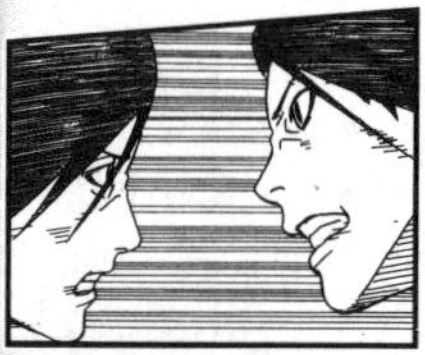

9th 44 votes Sasuke vs. Orochimaru

The day of parting finally comes. The Transference Technique is to be performed, but Sasuke hijacks the occasion.

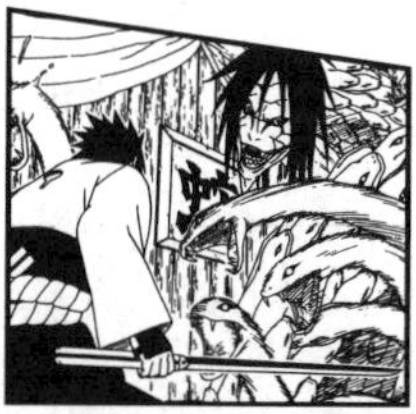

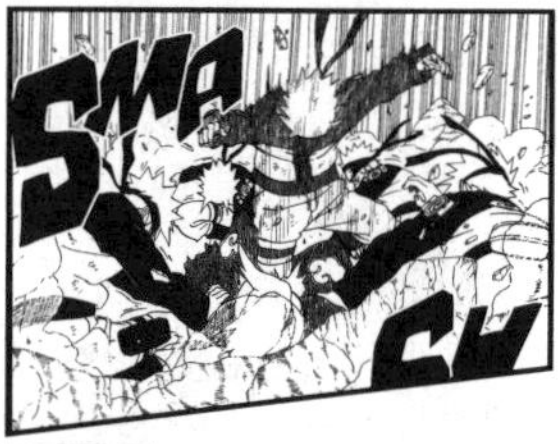

8th 45 votes Naruto & Kakashi vs. Deidara

Kakashi displays the power of his ocular jutsu on this mission to rescue Gaara. Naruto's lethal fist delighted many fans too.

Super maniac?! Key battles which got one vote!!

⬇ They fight like cats and dogs. But usually Karin drops Suigetsu first.

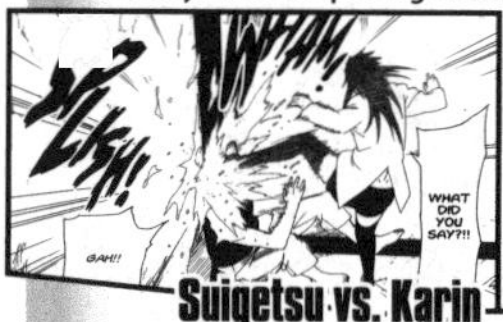
WHAT DID YOU SAY?!!
GAH!!
Suigetsu vs. Karin

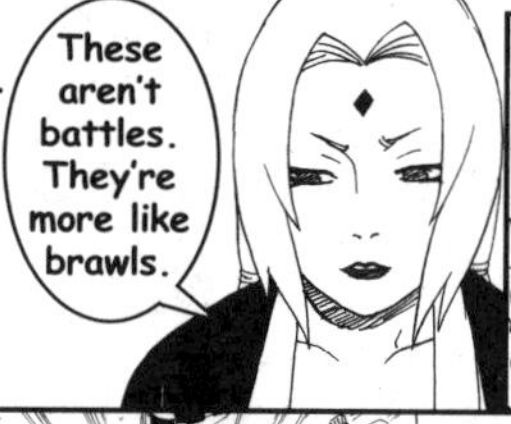
These aren't battles. They're more like brawls.

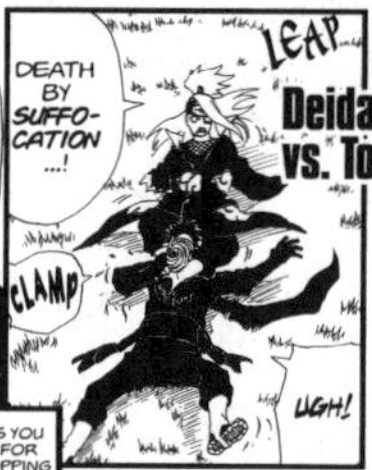
LEAP
DEATH BY SUFFOCATION ...!
Deidara vs. Tobi
CLAMP
UGH!

⬆ In a rage, Deidara chokes the overly talkative Tobi.

SURVEY RESULTS

Ratio of male to female: **3:7**
Average age: **17.2** years old
Total votes cast: **1,004**

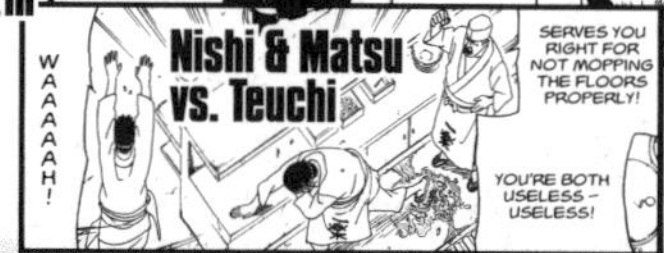
SERVES YOU RIGHT FOR NOT MOPPING THE FLOORS PROPERLY!
Nishi & Matsu vs. Teuchi
WAAAAAAH!
YOU'RE BOTH USELESS - USELESS!

⬆ Nishi faints?! It's not due to a Raiton by Teuchi . . . he's struck by lightning.

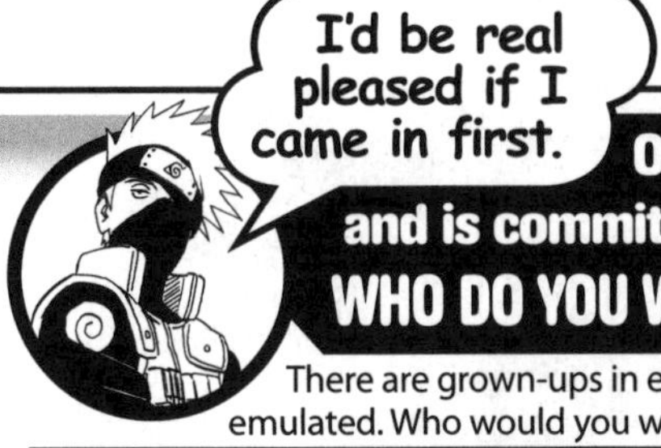
I'd be real pleased if I came in first.

One who excels in ninjutsu and is committed to the truth of Nindo. WHO DO YOU WANT AS YOUR TEACHER?

There are grown-ups in every generation who are admired and emulated. Who would you want as your guiding light and teacher?

1st — 268 votes — Kakashi

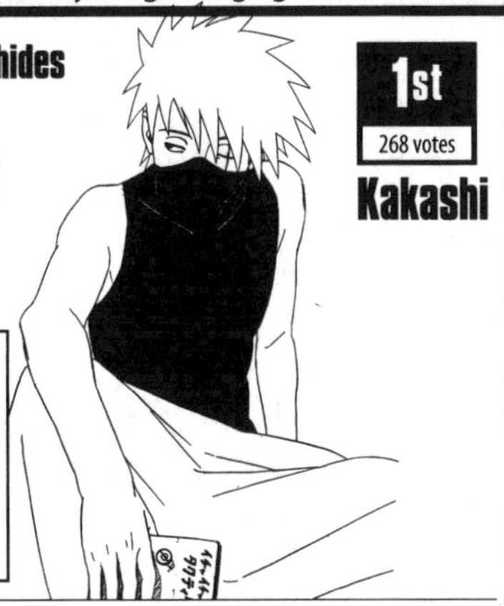

His easygoing personality hides his true inner strength.

He feigns ignorance, but he knows exactly what is going on and what he must do as a shinobi.

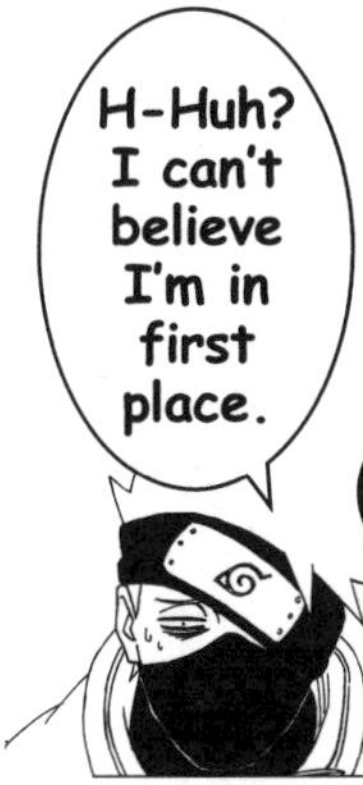
H-Huh? I can't believe I'm in first place.

Reader Comments

He would teach us to cherish our friends. (Y.M., Nara Prefecture) If you don't understand something, he seems the type who would work it out with you. (M.I., Shizuoka Prefecture)

2nd — 104 votes — Itachi

He seems to be very strict. But because he does it out of love, you would probably do your utmost for this taskmaster.

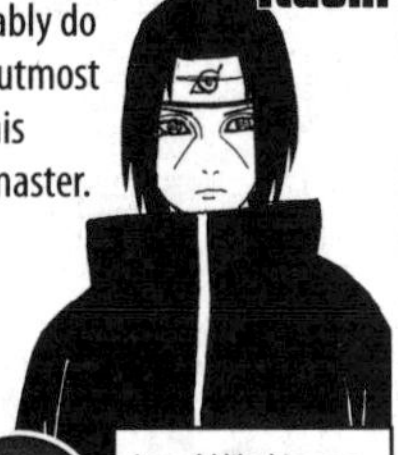

Reader Comments

I would like him as a teacher because he seems very diligent.

3rd — 100 votes — Jiraiya

Ninjutsu, academics, and of course, the perverted.
He is a teacher of life who knows it all.

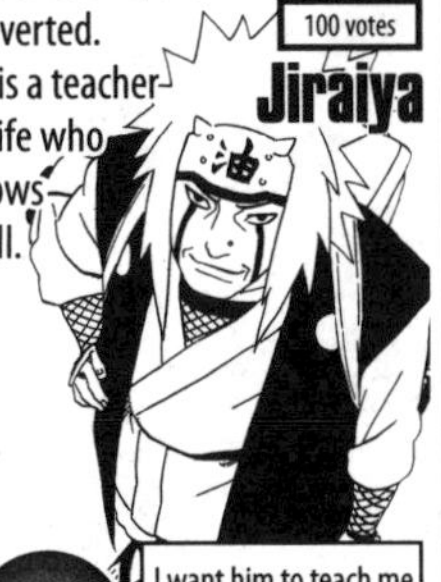

Reader Comments

I want him to teach me Summoning. (M.U., Aichi Prefecture)

4th — 84 votes — Hokage (The Fourth, Minato)

Minato has the most encouraging smile. You're sure to learn amazing ninjutsu, taijutsu and perseverance.

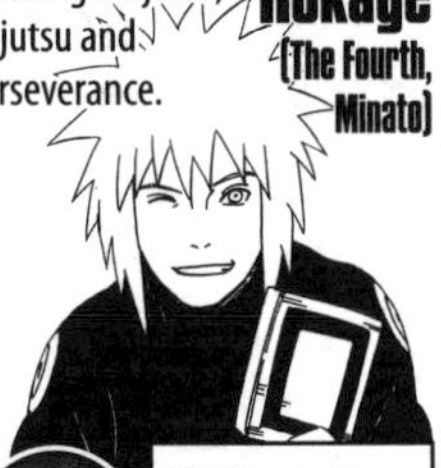

Reader Comments

I think he would overlook your failings. (A.T., Tokyo)

5th — 66 votes — Might Guy

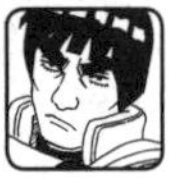

6th — 54 votes — Hokage (The Fifth, Tsunade)

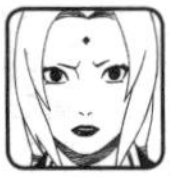

7th — 44 votes — Yamato

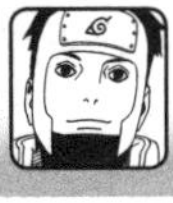

8th — 40 votes — Iruka

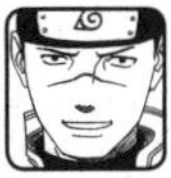

9th — 38 votes — Asuma

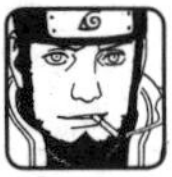

10th — 32 votes — Deidara

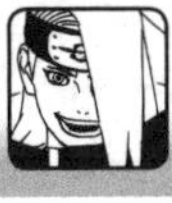

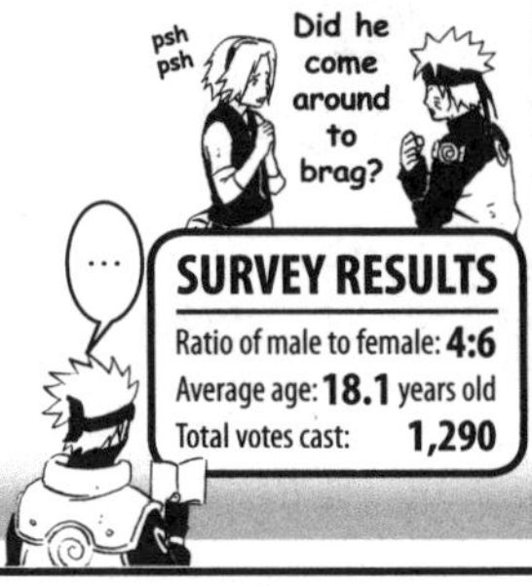
Did he come around to brag?
psh psh
...

SURVEY RESULTS

Ratio of male to female: **4:6**
Average age: **18.1** years old
Total votes cast: **1,290**

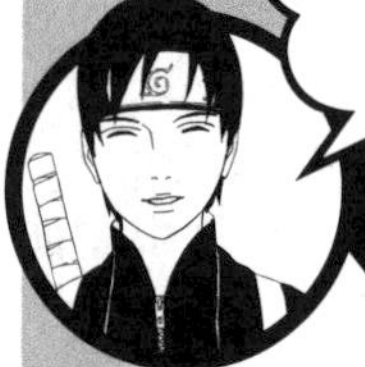
I wonder if these are called...*cool*?

Masterpieces! The Best Ten Top Frontispieces

Enduring art that will last forever in the museum of your imagination. Which had the most impact?

1st — 192 votes — From No. 384 — Two Paths...

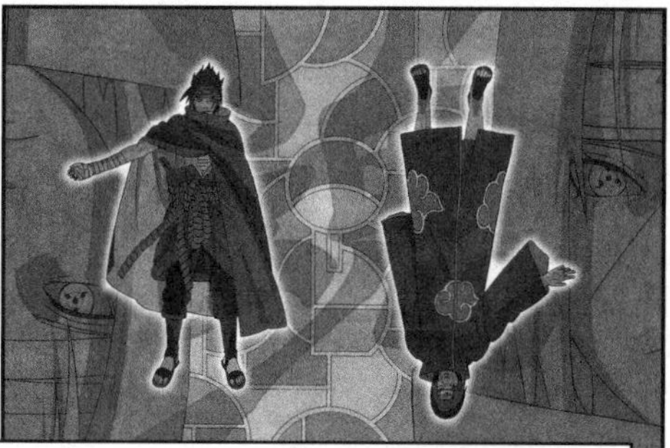

A predestined piece mixing love and hate!!

The face, the body, and the Uchiha crest at the center. It is a work of contrasts, illustrating how they keep passing each other by. Beautiful and heartbreaking.

Reader Comments: It conveys the quiet before the storm so perfectly. (S.M. Kochi Prefecture) It left an impression on me because the drawing matched the title so well. (R.T., Fukuoka Prefecture)

3rd — 128 votes — From No. 388 — Variance of Strength...!!

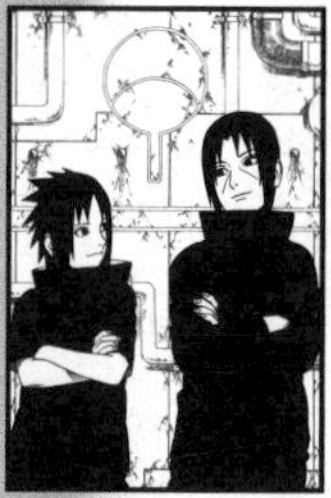

The bond of brotherhood will never be broken. If only one could return to those happy days…

Reader Comments: The warmth of their gazes breaks my heart. (T.T., Kyoto)

2nd — 144 votes — From No. 317 — Nightmares!

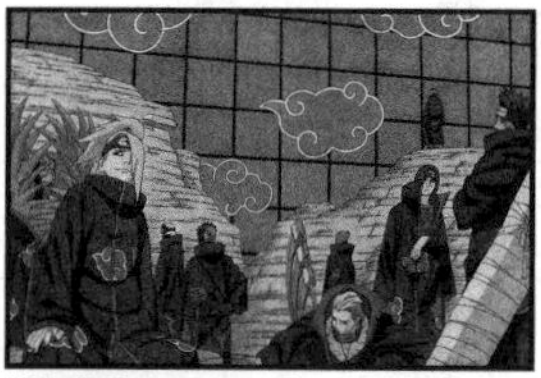

It's one of the few with every member of the Akatsuki. It has a visual depth which is interesting.

Reader Comments: It's so eerie, I love it. (S.O., Shimane Prefecture)

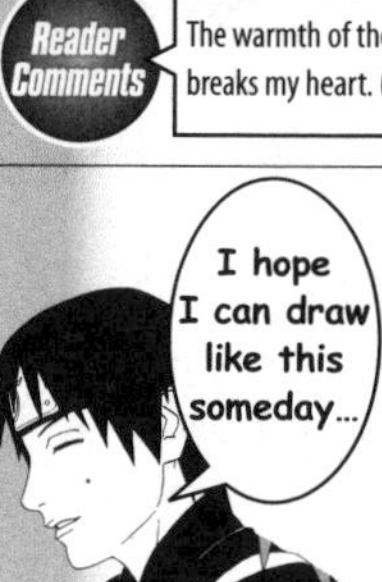
I hope I can draw like this someday...

Rank	Votes	From No.	Title
6th	51 votes	357	Deidara vs. Sasuke
7th	50 votes	294	The Fourth Tail...!!
8th	45 votes	332	Shikamaru's Fight!!
9th	36 votes	337	Shikamaru's Genius!!
10th	36 votes	364	The Target...!!

4th — 64 votes — From No. 341 — Practice Makes Perfect...!!

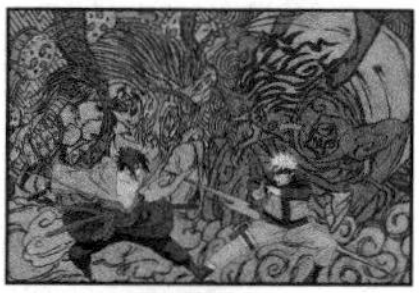

5th — 52 votes — From No. 377 — Honored Sage Mode!!

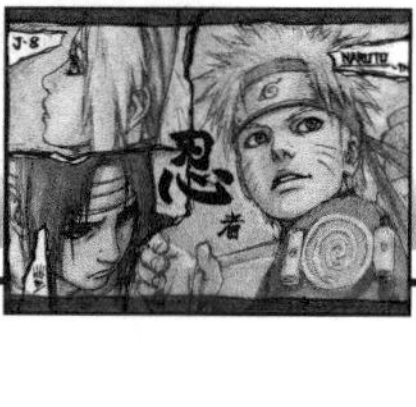

SURVEY RESULTS

Ratio of male to female: **3:7**
Average age: **18.2** years old
Total votes cast: **1,320**

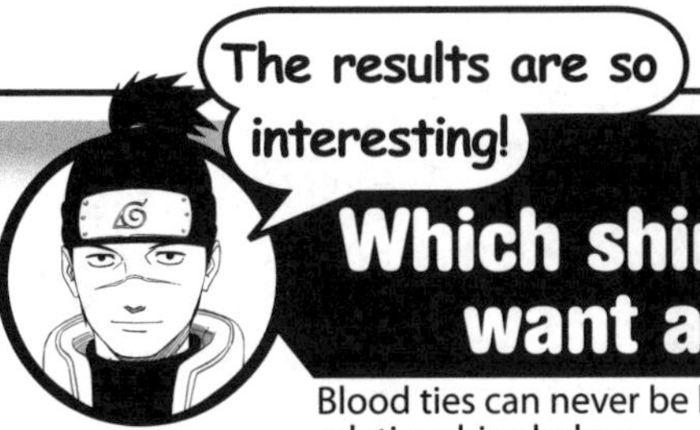
The results are so interesting!

Your Lifelong Bond!

Which shinobi would you want as your sibling?

Blood ties can never be broken. Check out the five relationships below.

Little Brother Category

He would follow you wherever you go. A cute little brother who is a bit of a rascal.

1st Naruto
92 votes

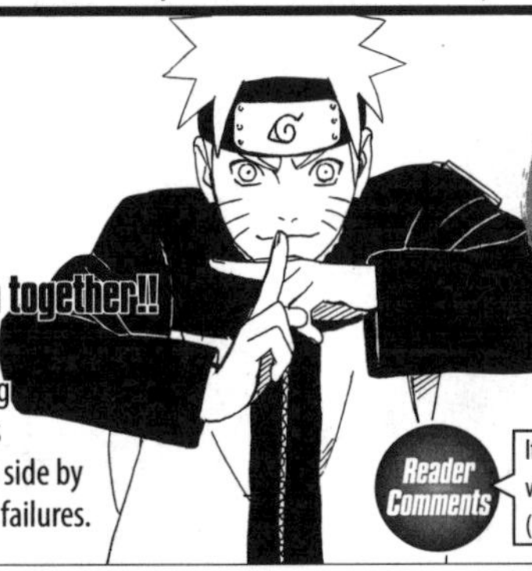

Happy moments,
Sad moments,
We can share them together!!

It would be a fun relationship with nothing hidden between us. Let's share lots of experiences side by side, both successes and failures.

Reader Comments If I'm feeling depressed, I think he would come and try to cheer me up. (K.N., Kyoto Prefecture)

2nd Sasuke
76 votes

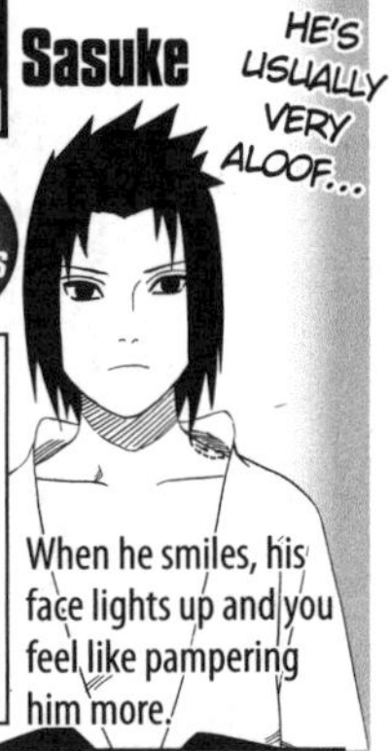
HE'S USUALLY VERY ALOOF...

Reader Comments He'd be a kid brother I could brag about. (M.K., Kanagawa Prefecture)

When he smiles, his face lights up and you feel like pampering him more.

3rd Deidara
48 votes

Little brothers are just right when they are a tad annoying?!

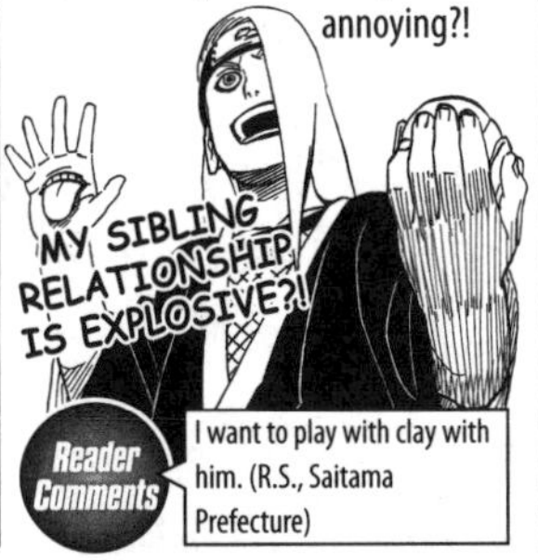
MY SIBLING RELATIONSHIP IS EXPLOSIVE?!

Reader Comments I want to play with clay with him. (R.S., Saitama Prefecture)

4th Gaara
26 votes

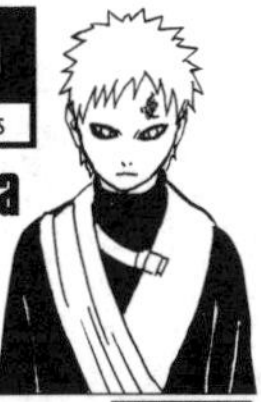

5th Sai
20 votes

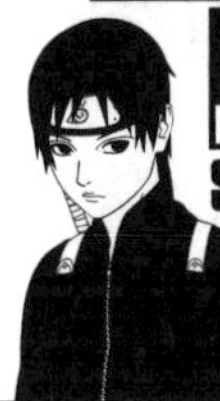

Big Sister Category

You can never catch up to her?! Someone who is closer too you than a friend, someone you can depend on.

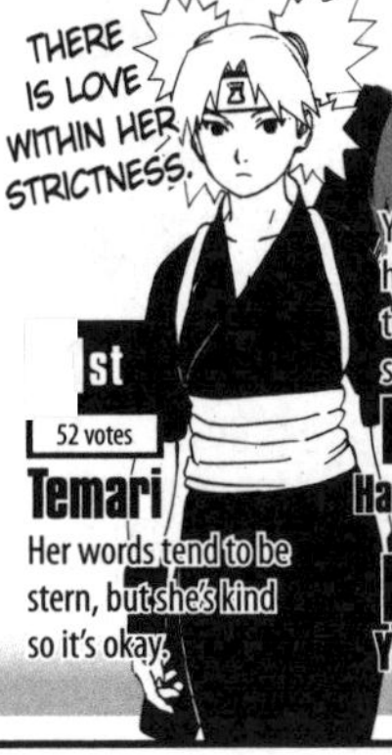
THERE IS LOVE WITHIN HER STRICTNESS.

1st Temari
52 votes

Her words tend to be stern, but she's kind so it's okay.

2nd Haruno Sakura 28 votes

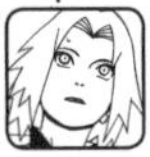

3rd Yamanaka Ino 21 votes

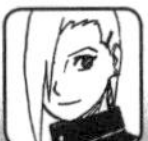

Little Sister Category

The way they try so hard to be grown-up makes them cute.

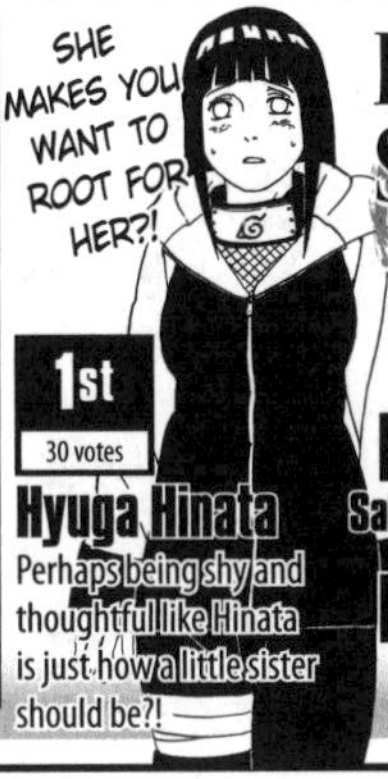
SHE MAKES YOU WANT TO ROOT FOR HER?!

1st Hyuga Hinata
30 votes

Perhaps being shy and thoughtful like Hinata is just how a little sister should be?!

2nd Sakura Haruno 16 votes

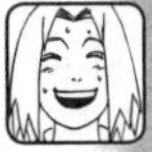

3rd Tenten 7 votes

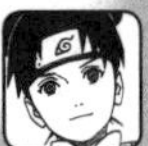

Big Brother Category

Someone you want to emulate all the time. Someone cool.

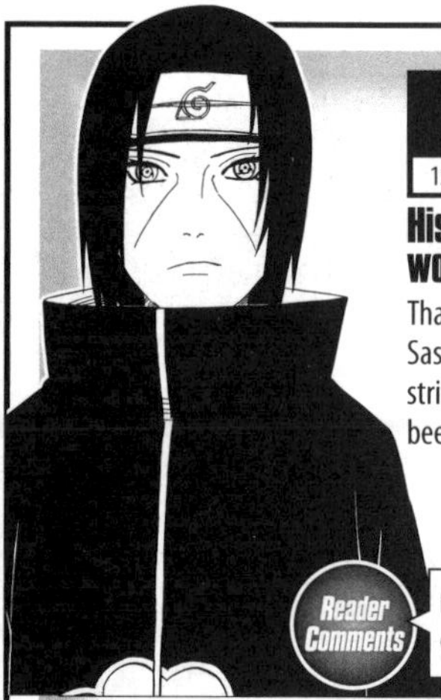

1st Itachi
158 votes

His love is strong and he would protect you!!

That he gave his life out of love for Sasuke is inspiring. If not for the strife within his clan, he would have been a happy big brother.

Reader Comments
He is a big brother you'd be proud of in every way. (K.Y., Kanagawa Prefecture)

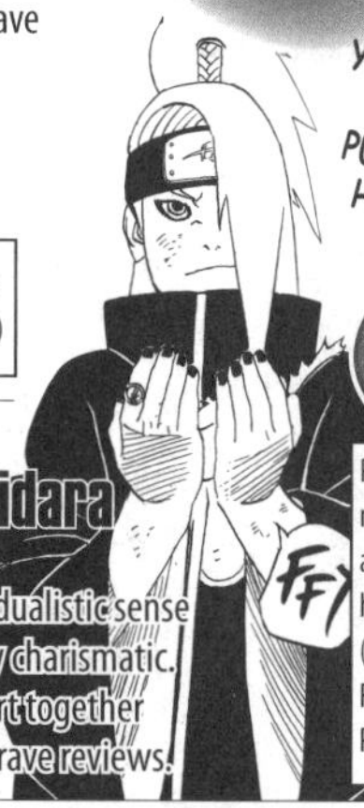
YOU WANT ME TO PULL YOU HARD?!
FF!

2nd Deidara
116 votes

He has an individualistic sense of art and is very charismatic. You can create art together that will garner rave reviews.

Reader Comments
Please help me with my art homework. (R.H., Fukuoka Prefecture)

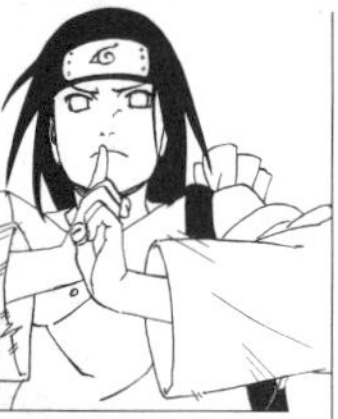

4th Neji
78 votes

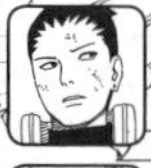

6th 31 votes Shikamaru

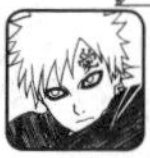

7th 30 votes Gaara

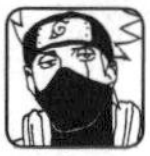

8th 29 votes Kakashi

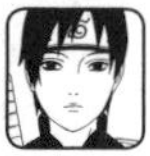

9th 24 votes Sai

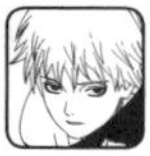

10th 16 votes Sasori

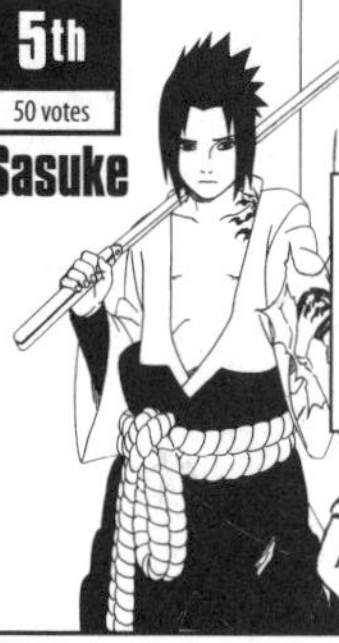

5th Sasuke
50 votes

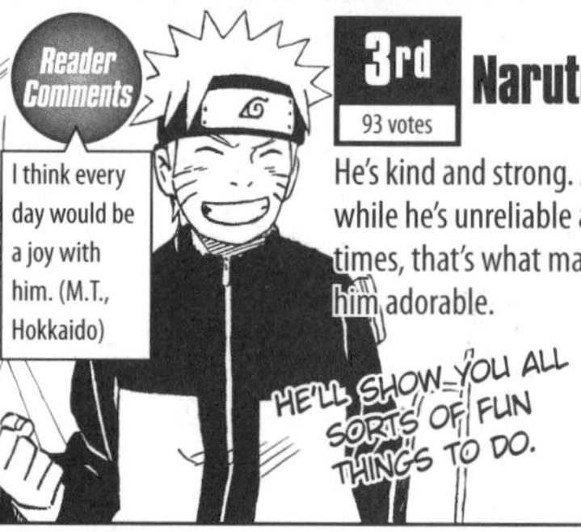
HE'LL SHOW YOU ALL SORTS OF FUN THINGS TO DO.

3rd Naruto
93 votes

He's kind and strong. And while he's unreliable at times, that's what makes him adorable.

Reader Comments
I think every day would be a joy with him. (M.T., Hokkaido)

Others

We had votes in other categories too. We present the top three here.

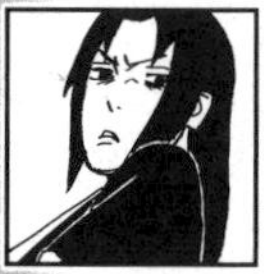

Mother Mikoto

She was chosen the best mother for her love and skill in raising Sasuke and Itachi.

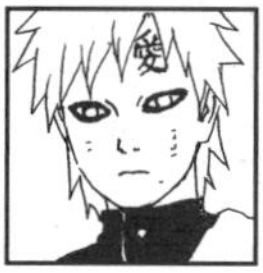

Son Gaara

Many sent in comments like, "If he were my son, I'd never make him a jinchûriki."

Twins Naruto

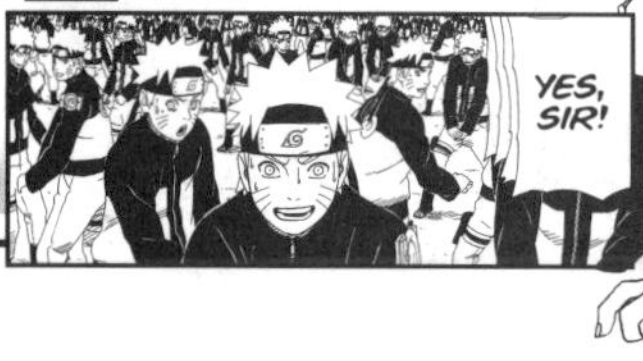
YES, SIR!

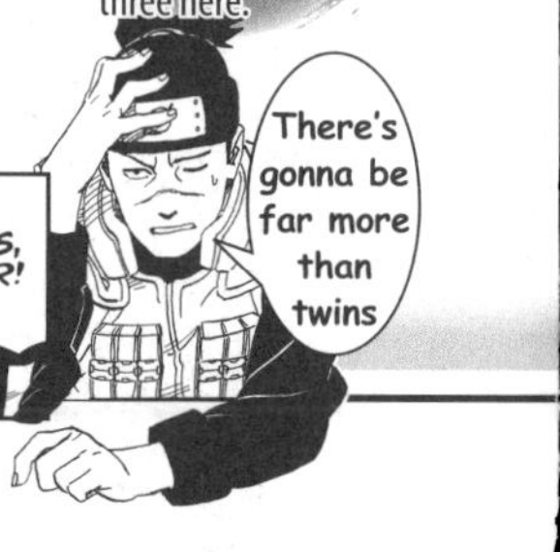
There's gonna be far more than twins

Naruto uses Multiple Shadow Doppleganger to be millenituplets!

SURVEY RESULTS

Ratio of male to female: **3:7**
Average age: **16.5** years old
Total votes cast: **1,160**

Of 300,000 votes from all six surveys, who ranked at the top?!

The Super-Popular Character Survey Results

We totaled every vote received at *Weekly Jump*, and the top 20 all-time most popular characters are ranked below.

Here are the results!!

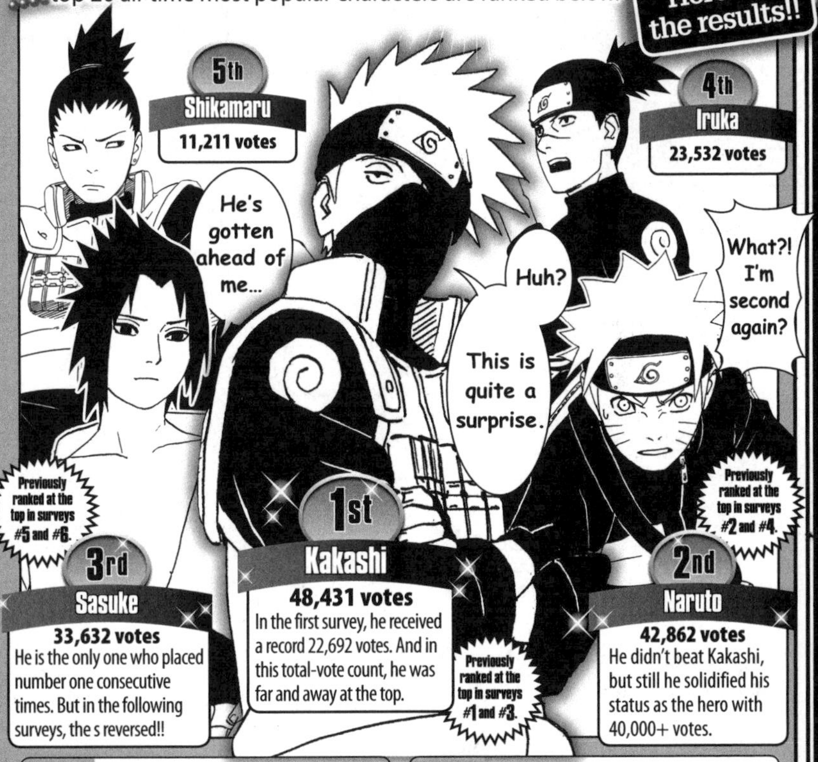

What?! I'm second again?
Huh?
This is quite a surprise.
He's gotten ahead of me...

5th Shikamaru
11,211 votes

4th Iruka
23,532 votes

Previously ranked at the top in surveys #2 and #4.

2nd Naruto
42,862 votes
He didn't beat Kakashi, but still he solidified his status as the hero with 40,000+ votes.

1st Kakashi
48,431 votes
In the first survey, he received a record 22,692 votes. And in this total-vote count, he was far and away at the top.

Previously ranked at the top in surveys #1 and #3.

Previously ranked at the top in surveys #5 and #6.

3rd Sasuke
33,632 votes
He is the only one who placed number one consecutive times. But in the following surveys, the s reversed!!

6th	Sakura	9,701 votes
7th	Neji	9,362 votes
8th	Gaara	8,660 votes
9th	Rock Lee	8,614 votes
10th	Itachi	7,067 votes
11th	Hinata	6,917 votes
12th	Haku	3,551 votes
13th	Might Guy	2,913 votes
14th	Temari	2,803 votes
15th	The Fourth Hokage	2,734 votes
16th	Deidara	2,555 votes
17th	Kiba	2,398 votes
18th	Hayate	2,183 votes
19th	Jiraiya	2,055 votes
20th	Shino	1,963 votes

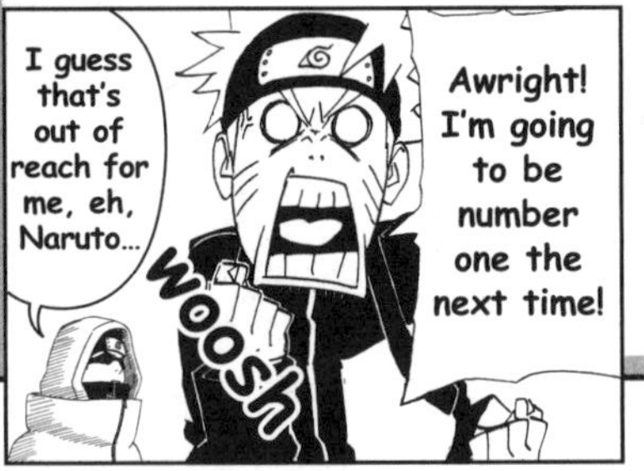

Awright! I'm going to be number one the next time!
I guess that's out of reach for me, eh, Naruto...
WOOSH

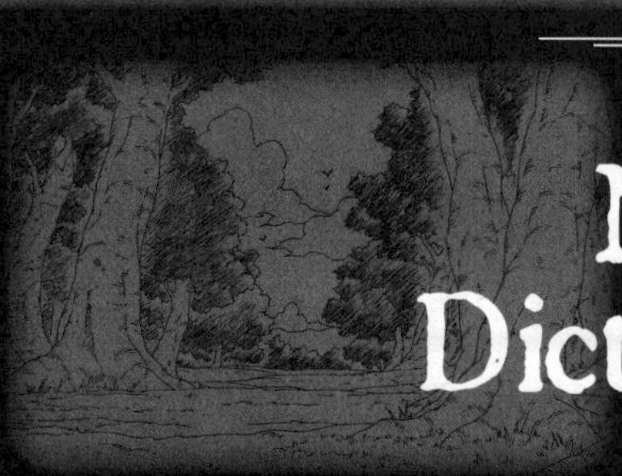

Naruto Dictionary

Listed here are immortal words that took root in giant trees and swayed in the winds.

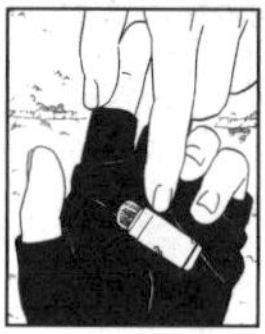

Blood Capsule: Shikamaru got this to use in the battle against Hidan and Kakuzu. It is a medical ninja tool meant for collecting blood samples.

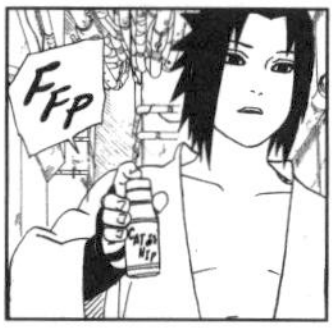
FFP

Bottle of Catnip: Something that ninja cats love. The finest grade catnip is refined and reduced to a concentrated extract. A single drop can soften up any ninja cat.

Boy After All: One of the reasons why Sai and Naruto were fighting was that Sai referred to him as a little boy. Later, he says he's a boy after all. But still with disrespect.

C

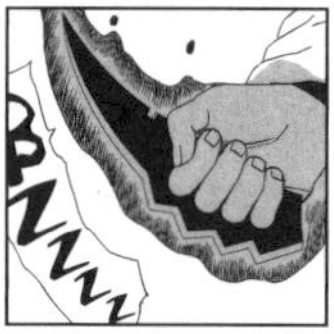

Chakra Blade: Made of a metal that absorbs chakra nature. Asuma and Shikamaru both use one.

A

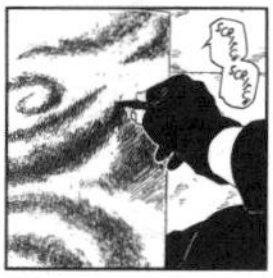

Artistic Type: Knowledge of art. It exists within the creators and the viewer. Sai's Art of Cartoon Beast Mimicry is impossible to use without being an artistic type.

Badgers in Same Hole: They are the same! Konohamaru says this to Naruto and Sakura when they get worked up over seeing his Ninja Centerfold.

Beautiful: What Sai called Ino when he was told to say the opposite of what he thought. Sakura was hurt. Sai called her homely.

Beauty of all Eternity: The opposite of momentary beauty. Sasori's ideal that art "is the beauty of all eternity."

Black Market Bounty: The price for shinobi heads on the black market. The prices are set based on past military achievements and history, as well as current strength and position. Asuma, a former member of the Guardian Shinobi Twelve and a Konoha jônin, is priced at 35 million ryo.

False Senility: Granny Chiyo's excuse for mistaking Kakashi for her son's killer. Her fake-out ability to even use her age as a weapon is impressive.

Fear Tactics: A tactic that platoon leader Yamato doesn't mind using. He mentions this when Naruto and the others are fighting. It is unclear whether he is just bluffing or whether he is serious.

Four-Man Cell: The basic number of members in a Konoha platoon. Ideally, there is an experienced captain and a medical ninja in the group.

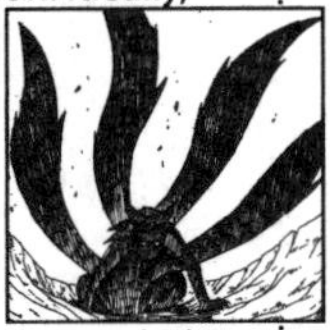

Fourth Tail: A state in which Naruto is in danger of transforming into the Nine Tails. Naruto's body is surrounded by highly dense chakra which doesn't protect his body, but causes serious damage to it instead.

Friends: Before Sai had met Naruto and Sakura, it was just a word. Now it's a keyword that represents a bond.

Fuma Clan: A group that fights using giant shuriken. They show their aggressive side when they attacked Jiraiya during his travels across the nation when he was younger.

Gift of the Sages: A special power that the priests of the Fire Temple have. Persistent training is needed to develop this talent that only a few people have.

Great Lord Elder: The popular term used to refer to the Great Toad Sage, the leader of the toads. At Mt. Myoboku, the toad village, everyone uses this term as a sign of respect and familiarity.

Great Naruto Bridge: The bridge that Naruto and Sasuke worked hard to lead to completion. Sasuke makes a visit with Suigetsu, who is after the Executioner's Blade.

Grotesque Puppet Show: Deidara described Sasori's puppet arts as such. He said it in an argument with the intent to anger Sasori.

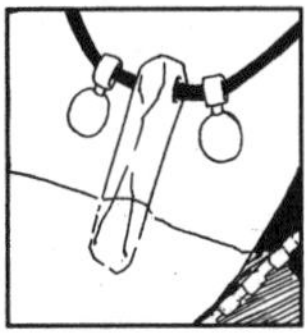

Chakra Crystal: A stone that resonates with the First Hokage's chakra and controls the powers of jinchûriki. There is one on the necklace that Tsunade gave to Naruto.

Child of Prophecy: The child whom the Great Toad Sage told Jiraiya would bring a revolution to the shinobi world. Jiraiya thought it was Nagato, but later, he was sure that it was Naruto.

Chûnin Commemoration Gift: The earring that Asuma gave to Shikamaru and his other students. It is a reminder to never forget Cell Number Ten.

Chûnin Exam Proctors: This committee of proctors which oversees the Chûnin Exams is led by Shikamaru and Temari. It is comprised of representatives from the major villages.

Climbing Silver: A shogi tactic in which you can thrust your silver general into enemy territory. In order to protect the king, which represents all future generations, Asuma charges into enemy territory.

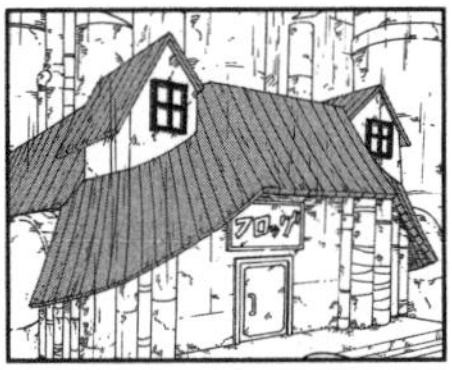

Club Toad: A bar that Jiraiya made that looks like a toad. For 500 ryo, you can drink all you want. On its opening day, as a special treat (?), a free interrogation was thrown in as well.

Collection Office: A place where bounties can be traded in for money. It is known that there are several of them, but their existence is hidden from the general public with secret entrances in the walls of public bathrooms and other such places.

Corrosion Style: A special ninjutsu that Roshi, the Four Tails jinchûriki, used. He combined Fire Style with Earth Style to create lava that can melt anything.

to guide the one who will bring forth a revolution.

King: In shogi, you lose when this piece is taken from you. If the Konoha shinobi were shogi pieces, the Black King would be the young children to whom the future is being left.

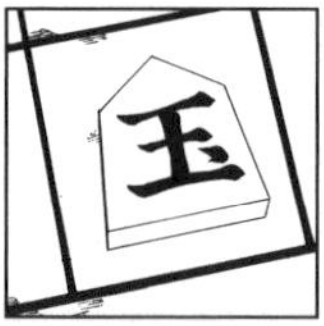
玉

Knight: The shogi piece that Asuma compared Shikamaru to. Its unique movements are similar to Shikamaru's flexible reasoning.

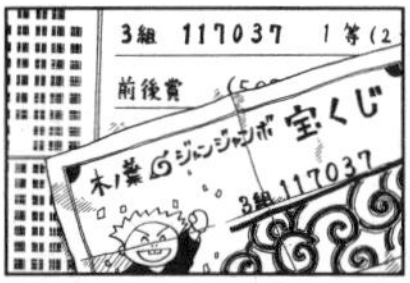
3組 117037
前後賞
宝くじ

Konoha Jumbo Lottery: First prize is 20,000,000 ryo. For Tsunade, good fortune is an omen of bad things to come, so when she won first prize, Gaara has been abducted.

Konohagakure Training Program: The curriculum for raising new recruits. Recently, the Village Hidden in the Sand has adopted it with great results.

Level-10 Medicine: A few days after using his Transference Technique, Orochimaru's body begins to reject him. This is the strongest dosage of medicine that he is given to suppress the reaction.

Little Boy: Sai's view of Naruto. He uses this derogatory term to refer to people who need help in battle.

M

Make-Out Tactics: The newest volume of the *Make-Out* series. A popular book about passionate love between a man and a woman, full of strategies and how-to tips.

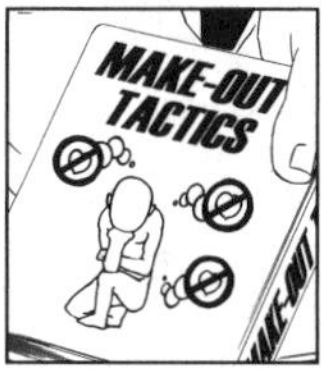
MAKE-OUT TACTICS

Manner of Death: The shinobi world's view of death. The value of one's death is not determined by how one lived, but by what one was doing at the time of one's death.

Guardian Shinobi Twelve: The collective name of the twelve elite ninja who guard the lord of the Land of Fire. A waistcloth with the nation's crest is proof of their position. Skilled ninja like Asuma and Chiriku once belonged to this group.

H

High Density Chakra: What Naruto released when his fourth tail emerged. It is so concentrated that even Orochimaru said that he would die if he got hit by it.

Homely: How Sai views Sakura. It is tactless, but Sai meant no harm by it. He also doesn't regret saying it. But it does cause girls to be angry with him.

Hozuki Brothers: A reference to Mangetsu and Suigetsu, two brothers from the Hidden Mist. The younger, Suigetsu, is a prodigy and is said to be the second coming of the Zabuza, the Demon. Zetsu even calls him a troublesome shinobi.

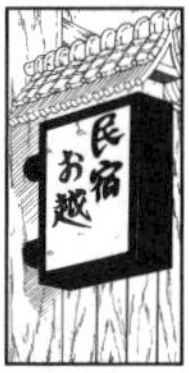
民宿
お越

Inn Okoshi: The old inn where Sasuke and his friends stayed. The building is in terrible shape, but the view from its giant window is magnificent.

Insanely Rough Estimates: Saying spontaneous things like "we'll get there in a day" or "we'll get there in half a day" about a trip that takes at least three days. A conversational technique that Guy and Lee excel at.

Intellectual Ninja Technique: A jutsu that requires extensive knowledge and precise chakra control. Advanced illusions are referred to as this.

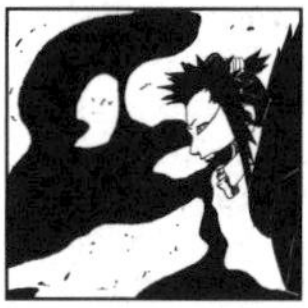

Iron Sand: The weapon used by the Third Kazekage, who is said to be the strongest in history. It is transformed into many shapes to fit the situation.

Jiraiya's Critical Selection: A choice that the Great Toad Sage predicted would bring stability or destruction to the ninja world. Jiraiya is given the task

Pop Art: A type of art that has the theme of mass production. But according to Deidara, pop is dead.

Power of Youth: A term that Guy uses when he gets worked up. It means to do your best like when you were a single-minded youth.

Puppet Hiruko: One of the puppets that Sasori controls. It is built to be worn by its user and functions as armor. Its special features are its thick, defensive outer shell and its scorpion-like tail.

Quota: The number of jinchûriki that the Akatsuki needs to find. Each member is required to collect one Biju.

Rejection Makes Men Stronger: A proverb that Jiraiya created based on his experiences of being rejected by Tsunade. It is a message to all boys who fear being rejected.

R

Ritual: A procedure that is carried out in a specific way. Hidan, who follows the way of Jashin, often performs rituals. Some of them take very long, which often annoys those around him.

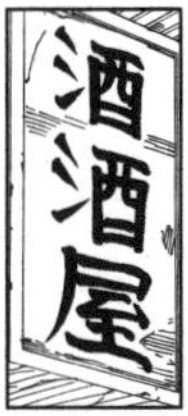
酒酒屋

Sake Sake Ya: A pub in Konoha. They're open even during the day. Jiraiya invited Tsunade here while she was working. It is popular for its Japanese sake and charcoal-grilled chicken.

Sasori of the Red Sand: The nickname of Sasori, a puppet master with no equal. He received this name during the Great Ninja War, when his puppets dyed the sand red with blood.

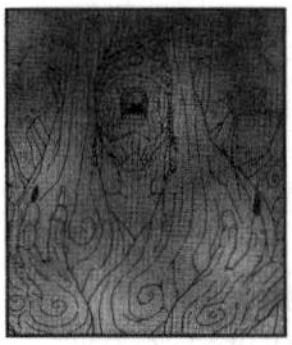

Sealing Statue: A giant, ominous statue that can seal away the giant power of the Biju. It has nine eyes and whenever one Biju is sealed away, one of the eyes opens.

Senju Clan: The most powerful clan during the feudal period. They helped in the founding of Konoha Village. Their leader, Hashirama Senju, was adored by all, and was appointed First Hokage.

Monzaemon: The first performer of the Art of the Puppet Master. He is the creator of the masterpiece Secret White Move: Chikamatsu's Ten Puppets.

N

New Pervy Ninjutsu: Naruto learned this after two and a half years of training. Sakura gets in the way of its unveiling.

Nikko Relay Station: A health resort with many hotels and restaurants. Sasuke rested here after being injured in his battle with Deidara.

Nine Tails' Aura: The state in which the Nine Tails' chakra overflows from Naruto and surrounds his body like a cloak. This chakra is uncontrollable and is very taxing on Naruto. At the moment, the only one who can suppress its power is Yamato.

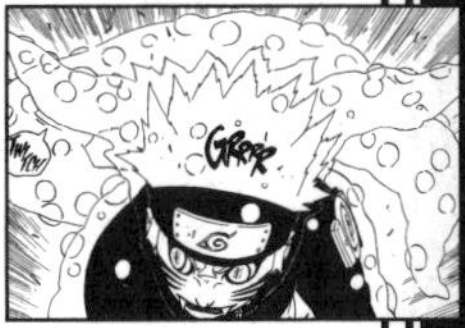

Ninja Temple: The term for temples that have shinobi working as priests. The Fire Temple in the Land of Fire is especially famous and well known throughout the land.

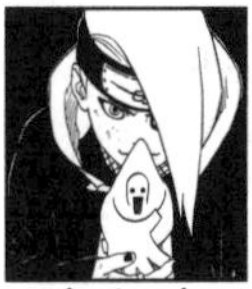

Ohako, "My Prize Masterpiece": One of Deidara's signature pieces is a highest level Clay Bomb with C3 chakra mixed into it. Its explosion has a giant radius and causes enormous damage.

Patience Breaking Point: A phrase that depicts the limit of one's patience as a bag. Everyone has one, but according to Tobi, Deidara has a Bag of Explosions.

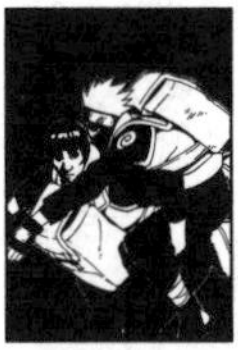

Piggyback: A childlike act that's a little disturbing when performed by two men who are not so young like Kakashi and Guy.

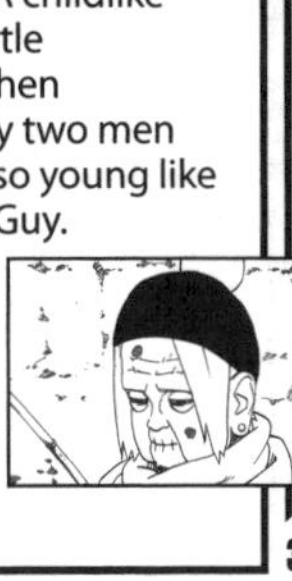

Playing Possum: A jutsu (?) meant to surprise people by doing nothing. The older you get, the more realistic it becomes.

when he saw the Nine Tails' fourth tail and the other when he was peeping on Tsunade while she was bathing at a hot spring resort.

Teleportation Ninjutsu: High-level ninjutsu that surpass the concepts of space and distance. It allows one to move into a subspace and appear at a specific destination with a jutsu formula.

Tenchi Bridge: A bridge that spans a deep ravine. Sasori chooses this place to secretly meet with Kabuto because it is in a remote area.

Tenzo: The codename that Yamato once had. Kakashi, a former Anbu, sometimes refers to Yamato by this name he is more familiar with.

The Akatsuki's Purse-Holder: Kakuzu, who manages the Akatsuki's funds, calls himself this. He was appointed to this task because of his sense of responsibility and loyalty.

The Land of Eddies: The land that Naruto's mother, Kushina, hails from. There are a lot of people here with the last name Uzumaki.

The Land of Rivers: A small verdant nation surrounded by wondrous nature, almost as though to isolate it from the rest of the world. They are skilled at building hide-outs and the Akatsuki is based there.

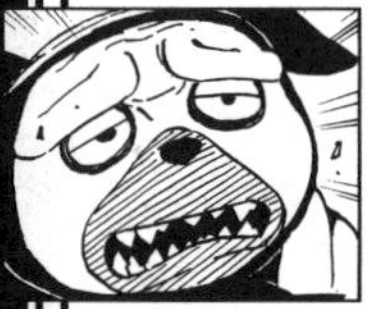

The Ninja Dogs Eight: The eight ninja dogs that Kakashi has a contract with. With Pakkun as their leader, they are all excellent ninja dogs. They are good at finding their targets with their acute sense of smell.

The Tale of Jiraiya the Gallant: A story based on Jiraiya's own life story. It ends with Jiraiya figuring out Pain's mystery and sending word to his village.

Tomoshiri Grass: A valuable medicinal herb that is used to make antidotes. It is difficult to grow and there are only a few of them in the Sand Village.

Shiny Happy Feelings: How Sakura feels for a moment when Naruto returns to the village after two years. But when she sees him show off his new pervy ninjutsu, he shatters those thoughts pretty fast.

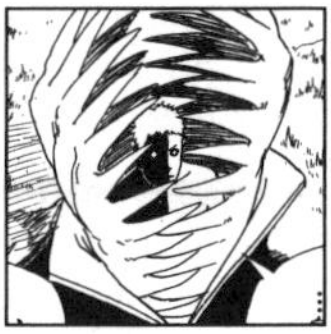

Spiky Aloe Fellow: A nickname (?) that Naruto gave to Zetsu. Judging from how angry Zetsu got by being called this, it seems he's not an aloe plant.

Spirit Weapon: Weapons that have no physical form like the Totsuka Blade and the Yata Mirror are referred to as this. Few have ever actually seen them and people question whether they actually exist.

Strange Beast: The word that Kisame used to describe Guy. Guy seems odd even to a monster like Kisame!

Superflat: Deidara claims it is a new innovation in pop art. It prefers an object to have a two-dimensional look over a three-dimensional look.

Survivors of the Former Hidden Rain: The shinobi who were defeated in the rebellion that split the Hidden Rain in two. They are still engaging in guerrilla activities.

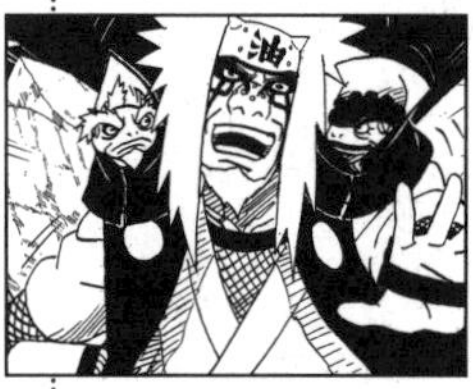

Swagger: Expressing a strong emotion in a single action. In other words, showing off. Jiraiya tries to do this many times during his battle with Pain, but he keeps getting interrupted.

Switch Hook Entry: A method of storming in by destroying entry to the enemy's territory and charging in all at once. It is the tactic used to break into the Akatsuki's hideout.

T

Tango with Death (Twice!): The times that Jiraiya sensed he was going to die. Once was won't die even if his head is cut off. They show off their high battle power by defeating powerful opponents like Chiriku and Asuma.

Urge to Slaughter: Strong feelings that drive one to kill someone. Jugo has especially strong urges that will suddenly appear and take control of his entire body.

Way of Jashin: Hidan follows this way of belief. It has extremely harsh qualities, including the belief in mass murder. Followers adhere to strict philosophical guidelines.

White Snake: A symbol of fortune and rebirth. Its molted skin is a rare sight. A young Orochimaru found one and stared at it curiously.

Will of Fire: The ideals the Konoha shinobi adhere to. Treat one's great predecessors as gods and fight with pride in their memory. And tell their beliefs to future generations.

Will of the Foundation: "Support the giant tree called Konoha from the unseen depths of the ground." The shared mindset of the organization.

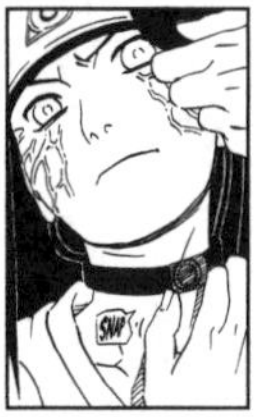

Wireless: Guy's platoon uses this to contact each other. It can make transmissions within a radius of 800 meters.

Yata Mirror: A mirror that can deflect anything. It is stored in Susano'o's left hand and has no physical form.

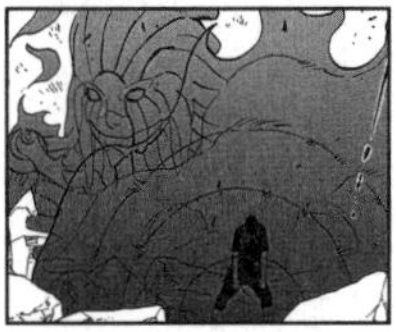

You're...who?: What Guy said when he couldn't remember who Kisame was despite having fought him once before. With Kisame's unique looks, it was probably the first time anyone ever asked him this.

Z

Top Secret Mission: "My Top Secret Mission was to kill Sasuke" (before he could be possessed by Orochimaru). That was the true mission that Danzo gave Sai.

Totsuka Blade: Its other name is the Sakegari Blade. The sword is covered in sealing spells, and those who are stabbed by it are drawn into a genjutsu world of drunken dreams. Itachi owned this sword.

Traitorous Cockroach: The term that Sai used to refer to Sasuke. Naruto and Sakura are furious upon hearing this.

Transient Beauty: Deidara's artistic ideal that "Art is the transient beauty that fades after just a moment."

True Art Is an Explosion: An expression of Deidara's artistic ideal of momentary beauty. He said these words when he blew himself up.

Tsunade Junior: Jiraiya named Sakura this when he noticed her temper and super strength. It is a name filled with great respect and fear.

Tsunade, The Slug Princess: Tsunade's name during the Great Ninja War. She was named this because she can summon a giant slug.

Tsunade's Rock Face: The giant rock sculpture that proves that one is Hokage. When Naruto returns home, the face of Tsunade, the fifth Hokage, has been completed.

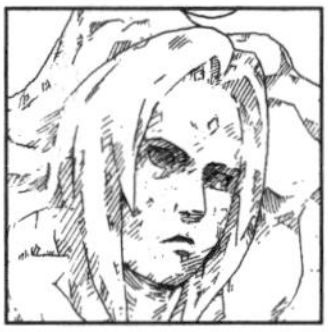

Two O'clock Direction: A direction as likened to a clock with the speaker facing directly at 12 o'clock. Two o'clock direction is front right.

Ultimate New Jutsu: A new jutsu involving the Mangekyo Sharingan. Naruto's growling stomach drowned out the explanation of this jutsu.

Unkillable Partnership: A reference to the two-man cell that has Kakuzu, who can stock up on hearts, and Hidan, who

Illustrations Data

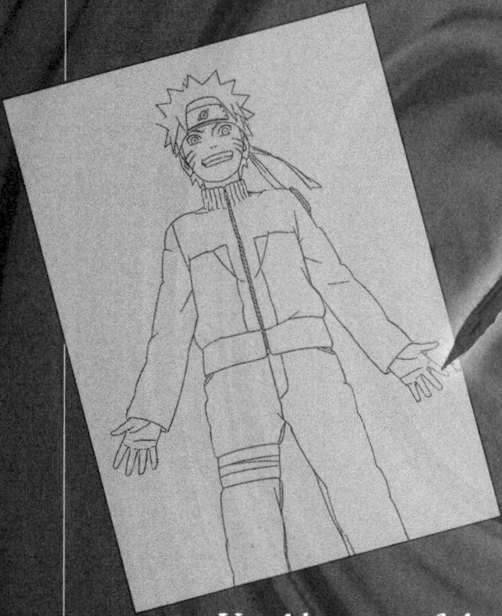

Untold secrets of the creation of *Naruto*!
When *Naruto* was a work in progress!
In Kishimoto Sensei's own words!

Masashi Kishimoto's Secret NARUTO Artwork Collection

Uzumaki Naruto

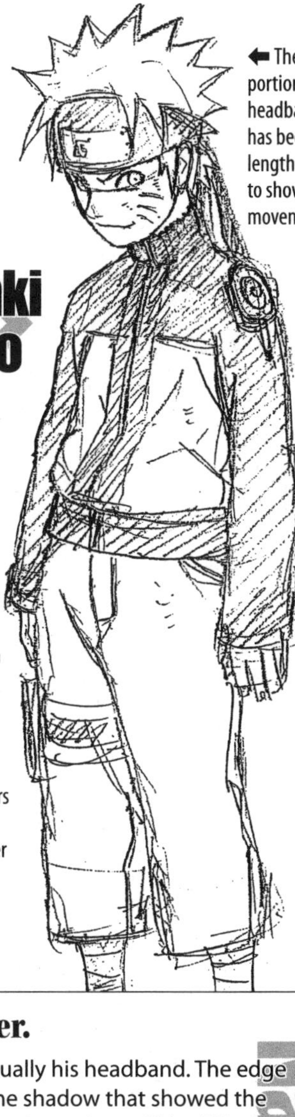

⬅ The band portion of his headband has been lengthened to show movement.

➡ Raising his collar and reducing the amount of skin he shows give him a mature look.

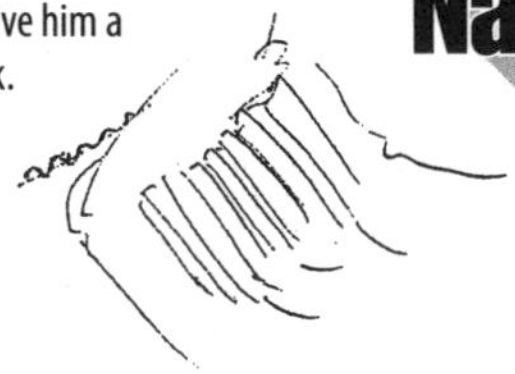

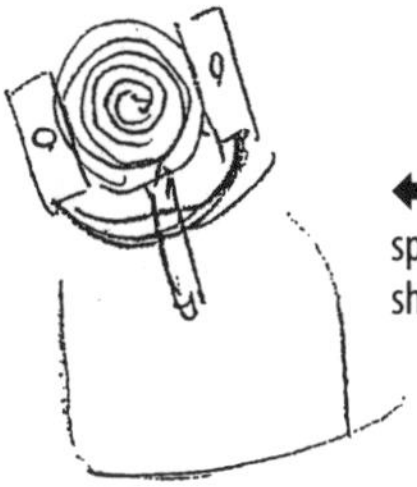

⬅ The strap attached to the spiral on his shoulder has been shortened.

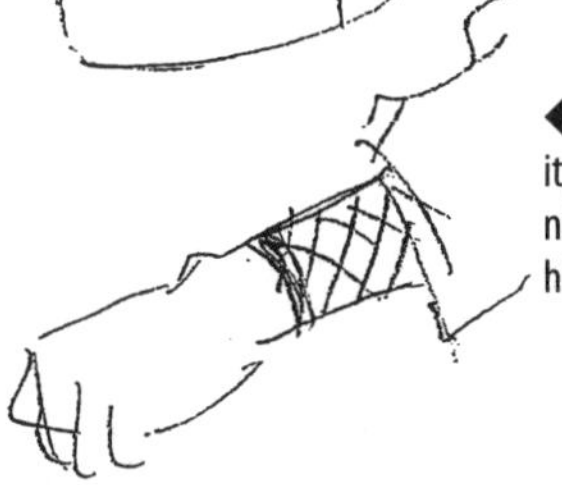

⬅ He usually covers it, but he wears a ninja costume under his jacket.

His headband is slightly larger.

The biggest feature of Naruto's outfit is actually his headband. The edge of his headband used to be very close to the shadow that showed the thickness of the metal plate. Because of that, it was incredibly difficult to draw the border between the two, as well as Naruto's eyebrows underneath the cloth. So I made the band a little larger. By doing this, the metal plate as well as the band appeared thicker. His eyebrows became very easy to draw. I also made his pants unrolled, and made his sandals high like boots. Showing off too much of his ankle would look childish, so I tried to cut down on that.

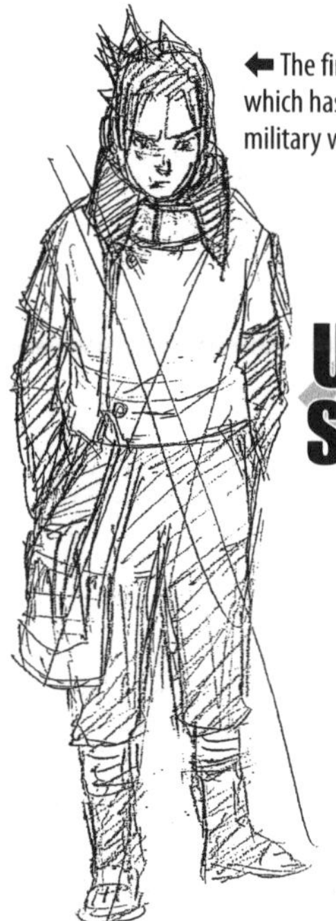

⬅ The first design, which has a casual military wear concept.

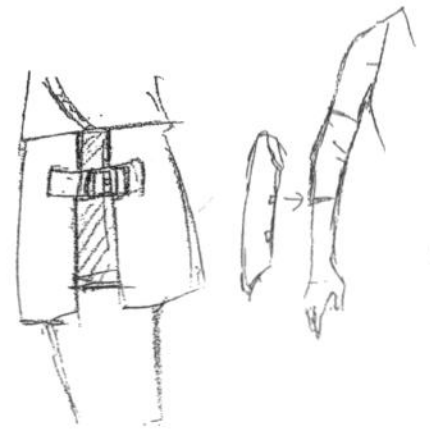

⬅ In order to combine mobility and femininity, her hair was shortened and her outfit was made to resemble a karate uniform.

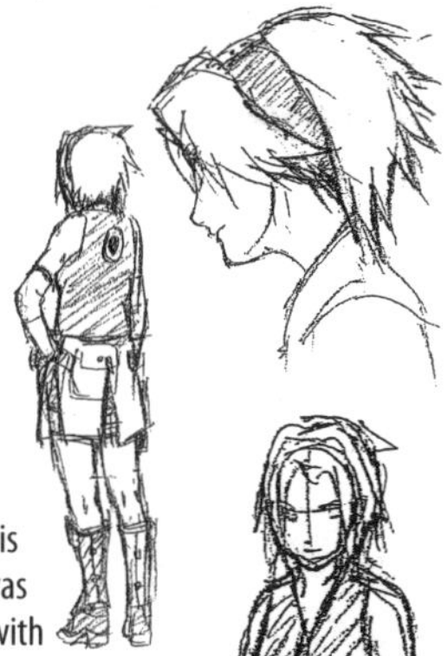

Uchiha Sasuke

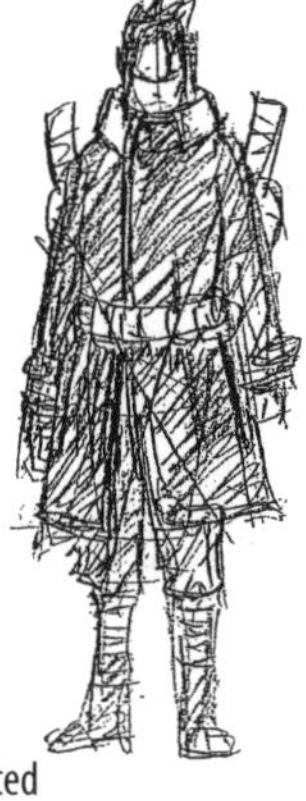

⬅ When his old outfit was combined with Orochimaru's rope belt, it looked like cold weather clothing.

Haruno Sakura

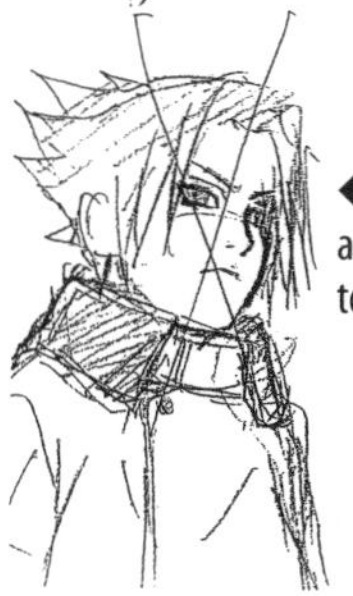

⬅ I wanted adult Sasuke to shine.

⬇ A gloved hand peeks out from a sleeve.

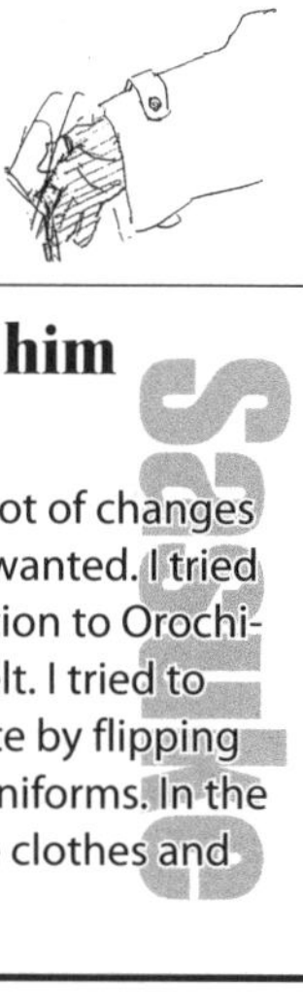

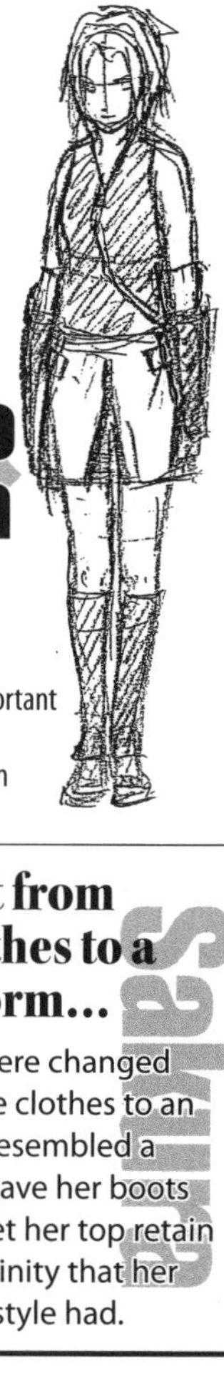

➡ To make her an important fighter, her outfit was designed with a focus on close-range combat.

I wanted to make him look cool!

He went through quite a lot of changes to achieve the coolness I wanted. I tried incorporating his connection to Orochimaru by adding a rope belt. I tried to make him look immaculate by flipping his collar. I tried military uniforms. In the end, I went with Japanese clothes and exposed his chest. (*laugh*)

Sakura went from Chinese clothes to a karate uniform...

Sakura's clothes were changed from Chinese-style clothes to an active outfit that resembled a karate uniform. I gave her boots and gloves. But I let her top retain some of the femininity that her previous Chinese style had.

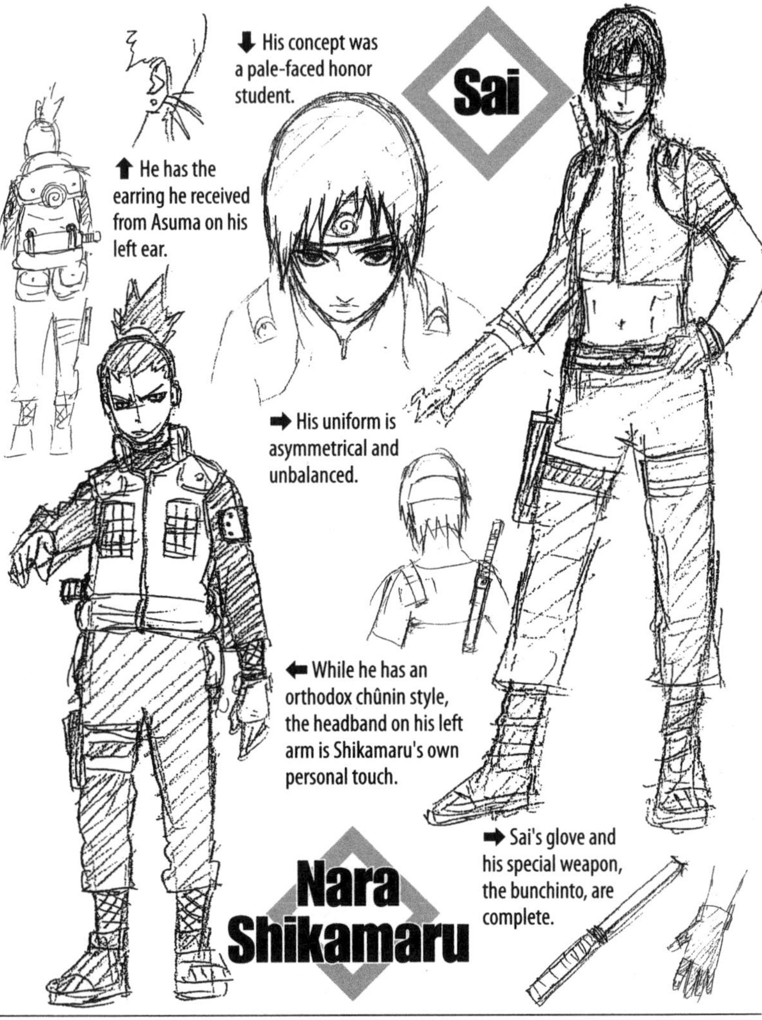
Sai
His concept was a pale-faced honor student.
He has the earring he received from Asuma on his left ear.
His uniform is asymmetrical and unbalanced.
While he has an orthodox chûnin style, the headband on his left arm is Shikamaru's own personal touch.
Sai's glove and his special weapon, the bunchinto, are complete.
Nara Shikamaru

The headband on his shoulder is important.

Even though he's wearing a chûnin vest, I tried to make sure he didn't look like other chûnin. That's why it was important to place his headband on his arm so that Shikamaru's main feature, his hair, wouldn't be hidden.

I wanted for him to shine a little with an open midriff. (*laugh*)

He was meant to take Sasuke's place, so I figured I needed to make him shine. As a result, I made him bare his midriff. (*laugh*) I changed the length of his gloves and tried to make him unbalanced.

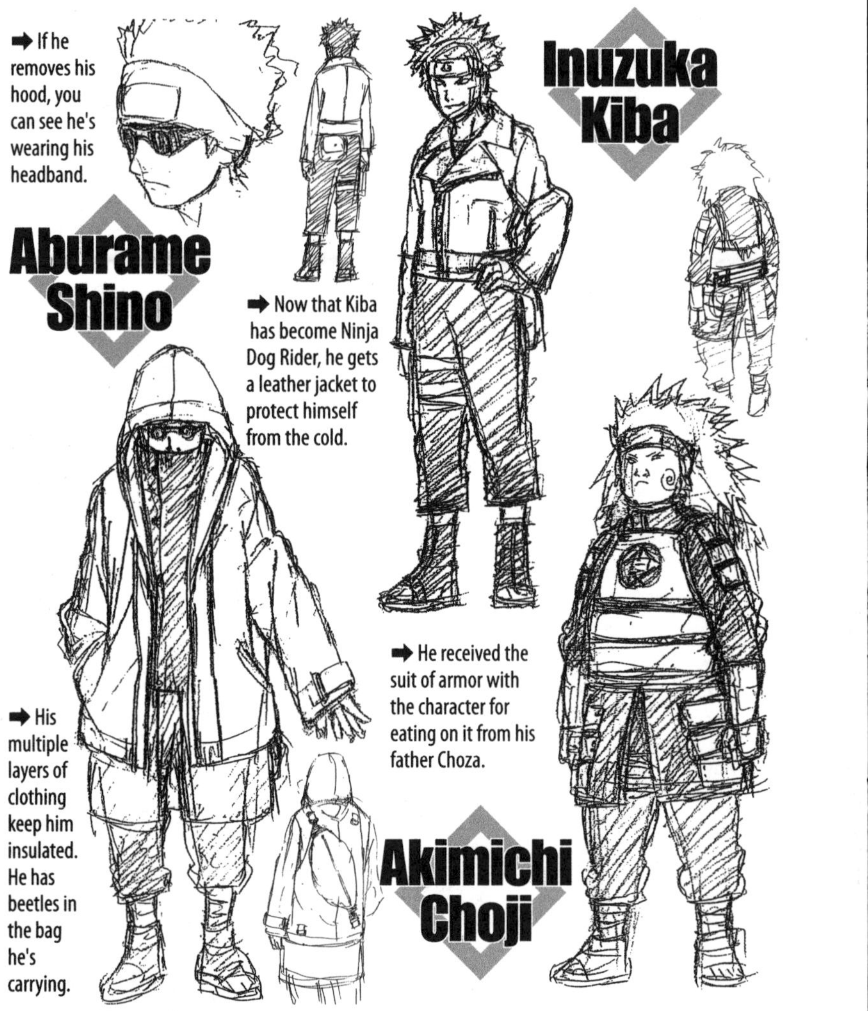
➡ If he removes his hood, you can see he's wearing his headband.
Aburame Shino
Inuzuka Kiba
➡ Now that Kiba has become Ninja Dog Rider, he gets a leather jacket to protect himself from the cold.
➡ He received the suit of armor with the character for eating on it from his father Choza.
➡ His multiple layers of clothing keep him insulated. He has beetles in the bag he's carrying.
Akimichi Choji

Shino has beetles stuffed in his backpack.

Shino

I made Shino wear even more layers of clothes. (*laugh*) In order to give him a creepy feel, I decided to keep his face and anything else hidden. Also, he's a beetle user, so he has beetles in the bag he's carrying.

Paternal Inheritance and Ninja Dog Rider.

Choji/Kiba

I drew Choji's father, Choza, a while ago, so I decided Choji would follow in his footsteps. Kiba rides on Akamaru, so I gave him cold weather clothing fit for Ninja Dog Rider. (*laugh*)

➡ Her pants are based on Chinese clothes. The way the end of her pant legs are cuffed is peculiar.

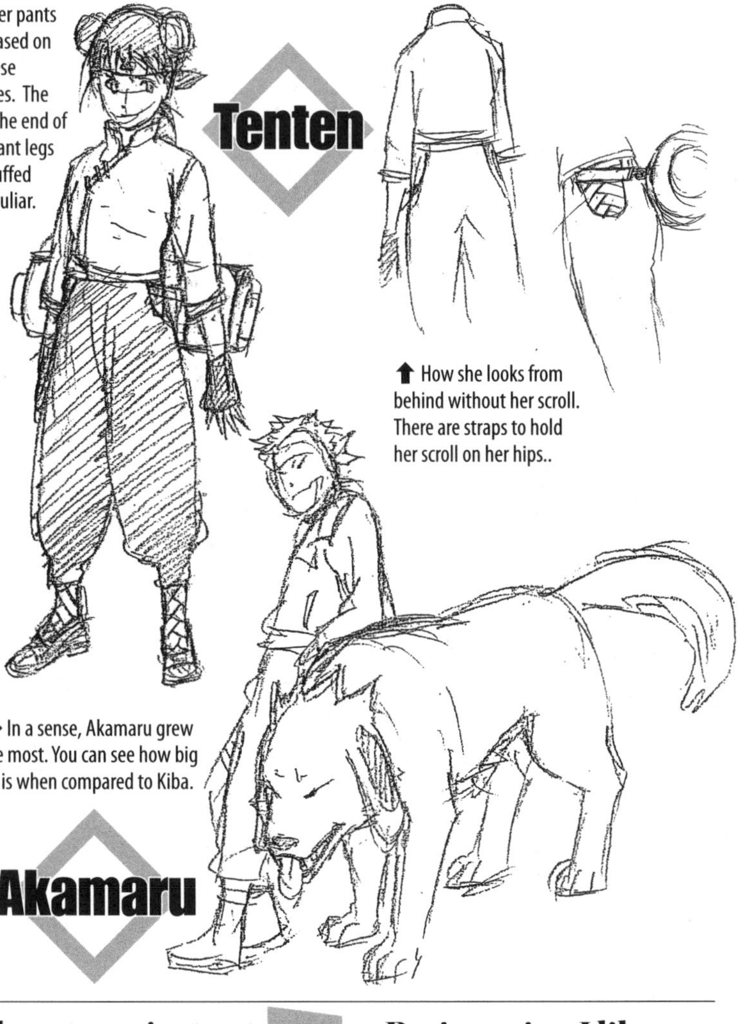
Tenten
Akamaru

⬆ How she looks from behind without her scroll. There are straps to hold her scroll on her hips..

➡ In a sense, Akamaru grew the most. You can see how big he is when compared to Kiba.

Akamaru...just got bigger.

I just made Akamaru bigger. (laugh) His face looks the same as before. I haven't decided what kind of dog he is. All I decided on was that he was a dog that keeps on getting bigger and that he would be big enough to carry Kiba.

Design-wise, I like her the best.

Tenten's concept was to have her do action scenes in three-quarter-sleeve Chinese clothes. I took ease of movement into consideration when I drew her.

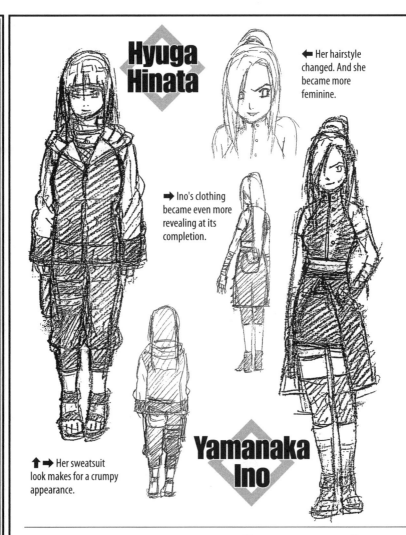

Hyuga Hinata

← Her hairstyle changed. And she became more feminine.

➡ Ino's clothing became even more revealing at its completion.

⬆➡ Her sweatsuit look makes for a crumpy appearance.

Yamanaka Ino

Hinata is *crumpy*. (*laugh*)

Hinata has a bland appearance. I tried to make her frumpy by reducing the amount of skin she shows. She's not too interested in fashion. I wanted to make her cute, but frumpy. *Crumpy*. (*laugh*)

She was covered in bandages, so I removed them.

I removed Ino's bandages and gave her clothes that were easier to move in, and since she's a girl, I tried to show more skin by baring her legs.

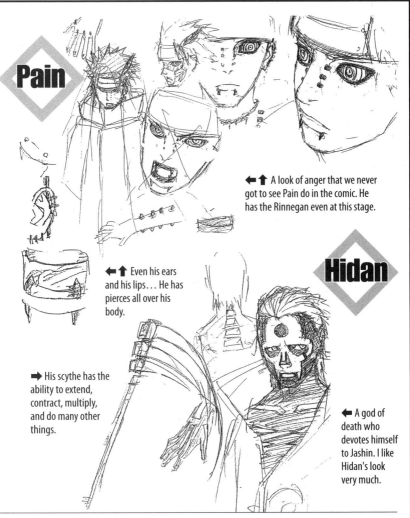

Pain

← ↑ A look of anger that we never got to see Pain do in the comic. He has the Rinnegan even at this stage.

← ↑ Even his ears and his lips… He has pierces all over his body.

Hidan

➡ His scythe has the ability to extend, contract, multiply, and do many other things.

← A god of death who devotes himself to Jashin. I like Hidan's look very much.

His concept was a god of death made of bones and holding a scythe.

I wanted Hidan to look curse arts focused, or rather, like a god of death. That's why he looks like he's made of bones and carries a scythe. His scythe can actually do all sorts of tricks, but I never got to show all of them. (*laugh*)

I wanted him to look cool and dangerous.

Since he was the Akatsuki leader, he needed to be cool, but I wanted him to also look dangerous. His name is Pain, so I gave him pierces. It makes it look like he was giving himself pain.

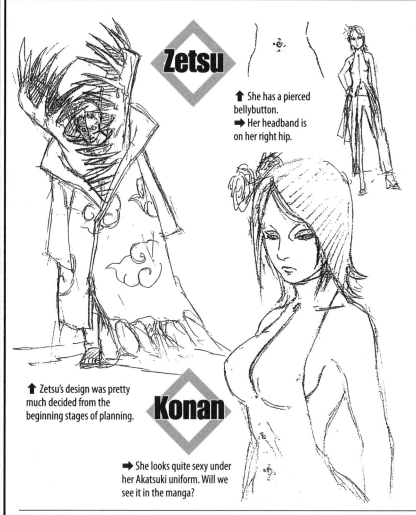

Zetsu

⬆ She has a pierced bellybutton.
➡ Her headband is on her right hip.

⬆ Zetsu's design was pretty much decided from the beginning stages of planning.

Konan

➡ She looks quite sexy under her Akatsuki uniform. Will we see it in the manga?

I wanted to make the Akatsuki a gang of monsters.

Zetsu's concept was a carnivorous plant. I wanted to make the Akatsuki a gang of non-human beings. He is split black and white down the center to show his two-faced nature.)

She's sexy, but she's wearing clothes. (*laugh*)

I wanted to make Konan the only woman in the group from the beginning, so I made her clothes a little sexy. But when I thought about it, she'd be wearing the Akatsuki uniform over it. (*laugh*) And also, she'd just turn into paper.

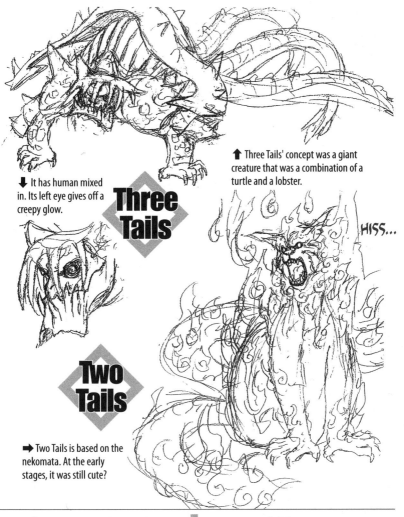

⬆ Three Tails' concept was a giant creature that was a combination of a turtle and a lobster.

⬇ It has human mixed in. Its left eye gives off a creepy glow.

Three Tails

HISS...

Two Tails

➡ Two Tails is based on the nekomata. At the early stages, it was still cute?

I've always loved giant monsters. (*laugh*)

I've always loved giant monsters or demons. Three Tails is a combination of those concepts. Its body is based on a turtle and its tail is based on a lobster.

It would be too cute as a regular cat.

There is a monster known as the *nekomata*, so it was easy to imagine what Two Tails would look like. It would have two tails. But it would be too cute as a regular cat, so I gave it some of the ferocity like that of a tiger or a lion.

Behind the Scenes Q&A!! With Masashi Kishimoto

About Sensei

Q. How do you choose a name for a character?

A. I choose Japanese nouns that sound good as a name.

Q. Which female character would you like as a girlfriend?

A. None. After all, I created them.

Q. How about if you were a girl, who would you pick as a boyfriend?

A. Shikamaru because he's intelligent and I think he'd succeed in life.

About the Characters

Q. The Akatsuki operates in two-man cells. What type of room do they get at hotels?

A. Two singles.

Q. Since the One Tail has been extracted from Gaara, is he unable to control sand?

A. Once it's ingrained in you, you can't take anything away, not even sand.

Q. What happens to the eyes of a baby who has Hyuga and Uchiha blood?

A. The right eye will have Sharingan. The left eye will have Byakugan! (*laughing*)

Q. If you drink Suigetsu (moon water), will you get a bellyache?

A. You'll have the runs.

Q. Naruto has a contract with Gamabunta, but how can he summon Gamakichi without a contract?

A. The contract with Gamabunta is a contract with all toads.

Q. Can you describe Naruto's New Pervy Ninjutsu?

A. I want to draw it and I'll do so as soon as I get the go-ahead from Editorial.

Explosive Unknown Facts

Q. Why has the seal on the Nine Tails begun to weaken?

Q. How come Naruto was able to reach the fourth tail of the Nine-Tails' chakra?

Q. What is it that Karin did to Sasuke in the past?

Q. Is Kushina alive?

Q. How did Kakashi awaken his Mangekyo Sharingan?

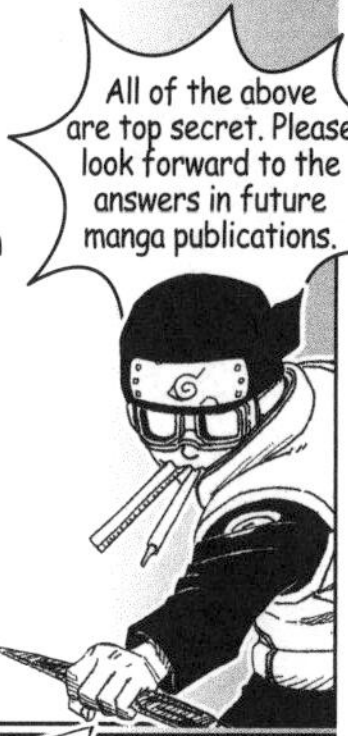
All of the above are top secret. Please look forward to the answers in future manga publications.

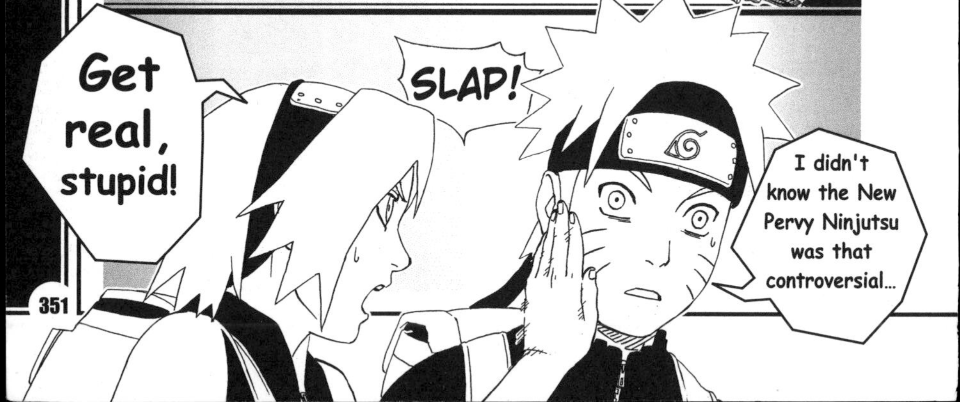
Get real, stupid!
SLAP!
I didn't know the New Pervy Ninjutsu was that controversial...

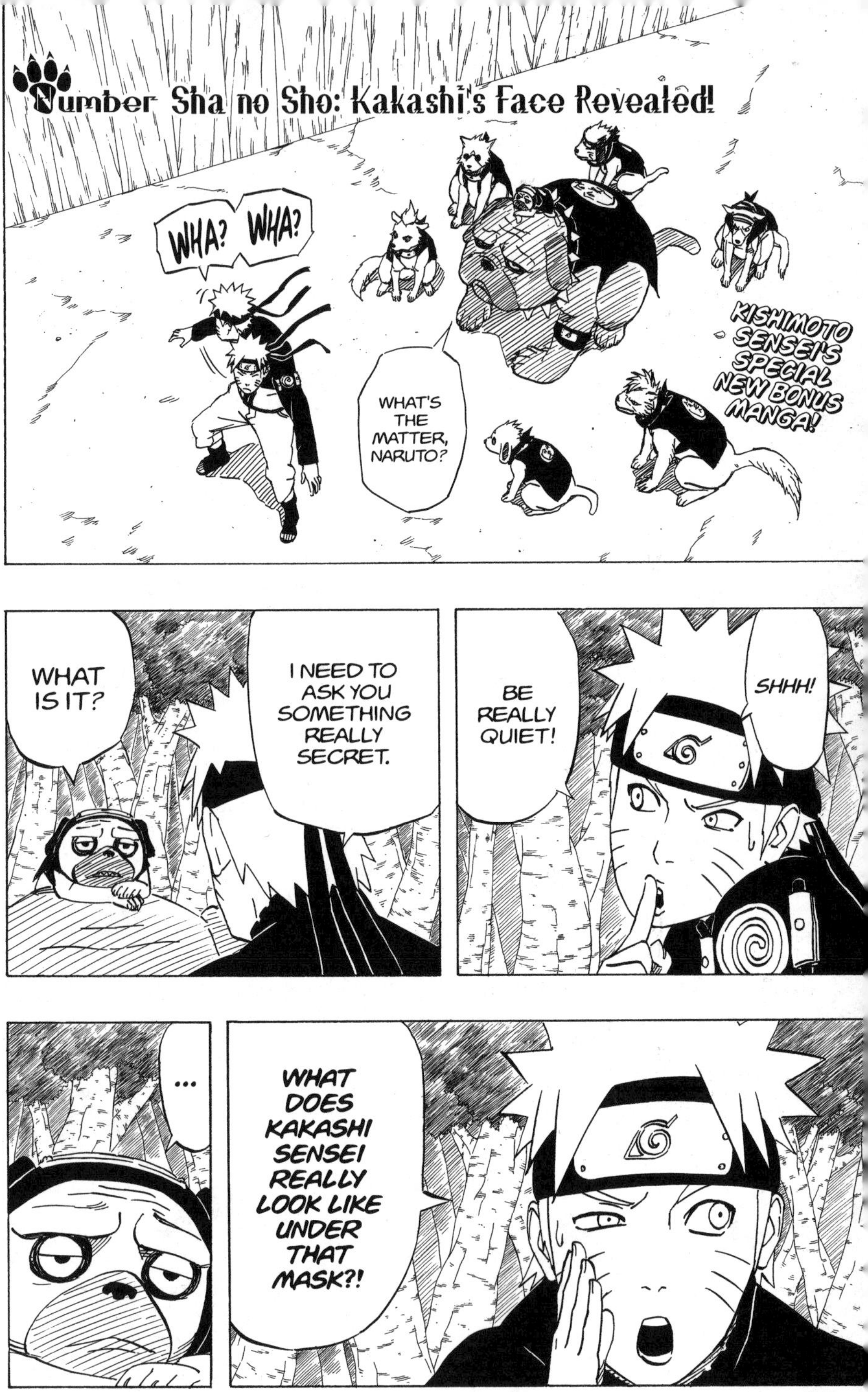
Number Sha no Sho: Kakashi's Face Revealed!
KISHIMOTO SENSEI'S SPECIAL NEW BONUS MANGA!
WHA? WHA?
WHAT'S THE MATTER, NARUTO?
SHHH!
BE REALLY QUIET!
I NEED TO ASK YOU SOMETHING REALLY SECRET.
WHAT IS IT?
WHAT DOES KAKASHI SENSEI REALLY LOOK LIKE UNDER THAT MASK?!
...

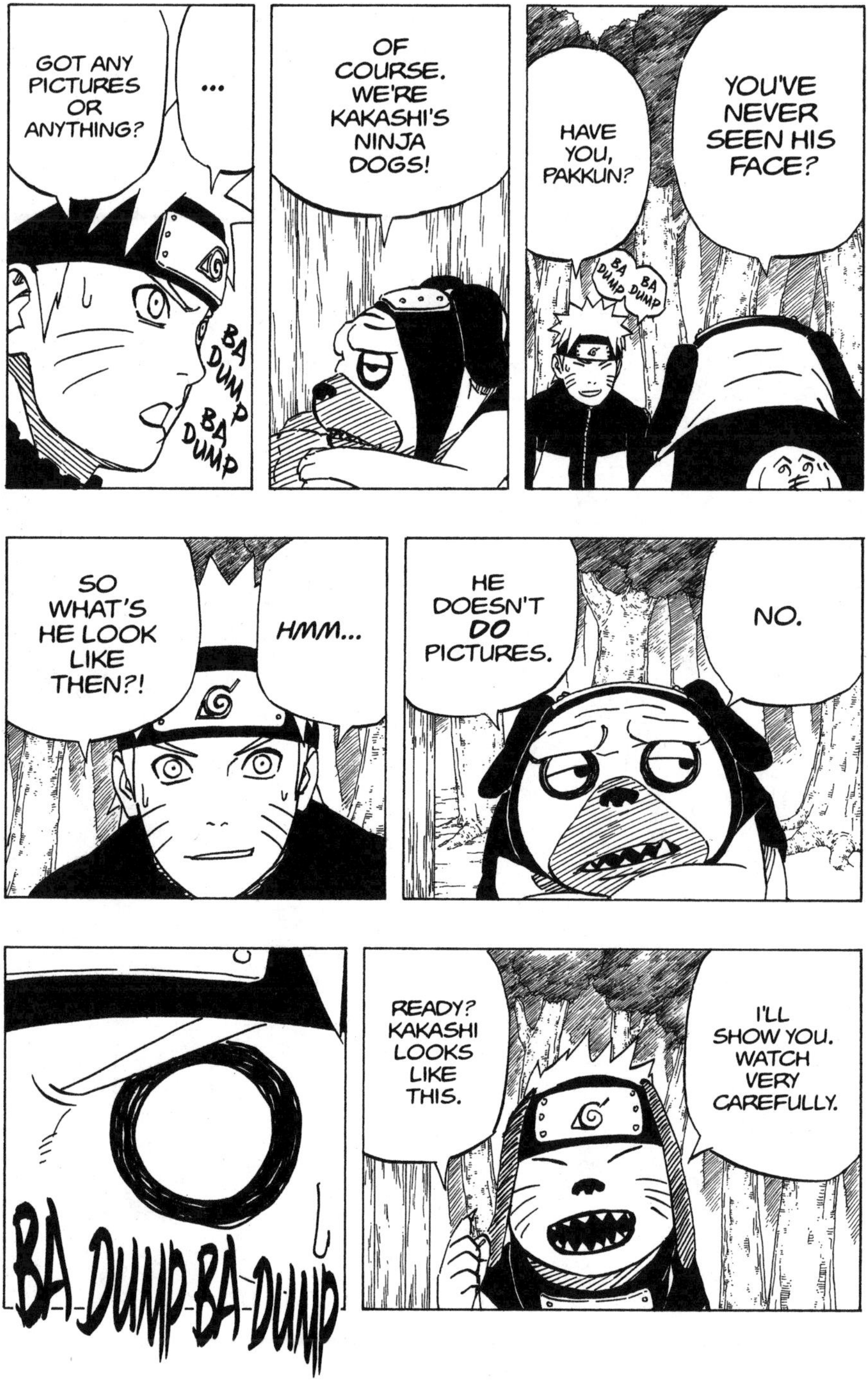
YOU'VE NEVER SEEN HIS FACE?
HAVE YOU, PAKKUN?
BA DUMP
BA DUMP
OF COURSE. WE'RE KAKASHI'S NINJA DOGS!
...
GOT ANY PICTURES OR ANYTHING?
BA DUMP
BA DUMP
NO.
HE DOESN'T **DO** PICTURES.
HMM...
SO WHAT'S HE LOOK LIKE THEN?!
I'LL SHOW YOU. WATCH VERY CAREFULLY.
READY? KAKASHI LOOKS LIKE THIS.
BA DUMP BA DUMP

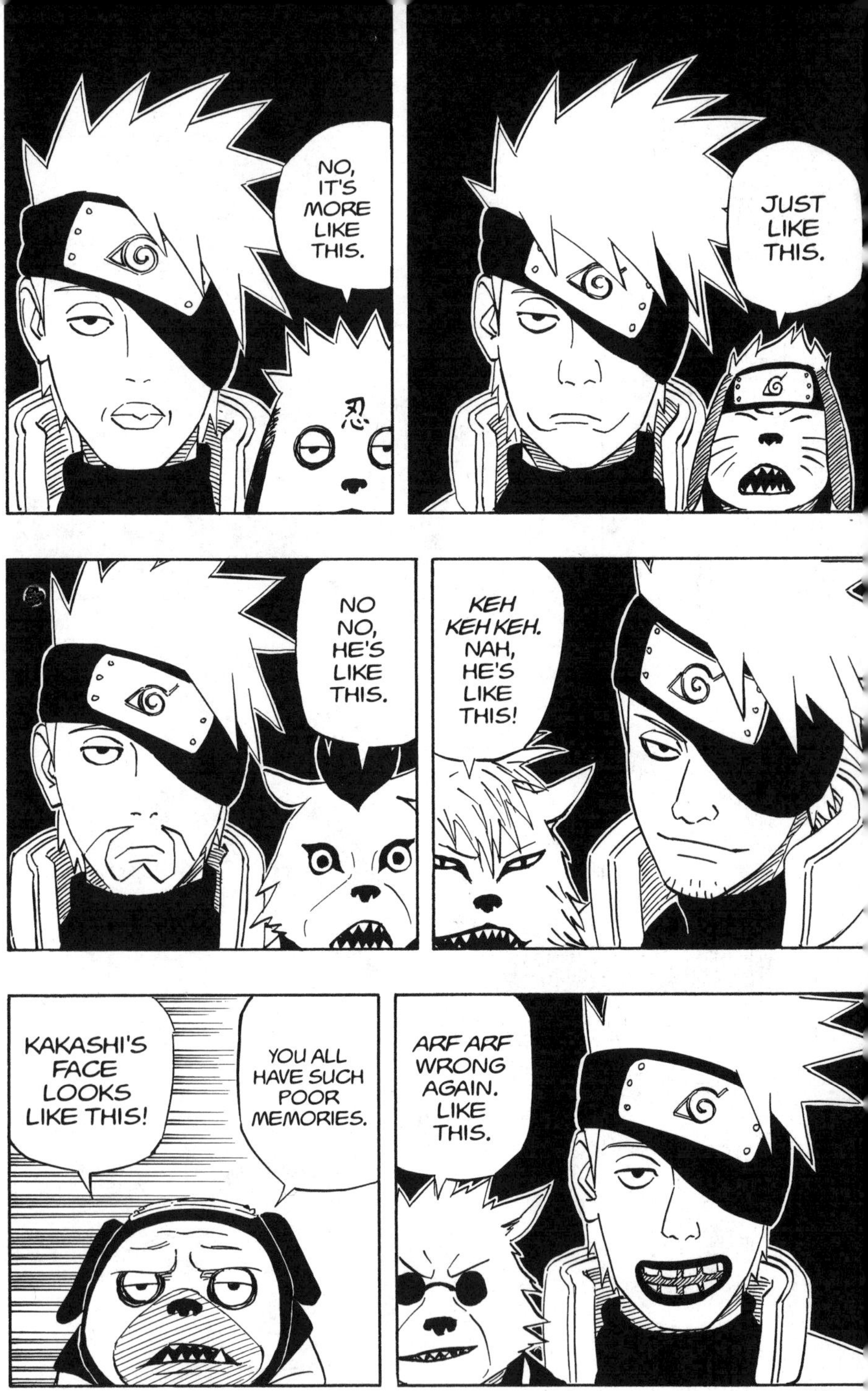
JUST LIKE THIS.
NO, IT'S MORE LIKE THIS.
KEH KEH KEH. NAH, HE'S LIKE THIS!
NO NO, HE'S LIKE THIS.
ARF ARF WRONG AGAIN. LIKE THIS.
YOU ALL HAVE SUCH POOR MEMORIES.
KAKASHI'S FACE LOOKS LIKE THIS!

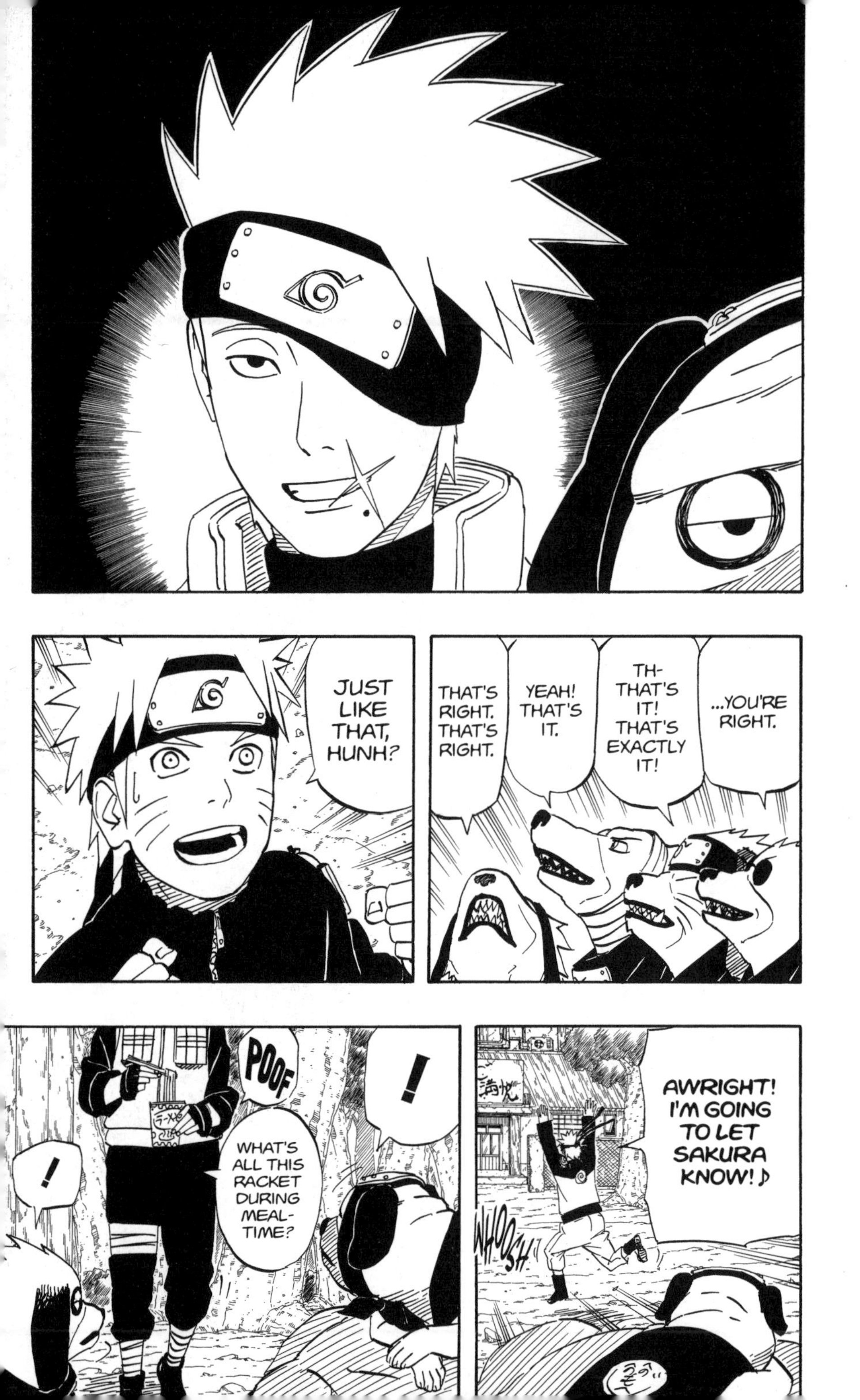
...YOU'RE RIGHT.
TH- THAT'S IT! THAT'S EXACTLY IT!
YEAH! THAT'S IT.
THAT'S RIGHT. THAT'S RIGHT.
JUST LIKE THAT, HUNH?
AWRIGHT! I'M GOING TO LET SAKURA KNOW! ♪
WHOOSH
!
POOF
WHAT'S ALL THIS RACKET DURING MEAL-TIME?
!

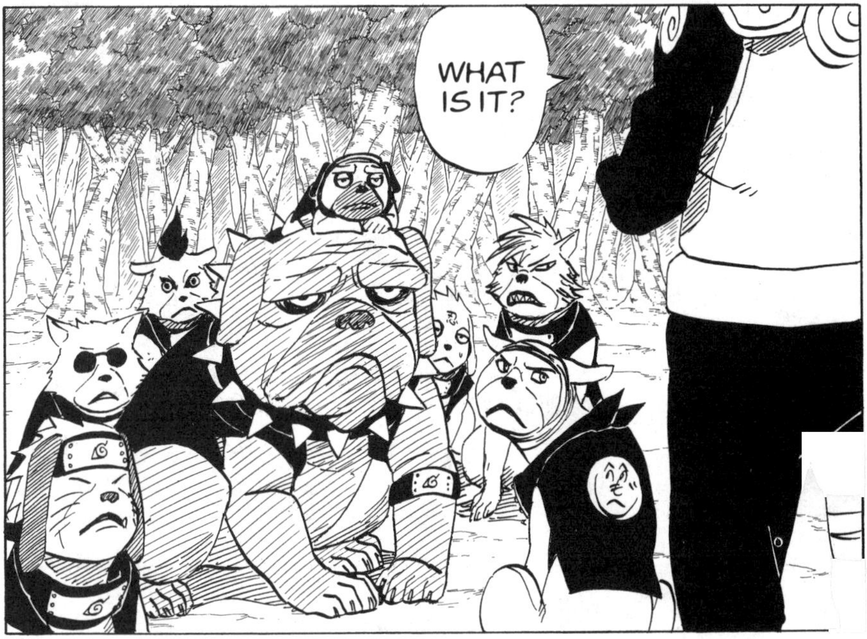
WHAT IS IT?

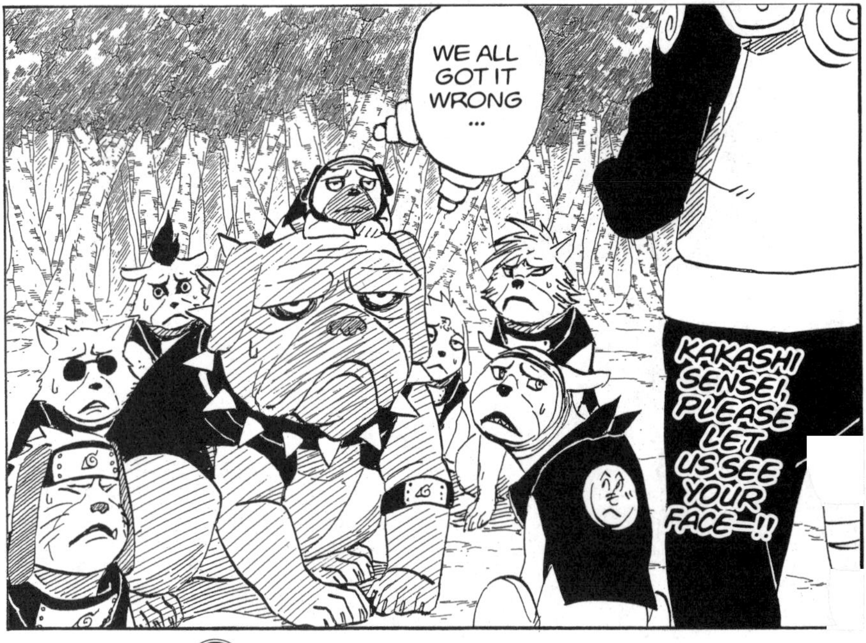
WE ALL GOT IT WRONG ...
KAKASHI SENSEI, PLEASE LET US SEE YOUR FACE—!!

NARUTO NO. SHA NO SHO / THE END

From Masashi Kishimoto...

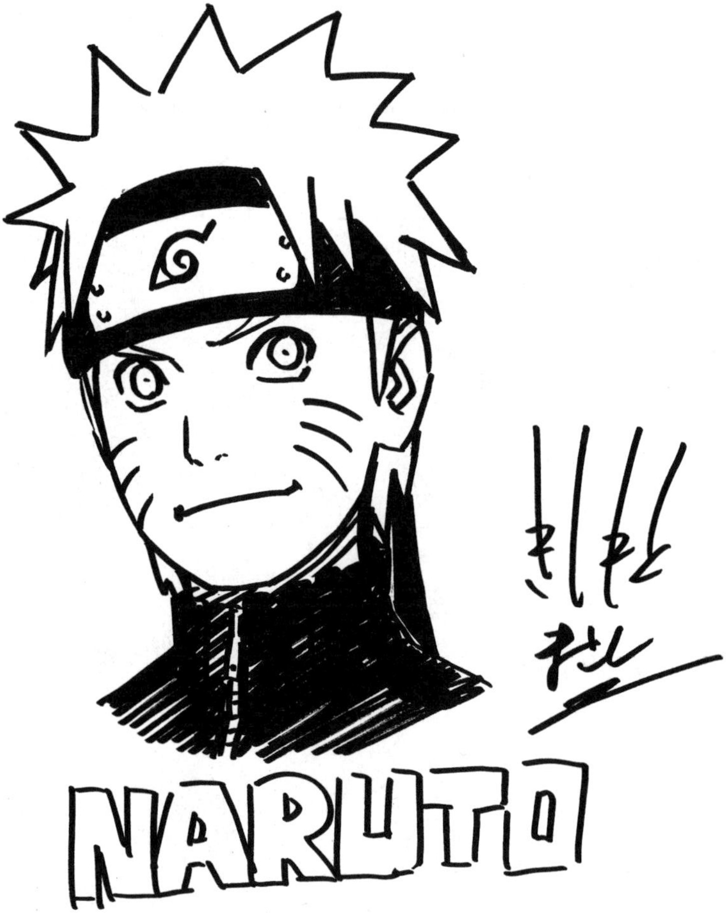
NARUTO

Thank you, everyone, for reading this book.
To each and every person who was involved in the completion of this book, thank you very much!

THE 4TH GREAT NINJA WAR AWAITS!

SHONEN JUMP NARUTO SHIPPUDEN
ULTIMATE NINJA STORM 3

THE MOST EPIC NARUTO GAME EVER!
AVAILABLE NOW!

- LEAD THE NINJA ALLIANCE ULTIMATE CONFRONTATION AGAINST AKATSUKI'S DEVASTATING ARMY

- CONFRONT OVERPOWERING BOSSES IN MEMORABLE BATTLES DEFYING TIME & DEATH

- NARUTO STORM SERIES ENTIRELY REVISITED THROUGH TOTALLY REVAMPED STORY MODE & COMBAT SYSTEM

- 80+ PLAYABLE CHARACTERS – THE BIGGEST ROSTER EVER!